TWENTIETH-CENTURY

YOUNG ADULT

WRITERS

Twentieth-Century Writers Series

TWENTIETH-CENTURY
YOUNG ADULT
WRITERS

FIRST EDITION

WITH AN INTRODUCTORY ESSAY BY
ROBERT CORMIER

EDITOR
LAURA STANDLEY BERGER

ASSOCIATE EDITORS
SHELLY ANDREWS
MOTOKO FUJISHIRO HUTHWAITE

ASSISTANT EDITORS
LINDA R. ANDRES
MICHAEL J. TYRKUS

—S^tJ—

S_T. J_{AMES} P_{RESS}

DETROIT • LONDON • WASHINGTON, D.C.

CONTENTS

PREFACE

Twentieth-Century Young Adult Writers continues the St. James Press Twentieth-Century Writers Series tradition by providing essential biographical, bibliographical, and critical information on more than 400 authors of fiction, poetry, and drama for young adults published in the English language. Authors whose works have been published in translation and selected authors of nonfiction works are also included.

Biographical and bibliographical information for each author was compiled through research and, whenever possible, verified with the listee; living entrants were also invited to make comments on their works for young adults. Critical essays were written especially for this book by professors of English and young adult literature, librarians, teachers, book reviewers, critics, and other individuals knowledgeable in the field.

For the purpose of determining inclusion, "young adult" has been defined as readers between the ages of eleven and nineteen—a wide age range, which helped ensure thorough coverage of authors. In addition to writers traditionally identified as "young adult" authors, such as Robert Cormier, S.E. Hinton, and Paul Zindel, users will also find authors of works written primarily for an older audience but often read by young adults—Ken Kesey, Terry McMillan, and Alice Walker, for example. Authors of adult works of science fiction, fantasy, and horror popular with young adult readers, including Michael Crichton, Stephen King, and Anne Rice, are also listed. In addition, authors of classic works studied in middle schools and high schools are featured, including Maya Angelou, Aldous Huxley, and John Steinbeck. A handful of authors whose works were published prior to this century, such as Jack London and Mark Twain, are also included due to their continuing literary significance and appeal to young adult readers.

Every effort has been made to identify those titles an author has written specifically for the young adult audience or which are appropriate for that audience; however, the inclusion of nontraditional young adult authors makes the categorization of bibliographical listings a challenging one, especially when an author writes for several age groups. For example, in cases where an author has written adult books that are also enjoyed by young adults, and has also written titles for the very young reader, the works read by adults and young adults are listed under "Publications for Adults and Young Adults," while works specifically intended for a younger audience are listed under "Publications for Children." Authors who write only works primarily intended for an older audience, but which appeal to young adults, are listed under "Publications."

As Robert Cormier writes in the following introductory essay, "The Gradual Education of a YA Novelist," "YA books are those that appeal to young readers, whether they were written specifically for that audience or for a general readership." With this far-reaching definition of YA literature, *Twentieth-Century Young Adult Writers* attempts to provide users with a comprehensive source of information on the authors read and enjoyed by young adults.

"The Gradual Education of a YA Novelist"

by Robert Cormier

Not so long ago, I was invited to a library near my home to hear a professor from a nearby college read from his unpublished novel. Not my idea of a terrific evening, but the librarian was an old friend and the professor was someone I had met casually some time before. He seemed like a nice guy. He turned out to be a superb reader. The selections he read aloud involved a young brother and sister and their mother. The characters were vibrant, the dialogue sizzling, the descriptions evocative of time and place.

The turnout on a snowy New England evening was small—six or seven of us gathered around a polished oak table. The writer asked for comments and suggestions. The comments were almost extravagantly favorable. What kind of suggestions did he want? He was quick to answer: he wanted to know where he could send the manuscript for possible publication. I remained silent as suggestions flew around about literary agents, small publishers, large publishers, the various writer-market publications. Finally, I asked whether he had considered the Young Adult market. He regarded me with something like horror in his eyes. "Young Adult?" Horror, too, in his rising voice. "But I didn't write it that way."

What way?

Before even trying to answer that question, let me say that his horrified response echoed my own, more than twenty years ago when my literary agent, Marilyn Marlow, listening to me talk about the first few chapters of what eventually became *The Chocolate War,* said that I seemed to be writing a YA novel. "What's a YA novel?" I asked in all innocence.

She explained what a YA novel was and scared me to death. How do you write for that strange category of people called Young Adults? Would I have to start my novel all over from page one? Simplify my plot? Dilute my characterizations? Wise agent that she is, Marilyn said to forget our conversation, continue the novel as I originally planned, and let her worry about the marketing.

I found out subsequently what that college professor had yet to find out, that Young Adult novels are contributing some of the finest writing to the world of children's literature and even beyond that world.

Although YA literature continues to be neglected or misunderstood, the gains made in the field are truly astonishing, considering that S.E. Hinton's *The Outsiders,* the first major work to be labeled YA, was published as recently as 1967, less than thirty years ago. In the blink of an eye those three decades represent in the long history of literature, YA writing has reached dazzling heights. The fact that the book you are holding in your hands exists at all is testimony to this glistening fact.

After Hinton opened the doors to YA literature, a giant walked in. Paul Zindel fulfilled her promise with his memorable novel *The Pigman,* written specifically for the YA market. Literature for young people was truly on its way. Such fine writers as John Donovan (*I'll Get There, It Better Be Worth the Trip*); M.E. Kerr (*Dinky Hocker Shoots Smack!*); Alice Childress (*A Hero Ain't Nothin' but a Sandwich*); and Bette Greene (*Summer of My German Soldier*) followed quickly. Their books were gobbled up by avid teenage readers, praised as serious efforts by critics and reviewers, and taught in classrooms by teachers grateful for books with characters and themes with whom their students could identify, books that created a bridge to the classics.

No longer did books written for young people have to deal with boys playing games or girls becoming cheerleaders, hoping for a date for the prom. The emergence of the YA genre prompted talented writers to tackle what formerly had been "taboo" subjects, ranging from drug use to homosexuality, violence to suicide. There was still room, of course, for romance and adventure and mystery but even these books received a more realistic treatment. Despite the sudden seriousness, writers found that whatever they were producing had to succeed first as entertaining stories. The magic of "Once upon a time..." still prevailed, whether the topic dealt with street gangs or vampires stalking the night.

Yet, doubt and confusion still exist about those strange denizens of today's literature—the Young Adult authors. Who are they, anyway? A glance at the writers in this biographical volume emphasizes that enigma. What are Stephen King, Agatha Christie, George Orwell, and John Steinbeck doing here with such YA standouts as Avi, Harry Mazer, Virginia Hamilton, and Christopher Crutcher?

The answer is a clue to the richness and variety of the field, and what Young Adult literature is all about. A book jacket may proclaim that a particular book is aimed at a "12 to 16" audience but unless storytelling magic is present, those designations are worthless. Simply put, YA books are those that appeal to young readers, whether they were written specifically for that audience or for a general readership.

Looking back, I realize that I have been influenced by three superb YA novels long before the label had ever been used: Mark Twain's *The Adventures of Tom Sawyer;* J.D. Salinger's *The Catcher in the Rye;* and John Knowles's *A Separate Peace.* These books opened wide vistas for me. My first fumbling attempts at writing centered on childhood and adolescence. These novels told me I was on the right path. I still read them with delight. If they were published for the first time today, would they be classified as YA novels? Perhaps, perhaps not. This probably underlines the confusion that exists about the genre—what it is and what it isn't. So the misconceptions continue.

Recently, I corresponded with Donald R. Gallo, a professor of English at Central Connecticut State University who not only teaches courses in literature for young adults but has edited several anthologies of works by YA writers. He regrets that many people remain entirely ignorant of the genre and thus are missing some of the best books being written today for any age group. He told me that once readers put aside their mistaken notions about YA novels—nice, safe stories like the "Sweet Valley High" series—they are free to discover the quality writing of Richard Peck, Sue Ellen Bridgers, Cynthia Voigt, Walter Dean Myers, and such newer writers in the field as Annette Curtis Klause and Linda Crew.

Don writes that many of the experienced teachers who enroll (often reluctantly) in his Literature for Young Adults courses find that the books in that course are among the best books they have *ever* read! "They are surprised to find themselves crying over the death of Johnny in S.E. Hinton's *The Outsiders,* being moved by the relationship between Rob and his father in Robert Newton Peck's *A Day No Pigs Would Die,* frustrated and fearful along with the narrator of Ouida Sebestyen's *The Girl in the Box,* and delighted by the outcome of Jean Davies Okimoto's *Molly by Any Other Name."*

Not only do these teachers feel better prepared to recommend books to the teenage readers in their classes but they begin to recommend those same "kids' books" to their spouses and other adult friends who are educators.

M. Jerry Weiss, Distinguished Service Professor at Jersey City State College, who is an acknowledged expert on the genre and irrepressibly enthusiastic, is irritated by those who consider YA books as narrow, trivial, and simplistic. The genre, in fact, represents *all* genres, he says—romance, mystery, fantasy, humor, drama, biography, and autobiography. Yet, the fact that these and other authorities must constantly come to its defense shows that mistaken notions about the genre continue. There is one aspect about which there is no mistake, however. That is its ability to touch off sparks of anger and indignation. Ironically, a genre that had once been regarded as mild and inoffensive has often been cast these days as a villain, a threat to young minds and hearts, and as a result, the object of censorship.

In a list compiled each year by People for the American Way of books that have faced the most challenges in courts, YA books make consistent appearances. The novels of Judy Blume (*Forever; Then Again, Maybe I Won't*), *Go Ask Alice,* and *The Chocolate War* always rank high on the roster of books under attack. They are usually in the company of *The Catcher in the Rye, The Diary of Anne Frank,* and *To Kill a Mockingbird.* Countless YA books have been subject to censorship attempts. The list, in fact, seems endless. Any book that dares to approach scene and character with a degree of realism is assaulted sooner or later.

The battle continues to this moment, in the spring of 1993. As I prepared to write this introduction, my telephone rang. A teacher from Worthington, Ohio, was on the line. She told me about a censorship problem she is having with my novel *We All Fall Down.* Her call was a plea for help. As usual in cases like this, I pledged my assistance, promised to send her supportive material, asked her to keep in touch. This kind of telephone call occurs several times a year. I always try to help—and I am always angry. Angry at those who seek to prevent my books from being read, angry at having to defend what I have written. Shouldn't the book stand by itself? Why should a writer have to defend it? Yet, how can I *not* come to its defense, not support someone who is fighting for the right of students to read my book? After all, it is *my* book, not the teacher's.

The agonies of censorship inflicted on teachers, librarians, students, publishers, and, of course, writers would consume this introduction if given full treatment. Its scope can't even be suggested in a few paragraphs. Yet, censorship cannot be ignored in any essay about Young Adult literature. My best response—and I think the best response of all writers—is simply to keep on writing.

Where is all this taking us? Where is YA literature going?

For an answer, I turned to Patty Campbell, general editor of Twayne's Young Adult Authors Series and winner of ALA's Grolier Foundation award for "an unusual contribution to the stimulation and guidance of reading by children and young people." It's going "to outer space and beyond," she writes, "or so it seems to me. Science fiction, horror, and particularly fantasy have grown in recent years from a specialized taste to a major part of young adult literature, and even standard writers who formerly dealt only with realism, have begun to add magical elements to their plots." She notes that "YA publishing and bookselling are being aimed at younger and younger readers, with the increasing sophistication of adolescents and the decreasing number of people in the 13-17 age range. But this last is a statistic that will soon change as the children of the boomers approach adolescence ready to dig in to their own literary feast." Thus will the genre continue to change and grow.

My own growth as a Young Adult writer virtually parallels the growth of the genre which I entered in 1974 with the publication of *The Chocolate War.* Like that college professor mentioned earlier, I was wary of and tentative about this new label, convinced that I had written a novel *about* teenagers and not *for* them. How could that novel be directed at young readers? It was concerned with physical and psychological violence, did not ignore masturbation and homosexuality, lacked role models. The bad guys won; the good guys lost. No one rode off into the sunset; instead an ambulance howled its way to the hospital. Yet, I opened the *New York Times* one Sunday morning and found *The Chocolate War* being reviewed on the front page of the Children's Book Section, praised as a Young Adult novel and "an ideal study for the high school classroom." I was delighted and confused and also uneasy about a novel of mine being studied by students, remembering how I had struggled years ago with *Silas Marner.* Would millions of kids hate me because they'd be forced to read my novel? I also was dismayed when I visited bookstores and found *The Chocolate War* among the children's books. What kind of writer had I become?

In the months following publication, I was caught up in a world illuminated by intelligence, wit, and enthusiasm, was introduced to the works of wonderful writers like Norma Klein (*Mom, the Wolf Man, and Me*); Robert Lipsyte (*The Contender*); and M.E. Kerr (*Is That You, Miss Blue?*). These and other writers I would read with such pleasure in the years ahead made me realize I had joined a caravan of stunningly talented people.

The fact that *The Chocolate War* and my subsequent novels found their way to classrooms made me a better writer. Spurred on by hundreds of letters from young readers, teachers, and librarians, ignited by the knowledge that my work would be studied, dissected, and probed in classrooms—these facts demanded that I seek the best within myself. One cannot write casually or carelessly for that kind of readership. The beauty of it all, I discovered, is that I could use all the craft at my command, could be sly and subtle, complex and confounding, and still have a young audience turning the pages of my books.

Thus went my education as a Young Adult writer, which I am certain mirrors the experience of many others who set out simply to tell a good story and find themselves with the YA label, grateful for its boundless graces. So, too, did that college professor become educated to the world of Young Adult literature. I know this because my telephone rang a few days after that library reading.

Could I recommend, he asked, a Young Adult editor to whom he could send his manuscript?

ADVISORY BOARD

READING LIST

Authors and Artists for Young Adults (continuing series). Detroit, Gale.

Breedlove, Wanda G., *Contemporary Trends in Children's and Young Adults' Literature: Research Perspectives.* South Carolina State Council of the International Reading Association, 1990.

Chambers, Aidan, *Reluctant Reader.* London, Pergamon Press, 1969.

Children's Literature Review (continuing series). Detroit, Gale.

Contemporary Literary Criticism (continuing series). Detroit, Gale.

Cuseo, Allan A., *Homosexual Characters in YA Novels: A Literary Analysis, 1969-1982.* Metuchen, New Jersey, Scarecrow Press, 1992.

Dixon, Bob. *Catching Them Young: Political Ideas in Children's Fiction.* London, Pluto Press, 1977.

Dixon, Bob. *Catching Them Young: Sex, Race and Class in Children's Fiction.* London, Pluto Press, 1977.

Donelson, Kenneth L., and Alleen Pace Nilsen, *Literature for Today's Young Adults,* fourth edition. Glenview, Illinois, Scott, Foresman, 1993.

Egoff, Sheila A., *Thursday's Child: Trends and Patterns in Contemporary Children's Literature.* Chicago, American Library Association, 1981.

Gallagher, Mary E, *Young Adult Literature: Issues and Perspectives.* Haverford, Pennsylvania, Catholic Library Association, 1988.

Harrison, Barbara, and Gregory Maguire, editors, *Innocence and Experience: Essays and Conversations on Children's Literature.* New York, Lothrop, Lee, and Shepard, 1987.

Hearne, Betsy, and Marilyn Kaye, editors, *Celebrating Children's Books: Essays on Children's Literature in Honor of Zena Sutherland.* New York, Lothrop, Lee, and Shepard, 1981.

Lenz, Millicent, and Ramona M. Mahood, editors, *Young Adult Literature: Background and Criticism.* Chicago, American Library Association, 1980.

MacCann, Donnarae, and Gloria Woodward, editors, *The Black American in Books for Children: Readings on Racism.* Metuchen, New Jersey, Scarecrow Press, 1972.

McVitty, Walter, *Innocence and Experience: Essays on Contemporary Australian Children's Writers.* Melbourne, Nelson, 1982.

Rees, David, *The Marble in the Water: Essays on Contemporary Writers of Fiction for Children and Young People.* Boston, Horn Book, 1980.

Roginski, Jim, *Behind the Covers: Interviews with Authors and Illustrators of Books for Children and Young Adults.* Littleton, Colorado, Libraries Unlimited, 1985.

Shapiro, Lillian L., editor, *Fiction for Youth: A Guide to Recommended Books.* New York, Neal-Schuman, 1980.

Snodgrass, Mary E., *Characters from Young Adult Literature.* Littleton, Colorado, Libraries Unlimited, 1991.

Stanford, Barbara Dodds, and Karima Amin, editors, *Black Literature for High School Students.* Urbana, Illinois, National Council of Teachers of English, 1978.

Sullivan, C.W., III, editor, *Science Fiction for Young Readers.* Westport, Connecticut, Greenwood Press, 1993.

Varlejs, Jhana, editor, *Young Adult Literature in the Seventies: A Selection of Readings.* Metuchen, New Jersey, Scarecrow Press, 1982.

CONTRIBUTORS

Hugh Agee
Janice M. Alberghene
Janice Antczak
Marilyn F. Apseloff
Judith Atkinson
Keith Barker
Henry J. Baron
Craig W. Barrow
Melanie Belviso
Linda G. Benson
Sharon Clontz Bernstein
Susan P. Bloom
Patricia L. Bradley
Bill Buchanan
Dennis Butts
Michael Cart
Rosemary Chance
Edgar L. Chapman
Joel D. Chaston
Cathy Chauvette
Ruth K.J. Cline
Carol Jones Collins
Hilary S. Crew
Hazel K. Davis
J. Madison Davis
Lesa Dill
Robert Dingley
Ruth E. Dishnow
Carol Doxey
William Ryland Drennan
Charles R. Duke
Eileen Dunlop
Audrey Eaglen
Edna Earl Edwards
Barbara Elleman
Laurie Ann Eno
Bonnie O. Ericson
Mary D. Esselman
Gwyneth Evans
Ron Evans
Jack Forman
Lawrence B. Fuller
Linda Garrett
Lois Rauch Gibson
Virginia L. Gleason
Karen J. Gould
M. Jean Greenlaw

Marlene San Miguel Groner
Laurie Schwartz Guttenberg
Lyman B. Hagen
Dennis Hamley
Jane Anne Hannigan
Terry Heller
James E. Higgins
Elbert R. Hill
Patricia Hill
Maryclare O'Donnell
Himmel
Peter Hollindale
Caroline C. Hunt
Sylvia Patterson Iskander
David Jenkinson
Judith Gero John
Deidre Johnson
Susanne L. Johnston
Patrick Jones
Antony Kamm
Joan F. Kaywell
Hugh T. Keenan
Donald J. Kenney
Cosette Kies
Lee Kingman
Fiona Lafferty
Keith Lawrence
Kate Lentz
Teri S. Lesesne
Leon Lewis
Myra Cohn Livingston
Mary Lowe-Evans
Hollis Lowery-Moore
Mary Lystad
Alf Mappin
Cathryn M. Mercier
Etta Miller
Joseph R. Millichap
Christian H. Moe
Karen Ferris Morgan
Gerald W. Morton
Charmaine Allmon Mosby
Mattie J. Mosley
John Murray
Claudia Nelson
Harold Nelson
Linda Newbery

Agnes Nieuwenhuizen
Alleen Pace Nilsen
Jill Paton Walsh
Jenny Pausacker
Pat Pflieger
Kathy Piehl
Reba Pinney
Elizabeth A. Poe
Catherine Price
Robert Protherough
Nicholas Ranson
Sheila Ray
Arthea J.S. Reed
John Reiss
Garyn G. Roberts
Linda Ross
Leonie Margaret Rutherford
Walker Rutledge
Maurice Saxby
Gary D. Schmidt
Richard D. Seiter
Pamela L. Shelton
Karen Patricia Smith
Mary Snyder
Albert F. Spencer
J.D. Stahl
Madeleine B. Stern
Michael Stone
Robbie W. Strickland
Tracy J. Sukraw
Zena Sutherland
Gillian Thomas
John Rowe Townsend
Jan Tyler
Michael J. Tyrkus
Suzanne M. Valentic
Kay E. Vandergrift
Karen E. Walsh
Donna R. White
Kerry White
Frank Whitehead
Angela Wigan
Linda Wilson
Louise J. Winters
Lisa A. Wroble
Jessica Yates
Laura M. Zaidman

TWENTIETH-CENTURY
YOUNG ADULT WRITERS

Richard Adams
C.S. Adler
Arnold Adoff
Joan Aiken
Vivien Alcock
Louisa May Alcott
James Aldridge
Lloyd Alexander
V.C. Andrews
Maya Angelou
Anonymous (*Go Ask Alice*)
Piers Anthony
William H. Armstrong
Brent Ashabranner
Sandy Asher
Bernard Ashley
Isaac Asimov
Margaret Atwood
Avi

Alice Bach
Allan Baillie
James Baldwin
Marion Dane Bauer
Nina Bawden
Peter S. Beagle
Harry Behn
Nathaniel Benchley
Jay Bennett
Francesca Lia Block
Joan W. Blos
Judy Blume
Janet Bode
Janine Boissard
Nancy Bond
Frank Bonham
L.M. Boston
Ray Bradbury
Marion Zimmer Bradley
Robin F. Brancato
Robbie Branscum
Sue Ellen Bridgers
Bruce Brooks
Terry Brooks
Eve Bunting
Robert J. Burch
Anthony Burgess
Olive Ann Burns
Edgar Rice Burroughs
Hester Burton
Octavia E. Butler
Betsy Byars

Patricia Calvert
Eleanor Cameron

Philip Caputo
Orson Scott Card
Alden R. Carter
Sylvia Cassedy
Rebecca Caudill
Betty Cavanna
Aidan Chambers
C.J. Cherryh
Grace Chetwin
Alice Childress
Agatha Christie
John Christopher
Marchette Chute
Sandra Cisneros
Patricia Clapp
Mary Higgins Clark
Arthur C. Clarke
Eldridge Cleaver
Vera and Bill Cleaver
Bruce Clements
Elizabeth Coatsworth
Brock Cole
Christopher Collier and
    James Lincoln Collier
Hila Colman
Ellen Conford
Jane Leslie Conly
Pam Conrad
Susan Cooper
Robert Cormier
Gary Crew
Linda Crew
Michael Crichton
Gillian Cross
Kevin Crossley-Holland
Chris Crutcher
Richie Tankersley Cusick

Roald Dahl
Maureen Daly
Paula Danziger
Jenny Davis
Terry Davis
Julie Reece Deaver
Farrukh Dhondy
Peter Dickinson
Eilis Dillon
Berlie Doherty
John Donovan
Michael Anthony Dorris
Arthur Conan Doyle
Brian Doyle
Diane Duane
Lois Duncan

Eileen Dunlop
Clyde Edgerton
Amy Ehrlich
Sarah Ellis
Ralph Ellison
Sylvia Louise Engdahl
Jeannette Hyde Eyerly

Walter Farley
Penelope Farmer
Howard Fast
Nicholas Fisk
Paul Fleischman
Ian Fleming
June Foley
Esther Forbes
Paula Fox
Anne Frank
Russell Freedman
Paul French
Jean Fritz
Monica Furlong

Ernest J. Gaines
Jane Gardam
Nancy Garden
Leon Garfield
Alan Garner
Eve Garnett
Jean Craighead George
Adèle Geras
William Gibson
Nikki Giovanni
Fred Gipson
Mel Glenn
William Golding
Nadine Gordimer
Lorenz Graham
Cynthia D. Grant
Joanne Greenberg
Bette Greene
Sheila Greenwald
Rosa Guy

Ann Halam
Barbara Hall
Lynn Hall
Virginia Hamilton
Cynthia Harnett
James S. Haskins
Esther Hautzig
Ann Head
Robert A. Heinlein
Joseph Heller
Nat Hentoff

Frank Herbert
Patricia Hermes
James Herriot
Douglas Hill
Tony Hillerman
S.E. Hinton
Minfong Ho
Will Hobbs
Anne Holm
Felice Holman
H.M. Hoover
James A. Houston
Janni Howker
Linda Hoy
Dean Hughes
Langston Hughes
Monica Hughes
Ted Hughes
Irene Hunt
Kristin Hunter
Mollie Hunter
Zora Neale Hurston
Johanna Hurwitz
Aldous Huxley

Hadley Irwin

Brian Jacques
Paul B. Janeczko
Annabel and Edgar Johnson
Allan Frewin Jones
Diana Wynne Jones
June Jordan
Norton Juster

Josephine Kamm
Harold Keith
Victor Kelleher
Carol Kendall
M.E. Kerr
Ken Kesey
Jamaica Kincaid
Stephen King
Annette Curtis Klause
Norma Klein
Robin Klein
John Knowles
R.R. Knudson
Ron Koertge
E.L. Konigsburg
Dean R. Koontz
Joseph Krumgold

Mercedes R. Lackey
Jane Langton
Kathryn Lasky

Jean Lee Latham
Louise Lawrence
Ursula K. Le Guin
Harper Lee
Mildred Lee
Tanith Lee
Robert Leeson
Madeleine L'Engle
Julius Lester
Steven Levenkron
Sonia Levitin
Myron Levoy
C.S. Lewis
Elizabeth Foreman Lewis
Kenneth Lillington
Joan Lingard
Robert Lipsyte
Jean Little
Jack London
Lois Lowry
Katie Letcher Lyle

R.A. MacAvoy
Michelle Magorian
Margaret Mahy
Kevin Major
Jan Mark
John Marsden
Bobbie Ann Mason
Mark Mathabane
Sharon Bell Mathis
William Mayne
Harry Mazer
Norma Fox Mazer
Anne McCaffrey
Geraldine McCaughrean
Carson McCullers
Eloise Jarvis McGraw
Vonda N. McIntyre
Patricia A. McKillip
Robin McKinley
Terry McMillan
Florence Crannell Means
Cornelia Lynde Meigs
Milton Meltzer
Eve Merriam
Carolyn Meyer
Gloria D. Miklowitz
Betty Miles
Frances A. Miller
Jim Wayne Miller
Margaret Mitchell
Louise Moeri
Nicholasa Mohr
N. Scott Momaday

Toni Morrison
Farley Mowat
Patricia Moyes
Shirley Rousseau Murphy
Walter Dean Myers

Beverley Naidoo
Lensey Namioka
Phyllis Reynolds Naylor
Jan Needle
John Neufeld
Emily Cheney Neville
Joan Lowery Nixon
Sterling North
Andre Norton
Christine Nöstlinger

Robert C. O'Brien
Scott O'Dell
Jean Davies Okimoto
Zibby Oneal
Judith O'Neill
Doris Orgel
Uri Orlev
George Orwell

Ruth Park
Katherine Paterson
Jill Paton Walsh
Gary Paulsen
Kit Pearson
Richard Peck
Robert Newton Peck
P.J. Petersen
K.M. Peyton
Joan Phipson
Meredith Ann Pierce
Tamora Pierce
Christopher Pike
Daniel Manus Pinkwater
Sylvia Plath
Chaim Potok
Philip Pullman
Howard Pyle

Ayn Rand
Ellen Raskin
Marjorie Kinnan Rawlings
Chap Reaver
Lynne Reid Banks
Anne Rice
Conrad Richter
Hans Peter Richter
Ann Rinaldi
Willo Davis Roberts

Keith Robertson
Spider Robinson
Barbara Rogasky
Margaret I. Rostkowski
Gillian Rubinstein
Lois Ruby
Cynthia Rylant

Marilyn Sachs
J.D. Salinger
Pamela Sargent
Harriet May Savitz
Sandra Scoppettone
Ouida Sebestyen
Ian Serraillier
Pamela Service
Ntozake Shange
Zoa Sherburne
Upton Sinclair
Marilyn Singer
William Sleator
Jan Slepian
Doris Buchanan Smith
Zilpha Keatley Snyder
Gary Soto
Ivan Southall
Muriel Spark
Elizabeth George Speare
Eleanor Spence
Art Spiegelman
Jerry Spinelli
Suzanne Fisher Staples
John Steinbeck
Robert Louis Stevenson
Mary Stewart
R.L. Stine
Mary Stolz
Rosemary Sutcliff
Glendon Swarthout
Robert Swindells

Amy Tan
Eleanora E. Tate
Mildred D. Taylor
Theodore Taylor
Stephen N. Tchudi
Colin Thiele
Joyce Carol Thomas
J.R.R. Tolkien
John Rowe Townsend
Sue Townsend
Geoffrey Trease
Henry Treece
Dalton Trumbo
John R. Tunis

Mark Twain
Anne Tyler

Jean Ure

Joan D. Vinge
Elizabeth Gray Vining
Cynthia Voigt
Kurt Vonnegut, Jr.

Amelia Elizabeth Walden
Alice Walker
Mildred Pitts Walter
Walter Wangerin, Jr.
Maureen Crane Wartski
Sally Watson
H.G. Wells
Rosemary Wells
Barbara Wersba
Jessamyn West
Robert Westall
Ellen Emerson White
Robb White
T.H. White
Phyllis A. Whitney
Elie Wiesel
Brenda Wilkinson
Barbara Willard
Margaret Willey
Rita Williams-Garcia
Patricia Windsor
Maia Wojciechowska
Virginia Euwer Wolff
Hilma Wolitzer
Patricia C. Wrede
Richard Wright
Patricia Wrightson

Elizabeth Yates
Laurence Yep
Jane Yolen

Jane Breskin Zalben
Paul Zindel

A

ADAMS, Richard (George). British. Born in Newbury, Berkshire, England, 9 May 1920. Educated at Bradfield College, Berkshire, 1933-38; Worcester College, Oxford, 1938-39, 1946-48, B.A. in modern history 1948, M.A. 1953. Served in the British Army, 1940-45. Married Barbara Elizabeth Acland in 1949; two daughters. Worked in Ministry of Housing and Local Government, London, 1948-68; Assistant Secretary, Department of the Environment, London, 1968-74; full-time writer, since 1974. Writer-in-residence, University of Florida, Gainesville, 1975, and Hollins College, Virginia, 1976. President, Royal Society for the Prevention of Cruelty to Animals, 1980-82 (resigned). Independent Conservative parliamentary candidate for Spelthorne, 1983. Recipient: Carnegie Medal, 1972, and Guardian award, 1973, both for *Watership Down;* Fellow, Royal Society of Literature, 1975; California Young Readers' Association award, 1977. Agent: David Higham Associates Ltd., 5-8 Lower John St., London W1R 4HA. Address: 26 Church Street, Whitchurch, Hampshire RG28 7AR, England.

PUBLICATIONS FOR YOUNG ADULTS

Fiction

Watership Down. London, Collings, 1972; New York, Macmillan, 1974.
Shardik. London, Allen Lane-Collings, 1974; New York, Simon & Schuster, 1975.
The Plague Dogs, illustrated by A. Wainwright. London, Allen Lane-Collings, 1977; New York, Knopf, 1978.
The Bureaucats, illustrated by Robin Jacques. Viking Kestrel, 1985.
Traveller. New York, Knopf, 1988; London, Hutchinson, 1989.

Poetry

The Tyger Voyage, illustrated by Nicola Bayley. London, Cape, and New York, Knopf, 1976.
The Adventures and Brave Deeds of the Ship's Cat on the Spanish Maine: Together with the Most Lamentable Losse of the Alcestis and Triumphant Firing of the Port of Chagres, illustrated by Alan Aldridge and Harry Willock. New York, Knopf, 1977.

Other

Nature through the Seasons, with Max Hooper, illustrated by David Goddard and Adrian Williams. London, Kestrel, and New York, Simon & Schuster, 1975.
Nature Day and Night, with Max Hooper, illustrated by David Goddard and Stephen Lee. London, Kestrel, and New York, Viking, 1978.
The Watership Down Film Picture Book. London, Allen Lane, and New York, Macmillan, 1978.
The Iron Wolf and Other Stories (folktales), illustrated by Yvonne Gilbert and Jennifer Campbell. London, Allen Lane, 1980; as *The Unbroken Web,* New York, Crown, 1980.
Editor, *Grimm's Fairy Tales,* illustrated by Pauline Ellison. London, Routledge, 1981.

Editor, *Richard Adams's Favorite Animal Stories,* illustrated by Beverly Butcher. London, Octopus, 1981.
Editor, *The Best of Ernest Thompson Seton.* London, Fontana, 1982.

PUBLICATIONS FOR ADULTS

Novels

The Girl in a Swing. London, Allen Lane, and New York, Knopf, 1980.
Maia. London, Viking, 1984; New York, Knopf, 1985.

Poetry

The Legend of Te Tuna. Los Angeles, Sylvester and Orphanos, 1982; London, Sidgwick and Jackson, 1986.

Other

Voyage through the Antarctic, with Ronald Lockley. London, Allen Lane, 1982; New York, Viking, 1986.
A Nature Diary. London, Viking, 1985; New York, Viking, 1986.
Editor and contributor, *Occasional Poets: An Anthology.* London, Viking, 1986.
The Day Gone By: An Autobiography. London, Hutchinson, 1990; New York, Knopf, 1991.

*

Media Adaptations: *Watership Down* (animated film), Avco-Embassy, 1978.

Critical Study: Entry in *Children's Literature Review,* Volume 20, Detroit, Gale, 1990, pp. 10-32.

*   *   *

Richard Adams is probably best known for his classic novel *Watership Down,* marketed for juveniles in England and for adults in America. He reportedly composed the book to amuse his two daughters who insisted that he write the tale down. It took Adams two years to complete the novel, whereafter it was rejected by four publishers and three agents. Since Adams wished to present his daughters with a published version, he was almost at the point of publishing it at his own expense when he read of a small publisher who had just reissued an animal fantasy. Rex Collins accepted *Watership Down* for a limited printing of 2,000 copies. Reprinted later by Penguin, the novel was a surprising financial success.

Watership Down tells of the exploits of a group of rabbits who seek a new home when their old one is leveled by developers who plan to gas all animal life. Even though older readers are tempted to read the novel as allegory or fable, Adams comments it is merely a story about rabbits and as such can be enjoyed by a younger readership. In addition to being a novel of tremendous imagination, describing a civilization with its own language, politics, history, and mythology, *Watership Down* is a well-crafted novel in the traditional sense with cliff-hanging chapter endings, excellent controlled tone, and a vast array of character types.

Adams's second novel, *Shardik*, is set in a mythical country and time. Shardik is a giant bear, respected and worshipped by the inhabitants of the country. Allison Lurie of the *New York Review of Books* views the novel as an ecological allegory of how humans choose and follow their gods. Belief causes cruel and destructive acts, as well as novel ones. The language of the novel is descriptive. It shows Adams's love of similes. Some critiques believe it to be a colorless facsimile of an epic, grim, obsessed with virginity, and full of the weakly supernatural.

The third novel by Adams, *The Plague Dogs*, is a return to the anthropomorphic use of animals. This novel is about two dogs who escape from an experimental laboratory in the English Lake District. The novel is criticized as being too literarily self-conscious and replete with tantrums, puns, parody and, perhaps worst of all, bitter contempt. Even when being praised, the novel is viewed by most as savage satire.

The Girl in a Swing relates the meeting and marriage of Alan Desland and the mysterious German woman, Kaethe. It is both supernatural and erotic, and may be viewed as both too mature and too intense for younger readers.

Maia is a tale of adventure and romance set in the Berklan Empire, a magical land. It deals with the life and adventures of a beautiful girl sold into slavery. Although degraded, the girl survives and becomes a heroine to her people. The novel has been praised as delightful and full of suspense.

The hero of Adams's novel *Traveller* is General Robert E. Lee's horse. Seen through the horse's eyes, the events of the Civil War are recounted. Once again a wise animal laments the follies of humans, especially their tendency to kill one another. The novel is composed as a conversation between Traveller and his stablemate, a cat named Tom. Amidst the horse's tales of the agony of defeat and the sweetness of victory is a tribute to Robert E. Lee.

A giant among contemporary English writers of fantasy, Adams will be remembered not only for his originality, epic scope, and masterful storytelling skills, but for his faith that youth and children will understand and appreciate the values inherent in his timeless stories.

—Lesa Dill

ADLER, C(arole) S(chwerdtfeger). American. Born in Rockaway Beach, Long Island, New York, 23 February 1932. Educated at Hunter College (now the City University of New York), B.A. (cum laude) 1953; Russell Sage College, Troy, New York, M.S. 1964. Married Arnold R. Adler in 1952; three sons, one deceased. Advertising assistant, 1952-54, Worthington Corp., Harrison, New Jersey; English teacher, 1967-77, Niskayuna Middle Schools, New York. Since 1977, writer. Recipient: Golden Kite award from Society of Children's Book Writers, and "Book of the Year" citation from Child Study Association, both 1979, and William Allen White Children's Book award, 1982, all for *The Magic of the Glits;* "Best Young Adult Book of the Year" citation, American Library Association, 1983, for *The Shell Lady's Daughter;* Children's Book award from Child Study Children's Book Committee, Bank St. College of

Education, 1985, for *With Westie and the Tin Man;* "Children's Choice" citation from International Reading Association and Children's Book Council, 1979, for *The Magic of the Glits,* 1987, for *Split Sisters,* and 1991, for *One Sister Too Many* and *Ghost Brother.* Address: 1350 Ruffner Rd., Schenectady, NY 12309, U.S.A.

PUBLICATIONS FOR YOUNG ADULTS

Fiction

The Magic of the Glits, illustrated by Ati Forberg. New York, Macmillan, 1979.
The Silver Coach. New York, Coward, 1979.
In Our House Scott Is My Brother. New York, Macmillan, 1980.
Shelter on Blue Barns Road. New York, Macmillan, 1981.
The Cat That Was Left Behind. New York, Clarion Books, 1981.
Down by the River. New York, Coward, 1981.
Footsteps on the Stairs. New York, Delacorte, 1982.
Some Other Summer (sequel to *The Magic of the Glits*). New York, Macmillan, 1982.
The Evidence That Wasn't There. New York, Clarion Books, 1982.
The Once in a While Hero. New York, Coward, 1982.
Binding Ties. New York, Delacorte, 1983.
Get Lost, Little Brother. New York, Clarion Books, 1983.
Roadside Valentine. New York, Macmillan, 1983.
The Shell Lady's Daughter. New York, Coward, 1983.
Fly Free. New York, Coward, 1984.
Good-bye, Pink Pig. New York, Putnam, 1985.
Shadows on Little Reef Bay. New York, Clarion Books, 1985.
With Westie and the Tin Man. New York, Macmillan, 1985.
Split Sisters, illustrated by Mike Wimmer. New York, Macmillan, 1986.
Kiss the Clown. New York, Clarion Books, 1986.
If You Need Me. New York, Macmillan, 1987.
Carly's Buck. New York, Clarion Books, 1987.
Eddie's Blue-Winged Dragon. New York, Putnam, 1988.
Always and Forever Friends. New York, Clarion Books, 1988.
One Sister Too Many (sequel to *Split Sisters*). New York, Macmillan, 1989.
The Lump in the Middle. New York, Clarion Books, 1989.
Ghost Brother. New York, Clarion Books, 1990.
Help, Pink Pig! (sequel to *Good-Bye, Pink Pig*). New York, Putnam, 1990.
Mismatched Summer. New York, Putnam, 1991.
A Tribe for Lexi. New York, Macmillan, 1991.
Tuna Fish Thanksgiving. New York, Clarion Books, 1992.
Daddy's Climbing Tree. New York, Clarion Books, 1993.
Willie, the Frog Prince. New York, Clarion Books, 1994.

*

Media Adaptations: *Get Lost, Little Brother* (cassette), Talking Books, 1983.

Biography: Entry in *Sixth Book of Junior Authors,* New York, H.W. Wilson, 1989; essay in *Authors and Artists for Young Adults,* Volume 4, Gale, 1990; essay in *Something About the Author Autobiography Series,* Volume 15, Detroit, Gale, 1993; essay in *Speaking for Ourselves, Too* compiled and edited by Donald R. Gallo, National Council of Teachers of English, 1993.

Critical Study: Entry in *Contemporary Literary Criticism,* Volume 35, Detroit, Gale, 1985.

C. S. Adler comments:

I'm not one of those adventuresome writers who take to sea on a blank page without first charting their courses. Before I sit down to that emptiness, which is now for me a computer screen, I know who my characters are and have probably done a written portrait of the main ones. I know the theme of the story I'm going to tell and I've sketched out a plot in a sequence of events that will each become a chapter. I know my destination before I start telling myself the story in the first draft of the book, but that doesn't mean there's no adventure for me in the telling. There are minor characters and incidents that surprise me, quirks of my characters that are revealed to me by what they suddenly say or do, bits of interesting dialogue that can't possibly have come from my head.

Each of the five or six drafts I go through before I subject my book to the keen eye of an editor has some challenge and pleasure in accomplishment for me. I just plain like writing—all aspects of it. Although, something I like even better is reading a wonderful book some other author has written.

*   *   *

A sensitive, sympathetic writer, skillfully dealing with problems facing adolescents, C.S. Adler ranks high on the list of young adult writers. She has received many awards and honors, including Best Young Adult Book of the Year citation in 1983 from the American Library Association for *The Shell Lady's Daughter,* besides recognition for her books for younger readers.

Ms. Adler's award-winning *The Magic of the Glits,* Junior Literary Guild selection *The Silver Coach,* along with *Good-bye, Pink Pig* and *Help, Pink Pig!,* weave a little magic throughout endearing, entertaining stories. The Glits are magical, sparkling creatures with the capability of granting wishes and filling humans with fuzzy joy. The Glits make the summer bearable for twelve-year-old Jeremy with his broken leg and Lynette who has recently lost her mother and has been pushed off on Jeremy and his family because her stepfather doesn't know how to cope with her. In *The Silver Coach,* Grandma Wallace has a small silver coach that shimmers and grows big enough to take twelve-year-old Chris and younger sister Jackie places far away to escape the trauma of their parents' divorce. A pink quartz pig figurine is the magical means of helping Amanda escape to an imaginary world in the pink pig stories where she battles dangers, but wins even in the real world with help from the pink pig. Sometimes young people need imagination and magic to help deal with reality, and these stories fufill that need while conveying love, caring, sharing and growing, and learning to face problems of divorce, death, and other obstacles while growing up in the real world.

In *Some Other Summer*, a sequel to *The Magic of the Glits,* Jeremy comes to the ranch where Lynette is living with her Uncle Josh who has adopted her. Lynette is going on thirteen and Jeremy is going on eighteen, and Lynette finds she has a crush on Jeremy. Unfortunately, her feelings are not returned because Lynette's pretty cousin has captured his eye. But Lynette learns that she is still an important part of Jeremy's life as well as that of her uncle, and she faces reality.

In *Carly's Buck,* Carly Alinsky goes to stay with her aunt and uncle in the Adirondack Mountains of upstate New York after her mother dies of cancer, and she decides she doesn't want to stay with her seemingly uncaring father. When Carly decides to protect a family of deer just before the hunting season, her favorite buck is accidentally shot and killed by a neighbor boy's father. It is difficult for Carly to realize that everyone makes mistakes, including herself, and that she is just as guilty as her father of not showing enough love and affection in their lives. This is a warm, loving story of a young girl coming to grips with reality and with herself, learning to face her shortcomings and vowing to do something about them. Young adults will learn from this book, while enjoying a light romance.

With Westie and the Tin Man portrays fifteen-year-old Greg Wightman, just released from a juvenile detention center after spending a year there for shoplifting. He goes home to two recovering alcoholics, his mother and her business partner, Manny. Greg becomes friends with Annabelle Waks, an honest, responsible young girl who is having problems of her own at home with a mother and father talking of divorce. Greg learns, like recovering alcoholics, that he must stop lying to himself as well as to others, stop rationalizing and denying things that make him look bad, and stop feeling guilty about the past. Ms. Adler has written an informative book about AA and recovering alcoholics, but has used this information to show that the AA concepts can be applied to the problems of an adolescent recovering from a history of shoplifting and a stint in a correctional facility. An enlightening book, young adults will gain from the information to influence their own lives.

Split Sisters and *One Sister Too Many* are about sisters Case and Jen living in Connecticut with a mother and stepfather who split up and then get back together. Then an unexpected member arrives in the form of a screaming, howling baby girl who keeps the family on edge with her squalling. A babysitter is hired to help, but the babysitter turns out to have mental problems and kidnaps the baby. Once more the family is faced with a crisis, but sticks together and faces it head-on. With Case's help and sharp insight, the baby is found, and once more the family is happy. Spell-binding books that keep the reader's nose glued to the tension-filled pages, the books are highly recommended for young adults, especially those with family problems.

In *Mismatched Summer* two seventh-grade girls, totally different from each other, are forced to spend a summer together, but after exuberant, fun-loving Mikale causes shy, orderly Meg the devastating embarrassment of losing her pants in the middle of a Fourth of July parade, the girls work out their differences. They learn to blend together, growing and learning by allowing a bit of each to rub off on the other during their sandpaper-like summer. A treat for young adults, the book is warm and humorous, delightfully realistic.

Thirteen-year-old Kelsey Morris and her family are uprooted from their home when Mr. Morris loses his job in *The Lump in the Middle.* Kelsey, a middle child, is blamed for everything that goes wrong and feels neglected, awkward, and unwanted. With the help of her friend Gabe whose father is dying of cancer, Kelsy learns that life would be easier for her if she tried harder to get along with others, particularly her own family. This is a thought-provoking story that middle children especially will enjoy.

C.S. Adler writes about many problems facing young people, including terminal illnesses, death, alcoholism, being left out, having parents that seem uncaring and unfeeling, and on and on. She handles these problems in a warm and positive manner, showing that young people are capable of facing these problems and becoming stronger because of them.

—Carol Doxey

ADOFF, Arnold. American. Born in New York City, 16 July 1935. Educated at City College of New York (now City College of the City University of New York), B.A. 1956; Columbia University, New York, 1956-58; New School for Social Research, New York, 1965-67. Served in the New York National Guard. Married Virginia Hamilton in 1960; one daughter and one son. Poet, anthologist, and fiction writer. Teacher in New York City public schools, 1957-69; literary agent, Arnold Adoff Agency, Yellow Springs, Ohio, since 1977. Instructor in federal projects at New York University, Connecticut College, and other institutions; visiting professor, Queens College, Flushing, New York, 1986-87. Lecturer at colleges throughout the United States; consultant in children's literature, poetry, and creative writing. Member of planning commission, Yellow Springs. Recipient: "Children's Books of the Year" citation, Child Study Association of America, 1968, for *I Am the Darker Brother,* 1969, for *City in All Directions,* and 1986, for *Sports Pages;* "Best Children's Books" citation, School Library Journal, 1971, for *It Is the Poem Singing into Your Eyes,* and 1973, for *Black Is Brown Is Tan;* "Notable Children's Trade Book" citation, Children's Book Council/National Council for Social Studies, 1974, and "Children's Choice" citation, International Reading Association/Children's Book Council, 1985, both for *My Black Me: A Beginning Book of Black Poetry;* "Books for the Teen Age" citation, New York Public Library, 1980, 1981, and 1982, all for *It Is the Poem Singing into Your Eyes;* special recognition, Jane Addams Children's Book award, 1983, for *All the Colors of the Race;* poetry award, National Council of Teachers of English, 1988. Address: Box 293, Yellow Springs, OH 45387, U.S.A.

PUBLICATIONS FOR YOUNG ADULTS

Poetry

Editor, *I Am the Darker Brother: An Anthology of Modern Poems by Negro Americans.* New York, Macmillan, 1968.
Editor, *Black on Black: Commentaries by Negro Americans.* New York, Macmillan, 1968.
Editor, *City in All Directions: An Anthology of Modern Poems.* New York, Macmillan, 1969.
Editor, *Black Out Loud: An Anthology of Modern Poems by Black Americans,* illustrated by Alvin Hollingsworth. New York, Macmillan, 1970.
Editor, *Brothers and Sisters: Modern Stories by Black Americans.* New York, Macmillan, 1970.
Malcolm X, illustrated by John Wilson. New York, Crowell, 1970.
Editor, *It Is the Poem Singing in Your Eyes: An Anthology of New Young Poets.* New York, Harper, 1971.
Editor, *The Poetry of Black America: An Anthology of the 20th Century.* New York, Harper, 1973.
Editor, *My Black Me: A Beginning Book of Black Poetry.* New York, Dutton, 1974.
Editor, *Celebrations: A New Anthology of Black American Poetry.* Chicago, Follett, 1977.
Editor, *The Next America,* forthcoming.
Slow Dance Heartbreak Blues, forthcoming.

PUBLICATIONS FOR CHILDREN

Poetry

MA nDA LA, illustrated by Emily McCully. New York, Harper, 1971.

Black Is Brown Is Tan, illustrated by Emily McCully. New York, Harper, 1973.
Make a Circle Keep Us In: Poems for a Good Day, illustrated by Ronald Himler. New York, Delacorte, 1975.
Big Sister Tells Me That I'm Black, illustrated by Lorenzo Lynch. New York, Holt, 1976.
Tornado!, illustrated by Ronald Himler. New York, Delacorte, 1977.
Under the Early Morning Trees, illustrated by Ronald Himler. New York, Dutton, 1978.
Where Wild Willie, illustrated by Emily McCully. New York, Harper, 1978.
Eats, illustrated by Susan Russo. New York, Lothrop, 1979.
I Am the Running Girl, illustrated by Ronald Himler. New York, Harper, 1979.
Friend Dog, illustrated by Troy Howell. New York, Lippincott, 1980.
OUTside INside Poems, illustrated by John Steptoe. New York, Lothrop, 1981.
Today We Are Brother and Sister, illustrated by Glo Coalson. New York, Lothrop, 1981.
All the Colors of the Race, illustrated by John Steptoe. New York, Lothrop, 1982.
Birds, illustrated by Troy Howell. New York, Lippincott, 1982.
The Cabbages Are Chasing the Rabbits, illustrated by Janet Stevens. San Diego, Harcourt, 1985.
Sports Pages, illustrated by Steven Kuzma. New York, Lippincott, 1986.
Chocolate Dreams, illustrated by Turi MacCombie. New York, Lothrop, 1988.
Flamboyan, illustrated by Karen Barbour. San Diego, Harcourt, 1988.
Greens, illustrated by Betsy Lewin. New York, Lothrop, 1988.
Hard to Be Six, illustrated by Cheryl Hanna. New York, Lothrop, 1990.
In for Winter, Out for Spring, illustrated by Jerry Pinkney. San Diego, Harcourt, 1991.
The Return of Rex and Ethel. San Diego, Harcourt, 1993.

*

Biography: Entry in *Fourth Book of Junior Authors and Illustrators,* New York, Wilson, 1978; essay in *Something about the Author Autobiography Series,* Volume 15, Detroit, Gale, 1993.

Critical Study: Entry in *Children's Literature Review,* Volume 7, Detroit, Gale, 1984.

*   *   *

With the current emphasis on multiculturalism in the children's book world, it is fascinating to remember what Arnold Adoff regarded in the late sixties, seventies, and eighties as "the safe and traditional versified bunny and the ossified narrative" of children's literature, a condition which Nancy Larrick partially touched upon in her landmark article, "The All White World of Children's Books." It was the late sixties when Adoff began publishing his anthologies, *I Am the Darker Brother: An Anthology of Modern Poems by Negro Americans* and *City in All Directions,* a book dedicated to the memory of Malcolm X whose poems, as Adoff wrote, "will help us understand cities, their inhabitants and some of the changes that are taking place." Although Adoff was not the first to include poets of all colors and countries, his own New York background (teaching and counseling in the New York public schools for twelve years and his marriage to Virginia Hamilton) made him an advocate for the appreciation of the rich and often overlooked contributions of black poets.

Adoff's goal "to create collections of Black American poetry for young readers...to help us reach some level of multi-racial/multi-cultural reality in our culture, in our literature—to go beyond the so-called American literature texts" would seem rooted in a view of himself as "the ultimate integrationist in my own life." Adoff includes such well-known poets as Langston Hughes, Paul Laurence Dunbar, Gwendolyn Brooks, and Arna Bontemps; but his greater contribution is making his readers aware of Sterling Brown, Ray Durem, Mari Evans, Robert Hayden and dozens of others whose names were/are unknown among the children (and very possibly the parents, teachers, and librarians) he reaches. These, and others, are anthologies compiled to introduce poetry beyond the range of the "aproned bears and the quick and easy rhyme," to pay tribute to black poets, and to make all readers aware of the wealth of literature beyond "a replication of the existing, a literature and education for the unimaginative and unjust status quo; a reactive 'moving backward, retrenching into materials and methods,' as James Moffett has written, 'long since tried and found untrue.'"

The manifestations of what he regards as true is both the subject, object, and heart of Arnold Adoff's work, whether it presents itself in further anthologies or in his own poetry. Stressing his belief in the "possibility, and potential for change" he becomes the inventor of change as he views/viewed it in the very process of writing, demonstrating to children and adults alike how he fashions his poems on long scrolls of paper, juxtaposing lines and words in phrases and sentences which demand unusual attention to seeing, speaking and breathing, and writing and rewriting. Oftentimes he dares the reader to unlock the meaning of what he is saying in an arch display of unusual configurations. Adoff makes a metaphor for his life and work as "some juggling, shuffling, middle-class/ middle-aged clown on the low slack rope, juggling those Indian clubs: of meaning/music; balancing symmetrical form, truth, beauty and some new American way!" In this description alone can be found the flavor of his speaking and writing. "If all the parallel cultures and literatures of all the Americas are not presented with force and conviction, he writes, "then no part of the so-called American children's literature is true; all must fall like some house of cards built on partial foundations."

Adoff's poems are notable for their great sense of earthiness—those feelings and things which nourish both the body and mind whether in such wonders as the grass, hoses, beans, and pea soup of *Greens,* the chocolate chip cookies, chocolate-covered marshmallows, a "100% solid milk chocolate delicious rabbit" of *Chocolate Dreams,* or the "great goblets of pudding powder in milk," pepperoni slices and a recipe for Sunday morning toast of *Eats.* Throughout his work runs a deep feeling for the sanctity of family life—its roots, its everyday joys. The family, he writes in *Make a Circle Keep Us In* is "safe and warm / and full / and banging into beds / to slee / p / we are / each with each / and stronger than a show / off / storm / we are / we."

In *All the Colors of the Race,* (1985), the narrator tells us that "Mama is chocolate" and "Daddy is vanilla" whereas "...I must be pecans / roasted / toasted; / almond / wal nut three / scoop combination / cone: / melting under / kisses. / It is a new color. / It is a new flavor / For / love."

An idiosyncratic use of punctuation and capitalization, which he believes affects the rhythm and movement of a poem, characterizes Adoff's writing, often (deliberately?) surprising the eye and ear of those accustomed to some codification for reading. Adoff uses rhyme very sparingly, and according to no formal pattern; each book promises and delivers something new, fresh, and challenging.

Winner of the National Council of Teachers of English (NCTE) Excellence in Poetry Award in 1988, he strives to present a poetry of "shaped speech" that is colloquial, that is relevant, short, and exciting. He does this with a variety of masks: sometimes boy, sometimes girl, and sometimes an androgynous voice. But always he fulfills his own code, the "need of the poet to help mold a complete reality through control of technique and imagination..." in which he most assuredly excels.

—Myra Cohn Livingston

———

AFFABEE, Eric. See **STINE, R(obert) L(awrence).**

———

AIKEN, Joan (Delano). British. Born in Rye, Sussex, 4 September 1924. Educated at Wychwood School, Oxford, 1936-40. Married 1) Ronald George Brown in 1945 (died 1955), one son and one daughter; 2) Julius Goldstein in 1976. Worked for the BBC, 1942-43; information officer, then librarian, United Nations Information Centre, London, 1943-49; sub-editor and features editor, *Argosy,* London, 1955-60; copywriter, J. Walter Thompson, London, 1960-61. Recipient: *Guardian* award, and runner-up for Carnegie award, 1969, both for *The Whispering Mountain;* Mystery Writers of America Edgar Allan Poe award, 1972, for *Night Fall.* Agent: A.M. Heath, 40-42 William IV Street, London WC2N 4DD. Address: The Hermitage, East Street, Petworth, West Sussex GU28 0AB, England.

PUBLICATIONS FOR YOUNG ADULTS

Fiction

All You've Ever Wanted and Other Stories, illustrated by Pat Marriott. London, Cape, 1953.
More Than You Bargained For and Other Stories, illustrated by Pat Marriott. London, Cape, 1955; New York, Abelard Schuman, 1957.
The Kingdom and the Cave, illustrated by Dick Hart. London, Abelard Schuman, 1960; New York, Doubleday, 1974.
The Wolves of Willoughby Chase, illustrated by Pat Marriott. London, Cape, 1962; New York, Doubleday, 1963.
Black Hearts in Battersea, illustrated by Robin Jacques. New York, Doubleday, 1964; London, Cape, 1965.
Nightbirds on Nantucket, illustrated by Pat Marriott. London, Cape, and New York, Doubleday, 1966.
The Whispering Mountain. London, Cape, 1968; New York, Doubleday, 1969.

A Necklace of Raindrops and Other Stories, illustrated by Jan Pienkowski. London, Cape, and New York, Doubleday, 1968.

Armitage, Armitage, Fly Away Home, illustrated by Betty Fraser. New York, Doubleday, 1968.

A Small Pinch of Weather and Other Stories, illustrated by Pat Marriott. London, Cape, 1969.

Night Fall. London, Macmillan, 1969; New York, Holt Rinehart, 1971.

Smoke from Cromwell's Time and Other Stories. New York, Doubleday, 1970.

The Green Flash and Other Tales of Horror, Suspense, and Fantasy. New York, Holt Rinehart, 1971.

The Cuckoo Tree, illustrated by Pat Marriott. London, Cape, and New York, Doubleday, 1971.

All and More, illustrated by Pat Marriott. London, Cape, 1971.

A Harp of Fishbones and Other Stories, illustrated by Pat Marriott. London, Cape, 1972.

Arabel's Raven, illustrated by Quentin Blake. London, BBC Publications, 1972; New York, Doubleday, 1974.

The Escaped Black Mamba, illustrated by Quentin Blake. London, BBC Publications, 1973.

All But a Few. London, Penguin, 1974.

The Bread Bin, illustrated by Quentin Blake. London, BBC Publications, 1974.

Midnight Is a Place. London, Cape, and New York, Viking Press, 1974.

Not What You Expected: A Collection of Short Stories. New York, Doubleday, 1974.

Mortimer's Tie, illustrated by Quentin Blake. London, BBC Publications, 1976.

A Bundle of Nerves: Stories of Horror, Suspense, and Fantasy. London, Gollancz, 1976.

The Faithless Lollybird and Other Stories, illustrated by Pat Marriott. London, Cape, 1977; New York, Doubleday, 1978.

The Far Forests: Tales of Romance, Fantasy, and Suspense. New York, Viking Press, 1977.

Go Saddle the Sea, illustrated by Pat Marriott. New York, Doubleday, 1977; London, Cape, 1978.

Tale of a One-Way Street and Other Stories, illustrated by Jan Pienkowski. London, Cape, 1978; New York, Doubleday, 1979.

Mice and Mendelson, music by John Sebastian Brown, illustrated by Babette Cole. London, Cape, 1978.

Mortimer and the Sword Excalibur, illustrated by Quentin Blake. London, BBC Publications, 1979.

The Spiral Stair, illustrated by Quentin Blake. London, BBC Publications, 1979.

A Touch of Chill: Stories of Horror, Suspense, and Fantasy. London, Gollancz, 1979; New York, Delacorte Press, 1980.

Arabel and Mortimer (includes *Mortimer's Tie, The Spiral Stair, Mortimer and the Sword Excalibur*), illustrated by Quentin Blake. London, Cape, 1980; New York, Doubleday, 1981.

The Shadow Guests. London, Cape, and New York, Delacorte Press, 1980.

Mortimer's Portrait on Glass, illustrated by Quentin Blake. London, Hodder and Stoughton, 1981.

The Stolen Lake, illustrated by Pat Marriott. London, Cape, and New York, Delacorte Press, 1981.

The Mystery of Mr. Jones's Disappearing Taxi, illustrated by Quentin Blake. London, Hodder and Stoughton, 1982.

A Whisper in the Night: Stories of Horror, Suspense, and Fantasy. London, Gollancz, 1982; New York, Delacorte Press, 1984.

Mortimer's Cross, illustrated by Quentin Blake. London, Cape, 1983; New York, Harper, 1984.

Bridle the Wind, illustrated by Pat Marriott. London, Cape, and New York, Delacorte Press, 1983.

The Kitchen Warriors, illustrated by Jo Worth. London, BBC Publications, 1983.

Up the Chimney Down (stories), illustrated by Pat Marriott. London, Cape, and New York, Harper, 1984.

Fog Hounds, Wind Cat, Sea Mice. London, Macmillan, 1984.

Mortimer Says Nothing and Other Stories, illustrated by Quentin Blake. London, Cape, 1985; New York, Harper, 1987.

The Last Slice of Rainbow and Other Stories, illustrated by Margaret Walty. London, Cape, 1985; New York, Harper, 1988.

Dido and Pa, illustrated by Pat Marriott. London, Cape, and New York, Delacorte Press, 1986.

Past Eight O'Clock: Goodnight Stories, illustrated by Jan Pienkowski. London, Cape, 1986.

A Goose on Your Grave. London, Gollancz, 1987.

The Moon's Revenge, illustrated by Alan Lee. London, Cape, and New York, Knopf, 1987.

The Teeth of the Gale, illustrated by Pat Marriott. London, Cape, and New York, Harper, 1988.

The Erl King's Daughter, illustrated by Paul Warren. London, Heinemann, 1988.

Voices. London, Hippo, 1988.

Give Yourself a Fright: Thirteen Tales of the Supernatural. New York, Delacorte Press, 1989.

A Fit of Shivers: Tales for Late at Night. London, Gollancz, 1990; New York, Delacorte, 1992.

A Foot in the Grave. London, Cape, 1990.

Jane Fairfax. London, Gollancz, 1990; New York, St. Martin's 1991.

The Haunting of Lamb House. London, Gollancz, 1991.

Is. London, Cape, 1992; as *Is Underground,* New York, Delecorte, 1993.

Plays

Winterthing, music by John Sebastian Brown, illustrated by Arvis Stewart (produced Albany, New York, 1977). New York, Holt Rinehart, 1972; included in *Winterthing, and The Mooncusser's Daughter,* 1973.

Winterthing, and The Mooncusser's Daughter, music by John Sebastian Brown. London, Cape, 1973; *The Mooncusser's Daughter* published separately, New York, Viking Press, 1974.

Street, music by John Sebastian Brown, illustrated by Arvis Stewart (produced London, 1977). New York, Viking Press, 1978.

Moon Mill (produced London, 1982).

Television Plays: *The Dark Streets of Kimballs Green,* 1976; *The Apple of Trouble,* 1977; *Midnight Is a Place* (serial), from her own story, 1977; *The Rose of Puddle Fratrum,* 1978; *Armitage, Armitage, Fly Away Home,* from her own story, 1978.

Poetry

The Skin Spinners, illustrated by Ken Rinciari. New York, Viking Press, 1976.

Other

Reteller, *The Kingdom under the Sea and Other Stories,* illustrated by Jan Pienkowski. London, Cape, 1971.

Translator, *The Angel Inn,* by Contessa de Ségur, illustrated by Pat Marriott. London, Cape, 1976; Owings Mills, Maryland, Stemmer House, 1978.

PUBLICATIONS FOR ADULTS

Novels

The Silence of Herondale. New York, Doubleday, 1964; London, Gollancz, 1965.

The Fortune Hunters. New York, Doubleday, 1965.

Trouble with Product X. London, Gollancz, 1966; as *Beware of the Bouquet,* New York, Doubleday, 1966.

Hate Begins at Home. London, Gollancz, 1967; as *Dark Interval,* New York, Doubleday, 1967.

The Ribs of Death. London, Gollancz, 1967; as *The Crystal Crow,* New York, Doubleday, 1968.

The Embroidered Sunset. London, Gollancz, and New York, Doubleday, 1970.

Died on a Rainy Sunday. London, Gollancz, and New York, Holt Rinehart, 1972.

The Butterfly Picnic. London, Gollancz, 1972; as *A Cluster of Separate Sparks,* New York, Doubleday, 1972.

Voices in an Empty House. London, Gollancz, and New York, Doubleday, 1975.

Castle Barebane. London, Gollancz, and New York, Viking Press, 1976.

Last Movement. London, Gollancz, and New York, Doubleday, 1977.

The Five-Minute Marriage. London, Gollancz, 1977; New York, Doubleday, 1978.

The Smile of the Stranger. London, Gollancz, and New York, Doubleday, 1978.

The Lightning Tree. London, Gollancz, 1980; as *The Weeping Ash,* New York, Doubleday, 1980.

The Young Lady from Paris. London, Gollancz, 1982; as *The Girl from Paris,* New York, Doubleday, 1982.

Foul Matter. London, Gollancz, and New York, Doubleday, 1983.

Mansfield Revisited. London, Gollancz, 1984; New York, Doubleday, 1985.

Deception. London, Gollancz, 1987; as *If I Were You,* New York, Doubleday, 1987.

Blackground. London, Gollancz, and New York, Doubleday, 1989.

Short Stories

The Windscreen Weepers and Other Tales of Horror and Suspense. London, Gollancz, 1969.

Other

The Way to Write for Children. London, Elm Tree, 1982; New York, St. Martin's Press, 1983.

Contributor, *Sixteen: Short Stories by Outstanding Writers for Young Adults,* edited by Donald R. Gallo. New York, Dell, 1984.

Media Adaptations: *Midnight Is a Place* (television series), Southern Television, 1977; *Armitage, Armitage, Fly Away Home* (television play), BBC, 1978; *The Wolves of Willoughby Chase* (cassette), Caedmon, 1978; (film), Atlantic/Zenith, 1988; *A Necklace of Raindrops and Other Stories* (cassette), Caedmon, 1978; *Apple of Discord* (play), BBC-TV; *The Rose of Puddle Fratrum* (play), BBC-TV.

Biography: Essay in *Something about the Author Autobiography Series,* Volume 1, Detroit, Gale, 1986; entry in *Authors and Artists for Young Adults,* Volume 1, Detroit, Gale, 1989; essay in *Speaking for Ourselves: Autobiographical Sketches by Notable Authors of Books for Young Adults,* Volume 1, compiled and edited by Donald R. Gallo, National Council of Teachers of English, 1990.

Critical Study: Entry in *Children's Literature Review,* Volume 1, Detroit, Gale, 1976; Volume 19, 1990; entry in *Contemporary Literary Criticism,* Volume 35, Detroit, Gale, 1985.

*   *   *

Joan Aiken's prolific writings showcase her marvelous imagination, spiced with wit and wisdom. Her stories for young adults are rich in bizarre situations and startling surprises. Ghosts, monsters, witches, and demons are often found in both her novels and short stories.

Many of Aiken's stories combine elements of historical fiction and gothic romance and quite a few are set in Aiken's own fictitious nineteenth-century England, where a Stuart king reigns over a country beset by constant threats, including wild wolves which not only roam the countryside but close in on London. This setting appears in such novels as *The Wolves of Willoughby Chase, Black Hearts in Battersea, The Cuckoo Tree, The Stolen Lake,* and *Dido and Pa.*

The Wolves of Willoughby Chase, is a Victorian melodrama that pits good against evil and provides a just and happy ending. Young Bonnie and her cousin Sylvia are left in the care of a wicked governess when Bonnie's sick mother and her wealthy father have to go on a long, recuperative cruise. The great English country estate, Willoughby Chase, seems like a warm and safe stronghold for Bonnie and Sylvia. But as soon as the parents leave, the two girls are terrorized by wolves outside and their evil governess within. It is the young Simon, who lives in a cave near the estate, who assists them throughout each misadventure.

Twenty years later Aiken still writes in this historical vein. In *Dido and Pa* Simon appears as the sixth Duke of Battersea. He is joined by another recurring character in Aiken's stories, Dido Twite, a forthright, tough young lady, resourceful in adversity and intolerant of evil. In this book Dido is placed in the midst of a dastardly Hanoverian conspiracy, which involves skullduggery all around.

Armitage, Armitage, Fly Away Home is a funny fantasy that begins with Mr. and Mrs. Armitage honeymooning at the beach, where Mrs. Armitage finds a wishing stone. She wishes for two children who will never be bored, who will have lots of interesting and unusual experiences and her wishes come true with the births of Mark and Harriet.

Aiken has written a number of suspenseful short stories. They are filled with all manner of supernatural beings as well as natural beings with unconventional behaviors. *A Fit of Shivers: Tales for Late at Night* contains ten such stories. In "Number Four, Bowstring Lane" a TV personality, Marcus Fantail, buys a country retirement home and orders up a ghost for company, to disastrous consequences. In "An L-Shaped Grave" the artist Luna Knox knocks off the art critic of a bad review with a full-size pair of elk's antlers. And in "Something" a ninety-year-old grandfather, lying cold in his bier, has one last nightmare and falls out of his box onto the stone church floor.

Joan Aiken is a wonderful storyteller. Her characters, even the ghoulies and ghosties, are great fun and have amazing adventures. The reader who finishes one Aiken book will look for more, to see what else she has conjured up.

—Mary Lystad

* * *

ALCOCK, Vivien (Dolores). British. Born in Worthing, Sussex, 23 September 1924. Educated at Devizes High School, Wiltshire; Oxford School of Art, 1940-42. Served as an ambulance driver in the Auxiliary Territorial Service, 1942-46. Married Leon Garfield in 1948; one adopted daughter. Artist, Gestetner Ltd., London, 1947-53; secretary, Whittington Hospital, London, 1953-58. Recipient: *Travellers by Night* was named to the *Horn Book* Honor List and named ALA notable book of the year, both 1985; *The Cuckoo Sister* was named ALA notable book of the year, 1986; *The Monster Garden* was named *Voice of Youth Advocate* best science fiction/fantasy book and ALA notable book of the year, both 1988. Agent: John Johnson Ltd., 45-47 Clerkenwell Green, London EC1R 0HT. Address: 59 Wood Lane, London N6 5UD, England.

PUBLICATIONS FOR YOUNG ADULTS

Fiction

The Haunting of Cassie Palmer. London, Methuen, 1980; New York, Delacorte Press, 1982.
The Stonewalkers. London, Methuen, 1981; New York, Delacorte Press, 1983.
The Sylvia Game. London, Methuen, 1982; New York, Delacorte Press, 1984.
Travellers by Night. London, Methuen, 1983; New York, Delacorte Press, 1985.
Ghostly Companions, illustrated by Jane Lydbury. London, Methuen, 1984; New York, Delacorte Press, 1987.
The Cuckoo Sister. London, Methuen, and New York, Delacorte Press, 1985.
Wait and See, illustrated by Jill Bennett. London, Deutsch, 1986.
The Mysterious Mr. Ross. London, Methuen, and New York, Delacorte Press, 1987.
The Monster Garden. London, Methuen, and New York, Delacorte Press, 1988.
The Thing in the Woods, illustrated by Sally Holmes. London, Hamish Hamilton, 1989.
The Trial of Anna Cotman. London, Methuen, 1989; London, Delacorte, 1990.
A Kind of Thief. New York, Delacorte, 1991.
Singer to the Sea God. New York, Delacorte, 1993.

*

Media Adaptations: *The Sylvia Game* (television movie), BBC-TV, 1983; *The Haunting of Cassie Palmer* (television series), Television South, 1984; *Travellers by Night* (television movie), BBC-TV, 1984; (television series), Television South, 1985.

Biography: Essay in *Authors and Artists for Young Adults,* Volume 8, Detroit, Gale, 1992; essay in *Speaking for Ourselves, Too* compiled and edited by Donald R. Gallo, National Council of Teachers of English, 1993.

Critical Study: Entry in *Children's Literature Review,* Volume 26, Detroit, Gale, 1992.

* * *

Vivien Alcock's books, whether for young adults or for readers in the middle grades, explore boundaries: between childhood and adolescence, between reality and imagination, between natural and supernatural, between good and evil. Her prolific output falls into three distinct periods: an early one emphasizing the question of reality, a middle period in which more realistic mysteries and family relationships come to the fore, and a more recent group in which ethical and social issues are developed.

The Haunting of Cassie Palmer, Alcock's first novel, introduces many of the author's major themes: reality versus imagination, parent-child conflict, and ethical dilemmas. Does Cassie, seventh child of a seventh child, have the "gift" that will enable her to deal with the spirit world more successfully than her mother, a fraudulent medium whose failures force the family to move each time she is exposed? Is Deverill, the dark shadowy figure Cassie meets in a cemetery, really a ghost—or a figment of her early adolescent mind? Cassie's human sympathy and strong imagination bring a happy ending both for Deverill and for herself. Ironically, it is her success in bringing peace to Deverill's troubled spirit that enables Cassie to grow beyond the world of her mother's spiritualism and prepare for a healing career in the ordinary world. More melodramatic than *The Haunting of Cassie Palmer,* Alcock's second novel for young adults, *The Stonewalkers,* presents a different view of the boundaries of reality: Poppy Brown and two of her friends realize that some local statues have come to life, but no one believes them. An exciting chase scene and a long period of captivity in a cave with the dangerous statues mark high points in this book, a favorite with young readers. Other themes from Alcock's first novel recur: again, the main character's difficult relationship with her mother is explored and shown capable of improvement through love; again, the implications of dishonesty (in this case, telling lies) are explored.

After these successful forays into the supernatural, Alcock turned toward a more direct focus on family and values. *The Sylvia Game* presents another irresponsible parent, a painter whose daughter Emily suspects him of complicity in a forgery scheme. Emily's remarkable resemblance to a portrait by Renoir involves her in an odd friendship with two very different boys: Oliver, heir to the Mallerton estates, and the illegitimate, colorful Kevin. For all three, loyalty to a very imperfect parent collides with the demands of honor. Although the parents in this novel do not change as much as those in the earlier ones, Oliver and Emily come to accept their fathers as people. The examination of class differences is both accurate and unsentimental. In *The Cuckoo Sister,* a stolen child returns years later—but is she really Emma, kidnapped years ago as a baby, or an imposter? Personality problems, class differences, and the lingering possibility of fraud combine to create tension and uncertainty in Kate's comfortable Hampstead family before the question of Emma's true identity is cleared up. Several Alcock novels of the 1980s aim at a slightly younger adolescent readership, such as the charming quest story *Travellers by Night,* with its brother and sister seeking refuge for a circus elephant, and the Carnegie Medal nominee, *The Monster Garden,* which approximates the science fiction and fantasy genres more than is usual for Alcock. Although *The Monster Garden* raises the issue of responsible laboratory experimentation with genetic materials, it concentrates on the fate of the charming Monnie more than on the ethical problems involved in his creation.

In recent years Alcock's books have become darker in mood. *The Trial of Anna Cotman* pits a lonely girl against a secret society whose rituals fascinate and degrade her. Alcock deftly contrasts the colorful costumes, imaginative hierarchy, and compelling ceremonies of the group to Anna's drab surroundings. Her stand against the group's corruption occurs naturally and inevitably, rather than as the result of any simplistic decision or fearless heroics. That she prevails almost by chance, and then only with adult help, is a suitable ending to this somber and convincing tale of group psychology.

A Kind of Thief presents once again the trials of an early adolescent with a socially unacceptable parent. Unlike the deceptive parents of Cassie Palmer and Emily Dodd, even more unlike the largely absent parents in many of Alcock's other young adult books, this story examines the effects of having a father who is actually in jail. The predictable breakup of Elinor's step family, which might have formed the climax of a less skilled writer's plot, occurs near the beginning. Though victims, Ellie's young stepmother and Ellie herself do not always behave well; indeed, the efforts to rescue and preserve her father's hidden suitcase make her into "a kind of thief," as culpable in her own way as he is. All the characters in *A Kind of Thief* are flawed, from the young stepmother Sophia to elderly Mrs. Carter, the children's great aunt; yet nearly all are resourceful and capable of sometimes surprising generosity. The slow realization of human strength and human weakness leads Ellie finally to accept herself as she is and to accept her family also.

—Caroline C. Hunt

ALCOTT, Louisa May. American. Born in Germantown, Philadelphia, Pennsylvania, 29 November 1832. Daughter of the philosopher Armos Bronson Alcott; grew up in Boston, and Concord, Massachusetts. Educated at home by her father, with instruction from Thoreau, Emerson, and Theodore Parker. Began to write for publication (author of novels, short stories, and poems), 1848; also worked as a teacher, seamstress, and domestic servant; army nurse at the Union Hospital, Georgetown, Washington, D.C., during the Civil War, 1862-63; editor of the children's magazine *Merry's Museum,* 1867. *Died 6 March 1888.*

Publications for Young Adults

Fiction

The Rose Family: A Fairy Tale. Boston, James Redpath, 1864.

Moods. A.K. Loring, 1865.
Nelly's Hospital. U.S. Sanitary Commission, 1865.
The Mysterious Key, and What It Opened. Boston, Elliott, Thomes & Talbot, 1867.
Aunt Kipp. A. K. Loring, 1868.
Kitty's Class Day. A. K. Loring, 1868.
Little Women or, Meg, Jo, Beth and Amy, two volumes, Boston, Roberts Brothers, 1868-69; volume 2 republished as *Little Women Wedded,* London, Low, 1872, as *Little Women Married,* London, Routledge, 1873; as *Nice Wives,* London, Weldon, 1875; both volumes republished as *Little Women and Good Wives,* London, Nisbet, 1895.
Psyche's Art. A. K. Loring, 1868.
An Old-Fashioned Girl. Boston, Roberts Brothers, 1870.
Will's Wonder Book. Boston, Horace B. Fuller, 1870; as *Louisa's Wonder Book: An Unknown Alcott Juvenile,* edited by Madeleine B. Stern, Mount Pleasant, Central Michigan University/Clark Historical Library, 1975.
Little Men: Life at Plumfield with Jo's Boys. Boston, Roberts Brothers, 1871.
Work: A Story of Experience. Boston, Roberts Brothers, 1873.
Eight Cousins; or, The Aunt-Hill. Boston, Roberts Brothers, 1875.
Rose in Bloom: A Sequel to "Eight Cousins." Boston, Roberts Brothers, 1876.
A Modern Mephistopheles (published anonymously). Boston, Roberts Brothers, 1877.
Under the Lilacs. Boston, Roberts Brothers, 1878.
Meadow Blossoms. New York, Crowell, 1879.
Sparkles for Bright Eyes. New York, Crowell, 1879.
Water Cresses. New York, Crowell, 1879.
Jack and Jill: A Village Story. Boston, Roberts Brothers, 1880.
Jo's Boys, and How They Turned Out: A Sequel to "Little Men." Boston, Roberts Brothers, 1886.
A Garland for Girls. Boston, Roberts Brothers, 1887.
An Old-fashioned Thanksgiving, illustrated by Holly Johnson. Philadelphia, Lippincott, 1974.
Trudel's Siege, art by Stan Skardinski. New York, McGraw-Hill, 1976.
Diana and Persis, edited by Sarah Elbert. Salem, New Hampshire, Ayer Company, 1978.
The Faded Banners: A Treasury of Nineteenth Century Civil War Fiction, edited by Eric Soloman. New York, Promontory Press, 1986.

Short Stories

Flower Fables. Boston, George W. Briggs, 1855.
On Picket Duty, and Other Tales. Boston, James Redpath, 1864.
Louisa M. Alcott's Proverb Stories (contains *Kitty's Class Day, Aunt Kipp,* and *Psyche's Art*), A. K. Loring, 1868.
Morning-Glories, and Other Stories. Boston, Horace B. Fuller, 1868.
Hospital Sketches [and] Camp and Fireside Stories. Boston, Roberts Brothers, 1869.
Aunt Jo's Scrap-Bag. Boston, Roberts Brothers, Volume 1, 1872, Volume 2, 1872, Volume 3, 1874, Volume 4, 1878, Volume 5, 1879, Volume 6, 1882.
Something to Do (contains *Proverb Stories*). London, Ward, Lock & Tyler, 1873.
Silver Pitchers [and] Independence, a Centennial Love Story. Boston, Roberts Brothers, 1876.

Spinning-Wheel Stories. Boston, Roberts Brothers, 1884.

Lulu's Library. Boston, Roberts Brothers, Volume 1: *A Christmas Dream,* 1886, Volume 2: *The Frost King,* 1887, Volume 3: *Recollections,* 1889.

A Modern Mephistopheles [and] A Whisper in the Dark. Boston, Roberts Brothers, 1889.

Comic Tragedies Written by "Jo" and "Meg" and Acted by the Little Women. Boston, Roberts Brothers, 1893.

A Round Dozen: Stories, edited by Anne Thaxter Eaton. New York, Viking, 1963.

Glimpses of Louisa: A Centennial Sampling of the Best Short Stories by Louisa May Alcott, edited by Cornelia Meigs. Boston, Little, Brown, 1968.

Behind a Mask: The Unknown Thrillers of Louisa May Alcott, edited by Madeleine B. Stern. New York, Morrow, 1975.

Plots and Counterplots: More Unknown Thrillers of Louisa May Alcott, edited by Madeleine B. Stern. (As A.M. Barnard), Boston, Thomes and Talbot, c. 1870; New York, Morrow, 1976.

The Hidden Louisa May Alcott: A Collection of her Unknown Thrillers, edited by Madeleine Stern. New York, Avenel Books, 1984.

The Works of Louisa May Alcott, 1832-1888. Kent, Connecticut, Reprint Services Corp., 1987.

Alternative Alcott, edited by Elaine Showalter. New Brunswick, New Jersey, Rutgers University Press, 1988.

A Double Life: Newly Discovered Thrillers of Louisa May Alcott, edited by Madeleine B. Stern. Boston, Little, Brown, 1988.

Freaks of Genius: Unknown Thrillers of Louisa May Alcott. edited by Daniel Shealy, Madeleine B. Stern, and Joel Myerson. New York, Greenwood Press, 1991.

Louisa May Alcott's Fairy Tales and Fantasy Stories, edited by Daniel Shealy. Knoxville, University of Tennessee Press, 1992.

Nonfiction

Hospital Sketches. Boston, James Redpath, 1863.

Louisa May Alcott: Her Life, Letters and Journals, edited by Ednah D. Cheney. Boston, Roberts Brothers, 1889.

Transcendental Wild Oats and Excerpts from the Fruitlands Diary, illustrated by J. Streeter Fowke. Harvard, Massachusetts, Harvard Common Press, 1975.

The Selected Letters of Louisa May Alcott, edited by Joel Myerson. Boston, Little, Brown, 1987.

*

Media Adaptations: *Little Women* (film), Famous Players, Lasky Corp., 1919; *Little Women* (play), RKO, 1933; *Little Women* (film), Metro-Goldwyn-Mayer, 1949; *Little Men* (film), Mascott, 1934; *Little Men* (film), RKO, 1940; and *An Old-Fashioned Girl* (film), Pathe Industries, 1949. Several recordings of Alcott's work have also been made.

Manuscript Collection: Family papers at Houghton Library, Harvard University, Cambridge, Massachusetts.

Biography: Entry in *Dictionary of Literary Biography,* Detroit, Gale, Volume 1: *The American Renaissance in New England,* edited by Joel Myerson, 1978, Volume 79: *American Magazine Journalists, 1850-1900,* edited by Sam G. Riley, 1989; entry in *Dictionary of Literary Biography,* Volume 42: *American Writers for Children before 1900,* edited by Glenn E. Estes, Detroit, Gale, 1985.

Bibliography: *Louisa May Alcott: Her Life, Letters and Journals,* edited by Ednah D. Cheney, Boston, Roberts Brothers, 1889; *Louisa May Alcott* by Katharine S. Anthony, New York, Knopf, 1938; *Louisa May Alcott: The Children's Friend* by Ednah D. Cheney, Sandusky, Ohio, Prang, 1888; *We Alcotts: The Story of Louisa May Alcott's Family as Seen through the Eyes of "Marmee," Mother of Little Women* by Aileen Fisher and Olive Rabe, New York, Atheneum, 1968; *The Story of the Author of "Little Women": Invincible Louisa* by Cornelia Meigs, New York, Little, Brown, 1933; *Louisa May Alcott* by Madeleine B. Stern, Norman, University of Oklahoma Press, 1950.

Critical Study: Entry in *Children's Literature Review,* Volume 1, Detroit, Gale, 1976.

*   *   *

In 1868 when, at the request of Thomas Niles of Roberts Brothers, Louisa May Alcott sat down to write a household story for girls, the domestic novel as evolved by Susan Warner, Maria Cummins, Ann Stephens, and Mrs. E.D.E.N. Southworth consisted of commonplace episodes worked into a trite plot involving pious and insipid characters. Bronson Alcott's opinion of juvenile literature, recorded in his diary for 1839, had, in the generation that followed, been given no cause for alteration. In 1868 it was still true that the "literature of childhood" had not been written. If such extraordinary moral tales as *The Wide, Wide World,* the Rollo books, the Lucy books, and the first of the Elsie books became unbearable, there was compensation for a youthful reader only in grave-and-horror stories, Hawthorne's legendary tales, or "Peter Parley's" edifying descriptions of natural wonders.

The times were ripe for Alcott and she was well equipped to fill the gap in domestic literature. With the publication of *Little Women* (1868-69) she created a domestic novel for young people destined to influence writers in that genre for generations to come. Responding to her publisher's request, she drew her characters from those of her own sisters, her scenes from the New England where she had grown up, and many of her episodes from those she and her family had experienced. In all this she was something of a pioneer, adapting her autobiography to the creation of a juvenile novel and achieving a realistic but wholesome picture of family life with which young readers could readily identify.

The literary influence of Bunyan and Dickens, Carlyle and Hawthorne, Emerson, Theodore Parker, and Thoreau can be traced in her work, but primarily she drew upon autobiographical sources for her plot and her characters, finding in her family and neighbors the groundwork for her three-dimensional characters. Her perceptively drawn adolescents, the Marches, modeled upon her sisters and herself, were not merely lifelike but alive. Her episodes, from the opening selection of a Christmas gift to the plays in the barn, from Jo March's literary career to Beth's death, were thoroughly believable for they had been lived. The Alcott humor which induced a chuckle at a homely phrase was appreciated by children. The Alcott poverty was sentimentalized; the eccentric Alcott father was an adumbrated shadow; yet, for all the glossing over, the core of the domestic drama was apparent. Reported simply and directly in a style that obeyed her injunction "Never use a long word, when a short one will do as well," the narrative embodied the simple facts and persons of a family and so filled a gap in the literature of childhood. Alcott had unlatched the door to one house, and "all find it is their own house which they enter." Twentieth-century writers for young people who aim at credibility and verisimilitude in their reconstructions of contemporary family life are all, in one way or another, indebted to Alcott.

By the time she created *Little Women* she had served a long apprenticeship and was already a professional writer. She had edited a juvenile monthly, *Merry's Museum,* and produced several books aimed at a juvenile readership: her first published book, *Flower Fables,* "legends of faery land"; *The Rose Family: A Fairy Tale;* and *Morning-Glories and Other Stories,* readable short stories in which autobiographical details were combined with nature lore and moral tidbits.

Alcott had also written in a variety of genres for a wide range of adult readers, weaving stories of sweetness and light, dramatic narratives of strong-minded women and poor lost creatures, realistic episodes of the Civil War, and blood-and-thunder thrillers of revenge and passion whose leading character was usually a vindictive and manipulating heroine. From the exigencies of serialization for magazines she had developed the skills of the cliffhanger and the page-turner. Her first full-length novel, *Moods* (1865), was a narrative of stormy passion and violence, death and intellectual love in which she attempted to apply Emerson's remark: "life is a train of moods like a string of beads." Off and on, she had worked at her autobiographical and feminist novel *Success,* subsequently renamed *Work: A Story of Experience.* By 1868, Alcott had run a gamut of literary experimentation from stories of virtue rewarded to stories of vice unpunished. She had attempted tales of escape and realism and stirred her literary ingredients in a witch's cauldron before she kindled the fire in a family hearth.

With few exceptions—notably *A Modern Mephistopheles* (1877) in which she reverted to the sensational themes of her earlier blood-and-thunders—Alcott clung to that family hearth during the remainder of her career. Between 1868 when Part One of *Little Women* appeared and 1888 when she died, she produced in her so-called *Little Women Series* a string of wholesome domestic narratives more or less autobiographical in origin, simple and direct in style, perceptive in the characterization of adolescents. *An Old-Fashioned Girl, Little Men, Eight Cousins, Rose in Bloom, Under the Lilacs, Jack and Jill,* and *Jo's Boys* are all in a sense sequels to *Little Women* though none of them quite rises to its level. *An Old-Fashioned Girl* is a domestic drama in reverse, exposing the fashionable absurdities of the Shaw home by contrast with Polly, the wholesome representative of domesticity. The Campbell clan of *Eight Cousins* exalts the family hearth again. In *Jack and Jill* the author enlarges upon the theme of domesticity, describing the home life of a New England village rather than of a single family.

Despite her experimentation with a diversity of literary techniques, despite the fact that she was a complex writer drawn to a variety of themes, Alcott has inevitably achieved fame as the author of a single masterpiece. Thanks to its psychological perceptions, its realistic characterizations, and its honest domesticity, *Little Women* has become an embodiment of the American home at its best. Consciously or unconsciously all subsequent writers who have attempted the domestic novel for young people have felt its influence, for in *Little Women* the local has been transmuted into the universal and the incidents of family life have been translated to the domain of literature.

Today not only *Little Women* but the entire Alcott oeuvre are being subjected to critical re-evaluation. For this the reprinting of her previously unknown thrillers (written in secret during the 1860s and published anonymously or pseudonymously) is largely responsible. Their themes (mind control and madness, hashish ex-

perimentation and opium addiction, mesmerism, and a powerful feminism) are leading critics to re-examine the simplistic interpretation of "America's best-loved author of juveniles."

—Madeleine B. Stern

———

ALDON, Adair. See **MEIGS, Cornelia Lynde.**

———

ALDRICH, Ann. See **KERR, M.E.**

———

ALDRIDGE, (Harold Edward) James. Australian. Born in White Hills, Victoria, 10 July 1918. Educated at Swan Hill High School; London School of Economics; Oxford University, 1939. Married Dina Mitchnik in 1942; two sons. Free-lance writer; office boy and file clerk, 1934-37, reporter, 1937-38, both for Melbourne *Herald;* reporter, Melbourne *Sun,* 1937-38; feature writer, London *Daily Sketch* and *Sunday Dispatch,* 1939; European and Middle East war correspondent, Australian Newspaper Service and North American Newspaper Alliance (in Finland, Norway, Greece, the Middle East, and the Soviet Union), 1939-44; Tehran correspondent, *Time* and *Life,* 1944. Recipient: Rhys Memorial prize, 1945; World Peace Council gold medal; International Organization of Journalist prize, 1967; Lenin Memorial Peace prize, 1972; Australian Children's Book Council Book of the Year award, 1985; *Guardian* award, for children's book, 1987. Agent: Curtis Brown, 162-168 Regent Street, London W1R 5TB, England. Address: 21 Kersley St., London SW11, England.

PUBLICATIONS FOR YOUNG ADULTS

Fiction

The Flying 19. London. Hamish Hamilton, 1966.
The Marvellous Mongolian. Boston, Little, Brown, and London, Macmillan, 1974.
The Broken Saddle. London, MacRae, 1982; New York, Watts, 1983.
The True Story of Lilli Stubeck. South Yarra, Victoria, Hyland House, 1984; London, Penguin, 1986.
The True Story of Spit MacPhee. Ringwood, Victoria, Viking, and London, Viking Kestrel, 1986.
The True Story of Lola Mackeller, forthcoming.

PUBLICATIONS FOR ADULTS

Novels

Signed with Their Honour. London, Joseph, and Boston, Little, Brown, 1942.

The Sea Eagle. London, Joseph, and Boston, Little, Brown, 1944.
Of Many Men. London, Joseph, and Boston, Little, Brown, 1946.
The Diplomat. London, Lane, 1949; Boston, Little, Brown, 1950.
The Hunter. London, Lane, 1950; Boston, Little, Brown, 1951.
Heroes of the Empty View. London, Lane, and New York, Knopf, 1954.
I Wish He Would Not Die. London, Bodley Head, 1957; New York, Doubleday, 1958.
The Last Exile. London, Hamish Hamilton, and New York, Doubleday, 1961.
A Captive in the Land. London, Hamish Hamilton, 1962; New York, Doubleday, 1963.
My Brother Tom. London, Hamish Hamilton, 1966; as *My Brother Tom: A Love Story,* Boston, Little, Brown, 1967.
The Statesman's Game. London, Hamish Hamilton, and New York, 1966.
A Sporting Proposition. London, Joseph, and Boston, Little, Brown, 1973; as *Ride a Wild Pony,* London, Penguin, 1976.
Mockery in Arms. London, Joseph, 1974; Boston, Little, Brown, 1975.
The Untouchable Juli. London, Joseph, 1975; Boston, Little, Brown, 1976.
One Last Glimpse. London, Joseph, and Boston, Little, Brown, 1977.
Flying. London, Pan, 1979.
Goodbye Un-America. London, Joseph, and Boston, Little, Brown, 1979.

Short Stories

Gold and Sand. London, Bodley Head, 1960.

Plays

The 49th State (produced London, 1947).
One Last Glimpse (produced Prague, 1981).

Television Plays: Scripts for *Robin Hood* series.

Other

Undersea Hunting for Inexperienced Englishmen. London, Allen & Unwin, 1955.
Cairo: Biography of a City. Boston, Little, Brown, 1969; London, Macmillan, 1970.
Living Egypt, photographs by Paul Strand. London, MacGibbon and Kee, and New York, Horizon Press, 1969.
Contributor, *Winter's Tales 15,* edited by A.D. Maclean. London, Macmillan, 1969; New York, St. Martin's, 1970.
Security Closed Circuit Television Handbook: Applications and Technical, with Thomas G. Kyle. Springfield, Illinois, C.C. Thomas, 1992.

*   *   *

James Aldridge began his career as a journalist reporting from the front lines during the Second World War. While working as a war correspondent he published two novels about the war, *Signed with Their Honour* and *The Sea Eagle,* and following their success gave up journalism to become a full-time writer, publishing many successful novels for adults—*The Diplomat* published in 1950 was

translated into twenty-five languages and was a best-seller in Russia.

In 1966 James Aldridge turned from these novels with international settings to writing young adult books situated in Australia. "I can't escape Australia, and I don't want to," he once remarked. He published seven novels set in the town of St. Helen, fictional counterpart of Swan Hill, a town he was born near and which he had left as a young man of nineteen. St. Helen, like Swan Hill, is situated on the banks of the Murray River, a river that is to Australians what the Mississippi is to Americans. Aldridge himself associates the two rivers when one of his characters talks about an idyllic "adventuresome Tom Sawyerian sort of boyhood on our lazy Murray River which had steamboats, floods, good fishing, hunting and the sort of adventure that lasted as a faint and unbelievable nostalgia for the rest of my life."

My Brother Tom, the first of the St. Helen novels, tells the love story of Tom Quayle and Peggy MacGibbon against the background of the Depression and the coming threat of the Second World War. Their fathers are archenemies and the couple have to cope with the prejudice of a small town divided by religious bigotry.

The True Story of Lilli Stubeck tells the story of Lilli, daughter of an itinerant family who sell her to a wealthy spinster for twenty-five pounds. The story concerns Lilli's determination to remain true to her own nature. *The True Story of Spit MacPhee* is another story of a tough individual who becomes the subject of a legal tussle between two couples when his grandfather becomes too old to care for him. Again there is religious division—Catholic versus Protestant—and the individual is pitted against a well-meaning town and the law. Paramount in the story is the question of what is best for the individual.

James Aldridge's most recent novel is another of his "true" stories, *The True Story of Lola Mackellar.* Like Spit MacPhee and Lilli Stubeck who arrive in St. Helen with incomplete backgrounds, Lola Mackellar (real name Lorelei), arrives from a foster home in Melbourne. This story, like other St. Helen novels, centres upon the question of identity; why does the wealthy landowning family bring Lola to the town but settle her with a poorer family like an outcast? When Lola's twin from Germany arrives, the question of identity becomes all important and the subtext of the novel raises issues about Australia's European heritage and the development of a national culture.

St. Helen itself has an important character of its own in these books. As individuals the townspeople are basically kind but collectively they are intolerant. One issue that plays an important role in the novels is the damaging effect of gossip. The novels take place in Australia in the 1930s and the town is divided by different levels of social self-interest. The social rules are written by the shopkeepers; the lawyers, doctors, and chemists are its decorative gentry, while the sheep farmers along the plains are the aristocracy, no less feudal for their easy link with the town. Middle-class mentality and morality prevail. In this situation, where materialism and money are emphasised, the fear of justice operating for the rich becomes a threat, but the principle of equality before the law always succeeds.

The novel *Ride a Wild Pony* (originally published as *A Sporting Proposition*) tells the story of thirteen-year-old Scott Pirie, a poor but fiercely independent spirit, whose Welsh pony, Taff, is an extension of himself. As one character puts it, the horses "know they are the centre of attention and obviously enjoy it." Conflict develops when Scott loses the pony and believes it has come into the possession of the wealthy but crippled daughter of a rich land-owner. The whole town becomes involved in the struggle for the pony's ownership and Aldridge offers no neat solution to the problem. The right to equality before the law is an important theme for the St. Helen novels and has its place here. *Ride a Wild Pony* was made into a Disney film in the late seventies, and this story along with Aldridge's *The Broken Saddle* and *The Marvellous Mongolian* are considered among the finest horse stories written by an Australian.

Through his novels James Aldridge seeks to answer age-old questions that have concerned humanity since Plato and Aristotle: how people ought to live in communities and how best to organise their political and social life. Aldridge is concerned with the betterment of life through the search for moral and religious understandings. The St. Helen novels take up these questions no less than his adult books, and because the prose is so concentrated with meaning in his young adult books, the points are effectively made. The characters are urged to overcome "the impoverishments of their generation," "the bigotry of dead morals," and "the violence of violent systems." Aldridge invites us to align with those characters of his who strive at "the frontiers of hope."

—Michael Stone

ALEXANDER, Lloyd (Chudley). American. Born in Philadelphia, Pennsylvania, 30 January 1924. Educated at West Chester State College and Lafayette College, Pennsylvania, 1942-43; the Sorbonne, Paris, 1946. Married Janine Denni in 1946; one daughter. Since 1946, writer and translator. Author-in-residence, schools in Springfield, Pennsylvania, 1967-68, and Temple University, 1970-74. Cartoonist, layout artist, advertising copywriter, and editor of industrial magazine, 1947-70. Since 1970 director, Carpenter Lane Chamber Music Society, Philadelphia; since 1973 member of the Editorial Advisory Board, *Cricket* magazine, Peru, Illinois. Served in the U.S. Army Combat Intelligence and Counter-Intelligence corps, 1942-46: Staff Sergeant. Recipient: Isaac Siegel Memorial Juvenile award, 1959, for *Border Hawk: August Bondi;* ALA notable book citation, 1964, for *The Book of Three;* Newbery Honor Book, 1965, for *The Black Cauldron;* "Best Books" citations, *School Library Journal,* 1967, for *Taran Wanderer,* 1971, for *The King's Fountain,* and 1982, for *Westmark;* citation from American Institute of Graphic Arts Children's Books, 1967-68, for *The Truthful Harp;* "Children's Book of the Year" citation, Child Study Association of America, 1968, for *The High King,* 1971, for *The King's Fountain,* 1973, for *The Cat Who Wished to Be A Man,* 1974, for *The Foundling and Other Tales of Prydain,* 1975, for *The Wizard in the Tree,* 1982, for *The Kestrel,* and 1985, for *The Black Cauldron* and *Time Cat;* Newbery Medal, National Book award nomination, both 1969, both for *The High King;* "Best Books of the Year" citation, Library of Congress, 1970, and National Book Award, 1971, both for *The Marvelous Misadventures of Sebastian;* Drexel award, 1972 and 1976, for outstanding contributions to literature for children; *Boston Globe-Horn Book* award, 1973, for *The Cat Who Wished to Be a Man;* "Outstanding Books of the Year" citation, *New York Times,* 1973, for *The Foundling and Other Tales of Prydain;* Laura Ingalls Wilder award nomination, 1975; National Book award nomination, 1979, Silver Pencil award, 1981, and Aus-

trian Children's Book award, 1984, all for *The First Two Lives of Lukas-Kasha;* American Book Award nomination, 1980, for *The High King,* and 1982, for *The Wizard in the Tree;* ALA "Best Books for Young Adults" citation, 1981, for *Westmark,* 1982, for *The Kestrel,* and 1984, for *The Beggar Queen;* American Book award, 1982, for *Westmark;* Parents' Choice award, 1982, for *The Kestrel,* 1984, for *The Beggar Queen,* and 1986, for *The Illyrian Adventure;* Golden Cat award, Sjoestrands Foerlag (Sweden), 1984, for excellence in children's literature; Regina Medal, Catholic Library Association, 1986; Church and Synagogue Library Association award, 1987; Field award, Pennsylvania Library Association, 1987, for *The Illyrian Adventure;* Lifetime Achievement award, Pennsylvania Center for The Book in Philadelphia, 1991; "Best Book" Citations from *Booklist, School Library Journal,* and Parents' Choice award, all 1991, all for *The Remarkable Journey of Prince Jen;* Parents' Choice award, *Parenting* award, both 1992, both for *The Fortune-Tellers;* *Boston Globe-Horn Book* award for *The Fortune-Tellers,* 1993. Agent: Brandt & Brandt, 1501 Broadway, New York, NY 10036. Address: 1005 Drexel Ave., Drexel Hill, PA 19026, U.S.A.

PUBLICATIONS FOR YOUNG ADULTS

Fiction

The Marvelous Misadventures of Sebastian. New York, Dutton, 1970.
The First Two Lives of Lukas-Kasha. New York, Dutton, 1978.
The Remarkable Journey of Prince Jen. New York, Dutton, 1991.

Prydain series:

The Book of Three. New York, Holt Rinehart, 1964; London, Heinemann, 1966.
The Black Cauldron. New York, Holt Rinehart, 1965; London, Heinemann, 1967.
The Castle of Llyr. New York, Holt Rinehart, 1966; London, Heinemann, 1968.
Taran Wanderer. New York, Holt Rinehart, 1967; London, Fontana, 1979.
The High King. New York, Holt Rinehart, 1968; London, Fontana, 1979.

The Westmark Trilogy:

Westmark. New York, Dutton, 1981.
The Kestrel. New York, Dutton, 1982.
The Beggar Queen. New York, Dutton, 1984.

The Vesper Holly Adventures:

The Illyrian Adventure. New York, Dutton, 1986.
The El Dorado Adventure. New York, Dutton, 1987.
The Drackenberg Adventure. New York, Dutton, 1988.
The Jedera Adventure. New York, Dutton, 1989.
The Philadelphia Adventure. New York, Dutton, 1990.

Biographies

Border Hawk: August Bondi, illustrated by Bernard Krigstein. New
York, Farrar, Straus, 1958.
The Flagship Hope: Aaron Lopez, illustrated by Bernard Krigstein.
Philadelphia, Jewish Publication Society, 1960.

PUBLICATIONS FOR CHILDREN

Fiction

Time Cat: The Remarkable Journeys of Jason and Gareth, illus-
trated by Bill Sokol. New York, Holt Rinehart, 1963; as *Nine
Lives,* London, Cassell, 1963.
Coll and His White Pig, illustrated by Evaline Ness. New York,
Holt Rinehart, 1965.
The Truthful Harp, illustrated by Evaline Ness. New York, Holt
Rinehart, 1967.
The King's Fountain, illustrated by Ezra Jack Keats. New York,
Dutton, 1971.
The Four Donkeys, illustrated by Lester Abrams. New York, Holt
Rinehart, 1972; Kingswood, Surrey, World's Work, 1974.
The Foundling and Other Tales of Prydain, illustrated by Margot
Zemach. New York, Holt Rinehart, 1973.
The Cat Who Wished to Be a Man. New York, Dutton, 1973.
The Wizard in the Tree, illustrated by Laszlo Kubinyi. New York,
Dutton, 1975.
The Town Cats and Other Tales, illustrated by Laszlo Kubinyi.
New York, Dutton, 1977.
The Fortune-Tellers, illustrated by Trina Schart Hyman. New York,
Dutton, 1992.

PUBLICATIONS FOR ADULTS

And Let the Credit Go (novel). New York, Crowell, 1955.
My Five Tigers. New York, Crowell, and London, Cassell, 1956.
Janine Is French. New York, Crowell, 1958; London, Cassell, 1960.
My Love Affair with Music. New York, Crowell, 1960; London,
Cassell, 1961.
Park Avenue Vet, with Dr. Louis Camuti. New York, Holt Rinehart,
and London, Deutsch, 1962.
Fifty Years in the Doghouse. New York, Putnam, 1963; as *Send for
Ryan!,* London, W. H. Allen, 1965.
My Cats and Me: The Story of an Understanding. Philadelphia,
Running Press, 1989.

Translator from the French

The Wall and Other Stories, by Jean-Paul Sartre. New York, New
Directions, 1948; as *Intimacy and Other Stories,* London, Peter
Nevill, 1949.
Nausea, by Jean-Paul Sartre. New York, New Directions, 1949; as
The Diary of Antoine Roquentin, London, Lehmann, 1949.
Selected Writings, by Paul Eluard. New York, New Directions, 1951;
as *Uninterrupted Poetry: Selected Writings,* New York, New Di-
rections, 1975.
The Sea Rose, by Paul Vialar. London and New York, Neville
Spearman, 1951.

Contributor

Horn Book Reflections on Children's Books and Reading, edited by
Elinor Whitney Field. Boston, Horn Book, 1969.
Cricket's Choice. Chicago, Open Court, 1974.
Celebrating Children's Books, edited by Betsy Hearne and Marilyn
Kaye. New York, Lothrop, 1981.
Innocence and Experience, edited by Barbara Harrison and Gregory
Macguire. New York, Lothrop, 1987.
The Voice of the Narrator in Children's Literature, edited by Char-
lotte F. Otten and Gary D. Schmidt. Westport, Connecticut,
Greenwood, 1989.
The Big Book for Peace, edited by Ann Durell and Margaret Sachs.
New York, Dutton, 1990.
The Cat on My Shoulder, edited by Lisa Angowski. Stamford, Con-
necticut, 1993.
The Zena Sutherland Lectures, 1983-1992, edited by Betsy Hearne.
New York, Clarion, 1993.

*

Media Adaptations: Stage versions of *The Cat Who Wished to Be a
Man* and *The Wizard in the Tree.* produced in Japan; television serial
version of *The Marvelous Misadventures of Sebastian.* produced in
Japan; *The Black Cauldron* (film based on the Prydain novels),
Walt Disney Productions, 1985.

Biography: Entry in *Third Book of Junior Authors,* New York,
H.W. Wilson, 1972; entry in *Dictionary of Literary Biography,*
Volume 52, Detroit, Gale, 1986; essay in *Authors and Artists for
Young Adults,* Volume 1, Detroit, Gale, 1989; essay in *Speaking for
Ourselves: Autobiographical Sketches by Notable Authors of Books
for Young Adults,* Volume 1, compiled and edited by Donald R.
Gallo, National Council of Teachers of English, 1990; *Lloyd
Alexander* by Jill P. May, Boston, Twayne, 1991.

Bibliography: *Lloyd Alexander, Evangeline Walton Ensley, Kenneth
Morris: A Primary and Secondary Bibliography* by Kenneth J.
Zahorski, Boston, Hall, 1981; *Lloyd Alexander: A Bio-Bibliogra-
phy* by James S. Jacobs and Michael O. Tunnell, Westport, Connecticut, Greenwood, 1991.

Critical Study: *Children's Literature Review,* Detroit, Gale, Volume
1, 1976, Volume 5, 1983; *A Tribute to Lloyd Alexander* by Myra
Cohn Livingston, Philadelphia, Drexel Institute, 1976; *Lloyd
Alexander: A Critical Biography* by James S. Jacobs, unpublished
dissertation, University of Georgia, 1978; *Contemporary Literary
Criticism,* Detroit, Gale, Volume 35, 1985; *The Prydain Companion*
by Michael O. Tunnell, Westport, Connecticut, Greenwood, 1989.

Lloyd Alexander comments:
    Although most of my books have been in the form of fantasy, I
have always hoped to use this genre in a most personal way, to
express my warm feelings and attitudes toward the real world and
the real people in it. Writing realism or fantasy, my concerns are the
same: how we learn to be genuine human beings.

*   *   *

The adjective that best describes Lloyd Alexander's work is
"American." Whether he is writing about legendary Welsh sorcer-

ers, turn-of-the-century adventurers, or ancient Chinese princes, Alexander's themes and outlook are clearly American. His favorite plot involves freeing an oppressed society and reordering it along democratic principles. During this democratization, Alexander's feisty young heroines and heroes grow up as their youthful idealism becomes tempered by a sometimes grim reality.

Alexander's most noted works are the five volumes of "The Chronicles of Prydain"—*The Book of Three, The Black Cauldron, The Castle of Llyr, Taran Wanderer,* and *The High King.* Although the characters and plots are inspired by Welsh legends, American values permeate the books. The orphaned Taran, whose family background remains a mystery, becomes high king of Prydain in a medieval version of the "any boy can be President" myth, and the self-ruled Free Commots are held up as the ideal democratic society. After many magical adventures and epic battles between good and evil, magic itself must depart Prydain so that a new human order can be established. "The Chronicles of Prydain" not only established Alexander's reputation as a fantasy writer, but they also reinvented American fantasy, bringing the genre critical respect as a serious dramatic form and setting high standards for other fantasy writers as well. This series represents Alexander at his best and highlights his gift for blending humor with high fantasy or other dramatic forms.

The "Westmark" trilogy displays a darker approach to Alexander's main themes of growing up and democratizing society. Political issues come to the fore as a printer's apprentice joins a rebellion against a tyrannical ruler in *Westmark,* the first volume of the series. *The Kestrel* and *The Beggar Queen* continue to raise issues about war, freedom of speech, and the right of self-government. Alexander makes no clear division between good and evil; moral choices are ambiguous, and characters must live with the often difficult consequences of their decisions. At the end of the series the young queen—an enlightened monarch—abdicates her throne in favor of a democratic government. Although Westmark and its neighbors are invented countries, this is not technically a fantasy series; indeed, the first volume is more of a picaresque adventure tale. Altogether, however, the three books are serious novels that explore painful questions of conscience for which there are no easy answers.

The "Vesper Holly" books comprise a much more light hearted series. Set at the turn of the century, these stories recount the adventures of a young lady from Philadelphia and her adoring, slightly stuffy guardian as they pursue their scientific interests to obscure corners of the world. Beginning with *The Illyrian Adventure* and continuing through *The El Dorado Adventure, The Drackenberg Adventure, The Jedera Adventure,* and *The Philadelphia Adventure,* Vesper and Brinnie use their American ingenuity and democratic principles to foil villains, join uprisings, uncover lost treasures, and restore stability in a number of imaginary countries. The series boasts a fast-paced vitality reminiscent of the best Victorian adventures; it's as if Sherlock Holmes and Dr. Watson were racing Captain Nemo to King Solomon's mines. These books represent a departure for Alexander: there are no lessons in growing up, no heavy political issues, and nothing serious to interfere with the humor and adventure.

Aside from these three series, Alexander has written a number of independent novels and biographies for young readers. His two biographies are *Border Hawk: August Bondi* and *Flagship Hope: Aaron Lopez.* Most of his other works are fantasies that rework his favorite themes. *Time Cat,* Alexander's first fantasy, follows the adventures of a cat and his boy as they travel through time to nine

different countries. Another feline fantasy, *The Cat Who Wished to Be a Man,* is as light hearted as the "Vesper Holly" tales. Lionel, the cat of the title, convinces his master—a wizard—to transform him into a man so that he may see how humans live. Most of the action takes place in a small town ruled by a despotic mayor. Although Alexander paints on a smaller canvas in this book, he still employs his favorite themes: Lionel matures as he becomes more human, and the tyrannical mayor is overthrown by the democratic town council.

Three other fantasies deal with young men who grow up through travel and adventure, saving various kingdoms from tyranny along the way. The adventure in *The First Two Lives of Lukas-Kasha* takes place in the main character's mind, but when his fantasy adventure casts him as a king, his goal for his country is to make the monarchy obsolete. Similarly, the young musician in *The Marvelous Misadventures of Sebastian* helps a princess free her country from a ruthless regent, and the book concludes with the princess planning to convert her monarchy into a democracy. *The Remarkable Journey of Prince Jen* tells a similar story of ancient China. In this case, however, the hero is the highborn character and the heroine is the commoner—a reversal of Alexander's usual pattern. Totally isolated in the royal palace, Prince Jen has no idea what life is like in his country. A quest to find a mythical kingdom brings him and his companions face to face with the greed, petty tyranny, poverty, and despair that is crippling their country. Like other Alexander heroes, Jen must learn harsh lessons before he is fit to rule himself, let alone his people, but eventually he and his friends succeed in establishing a fair and equitable monarchy.

Although his underlying themes are serious and complex political issues, Alexander invariably leavens them with humor, thus making them more palatable. He is a master at creating memorable characters with a comic twist. But above all, he is a Philadelphian, and everything he writes reflects the values of the cradle of liberty.

—Donna R. White

———

ALLEN, Betsy. See **CAVANNA, Betty.**

———

ANDREWS, V(irginia C(leo). American. Born in Portsmouth, Virginia. Educated in Portsmouth, Virginia. Writer. Formerly worked as a fashion illustrator, commercial artist, portrait artist, and gallery exhibitor. *Died 19 December 1986.*

PUBLICATIONS

Novels

Flowers in the Attic. New York, Pocket Books, 1979.
Petals on the Wind. New York, Simon and Schuster, 1980.
If There Be Thorns. New York, Simon and Schuster, 1981.
My Sweet Audrina. New York, Poseidon Press, 1982.
Seeds of Yesterday. New York, Poseidon Press, 1984.

Heaven. New York, Poseidon Press, 1985.
Dark Angel. New York, Poseidon Press, 1986.
Garden of Shadows. New York, Pocket Books, 1987.
Fallen Hearts. New York, Pocket Books, 1988.
Gates of Paradise. New York, Pocket Books, 1989.
Dawn. New York, Pocket Books, 1990.
Web of Dreams. Boston, G.K. Hall, 1990.
Secrets of the Morning. Boston, G.K. Hall, 1991.
Jardin Sombrio. La Costa Press, 1992.
Midnight Whispers. New York, Pocket Books, 1992.
Twilight's Child. Boston, G.K. Hall, 1992.
Darkest Hour. New York, Pocket Books, 1993.

*

Media Adaptations: *Flowers in the Attic* (film), Fries Entertainment-New World Pictures, 1987.

Biography: Essay in *Authors and Artists for Young Adults,* Volume 4, Detroit, Gale, 1990.

*   *   *

V.C. Andrews wrote several, extremely popular Gothic novels and was reported as one of the fastest-selling authors in America. Her works were originally published in paperback by Pocket Books and were especially popular with adolescents.

Flowers in the Attic, published in 1979, is the story of the four Dollanganger children who are locked in the attic by their mother and tortured by their grandmother. These four beautiful children are the product of an incestuous union. Their imprisonment occurs because their mother fears that she will be excluded from their fundamentalist grandfather's will if he learns of their existence. The children create their own world and turn to each other for love. *Flowers in the Attic* was originally a 290,000-word story called *The Obsessed.* Pared down to ninety-eight pages, the book was very "reserved." Editors encouraged Andrews to write more from her imagination, so she began to tackle difficult subjects many had neglected. *Flowers in the Attic* was adapted into a movie in 1987 and filmed by Fries Entertainment—New World Pictures.

The lives of the Dollanganger children and their revenge continued in the next two novels—*Petals on the Wind* and *If There Be Thorns. Flowers in the Attic* was so popular that when readers found a sequel was forthcoming, demand became so great that Pocket Books advanced the publication date by several months. *Petals on the Wind* was so successful that it not only appeared on the best-seller list for nineteen weeks but also pulled *Flowers in the Attic* back on to the list for a time. Shocking and entrancing, *Petals on the Wind* continues *Flowers in the Attic*'s themes and may tax credibility. The last novel of the trilogy, *If There Be Thorns,* was also incredibly popular, reaching the number two slot only two weeks after its release. The "Dollanganger" series then continued with *Seeds of Yesterday* and *Garden of Shadows.*

The themes of the books—misogyny, rape, incest, and revenge—are touchy subjects to some readers and have provoked a degree of outrage. Adolescent girls still constitute a large portion of their readership. Some critics have called Andrews's plots unbelievable. A few critics, however, have praised her ability to captivate an audience with absorbing narrative and realistic point of view.

My Sweet Audrina was published in 1982. It relates the strange life of Audrina Adare who has been protected from the world by her parents. She has no sense of time or memory of the past. She is the second daughter of that name. The first was a beloved girl who died mysteriously at age nine. As the second Audrina grows up and falls in love, she is plagued by a jealous cousin and haunted by the memory of her dead older sister and her father's possessiveness. When she is grown, she confronts her father and learns of the intricate web of lies that protects her from a terrible truth.

Andrews's other novels continue with her themes of darkness and secrets. *Garden of Shadows* was published in 1987 after Andrews's death. This novel takes place before *Flowers in the Attic* and tells the story of forbidden passions and dreadful secrets. Its main character is Olivia, whose happiness becomes tainted when a jealous obsession threatens her two boys and beautiful girl, and the wicked curse of the Dollanganger family begins.

V.C. Andrews's "Casteel" series includes *Heaven, Dark Angel, Fallen Hearts, Gates of Paradise,* and *Web of Dreams.* After her death, Andrews's family chose a writer to complete her stories, beginning with her final books in the "Casteel" series. Much controversy has arisen from this ploy to keep a "dead" author writing other best-sellers.

Dawn, published in 1990, is solely the work of Andrew Neiderman. It tells the story of Dawn Longchamp and her brother, Jimmy, who have grown up in poverty. They are allowed to attend an exclusive private school because their father is a janitor there. When Dawn's mother dies, she discovers she was kidnapped at birth from a wealthy family. Humiliated and scorned, Dawn tries to find Jimmy and to rid herself of the awful lies that have changed their lives.

More novels in the "Dawn" series are promised. The Andrews family wrote the following in a letter prefaced to *Dawn:* "When Virginia became seriously ill while writing the 'Casteel' series, she began to work even harder, hoping to finish as many stories as possible so that her fans could one day share them. Just before she died we promised ourselves that we would take all of these wonderful stories and make them available to her readers."

—Lesa Dill

———

ANGELOU, Maya. Pseudonym for Marguerita Annie Johnson. American. Born in St. Louis, Missouri, 4 April 1928. Educated at schools in Arkansas and California; studied music privately, dance with Martha Graham, Pearl Primus, and Ann Halprin, and drama with Frank Silvera and Gene Frankel. Married 1) Tosh Angelos in 1950 (divorced); 2) Paul Du Feu in 1973 (divorced 1981), one son. Author, poet, playwright, educator, actress, dancer, and singer. Appeared in *Porgy and Bess* on twenty-two nation tour sponsored by the U.S. Department of State, 1954-55; appeared in Off-Broadway plays, *Calypso Heatwave,* 1957, and Jean Genet's *The Blacks,* 1960; with Godfrey Cambridge wrote, produced, and performed in *Cabaret for Freedom,* Off-Broadway, 1960; associate editor, *Arab Observer,* Cairo, 1961-62; assistant administrator, School of Music and Drama, University of Ghana Institute of African Studies, Legon and Accra, 1963-66; freelance writer for *Ghanaian Times* and Ghanaian Broadcasting Corporation, both Accra, 1963-65; appeared in *Mother Courage* at University of Ghana, 1964; feature editor, *African Review,* Accra, 1964-66; appeared in *Meda* in Hollywood, 1966; lecturer, University of California, Los Angeles, 1966;

made Broadway debut in *Look Away,* 1973; writer-in-residence or Visiting Professor, University of Kansas, Lawrence, 1970, Wake Forest University, Winston-Salem, North Carolina, 1974, Wichita State University, Kansas, 1974, and California State University, Sacramento, 1974; director *Moon on a Rainbow Shawl* by Errol John, London, 1988. Since 1981 Reynolds Professor, Wake Forest University. Also television host and interviewer, and composer. Writer for Oprah Winfrey television series *Brewster Place.* Northern coordinator, Southern Christian Leadership Conference, 1959-60; member, American Revolution Bicentennial Council, 1975-76; member of the advisory board, Women's Prison Association. Since 1975 member of the board of trustees, American Film Institute. Recipient: National Book Award nomination, 1970, for *I Know Why the Caged Bird Sings*; Yale University fellowship, 1970; Pulitzer Prize nomination, 1972, for *Just Give Me a Cool Drink of Water 'fore I Diiie*; Tony Award nomination, 1973, for performance in *Look Away*; Rockefeller grant, 1975; named Woman of the Year in Communications by *Ladies Home Journal,* 1976; Matrix Award in the field of books, Women in Communication, Inc., 1983. Honorary degrees: Smith College, Northampton, Massachusetts, 1975; Mills College, Oakland, California, 1975; Lawrence University, Appleton, Wisconsin, 1976. Agent: Lordly and Dame Inc., 51 Church Street, Boston, MA 02116. Lives in Sonoma California. Address: Department of Humanities, Wake Forest University, Reynolds Station, Winston Salem, NC 27109, U.S.A.

PUBLICATIONS

Novels

I Know Why the Caged Bird Sings. New York, Random House, 1970; London, Virago Press, 1984.
Gather Together in My Name. New York, Random House, 1974; London, Virago Press, 1985.
Singin' and Swingin' and Gettin' Merry Like Christmas. New York, Random House, 1976; London, Virago Press, 1985.
The Heart of a Woman. New York, Random House, 1981; London, Virago Press, 1986.
All God's Children Need Traveling Shoes. New York, Random House, 1986; London, Virago Press, 1987.

Poetry

Just Give Me a Cool Drink of Water 'fore I Diiie. New York, Random House, 1971; London, Virago Press, 1988.
Oh Pray My Wings Are Gonna Fit Me Well. New York, Random House, 1975.
Poems: Maya Angelou. New York, Bantam, 1981.
Shaker, Why Don't You Sing? New York, Random House, 1983.
Now Sheba Sings the Song, illustrated by Tom Feelings. New York, Dial Press, and London, Virago Press, 1987.
I Shall Not Be Moved. New York, Random House, 1990.

Recordings: *Miss Calypso,* Liberty Records, 1957; *The Poetry of Maya Angelou,* GWP Records, 1969; *An Evening with Maya Angelou,* Pacific Tape Library, 1975.

Plays

Cabaret for Freedom (revue), with Godfrey Cambridge (produced New York, 1960).
The Least of These (produced Los Angeles, 1966).
Ajax, from the play by Sophocles (produced Los Angeles, 1974).
And Still I Rise (also director: produced in Oakland, California, 1976). New York, Random House, 1978; London, Virago Press, 1986.
King (lyrics only, with Alistair Beaton), book by Lonne Elder III, music by Richard Blackford (produced London, 1990).

Screenplays: *Georgia, Georgia,* Independent-Cinerama, 1972; *All Day Long* (also director), American Film Institute, 1974.

Television Play: *Sister, Sister,* with John Berry, National Broadcasting Co., Inc., 1982.

Other

Mrs. Flowers: A Moment of Friendship (for children), illustrations by Etienne Delessert. Minneapolis, Redpath Press, 1986.
Conversations with Maya Angelou, edited by Jeffrey M. Elliot. University, University of Mississippi, and London, Virago Press, 1989.

*

Media Adaptations: *I Know Why the Caged Bird Sings* (audio cassette with filmstrip and teacher's guide), Center for Literary Review, 1978, abridged version read by Angelou, New York, Random House, 1986; *I Know Why the Caged Bird Sings* (television movie), Columbia Broadcasting System, Inc., 1979; *Women in Business,* University of Wisconsin, 1981; *And Still I Rise* (television special), Public Broadcasting Service, 1985; *Making Magic in the World,* New Dimensions, 1988.

Television Documentaries: *Black, Blues, Black,* National Educational Television, 1968; *Assignment America,* 1975; *The Legacy,* 1976; *The Inheritors,* 1976; *Trying to Make It Home* (*Byline* series), 1988; *Maya Angelou's America: A Journey of the Heart* (also host).

Biography: Entry in *Dictionary of Literary Biography,* Volume 38, Detroit, Gale, 1985.

Manuscript Collection: Wake Forest University, Winston-Salem, North Carolina.

Critical Study: Entry in *Contemporary Literary Criticism,* Detroit, Gale, Volume 12, 1980, Volume 35, 1985.

*   *   *

Maya Angelou is perhaps right to claim that she is "the only serious writer who has chosen the autobiographical form to carry her work, her expression." She has been duly recognized as being one of the most successful serial writers of black autobiography. In her five autobiographies (and also in her poetry), she dramatizes both the pleasure and the plight of a young black female in America's socially segregated society.

The sequential books written by Angelou tell not just what has happened to her but the effect upon her of these happenings. She relates things she has learned, how she has grown, and how she has moved along the trail of self-discovery. Her stories seem to tell themselves and from them emerge the exposition of her themes. Angelou's dedication to personal growth and self-evaluation comes up repeatedly and she continually modifies her ideas about black/white relationships over time. Despite early enviromental conditioning, she eventually realizes, as did her friend Malcolm X, that not all whites are devils. Three familiar themes of black autobiography are found in both Angelou's prose and her poetry: repeated triumphs over obstacles, a search for identity, and the value of literacy and learning.

Angelou examines her childhood and responds to the problems of that childhood by creating a persona. She has said she invented herself because she was tired of society inventing her, of distorting her personality, of turning a stereotype into reality, of bestowing upon her a label she rejected.

The biographical facts of Angelou's early life in Stamps, Arkansas, in the 1930s, where she lived from the age of three to thirteen with Grandmother "Momma" Henderson after the divorce of her parents, are interwoven with many accounts about that life in her first autobiography, the highly successful and immensely popular *I Know Why the Caged Bird Sings* (1970). This book contains a series of anecdotes linked together by a theme of displacement: "If growing up is painful for the Southern Black girl, being aware of her displacement is the rust on the razor that threatens the throat. It is an unnecessary insult." *Caged Bird* takes Angelou through high school graduation and the birth of her son. It includes most of the general elements of childhood autobiographies. A lack of self-esteem and a sense of insignificance show when Angelou says she is "Awful" because she is a "too-big Negro girl, with nappy black hair, broad feet and a space between her teeth that would hold a number-two pencil," and she wears hand-me-down clothes. Rejection is a factor related to the mostly absent mother and father. The father is never depicted as affectionate. Being black in a segregated society, Angelou sees herself as dependent, ineffective, and small. She had to rely on ministrations of others—mainly her grandmother.

Angelou's four subsequent autobiographies proceed chronologically. Covering her life as a teenage mother, her introduction to drugs and illicit activities, and the basics of economic survival is the thrust of volume two, *Gather Together in My Name* (1974). Focusing on her young adult years as a show business personality is *Singin' and Swingin' and Gettin' Merry Like Christmas* (1976). Most of the book tells about her adventures while on a *Porgy and Bess* tour for the U.S. State Department. Her life as an activist embroiled in social causes reflects a maturing Angelou in *The Heart of a Woman* (1981). The fifth book, *All God's Children Need Traveling Shoes* (1986), relates her experiences as an expatriate in Ghana.

Maya Angelou's stories are aptly called testimonials. She "testifies" not only for herself but also for her community. She seems to speak for black consciousness. Her voice as a writer is the voice of her people. What her community endures, she endures. She writes about what she knows: the black experience. The universals contained in her work serve to underscore her frequently expressed thesis: that as people, we are more alike than unalike.

—Lyman B. Hagen

ANONYMOUS (*Go Ask Alice*).

*   *   *

In 1971 a book for young adult readers was published and became an immediate success. Today, more than two decades later, *Go Ask Alice* is still going strong, with some three million copies in print, seventy-seven printings at this writing, translation into sixteen languages, and a made-for-TV movie based on it that still shows up regularly on late-night video. Many people who have expertise or interest in YA books, however, believe that *Alice*'s greatest success is that it probably is one of the biggest hoaxes in publishing history.

When Prentice-Hall published the book, the author was listed as "Anonymous," ostensibly to protect the identity of the fifteen-year-old drug addict whose diary it was. The original diary, P-H claimed, was hidden in a secure place and would not he released to anyone even though the girl was supposed to have died of an overdose, either accidental or intentional, only a few weeks after the last entry in her diary. A few years later, however, P-H ran an ad in *Publishers Weekly* describing their fall 1977 list of titles for young readers. One of the titles was *Voices,* and the annotation mentioned that its author, Beatrice Sparks, was "the *author* [italics mine] of *Go Ask Alice.*" Curious, a number of librarians asked P-H how this could be, since the Epilogue to *Alice* clearly stated that the diarist had died of an overdose six years earlier. No response was forthcoming, but when the book finally appeared, its jacket stated that it was "from Beatrice Sparks...the author who brought you *Go Ask Alice.*" A year later, another Sparks title appeared, *Jay's Journal,* and this one also claimed to be "edited by Beatrice Sparks, who brought you...*Alice.*"

Needless to say, YA literature mavens were puzzled. One of these people, Alleen Pace Nilsen of Arizona State University, was puzzled enough to seek Sparks out and interview her about *Alice;* the interview, entitled "The House That Alice Built," appeared in the October 1979 issue of *School Library Journal* and a fascinating interview it was—and still is. Suffice it to say that after it appeared in *SLJ* very few people believed that *Alice* was a teenager's true tale.

The discussion above is given to illustrate how controversial *Go Ask Alice* is and has been, while at the same time a whole generation of young readers has bought it hook, line, and sinker, believing that they are reading a true story about someone very much like themselves. This goes a long way toward proving just how foolish the old saw about how you can't really fool the young is, because they are and always have been fooled by this book. And it is a dreadful book in almost every way. Not a line rings true as the word of a young person, but instead is blatantly the work of an adult trying mightily to sound like a kid but unable to do it. And there is a great deal of extremely clumsy swearing; anyone who knows young people knows that they know how to use cuss words very realistically and appropriately. Finally, the book is as didactic as any nineteenth-century religious tract; Sparks bludgeons the reader on nearly every page with pietistic preaching. A few passages from the book should illustrate these criticisms:

> Oh to be stoned, to have someone tie me off and give me
> a shot of anything. I've heard paregoric is great. Oh hell, I
> wish I had enough anything to end the whole shitty mess.

July 27

Dear Diary,

I truly must have lost my mind or at least control of it, for I have just tried to pray. I wanted to ask God to help me but I could utter only words, dark, useless words which fell on the floor beside me and rolled off into the corners and underneath the bed. I tried. I really tried to remember what I should say after "Now I lay me down to sleep," but they are only words, useless, artificial, heavy words which have no meaning and no powers. They are like the ravings of the idiotic spewing woman who is now part of my inmate family. Verbal rantings, useless, groping, unimportant, with no power and no glory. Sometimes I think death is the only way out of this room.

If there were still doubts in anyone's mind about whether *Alice* was fact or fiction after Nilsen's damning interview in *SLJ* and the profound shallowness and phoniness of the book itself, they were surely dissolved by Sparks's next two books. Both purported to be true stories of real young people, told in their own words; each is as clumsy, shallow, phony, and didactic as *Alice,* with, if such is possible, a writing style that is simply unbelievably bad. *Voices* is supposed to be the stories of four teenagers who fall victim to some awful conditions of modern life. Mary, a bored sophomore in high school, takes up with Dawn, "a clear-eyed quiet smiling girl," who inspires Mary to run off with her and join a cult called Heaven House presided over by the stereotypical guru, Sky, who soon sends Mary out to panhandle in the big city. At one point, Mary is rhapsodizing in her mind about her new life, which is "too wonderful, too special, too yummy" for words. A half dozen lines later she is "flipping the bird" at "a couple of cute dudes in a convertible." She is finally rescued (near death from starvation) from the satanic Sky, but not before the reader has been subjected to about eighty pages of totally unbelievable as well as totally bad prose.

Mark, whose story is subtitled "the lure of suicide," begins his turgid account with this statement: "As I think about the whole a-hole concept of life, I wonder if it's worth the hassle. Man, what a grind, what a hassle." Four lines later, he is telling about an incident when he was a little kid: "Like the time we made our Christmas home movie [and] the dad-gummed donkey we borrowed from someone wouldn't go." No teenager in the twentieth century has used the expression "dad-gummed" and probably their grandparents haven't either. Millie gets into what Sparks calls "the homosexual alternative" but what Millie calls "the Lizzie set," when Mrs. Stephens, Millie's typing teacher, takes an interest in her. In Millie's words, "Now that I'm an 'into it' person. I can't believe the time and patience she took to turn me on. Actually she softened me up for over three months before she finally laid it to me. Man, when I want someone, I want them now! I don't want to fool around. I guess you know most gays are real single shots, picking up numbers in gas station rest rooms and stuff, but her. I dunno...I guess it was the big conquest bit or something..." (Author's note: Millie is thirteen at this time.) Millie is finally sent to a private girls' school, which of course is a hotbed of young "Lizzies." Jane, the last speaker in the book, pays "the price of peer pressure," which in her case means getting "hooked on sex." At one point she describes her life: "Once I went home with Marty, whose Mother [sic] worked. He was only twelve years old and I raped him—actually raped him! Can you believe that of a girl from a nice family like mine?" Merci-

fully, Jane's entire story takes only ten and one half pages to tell, because it's even sillier than the three which preceded it.

Two years after *Voices,* Sparks's final book was published. Called *Jay's Journal,* the book's cover says it is "The haunting diary of a sixteen-year-old in the world of witchcraft..." This is another of her "true" stories, given to her in the form of a journal/diary such as the one Alice kept. Jay is her usual unhappy teenager, lonely and anxious until he enters "the eerie and dangerous world of the occult...a weird world of levitation and psychic forces, 'wangas' or feathered voodoo charms, auras and black presences, and grisly mystic rites like the Bootan ritual of cattle mutilation and baptism by blood." The book is pure Sparks; full of florid prose, outdated slang, teenage *angst,* and a message with a capital M—voodoo will get you just like drugs and cults and Lizzies and suicide and peer pressure, as it got Jay, who committed suicide. To no one's surprise except perhaps Sparks and her publisher, even the Library of Congress came to its senses with *Voices* and *Jay's Journal* and catalogued them as fiction (as which they later recatalogued *Alice* as well). Mercifully, both books have long been out of print, even though *Alice* goes on and on and on fooling the vulnerable young—and that's the real tragedy of *Go Ask Alice.*

—Audrey Eaglen

———

ANTHONY, Piers (Piers Anthony Dillingham Jacob). Also writes as Robert Piers (a joint pseudonym). American. Born in Oxford, England, 6 August 1934; became United States citizen, 1958. Educated at Goddard College, Plainfield, Vermont, B.A. 1956; University of South Florida, Tampa, teaching certificate 1964. Served in the United States Army, 1957-59. Married Carol Marble in 1956; two daughters. Technical writer, Electronic Communications Inc., St. Petersburg, Florida, 1959-62; English teacher, Admiral Farragut Academy, St. Petersburg, 1965-66. Since 1966 freelance writer. Recipient: August Derleth award, 1977; British Fantasy award, 1977, for *A Spell for Chameleon.* Address: c/o HI Piers, Suite 206E, 13540 North Florida Avenue, Tampa, FL 33613, U.S.A.

PUBLICATIONS FOR YOUNG ADULTS

Novels

Omnivore. New York, Ballantine, 1968; London, Faber, 1969.
Sos the Rope. New York, Pyramid, 1968; London, Faber, 1970.
The Ring, with Robert E. Margroff. New York, Ace, 1968; London, Macdonald, 1969.
The E.S.P. Worm, with Robert E. Margroff. New York, Paperback Library, 1970.
Orn. New York, Avon, 1971; London, Corgi, 1977.
Var the Stick. London, Faber, 1972; New York, Bantam, 1973.
Rings of Ice. New York, Avon, 1974; London, Millington, 1975.
Triple Détente. New York, DAW, 1974; London, Sphere, 1975.
Neq the Sword. London, Corgi, 1975.
But What of Earth?, with Robert Coulson. Toronto, Laser, 1976; revised edition, New York, Tor, 1989.
Ox. New York, Avon, 1976; London, Corgi, 1977.
Steppe. London, Millington, 1976; New York, Tor, 1985.

Cluster. New York, Avon, 1977; London, Millington, 1978; as *Vicinity Cluster,* London, Panther, 1979.

Hasan, with Roberto Fuentes. San Bernardino, California, Borgo Press, 1977.

A Spell for Chameleon. New York, Ballantine, 1977; London, Macdonald, 1984.

Chaining the Lady. New York, Avon, and London, Millington, 1978.

Kirlian Quest. New York, Avon, and London, Millington, 1978.

Castle Roogna. New York, Ballantine, 1979; London, Macdonald, 1984.

The Pretender, with Frances Hall. San Bernardino, California, Borgo Press, 1979.

The Source of Magic. New York, Ballantine, 1979; London, Macdonald, 1984.

God of Tarot. New York, Jove, 1979.

Faith of Tarot. New York, Berkley, 1980.

Vision of Tarot. New York, Berkley, 1980.

Split Infinity. New York, Ballantine, 1980; London, Granada, 1983.

Thousandstar. New York, Avon, 1980; London, Panther, 1984.

Blue Adept. New York, Ballantine, 1981; London, Granada, 1983.

Mute. New York, Avon, 1981; London, New English Library, 1984.

Centaur Aisle. New York, Ballantine, 1982; London, Macdonald, 1984.

Juxtaposition. New York, Ballantine, 1982.

Ogre, Ogre. New York, Ballantine, 1982; London, Futura, 1984.

Viscous Circle. New York, Avon, 1982; London, Panther, 1984.

Dragon on a Pedestal. New York, Ballantine, 1983; London, Futura, 1984.

Night Mare. New York, Ballantine, 1983; London, Futura, 1984.

Bearing an Hourglass. New York, Ballantine, and London, Severn House, 1984.

On a Pale Horse. New York, Ballantine, 1984; London, Panther, 1985.

Bio of a Space Tyrant. Boston, Gregg Press, 1985.

Crewel Lye: A Caustic Yarn. New York, Ballantine, 1985; London, Futura, 1986.

With a Tangled Skein. New York, Ballantine, 1985; London, Panther, 1986.

Golem in the Gears. New York, Ballantine, and London, Futura, 1986.

Of Man and Mantra: A Trilogy (includes *Omnivore, Orn,* and *Ox*). London, Corgi, 1986.

Shade of the Tree. New York, St. Martin's, 1986; London, Grafton, 1987.

Wielding a Red Sword. New York, Ballantine, 1986; London, Grafton, 1987.

Being a Green Mother. New York, Ballantine, 1987; London, Grafton, 1988.

Dragon's Gold, with Robert E. Margroff. New York, Tor, 1987.

Out of Phaze. New York, Putnam, 1987; London, New English Library, 1989.

Tarot (includes *God of Tarot, Vision of Tarot,* and *Faith of Tarot*). New York, Ace, and London, Grafton, 1987.

Vale of the Vole. New York, Avon, 1987; London, New English Library, 1988.

Heaven Cent. New York, Avon, 1988; London, New English Library, 1989.

For Love of Evil. New York, Morrow, 1988; London, Grafton, 1989.

Robot Adept. New York, Putnam, 1988; London, New English Library, 1989.

Serpent's Silver, with Robert E. Margroff. New York, Tor, 1988.

Man from Mundania. New York, Avon, 1989; London, New English Library, 1990.

Unicorn Point. New York, Putnam, 1989; London, New English Library, 1990.

And Eternity. New York, Morrow, and London, Severn House, 1990.

Balook. Lancaster, Pennsylvania, Underwood Miller, 1990.

Chimaera's Cooper, with Robert E. Margroff. New York, Tor, 1990.

Hard Sell. Houston, Texas, Tafford, 1990.

Isle of View. New York, Morrow, 1990.

Orc's Opal, with Robert E. Margroff. New York, Tor, 1990.

Phaze Doubt. New York, Putnam, 1990.

Through the Ice (completion of work by Robert Kornwise). Lancaster, Pennsylvania, Underwood Miller, 1990.

MerCycle, illustrated by Ron Lindham and Val Lindham. Houston, Texas, Tafford, 1991.

Question Quest. New York, Morrow, 1991.

Virtual Mode. New York, Putnam, 1991.

The Caterpillar's Question, with Philip Jose Farmer. New York, Ace, 1992.

The Color of Her Panties. New York, Morrow, 1992.

Fractal Mode. New York, Putnam, 1992.

Mouvar's Magic, with Robert E. Margroff. New York, Tor, 1992.

Demons Don't Dream. New York, Tor, 1993.

If I Pay Thee Not in Gold, with Mercedes Lackey. Riverdale, New York, Baen, 1993.

Killobyte. New York, Putnam, 1993.

Letters to Jenny. New York, Tor, 1993.

Isle of Woman. New York, Tor, 1993.

Short Stories

Prostho Plus. London, Gollancz, 1971; New York, Bantam, 1973.

Anthonology (collection). New York, Tor, 1985; London, Grafton, 1986.

Other

Contributor, *Science against Man,* edited by Anthony Cheetham. New York, Avon, 1970.

Contributor, *Nova One: An Anthology of Original Science Fiction,* edited by Harry Harrison. New York, Delacorte Press, 1970.

Contributor, *Again, Dangerous Visions,* edited by Harlan Ellison. New York, Doubleday, 1972.

Contributor, *Generation,* edited by David Gerrold. New York, Dell, 1972.

Race against Time (for children). New York, Hawthorn, 1973.

Battle Circle (includes *Sos the Rope, Var the Stick,* and *Neq the Sword*). New York, Avon, 1978; London, Corgi, 1984.

Contributor, *The Berkley Showcase,* edited by Victoria Schochet and John Silbersack. New York, 1981.

The Magic of Xanth. New York, Doubleday, 1981.

Double Exposure (includes *Split Infinity, Blue Adept,* and *Juxtaposition*). New York, Doubleday, 1982.

Editor, with Barry N. Malzberg, Martin H. Greenberg, and Charles G. Waugh, *Uncollected Stars.* New York, Avon, 1986.

Bio of an Ogre: The Autobiography of Piers Anthony to Age 50. New York, Ace, 1988.

Pier Anthony's Visual Guide to Xanth, with Jody Lynn Nye, illustrated by Todd Cameron Hamilton and James Clouse. New York, Avon, 1989.

Alien Plot (collection). New York, Doherty, 1992.
Chaos Mode. New York, Putnam, 1993.
Happy Thyme. England, New England Library, 1993.

PUBLICATIONS FOR ADULTS

Novels

Chthon. New York, Ballantine, 1967; London, Macdonald, 1970.
Macroscope. New York, Avon, 1969; London, Sphere, 1972.
Kiai!, with Roberto Fuentes. New York, Berkley, 1974.
Mistress of Death, with Roberto Fuentes. New York, Berkley, 1974.
The Bamboo Bloodbath, with Roberto Fuentes. New York, Berkley, 1975.
Ninja's Revenge, with Roberto Fuentes. New York, Berkley, 1975.
Phthor. New York, Berkley, 1975; London, Panther, 1978.
Amazon Slaughter, with Roberto Fuentes. New York, Berkley, 1976.
Refugee. New York, Avon, 1983.
Mercenary. New York, Avon, 1984.
Executive. New York, Avon, 1985.
Politician. New York, Avon, 1985.
Ghost. New York, Tor, 1986.
Statesman. New York, Avon, 1986.
Pornucopia. Houston, Texas, Tafford, 1989.
Total Recall. New York, Morrow, 1989; London, Legend, 1990.
Dead Morn, with Roberto Fuentes. Houston, Texas, Tafford, 1990.
Firefly. New York, Morrow, 1990.
Tatham Mound. New York, Morrow, 1991.

Also contributor, with Robert Margroff, under joint pseudonym Robert Piers, of a short story to *Adam Bedside Reader.* Also contributor of short stories to science fiction periodicals, including *Analog, Fantastic, Worlds of If, Worlds of Tomorrow, Amazing, Magazine of Fantasy and Science Fiction,* and *Pandora.*

*

Biography: Entry in *Dictionary of Literary Biography,* Volume 8, Detroit, Gale, 1981.

Manuscript Collection: Syracuse University, New York; University of South Florida, Florida.

Critical Study: *Piers Anthony* by Michael R. Collings, Mercer Island, Washington, Starmont House, 1983; Entry in *Contemporary Literary Criticism,* Volume 35, Detroit, Gale, 1985.

*   *   *

Known as a prolific and controversial writer of fantasy and science fiction for young adults, Piers Anthony himself suggests that his works are merely entertaining and relaxing. Even though his plots may sound familiar, Anthony is capable of making the ordinary extraordinary with his unique plot twists and unusual phrasings.

Among the myriad novels to his credit are several series. The first novel to be published, *Chthon,* was a Nebula and Hugo Award nominee. It has a sequel called *Phthor.* Both novels share Anthony's characteristic motifs and organization. They contain a mixture of classical myth and legend, modern psychoanalysis, more traditional literary themes, and folk tales. *Chthon* tells of Anton Five and his

fellow prisoners in the garnet mines inside the planet Chthon. *Phthor* continues with the tale of Arlo, Anton's son, and concludes with a major conflict between mineral and organic intelligence. While Anton's imprisonment is symbolic of humanity's status today, his escape foreshadows hope for mankind.

In the "Omnivore" series (*Omnivore, Orn, Ox*), three space explorers from Earth—Veg, Cal, and Aquilon—explore alternate worlds. Through their adventures, the human race is assessed to its detriment as Anthony examines man's role in the natural world. The "Battle Circle" trilogy (*Sos the Rope, Var the Stick, Neq the Sword*) takes place after the devastation of nuclear war has reduced America to barbaric nomads and an underground of technological experts who have survived. *Macroscope,* considered Anthony's best work by some critics, features a mechanical device that enables man to penetrate the mysteries of the universe and the human consciousness so that humanity loses significance in relation to the universe, even as an individual might lose meaning versus mass society.

The Tarot novels—originally *God of Tarot, Vision of Tarot,* and *Faith of Tarot* —again question humanity, this time in the form of questioning the beliefs of the individual. Brother Paul of the secular Holy Order of Vision investigates odd tarot animations that may imply the existence of a deity and at the same time makes discoveries of his own.

The "Apprentice Adept" novels (*Split Infinity, Blue Adept, Juxtaposition, Out of Phaze, Robot Adept, Unicorn Point, Phaze Doubt*) attempt to combine fantasy and science fiction. Science fiction is sprinkled with magic and the natural in *Out of Phaze.* The world of Phaze is contrasted to Proton. The former is magical but still natural, while the latter is scientific and ecologically controlled.

The "Magic of Xanth" series (*A Spell for Chameleon, The Source of Magic, Castle Roogna, Centaur Aisle, Ogre, Ogre, Night Mare, Dragon on a Pedestal, Crewel Lye: A Caustic Yarn, Golem in the Gears, Vale of the Vole, Heaven Cent, Man from Mundania*), the most popular of Anthony's writings, is light-hearted and pun-filled. Xanth is a fairy-tale peninsula populated by dragons, ogres, centaurs, and nymphs. These episodic novels, filled with references to classical myths, reflect Anthony's environmental concerns. Some readers, however, are troubled by their over-reliance on word play and by their use of sexist humor.

The "Bio of a Space Tyrant" series (*Refugee, Mercenary, Politician, Executive, Statesman*) and the "Incarnations of Immortality" series (*On a Pale Horse, Bearing an Hourglass, With a Tangled Skein, Wielding a Red Sword, Being a Green Mother, For Love of Evil,* and *And Eternity* comprise Anthony's "serious" phase and express his views on society. In "Incarnations," personifications of Death, Time, Space, War, and Nature battle Satan. The "Bio" novels show the rise to power of a space refugee on the planet Jupiter.

Anthony's prodigious output includes a number of individual novels of science fiction and fantasy, a collection of short stories *Anthology,* an autobiography entitled *Bio of an Ogre,* and *Race against Time,* specifically marketed as juvenile fiction. While entertaining his readers with his inventive word play, numerous literary allusions, apt symbolism, humorous satire, and wild adventures, Anthony effectively conveys his personal convictions about man's responsibilities in and to the universe.

—Lesa Dill

ARMSTRONG, William H(oward). American. Born in Lexington, Virginia, 14 September 1914. Educated at Hampden-Sydney College, A.B. (cum laude) 1936; graduate study at University of Virginia, Charlottesville, 1937-38. Married Martha Stone Street Williams in 1943 (died, 1953); two sons, one daughter. History teacher, Virginia Episcopal School, 1939-44; history master, Kent School, Kent, Connecticut, beginning 1945; farmer, writer, real estate agent. Recipient: National School Bell Award of National Association of School Administrators, 1963, for distinguished service in the interpretation of education; Lewis Carroll Book Shelf Award, 1970; John Newbery Medal from American Library Association, 1970, Mark Twain Award from Missouri Association of School Librarians, 1972, and Nene Award from Hawaii Association of School Librarians and Hawaii Library Association, all for *Sounder;* Academy Award nomination for the media adaptation of *Sounder,* 1972; Jewish-Christian Brotherhood award, 1972; Sue Hefley Award, 1976; D. Litt, Hampden-Sydney College, 1986. Address: Kimadee Hill, Kent, CT 06757, U.S.A.

PUBLICATIONS FOR YOUNG ADULTS

Fiction

Sounder, illustrated by James Barkley. New York, Harper, 1969; London, Gollancz, 1971.
Sour Land, illustrated by David B. Armstrong. New York, Harper, 1971.
The MacLeod Place, illustrated by Eros Keith. New York, Coward, 1972.
The Mills of God, illustrated David B. Armstrong. New York, Doubleday, 1973.
JoAnna's Miracle. Nashville, Broadman, 1978.
The Tale of Tawny and Dingo, illustrated by Charles Mikolaycak. New York, Harper, 1979.

Other

Tools of Thinking: A Self-Help Workbook for Students in Grades 5-9. Woodbury, New York, Barron's, 1968; as *Word Power in 5 Easy Lessons: A Simplified Approach to Excellence in Grammar, Punctuation, Sentence Structure, Spelling and Penmanship,* 1969.
Barefoot in the Grass: The Story of Grandma Moses. New York, Doubleday, 1970.
Adapter, with Hana Doskocilova, *Animal Tales,* illustrated by Mirko Hanak, translated from the Czechoslovakian by Eve Merriam. New York, Doubleday, 1970.
Hadassah: Esther the Orphan Queen, illustrated by Barbara Byfield. New York, Doubleday, 1972.
My Animals, illustrated by Mirko Hanak. New York, Doubleday, 1973.
The Education of Abraham Lincoln, illustrated by William Plummer. New York, Coward, 1974.

PUBLICATIONS FOR ADULTS

Other

Study Is Hard Work. New York, Harper, 1956.
Through Troubled Waters, New York, Harper, 1957.

Peoples of the Ancient World, with Joseph W. Swain. New York, Harper, 1959.
87 Ways to Help Your Child in School. Great Neck, New York, Barron's, 1961.
Study Tapes. Woodbury, New York, Barron's. 1975.
Study Tips: How to Improve Your Study Habits and Improve Your Grades. Woodbury, New York, Barron's, 1976; revised edition, as *Study Tactics,* 1983.

*

Media Adaptations: *Sounder* (film), Twentieth Century-Fox, 1972.

Biography: Entry in *More Books by More People* by Lee Bennett Hopkins, Citation, 1974; essay in *Something about the Author Autobiography Series,* Volume 7, Detroit, Gale, 1988, pp. 1-16.

Manuscript Collection: Kerlan Collection, University of Minnesota.

Critical Study: Entry in *Children's Literature Review,* Volume 1, Detroit, Gale, 1976.

*   *   *

William Armstrong was for over thirty years a high school history teacher. His perspective of the past, his interest in social change, and his deep concern for individuals are reflected in both the biographical and the fictional books he writes. Armstrong has written about ancient times in *The MacLeod Place,* and about great Americans, in *The Education of Abraham Lincoln* and *Barefoot in the Grass* (the life of Grandma Moses). But it is his writings about the twentieth century—its social values and institutions, its social problems—that are particularly compelling and for which he is best known.

His most successful book is the novel *Sounder,* which reflects two developments in mid-twentieth-century American literature for children: a willingness to look at the presence and the pain of racial and ethnic injustices in society and a willingness to look at adolescent development—at the growing up process, including the joys and the hurts that accompany transition from childhood to adulthood.

Sounder is one of the few books of mid-century focused on black adolescents in the South. Armstrong tells us that *Sounder* is the black man's story, told to him by an elderly teacher who ran the one-room black school several miles from Armstrong's childhood home in Virginia. This man worked for Armstrong's father after school and in the summer, and attended Armstrong's white church because there was seldom a preacher for the church in his black district. In the evening the teacher told the Armstrong children stories from Aesop, the Old Testament, and Homer. One night at the table after he had told the story of Argus, the faithful dog of Odysseus, he told the story of Sounder, a faithful coon dog. This story was not from Aesop, the Old Testament, or Homer, but from his own history.

Sounder describes the rural South at the turn of the century, a society caught up in a web of ignorance, prejudice, and great poverty. The focus is on one nameless black family: its isolation from society but its love for one another, its lack of opportunity and its determination, its despair and its hope. It begins with the father, the coon dog, and the oldest child (a boy) going hunting. Later the father, a sharecropper, steals food for his hungry family and is imprisoned in a terrible criminal justice system. The mother then toils alone, with determination and skill, to provide for her children. The boy does as much as he can for the family. He does something else as well; he goes to school. He walks for miles and miles to find an education.

The father comes home to die after being seriously wounded in a dynamite blast in the prison quarry—one side of his body crushed under an avalanche of limestone. The old dog Sounder, crushed in spirit, also dies. But the boy returns to school and learns to read. His teacher helps him, through a discussion of literature, to understand that love does not die but continues for whoever has known it.

In *Sounder* Armstrong engages the reader in a history of brave and caring people who do not cry out against the wrongs meted them, but who continue in whatever way they are able, to survive with dignity and rightness. The book with stunning clarity points out the devastating consequences of racial discrimination to members of minority and majority groups.

Armstrong has received many book awards, including the John Newbery Medal and the Mark Twain award for *Sounder*. *Sounder* was the basis of a compelling movie of that name, produced by Twentieth Century Fox in 1972. Armstrong has also received awards for distinguished service in education, including the National School Bell Award.

Armstrong writes about complicated characters and cultures in a careful, deliberate style, elegant in its simplicity and honesty. His stories are for adolescents, but adults are welcome to read them for they offer extraordinarily moving picture of people and their changing places in the world. They extol human resilience and raise questions of human responsibility.

—Mary Lystad

ASHABRANNER, Brent (Kenneth). American. Born in Shawnee, Oklahoma, 3 November 1921. Educated at Oklahoma State University, B.S. 1948, M.A. 1951; additional study at University of Michigan, Ann Arbor, 1955, and Boston University, Massachusetts, and Oxford University, 1959-60. Served in the U.S. Navy, 1942-45. Married Martha White in 1941; two daughters. Oklahoma State University, Stillwater, instructor in English, 1952-55; Ministry of Education, Technical Cooperation Administration, Addis Ababa, Ethiopia, educational materials adviser, 1955-57; International Cooperation Administration, Tripoli, Libya, chief of Education Materials Development Division, 1957-59; Agency for International Development, Lagos, Nigeria, education program officer, 1960-61; Peace Corps, Washington, DC, acting director of program in Nigeria, 1961-62, deputy director of program in India, 1962-64, director of program in India, 1964-66, director of Office of Training, 1966-67, deputy director of Peace Corps, 1967-69; Harvard University, Center for Studies in Education and Development, Cambridge, Massachusetts, research associate, 1969-70; Pathfinder Fund, Boston, Massachusetts, director of Near East-South Asia Population Program, 1970-71; director of project development for World Population International Assistance Division, Planned Parenthood, 1971-72; Ford Foundation, New York City, associate representa-

tive and population program officer, 1972-80, deputy representative to Philippines, 1972-75, deputy representative to Indonesia, 1975-80; writer, 1980—. Recipient: National Civil Service League career service award, 1968; Notable Children's Trade Book in the Field of Social Studies, 1982, and Carter G. Woodson Book Award, National Council for the Social Studies, 1983, both for *Morning Star, Black Sun: The Northern Cheyenne Indians and America's Energy Crisis;* Notable Children's Trade Book in the Field of Social Studies, American Library Association (ALA) Notable Book, and Books for the Teen Age, New York Public Library, all 1983, all for *The New Americans: Changing Patterns in U.S. Immigration;* Notable Children's Trade Book in the Field of Social Studies, 1984, ALA Best Book for Young Adults, 1984, and Carter G. Woodson Book Award, 1985, all for *To Live in Two Worlds: American Indian Youth Today;* Notable Children's Book in the Field of Social Studies and ALA Notable Book, both 1984, both for *Gavriel and Jemal: Two Boys of Jerusalem;* ALA Notable Book, 1985, *Boston Horn-Globe* Honor Book, 1986, and Carter G. Woodson Book Award, 1986, all for *Dark Harvest: Migrant Farmworkers in America;* ALA Notable Book and *School Library Journal* Best Book of the Year, both 1986, both for *Children of the Maya: A Guatemalan Indian Odyssey;* Notable Children's Trade Book in the Field of Social Studies, *School Library Journal* Best Book of the Year, ALA Notable Book, and Christopher Award, all 1987, all for *Into a Strange Land: Unaccompanied Refugee Youth in America;* Notable Children's Trade Book in the Field of Social Studies, 1987, for *The Vanishing Border: A Photographic Journey along Our Frontier with Mexico;* ALA Notable Book and ALA Best Book for Young Adults, both 1988, both for *Always to Remember: The Story of the Vietnam Veterans Memorial; Born to the Land: An American Portrait, Counting America: The Story of the United States Census, People Who Make a Difference,* and *The Times of My Life: A Memoir* were named Books for the Teen Age by New York Public Library. Address: 15 Spring W., Williamsburg, VA 23188, U.S.A.

PUBLICATIONS FOR YOUNG ADULTS

Fiction

The Lion's Whiskers, with Russell Davis. Boston, Little, Brown, 1959.
Ten Thousand Desert Swords, with Russell Davis. Boston, Little, Brown, 1960.
The Choctaw Code, with Russell Davis. New York, McGraw, 1961.
Strangers in Africa, with Russell Davis. New York, McGraw, 1963.

Nonfiction

Point Four Assignment: Stories from the Records of Those Who Work in Foreign Fields for the Mutual Security of Free Nations, with Russell Davis. Boston, Little, Brown, 1959.
Chief Joseph: War Chief of the Nez Perce, with Russell Davis. New York, McGraw, 1962.
Land in the Sun: The Story of West Africa, with Russell Davis. Boston, Little, Brown, 1963.
Morning Star, Black Sun: The Northern Cheyenne Indians and America's Energy Crisis, photographs by Paul Conklin. New York, Dodd, 1982.
The New Americans: Changing Patterns in U.S. Immigration, photographs by Paul Conklin. New York, Dodd, 1983.

To Live in Two Worlds: American Indian Youth Today, photographs by Paul Conklin. New York, Dodd, 1984.

Gavriel and Jemal: Two Boys of Jerusalem, photographs by Paul Conklin. New York, Dodd, 1984.

Dark Harvest: Migrant Farmworkers in America, photographs by Paul Conklin. New York, Dodd, 1985.

Children of the Maya: A Guatemalan Indian Odyssey. photographs by Paul Conklin. New York, Dodd, 1986.

Into a Strange Land: Unaccompanied Refugee Youth in America, with Melissa Ashabranner. New York, Dodd, 1987.

The Vanishing Border: A Photographic Journey along Our Frontier with Mexico, photographs by Paul Conklin. New York, Dodd, 1987.

Always to Remember: The Story of the Vietnam Veterans Memorial, photographs by Jennifer Ashabranner. New York, Dodd, 1988.

Born to the Land: An American Portrait, photographs by Paul Conklin. New York, Putnam, 1989.

I'm in the Zoo, Too!, illustrated by Janet Stevens. New York, Cobblehill Books, 1989.

Counting America: The Story of the United States Census, with Melissa Ashabranner. New York, Putnam, 1989.

People Who Make a Difference, photographs by Paul Conklin. New York, Cobblehill Books, 1989.

A Grateful Nation: The Story of Arlington National Cemetery, photographs by Jennifer Ashabranner. New York, Putnam, 1990.

The Times of My Life: A Memoir. New York, Dutton, 1990.

Crazy about German Shepherds, photographs by Jennifer Ashabranner. New York, Dutton, 1990.

An Ancient Heritage: The Arab-American Minority, photographs by Paul Conklin. New York, Harper, 1991.

Land of Yesterday, Land of Tomorrow: Discovering Chinese Central Asia, photographs by Paul Conklin. New York, Dutton, 1992.

A Memorial for Mr. Lincoln, photographs by Jennifer Ashabranner. New York, Putnam, 1992.

Still a Nation of Immigrants, photographs by Jennifer Ashabranner. New York. Dutton, 1993.

A New Frontier: The Peace Corps in Eastern Europe, photographs by Paul Conklin. New York, Dutton, 1994.

Other

Editor, *The Stakes Are High.* New York, Bantam, 1954.

A First Course in College English (textbook), with Judson Milburn and Cecil B. Williams. Boston, Houghton, 1962.

A Moment in History: The First Ten Years of the Peace Corps. New York, Doubleday, 1971.

*

Biography: Entry in *Sixth Book of Junior Authors and Illustrators,* New York, H.W. Wilson, 1989; essay in *Authors and Artists for Young Adults,* Volume 6, Detroit, Gale, 1991; essay in *Something about the Author Autobiography Series,* Volume 14, Detroit, Gale, 1992.

Critical Study: Entry in *Children's Literature Review,* Volume 28, Detroit, Gale, 1992.

Brent Ashabranner comments:

Much of my nonfiction is about immigrants, refugees, Native Americans, and young adults in crisis. No matter what ethnic minority or disadvantaged social group my books may deal with, I have one overriding hope for each of them that the people I write about will emerge as human beings who have lives that are real and valuable and who have a right to strive for decent lives.

*   *   *

A personal and professional commitment to furthering cross cultural awareness and understanding characterizes the informational books of Brent Ashabranner. By combining timely social issues with individual life experience through case studies, anecdotes, and interviews, Ashabranner draws compelling portraits of adversity and triumph, of difference and commonality, of conflict and resolution. A common theme throughout much of Ashabranner's work concerns the power of the individual's commitment to effect change. The author evokes images of real-life role models confronting difficult social and cultural issues while maintaining and strengthening the bonds of the land, the home, and the family. Ashabranner's award winning books address many of the fundamental social issues of our times, providing the reader with both factual information and personal narrative.

Drawing upon his own extensive experience of living and working outside of the United States, Ashabranner incorporates various journalistic techniques into his work. Documented historical information and factual data temper personal memoirs and interviews. His lucid writing style and attention to detail reflect his commitment to effective communication and scholarly research. The tone of much of Ashabranner's work reflects his extensive professional experience working with diverse societies and his intense personal respect for these cultures. His talent for letting his subjects speak for themselves provides readers with a human voice to associate the larger societal issues at hand with. In using this voice, Ashabranner builds a bridge from simple awareness to more complex reactions of empathy and understanding. Black and white photographs of many of his featured subjects and of diverse locales and situations expand the text and amplify the human element so pervasive in Ashabranner's work. These essential elements all contribute to the work's effectiveness, both in factual and in aesthetic terms.

Ashabranner's first young adult effort, *Morning Star Black Sun: The Northern Cheyenne Indians and America's Energy Crisis,* combines cultural, social, and historical perspectives with questions of ethical rights and responsibilities. Ashabranner draws parallels between the past history of government relations with the Montana tribe and the present need to mine coal for energy production. The conflicts between the northern Cheyenne people, government agencies, and the power and oil companies reflect the fundamental desire of the tribe to control their land and maintain their ancient heritage in the face of complicated modern problems involving financial and environmental concerns.

The struggle to reach the United States and then establish a productive, healthy life characterizes many of the personal histories presented in *The New Americans: Changing Patterns of U.S. Immigration.* In tracing the early history of immigration, Ashabranner establishes a factual base for further investigation of immigration patterns and the discussion of issues of diverse peoples. Their desire for freedom and safety and need for education and training are common themes explored. *Into a Strange Land: Unaccompanied Refugee Youth in America* also addresses the complex issues of refugees in American life by examining the linguistic, cultural, historical, and societal dilemmas facing young people caught up in political turmoil. The book describes the plight of youth who are faced with making a new life, alone, in an alien environment. Despite the emotional reactions, cultural differences, and humanitarian concerns, Ashabranner manages to effectively convey the hope, courage, and determination of the protagonists.

The tabulation and interpretation of census data is explored in a collaborative effort with Melissa Ashabranner, *Counting America: The Story of the United States Census.* The Ashabranner's offer a history of the census, a look at its use in business, education, and government, and a review of the complicated procedures involved in gathering, compiling, and interpreting demographic data. Inclusion of reproductions and archival photographs of early history and techniques gives a real sense of the effects of technology on data collection.

The acclaimed *Always to Remember: The Story of the Vietnam Veterans Memorial* captures the spirit and resolve of the veterans and others involved in the monument's planning, design, and construction. Ashabranner effectively draws parallels between the sense of continuing controversy and divisiveness surrounding the memorial's design and the conduct of the Vietnam War. The themes of conflict and resolution resonate throughout the work, from the perseverance of Jan Scruggs, the activist behind the Vietnam Veterans Memorial Fund, to the determination of Maya Lin, the designer of the memorial, to the simple and eloquent statements of the visitors to the monument. An interview with the curator of the mementos left behind at the memorial provides insight into the depth of feeling expressed by the Memorial's visitors.

In *A Grateful Nation: The Story of Arlington National Cemetery,* Ashabranner considers "the forces of reconciliation." Complemented with photographs by Jennifer Ashabranner and by historical artifacts, the book traces the history and administration of the grounds, and details the exacting military ceremonies which honor the interred. Another historical work set in the nation's capitol is *A Memorial for Mr. Lincoln,* which also features the photographs of Jennifer Ashabranner. A brief treatment of Lincoln's presidency and his contributions leads to a discussion of the search for a fitting tribute to the man. Ashabranner effectively portrays the motives and visions of the memorial's designers and craftsmen and carefully details the exacting work required for its production. The dedication and subsequent influence of the monument as a focal point for events such as the 1963 "March on Washington" serve as fitting reminders of the symbolic importance of the memorial in American history.

Conflict and resolution are again present in the biographical sketches of *Gavriel and Jemal: Two Boys of Jerusalem.* Both the content and the structure of the work emphasize the shared history and traditions of the two protagonists. By moving back and forth between the households of the Palestinian youth and his Jewish counterpart, Ashabranner presents the parallels which characterize life in the Middle East. The love of family, the devotion to religious beliefs and rituals, the significance of traditional education, and the concern for the future are graphically expressed by Ashabranner's facile text and through the dynamic photographs of Paul Conklin. Ashabranner's style, once again, provides an effective framework which allows the reader to reach conclusions about the future of the conflict through the lives and feelings of two young men. A related book, *An Ancient Heritage: The Arab American Minority* chronicles the lives and influence of Arab Americans as a cultural, artistic, and economic force. It offers a positive view of the history of immigra-

tion patterns and the subsequent assimilation of Arab peoples into American culture.

Several of Ashabranner's books address the conflict of tradition and life in the modern world. In *To Live in Two Worlds: American Indian Youth Today,* the personal stories of the young men and women featured reflect the struggle to establish a meaningful place in modern society while retaining the essential knowledge and traditions of the past. Through interviews, personal histories, and statistics, the author's portrait of Native American life balances the sense of traditional tribal pride with the reality of unemployment, poverty, and lack of educational opportunity. A view of farm and family life in New Mexico is found in Ashabranner's *Born to the Land: An American Portrait.* Concentrating on ranching families, the author describes the problems of working the land, the effects of the environment, and the need for a strong sense of family and community. The importance of community highlights a shortcoming of this work, which gives too little emphasis on the contributions of the local Hispanics in the overall development of the region. *The Vanishing Border: A Photographic Journey Along Our Frontier with Mexico* provides an additional perspective on life near the U.S.-Mexican border, dealing primarily with immigration and work related issues.

A starker view of family life is presented in the 1986 publication *Children of the Maya: A Guatemalan Indian Odyssey,* which traces the flight of Mayan Indians from violence and death in their own country to a new life in rural Florida. The examples of the desperate living conditions in their homeland and in the refugee camps serve as a powerful testament to the plight of the Mayas. Conklin's black and white photographs provide the essential human face to personalize both the suffering and the perseverance of the subjects featured. Another title dealing with the lives of migrant workers is *Dark Harvest: Migrant Farmworkers in America.* In this book, Ashabranner chronicles the typical lack of educational, housing, and health facilities, and the enormous desire of many workers to break the cycle of poverty and isolation. Community efforts to improve opportunities and living conditions by organizing workers serve as examples of how change can occur. Paul Conklin's photographic contributions focus particular attention to the role of the entire family, even young children, in the field work.

People Who Make a Difference exemplifies Ashabranner's talent for social commentary and emphasis on the power of the individual. This title describes, in a series of brief biographical sketches and interviews, the efforts of individuals who have dedicated themselves to service, working in a variety of settings and attacking problems with unique and innovative solutions. Their human voices resound with resolve, patience, and persistence. Photographs of each subject add an additional personal dimension to this powerful and up-beat work.

Ashabranner has also written an illustrated autobiography, *The Times of My Life: A Memoir.* In which Ashabranner gives a personal account of his early life during the Depression, his military service, his subsequent careers in government and as an author. His work in the Peace Corps and the civil rights movement verify his lifelong interest in humanitarian concerns and establish his credentials as an author who offers young people a unique and valuable perspective on some of the most volatile and complicated issues of our times. Through history and personal anecdotes, Ashabranner downplays his accomplishments with the specific intention of focusing the reader on the overriding themes of his life—those of the need for genuine compassion for and service to humanity. This work exemplifies both the writing style and the personal commitment which make Ashabranner's a unique and valuable human voice in the world of informational books for young people.

—Mary Snyder

————

ASHER, Sandy. Also writes as Sandra Fenichel Asher. American. Born in Philadelphia, Pennsylvania, 16 October 1942. Educated at University of Pennsylvania, 1960-62; Indiana University, B.A. 1964; graduate study at University of Connecticut, Storrs, Connecticut, 1973; Drury College, Springfield, Missouri, elementary education certificate, 1974. Married Harvey Asher in 1965; one daughter and one son. Novelist and playwright. WFIU-Radio, Bloomington, Indiana, scriptwriter, 1963-64; Ball Associates (advertising agency), Philadelphia, Pennsylvania, copywriter, 1964; *Spectator,* Bloomington, Indiana, drama critic, 1966-67; Drury College, Springfield, Missouri, instructor in creative writing, 1978-85, writer in residence, 1985—. Instructor, Institute of Children's Literature, 1986—. Instructor in creative writing for children's summer programs, Summerscape, 1981-82, and Artworks, 1982. Frequent guest speaker at conferences, workshops, and schools. Recipient: Honorable mention from *Envoi* magazine, 1970, for poem, "Emancipation"; award of excellence from Festival of Missouri Women in the Arts, 1974, for *Come Join the Circus;* creative writing fellowship grant in playwriting from National Endowment for the Arts, 1978, for *God and a Woman;* first prize in one-act play contest from Little Theatre of Alexandria, 1983, and Street Players Theatre, 1989, for *The Grand Canyon;* first prize from Children's Musical Theater of Mobile contest and Dubuque Fine Arts Players contest, both 1984, both for *East of the Sun/West of the Moon; Just Like Jenny* was nominated for the Mark Twain Award, 1984; included on the University of Iowa Outstanding Books for Young Adults List and Child Study Association Best Books List, both 1985, both for *Missing Pieces; Little Old Ladies in Tennis Shoes* was named best new play of the season by Maxwell Anderson Playwriting Series, 1985-86, and was a finalist for the 1988 Ellis Memorial Award, Theatre Americana; *God and a Woman* won Center Stage New Horizons contest in 1986, Mercyhurst College National Playwrights Showcase, 1986-87, and the Unpublished Play Project of the American Alliance for Theatre in Education, 1987-88; *Things Are Seldom What They Seem* was nominated for Iowa Teen Award and Young Hoosier Award, both 1986-87; Indianapolis Children's Theatre Symposium playwriting awards, from Indiana University/Purdue University, 1987, for *Prince Alexis and the Silver Saucer,* and 1989, for *A Woman Called Truth; Dancing with Strangers* won playwriting contests sponsored by TADA!, 1991, and Choate Rosemary Hall, 1993; Joseph Campbell Memorial Fund Award from the Open Eye, 1991-92, for *A Woman Called Truth;* New Play Festival Award from the Actors' Guild of Lexington, Inc., 1992, for *Sunday, Sunday; Once, In the Time of Trolls* won a playwriting contest sponsored by East Central College in Union, Missouri, 1993; *A Woman Called Truth* was voted an Outstanding Play for Young Audiences by the U.S. Center of the International Association of Theatres for Children ad Young People, 1993. Agent: Harold Ober Associates, Inc., 425 Madison Ave., New York, NY 10017, U.S.A.

PUBLICATIONS FOR YOUNG ADULTS

Novels as Sandy Asher

Summer Begins. Elsevier-Nelson, 1980; as *Summer Smith Begins.* New York, Bantam, 1986.

Daughters of the Law. New York, Beaufort Books, 1980; as *Friends and Sisters.* London, Gollancz, 1982.
Just Like Jenny. New York, Delacorte, 1982; London, Gollancz, 1985.
Things Are Seldom What They Seem. New York, Delacorte, 1983; London, Gollancz, 1985.
Missing Pieces. New York, Delacorte, 1984.
Teddy Teabury's Fabulous Fact. New York, Dell, 1985.
Everything Is Not Enough. New York, Delacorte, 1987; London, Macmillan, 1987; as *Sunnyboy und Aschenputtel,* Bergisch Gladbach, Bastei-Verlag, 1990.
Teddy Teabury's Peanutty Problems. New York, Dell, 1987.
Out of Here: A Senior Class Yearbook. New York, Dutton/Lodestar, 1993.

"Ballet One" Series:

Best Friends Get Better. New York, Scholastic, 1989.
Mary-in-the-Middle. New York, Scholastic, 1990.
Pat's Promise. New York, Scholastic, 1990.
Can David Do It?. New York, Scholastic, 1991.

Nonfiction as Sandy Asher

Where Do You Get Your Ideas? Helping Young Writers Begin, illustrated by Susan Hellard. New York, Walker and Co., 1987.
Wild Words! How to Train Them to Tell Stories, illustrated by Dennis Kendrick. New York, Walker and Co., 1989.

Plays as Sandra Fenichel Asher

Come Join the Circus (one-act), (first produced Springfield, Missouri, 1973).
Afterthoughts in Eden (one-act), (first produced Los Angeles, 1975).
A Song of Sixpence (one-act), Orem, Utah, Encore Performance Publishing Co., 1976.
The Ballad of Two Who Flew (one-act), *Plays,* March, 1976.
How I Nearly Changed the World, but Didn't (one-act), (first produced Springfield, Missouri, 1977).
Witling and the Stone Princess, Plays, 1979.
The Insulting Princess (one-act), (first produced Interlochen, Michigan, 1979), Orem, Utah, Encore Performance Publishing, 1988.
Food Is Love (one-act), (first produced Springfield, Missouri, 1979).
The Mermaid's Tale (one-act), (first produced Interlochen, Mississippi, 1979), Vacaville, California, Encore Performance Publishing, 1988.
Dover's Domain, Denver, Colorado, Pioneer Drama Service, 1980.
The Golden Cow of Chelm (one-act), *Plays,* 1980.
Sunday, Sunday (two-act), (first produced Lafayette, Indiana, 1981).
The Grand Canyon (one-act), (first produced Alexandria, Virginia, 1983).
Little Old Ladies in Tennis Shoes (two-act), (first produced Philadelphia, Pennsylvania, 1985), Woodstock, Illinois, Dramatic Publishing Co., 1989.
East of the Sun/West of the Moon (one-act), (first produced Mobile, Alabama, 1985).
God and a Woman (two-act), (first produced Erie, Pennsylvania, 1987).
Prince Alexis and the Silver Saucer (one-act), (first produced Springfield, Missouri, 1987).

A Woman Called Truth (one-act), (first produced Houston, Texas, 1989), Woodstock, Illinois, Dramatic Publishing Co., 1989.

The Wise Men of Chelm (one-act), (first produced Louisville, Kentucky, 1991), Woodstock, Illinois, Dramatic Publishing Co., 1992.

All on a Saturday Morning (one act), (first produced Columbia, Missouri, 1992).

Blind Dating (one-act), (first produced New York, 1992).

Perfect (one-act), (first produced New York, 1992).

Dancing with Strangers (three one-acts), (first produced Wallingford, Connecticut, 1993).

Where Do You Get Your Ideas? (adapted for stage from book of same title), (first produced Chester, New Jersey, 1993).

Nonfiction as Sandra Fenichel Asher

The Great American Peanut Book, illustrated by Jo Anne Metsch Bonnell. New York, Tempo, 1977.

PUBLICATIONS FOR CHILDREN

Fiction

Princess Bee and the Royal Good-night Story (picture book), illustrated by Cat Bowman Smith. Niles, Illinois, A. Whitman, 1990.

Contributor of plays to anthologies, including *Center Stage,* Harper, 1990. Contributor of stories and articles to books, including *Visions,* edited by Donald Gallo, Delacorte/Dell, 1987; *Writers in the Classroom,* edited by Ruth Nathan, Christopher-Gordon, 1991; *Performing the Text: Reading, Writing, and Teaching the Young Adult Novel,* edited by Virginia Monseau and Gary Salvner, Heinemann-Boynton/Cook, 1992; *Authors' Perspectives: Turning Teenagers into Readers and Writers,* edited by Donald Gallo, Heinemann-Boynton/Cook, 1992. Contributor of stories and articles to magazines, including *The ALAN Review, The Journal of Reading, Spark!,* and *Theater for Young Audiences Today.*

*

Biography: Entry in *Dictionary of Literary Biography Yearbook: 1983* by Judith S. Baughman, Detroit, Gale, 1984; essay in *Speaking for Ourselves: Autobiographical Sketches by Notable Authors of Books for Young Adults,* Volume 1, compiled and edited by Donald R. Gallo, National Council of Teachers of English, 1990; essay in *Something about the Author Autobiography Series* by Sandy Asher, Detroit, Gale, Volume 13, 1991.

Sandy Asher comments:

I've centered my work on "nice kids"—the ones who rarely give a teacher a minute's trouble, who would never confront a police officer except to ask directions, who might never attract the attention of social workers, sociologists, journalists, and so on. I'm not talking about saints here, just decent young people who are trying to figure out how to lead productive, meaningful lives.

Like the characters in my books, these young adults learn to deal with grief, loneliness, fear, jealousy, anger, frustration, confusion, love—and the lack of it—because nice kids must, and nice kids do. And they need and deserve books that cheer them on, that encourage them to go with their own best instincts, and that assure them

there is a cure for adolescence: equal parts of time, understanding, and laughter.

* * *

Sandy Asher has the ability to climb inside the heads of her characters and see the world from their points of view. Her writing style of showing, not telling, makes her stories come alive and the characters and their relationships convincing.

Preteens and young teens face change and stress as they strive toward maturity, and Asher, reflecting on some of her experiences from her own early years, skillfully portrays realistic characters dealing with and handling such challenges as they approach and struggle through their teenage years, ranking her as very popular with young adult readers.

Just Like Jenny, a story with a ballet theme, but more importantly portraying a struggle of two young dancers maintaining a true friendship regardless of competition and differences of abilities, proves that true friendship can survive during a difficult period of maturing and changing. The book also provides authentic knowledge of ballet, of the fatiguing, demanding work required, leaving little time for extracurricular activities.

Asher's vivid, precise descriptions, strong nouns and verbs, clear sensory details, and specifics rather than generalizations are tools she uses in all her books. *Things Are Seldom What They Seem* grabs the reader's attention and holds it as tension and suspense fill the entire book. Debbie's sister, Maggie, is enamoured with her handsome high school drama coach, to the point where she doesn't realize the effect he is having upon her.

Debbie's friend Karen joins the drama club, and she, like Maggie, changes, spending all her spare time with the "wonderful" Mr. Carraway. Debbie feels left out, but she also feels something is terribly wrong. With the help of her friend Murray, Debbie discovers that Mr. Carraway has been making sexual advances toward his students, including Debbie's sister, Maggie. Sexual abuse is a tough subject to write about and is an ugly topic, but Ms. Asher deals with it head-on in a bold yet sensitive way, showing that young people can handle such predicaments with or without support from adults.

Everything Is Not Enough is a good example of change and growing up. Michael, seventeen years old, with everything he could possibly want including money, popularity, and a great future, decides that this is what his parents want for him and not what he himself wants. While spending the summer by the sea, Michael goes to work at the Jolly Mackerel, a local restaurant, working hard as a busboy for minimum wage and enduring the cold shoulder and sarcasm from co-workers and local residents, but proving that he can be what he wants to be. Linda, a local girl also working at the Jolly Mackerel, determined to save enough money to move to New York where she can begin a career in fashion design, wants nothing to stand in the way of her future, and that includes Michael. But the two of them are drawn together when Linda's friend Traci is beaten and abused by her boyfriend. Dealing with a tragic social issue, violence against women, Ms. Asher skillfully and realistically presents the problem, creating a spine-tingling story, portraying young people courageously facing the real world with their eyes wide open.

A story in a lighter vein, *Summer Begins,* also published in paperback as *Summer Smith Begins,* portrays a young girl, Summer Smith, who detests making waves and prefers to keep a low profile. An editorial she writes for the school newspaper, however, sets off unexpected fireworks. Summer finds herself in the middle of an uproar centering on the annual Christmas program, a boring tradition that is the same every year. Summer's editorial suggests the program include ALL religious traditions, and not just Christian as in the past. A heartwarming story about a sensitive young girl striving to overcome her shyness and standing up for what she believes, it is also about coping with a frustrated mother going through menopause. The writer, without the reader even being aware of it, delivers her message that young people can overcome damaging peer pressure as well as adult bigotry.

Ideas for writing stories, poems, and plays may be found in Asher's *Where Do You Get Your Ideas? Helping Young Writers Begin.* According to this instructive book, ideas are found everywhere, and, when found, should be written in a journal to be used when needed. Also in the book are over two dozen views from other authors that briefly describe how they, too, get their ideas for stories. The budding author is encouraged, and many practical suggestions are provided for writers young and old.

Missing Pieces deals with many losses of loved ones. Heather loses her brother when he gets married, her father when he dies, her mother when she withdraws after the death of her husband, and her boyfriend when he runs away. The girl overcomes a lack of communication as well as the feeling of overwhelming loneliness and deals effectively with family problems and self-preservation. Asher's sympathetic story of grief and conflict once again proves her competence and popularity.

With numerous awards and honors for her many plays and novels, Sandy Asher ranks high in the field of writers for young adults, skillfully portraying characters who deal realistically with problems facing young people as they strive toward maturity, ever changing, growing, and learning as they go.

—Carol Doxey

ASHLEY, Bernard. British. Born in London, 2 April 1935. Educated at Roan School, Blackheath, London, and Sir Joseph Williamson's School, Rochester, Kent, 1947-53; Trent Park College of Education, 1955-57, Cert. Ed. 1957; Cambridge Institute of Education, 1970-71, associate diploma in primary education, 1971. Served in the Royal Air Force, 1953-55; became senior aircraftman. Married Iris Holbrook in 1958; three sons. Teacher, Kent Educational Committee, Gravesend, 1957-65, Hertfordshire Educational Committee, Hertford Heath, 1965-71, and Hartley Junior School, Newham, London, 1971-76. Since 1977, headteacher, Charlton Manor Junior School, London. Recipient: Other award, Children's Rights Workshop, 1976, for *The Trouble with Donovan Croft;* Carnegie Medal commendation, 1979, for *A Kind of Wild Justice,* and 1987, for *Running Scared.* Address: 128 Heathwood Gardens, London SE7 8ER, England.

PUBLICATIONS FOR YOUNG ADULTS

Fiction

The Trouble with Donovan Croft, illustrated by Fermin Rocker. London, Oxford University Press, 1974.

Terry on the Fence, illustrated by Charles Keeping. London, Oxford University Press, 1975; New York, Phillips, 1977.

All My Men. London, Oxford University Press, 1977; New York, Phillips, 1978.

A Kind of Wild Justice, illustrated by Charles Keeping. London, Oxford University Press, 1978; New York, Phillips, 1979.

Break in the Sun, illustrated by Charles Keeping. London, Oxford University Press, and New York, Phillips, 1980.

Dinner Ladies Don't Count, illustrated by Janet Duchesne. London, MacRae, and New York, Watts, 1981.

Dodgem (novel). London, MacRae, 1981; New York, Watts, 1982.

I'm Trying to Tell You, illustrated by Lyn Jones. London, Kestrel Books, 1981.

Linda's Lie, illustrated by Janet Duchesne. London, MacRae, and New York, Watts, 1982.

High Pavement Blues. London, MacRae, and New York, Watts, 1983.

Your Guess Is as Good as Mine, illustrated by Steven Cain. London, MacRae, and New York, Watts, 1983.

A Bit of Give and Take, illustrated by Trevor Stubley. London, Hamish Hamilton, 1984.

Janey. London, MacRae, 1985.

Running Scared. London, MacRae, 1986.

Clipper Street Stories (Calling for Sam, Taller Than Before, Down and Out, The Royal Visit, All I Ever Ask..., Sally Cinderella), illustrated by Jane Cope. London, Orchard, 6 vols., 1987-89.

Bad Blood. London, MacRae, 1988.

The Country Boy (novelization of his own television series). London, MacRae, 1989.

The Dockside School Stories (Boat Girl, The Ghost of Dockside School, Getting In, The Cartaker's Car). London, MacRae, 4 vols., 1990.

Seeing Off Uncle Jack. London, Viking, 1991.

Cleversticks, illustrated by Derek Brazell. New York, Crown, 1992.

Plays

Television Plays: *Running Scared,* from his own story, 1986; *The Country Boy* series, 1989.

The Old Woman Who Lived in a Cola Can, music by David Smith (produced on tour, 1988).

The Secret of Theodore Brown (produced, 1989).

Dodgem (produced, 1991).

Other

The Men and the Boats: Britain's Life-Boat Service. London, Allman, 1968.

Weather Men. London, Allman, 1970; revised edition, 1974.

PUBLICATIONS FOR CHILDREN

Other

Don't Run Away (reader), illustrated by Ray Whittaker. London, Allman, 1965.

Wall of Death (reader), illustrated by Ray Whittaker. London, Allman, 1966.

The Big Escape (reader), illustrated by James Hunt. London, Allman, 1967.

Space Shot (reader), illustrated by Laszlo Acs. London, Allman, 1967.

*

Critical Study: Entry in *Children's Literature Review,* Volume 4, Detroit, Gale, 1984.

*   *   *

Drawing on his extensive experience as a classroom teacher and headmaster in primary schools, Bernard Ashley first claimed attention as the author of books for young children, but he has turned increasingly to writing for young adults. *The Trouble with Donovan Croft* was hailed as one of the first British books to give a central role to a black child, a West Indian boy who becomes mute when separated from his parents and put in a foster home with a white family. In a number of ways this novel foreshadowed the course of Ashley's later writing: a young person isolated and misunderstood by adults, a concern for social conflict, and a convincing presentation of young people's behaviour and language in urban, multicultural settings.

In 1978 Ashley began a sequence of tough stories about contemporary life, combining features of the thriller with those of the "problem" novel. The young protagonists, like Donovan, have problems (they include a grubby nonreader and a bed wetter) and lead secret, dangerous lives. Ronnie, in *A Kind of Wild Justice,* exists dangerously on the fringe of violent crime; Kevin has to guard the family's market stall against takeover in *High Pavement Blues;* and the title character in *Janey* acts as a lookout for thieves. Conventional relationships between parent and child are frequently reversed; the young people have to take on the active, caring role. In *Dodgem,* Simon struggles to care for his father who was paralysed in the car crash that killed his mother. Kevin, in *High Pavement Blues,* tries to look after his mother and to bring back his father, who deserted them both.

Ritchie in *Bad Blood* attempts to get the transplant that may save his father's life. Largely ignored by the adult world, these young people have to grow up quickly. They struggle to reconcile the conflicting demands made on them by the different worlds in which they exist: home and school, black and white communities, criminal groups and the rule of law. A repeated theme is the experience of a character uprooted from one environment to be plunged into another. It may simply be a change to a different kind of school (as in *All My Men*), or the more dramatic changes of Patsy in *Break in the Sun,* escaping with a barge load of amateur actors, or Simon being hidden in a travelling fair in *Dodgem.*

Ashley is an excellent storyteller. In the later novels he cuts cinematically from scene to scene, the descriptions are vivid and convincing, and the dialogue is appropriate to the characters—racy and immediate (and therefore, inevitably dated in places). The titles and themes are frequently symbolic but at a level appropriate to young readers. Simon describes himself as a dodgem, "bashed into from all angles"; the "bad blood" refers to heredity and to fraternal antipathy as well as to leukemia. The lessons of the novels are rarely cut and dried. Few characters are shown as straightforwardly good or bad, and they rarely understand the whole truth of the situations. Issues are seen as complex and ambiguous. Some readers have been unhappy about Ashley's realism; figures of authority (like the social services in *Dodgem*) are not always presented sympathetically, and sexual relationships are presented frankly. How-

ever, without much sense of contrivance, the books do convey clear moral positives. The central characters move through painful experiences towards greater understanding of themselves and of the world. Much of this learning comes about through significant contacts with other people who are very different from themselves. Paul learns from Lorraine, Ronnie from the Pakistani girl Margit, and Janey from the elderly Mrs. Woodcroft.

These qualities of Ashley's writing are shown clearly in *Running Scared,* the novel he based on his British Broadcasting Channel television series for young people. The story centres on the relationship between a London schoolgirl, Paula Prescott and her best friend Narinder, a member of a Sikh family settled in England for some years. They live in an area where crime is common, and Paula's cabbie grandfather is the innocent witness of a robbery that goes wrong. Paula's cousin Brian is one of the local gang, extorting protection money from local Asians, and under this pressure Narinder's father thinks of taking his family back to India. Paula discovers that her grandfather died leaving a clue to the whereabouts of a vital piece of evidence and the girls work together, ultimately finding it in a Sikh temple. She then faces a difficult choice: to be responsible for sending her cousin to prison or to condone evil. There is an effective and plausible climax to the book, which combines an exciting plot and strong characters with moral seriousness that is not overly didactic.

Ashley's novels are not for passive readers. They demand that readers interpret events, assess characters, and judge motives much as they would do in real life. It is not surprising that his books have proved so popular, both in school and with young people choosing books for themselves.

—Robert Protherough

———

ASIMOV, Isaac. Also writes as George E. Dale; Dr. A; Paul French. American. Born in Petrovichi, U.S.S.R., 2 January 1920; immigrated to the United States in 1923; became citizen 1928. Educated at Columbia University, New York, B.S. 1939, M.A. 1941, Ph.D. in chemistry 1948. Served in the United States Army, 1945-46. Married 1) Gertrude Blugerman in 1942 (divorced 1973), one son and one daughter; 2) Janet Opal Jeppson in 1973. Writer. Instructor, 1949-51, Assistant Professor, 1951-55, Associate Professor, 1955-79, and since 1979 Professor of Biochemistry, Boston University School of Medicine, Boston, Massachusetts. Worked as a civilian chemist at U.S. Navy Air Experimental Station, Philadelphia, 1942-45. Recipient: Edison Foundation National Mass Media award, 1958; Blakeslee award for nonfiction, 1960; special Hugo award for distinguished contributions to the field, 1963, for science articles in the *Magazine of Fantasy and Science Fiction,* special Hugo award for best all-time science fiction series, 1966, for *Foundation, Foundation and Empire,* and *Second Foundation,* Hugo award for best novel, 1973, for *The Gods Themselves,* and 1983, for *Foundation's Edge,* Hugo award for best short story, 1977, for "The Bicentennial Man," Hugo award, 1983, all from World Science Fiction Conventions; World Science Fiction Convention citation, 1963; American Chemical Society James T. Grady award, 1965; American Association for the Advancement of Science-Westinghouse award for science writing, 1967; Nebula award, Science Fiction Writers of America, 1973, for *The Gods Themselves,* and 1977, for "The Bicentennial Man"; Glenn Seabord award, International Platform Association, 1979; *Locus* award, for non-fiction, 1981, for fiction, 1983; Washington *Post* Children's Book Guild award, for non-fiction, 1985; "Nightfall" was chosen the best science fiction story of all time in a Science Fiction Writers of America poll. Guest of Honor, Thirteenth World Science Fiction Convention, 1955. *Died 6 April 1992.*

PUBLICATIONS FOR YOUNG ADULTS

Nonfiction

Building Blocks of the Universe. New York, Abelard Schuman, 1957; London, Abelard Schuman, 1958; revised edition, 1961, 1974.
Breakthroughs in Science, illustrated by Karoly and Szanto. Boston, Houghton Mifflin, 1960.
Satellites in Outer Space, illustrated by John Polgreen. New York, Random House, 1960; revised edition, 1964, 1973.
The Kite That Won the Revolution. Boston, Houghton Mifflin, 1963.
The Moon, illustrated by Alex Ebel. Chicago, Follett, 1967; London, University of London Press, 1969.
To the Ends of the Universe. New York, Walker, 1967; revised edition, 1976.
Mars, illustrated by Herb Herrick. Chicago, Follett, 1967; London, University of London Press, 1971.
Stars, illustrated by Herb Herrick, diagrams by Mike Gordon. Chicago, Follett, 1968.
Galaxies, illustrated by Alex Ebel and Denny McMains. Chicago, Follett, 1968; London, University of London Press, 1971.
ABC's of Space. New York, Walker, 1969; as *Space Dictionary,* New York, Scholastic, 1970.
Great Ideas of Science, illustrated by Lee Ames. Boston, Houghton Mifflin, 1969.
The ABC's of the Ocean. New York, Walker, 1970.
The Heavenly Host, illustrated by Bernard Colonna. New York, Walker, 1975; London, Penguin, 1978.
Light, photography by Allen Carr. Chicago, Follett, 1970.
What Makes the Sun Shine?, illustrated by Marc Brown. Boston, Little Brown, 1971.
ABC's of the Earth. New York, Walker, 1971.
ABC's of Ecology. New York, Walker, 1972.
Ginn Science Program. Boston, Ginn, 5 vols., 1972-73.
Comets and Meteors, illustrated by Raul Mina Mora. Chicago, Follett, 1972.
The Sun, illustrated by Alex Ebel. Chicago, Follett, 1972.
Jupiter, the Largest Planet. New York, Lothrop, 1973; revised edition, 1976.
Please Explain, illustrated by Michael McCurdy. Boston, Houghton Mifflin, 1973; London, Abelard Schuman, 1975.
Earth: Our Crowded Spaceship. New York, Day, and London, Abelard Schuman, 1974.
The Solar System, illustrated by David Cunnigham. Chicago, Follett, 1975.
Alpha Centauri, the Nearest Star. New York, Lothrop, 1976.
Mars, the Red Planet. New York, Lothrop, 1977.
Saturn and Beyond, diagrams by Giulio Maestro. New York, Lothrop, 1979.
Venus: Near Neighbor of the Sun, diagrams by Yukio Kondo. New York, Lothrop, 1981.

Beginnings: The Story of Origins—Of Mankind, Life, the Earth, the Universe. New York, Walker, 1987.
Franchise. Mankato, Minnesota, Creative Education, 1988.
All the Troubles of World. Mankato, Minnesota, Creative Education, 1988.
Little Treasury of Dinosaurs, illustrated by Christopher Santoro. New York, Crown, 1989.
Think about Space: Where Have We Been and Where Are We Going, with Frank White. New York, Walker, 1989.
Isaac Asimov's Pioneers of Science and Explorations (Christopher Columbus: Navigator to the New World; Ferdinand Magellan: Opening the Door to World Exploration; Henry Hudson: Arctic Explorer and North American Adventurer). Milwaukee, Stevens, 1991.

PUBLICATIONS FOR CHILDREN

Fiction

The Key Word and Other Mysteries, illustrated by Rod Burke. New York, Walker, 1977.
Norby, the Mixed-Up Robot, with Janet Asimov. New York, Walker, 1983; London, Methuen, 1984.
Norby's Other Secret, with Janet Asimov. New York, Walker, 1984; London, Methuen, 1985.
Norby and the Invaders, with Janet Asimov. New York, Walker, 1985.
Norby and the Lost Princess, with Janet Asimov. New York, Walker, 1985.
The Norby Chronicles (includes *Norby, the Mixed-Up Robot* and *Norby's Other Secret),* with Janet Asimov. New York, Ace, 1986.
Norby and the Queen's Necklace, New York, Walker, 1986.
Norby: Robot for Hire (includes *Norby and the Lost Princess* and *Norby and the Invaders),* with Janet Asimov. New York, Ace, 1987.
Norby Finds a Villain, with Janet Asimov. New York, Walker, 1987.
Norby through Time and Space (includes *Norby and the Queen's Necklace* and *Norby Finds a Villain),* with Janet Asimov. New York, Ace, 1988.
All the Troubles of the World, illustrated by David Shannon. Mankato, Minnesota, Creative Education, 1989.
Franchise, illustrated by David Shannon. Mankato, Minnesota, Creative Education, 1989.
Norby Down to Earth, with Janet Asimov. New York, Walker, 1989.
Norby and Yobo's Great Adventure, with Janet Asimov. New York, Walker, 1989.
Robbie, illustrated by David Shannon. Mankato, Minnesota, Creative Education, 1989.
Sally, illustrated by David Shannon. Mankato, Minnesota, Creative Education, 1989.
Norby and the Oldest Dragon, with Janet Asimov. New York, Walker, 1990.
Norby and the Court Jester, with Janet Asimov. New York, Walker, 1991.

Fiction as Paul French

David Starr, Space Ranger. New York, Doubleday, 1952; Kingswood, Surrey, World's Work, 1953; as Isaac Asimov, Boston, Twayne, 1978.

Lucky Starr and the Pirates of the Asteroids. New York, Doubleday, 1953; Kingswood, Surrey, World's Work, 1954; as Isaac Asimov, Boston, Twayne, 1978.

Lucky Starr and the Oceans of Venus. New York, Doubleday, 1954; as *The Oceans of Venus* (as Isaac Asimov), London, New English Library, 1973; as Isaac Asimov, Boston, Twayne, 1978.

Lucky Starr and the Big Sun of Mercury. New York, Doubleday, 1956; as *The Big Sun of Mercury* (as Isaac Asimov), London, New English Library, 1974; as Isaac Asimov, Boston, Twayne, 1978.

Lucky Starr and the Moons of Jupiter. New York, Doubleday, 1957; as *The Moons of Jupiter* (as Isaac Asimov), London, New English Library, 1974; as Isaac Asimov, Boston, Twayne, 1978.

Lucky Starr and the Rings of Saturn. New York, Doubleday, 1958; as *The Rings of Saturn* (as Isaac Asimov), London, New English Library, 1974; as Isaac Asimov, Boston, Twayne, 1978.

Poetry

Isaac Asimov's Limericks for Children, illustrated by Wally Neibart. New York, Caedmon, 1984.

Nonfiction

Twentieth Century Discovery. New York, Doubleday, and London, Macdonald, 1969.

The Best New Thing, illustrated by Symeon Shimin. Cleveland, World, 1971.

How Did We Find Out about Dinosaurs [the Earth Is Round, Electricity, Vitamins, Germs, Comets, Energy, Atoms, Nuclear Power, Numbers, Outer Space, Earthquakes, Black Holes, Our Human Roots, Antarctica, Coal, Solar Power, Volcanoes, Life in the Deep Sea, Our Genes, the Universe, Computers, Robots, the Atmosphere, DNA, the Speed of Light, Blood, Sunshine, the Brain, Super Conductivity, Microwaves, Photosynthesis], illustrated by David Wool and others. New York, Walker, 32 vols., 1973-89; 6 vols. published London, White Lion, 1975-76; 1 vol., published London, Pan, 1980; 7 vols. published (as *How We Found Out...* series), London, Longman, 1982.

I, Rabbi. New York, Walker, 1976.

Animals of the Bible. New York, Doubleday, 1978.

Those Amazing Electronic Thinking Machines! New York, Watts, 1983.

Editor, with Martin H. Greenberg and Charles G. Waugh, *Young Mutants, Extraterrestrials, Ghosts, Monsters, Star Travelers, Witches and Warlocks.* New York, Harper, 6 vols., 1984-87.

Bare Bones: Dinosaur, with David Hawcock. New York, Holt, 1986; London, Methuen, 1987.

Ask Isaac Asimov (What Is a Shooting Star?; What Is an Eclipse?; Why Do Stars Twinkle?; Why Does the Moon Change Shape?; Why Do We Have Different Seasons?; What Causes Acid Rain?; Is Our Planet Warming Up?; Why Are Whales Vanishing?; Why Are Some Beaches Oily?; Why Is the Air Dirty?; Where Does Garbage Go?; Why Does Litter Cause Problems?; Why Are Rain Forests Vanishing?; What's Happening to the Ozone Layer?; Why Are Animals Endangered?; How Is Paper Made?; What Happens When I Flush the Toilet?; How Does a TV Work?; How Do Airplanes Fly?; How Do Big Ships Float?), some titles written with Elizabeth Kaplan. Milwaukee, Stevens, vols., 1991-93.

How Did We Find Out About Pluto?, illustrated by Erika Kors. New York, Walker, 1991.

Other

An Isaac Asimov Double: "Space Ranger" and "Pirates of the Asteroids." London, New English Library, 1972.

A Second Isaac Asimov Double: "The Big Sun of Mercury" and "The Oceans of Venus." London, New English Library, 1973.

The Third Isaac Asimov Double. London, New English Library/ Times Mirror, 1973.

Editor, with Martin H. Greenberg and Charles G. Waugh, *Science Fiction Shorts* series (includes *After the End, Thinking Machines, Travels Through Time, Wild Inventions, Mad Scientists, Mutants, Tomorrow's TV, Earth Invaded, Bug Awful, Children of the Future, The Immortals, Time Warps),* illustrated by various artists. Milwaukee, Raintree, 12 vols., 1981-84.

PUBLICATIONS FOR ADULTS

Novels

Pebble In the Sky. New York, Doubleday, 1950; London, Corgi, 1958.

The Stars, Like Dust. New York, Doubleday, 1951; London, Panther, 1958; abridged edition, as *The Rebellious Stars,* New York, Ace, 1954.

Foundation. New York, Gnome Press, 1951; London, Weidenfeld and Nicolson, 1953; abridged edition, as *The Thousand-Year Plan,* New York, Ace, 1955.

Foundation and Empire. New York, Gnome Press, 1952; London, Panther, 1962; as *The Man Who Upset the Universe,* New York, Ace, 1955.

The Currents of Space. New York, Doubleday, 1952; London, Boardman, 1955.

Second Foundation. New York, Gnome Press, 1953.

The Caves of Steel. New York, Doubleday, and London, Boardman, 1954.

The End of Eternity. New York, Doubleday, 1955; London, Panther, 1958.

The Naked Sun. New York, Doubleday, 1957; London, Joseph, 1958.

The Robot Novels (includes *The Caves of Steel* and *The Naked Sun).* New York, Doubleday, 1957.

The Death Dealers. New York, Avon, 1958; as *A Whiff of Death,* New York, Walker, and London, Gollancz, 1968.

Triangle: "The Currents of Space," "Pebble In the Sky," and "The Stars, Like Dust." New York, Doubleday, 1961; as *An Isaac Asimov Second Omnibus,* London, Sidgwick and Jackson, 1969.

The Foundation Trilogy: Three Classics of Science Fiction (includes *Foundation, Foundation and Empire,* and *Second Foundation).* New York, Doubleday, 1963; as *An Isaac Asimov Omnibus,* London, Sidgwick and Jackson, 1966.

Fantastic Voyage (novelization of screenplay). Boston, Houghton Mifflin, and London, Dobson, 1966.

The Gods Themselves. New York, Doubleday, and London, Gollancz, 1972.

Murder at the ABA: A Puzzle in Four Days and Sixty Scenes. New York, Doubleday, 1976; as *Authorized Murder: A Puzzle in Four Days and Sixty Scenes,* London, Gollancz, 1976.

The Collected Fiction of Isaac Asimov: The Far Ends of Time and Earth (includes *Pebble in the Sky, Earth Is Room Enough,* and *The End of Eternity).* New York, Doubleday, 1979.

The Collected Fiction of Isaac Asimov: Prisoners of the Stars (includes *The Stars, Like Dust, The Martian Way and Other Stories,* and *The Currents of Space*). New York, Doubleday, 1979.
Foundation's Edge. New York, Doubleday, 1982; London, Granada, 1983.
The Robots of Dawn. New York, Doubleday, 1983; London, Granada, 1984.
Robots and Empire. New York, Doubleday, and London, Granada, 1985.
Foundation and Earth. New York, Doubleday, and London, Grafton, 1986.
Fantastic Voyage II: Destination Brain. New York, Doubleday, and London, Grafton, 1987.
Azazel. New York, Doubleday, 1988; London, Doubleday, 1989.
Prelude to Foundation, illustrated by Vincent DiFate. New York, Doubleday, and London, Grafton, 1988.
Nemesis. New York, Doubleday, and London, Doubleday, 1989.
Invasions. New York, New American Library, 1990.
Nightfall, with Robert Silverberg. New York, Doubleday, and London, Gollancz, 1990.
Forward the Foundation. New York, Doubleday, 1993.

Short Stories

I, Robot. New York, Gnome Press, 1950; London, Grayson, 1952.
The Martian Way and Other Stories. New York, Doubleday, 1955; London, Dobson, 1964.
Earth Is Room Enough: Science Fiction Tales of Our Own Planet. New York, Doubleday, 1957; London, Panther, 1960.
Nine Tomorrows: Tales of the Near Future. New York, Doubleday, 1959; London, Dobson, 1963.
The Rest of the Robots. New York, Doubleday, 1964; as *Eight Stories from the Rest of the Robots,* San Diego, California, Pyramid, 1966; London, Dobson, 1967.
Through a Glass Clearly. London, New English Library, 1967.
Asimov's Mysteries. New York, Doubleday, and London, Rapp and Whiting, 1968.
Nightfall and Other Stories. New York, Doubleday, 1969; as *Nightfall One* and *Nightfall Two,* London, Panther, 1969; as *Nightfall: Twenty SF Stories,* London, Rapp and Whiting, 1971.
The Early Asimov: Or, Eleven Years of Trying. New York, Doubleday, 1972; London, Gollancz, 1973.
The Best of Isaac Asimov (1939-1972), edited by Angus Wells. London, Sidgwick and Jackson, 1973; New York, Doubleday, 1974.
Have You Seen These? Cambridge, Massachusetts, NESFA Press, 1974.
Tales of the Black Widowers. New York, Doubleday, 1974; London, Gollancz, 1975.
Buy Jupiter and Other Stories. New York, Doubleday, 1975; London, Gollancz, 1976.
The Dream, Benjamin's Dream, Benjamin's Bicentennial Blast: Three Short Stories. Privately printed, 1976.
The Bicentennial Man and Other Stories. New York, Doubleday, 1976; London, Gollancz, 1977.
More Tales of the Black Widowers. New York, Doubleday, 1976; London, Gollancz, 1977.
Good Taste, illustrated by Brent Garrett. Topeka, Kansas, Apocalypse Press, 1977.
Casebook of the Black Widowers. New York, Doubleday, and London, Gollancz, 1980.

Three by Asimov. New York, Targ, 1981.
The Complete Robot. New York, Doubleday, and London, Granada, 1982.
The Union Club Mysteries. New York, Doubleday, 1983; London, Granada, 1984.
The Winds of Change and Other Stories. New York, Doubleday, and London, Granada, 1983.
Banquets of the Black Widowers. New York, Doubleday, 1984; London, Gollancz, 1985.
The Disappearing Man and Other Mysteries, illustrated by Yoshi Miyake. New York, Walker, 1985.
The Edge of Tomorrow. New York, Tor, 1985.
The Best Science Fiction of Isaac Asimov. New York, Doubleday, 1986; London, Grafton, 1987.
The Alternative Asimovs. New York, Doubleday, 1986.
The Best Mysteries of Isaac Asimov. New York, Doubleday, 1986; London, Grafton, 1987.
Robot Dreams, edited by Bryon Preiss, illustrated by Ralph McQuarrie. New York, Berkley, 1986; London, Gollancz, 1987.
The Asimov Chronicles: Fifty Years of Isaac Asimov, edited by Martin H. Greenberg. New York, Dark Harvest, 1989.
Isaac Asimov: The Complete Stories. New York, Doubleday, 1990.
Puzzles of the Black Widowers. New York, Doubleday, 1990.
Robot Visions, illustrated by Ralph McQuarrie. New York, New American Library, and London, Gollancz, 1990.
The Asimov Chronicles. New York, Ace, 3 vols., 1990.
The Asimov Chronicles. New York, Dell, 1991.

Poetry

Lecherous Limericks, illustrated by Julien Dedman. New York, Walker, 1975; London, Corgi, 1977.
More Lecherous Limericks, illustrated by Julien Dedman. New York, Walker, 1976.
Still More Lecherous Limericks, illustrated by Mel Brofman. New York, Walker, 1977.
Asimov's Sherlockian Limericks. Yonkers, New York, New Mysterious Press, 1978.
Limericks Too Gross, with John Ciardi. New York, Norton, 1978.
A Grossery of Limericks, with John Ciardi. New York, Norton, 1981.

Nonfiction

Biochemistry and Human Metabolism, with Burnham Walker and William C. Boyd. Baltimore, Williams and Wilkins, 1952; revised edition, 1954, 1957; London, Ballière Tindall and Cox, 1955.
The Chemicals of Life: Enzymes, Vitamins, Hormones. New York, Abelard Schuman, 1954; London, Bell, 1956.
Races and Peoples, with William C. Boyd. New York, Abelard Schuman, 1955; London, Abelard Schuman, 1958.
Chemistry and Human Health, with Burnham Walker and Mary K. Nicholas. New York, McGraw Hill, 1956.
Inside the Atom, illustrated by John Bradford. New York and London, Abelard Schuman, 1956; revised edition, Abelard Schuman, 1958, 1961, 1966, 1974.
Only a Trillion. New York and London, Abelard Schuman, 1957; as *Marvels of Science: Essays of Fact and Fancy on Life, Its Environment, Its Possibilities,* New York, Collier, 1962.

The World of Carbon. New York and London, Abelard Schuman, 1958; revised edition, New York, Collier, 1962.

The World of Nitrogen. New York and London, Abelard Schuman, 1958; revised edition, New York, Collier, 1962.

The Clock We Live On. New York and London, Abelard Schuman, 1959; revised edition, New York, Collier, 1962; Abelard Schuman, 1965.

The Living River. New York and London, Abelard Schuman, 1959; revised edition, as *The Bloodstream: River of Life,* New York, Collier, 1961.

Realm of Numbers, diagrams by Robert Belmore. Boston, Houghton Mifflin, 1959; London, Gollancz, 1963.

Words of Science and the History behind Them, illustrated by William Barss. Boston, Houghton Mifflin, 1959; London, Harrap, 1974.

The Double Planet, illustrated by John Bradford. New York, Abelard Schuman, 1960; London, Abelard Schuman, 1962; revised edition, 1966.

The Intelligent Man's Guide to Science. New York, Basic Books, 2 vols., 1960; published separately as *The Intelligent Man's Guide to the Physical Sciences* and *The Intelligent Man's Guide to the Biological Sciences,* New York, Pocket Books, 1964; revised edition as *The New Intelligent Man's Guide to Science,* 1 vol., New York, Basic Books, 1965; London, Nelson, 1967; as *Asimov's Guide to Science,* New York, Basic Books, 1972; London, Penguin, 2 vols., as *Asimov's New Guide to Science,* New York, Basic Books, 1984.

The Kingdom of the Sun. New York and London, Abelard Schuman, 1960; revised edition, New York, Collier, 1962; Abelard Schuman, 1963.

Realm of Measure, diagrams by Robert Belmore. Boston, Houghton Mifflin, 1960.

The Wellsprings of Life. New York and London, Abelard Schuman, 1960.

Realm of Algebra, diagrams by Robert Belmore. Boston, Houghton Mifflin, 1961; London, Gollancz, 1964.

Life and Energy. New York, Doubleday, 1962; London, Dobson, 1963.

Fact and Fancy New York, Doubleday, 1962; London, Dobson, 1963.

The Search for the Elements. New York, Basic Books, 1962.

The Genetic Code. New York, Orion Press, 1963; London, Murray, 1964.

The Human Body: Its Structure and Operation, illustrated by Anthony Ravielli. Boston, Houghton Mifflin, 1963; London, Nelson, 1965.

View from a Height. New York, Doubleday, 1963; London, Dobson, 1964.

The Human Brain: Its Capacities and Functions. Boston, Houghton Mifflin, 1964; London, Nelson, 1965.

A Short History of Biology. Garden City, New York, Natural History Press, 1964; London, Nelson, 1965.

Quick and Easy Math. Boston, Houghton Mifflin, 1964; London, Whiting and Wheaton, 1967.

Adding a Dimension: Seventeen Essays on the History of Science. New York, Doubleday, 1964; London, Dobson, 1966.

Planets for Man, with Stephen H. Dole. New York, Random House, 1964.

Asimov's Biographical Encyclopedia of Science and Technology. New York, Doubleday, 1964; London, Allen and Unwin, 1966; revised edition, Doubleday, 1972, 1982; London, Pan, 1975.

The Greeks: A Great Adventure. Boston, Houghton Mifflin, 1965.

A Short History of Chemistry, illustrated by Robert Yaffe. New York, Doubleday, 1965; London, Heinemann, 1972.

Of Time and Space and Other Things. New York, Doubleday, 1965; London, Dobson, 1967.

An Easy Introduction to the Slide Rule, diagrams by William Barss. Boston, Houghton Mifflin, 1965; London, Whiting and Wheaton, 1967.

The Noble Gasses. New York, Basic Books, 1966.

The Neutrino: Ghost Particle of the Atom. New York, Doubleday, and London, Dobson, 1966.

The Roman Republic. Boston, Houghton Mifflin, 1966.

Understanding Physics. New York, Walker, 3 vols., 1966; London, Allen and Unwin, 3 vols., 1967; as *The History of Physics,* New York, Walker, 1 vol., 1984.

The Genetic Effects of Radiation, with Theodosius Dobzhansky. Washington, D.C., Atomic Energy Commission, 1966.

The Universe: From Flat Earth to Quasar. New York, Walker, 1966; London, Penguin, 1967; revised edition, Walker, and Penguin, 1971; revised edition, as *The Universe: From Flat Earth to Black Holes—and Beyond,* Walker, 1980; Penguin, 1983.

From Earth to Heaven: Seventeen Essays on Science. New York, Doubleday, 1966.

The Egyptians. Boston, Houghton Mifflin, 1967.

Environments Out There. New York, Abelard Schuman, 1967; London, Abelard Schuman, 1968.

From Earth to Heaven: Seventeen Essays on Science. New York, Doubleday, 1967; London, Dobson, 1968.

Is Anyone There? (essays). New York, Doubleday, 1967; London, Rapp and Whiting, 1968.

The Roman Empire. Boston, Houghton Mifflin, 1967.

The Dark Ages. Boston, Houghton Mifflin, 1968.

The Near East: Ten Thousand Years of History. Boston, Houghton Mifflin, 1968.

Photosynthesis. New York, Basic Books, 1968; London, Allen and Unwin, 1970.

Science, Numbers and I: Essays on Science. New York, Doubleday, 1968; London, Rapp and Whiting, 1969.

Words from History, illustrated by William Barss. Boston, Houghton Mifflin, 1968.

The Shaping of England. Boston, Houghton Mifflin, 1969.

Constantinople: The Forgotten Empire. Boston, Houghton Mifflin, 1970.

The Land of Canaan. Boston, Houghton Mifflin, 1970.

To the Solar System and Back. New York, Doubleday, 1970.

The Space Dictionary. New York, Starline, 1971.

The Stars in Their Courses. New York, Doubleday, 1971; London, White Lion, 1974.

The Left Hand of the Electron (essays). New York, Doubleday, 1972; London, White Lion, 1975.

Electricity and Man. Washington, D.C., Atomic Energy Commission, 1972.

The Shaping of France. Boston, Houghton Mifflin, 1972.

Worlds within Worlds: The Story of Nuclear Energy. Washington, D.C., Atomic Energy Commission, 3 vols., 1972.

Physical Science Today. Del Mar, California, CRM, 1973.

The Shaping of North America from Earliest Times to 1763. Boston, Houghton Mifflin, 1973; London, Dobson, 1975.

Today and Tomorrow and... New York, Doubleday, 1973; London, Abelard Schuman, 1974; as *Towards Tomorrow,* London, Hodder and Stoughton, 1977.

The Tragedy of the Moon (essays). New York, Doubleday, 1973; London, Abelard Schuman, 1974.

Asimov on Astronomy New York, Doubleday, and London, Macdonald, 1974.

Asimov on Chemistry (essays). New York, Doubleday, 1974; London, Macdonald and Jane's, 1975.

The Birth of the United States, 1763-1816. Boston, Houghton Mifflin, 1974.

Our World in Space, illustrated by Robert McCall. Greenwich, Connecticut, New York Graphic Society, and Cambridge, Patrick Stephens, 1974.

Birth and Death of the Universe. New York, Walker, 1975.

Of Matters Great and Small. New York, Doubleday, 1975.

Our Federal Union: The United States from 1816 to 1865. Boston, Houghton Mifflin, and London, Dobson, 1975.

Science Past—Science Future. New York, Doubleday, 1975.

Eyes on the Universe: A History of the Telescope. Boston, Houghton Mifflin, 1975; London, Deutsch, 1976.

The Ends of the Earth: The Polar Regions of the World, illustrated by Bob Hines. New York, Weybright and Talley, 1975.

Asimov on Physics (essays). New York, Doubleday, 1976.

The Planet that Wasn't (essays). New York, Doubleday, 1976; London, Sphere, 1977.

Asimov on Numbers. (essays). New York, Doubleday, 1977.

The Beginning and the End (essays). New York, Doubleday, 1977.

The Collapsing Universe: The Story of Black Holes. New York, Walker, and London, Hutchinson, 1977.

The Golden Door: The United States from 1865 to 1918. Boston, Houghton Mifflin, and London, Dobson, 1977.

Quasar, Quasar, Burning Bright. New York, Doubleday, 1978.

Life and Time. New York, Doubleday, 1978.

The Road to Infinity (essays). New York, Doubleday, 1979.

A Choice of Catastrophes: The Disasters that Threaten Our World. New York, Simon and Schuster, 1979; London, Hutchinson, 1980.

Visions of the Universe, paintings by Kazuaki Iwasaki. Montrose, California, Cosmos Store, 1981.

The Sun Shines Bright (essays). New York, Doubleday, 1981; London, Granada, 1983.

Exploring the Earth and the Cosmos: The Growth and Future of Human Knowledge. New York, Crown, 1982; London, Allen Lane, 1983.

Counting the Eons. New York, Doubleday, 1983; London, Granada, 1984.

The Roving Mind. Buffalo, Prometheus, 1983.

The Measure of the Universe, illustrated by Roger Jones. New York, Harper, 1983.

Isaac Asimov on the Human Body and the Human Brain (includes *The Human Body: Its Structure and Operation* and *The Human Brain: Its Capacities and Functions).* Bonanza Books, 1984.

X Stands for Unknown. New York, Doubleday, 1984; London, Granada, 1985.

The Exploding Suns: The Secrets of the Supernovas, illustrated by D.F. Bach. New York, Dutton, and London, Joseph, 1985.

Asimov's Guide to Halley's Comet. New York, Walker, 1985.

Robots: Machines in Man's Image, with Karen Frenkel. New York, Harmony, 1985.

Robots: Where the Machine Ends and Life Begin, with Karen Frenkel. New York, Crown, 1985.

The Subatomic Monster: Essays on Science. New York, Doubleday, 1985; London, Grafton, 1986.

The Dangers of Intelligence and Other Science Essays. Boston, Houghton Mifflin, 1986.

Future Days: A Nineteenth-Century Vision of the Year 2000, illustrated by Jean Marc Cote. New York, Holt, and London, Virgin, 1986.

Isaac Asimov's Wonderful Worldwide Science Bazaar: Seventy-Two Up-to-Date Reports on the State of Everything from Inside the Atom to Outside the Universe. Boston, Houghton Mifflin, 1986.

As Far as Human Eye Could See (essays). New York, Doubleday, 1987; London, Grafton, 1988.

The Relativity of Wrong: Essays on the Solar System and Beyond. New York, Doubleday, 1988; Oxford, Oxford University Press, 1989.

Asimov on Science: A Thirty Year Retrospective. New York, Doubleday, 1989.

Asimov's Chronology of Science and Technology: How Science Has Shaped the World and How the World Has Affected Science from 4,000,000 B.C. to the Present. New York, Harper, 1989.

The Secret of the Universe. New York, Doubleday, 1989.

The Tyrannosaurus Prescription and One Hundred Other Essays. New York, Prometheus, 1989.

The March of the Millennia: A Key to Looking at History, with Frank White. New York, Walker, 1990.

The Next Millennium. New York, Walker, 1990.

Out of the Everywhere (essays). New York, Doubleday, 1990.

Asimov's Chronology of the World. New York, Harper, 1991.

Asimov's Guide to Earth and Space. New York, Random House, 1991.

Atom: Journey across the Subatomic Cosmos, illustrated by D.F. Bach. New York, Dutton, 1991.

Frontiers: New Discoveries about Man and His Planet, Outer Space, and the Universe. New York, Dutton, 1991.

Our Angry Earth. with Frederick Pohl. New York, Tor, 1991.

Frontiers II: More Recent Discoveries about Life, Earth, Space, and the Universe, with Janet Asimov. New York, Dutton, 1993.

The Future in Space, with Robert Giraud. Milwaukee, Stevens, 1993.

Other

Contributor, *Science Fiction Terror Tales by Isaac Asimov and Others,* edited by Groff Conklin. New York, Gnome Press, 1955.

Words from the Myths, illustrated by William Barss. Boston, Houghton Mifflin, 1961; London, Faber, 1963.

Words in Genesis, illustrated by William Barss. Boston, Houghton Mifflin, 1962.

Words on the Map. Boston, Houghton Mifflin, 1962.

Words from Exodus. Boston, Houghton Mifflin, 1963.

Asimov's Guide to the Bible: The Old Testament, The New Testament. New York, Doubleday, 2 vols., 1968-69.

Opus 100 (selection). Boston, Houghton Mifflin, 1969.

Asimov's Guide to Shakespeare: The Greek, Roman, and Italian Plays; The English Plays, illustrated by Rafael Palacios. New York, Doubleday, 2 vols., 1970.

Unseen World (teleplay). ABC-TV, 1970.

Isaac Asimov's Treasury of Humor: A Lifetime Collection of Favorite Jokes, Anecdotes, and Limericks with Copious Notes on How to Tell Them and Why. Boston, Houghton Mifflin, 1971; London, Vallentine Mitchell, 1972.

The History of Science Fiction from 1938 to the Present (filmscript), with James Gunn. Extramural Independent Study Center, University of Kansas, 1971.

The Sensuous Dirty Old Man (as Dr. A.). New York, Walker, 1971.

Contributor, *The Do-It-Yourself Bestseller*, edited by Tom Silberkleit and Jerry Biederman. New York, Doubleday, 1982.

More Words of Science, illustrated by William Barss. Boston, Houghton Mifflin, 1972.

Contributor, *Possible Tomorrows by Isaac Asimov and Others*, edited by Groff Conklin. London, Sidgwick and Jackson, 1972.

The Story of Ruth. New York, Doubleday, 1972.

Asimov's Annotated "Don Juan," illustrated by Milton Glaser. New York, Doubleday. 1972.

Asimov's Annotated "Paradise Lost." New York, Doubleday, 1974.

Familiar Poems Annotated. New York, Doubleday, 1977.

Opus 200 (selection). Boston, Houghton Mifflin, 1979.

In Memory Yet Green: The Autobiography of Isaac Asimov, 1920-1954. New York, Doubleday, 1979.

Extraterrestrial Civilizations. New York, Crown, 1979; London, Robson, 1980.

Isaac Asimov's Book of Facts. New York, Grosset and Dunlap, 1979; London, Hodder and Stoughton, 1980; abridged edition (for children), as *Would You Believe?* and *More...Would You Believe?*, illustrated by Sam Sirdofsky Haffner and Pat Schories. New York, Grosset and Dunlap, 2 vols., 1981-82.

In Joy Still Felt: The Autobiography of Isaac Asimov, 1954-1978. New York, Doubleday, 1980.

The Annotated "Gulliver's Travels." New York, Potter. 1980.

Opus (includes *Opus 100* and *Opus 200*). London, Deutsch, 1980.

In the Beginning: Science Faces God in the Book of Genesis. New York, Crown, and London, New English Library, 1981.

Asimov on Science Fiction. New York, Doubleday, 1981; London, Granada, 1983.

Change! Seventy-One Glimpses of the Future. Boston, Houghton Mifflin, 1981.

Isaac Asimov Presents Superquiz, with Ken Fisher. New York, Dembner, 1982.

Isaac Asimov Presents Superquiz 2, with Ken Fisher. New York, Dembner, 1983.

Isaac Asimov's Aliens and Outworlders, edited by Shawna McCarthy. New York, Dial, 1983.

Isaac Asimov's Space of Her Own, edited by Shawna McCarthy. New York, Dial, 1983.

The Robot Collection (includes *The Caves of Steel*, *The Naked Sun*, and *The Complete Robot*). New York, Doubleday. 1983.

Opus 300. Boston, Houghton Mifflin, 1984; London, Hale, 1985.

The Impact of Science on Society, with James Burke and Jules Bergman. Washington D.C., National Aeronautics and Space Administration, 1985.

Isaac Asimov's Fantasy!, edited by Shawna McCarthy. New York, Dial, 1985.

The Alternate Asimovs. New York, Doubleday, 1986.

Isaac Asimov. New York, Octopus Books, 1986.

Other Worlds of Isaac Asimov, edited by Martin H. Greenberg. Avenel, 1986.

Past, Present, and Future. Buffalo, New York, Prometheus, 1987.

How to Enjoy Writing: A Book of Aid and Comfort, with Janet Asimov, illustrated by Sidney Harris. New York, Walker, 1987.

Asimov's Annotated Gilbert and Sullivan. New York, Doubleday, 1988.

Library of the Universe (Did Comets Kill the Dinosaurs; The Asteroids; Ancient Astronomy; Is There Life On Other Planets?; Jupiter, the Spotted Giant; Mercury, the Quick Planet; Our Milky and Other Galaxies; How Was the Universe Born?; Saturn, the Ringed Beauty; The Space Spotter's Guide; Unidentified Flying Objects; Earth, Our Home Base; The Birth and Death of the Stars; Science Fiction, Science Fact; Space Garbage; Astronomy Today; Comets and Meteors; Mythology of the Universe; Pluto, A Double Planet?; Colonizing the Planets and Stars; Neptune, The Farthest Giant; Piloted Space Flights; Projects in Astronomy; Our Solar System; Uranus: The Sideways Planet; Astronomy Today; Quasars, Pulsars, and Black Holes; Venus, A Shrouded Mystery; The World's Space Programs). Milwaukee, Stevens, 24 vols., 1988-90.

Asimov's Galaxy: Reflections on Science Fiction. New York, Doubleday, 1989.

Foundation's Friends: Stories in Honor of Isaac Asimov, edited by Martin H. Greenberg. New York, T. Doherty Associates, 1989.

The Ugly Little Boy/The Widget, the Wadget, and Boff, with Theodore Sturgeon. New York, Tor, 1989.

Isaac Asimov Laughs Again. New York, Harper, 1991.

Contributor, *The John W. Campbell Letters with Isaac Asimov and A.E. van Vogt*. A.C. Projects, 1991.

The Ugly Little Boy, with Robert Silverberg. New York, Doubleday, 1992.

Editor

Isaac Asimov Presents the Golden Years of Science Fiction, with Martin H. Greenberg. New York, Crown, 1939.

Isaac Asimov Presents the Golden Years of Science Fiction: Twenty-Eight Stories and Novellas, with Martin H. Greenberg. New York, Bonanza, 1941.

Isaac Asimov Presents the Golden Years of Science Fiction: Twenty Stories and Novellas, with Martin H. Greenberg. New York, Crown, 1943.

Isaac Asimov Presents the Golden Years of Science Fiction: Twenty-Six Stories and Novellas, with Martin H. Greenberg. New York, Crown, 1945.

Isaac Asimov Presents the Golden Years of Science Fiction: Thirty-Three Stories and Novellas, with Martin H. Greenberg. New York, Crown, 1947.

Soviet Science Fiction and *More Soviet Science Fiction*. New York, Collier, 2 vols., 1962.

The Hugo Winners 1-4. New York, Doubleday, 4 vols., 1962-85; *Volume 1* and *Volume 3*, London, Dobson, 2 vols., 1963-67; *Volume 2*, London, Sphere, 1973.

Fifty Short Science Fiction Tales, with Groff Conklin. New York, Collier, 1963.

Four Futures: Four Original Novellas of Science Fiction. New York, Hawthorn, 1971.

Tomorrow's Children: Eighteen Tales of Fantasy and Science Fiction, illustrated by Emanuel Schongut. New York, Doubleday, 1966; London, Futura, 1974.

Where Do We Go from Here? New York, Doubleday, 1971; London, Joseph, 1973.

Nebula Award Stories 8. New York, Harper, and London, Gollancz, 1973.

Before the Golden Age: A Science Fiction Anthology of the 1930's. New York, Doubleday, and London, Robson, 1974.

100 Great Science Fiction Short-Short Stories, with Martin H. Greenberg and Joseph D. Olander. New York, Doubleday, and London, Robson, 1978.

The Science Fictional Solar System, with Martin H. Greenberg and Charles G. Waugh. New York, Harper, 1979; London, Sidgwick and Jackson, 1980.

The Thirteen Crime of Science Fiction, with Martin H. Greenberg and Charles G. Waugh. New York, Doubleday, 1979.

The Great SF Stories 1-20, with Martin H. Greenberg. New York, DAW, 1979-90.

Microcosmic Tales: 100 Wondrous Science Fiction Short-Short Stories, with Martin H. Greenberg and Joseph D. Olander. New York, Taplinger, 1980.

Space Mail 1, with Martin H. Greenberg and Joseph D. Olander. New York, Fawcett, 1980.

The Future in Question, with Martin H. Greenberg and Joseph D. Olander. New York, Fawcett, 1980.

Who Done It?, with Alice Laurance. Boston, Houghton Mifflin, 1980.

The Seven Deadly Sins of Science Fiction, edited by Martin H. Greenberg and Charles G. Waugh. New York, Fawcett, 1980.

Miniature Mysteries: 100 Malicious Little Mystery Stories, with Martin H. Greenberg and Joseph D. Olander. New York, Taplinger, 1981.

Fantastic Creature. New York, Watts, 1981.

The Best Science Fiction [Fantasy, Horror and Supernatural] of the 19th Century. New York, Beaufort, 3 vols., 1981-83; *Science Fiction,* London, Gollancz, 1983; *Fantasy and Horror and Supernatural,* London, Robson, 2 vols., 1985, all with Martin H. Greenberg and Charles G. Waugh.

Asimov's Marvels of Science Fiction. London, Hale, 1981.

The Twelve Crimes of Christmas, with Carol-Lynn Rössell Waugh and Martin H. Greenberg. New York, New York, Avon, 1981.

The Seven Cardinal Virtues of Science Fiction, with Charles G. Waugh and Martin H. Greenberg. New York, Fawcett, 1981.

TV: 2000, with Martin H. Greenberg and Charles G. Waugh. New York, Fawcett, 1982.

Last Man on Earth, with Martin H. Greenberg and Charles G. Waugh. New York, Fawcett, 1982.

Tantalizing Locked Room Mysteries, with Charles G. Waugh and Martin H. Greenberg. New York, Walker, 1982.

Space Mail 2, with Martin H. Greenberg and Charles G. Waugh. New York, Fawcett, 1982.

Laughing Space: Funny Science Fiction, with J.O. Jeppson. Boston, Houghton Mifflin, and London, Robson, 1982.

Speculations, with Alice Laurance. Boston, Houghton Mifflin, 1982.

Science Fiction from A to Z: A Dictionary of the Great Themes of Science Fiction, with Charles G. Waugh and Martin H. Greenberg. Boston, Houghton Mifflin, 1982.

Flying Saucers, with Martin H. Greenberg and Charles G. Waugh. New York, Fawcett, 1982.

Dragon Tales, with Martin H. Greenberg and Charles G. Waugh. New York, Fawcett, 1982.

Asimov's Worlds of Science Fiction. London, Hale, 1982.

Hallucination Orbit: Psychology in Science Fiction, with Martin H. Greenberg and Charles G. Waugh. New York, Farrar Straus, 1983.

Magical Worlds of Fantasy series (*Wizards, Witches*). New York, New American Library, 2 vols., 1983-84; 1 vol. edition, New York, Bonanza, 1985.

Caught in the Organ Draft: Biology in Science Fiction, with Martin H. Greenberg and Charles G. Waugh. New York, Farrar Straus, 1983.

The Big Apple Mysteries. New York, Avon, 1983.

The Science Fiction Weight-Loss Book, with George R. Martin and Martin H. Greenberg. New York, Crown, 1983.

Starships, with Martin H. Greenberg and Charles G. Waugh. New York, Ballantine, 1983.

Asimov's Wonders of the World. London, Hale, 1983.

Creations: The Quest for Origins in Story and Science, with Martin H. Greenberg and George Zebrowski. New York, Crown, 1983; London, Harrap, 1984.

Computer Crimes and Capers, with Martin H. Greenberg and Charles G. Waugh. Chicago, Academy, 1983; London, Viking, 1985.

Thirteen Horrors of Halloween. Avon, 1983.

Machines That Think, Patricia S. Warrick and Martin H. Greenberg. New York, Holt Rinehart, and London, Allen Lane, 1984.

100 Great Fantasy Short-Short Stories, with Terry Carr and Martin H. Greenberg. New York, Doubleday, and London, Robson, 1984.

The Great Science Fiction Firsts, with Charles G. Waugh and Martin H. Greenberg. New York, Beaufort, 1984; London, Robson, 1985.

Murder on the Menu, with others. New York, Avon, 1984.

Sherlock Holmes Through Time and Space, with Martin H. Greenberg and Charles G. Waugh. New York, Bluejay, 1984; London, Severn House, 1985.

Isaac Asimov's Wonderful World of Science Fiction 2: The Science Fictional Olympics, with Martin H. Greenberg. New York, New American Library, 1984.

Election Day 2084: A Science Fiction Anthology on the Politics of the Future, with Martin H. Greenberg. Buffalo, New York, Prometheus, 1984.

Baker's Dozen: Thirteen Short Fantasy Novels, with Martin H. Greenberg and Charles G. Waugh. New York, Greenwich House, 1984.

Amazing Stories: Sixty Years of the Best Science Fiction, with Martin H. Greenberg and Charles G. Waugh. Lake Geneva, Wisconsin, TRS, 1985.

Living in the Future. New York, Beaufort, 1985.

Great Science Fiction Stories by the World's Great Scientists, with Martin H. Greenberg and Charles G. Waugh. New York, Fine, 1985.

Giants, with Martin H. Greenberg and Charles G. Waugh. New York, New American Library, 1985.

Comets, with Martin H. Greenberg and Charles G. Waugh. New York, New American Library, 1986.

Mythical Beasties, with Martin H. Greenberg and Charles G. Waugh. New York, New American Library, 1986; as *Mythic Beasts,* London, Robinson, 1988.

The Mammoth Book of Short Fantasy Novels. London, Robinson, 1986.

The Mammoth Book of Short Science Fiction Novels. London, Robinson, 1986.

The Dark Void. London, Severn House, 1987.

Beyond the Stars. London, Severn House, 1987.

Hound Dunnit, with Carol-Lynn Rössell Waugh and Martin H. Greenberg. New York, Carroll and Graf, 1987; London, Robson, 1988.

Cosmic Knight, with Martin H. Greenberg and Charles G. Waugh. London, Robinson, 1987.

The Best Crime Stories of the 19th Century, with Martin H. Greenberg and Charles G. Waugh. New York, Dembner, 1988; London, Robson, 1989.

Isaac Asimov's Book of Science and Nature Quotations, with Jason A. Shulman. New York, Weidenfeld and Nicolson, 1988.

Ghosts, with Martin H. Greenberg and Charles G. Waugh. London, Collins, 1988.

The Best Detective Stories of the 19th Century, with Martin H. Greenberg and Charles G. Waugh. New York, Dembner, 1988.

The Mammoth Book of Classic Science Fiction: Short Novels of the 1930's, with Martin H. Greenberg and Charles G. Waugh. New York, Carroll and Graf, and London, Robinson, 1988.

Monsters, with Martin H. Greenberg and Charles G. Waugh. New York, New American Library, 1988; London, Robinson, 1989.

The Mammoth Book of Golden Age Science Fiction: Short Novels of the 1940's, with Martin H. Greenberg and Charles G. Waugh. New York, Carroll and Graf, and London, Robinson, 1989.

Curses, with Martin H. Greenberg and Charles G. Waugh. New York, New American Library, 1989.

Senior Sleuths, with Martin H. Greenberg and Carol-Lynn Rossel Waugh. Boston, G.K. Hall, 1989.

Tales of the Occult, with Martin H. Greenberg and Charles G. Waugh. Buffalo, New York, Prometheus, 1989.

Robots, with Martin H. Greenberg and Charles G. Waugh. London, Robinson, 1989.

The New Hugo Winners, with Martin H. Greenberg. New York, Wynwood Press, 1989.

Visions of Fantasy: Tales from the Masters, with Martin H. Greenberg, illustrated by Larry Elmore. New York, Doubleday, 1989.

The Mammoth Book of Vintage Science Fiction: Short Novels of the 1950's, with Martin H. Greenberg and Charles G. Waugh. New York, Carroll and Graf, and London, Robinson, 1990.

Cosmic Critiques: How and Why Ten Science Fiction Stories Work, with Martin H. Greenberg. Cincinnati, Writer's Digest, 1990.

*

Media Adaptations: *Foundation: The Psychohistorians* (recording of selected chapters of *Foundation* read by William Shatner, Caedmon, 1976; *The Mayors* (recording of Asimov reading *Foundation),* Caedmon, 1977; *The Ugly Little Boy* (film), Learning Corporation of America, 1977; *Nightfall* (film), MGM/UA, 1988.

Biography: Entry in *Dictionary of Literary Biography,* Volume 8, Detroit, Gale, 1981.

Bibliography: *Isaac Asimov: A Checklist of Works Published in the United States March 1939-May 1972* by Marjorie M. Miller, Kent, Ohio, Kent State University Press, 1972; in *In Joy Still Felt,* 1980.

Manuscript Collection: Mugar Memorial Library, Boston University.

Critical Study: *Asimov Analyzed* by Neil Goble, Baltimore, Mirage Press, 1972; entry in *Contemporary Literary Criticism,* Volume 1, Detroit, Gale, 1973; Volume 3, 1975; Volume 9, 1978; Volume 19, 1981; Volume 26, 1983; *Isaac Asimov Talks: An Interview* (recording), Writer's Voice, 1974; *The Science Fiction of Isaac Asimov* by Joseph F. Patrouch, Jr., New York, Doubleday, 1974, London, Panther, 1976; *Isaac Asimov* edited by Joseph D. Olander and Martin H. Greenberg, New York, Taplinger, and Edinburgh, Harris, 1977; *Asimov: The Foundations of His Science Fiction* by George Edgar Slusser, San Bernardino, California, Borgo Press, 1980; *Isaac*

Asimov: The Foundations of Science Fiction by James Gunn, New York and Oxford, Oxford University Press, 1982; *Isaac Asimov* by Jean Fiedler and Jim Mele, New York, Ungar, 1982; entry in *Children's Literature Review,* Volume 12, Detroit, Gale, 1987.

*   *   *

Isaac Asimov is the extraordinarily prolific writer of a prodigious number of works including science fiction, science fact, mystery, history, short stories, guides to the Bible and Shakespeare, and discussions of myth, humor, poems, limericks, as well as annotations of literary works. His wide-ranging interests, scholarship, and productivity should serve as inspiration to his readers.

Among Asimov's credits are several types of books for young readers and several other works written for adults but also suited for older juvenile readers. His science fiction for juveniles include a series of novels originally published under the pseudonym of Paul French and subsequently represented under Asimov's name. These are entitled *David Starr, Space Ranger* (1952); *Lucky Starr and the Pirates of the Asteroids* (1953); *Lucky Starr and the Oceans of Venus* (1954); *Lucky Starr and the Big Sun of Mercury* (1956), published under Asimov's name as *The Big Sun of Mercury* in 1974 and later under Asimov's name under original title in 1978; *Lucky Starr and the Moons of Jupiter* (1957); and *Lucky Starr and the Rings of Saturn* (1958).

David Starr, Space Ranger and the other novels listed are "space operas." In these novels, good prevails over evil, science always wins out over ignorance, and earthlings win over those from other parts of the galaxy. These books contain constant action, imaginative gadgetry, and brisk narrative. Not surprising considering Asimov's training as a scientist is that his novels are filled with prose passages explaining space phenomena and giving information about the galaxy. All of the sequels to *David Starr, Space Ranger* present a mystery that David and the readers must solve.

David Starr, who was later called Lucky, is an interesting character. He has brains, courage, and athletic ability. He is also modest. Bigman Jones is David's devoted companion; he is a small Martian who offers comic relief. The villains are sufficiently villainous.

The David Starr novels, written when the military rivalry with the U.S.S.R. was at its height, frequently flaunt the democratic ideal and present villains as evil would-be dictators. The reissued novels allows Asimov to report new scientific findings that have relevance to the works.

Other science fiction works for young people are *The Best New Thing* (1971), The *Heavenly Host* (1975) and the Norby novels: *Norby, the Mixed up Robot* (1983); *Norby and the Lost Princess* (1985); *Norby and the Invaders* (1985); *Norby and the Queen's Necklace* (1986); *Norby Finds a Villain* (1987); *Norby Down to Earth* (1989); and *Norby and the Oldest Dragon* (1990). The Norby novels are written with Asimov's wife Janet O. Jeppson as co-author. *Franchise, All the Troubles of the World, Sally,* and *Robbie* were all published in 1989 by creative education.

Several of Asimov's titles for adults have been widely read by a younger audience. These most notably include the Foundation Trilogy published from 1951 to 1953. The trilogy consists of three books of stories—*Foundation, Foundation and Empire,* and *Second Foundation.* These novels compose a history of the future loosely based on the events in the fall of the Roman Empire. Beyond that, the novels provide a powerful commentary on the nature of history. In the novels, the Roman Empire is the Galactic Empire. A new science called psychohistory allows people to predict what will happen in the future. This situation allows a venue for exploring historical trends, the conflict of determinism and free will, and the ability of one person or a group to control others and ultimately history. These are certainly adult subjects. Forty years after the original trilogy, in the 1980s, Asimov added a new volume, Foundation's Edge. He also linked the Foundation stories with his robot novels in *The Robots of Dawn, Robots and Empire, Foundation and Earth,* and *Prelude to Foundation.*

The novels are—in form—space operas, primarily adventure stories set in the future. As such, their appeal is wide. They have galaxy-spanning federations, fast ships that travel at above lightspeed, and atomic weaponry. The Foundation triumphs on the planet Terminus. Foundation is an island of scientific knowledge— an expressed wish perhaps for reason to triumph over the irrational.

Asimov's nonfiction works for young readers are as impressive as his fiction. He wrote a number of books on astronomy: *Building Blocks of the Universe, Satellites in Outer Space, The Moon, To the Ends of the Universe, Mars, Stars, Galaxies* and many more. In addition to astronomy topics, Asimov wrote about various aspects of science in general in *Breakthroughs in Science, Great Ideas of Science, Ginn Science Program, Please Explain,* and *Little Treasury of Dinosaurs.* All of these works are somewhat dated in their information, but are nonetheless classics of a sort. Asimov also wrote several histories, one of which was specifically designed for juveniles entitled *The Kite that Won the Revolution.*

Isaac Asimov's creativity and intelligence in presenting information both fiction and nonfiction will guarantee his place as one of the masters of science fiction.

—Lesa Dill

ATWOOD, Margaret (Eleanor). Canadian. Born in Ottawa, Ontario, Canada, 18 November 1939. Educated at Victoria College, University of Toronto, B.A. 1961; Radcliffe College, Cambridge, Massachusetts, A.M. 1962; Harvard University, Cambridge, Massachusetts, graduate study, 1962-63, and 1965-67. Married 1) James Polk (divorced); 2) Graeme Gibson, one daughter. Lecturer in English, University of British Columbia, Vancouver, 1964-65; Instructor in English, Sir George Williams University, Montreal, Quebec, 1967-68; teacher of creative writing, University of Alberta, Edmonton, 1969-70; Assistant Professor of English, York University, Toronto, Ontario, 1971-72; Editor and member of board of directors, House of Anansi Press, Toronto, 1971-73. Writer-in-residence, University of Toronto, Toronto, 1972-73, University of Alabama, Tuscaloosa, 1985, Macquarie University, North Ryde, New South Wales, 1987, and Trinity University, San Antonio, Texas, 1989; Berg Visiting Professor of English, New York University, New York, 1986. President, Writers Union of Canada, 1981-82, and PEN Canadian Centre, 1984-86. Recipient: E.J. Pratt medal, 1961, for *Double Persephone;* President's medal, University of Western Ontario, 1965; YWCA Women of Distinction award, 1966; Governor General's award, 1966, for *The Circle Game,* and 1986, for *The Handmaid's Tale;* first prize in Canadian Centennial Commission Poetry Competition, 1967; Union Prize, *Poetry,* 1969; Bess Hoskins Prize, *Poetry,* 1969 and 1974; City of Toronto award,

1976, 1989; Canadian Booksellers' Association award, 1977; Periodical Distributors of Canada Short Fiction award, 1977; St. Lawrence award for fiction, 1978; Radcliffe medal, 1980; *Life before Man* named notable book of 1980 by the American Library Association; Molson award, 1981; Guggenheim fellowship, 1981; International Writer's Prize, Welsh Arts Council, 1982; Book of the Year award, Periodical Distributors of Canada and the Foundation for the Advancement of Canadian Letters, 1983; Ida Nudel Humanitarian award, 1986; Toronto Arts award for writing and editing, 1986; *Los Angeles Times* Book award, 1986, for *The Handmaid's Tale;* named Woman of the Year, *Ms.* magazine, 1986; Arthur C. Clarke award, 1987; Commonwealth Literature Prize, 1987; Council for the Advancement and Support of Education silver medal, 1987; Humanist of the Year award, 1987; National Magazine award, for journalism, 1988; Harvard University Centennial medal, 1990; named *Chatelaine* magazine's Woman of the Year. D.Litt.: Trent University, Peterborough, Ontario, 1973; Concordia University, Montreal, 1980; Smith College, Northampton, Massachusetts, 1982; University of Toronto, 1983; Mount Holyoke College, South Hadley, Massachusetts, 1985; University of Waterloo, Ontario, 1985; University of Guelph, Ontario, 1985; Victoria College, 1987; LL.D.: Queen's University, Kingston, Ontario, 1974. Companion, Order of Canada, 1981. Fellow, Royal Society of Canada, 1987; Honorary Member, American Academy of Arts and Sciences, 1988. Address: c/o Oxford University Press, 70 Wynford Drive, Don Mills, Ontario M3C 1J9, Canada.

PUBLICATIONS

Novels

The Edible Woman. Toronto, McClelland and Stewart, and London, Deutsch, 1969; Boston, Little Brown, 1970.
Surfacing. Toronto, McClelland and Stewart, 1972; London, Deutsch, and New York, Simon and Schuster 1973.
Lady Oracle. Toronto, McClelland and Stewart, and New York, Simon and Schuster, 1976; London, Deutsch, 1977.
Life Before Man. Toronto, McClelland and Stewart, 1979; New York, Simon and Schuster, and London, Cape, 1980.
Bodily Harm. Toronto, McClelland and Stewart, 1981; New York, Simon and Schuster, and London, Cape, 1982.
Cat's Eye. Toronto, McClelland and Stewart, 1985; New York, Doubleday, and London, Bloomsbury, 1989.
The Handmaid's Tale. Toronto, McClelland and Stewart, 1985; Boston, Houghton Mifflin, and London, Cape, 1986.
The Robber Bride. Toronto, McClelland and Stewart, and New York, Doubleday, 1993.

Short Stories

Dancing Girls and Other Stories. Toronto, McClelland and Stewart, 1977; New York, Simon and Schuster, and London, Cape, 1982.
Encounters with the Element Man. Concord, New Hampshire, Ewert, 1982.
Bluebeard's Egg and Other Stories. Toronto, McClelland and Stewart, 1983; Boston, Houghton Mifflin, 1986; London, Cape, 1987..
Murder in the Dark: Short Fictions and Prose Poems. Toronto, Coach House Press, 1983; London, Cape, 1984.

Unearthing Suite. Toronto, Grand Union Press, 1983.
Hurricane Hazel and Other Stories. Helsinki, Eurographica, 1986.
Wilderness Tips. Hampton, New Hampshire, Chivers, 1991.
Good Bones. Toronto, Coach House Press, 1992.

Poetry

Double Persephone. Toronto, Hawkshead Press, 1961.
The Circle Game (single poem). Bloomfield Hills, Michigan,
    Cranbrook Academy of Art, 1964; revised edition, Contact Press,
    1966.
Kaleidoscopes Baroque: A Poem. Bloomfield Hills, Michigan,
    Cranbrook Academy of Art, 1965.
Talismans for Children. Bloomfield Hills, Michigan, Cranbrook
    Academy of Art, 1965.
Expeditions. Bloomfield Hills, Michigan, Cranbrook Academy of
    Art, 1966.
Speeches for Doctor Frankenstein. Bloomfield Hills, Michigan,
    Cranbrook Academy of Art, 1966.
The Animals in That Country. Toronto, Oxford University Press,
    1968; Boston, Little Brown, 1969.
Who Was in the Garden. Santa Barbara, California, Unicorn, 1969.
Five Modern Canadian Poets, with others, edited by Eli Mandel.
    Toronto, Holt Rinehart, 1970.
The Journals of Susanna Moodie. Toronto, Oxford University
    Press, 1970.
Oratorio for Sasquatch, Man and Two Androids: Poems for Voices.
    Toronto, Canadian Broadcasting Corporation, 1970.
Procedures for Underground. Toronto, Oxford University Press,
    and Boston, Little Brown, 1970.
Power Politics. Toronto, Anansi, 1971; New York, Harper, 1973.
You Are Happy. Toronto, Oxford University Press, and New York,
    Harper, 1974.
Selected Poems, 1965-1975. Toronto, Oxford University Press,
    1976; New York, Simon and Schuster, 1978.
Marsh Hawk. Toronto, Dreadnaught, 1977.
Two-Headed Poems. Toronto, Oxford University Press, 1978; New
    York, Simon and Schuster, 1981.
Notes Toward a Poem That Can Never Be Written. Toronto, Sala-
    mander Press, 1981.
True Stories. Toronto, Oxford University Press, 1981; New York,
    Simon and Schuster, and London, Cape, 1982.
Snake Poems. Toronto, Salamander Press, 1983.
Interlunar. Toronto, Oxford University Press, 1984; London, Cape,
    1988.
Selected Poems II: Poems Selected and New, 1976-1986. Toronto,
    Oxford University Press, 1986; Boston, Houghton Mifflin, 1987.
Selected Poems 1966-1984. Toronto, Oxford University Press, 1990.
Poems 1965-1975. London, Virago Press, 1991.

Plays

Radio Plays: *The Trumpets of Summer,* CBC, 1964.

Television Plays: *The Servant Girl,* CBC-TV, 1974; *Snowbird,* CBC-
TV, 1981; *Heaven on Earth,* with Peter Pearson, CBC-TV, 1986.

Other

Survival: A Thematic Guide to Canadian Literature. Toronto,
Anansi, 1972.

Contributor, *The Canadian Imagination: Dimensions of a Literary
    Culture.* Cambridge, Massachusetts, Harvard University Press,
    1977.
Days of the Rebels, 1815-1840. Toronto, Natural Science of Canada,
    1977.
Up in the Tree (for children). Toronto, McClelland and Stewart,
    1978.
Contributor, *To See Our World,* by Catherine M. Young. GLC
    Publishers, 1979; New York, Morrow, 1980.
Anna's Pet (for children), with Joyce Barkhouse, illustrated by Ann
    Blades. Toronto, Lorimer, 1980.
Second Words: Selected Critical Prose. Toronto, Anansi, 1982;
    Boston, Beacon Press, 1984.
Editor, *The New Oxford Book of Canadian Verse in English.* Toronto,
    New York, and Oxford, Oxford University Press, 1982.
Editor, with Robert Weaver, *The Oxford Book of Canadian Short
    Stories in English.* Toronto, Oxford, and New York, Oxford Uni-
    versity Press, 1986.
Editor, *The Canlit Foodbook: From Pen to Palate: A Collection of
    Tasty Literary Fare.* Toronto, Totem, 1987.
Editor, with Shannon Ravenel. *The Best American Short Stories,
    1989.* Boston, Houghton Mifflin, 1989.
Margaret Atwood: Conversations, edited by Earl G. Ingersoll.
    Princeton, New Jersey, Ontario Review Press, 1990.
For the Birds (for children). Toronto, Douglas and McIntyre, 1990.
Family Cooking Celebration: Kitchen Discoveries for All Ages!,
    with Victory Crealock. Seattle, Washington, Pepper Mill, 1991.

Contributor to anthologies, including *Women on Women,* 1978 and
to periodicals, including *Atlantic, Poetry, Kayak, New Yorker,
Harper's, New York Times Book Review, Saturday Night, Tamarack
Review, Canadian Forum,* and other publications.

*

Media Adaptations: *The Poetry and Voice of Margaret Atwood*
(recording), Caedmon, 1977; *The Handmaid's Tale* (film), Cinecom
Entertainment Group, 1990; *Margaret Atwood Reads from A
Handmaid's Tale,* Caedmon.

Biography: *Margaret Atwood* by Jerome H. Rosenberg, Boston,
Twayne, 1984; Entry in *Dictionary of Literary Biography,* Volume
53, Detroit, Gale, 1986; *Margaret Atwood* by Barbara Hill Rigney,
London, Macmillan, 1987.

Bibliography: "Margaret Atwood: An Annotated Bibliography"
(prose and poetry) by Alan J. Horne, in *The Annotated Bibliography of Canada's Major Authors 1-2* edited by Robert Lecker and
Jack David, Downsview, Ontario, ECW Press, 2 vols., 1929-80.

Manuscript Collection: Fisher Library, University of Toronto.

Critical Study: Entry in *Contemporary Literary Criticism,* Volume
2, Detroit, Gale, 1974; Volume 3, 1975; Volume 4, 1975; Volume 8,
1978; Volume 13, 1980; Volume 15, 1980; Volume 25, 1983; Volume
44, 1987; *Margaret Atwood: A Symposium* edited by Linda Sandler,
Victoria, British Columbia, University of Victoria, 1977; *A Violent
Duality* by Sherrill E. Grace, Montreal, Véhicule Press, 1979, and
Margaret Atwood: Language, Text, and System edited by Grace and
Lorraine Weir, Vancouver, University of British Columbia Press,
1983; *The Art of Margaret Atwood: Essays in Criticism* edited by
Arnold E. Davidson and Cathy N. Davidson, Toronto, Anansi,

1981; *Margaret Atwood: A Feminist Poet* by Frank Davey, Vancouver, Talonbooks, 1984; *Margaret Atwood: Reflection and Reality* by Beatrice Mendez-Egle, Edinburg, Texas, Pan American University, 1987; *Critical Essays on Margaret Atwood* edited by Judith McCombs, Boston, Hall, 1988; *Margaret Atwood: Vision and Forms* edited by Kathryn van Spanckeren and Jan Garden Castro, Carbondale, Southern Illinois University Press, 1988.

*   *   *

Margaret Atwood is best known for the Canadian nationalism and feminism that characterize her works. As controversial as she is versatile, however, she modifies both her national pride and her feminist sensibilities with a questioning attitude that often seems to subvert the very principles she sets out to establish.

In both her poetry collections and novels, Atwood's brand of feminism is one that views women as being generally double-minded about their status as daughters, mothers, wives. Realizing the inferiority with which society has endowed these positions, most women are willing to accept their inferior status in return for certain apparent goods, such as financial security, physical protection, and freedom from hard labor. In order to assure themselves of such goods, women learn to play the games men design for them and conspire in creating the male lovers/masters who rule them. They also learn to betray other women in the process. These themes, with variations, provide the energy for Atwood's most famous novel and one that will appeal to young adults, *The Handmaid's Tale.*

In the short time since its publication in 1985, *The Handmaid's Tale* has become a modern classic. Difficult to classify, it has been discussed as a futuristic fantasy, a cautionary tale, and a feminist tract. Indeed it is all three and more, for the dystopia that the narrator describes is a theocratic, patriarchal, nightmare world created by men, with the help of women, which proves to be equally restrictive for both sexes.

Although the narrator is thirty-three years old at the time the events of the novel occur (sometime near the turn of the twentieth century), she moves us into her past so that we begin to realize that the current sterile police state is the "fault" of myriad special-interest groups including even her mother's feminist activist organization. We also realize that women as well as men are willing to subordinate and betray one another for some perceived personal gain.

In spite of the conspiracy theory of female inferiority that underpins this novel, however, Atwood makes clear that men *do* hold the power that ultimately determines the quality of life. Thus she holds men more responsible for the depressing state of affairs in the fictional country of Gilead (formerly the United States) than women. An environment made toxic by the irresponsible use of chemicals has led to a dangerous level of male and female sterility (although *male* sterility is never openly admitted). The few women who are known to be fertile are rounded up and indoctrinated as Handmaids, women who will be impersonally impregnated by "Commanders" whose barren wives passively participate in the "Ceremony" of impregnation. The narrator is one of the Handmaids, and, like others of her class, she bears the name of the Commander to whom she is temporarily assigned. She is therefore known to us simply as Offred (Of Fred), a detail that vividly dramatizes a longstanding fact of our culture: that women derive their roles, their self-respect, even their identities, from the men who master them.

Young adults quickly become engaged in the philosophical issues raised in this novel. Because Atwood does not present a simplistic view of innocent females unwillingly victimized by men, young readers are alerted to the fact that the plight of women is a very complicated issue, inextricably bound with the plight of men and of the environment. Atwood adeptly reveals the multiplicity of forces that work toward controlling gender roles in our culture. The Bible, fairy tales (The Wives are dressed in the colors of the Blessed Virgin Mary; the Handmaids are dressed like Little Red Riding Hood), popular songs, classical literature, trendy crusades, even computer technology all can be made to pressure women's and men's behavior in ways considered to be appropriate to their gender, class, and role.

At the conclusion of the novel we learn that what we have taken to be the journal or diary of our heroine is a transcription of tapes that were discovered in the twenty-second century in a metal footlocker by a team of researchers who specialize in "Gileadean Studies." The tapes are being discussed at a typical academic conference. In spite of the fact that women are conspicuous at this conference, the very familiarity of its format suggests that conventions haven't changed as much as one might have hoped in two hundred years. The sense of familiarity conveyed by the proceedings of the conference is consistent with the déjà vu we experience throughout the novel. Attitudes about women and their roles seem to keep repeating themselves. In spite of all the technological advancements of two thousand years, it seems, women will be imprisoned by their biology if they conspire with men to be so.

—Mary Lowe-Evans

———

AVI (Avi Wortis). American. Born in New York City, 23 December 1937. Educated at Elisabeth Irwin High School, New York; University of Wisconsin, Madison, B.A. in history 1959, M.A. in drama 1962; Columbia University, New York, M.S. in library science 1964. Married 1) Joan Gabriner in 1963 (divorced), two sons; 2) Coppélia Kahn, one son. Staff member, Lincoln Center Library of the Performing Arts Theatre Collection, New York, 1962-70, and Lambeth Public Library, London, 1968; Assistant Professor and humanities librarian, Trenton State College, New Jersey, 1970-86. Since 1986 full-time writer. Regular reviewer, *Library Journal* and *School Library Journal,* both New York, 1965-73. Recipient: New York Public Library grant, 1969; New Jersey Council on the Arts grant, 1974, 1976, 1978; Mystery Writers of America Special award, 1975, for *No More Magic,* 1979, for *Emily Upham's Revenge,* and 1983, for *Shadrach's Crossing;* Christopher award, 1981, for *Encounter at Easton;* Children's Choice award, International Reading Association, 1980, for *Man from the Sky,* and 1988, for *Romeo and Juliet, Together (and Alive) at Last;* Authors award, for *Shadrach's Crossing,* 1983; Scott O'Dell award for historical fiction, from *Bulletin of the Center for Children's Books,* 1984, for *The Fighting Ground;* Virginia Young Readers' award, 1990, for *Wolf Rider;* John Newbery honor award, from American Library Association, *Horn Book*-Boston Globe award, and Golden Kite award, from Society of Children's Book Authors, all 1990, and Judy Lopez Memorial award, 1991, all for *The True Confessions of Charlotte Doyle;* Newbery honor award and Boston Globe-*Horn Book* Honor award, both 1992, both for *Nothing but the Truth; Snail Tale* was named best book of the year by the British Book Council, 1973; *School Library Journal,* best books of the year citations for *Night Jour-*

neys, 1980, *Wolf Rider,* 1987, and *The True Confessions of Charlotte Doyle,* 1990. American Library Association, best books for young adults citations, 1984, for *The Fighting Ground,* and 1986, for *Wolf Rider,* and notable book citation for *The True Confessions of Charlotte Doyle,* 1990. Library of Congress, best books of the year citations for *Something Upstairs,* 1989, and *The Man Who Was Poe,* 1990. Volunteer State award, 1991-92, for *Something Upstairs: A Tale of Ghosts.* Agent: Dorothy Markinko, McIntosh and Otis, 475 Fifth Avenue, New York, NY 10017. Address: 15 Sheldon Street, Providence, RI 02906, U.S.A.

PUBLICATIONS FOR YOUNG ADULTS

Fiction

Captain Grey. New York, Pantheon, 1977.
Emily Upham's Revenge, illustrated by Paul O. Zelinsky. New York, Pantheon, 1978.
Night Journeys. New York, Pantheon, 1979.
Encounter at Easton. New York, Pantheon, 1980.
The History of Helpless Harry, illustrated by Paul O. Zelinsky. New York, Pantheon, 1980.
A Place Called Ugly. New York, Pantheon, 1981.
Sometimes I Think I Hear My Name. New York, Pantheon, 1982.
Shadrach's Crossing. New York, Pantheon, 1983.
Devil's Race. New York, Lippincott, 1984.
The Fighting Ground. New York, Lippincott, 1984.
Bright Shadow. New York, Bradbury Press, 1985.
Wolf Rider. New York, Bradbury Press, 1986.
Something Upstairs: A Tale of Ghosts. New York, Orchard, 1988.
The Man Who Was Poe. New York, Orchard, 1989.
The True Confessions of Charlotte Doyle. New York, Orchard, 1990.
Nothing But the Truth. New York, Orchard, 1991.
Blue Heron. New York, Bradbury, 1992.
"Who Was That Masked Man, Anyway?" New York, Orchard, 1992.
Punch with Judy. New York, Bradbury, 1993.
City of Light, City of Dark. New York, Orchard, 1993.
The Barn. New York, Orchard, 1994.
The Bird, The Frog, and the Light. New York, Orchard, 1994.
Pip. New York, Orchard, 1995.
Tom, Babette & Simon. New York, Bradbury, 1995.

PUBLICATIONS FOR CHILDREN

Fiction

Things That Sometimes Happen (stories), illustrated by Jodi Robbin. New York, Doubleday, 1970.
Snail Tale, illustrated by Tom Kindron. New York, Pantheon, 1972; London, Hutchinson, 1973.
No More Magic. New York, Pantheon, 1975.
Man from the Sky, illustrated by David Wiesner. New York, Knopf, 1980.
Who Stole the Wizard of Oz?, illustrated by Derek James. New York, Knopf, 1981.
S.O.R. Losers. New York, Bradbury Press, 1984.
Romeo and Juliet, Together (and Alive!) at Last. New York, Orchard, 1987.
Windcatcher. New York, Bradbury, 1991.

Media Adaptations: *The Fighting Ground* (recording), Listening Library; *Emily Upham's Revenge, Shadrach's Crossing, Something Upstairs, The Fighting Ground,* and *The True Confessions of Charlotte Doyle* were produced on radio programs "Read to Me", Maine Public Radio, and "Books Aloud," WWON-Rhode Island.

Biography: Essay in *Speaking for Ourselves: Autobiographical Sketches by Notable Authors of Books for Young Adults,* Volume 1, compiled and edited by Donald R. Gallo, National Council of Teachers of English, 1990.

*   *   *

Avi has written over twenty books for young people and is often acclaimed for the wide variety of genres he covers, from historical fiction to contemporary realism. His best works are historical novels in which he creates a vivid sense of colonial America and captures the consciousness of young people coming of age. His success with this genre is evident—he has received two prominent awards for his work in this genre: *The Fighting Ground* won the Scott O'Dell Award for Historical Fiction in 1985, and he received a Newbery Honor as well as the 1991 Boston Globe-Horn Book Award for fiction for his historical fiction novel *The True Confessions of Charlotte Doyle.*

In *The Fighting Ground,* which takes place during the Revolutionary War, thirteen-year-old Jonathan is a self-doubting young man who lives on a farm near Trenton, New Jersey, with his parents and younger siblings. The entire novel takes place in the course of twenty-four hours. As the novel begins, Jonathan dreams of cannons, flags, drums, parades, and fighting the British, just as his elder brother and father do. He runs off to fight, joining a handful of Patriots under a domineering corporal. Once he finds himself caught up in battle, Jonathan begins to question why he is there and who the real enemy is. The themes of growth and war are timeless— Jonathan begins as a boy full of dreams of exciting battles and anticipation of heroic deeds; his experiences of the true horrors of war and death cause him to grow and mature as a man.

In *The True Confessions of Charlotte Doyle,* thirteen-year-old Charlotte begins as a docile, proper, mid-nineteenth-century school girl. By novel's end, she is a weather-cured sailor who agilely climbs masts and has survived more than a hurricane aboard the *Seahawk.* The story is told in first-person; the reader boards the *Seahawk* as Charlotte does, and sees, hears, and feels all that she experiences aboard ship. In the preface to the novel, which is called "An Important Warning," young Charlotte writes, "Not every thirteen-year-old girl is accused of murder, brought to trial, and found guilty. But I was just such a girl, and my story is worth relating even if it did happen years ago. Be warned, however, this is no "Story of a Bad Boy, no "What Katy Did." If strong ideas and action offend you, read no more. Find another companion to share your idle hours. For my part I intend to tell the truth as I lived it."

From the novel's riveting beginning to its surprise ending, *The True Confessions of Charlotte Doyle* is destined to be a favorite of young readers. Avi has included an appendix, with a sketched picture of the *Seahawk,* including illustrations of the brig, the bowspit, deck, and mainmast; he also includes a list of ship times and bells. These additions make the story even more appealing and realistic to young readers.

Sometimes I Think I Hear My Name covers one week in the life of thirteen-year-old Conrad. He is portrayed as an adolescent victim of the adult world. Conrad lives with Aunt Lu and Uncle Carl, two kind but overly sensitive relatives with whom he has lived since his parents divorced when he has nine. Since the divorce, Conrad's parents have made little effort to maintain their relationship with their son, leaving Conrad confused and disappointed. In an attempt to ease his disappointment, his aunt and uncle plan a surprise trip to England over Conrad's spring vacation. While in New York to pick up plane tickets for the trip, Conrad meets Nancy, with whom he shares many of the same adolescent fears and dreams, and they quickly establish a close relationship. With Nancy's help, he tries to locate his parents, with whom he has had little contact since they divorced. After finding his parents, it becomes clear to Conrad that they have little interest in assuming a parental relationship with him. Conrad comes to realize that his life with his aunt and uncle in St. Louis is not so bad after all. Avi treats the serious issues dealt with in this novel with a touch of humor, and writes about adolescent experiences with great sensitivity, which is why his works are so appealing to young people.

Avi once noted, "a good children's book is a book of promises. Promises are meant to be kept." Avi keeps his promises, giving young people characters they can relate to and stories that hold their interest.

—Robbie W. Strickland

————

AXTON, David. See KOONTZ, Dean R.

————

B

BACH, Alice (Hendricks). American. Born in New York City, 6 April 1942. Educated at Barnard College, New York, B.A. 1963. Assistant editor, Random House, New York, 1964-66; associate editor, Harper and Row Publishers Incorporated, New York, 1966-69; senior editor of books for young readers, Dial Press, New York, 1969-71; Consultant, Bedford-Stuyvesant Writers Workshop, 1973-76. Adjunct professor of creative writing, School for Continuing Education, New York University, 1977-79. Recipient: *New York Times* cited *Mollie Make-Believe* as one of the best books of the year, 1974; MacDowell Colony fellowship, 1976, 1977; American Library Association Notable Book award, 1980, for *Waiting for Johnny Miracle.* Agent: Joan Daves, 59 East 54th Street, New York, NY 10022. Address: 175 East 79th Street, New York, NY 10021, U.S.A.

PUBLICATIONS FOR YOUNG ADULTS

Novels

They'll Never Make a Movie Starring Me. New York, Harper, 1973.
Mollie Make-Believe. New York, Harper, 1974.
The Meat in the Sandwich. New York, Harper, 1975.
A Father Every Few Years. New York, Harper, 1977.
Waiting for Johnny Miracle. New York, Harper, 1980.
The Grouter Connection. New York, Bantam, 1983.
When the Sky Began to Roar. Boston, Houghton Mifflin, 1984.
He Will Not Walk With Me. New York, Delacorte, 1985.
Double Bucky Shanghai. New York, Dell, 1987.
Parrot Woman. New York, Dell, 1987.
Ragwars. New York, Dell, 1987.
The Bully of Library Place. New York, Dell, 1988.

Other

Editor, *Ad Feminam.* Union Seminary Quarterly Review, 1989.
Editor, *The Pleasure of Her Text: Feminist Readings of Biblical and Historical Text.* Philadelphia, Trinity, 1990.

PUBLICATIONS FOR CHILDREN

Fiction

Translator, *How Artists Work: An Introduction to Techniques of Art,* by Pierre Belves and Francois Mathey. Rochester, New York, Lion Press, 1968.
The Day After Christmas, illustrated by Mary Chalmers. New York, Harper, 1975.
The Smartest Bear and His Brother Oliver, illustrated by Steven Kellogg. New York, Harper, 1975.
The Most Delicious Camping Trip Ever, illustrated by Steven Kellogg. New York, Harper, 1976.
Grouchy Uncle Otto, illustrated by Steven Kellogg. New York, Harper, 1977.

Millicent the Magnificent, illustrated by Steven Kellogg. New York, Harper, 1978.
Warren Weasle's Worse than Measles, illustrated by Hilary Knight. New York, Harper, 1980.
Moses' Ark: Stories from the Bible, with J. Cheryl Exum, illustrated by Leo Dillon and Diane Dillon. New York, Delacorte, 1989.
Miriam's Well: Stories About Women in the Bible, with J. Cheryl Exum, illustrated by Leo Dillon and Diane Dillon. New York, Delacorte, 1991.

*   *   *

One of the common criticisms of young adult novels is that so many of them are so-called problem books—that is, they are one-dimensional, focusing only on issues or problems to the exclusion of other literary elements such as characterization or theme development. One outspoken critic of young adult problem novels is Alice Bach, also the author of more than twenty books for children and young adults. In an entry in *Something about the Author,* Bach wrote, "I believe it is critical for writers of children's books to be honest about the hardships as well as the joys of life, and never to provide easy answers to questions about abandonment, hurt, rejection, love, betrayal, seduction, winning, losing, etc., that all people, children and adults, feel. So many of today's supposed 'realistic novels' for young adults are realistic in setting and then supply meretricious reassurance about the genuine puzzlements of life."

It seems appropriate to examine Bach's writing for young adults in the light of her own literary standards. It can certainly be argued that a number of her novels fall within the problem novel category. For example *Waiting for Johnny Miracle* is a story about a teenage girl with cancer, and *A Father Every Few Years* deals with the effect of desertion on a younger boy. According to Jack Forman who reviewed Bach's novel *When the Sky Began to Roar* in the January/February 1985 issue of *Horn Book,* one criterion of whether or not young adult fiction transcends the common definition of problem novel is whether or not the main characters "know that there are consequences to their actions affecting other people and that there is a price paid for their mistakes—even if they learn the right lessons."

Applying this standard to Bach's own writing yields mixed results. In the two novels which have received the most critical acclaim, she has skillfully woven complex relationships among her characters. In *Waiting for Johnny Miracle,* she turns an unflinching eye on a children's cancer ward based on her own experience as a volunteer at a cancer-treatment facility. Becky and Theo are seventeen-year-old twin sisters whose typical high school world is shattered when Becky is diagnosed with bone cancer.

The fact that they are twins provides Bach with a rich opportunity to explore the closest kind of relationship under an unusual amount of strain. Theo experiences jealousy because Becky is the focus of her parents' attention and energy; guilt because she is jealous and because she is healthy; and rejection because Becky feels more comfortable discussing her illness with the other cancer patients instead of confiding in Theo. Becky, on the other hand, experiences fear and uncertainty due to the illness; rejection and betrayal because her boyfriend cannot deal with her illness; and alienation from her classmates because her world has changed suddenly and completely. Bach does not take the easy route; her characters in this novel, including the parents and other siblings, do not always display courage. They get tired, they snap at one another, they suffer.

In *Mollie Make-Believe,* another well received novel, Mollie Fields, an upper-middle-class teenager, suffers severe guilt pangs when she spends time with Jaimie, a young man she has met, instead of staying at her ill grandmother's bedside. Once again, there are no miraculous cures for removing the guilt, only gradual insights, acceptance, and partial resolution. Her remaining novels are not as successful in terms of character development, and it can be said of at least one, *A Father Every Few Years,* that it matches the definition of the stereotypical problem novel in which problems eclipse all other literary elements.

In recent years, Bach has earned a doctorate at Union Theological Seminary and now teaches religious studies at Stanford University. Using her expertise in this field, she has turned her writing talents toward two nonfiction books for intermediate grades and above: *Moses' Ark: Stories from the Bible* and *Miriam's Well: Stories about Women in the Bible.* Together with coauthor J. Cheryl Exum and illustrators Leo and Diane Dillon, Bach has creatively woven together historical, literary, archeological, and anecdotal evidence to recreate biblical stories. These handsome books are a blend of impeccable scholarship—apparent in the notes at the end of each story—and vigorous prose, appealing to a wide audience.

—Linda J. Wilson

BACHMAN, Richard. See **KING, Stephen (Edwin).**

BAILLIE, Allan. Scottish. Born in Prestwick, Scotland, 29 January 1943. Educated at University of Melbourne, 1962-63. Married Agnes Chow in 1972; one daughter and one son. Reporter, *Herald/Sun,* Melbourne, Australia, 1962-65; subeditor, *Middlesex Advertiser,* London, 1967-68; Australian Consolidated Press, Sydney, 1970-73 and 1978-80; Australian Broadcasting Commission, Sydney, 1973-77; John Fairfax and Sons, Sydney, 1980—. Recipient: Kathleen Fidler award from the National Book League, 1982, for *Adrift.* Address: John Fairfax and Sons, Jones Street, Sydney, NSW 2001, Australia.

PUBLICATIONS FOR YOUNG ADULTS

Fiction

Mask Maker. London, Macmillan, 1975.
Adrift. Blackie and Son, 1983.
Little Brother. Blackie and Son, 1985.
Riverman. Blackie and Son, 1986.
Eagle Island. Blackie and Son, n.d.
Drac and the Gremlin, illustrated by Jane Tanner. Melbourne, Australia, Nelson, 1989.

Megan's Star. Blackie and Son, 1990.
Bawshou Rescues the Sun: A Han Folktale, with Chun-Chan Yeh, illustrated by Michelle Powell. New York, Scholastic, 1991.
Hero. Blackie and Son, 1991.
The Boss, illustrated by Fiona O'Beirne. New York, Scholastic, 1992.
The China Coin. Blackie and Son, 1992.
Magician, forthcoming.

Work represented in anthologies, including *Under Twenty-Five, Transition,* and *Bad Deeds Gang.* Contributor to magazines, including *Child Life, Pursuit, School,* and *Meanjin.*

*   *   *

Allan Baillie's most significant works for the young adult reader demonstrate the fact that he graduated from journalism into writing books for child readers.

These books are characterised by their plots being centred around some significant element, either political (*The China Coin*—the 1989 events in Tiananmen Square) or natural disaster (*Hero*—the Sydney floods of 1986). The settings of these events are strongly realised through the author's actual experience of them—on-site reporting, as it were. In some novels, such as *The China Coin,* the author has actually experienced the event itself as well as explored the setting. It would appear that these two elements, event and setting, together with the author's involvement with either or both of them, are the dominant features of these particular novels.

Using the events as the backgrounds for the novels, Baillie presents within the structure of an adventure story the maturation of his particular characters, generally at the climactic moment of the base events. However, frequently it is the events themselves which carry more significance and it would seem that the author is propelled more by the desire to explore these fully and to make readers aware of their significance.

After a novel for younger readers, *Adrift,* which won him the 1983 Kathleen Fidler award, thus guaranteeing the manuscript would go into print and setting him on the road to this particular form of authorship, Baillie wrote *Little Brother.* The plot concerns a Kampuchean boy whose parents have been killed in the war. He now travels alone searching for his older brother.

Basically the plot is one of the adventure quest, Mang overcoming one obstacle after another as he travels throughout war-torn Kampuchea. The simple structure allows the author to expose the dreadful hardships experienced by people as the war raged about them. While the story carries a certain sense of melodrama and a rather too pat, though probably necessary (considering its audience) happy ending, Mang is one of the more memorable of the Baillie characters. His hope and indefatigable determination that his brother is still alive and will be found, and his ability to somehow still remain childishly unblemished from all that happens to him give him a humanity that extends the writer's compassion for his subject to the reader.

This is also one of Baillie's more popular reads. He has managed to balance nicely the mix of explanation of events, description of the environment and narrative so that the reader does not feel unnecessarily held up.

Some of the later novels, though they show a demonstrably greater writing skill, also move much slower, the narrative waiting for the author to tell all he knows about the setting and the "real" events. Such a novel is *Riverman,* the one that followed *Little Brother.*

Riverman, an excellent novel, was shortlisted for both the Australian Children's Book of the Year award and the Guardian Children's Fiction award and won the IBBY Honour Diploma (Australia). No doubt influenced by the battle raging in Tasmania by conservationists to preserve the wilderness around the Franklin River which the government was proposing to dam, *Riverman* is set partly on the wild Franklin River itself.

Baillie, relating events of 1912 though wanting to connect them to the current conservationist struggle, adopted the symbol of a huge Huon pine, using its long life to link the past with the present. Structurally the story is set within the confines of a prologue and epilogue in the present day wherein Great Uncle Tim tries to show young Brian the importance of the pine and the forest. The story proper is in two sections, the first relating the story of a Tasmanian mining disaster in 1912 and the effect it had upon twelve-year-old Tim, the second section telling of his life with the rivermen on the Franklin River and of how he comes to know the great Huon pine which is so significant to the narrative.

Baillie has a splendid prose, especially when he describes the things he knows at first hand: "But the creaking increased and became a savage squeal as the wood at the heart of the trunk was slowly torn apart. A cloud passed over the tree, then the tip followed the cloud and overtook it. The tree cracked, rolled a little on its stump and crashed down into the forest. It splintered a tall blackwood tree, snapped the stump of a young celery-top pine six feet from the ground, and brought a shriek from a few birds." Occasionally though, there are sections wherein the desire to tell produces a slightly didactic feel, especially in some of the direct speech. However, all in all, this is a particularly fine novel, setting the coming of age of a young boy against the almost ageless trees of the Tasmanian wilderness.

Eagle Island, while having a real setting on an island on the Great Barrier Reef, is not based on any real event and somehow lacks the emotional power which human conflicts obviously stir the author's passions to relate. However, as a straight adventure story of a boy outwitting a pair of crooks it works well.

Hero, based upon floods in an outer suburb of Sydney and giving an excellent depiction of such a disaster in action, focuses the reader's attention on three children: Darcy, a rebellious boy who in a mad fling steals a trail bike; Pam, a new girl to the district and somewhat critical of anyone who has not her wealthy status; and Barney, a serious-minded farmer. During the events of the story the three children come together in a highly exciting climax which tests the mettle of them all. The story leaves us with the question of which one of them is the hero, for the title is singular. Heroism and what constitutes it is featured in Baillie's novels, for his characters are those of the ordinary person caught up in the extraordinary.

In 1987 Baillie was part of a five-person team to visit China on invitation from the government to talk on children's literature. He was intrigued enough to return to learn more about the country, and, of course, to search out material for a book. While he was there he was in Beijing at the time of the Tiananmen Square uprising. This was to form the basis for *The China Coin.* It is a totally absorbing long read and supplies much background to present-day China and its people while relating the story of a part Chinese, part Australian girl searching out her Chinese family and her own identity through a broken coin. The writing is at times dense, with so much background information having to be supplied, but it is a fascinating read. Again it is in quest mode, as the search for the mystery of the coin leads the protagonists to Beijing at the time of the uprising.

Two other books for young adults are fantasy: *Megan's Star* and *Magician.* Both being set in the future, they must necessarily not have event bases though Baillie quite clearly shows events of the future as the results of happenings today. *Megan's Star* contains quite magical moments of mind star travel, unique in children's literature.

Allan Baillie is a significant and important writer for young adults. His particular method of taking events and setting adventure narratives within them gives his YA readers a sense of the values of humanity in today's world, wherein individuals must come to grips with a sense of themselves against the larger problems of survival in a sometimes difficult modern world.

—Alf Mappin

BALDWIN, James (Arthur). American. Born in New York City, 2 August 1924. Educated at Public School 139, Harlem, New York, and De Witt Clinton High School, Bronx, New York, graduated 1942. Worked as handyman, dishwasher, waiter, and office boy in New York, and in defense work, Belle Meade, New Jersey, in early 1940s; full-time writer from 1943; lived in Europe, mainly in Paris, 1948-56. Recipient: Saxton fellowship, 1945; Rosenwald fellowship, 1948; Guggenheim fellowship, 1954; American Academy award, 1956; National Institute of Arts and Letters grant in literature, 1956; *Partisan Review* fellowship, 1956; Ford fellowship, 1958; National Conference of Christians and Jews Brotherhood Award, 1962, for *Nobody Knows My Name: More Notes of a Native Son*; George Polk Award, 1963, for magazine articles; Foreign Drama Critics award, 1964, for *Blues for Mister Charlie*; National Association of Independent Schools Award, 1964, for *The Fire Next Time*; Martin Luther King, Jr., Award (City University of New York), 1978; American Book Award nomination, 1980, for *Just above My Head*; named Commander of the Legion of Honor (France), 1986. D.Litt.: University of British Columbia, Vancouver, 1963. *Died 30 November 1987.*

PUBLICATIONS

Novels

Go Tell It on the Mountain. New York, Knopf, 1953; London, Joseph, 1954.
Giovanni's Room. New York, Dial Press, 1956; London, Joseph, 1957.
Another Country. New York, Dial Press, 1962; London, Joseph, 1963.
Tell Me How Long the Train's Been Gone. New York, Dial Press, and London, Joseph, 1968.
If Beale Street Could Talk. New York, Dial Press, and London, Joseph, 1974.
Little Man, Little Man: A Story of Childhood. London, Joseph, 1976; New York, Dial Press, 1977.
Just above My Head. New York, Dial Press, and London, Joseph, 1979.

Short Stories

Going to Meet the Man. New York, Dial Press, and London, Joseph, 1965.

Contributor, *American Negro Short Stories.* New York, Hill and Wang, 1966.

Uncollected Short Stories

"Any Day Now," in *Partisan Review* (New Brunswick, New Jersey), spring 1960.

"Exodus," in *American Negro Short Stories,* edited by John Henrik Clarke. New York, Hill and Wang, 1966.

"Equal in Parts," in *Travelers.* New York, Macmillan, 1972.

Poetry

Jimmy's Blues: Selected Poems. London, Joseph, 1983; New York, St. Martin's Press, 1985.

Plays

The Amen Corner (produced Washington, D.C. 1955; New York, Edinburgh, and London, 1965). New York, Dial Press, 1968.

Blues for Mister Charlie (produced New York, 1964; London, 1965). New York, Dial Press, 1964; London, Joseph, 1965.

One Day, When I Was Lost: A Scenario Based on "The Autobiography of Malcolm X." London, Joseph, 1972; New York, Dial Press, 1973.

A Deed for the King of Spain (produced New York, 1974).

Screenplay: *The Inheritance,* 1973.

Other

Autobiographical Notes. New York, Knopf, 1953.

Notes of a Native Son. Boston, Beacon Press, 1955; London, Joseph, 1964.

Nobody Knows My Name: More Notes of a Native Son. New York, Dial Press, 1961; London, Joseph, 1964.

The Fire Next Time. New York, Dial Press, and London, Joseph, 1963.

Nothing Personal, photographs by Richard Avedon. New York, Atheneum, and London, Penguin, 1964.

Black Anti-Semitism and Jewish Racism, with others. R.W. Baron, 1969.

Menschenwuerde und Gerechtigkeit (essays delivered at the fourth assembly of the World Council of Churches), with Kenneth Kaunda, edited by Carl Ordung. Union-Verlag, 1969.

A Rap on Race, with Margaret Mead. Philadelphia, Lippincott, and London, Joseph, 1971.

No Name in the Street. New York, Dial Press, and London, Joseph, 1972.

Cesar: Compressions d'or, with Francoise Giroud. Connecticut, Hachette, 1973.

A Dialogue: James Baldwin and Nikki Giovanni. Philadelphia, Lippincott, 1973; London, Joseph, 1975.

The Devil Finds Work: An Essay. New York, Dial Press, and London, Joseph, 1976.

Harlem, U.S.A.: The Story of a City within a City, with others, edited by John Henrik Clarke. Berlin, Seven Seas, 1976.

The Price of a Ticket: Collected Nonfiction 1948-1985. New York, St. Martin's Press, and London, Joseph, 1985.

The Evidence of Things Not Seen. New York, Holt Rinehart, 1985; as *Evidence of Things Not Seen,* London, Joseph, 1986.

Perspectives: Angles on African Art, with others, edited by Michael J. Weber. Center for African Art, 1987.

*

Media Adaptations: *Giovanni's Room* (play), first produced in New York City at Actors' Studio, 1957; *Amen Corner* (play), adapted by Garry Sherman, Peter Udell and Philip Rose, 1983; *Go Tell It on the Mountain* (television movie), PBS "American Playhouse" series, 1985.

Biography: Entry in *Dictionary of Literary Biography,* Detroit, Gale, Volume 2, 1978, Volume 7, 1981, Volume 33, 1984; entry in *Concise Dictionary of American Literary Biography: The New Consciousness, 1941-1968,* Detroit, Gale, 1987; entry in *Dictionary of Literary Biography Yearbook: 1987,* Detroit, Gale, 1988.

Bibliography: "James Baldwin: A Checklist 1947-1962" by Kathleen A. Kindt, and "James Baldwin: A Bibliography 1947-1962" by Russell G. Fischer, both in *Bulletin of Bibliography* (Boston), January-April 1965; *James Baldwin: A Reference Guide* by Fred L. and Nancy Standley, Boston, Hall, 1980.

Critical Study: *The Furious Passage of James Baldwin* by Fern Eckman, New York, Evans, 1966, London, Joseph, 1968; *Five Black Writers: Essays on Wright, Ellison, Baldwin, Hughes, and LeRoi Jones* edited by Donald B. Gibson, New York, New York University Press, 1970; entries in *Contemporary Literary Criticism,* Detroit, Gale, Volume 1, 1973, Volume 2, 1974, Volume 3, 1975, Volume 4, 1975, Volume 5, 1976, Volume 8, 1978, Volume 13, 1980, Volume 15, 1980, Volume 17, 1981, Volume 42, 1987, Volume 50, 1988, Volume 67, 1992; *James Baldwin: A Critical Study* by Stanley Macebuh, New York, Third Press, 1973, London, Joseph, 1975; *James Baldwin: A Collection of Critical Essays* edited by Keneth Kinnamon, Englewood Cliffs, New Jersey, Prentice Hall, 1974; *The Theme of Identity in the Essays of James Baldwin* by Karin Moeller, Acta Universitatis Gotoburgensis, 1975; *James Baldwin: A Critical Evaluation* edited by Therman B. O'Daniel, Washington, D.C., Howard University Press, 1977; *Squaring Off: Mailer vs. Baldwin* by William J. Weatherby, Mason/Charter, 1977; *James Baldwin* by Louis H. Pratt, Boston, Twayne, 1978; *James Baldwin* by Carolyn W. Sylvander, New York, Ungar, 1980; *Critical Essays on James Baldwin* edited by Nancy and Fred Standley, Boston, Hall, 1981; *Baldwin: Three Interview* by Kenneth B. Clarke and Malcolm King, Middletown, Connecticut, Wesleyan University Press, 1985; *Contemporary Authors Bibliographical Series,* Detroit, Gale, Volume 1, 1986.

*   *   *

Although James Baldwin believed that no one could be described, words such as genius, gifted, passionate, and intense have frequently been used to capture the essense of this man. A novelist, essayist, and playwright, James Baldwin was also a dedicated civil rights crusader and social critic. He was a preacher from the early age of fourteen; however, he left the church at seventeen and began writing what is considered one of his greatest novels, *Go Tell It on the*

Mountain. Although Baldwin wrote for an adult audience, young adults can appreciate reading this novel as well as his *If Beale Street Could Talk.*

Go Tell It on the Mountain, published in 1953, is largely autobiographical. Baldwin denied the novel was about life with his stepfather (to whom he referred as father) and said it was purely a product of his imagination. However, there are many parallels to Baldwin's real life.

The book begins the morning of John Grimes's fourteenth birthday. With its arrival comes the realization that John will become a preacher like his father, Gabriel Grimes, head deacon of Temple of the Fire Baptized in Harlem. Deacon Grimes is well-respected in the community and devoted to the church. But at home his faith does not ease the rage he feels for the prejudice he has endured. "Your daddy beats you...because he loves you," John's mother tells him. Is it a misguided attempt to prevent his children from succumbing to the temptations of the street, or has he *become* the hatred that is borne out of the racism he so bitterly rages against?

John didn't realize he was gifted. "You're a very bright boy, John Grimes," the principal of his school told him. With this, she had given him "if not a weapon at least a shield...he had in himself a power that other people lacked; that he could use this to save himself, to raise himself...with this power he might one day win that love which he so longed for." John would use his giftedness. It was both "part of that wickedness for which his father beat him and to which he clung in order to withstand his father." Perhaps he would be a preacher like his father, but he would not *be* his father. He would live differently.

Go Tell It on the Mountain explores not only the experience of growing up in poverty, gifted and black, but reveals the hypocrisy of a man devoted to religion, yet cruel and abusive to his own children. The novel, through several flashbacks, examines the struggling lives of John, his father and mother, other members of his family, and his Sunday school teacher, Elisha, for whom John has great admiration.

The novel ends the next morning, John having emerged from the church following a long and tumultuous evening of spiritual rebirth. "I'm on my way." The reader has witnessed the despair in Baldwin's characters. However, this final note of optimism, typical of Baldwin, leaves one with a powerful sense of hope.

If Beale Street Could Talk, published in 1974, was written from the perspective of nineteen-year-old Tish. She is pregnant and in love with the baby's father, Fonny, twenty-one, who is in love with her. Their plans to marry are shattered when Fonny is imprisoned after being falsely accused of rape—having been set up by a vindictive white cop. Tish's family stands together. Held together with a strong love and mutual respect, they fight back to win Fonny's freedom. Fonny's family, in contrast, has deteriorated, despite (or because of, Baldwin seems to be saying) his unloving mother's strong religious faith. Baldwin's point is, after all, that love is the key.

This is an important book for it reveals the reality of living in a divided world; a world where a system of justice can be corrupted to trap an innocent young man because of the color of his skin. It was based on Baldwin's involvement with the Tony Maynard case, where it took seven years for his friend to be proven innocent of a murder charge.

If Beale Street Could Talk is slightly outdated only in its use of some of the colloquialisms of the '70s (e.g., "I believe the cat would have split the scene") and for the misrepresentation that an occasional drink while pregnant is harmless, now proven to be quite dangerous. However, *If Beale Street Could Talk* is definitely worth reading for it involves the reader in the struggle against the injustice of racism that many have and continue to face. *Beale Street* also demonstrates the themes of self-reliance and the power of love.

Many criticized *Beale Street* saying that after six years in the making, it lacked the rage and fire for which Baldwin is known. However, examination of the times during which the novel was written reveals Baldwin was struggling with the death of Martin Luther King, Jr., six years earlier. Baldwin said of his relationship with King, "We had been young together, we had tramped all over the South together, we had even dared hope together.... I believed in him." The death of King was the death of a dream and the decline of the civil rights movement. To think Baldwin could continue to write unaffected is naive.

Tish could not forget the hopeful white rose she once saw in a church lady's hat. "It's funny what you hold onto to get through terror when terror surrounds you." The novel ends with the strong, persistent cry of their baby—a tiny voice that inherits an unjust world, but is, nonetheless, a voice of hope.

—Suzanne M. Valentic

———

BAUER, Marion Dane. American. Born in Oglesby, Illinois, 20 November 1938. Educated at La Salle-Peru-Oglesby Junior College, 1956-58, and University of Missouri, 1958-59; University of Oklahoma, B.A. 1962. Married Ronald Bauer in 1959 (divorced), one daughter and one son. Writer. High school teacher, Waukesha, Wisconsin, 1962-64; Hennepin Technical Center, Minneapolis, Minnesota, instructor in creative writing for adult education program, 1975-78; instructor, University of Minnesota Continuing Education for Women, 1978-85, Institute for Children's Literature, 1982-85, and The Loft, since 1987. Recipient: American Library Association Notable Book Award, 1976, and Japanese Library Association Award, both for *Shelter from the Wind;* Golden Kite Honor Book Award, Society of Children's Book Writers, 1979, for *Foster Child;* Jane Addams Peace Association Award, 1984, for *Rain of Fire;* Notable Children's Book Award, American Library Association, and Best Books list, *School Library Journal,* both 1986, both for *On My Honor;* Newbery Honor Book Award and British Children's Book Award runner-up, both 1987, both for *On My Honor;* Notable Children's Book Award, ALA, 1992, for *What's Your Story? A Young Person's Guide to Writing Fiction.* Address: 8861 Basswood Rd., Eden Prairie, MN 55344, U.S.A.

PUBLICATIONS FOR YOUNG ADULTS

Fiction

Shelter from the Wind. New York, Clarion, 1976.
Foster Child. New York, Clarion, 1977.
Tangled Butterfly. New York, Clarion, 1980.
Rain of Fire. New York, Clarion, 1983.
Like Mother, Like Daughter. New York, Clarion, 1985.
On My Honor. New York, Clarion, 1986.
Touch the Moon. New York, Clarion, 1987.
A Dream of Queens and Castles. New York, Clarion, 1990.

Face to Face. New York, Clarion, 1991.
Ghost Eye. New York, Scholastic, 1992.
A Taste of Smoke. New York, Clarion, 1993.
A Question of Trust. New York, Scholastic, forthcoming.
The Haunted Doll. New York, Scholastic, forthcoming.

Nonfiction

What's Your Story?: A Young Person's Guide to Writing Fiction. New York, Clarion, 1992.

Other

Editor, *Am I Blue? Coming out from the Silence.* New York, HarperCollins, forthcoming.
When I Go Camping with Grandma (picture book). Mahwah, New Jersey, BridgeWater Books, forthcoming.

*

Media Adaptations: *Rodeo Red and the Runaway* (television movie based on *Shelter from the Wind*); *On My Honor* (videocassette), Random House.

Biography: Essay in *Something about the Author Autobiography Series,* Detroit, Gale, Volume 9, 1990; essay in *Speaking for Ourselves, Too* compiled and edited by Donald R. Gallo, National Council of Teachers of English, 1993.

Marion Dane Bauer comments:

In the last few years I have been extending the range of my work, writing for younger children even to the point of producing my first picture book text. However, the most solid place my stories still emerge from are the transitional years, twelve and thirteen. The passage from childhood into the world of the young adult *feels* important to me—fraught with terror, and trembling with expectation. Both the terror and the expectation remain part of my reality. They are an energy, even a passion I can tap into at will.

There are times when I find myself wishing that I could write stories that are lighter, those people would refer to as "heartwarming." I do have, after all, a warm heart. And a sense of humor, too, though my stories rarely show it. (One of my favorite reviews refers to the "brisk humor" in *Ghost Eye.*) But growing up was, for me, a solemn undertaking, even a perilous one, and it is those feelings I return to when I look out at the world through twelve- and thirteen-year-old eyes...along with an absolutely determined hope. My most cherished dream is that emerging young adults who find their way to my stories will discover comfort in the midst of their own solemnity, reassurance in their own peril. And most important of all, I pray that they will be reaffirmed in their own determined hope.

*   *   *

Marion Dane Bauer is best known for her portrayal of the harsh realities that frequently accompany growing up in contemporary society. Her characters, who are convincingly drawn, often must make tough moral choices.

In *On My Honor* Joel is afraid to go to the rock bluffs with his friend Tony but he is more afraid of Tony's taunts of cowardice. So, his first choice is to ask his father for permission to go, feeling confident that his dad will refuse. To Joel's dismay his father assents. On the bike ride, Tony goads Joel into a swim in the river. Feeling resentful and angry, Joel is the one to make a dare—a race to the sandbar. A superior swimmer, Joel wins and looks for Tony but he has disappeared. Gradually, Joel comes to the horrifying realization that Tony has drowned. Overcome by shock, disbelief and guilt, Joel returns home and goes to his room as if nothing had happened. His father, who accepts some of the blame for the tragedy, is finally able to coax the story from Joel.

This is not a story about loss, but one of moral choices, reaction to tragedy and responsibility for actions. The characters in this story are realistic. Everyone knows an impulsive child like Tony who likes to live on the edge. Usually, they don't get hurt. Joel's feelings of impotence and anger are also understandable. The fear of being called a coward is powerful and leads young people to unpleasant choices—either behave in a way that causes anxiety or endure ridicule. Joel's father is a recognizable figure. He is a cautious parent who failed to read his son's apprehensions and who suffers, with his son, as a result of the tragedy. It is refreshing to find a supportive, caring parent in contemporary realistic fiction. They are a vanishing breed.

Another sympathetic parent can be found in *Like Mother, Like Daughter.* Leslie is revolted by her mother's laid-back Aquarian approach to life; she is a rescuer of strays. As an alternative role-model, Leslie selects the new journalism advisor at school who is bright, tough and assertive. The advisor encourages Leslie to report the results of her survey of student attitudes toward faculty in the school paper. Leslie derives a certain pleasure in getting revenge on a senior faculty member who resigns in the wake of her report. As the consequences of her actions become apparent, Leslie seeks the support of the journalism advisor, only to find that she has disappeared and that she is a fraud. A supportive mother helps Leslie make the appropriate decisions.

The mother-daughter interaction in this book is as realistic as Leslie's attraction to someone who is her mother's polar opposite. The conflict and resolution are also realistic and again Bauer has drawn attention to the morality of choices and responsibility for actions. She also illuminates how easily people can be persuaded to follow their baser instincts.

In *Rain of Fire* taunts of cowardice are leveled at Steve's brother Matthew, who has seen the horrors of Hiroshima and has returned home withdrawn and espousing antiwar sentiments. Defense of his brother's honor leads Steve into an escalating conflict with Ray, his brother's accuser. In a dramatic climax to the conflict, Steve takes Ray captive and plants an explosive nearby. He reconsiders his actions, attempts to kick away the explosive and is injured. While in the hospital Steve becomes closer to his brother as he gains understanding of Matthew's opposition to war. Although Bauer realistically portrays Steve's conflicting feelings of loyalty to his brother and frustration with his behavior, she is heavy-handed with her antiwar message.

In *Shelter from the Wind,* Bauer portrays a girl who feels unwelcome in her father's home when her stepmother becomes pregnant. She runs away in an attempt to find her own alcoholic mother but stumbles into the desert cabin of Ella, who shelters her. When Ella is hurt, Stacy must help Ella's beautiful shepherd dog whelp her pups. The birth is graphic but more so is Stacy's drowning of the abnormal puppy. The need for that bit of realism is unclear. Stacy's petulance is a recognizable trait of adolescence. Ella's reminiscences about her departed husband and lost children, however, tell a story that is less appropriate for young adult readers.

As a writer of realistic fiction, Bauer is at her best when the story lets the reader draw conclusions rather than preaching them. Overall, her books are inviting. She provides memorable characters who are involved in rapidly unfolding plots which deal with serious issues. Bauer illuminates the difficult choices with all their attendant consequences which may lie ahead for young adults. She also provides a view of problem-solving approaches which may enable them to navigate more successfully the treacherous waters of contemporary adolescent life.

—Anne Drolett Creany

———

BAWDEN, Nina (née Mabey). British. Born in London, England, 19 January 1925. Educated at Ilford County High School; Somerville College, Oxford, B.A. 1946, M.A. 1951; Salzburg Seminar in American Studies, 1960. Married 1) H.W. Bawden in 1946, two sons (one deceased); 2) the broadcast executive Austen Steven Kark in 1954, one daughter. Writer, since 1952. Assistant, Town and Country Planning Associates, 1946-47; Justice of the Peace, Surrey, 1968-76. Regular reviewer, *Daily Telegraph,* London. Member, PEN Executive Committee, 1968-71; President, Society of Women Writers and Journalists. Recipient: Carnegie commendation, 1973, for *Carrie's War; Guardian* award for children's fiction, 1975, for *The Peppermint Pig; Yorkshire Post* Novel of the Year award, 1977, for *Afternoon of a Good Woman;* Parents' Choice citation, 1982, and Edgar Allan Poe award nomination, 1983, both for *Kept in the Dark;* Parents' Choice citation, 1985, for *The Finding;* Booker Prize nomination, 1987, for *Circles of Deceit;* Phoenix award, 1993, for *Carrie's War.* Agent: Curtis Brown, Ltd., 575 Madison Ave., New York, NY 10022. Address: 22 Noel Rd., London N1 8HA, England.

PUBLICATIONS FOR YOUNG ADULTS

Fiction

Devil by the Sea. London, Collins, 1957; Philadelphia, Lippincott, 1959; abridged edition (for children), London, Gollancz, and Lippincott, 1976.
The Secret Passage. London, Gollancz, 1963; as *The House of Secrets,* Philadelphia, Lippincott, 1964.
On the Run. London, Gollancz, 1964; as *Three on the Run,* Philadelphia, Lippincott, 1965.
A Little Love, a Little Learning. London, Longmans, 1965; New York, Harper, 1966.
The White Horse Gang. London, Gollancz, and Philadelphia, Lippincott, 1966.
The Witch's Daughter. London, Gollancz, and Philadelphia, Lippincott, 1966.
A Handful of Thieves. London, Gollancz, and Philadelphia, Lippincott, 1967.
The Runaway Summer. London, Gollancz, and Philadelphia, Lippincott, 1969.
Squib, illustrated by Shirley Hughes. London, Gollancz, 1971; illustrated by Hank Blaustein, Philadelphia, Lippincott, 1971.
Carrie's War. London, Gollancz, and Philadelphia, Lippincott, 1973.

The Peppermint Pig. London, Gollancz, and Philadelphia, Lippincott, 1975.
Rebel on a Rock. London, Gollancz, and Philadelphia, Lippincott, 1978.
The Robbers. London, Gollancz, and New York, Lothrop, 1979.
Kept in the Dark. London, Gollancz, and New York, Lothrop, 1982.
The Finding. London, Gollancz, and New York, Lothrop, 1985.
Princess Alice. London, Deutsch, 1985.
Keeping Henry. London, Gollancz, 1988; as *Henry,* New York, Lothrop, 1988.
The Outside Child. London, Gollancz, and New York, Lothrop, 1989.
Humbug. New York, Clarion, 1992.
The Real Plato Jones. New York, Clarion, 1993.

Other

Adapter, *William Tell,* illustrated by Pascale Allamand. London, Cape, and New York, Lothrop, 1981.
St. Francis of Assisi. London, Cape, and New York, Lothrop, 1983.

PUBLICATIONS FOR ADULTS

Novels

Who Calls the Tune. London, Collins, 1953; as *Eyes of Green,* New York, Morrow, 1953.
The Odd Flamingo. London, Collins, 1954.
Change Here for Babylon. London, Collins, 1955.
The Solitary Child. London, Collins, 1956; New York, Lancer, 1966.
Just Like a Lady. London, Longmans, 1960; as *Glass Slippers Always Pinch,* Philadelphia, Lippincott, 1960.
In Honour Bound. London, Longmans, 1961.
Tortoise by Candlelight. London, Longmans, and New York, Harper, 1963.
Under the Skin. London, Longmans, and New York, Harper, 1964.
A Woman of My Age. London, Longmans, and New York, Harper, 1967.
The Grain of Truth. London, Longmans, and New York, Harper, 1968.
The Birds on the Trees. London, Longmans, and New York, Harper, 1970.
Anna Apparent. London, Longmans, and New York, Harper, 1972.
George beneath a Paper Moon. London, Allen Lane, and New York, Harper, 1974; as *On the Edge,* London, Sphere, 1985.
Afternoon of a Good Woman. London, Macmillan, and New York, Harper, 1976.
Familiar Passions. London, Macmillan, and New York, Morrow, 1979.
Walking Naked. London, Macmillan, and New York, St. Martin's, 1981.
The Ice House. New York, St. Martin's, 1983.
Circles of Deceit. London, Macmillan, and New York, St. Martin's, 1987.
Family Money. London, Gollancz, and New York, St. Martin's Press, 1991.

*

Media Adaptations: Many of Bawden's children's stories have

been adapted for television in Great Britain. A four-part adaptation of *Carrie's War* was shown on American Public Broadcasting in May, 1981; an adaptation of *The Finding* was broadcast in 1990 as part of the Public Broadcasting System's "Wonderworks" series.

Critical Studies: Entry in *Dictionary of Literary Biography,* Volume 14: *British Novelists since 1960,* Detroit, Gale, 1983, pp. 77-86; entry in *Children's Literature Review,* Volume 2, Detroit, Gale, 1976.

*   *   *

Nina Bawden is one of the very few writers for young people who will admit to making a conscious adjustment to writing for children. Perhaps because she also writes for adults she is singularly free from the temptation to write for adults on the children's list. Plot summaries of Bawden's early work might seem like run-of-the-mill escapism. The jewel thieves in *The Witch's Daughter,* the children-catch-villains theme of *A Handful of Thieves,* the Prime Minister's son saved from political kidnapping in *On the Run,* are typical examples. But Bawden is a subtle writer, who plays her themes with a difference. In *The Witch's Daughter* one of the children is blind; the Prime Minister's son in *On the Run* comes not from Ruritania but modern Africa; another of Bawden's runaways is an illegal Pakistani immigrant. Bawden's characters may have improbable adventures, but they never think, feel or say unchildlike or improbable things. Their preoccupations, their relationships with the adults around them, their faults as well as their innocence and courage are entirely realistic and believable. This is childhood seen with particular clarity. There is also a very distinctive tone to Bawden's sympathy—a particular tenderness for children having a rough time, and for not very likeable children. Mary in *The Runaway Summer* is a good example. Lonely and miserable because her parents are getting divorced, she is beastly to her kind aunt, and even steals, and yet we never lose sympathy with her.

It is this element in Bawden's work that flowers in *Squib,* the story of a grossly neglected child. There are brilliant insights in this book which overlie the awful knowledge that Squib has been shackled in a laundry basket—especially the pathetic muddle of half-baked fears—and simply confuse the children about what is real and what is not, so that they hardly know if they are playing or rescuing a real victim. However there is also a good deal of the apparatus of adventure that had been so strong an element in Bawden's work so far—a burning tower, a disastrous raid on Squib's caravan, and on to a happy ending that involves bringing in the adults to get things right. The emotional tone of this uncomplicated complication sits rather uneasily with the real subject of *Squib*—the compassion and fear of a young girl, the courage of a young boy, and the suffering of Squib himself.

With the appearance of *Carrie's War,* it became clear Squib had been a transitional book. Carrie and her brother are evacuees in a Welsh village with a narrow, bigoted shopkeeper and his kindly, browbeaten sister. They would be miserable without the friendship of other villagers, especially Hepzibah, who feeds them love, food and stories. Once more the plot concerns the precarious hold on reality of an imaginative child. Convinced by Hepzibah's tales Carrie comes to believe that she has committed a dreadful crime, and she carries the load of grief and guilt with her into adult life. Only when she brings her own children back with her to the village can the truth emerge and all be made well again. In this book we have dispensed with the drama of external situations—there are no crooks,

no villains, but Carrie's own guilty fears. In a notable shift of feeling, Carrie reaches a glimpse of sympathy and understanding even for the horrible tyrant Mr. Evans. This is a profound and affectionate book.

In *The Peppermint Pig,* the mature, subtle, and fundamentally sunny atmosphere of *Carrie's War* is brought to a peak of achievement. *The Peppermint Pig* is about the sojourn in a country village of an Edwardian family whose father has gone abroad to seek his fortune. But the true subject is the painful relationship of happiness, hope and the inexorable passing of time. These themes are delicately explored in the relationship of the children to their changed circumstances, the absence of their father, and the growth, flourishing and death of Johnny, the pet pig. All the while the book, with consummate skill, plays on the difference of scale in the life of children and adults, bringing the two perspectives into brilliant direct contrast only on the last page. *The Peppermint Pig* is a small masterpiece.

Since *The Peppermint Pig* Bawden has to some extent resumed her earlier style, though not without differences. In *Rebel on a Rock* Carrie and her family visit a foreign country (a thinly disguised Greece) in which a dictator is in power and a revolution is simmering into readiness. In *The Robbers,* a boy brought up with all the appurtenances of privilege makes friends with a boy deprived of all material wealth but rich in affection. Trying to help the poorer boy's family, they get into trouble, and the law takes a different view of them because of their different social class. In both these books there is a return to a simpler texture and characters of instant credibility, having child-sized adventures. But unlike Bawden's earlier books is the seriousness of the backgrounds—political revolution played against family loyalty, or the unfairness of justice—and the consequent large import of childish escapades. A sad, implied comment is made on children's adventure stories; this is what would really happen if children intervened in revolutions, or tried to restore the family fortunes.

With *Kept in the Dark,* Bawden returns to a subject explored earlier in *Devil by the Sea,* published originally for adults, and then republished for younger readers in a changed climate of opinion. The subject is the helplessness of young people if the adults around them are not both beneficent and competent. The children in *Kept in the Dark* are being looked after by grandparents who are themselves being preyed upon by a half-uncle who bullies and threatens with seeming impunity. The children's terror and confusion are strongly conveyed; locked in the child's viewpoint, the book conveys only partly the nature of the villain's badness, and his adult victims' weakness.

The Finding neatly inverts the typical Bawden statement of relations between adults and young people, which has gradually emerged as her quintessential theme. The fantasy of adults—the machinations of a lethally awful grandmother, and the scheming of incompetent crooks—gets Alex, an adopted foundling, into trouble. Only his sister's childish understanding of his inner world can provide the means to find him. Once again a thriller plot is combined with satisfying characterisation to provide Bawden's typical balance of readability and depth.

Keeping Henry is a new departure. It is not so much fiction as very lightly fictionalised recollection, in which the author appears as herself, in her own family, telling us the true story of Henry, the family's pet squirrel, which they kept on a Welsh farm where they spent part of the war. The story has the shapeliness and accessibility of Bawden's true fiction. Additionally it is fascinating to see the origins in the author's childhood experience of the material of both

Carrie's War and *The Peppermint Pig,* each of which is illuminated by *Keeping Henry,* and each of which in turn throws light on the later book. *The Outside Child* is based, like *Keeping Henry,* on an autobiographical recollection, this time one of considerable mystery and force. Jane is brought up by aunts while her father, a seaman, comes and goes on his ship. Visiting him she sees a picture of his other family, her secret brother and sister. Filled with love and yearning for them she is reduced to childish spying, abetted by her friend. At the heart of the story is the selfishness and silliness of an emotional adult; the ending can only be cautiously happy.

Bawden's latest work for young readers, *Humbug,* continues the exploration of the relationship of young people and adults—a theme which in Bawden's hands is inexhaustible. When her grandmother is taken suddenly into hospital, Cora is parted from her brother and sister and taken care of by a neighbour, finding herself at the mercy of a repulsive child, Angelica, and her smug, self-deceiving grownup. Angelica is Bawden's first wholly unlikeable child, but she is fearfully convincing. The terrifying gulf that opens below Cora's feet, as her grandfather forgives her with knowing understanding for a theft she did not commit, has likewise a nightmare plausibility.

Bawden can now command the gripping readability of her early work without resorting to anything but wholly credible psychological drama. Balancing the different views of young people and adults, whose relations have been gradually emerging over her whole career as a central subject of her writing on both adult and children's lists, she never unfairly prefers an adult view, and deeply ingrained in this story is the sense of what kind of moral benchmark it is for adults to have the care of children.

From *The Secret Passage* to *The Outside Child* there is a very large development and flowering of Bawden's talent; it can still be said of her that more than any other contemporary writer for the young she understands and respects the youth of her readers as well as that of her characters.

—Jill Paton Walsh

BEAGLE, Peter S(oyer). American. Born in New York City, 20 April 1939. Educated at University of Pittsburgh, B.A. 1959; Stanford University, 1960-61. Married 1) Enid Elaine Nordeen in 1964 (divorced 1980); 2) Padma Hejmadi in 1988, two daughters and one son. Writer. Recipient: Wallace Stegner Writing Fellowship, 1960-61; Guggenheim Foundation award, 1972-73; NEA Grant, 1977-78; Guest of Honor, Seventh World Fantasy Convention, 1981. Agent: McIntosh and Otis, Incorporated, 475 Fifth Avenue, New York, NY 10017, U.S.A.

PUBLICATIONS

Fiction

A Fine and Private Place. New York, Viking, 1960.
The Last Unicorn. New York, Viking, 1968; as *The Last Unicorn: A Fantastic Tale,* London, Bodley Head, 1968.
Lila the Werewolf. Santa Barbara, California, Capra Press, 1974; revised edition, Santa Barbara, California, Capra Press, 1976.
The Fantasy Worlds of Peter S. Beagle. New York, Viking, 1978.

The Folk of the Air. New York, Del Rey, 1987.
The Innkeeper's Song. New York, Roc, 1993.

Plays

Screenplays: *The Zoo,* Columbia Broadcasting System, 1973; *The Dove,* with Adam Kennedy, E.M.I., 1974; *The Greatest Thing That Almost Happened,* Fries, 1977; *The Lord of the Rings, Part One,* with Chris Conkling, United Artists, 1978; *The Last Unicorn,* Marble Arch/Rankin-Bass, 1982.

Nonfiction

I See by My Outfit. New York, Viking, 1965.
Author of introduction, *The Tolkien Reader,* by J.R.R. Tolkien. Boston, Houghton Mifflin, 1966.
The California Feeling, illustrated by Michael Bry and Ansel Adams. New York, Doubleday, 1969.
American Denim: A New Folks Art. Abrams/Warner, 1975.
The Lady and Her Tiger, with Pat Derby. New York, Dutton, 1976.
Author of foreword, *Adventures of Yemima, and Other Stories,* by Abraham Soyer, translated by Rebecca Beagle and Rebecca Soyer. New York, Viking, 1979.
Author of foreword, *The Best of Avram Davidson,* by Avram Davidson. New York, Doubleday, 1979.
The Garden of Earthly Delights. New York, Viking, 1981.

Other

Contributor, *Prize Stories: The O. Henry Awards,* edited by Williams Abrahams and Richard Poirier. New York, Dutton, 1965.
Contributor, *New Worlds of Fantasy,* edited by Terry Carr. New York, Ace, 1967.
Contributor, *New Worlds of Fantasy 3,* edited by Terry Carr. New York, Ace, 1971.
Contributor, *Phantasmagoria,* edited by Jane Mobley. Homer, Arkansas, Anchor, 1977.
Contributor, *The Fantastic Imagination: An Anthology of High Fantasy,* edited by Robert H. Boyer and Kenneth J. Zahorski. New York, Dell, 1978.
Contributor, *Dark Imaginings: A Collection of Gothic Fantasy,* edited by Robert H. Boyer and Kenneth J. Zahorski. New York, Dell, 1978.

*

Biography: Entry in *Dictionary of Literary Biography Yearbook,* Detroit, Gale, 1980; *Peter S. Beagle* by Kenneth J. Zahorski, Mercer Island, Washington, Starmont House, 1988.

Critical Study: Entry in *Contemporary Literary Criticism,* Volume 7, Detroit, Gale, 1977; *Science Fiction and Fantasy Literature* by R. Reginald, Volume 2, Detroit, Gale, 1979; "The Fantasy Worlds of Peter Beagle" by Ina Rae Hark, in *Survey of Modern Fantasy Literature* edited by Frank N. Magill, Englewood Cliffs, New Jersey, Salem Press, 1983.

*   *   *

Peter S. Beagle is a well-respected writer of fantasy with a relatively small body of work. His works notably include a novella, novels, and several screenplays. Though a common theme in his work is the sometimes blurry distinction between people living and dead, he treats the subject with humor. Much of his work holds appeal for young adult fans of fantasy and the supernatural.

Beagle's first novel, published in 1960, was *A Fine and Private Place*. This story is set in a Bronx cemetery and is about a bankrupt fifty-three-year-old druggist named Jonathan Rebeck. Rebeck becomes disenchanted by the commercialism of his neighborhood and moves to an isolated mausoleum. There he meets a middle-aged widow who visits her dead husband, two young ghosts, and a talking raven who steals food for him from a local deli. The plot becomes more than an account of Rebeck's mundane life of chess games and long walks with the appearance of Mrs. Gertrude Klapper and the supernatural couple, Michael Morgan and Laura Durand. The latter meet as ghosts in the cemetery, fall in love, and try to find a way to avoid drifting into oblivion. Rebeck becomes involved in the lovers' dilemma and seeks to resolve it with the support of Mrs. Klapper. The novel examines the distinctions between the living and the not living and finds them far from being clear-cut. The theme is not so much life after death as death in life. *A Fine and Private Place* was well-received because of its memorable characters, delightful humor, and significant allegorical truth. Beagle's style was praised as beautiful, confident, and charming—quite a feat since Beagle was only nineteen when he wrote the novel.

Beagle's second novel, *The Last Unicorn,* was heralded by *Fantasy Literature* as belonging to a list of the ten best in modern fantasy. The story is about the world's last surviving unicorn and her adventures in searching for others like her. She is helped in the quest by Schmendrick the Magician. Schmendrick is an inept wizard who usually cannot perform the simplest of tricks effectively, but every now and then is capable of the greatest of magic. The last unicorn is also aided by a peasant woman called Molly Grue, who finds true wonder and delight in the unicorn. The three set off in search of the lost unicorns and discover a wasteland ruled by King Haggard. The king has imprisoned the unicorns and has them under the guard of the Red Bull, a terrifying animal that frightens the unicorns and causes them to forget who and what they are. At the end of the novel, the unicorns are freed and the wasteland is transformed into a thriving community again. Like *A Fine and Private Place, The Last Unicorn* concerns death in life. King Haggard has captured the unicorns in an attempt to hold onto beauty and to possess it completely. The theme of the wasteland and its rebirth is potently retold with a degree of absurdity that makes it both a parody of traditional romantic fantasy and a reestablishment of the genre. The novel is also filled with literary allusions and contemporary colloquialisms. *The Last Unicorn* was made into an animated movie in 1982.

Lila the Werewolf and "Come, Lady Death" are examples of Beagle's short fiction. *Lila the Werewolf,* originally published as "Farrell and Lila the Werewolf," is about a young man who discovers that his lover is transformed into a werewolf with every full moon. Its linking of lycanthropy and sexuality is unique. "Come, Lady Death" is a short story about a society lady of eighteenth-century London. She invites Death to a party to liven up her boring existence. Beagle apparently wrote this last story in college to please Frank O'Connor, his professor, who hated fantasy.

The Folk of the Air was published in 1987, and was the winner of the Mythopoeic Fantasy Award. It concerns Farrell's return to Avincenna, California, after some years away. He finds his old friend Ben living with Sia, an older woman who is wild and magical. Ben has become involved in a group, the League for Archaic Plea-

sures, known to playact medieval chivalry. However, it is revealed that the group members are not merely playacting; instead they *are* the medieval characters that they portray. Sia's house contains rooms that appear and disappear, and Sia herself possesses power that she can exert at her will. While attending a League meeting, Farrell and his girlfriend Julie watch as the young witch Aiffe conjures up Nicholas Bonner, who had been sent into limbo five centuries earlier. Bonner and Aiffe cause much chaos and attempt to defeat Sia, as Farrell comes to realize that only Sia can stand against the power of Bonner and Aiffe to protect the world from their evil.

Though he is primarily recognized as an accomplished writer of fantasy, Peter Beagle's other credits include several screenplays, such as "The Dove" with Adam Kennedy in 1974 for E.M.I., and "The Lord of the Rings, Part One" with Chris Conkling in 1978 for United Artists. Beagle also did the screenplay for "The Last Unicorn" animated film for Marble Arch/Rankin-Bass.

—Lesa Dill

* * *

BEHN, Harry. Also wrote as Giles Behn. American. Born in Prescott, Arizona, 24 September 1898. Educated at Stanford University, California, 1918; Harvard University, Cambridge, Massachusetts, B.S. 1922. Married Alice Lawrence in 1925; one daughter and two sons. Scenario writer, Metro-Goldwyn-Mayer, Twentieth Century-Fox, and Universal studios, Hollywood, 1925-35; Professor of Creative Writing, University of Arizona, Tucson, 1938-47. Founding director, Phoenix Little Theatre, 1922-23; vice president, Tucson Regional Plan, 1940-47; founding editor, *Arizona Quarterly,* Tucson, 1942-47; founder and manager of radio bureau, 1938-47; founder, University of Arizona Press, 1960. Recipient: Fellowship for graduate study in Sweden, 1923-24; Graphic Arts awards for book design of *The Little Hill, All Kinds of Time,* and *The Painted Cave; All Kinds of Time* is one of thirty classics selected by New York Public Library and *Life;* honor award of Boys' Clubs of America for *Omen of the Birds;* award of merit of Claremont Graduate College for *Cricket Songs.* George G. Stone Center for Children's Books award, 1965. *Died 6 September 1973.*

PUBLICATIONS FOR YOUNG ADULTS

Fiction

The Faraway Lurs, illustrated by the author. Cleveland, World, 1963; as *The Distant Lurs,* London, Gollancz, 1965.

Poetry (illustrated by the author)

The Little Hill: Poems and Pictures. New York, Harcourt Brace, 1949.
All Kinds of Time. New York, Harcourt Brace, 1950.
Windy Morning: Poems and Pictures. New York, Harcourt Brace, 1953.
The House beyond the Meadow. New York, Pantheon, 1955.
The Wizard in the Well: Poems and Pictures. New York, Harcourt Brace, 1956.

The Golden Hive: Poems and Pictures. New York, Harcourt Brace, 1966.

What a Beautiful Noise, illustrated by Harold Berson. New York, World, 1970.

Crickets and Bullfrogs and Whispers of Thunder, edited by Lee Bennett Hopkins. New York, Harcourt Brace, 1984.

Trees, illustrated by James Endicott. New York, Holt, 1992.

Other

Translator, *Cricket Songs* [and *More Cricket Songs*]: *Japanese Haiku.* New York, Harcourt Brace, 2 vols., 1964-71.

PUBLICATIONS FOR CHILDREN

Fiction

The Painted Cave, illustrated by the author. New York, Harcourt Brace, 1957.

Timmy's Search, illustrated by Barbara Cooney. Greenwich, Connecticut, Seabury Press, 1958.

The Two Uncles of Pablo, illustrated by Mel Silverman. New York, Harcourt Brace, 1959; London, Macmillan, 1960.

Roderick, illustrated by Mel Silverman. New York, Harcourt Brace, 1961.

Omen of the Birds, illustrated by the author. Cleveland, World, 1964; London, Gollancz, 1965.

PUBLICATIONS FOR ADULTS

Plays

Screenplays: *The Big Parade,* 1925; *Proud Flesh,* with Agnes Christine Johnson, 1925; *La Bohème,* with Ray Doyle, 1926; *The Crowd,* with King Vidor and John V.A. Weaver, 1928; *The Racket,* with Del Andrews, 1928; *Frozen River,* 1929; *The Sin Sister,* with Andrew Bennison, 1929; *Hell's Angels,* with Howard Estabrook, 1930.

Poetry

Siesta. Phoenix, Golden Bough Press, 1931.

The Grand Canyon (as Giles Behn). Privately printed, 1935.

Sombra. Copenhagen, Christreu, 1961.

Other

Translator, *The Duino Elegies* by Rainer Maria Rilke. Mount Vernon, New York, Peter Pauper Press, 1957.

Translator, with Peter Beilenson, *Haiku Harvest.* Mount Vernon, New York, Peter Pauper Press, 1962.

Chrysalis: Concerning Children and Poetry. New York, Harcourt Brace, 1968.

*

Manuscript Collections: Kerlan Collection, University of Minnesota, Minneapolis; University of Oregon Library, Eugene.

*   *   *

It is a fascinating and far-flung legacy which Harry Behn has left to the young reader and to those interested in literature for children, characterized, perhaps, by his own words, "Innocence is hardly more than a willingness to wonder." How unusual it is to think of Behn as a man of innocence—born in Arizona when it was still a territory, educated at Harvard, and world-traveled! And yet it is the right phrase, for his willingness to wonder and wander, his enthusiasms, and curiosity moved within a changing world which he persisted in viewing, most often, through the eyes of the innocent.

His books, ranging from the child's poetic voice of *Windy Morning* through stories and novels and further poetry as well as translation of haiku, carry a thread of transcendentalism; it is the Indian Earth-Mother, the gods of the Sun People, the god Aplu, the rising of the sun, the "almost imperceptible experience of wonder, removed from knowledge." "When a child," he wrote in *Chrysalis,* "sees his first butterfly and becomes himself a flying flower, such innocence has in it more reality than any however heroic whiz around the planet." So it was that the language of a bug, a chicken, a crow, a storm, rain, or train could spellbind him into poem or prose-making.

Like Walter de la Mare, he found elves and wizards, fairies and magical beings of whom to write; like Robert Louis Stevenson he became the child speaking in "Swing Song" or "Pirates." Yet his was an American heritage, rooted in world history. *All Kinds of Time* clearly expressed that "Seconds are bugs / minutes are children / hours are people / days are postmen / weeks are Sunday School / months are / north / south / east / west / and in between / seasons are / wild flowers / tame flowers / golden leaves / and snow / years are / Santa Claus / centuries are / George / Washington / and forever is God." This and the poems within his other books of poetry for children are those of an American child and his particular wonder: "Tell me, tell me everything! / What makes it Winter / And then Spring?" he asks through the child in "Curiosity." Yet, the series of questions of the poem end with his own continuing questions, "Tell me! or don't even grown-ups know?" This search, therefore, led him on; it was not unusual that because of his love for seasons and simplicity he should turn to the translation of Japanese haiku, that he should examine the life of a crow in *Roderick,* or Dawn Boy, the Indian, in *The Painted Cave;* that his mother's childhood in Denmark should inspire him to write *The Faraway Lurs* or that his questioning of the correlation between Etruscan and American civilization spun itself out in *Omen of the Birds.*

Poetry, he wrote, "must be presented with careful incompleteness of information." Incompletion thus sustains curiosity; information is not a *raison d'être* for the poet, and "willingness to wonder" is Harry Behn's unique contribution to children's literature.

—Myra Cohn Livingston

———

BENCHLEY, Nathaniel (Goddard). American. Born in Newton, Massachusetts, 13 November 1915. Educated at Phillips Exeter Academy, Exeter, New Hampshire, 1931-34; Harvard University, Cambridge, Massachusetts, 1934-38, S.B. 1938. Served in the United States Naval Reserve, 1941-45. Married Marjorie Bradford in 1939; two sons. City reporter, New York *Herald Tribune,* 1939-41; assistant entertainment editor, *Newsweek,* New York, 1946-47. Recipient: Western Writers of America Spur award, 1973, for *Only Earth and Sky Last Forever; Bright Candles* was named an ALA notable book, 1974. *Died 14 December 1981.*

PUBLICATIONS FOR YOUNG ADULTS

Fiction

Gone and Back. New York, Harper, 1970.
Only Earth and Sky Last Forever. New York, Harper, 1972.
Bright Candles. New York, Harper, 1974; London, Deutsch, 1976.
Beyond the Mists. New York, Harper, 1975.
A Necessary End. New York, Harper, 1976; London, Deutsch, 1978.

PUBLICATIONS FOR CHILDREN

Fiction

Red Fox and His Canoe, illustrated by Arnold Lobel. New York, Harper, 1964; Kingswood, Surrey, World's Work, 1969.
Oscar Otter, illustrated by Arnold Lobel. New York, Harper, 1966; Kingswood, Surrey, World's Work, 1967.
The Strange Disappearance of Arthur Cluck, illustrated by Arnold Lobel. New York, Harper, 1967; Kingswood, Surrey, World's Work, 1968.
A Ghost Named Fred, illustrated by Ben Shecter. New York, Harper, 1968; Kingswood, Surrey, World's Work, 1969.
Sam the Minuteman, illustrated by Arnold Lobel. New York, Harper, 1969; Kingswood, Surrey, World's Work, 1976.
The Several Tricks of Edgar Dolphin, illustrated by Mamoru Funai. New York, Harper, and Kingswood, Surrey, World's Work, 1970.
The Flying Lesson of Gerald Pelican, illustrated by Mamoru Funai. New York, Harper, 1970.
Feldman Fieldmouse, illustrated by Hilary Knight. New York, Harper, 1971; London, Abelard Schuman, 1975.
Small Wolf, illustrated by Joan Sandin. New York, Harper, 1972; Kingswood, Surrey, World's Work, 1973.
The Magic Sled, illustrated by Mel Furukawa. New York, Harper, 1972; as *The Magic Sledge,* London, Deutsch, 1974.
The Deep Dives of Stanley Whale, illustrated by Mischa Richter. New York, Harper, 1973; Kingswood, Surrey, World's Work, 1976.
Snorri and the Strangers, illustrated by Don Bolognese. New York, Harper, 1976; Kingswood, Surrey, World's Work, 1978.
George, the Drummer Boy, illustrated by Don Bolognese. New York, Harper, 1977; Kingswood, Surrey, World's Work, 1978.
Kilroy and the Gull, illustrated by John Schoenherr. New York, Harper, 1977; London, Abelard Schuman, 1979.
Running Owl, the Hunter, illustrated by Mamoru Funai. New York, Harper, 1979.
Demo and the Dolphin, illustrated by Stephen Gammell. New York, Harper, 1981.
Snip, illustrated by Irene Trivas. New York, Doubleday, 1981.
Walter, the Homing Pigeon, illustrated by Whitney Darrow, Jr. New York, Harper, 1981.

Other

Sinbad the Sailor, illustrated by Tom O'Sullivan. New York, Random House, 1960; London, Muller, 1964.

PUBLICATIONS FOR ADULTS

Novels

Side Street. New York, Harcourt Brace, 1950.
One to Grow On. New York, McGraw Hill, 1958.
Sail a Crooked Ship. New York, McGraw Hill, 1960; London, Hutchinson, 1961.
The Off-Islanders. New York, McGraw Hill, 1961; London, Hutchinson, 1962; as *The Russians Are Coming! The Russians Are Coming!* New York, Popular Library, 1966.
Catch a Falling Spy. New York, McGraw Hill, and London, Hutchinson, 1963.
A Winter's Tale. New York, McGraw Hill, and London, Hutchinson, 1964.
The Visitors. New York, McGraw Hill, 1964; London, Hutchinson, 1965.
A Firm Word or Two. New York, McGraw Hill, 1965.
The Monument. New York, McGraw Hill, and London, Hutchinson, 1966.
Welcome to Xanadu. New York, Atheneum, and London, Hutchinson, 1968.
The Wake of Icarus. New York, Atheneum, 1969.
Lassiter's Folly. New York, Atheneum, 1971.
The Hunter's Moon. Boston, Little Brown, 1972.
Portrait of a Scoundrel. New York, Doubleday, 1979.
Sweet Anarchy. New York, Doubleday, 1979.
All Over Again. New York, Doubleday, 1981.
Speakeasy. New York, Doubleday, 1982.

Plays

The Frogs of Spring, adaptation of his novel *Side Street* (produced New York, 1953). New York, French, 1954.

Screenplay: *The Great American Pastime,* 1956.

Other

Robert Benchley: A Biography. New York, McGraw Hill, 1955; London, Cassell, 1956.
Editor, *The Benchley Roundup* (writings by Robert Benchley). New York, Harper, 1954; London, Cassell, 1956.
Humphrey Bogart. Boston, Little Brown, and London, Hutchinson, 1975.

*

Media Adaptations: *Sail a Crooked Ship* (film), Columbia, 1961; *The Russians Are Coming, the Russians Are Coming* (film adaptation of *The Off-Islanders),* United Artists, 1966; *The Spirit Is Willing* (film adaptation of *The Visitors),* Paramount, 1966.

Manuscript Collection: Mugar Memorial Library, Boston University.

*   *   *

An author of books for adults who for the last seventeen years of his life turned to writing for youth, Nathaniel Benchley produced a range of fiction for young children to teenagers. Often reflecting an interest in history or nature, his stories characteristically introduce animal or child protagonists who yearn to do grown-up deeds and undertake adventures that either caution them to wait for adulthood or thrust them faster into its early stages.

Believing in the need for the teenage novel to bridge the gap between children and adult fiction, Benchley in the 1970s produced five young-adult, historical novels all characterized by strong story-telling, detailed research, and interesting characters. Set in the nineteenth century, the award-winning *Gone and Back* compellingly chronicles young Obed Taylor's growth toward maturity and slow recognition of his father as a born loser as his family treks west from Nantucket to the Oklahoma Land Rush without striking success. Benchley skillfully integrates an authentic historical setting and a mature theme with Obed's experiences. In the superbly written *Only Earth and Sky Last Forever,* a nineteenth-century Cheyenne boy named Dark Elk, seeing the humiliation suffered by Agency Indians and wanting to prove himself a warrior, joins Crazy Horse in leading forays against the white man and fighting at Little Big Horn. Peopled with convincingly historical as well as fictional characters, the story vividly portrays the Indians' last struggle for survival. *Bright Candles* tells a fast-paced and well-researched story highlighting the Danish resistance during the Nazi regime through the figure of an adolescent boy who joins the Underground. Based on the eleventh-century sagas, the richly detailed and exciting *Beyond the Mists* centers on a Danish youth disenchanted with warring on murderous Viking raids who survives a shipwreck as a merchant seaman to join up with Leif Eriksson on a journey to North America. Plumbing his wartime Navy experience, Benchley writes a perceptive account of service aboard a World War II subchaser in training and Pacific combat in *A Necessary End.*

Not surprisingly, five of the author's fourteen adult novels hold appropriate appeal for the sixteen- to nineteen-year-old reader. The *Off-Islanders* (source of the screenplay *The Russians Are Coming! The Russians Are Coming!*), *Sail a Crooked Ship,* and *The Wake of the Icarus* are maritime adventures with a strong seasoning of melodrama, wry humor, and farce. *The Visitors* focuses on domestic issues, telling the story of the parents and son who occupy an old, reputedly haunted, house on the Atlantic coast where they encounter its ghosts and manage to exorcise them after several well-plotted comic complications. In *Welcome to Xanadu,* a bored, sixteen-year-old, New Mexico farmer's daughter is abducted and briefly held hostage by an erudite, mental-institution escapee who, during her captivity, teaches her to think and learn more about her life. The story is effectively suspenseful and not without humor.

Benchley produced a number of successful picture books and two works that appeal to the youngest of young adult readers: *Kilroy and the Gull,* about a restless captured orca who learns to communicate with humans once he escapes to sea, and *Demo and the Dolphin,* about a dolphin in ancient Greece who carries a boy seeking advice to Delphi, where both receive ambiguous advice but a better grasp of the mystical past.

Benchley once described an effective children's book as one which does not talk down to readers, offers humor and suspense, and, he added, "You need a page-turner." His overall canon admirably reflects these qualities, and upon his death in 1981, Benchley left a rich legacy indeed to young-adult fiction.

—Christian H. Moe

BENNETT, Jay. American. Born in New York, 24 December 1912. Educated at New York University. Married Sally Stern in 1937; two sons. Served as English features writer and editor, Office of War Information, 1942-45. Writer and lecturer. Has worked as a farmhand, factory worker, lifeguard, mailman, salesman, and senior editor of an encyclopedia. Recipient: Edgar Allan Poe award from Mystery Writers of America for best juvenile mystery novel, 1974, for *The Long Black Coat,* and 1975, for *The Dangling Witness.* Address: 64 Greensward Lane, Cherry Hill, NJ 08002, U.S.A.

PUBLICATIONS FOR YOUNG ADULTS

Fiction

Deathman, Do Not Follow Me. New York, Meredith Press, 1968.
The Deadly Gift. New York, Meredith Press, 1969.
The Killing Tree. New York, Franklin Watts, 1972.
Masks: A Love Story. New York, Franklin Watts, 1972.
The Long Black Coat. New York, Delacorte, 1973.
The Dangling Witness. New York, Delacorte, 1974.
Shadows Offstage. New York, Nelson, 1974.
Say Hello to the Hit Man. New York, Delacorte, 1976.
The Birthday Murder. New York, Delacorte, 1977.
The Pigeon. New York, Methuen, 1980.
The Executioner. New York, Avon, 1982.
Slowly, Slowly, I Raised the Gun. New York, Avon, 1983.
I Never Said I Loved You. New York, Avon, 1984.
The Death Ticket. New York, Avon, 1985.
To Be a Killer. New York, Scholastic, 1985.
The Skeleton Man. New York, Franklin Watts, 1986.
The Haunted One. New York, Fawcett, 1989.
The Dark Corridor. New York, Fawcett, 1990.
Sing Me a Death Song. New York, Franklin Watts, 1990.
Coverup. New York, Franklin Watts, 1991.
Skinhead. New York, Franklin Watts, 1991.
The Hooded Man. New York, Fawcett, 1992.
Death Grip. New York, Fawcett, 1993.

PUBLICATIONS FOR ADULTS

Fiction

Catacombs. New York, Abelard-Schuman, 1959.
Death Is a Silent Room. New York, Abelard-Schuman, 1965.
Murder Money. New York, Fawcett, 1963.

Plays

No Hiding Place (produced New York, 1949).
Lions after Slumber (produced London, 1951).

Also author of radio scripts, including *Miracle before Christmas* and *The Wind and Stars Are Witness;* author of television scripts for *Alfred Hitchcock Presents, Crime Syndicated, Wide, Wide World, Cameo Theater,* and *Monodrama Theatre.*

*

Biography: Essay in *Something about the Author Autobiography*

Series, Volume 4, Detroit, Gale, 1987; essay in *Speaking for Our-selves: Autobiographical Sketches by Notable Authors of Books for Young Adults,* Volume 1, compiled and edited by Donald R. Gallo, National Council of Teachers of English, 1990.

Critical Study: Entry in *Contemporary Literary Criticism,* Volume 35, Detroit, Gale, 1985.

*   *   *

Jay Bennett is a recognized master of mystery and suspense novels for young adult readers. He has twice won the Mystery Writers of America Edgar Allan Poe award for best juvenile mystery for *The Long Black Coat* and *The Dangling Witness.*

He is respected for his craft as a writer, especially his gift for creating and sustaining a mysterious atmosphere in which violence threatens the characters. His protagonists are frequently "outsiders." The "loner" character appeals to young adult readers, who often identify with that aspect of the character's personality. Yet Bennett's outsiders find through the course of the novels that it is difficult to survive alone, and it is this discovery that becomes the thematic framework for his stories.

Bennett's style tends to be an economical one. His writing is clear and simple, again appealing to many young readers; but his concise prose is rich in meaning and fully expressive. He once described himself as a "poetic realist" and this phrase truly characterizes his work. He holds himself to high standards of writing for young people, creating stories that entertain and enlighten.

Bennett has written seventeen novels for YA readers, the majority of them suspenseful thrillers with serious themes. Two recent novels clearly show the strength of Bennett's use of theme. In *Coverup: A Novel,* the issues of teenage drinking and the homeless combine to provide the chilling effect, when the hero Brad cannot remember what happened the night before when he had been drinking with his friend Alden, the judge's son. Alden and his father try to convince Brad that nothing happened to cause his nagging feeling of an awful event occurring when Alden drove them home. When Brad meets and tries to help Ellen search for her homeless father, he learns the terrible truth about the ability of those in power to cover up scandal, even death by auto. The truth emerges when Alden's mother turns in her son and husband, and justice (another favorite Bennett theme) is served.

White supremacy becomes the catalyst for suspense in *Skinhead.* Jonathan Atwood is summoned to the deathbed of a man, three thousand miles away in Seattle. Jonathan is the grandson of a millionaire and through him has access to power. His trip to Seattle brings him an anonymous death threat linked to the man whose death summoned him West. He meets Jenny in the airport while waiting for his flight back to New York. She knows him and the dead man, Alfred Kaplan. He decides to stay in Seattle, but Skinheads are watching his movements. Kaplan had been writing a book on the white supremacists. The Skinheads saw it as a threat and now Jonathan is one, too, and his life is in danger. Jonathan must confront the violence of the Skinheads, his true paternity, and his wealthy grandfather's bigotry to come to terms with his own sense of self and justice.

Bennett's earlier award-winning novels are more typically thrillers. In *The Long Black Coat,* Phil Brant is caught in the shadow of his older brother Vinnie's death. Vinnie had been part of a bank robbery, pulled before he left to serve in Vietnam. Vinnie's two accomplices menace Phil because they think he knows about the location of the stash. The secret lies in a cashmere coat and Vinnie who is alive and well after all.

The second Edgar winner, *The Dangling Witness,* uses murder as its core event. Matthew Garth, an usher at a movie theater, is the only witness to a murder. Matt is fearful of going to the police and of the killer who knows he knows, and of the Syndicate that may want his silence or his death. Matt's fear of violence, his own guilt over the death of a fellow football player, and his troubled relationship with his father make him an easy prey for the killer. Detective Anderson and Julie Leonard, the murder victim's sister, help Matt find his way through this moral crisis.

Another earlier novel, *The Deadly Gift,* combines suspense and another moral dilemma. John-Tom Dawes's father is a Mohawk high-steel worker in New York City. One rainy night, John-Tom picks up a briefcase left behind by a man waiting for a bus. The briefcase holds ten thousand dollars. It could be money for college. Does it now belong to him or does it belong to an underworld figure who wants it back under the threat of death? John-Tom abhors violence, even the violence in a game of football, but the money draws him more and more into it.

Murder and international terrorism in New York City provide the components of the thriller *The Pigeon.* Brian Cawley is the pigeon lured to his girlfriend's apartment where he finds her dead. A well-timed phone call's rough voice tells him he's been set up and the police are on the way. With the help of a former teacher, Brian tries to find the killers. His search leads him into a terrorist net of Neo-Nazis whose plans include bombing the Staten Island ferry. The novel explores a major Bennett theme of rejecting violence as a means to an end.

Other books combine murder with contemporary issues. *The Dark Corridor* grapples with an epidemic of teenage suicide. When Alicia Kent is reported as the latest suicide her boyfriend Kerry Lanson does not believe it. If it wasn't suicide, was Alicia a murder victim? In *Sing Me a Death Song,* Jason Feldman races against time to prove that his mother was framed for a murder. He has only days before her scheduled execution to prove her innocence. Again the young protagonists of these novels are looking for justice and an antidote to violence in the world.

In addition to the works of mystery, Bennett has published two YA romance novels: *Masks: A Love Story* and *I Never Said I Loved You. Masks* is a story of the interracial romance between Gonophore, a white teenager, and Peter Yeng, the son of a Chinese doctor. The story explores family dynamics and the parent's rejections of the young couple's relationship. *I Never Said I Loved You* explores another troubled relationship. Peter, an overachieving Princeton freshman with his eye on the family law firm, falls in love with unconventional, idealistic Alice. This mismatched pair seems to be the attraction of opposites, but their divergent views of life cannot be reconciled and the relationship is doomed.

Whether writing mystery or romance, Jay Bennett creates novels that young readers respond to. He understands and presents their concerns and provides thrills in crisp dialogue and prose that attracts even reluctant readers.

—Janice Antczak

———

BLACKLIN, Malcolm. See **CHAMBERS, Aidan**

———

BLOCK, Francesca Lia. American. Born in Hollywood, California, 3 December 1962. Educated at University of California, Berkeley, B.A. 1986. Writer. Recipient: University of California, Berkeley, short fiction award, 1986; Emily Chamberlin Cook award, 1986; *Weetzie Bat* was shortlisted as a book of the year by the American Library Association and was a Recommended Book for Reluctant Young Adult Readers; *Witch Baby* was a Recommended Book for Reluctant Young Adult Readers and a Cherokee Bat ALA Book of the Year. Agent: Julie Fallowfield, McIntosh and Otis Agency, 310 Madison Avenue, New York, NY 10017, U.S.A. Lives in Joshua Tree, California.

PUBLICATIONS FOR YOUNG ADULTS

Novels

Weetzie Bat. New York, Harper, 1989.
Witch Baby. New York, Harper, 1990.
Cherokee Bat and the Goat Guys. New York, Harper, 1991.
Missing Angel Juan. New York, HarperCollins, 1993.
Ecstasia. New York, ROC, 1993.

*

Biography: Essay in *Speaking for Ourselves, Too* compiled and edited by Donald R. Gallo, National Council of Teachers of English, 1993.

*   *   *

Most writers for young adults set their stories in places and times with which they are familiar. Judy Blume writes about life in the suburbs of New Jersey which is, of course, where she herself grew up. Norma Klein's books almost always take place in New York City and Robert Cormier's in small-town eastern Massachusetts, locales with which the respective authors are familiar from their own youth. But few young adult authors have dealt with life in the Southern California milieu of Los Angeles and the "punk" youth subculture that flourishes there—until Francesca Lia Block came along.

In 1989 Block's first book, *Weetzie Bat,* was published to the utter delight of most critics and the absolute consternation of the rest. It is a slight book of only eighty-eight pages. Block's writing style is simple and larded with contemporary slang; the book's plot is helped along by some wondrous events that could have come straight out of *The Red Fairy Book* but they are counterbalanced by Block's frequent allusions to Los Angeles's ambience and its pop culture. All these elements might make *Weetzie Bat* appear less than significant in the world of young adult literature, but it is in her characterizations that Block excels, creating a wonderful fable as well as a tender love story and an affirmation of the power of family—a somewhat different kind of family, perhaps, but a warm and caring one that nurtures and protects its members.

In the story, Weetzie Bat lives in Los Angeles with her dysfunctional parents and her pet, Slinkster Dog. She's unhappy in school and lonely until she meets Dirk, the school hunk, who sports a "shoe-polish black Mohawk" and drives a "slinkster-cool red '55 Pontiac." They become fast friends and drop out of school to "do" Los Angeles together and have a glorious time at it. But then one day Dirk confesses to Weetzie that he's gay, so they resolve to go

duck (lover) hunting together. Before long Dirk finds a partner (actually named Duck as it turns out) but Weetzie's ducks all turn out to be duds until My Secret Agent Lover Man (his real name too) comes along. Dirk's Grandma Fifi conveniently died and left her little cottage to Dirk, so the four of them—Dirk, Duck, Weetzie, and My Secret Agent Lover Man along with Slinkster Dog—set up housekeeping in their new home and are soon a warm and loving family. But Weetzie decides that the only thing missing in their little ménage is a baby. Lover Man refuses to go along with her because the horrors of the world are too overwhelming to bring a new life into it. Dirk and Duck come to the rescue; while Lover Man is away on a fishing trip they sleep with Weetzie and she conceives. When he hears the news on his return, Lover Man, shocked and angry, flees the cottage and doesn't return until after the birth of the baby girl they name Cherokee.

It turns out that during his absence, Lover Man managed to overcome his scruples about new lives. However, he took up with a beautiful but strange woman with whom he conceived a child. Soon after his return to the cottage, the woman drops the baby off there. The group decides to make the new baby a part of their family too and christen her Witch Baby. The family expands further when Go-Go Girl, a canine companion of Slinkster Dog, joins the group and has five puppies: Pee Wee, Wee Wee, Teenie Wee, Tiki Tee, and Tee Pee.

But their happy, loving family unit is sundered when Duck disappears one night, leaving a note saying that a dear friend is desperately ill (of AIDS presumably), and that he, Duck, must leave for a while because the world is just too scary "when loving someone can be the way you kill him." Dirk, frantic, resolves to find him and drives to San Francisco. He searches the places where they have been together and finally finds him in a bar. The next day they return to the cottage where the rest of the family is anxiously waiting. Block describes the reunion thusly:

> When they got home, it was a purple, smoggy L.A. twilight. Weetzie and My Secret Agent Lover Man and Cherokee and Witch Baby and Slinkster Dog and Go-Go Girl and the puppies Pee Wee, Wee Wee, Teenie Wee, Tiki Tee, and Tee Pee were waiting on the front porch drinking lemonade and listening to Iggy Pop's "Lust for Life" as the sky darkened and the barbecue summer smells filled the air.
>
> Weetzie ran up to them first and flung her arms around Duck and then Dirk. Then all six of them held on to one another in a football huddle and the dogs slunk around their feet.
>
> That night, they all ate linguini and clam sauce that My Secret Agent Lover Man made, and they drank wine and lit the candles.
>
> Weetzie looked around at everyone—she saw Dirk, tired, unshaven, his hair a mess; he hardly ever looked like this. But his eyes shone wet with love. Duck looked older, there were lines in his face she hadn't remembered seeing before, but he leaned against Dirk like a little boy. Weetzie looked at My Secret Agent Lover Man finishing his linguini, sucking it up with his pouty lips. Cherokee was pulling on his sleeve and he leaned over and kissed her and then put her onto his lap to help him finish the last bite of pasta. Witch Baby sat alone, mysterious and beautiful.
>
> Weetzie's heart felt so full with love, so full, as if it could hardly fit in her chest. She knew they were all afraid But love and disease are both like electricity, Weetzie thought.

They are always there—you can't see or smell or hear, touch, or taste them, but you know they are there like a current in the air. We can choose, Weetzie thought, we can choose to plug into the love current instead. And she looked around the table at Dirk and Duck and My Secret Agent Lover Man and Cherokee and Witch Baby—all of them lit up and golden like a wreath of lights.

I don't know about happily ever after...but I know about happily, Weetzie Bat thought.

This somewhat lengthy description of *Weetzie Bat* is only to give the reader some of the flavor of Block's unique writing style and her highly unconventional plotting and characterization. Most reviewers found the book "charming," "funny," "magical," "tender," "an affirmation of life," "a warm and loving look at an unconventional but strong family," etc. But some found it horrifying because of the kind of "family" it seemed to approve of, its casual treatment of extramarital sex and childbirth, its acceptance of homosexuality, its implied approval of wildly unconventional living arrangements, and of course its frank language. One reviewer went so far as to rebuke Block severely for not having her characters indulge in "safe" sex if they had to indulge at all, completely missing the point Block makes: there are a whole lot of young people about whom it probably can be said that safe sex is the last thing on their minds. Those critics notwithstanding, a host of others found a great deal of value in *Weetzie Bat*. Perhaps their attitude was best summed up in the review that appeared in *Booklist:* "This skinny book is almost a prose poem. Punks will love it, but it will also charm those who can see that what appears to be bizarre is also beautiful, delicate, and cozily domestic, 'a collage of glitter and petals.'" It is safe to say that *Weetzie Bat* is a unique contribution to young adult literature in the same way that Cormier's *The Chocolate War,* Blume's *Forever,* and Hinton's *The Outsiders* were; each broke entirely new ground and permanently changed the face of young adult literature in significant ways.

Block's next three books follow the same pattern as her first. *Witch Baby* picks up the story of the strange child left on the family's doorstep long ago, a child who has always felt that she is an "almost-member" of the family but who wants to be more than that. Her anguish finds release in obnoxious behavior and generally making the rest of the family miserable too. Finally in desperation she sets out to find her birth mother, but when she does meet her again she learns a painful lesson. Sadder but wiser, she realizes that her home has always been with the people who love her—Weetzie and the rest who chose to make her one of them many years before. But Witch Baby is still not a whole person and her story continues in *Cherokee Bat and the Goat Guys.* In this book Weetzie and the other family adults have gone off to film a movie, leaving Witch Baby and Cherokee in the somewhat casual care of a Native-American friend of the family, Coyote. When their two male friends, Raphael and Angel Juan, enter the scene, the four of them decide to form a rock band to have something to do and to help Witch Baby, who is once again becoming severely dysfunctional. Coyote helps them achieve success by giving them powerful tribal gifts, but that very success sends the four young people into a morass of sex, drugs, and alcohol so deep that Cherokee comes close to committing suicide. Just before they all self-destruct, however, Coyote returns and takes back his totems, which leaves them free to heal.

Missing Angel Juan, the most recent of Block's young adult books continues the story of Witch Baby's journey to wholeness. By the end of *Cherokee Bat and the Goat Guys* the members of the band had paired off, Cherokee with Raphael and Witch Baby with Angel Juan. At the beginning of *Missing Angel Juan,* Witch Baby, who is if anything totally besotted with Juan, finds that he is leaving for New York to find himself through his music. Devastated, she decides to follow him and locate him in that enormous city, with only a few vague clues as to where to begin on the one postcard he sent her. From this point on strange things begin to happen; Witch Baby's search at times is dreamlike and at other times it has a truly nightmarish quality as she combs the Borough from Harlem to the meatpacking district looking for Angel Juan. While all Block's books contain elements of the supernatural/magical, she has pulled out all the stops in this one, and the book is significantly weaker for it; much of the plot turns on coincidence that is simply unbelievable, and magic—both helpful and malevolent—just doesn't make it any less so. The fairy tale quality of the magic that Block used so charmingly in her earlier books seems heavy-handed and depressing in *Missing Angel Juan;* consequently the reader is not left with that warm glow that followed reading *Weetzie Bat, Witch Baby,* and *Cherokee Bat and the Goat Guys*—and it's missed.

In the few years that she has been writing books for young adults, Francesca Lia Block has established herself as a major talent. Her books have been honored as Young Adult Best Books by the American Library Association and have been lauded by most critics and reviewers for her unique voice and transcendent themes. Block, on the basis of four small books, has become, as one critic put it in *Horn Book,* "a brilliant addition to the canon of respected young adult authors."—and that's slinkster cool, to say the least.

—Audrey Eaglen

BLOS, Joan W(insor). American. Born in New York City, New York, 9 December 1928. Educated at Vassar College, Poughkeepsie, New York, B.A. 1949; City College (now of the City University of New York), M.A. 1956. Married Peter Blos, Jr., in 1953; one son (deceased), one daughter. Research assistant, Jewish Board of Guardians, New York City, 1949-50; assistant teacher of psychology, City College (now of the City University of New York), New York City, 1950-51; research assistant, Yale University, Child Study Center, New Haven, Connecticut, 1951-53; associate editor in publications division, Bank Street College of Education, New York City, 1959-66, instructor in teacher education division, 1960-70; research assistant and specialist in children's literature for the Department of Psychiatry, University of Michigan, Ann Arbor, 1970-73, lecturer for School of Education, 1973-80; writer and lecturer, 1980—. Volunteer reviewer of children's books for the Connecticut Association of Mental Health and chairperson of Children's Book Committee, 1954-56. Member of editorial board, *Children's Literature in Education,* London, 1973-77, U.S. editor, 1976-81. Recipient: John Newbery Medal from American Library Association, and American Book Award for children's hardcover fiction, both 1980, both for *A Gathering of Days: A New England Girl's Journal, 1830-32; A Gathering of Days* was also chosen as one of the Best Books of the Year by *School Library Journal* and as an Ambassador Book by the English-Speaking Union. Agent: Curtis Brown Ltd., 10 Astor Place, New York, NY 10003, U.S.A.

PUBLICATIONS FOR YOUNG ADULTS

Fiction

A Gathering of Days: A New England Girl's Journal, 1830-32 (historical fiction). New York, Scribner, 1979.
Brothers of the Heart: A Story of the Old Northwest, 1837-38 (historical fiction). New York, Scribner, 1985.
Brooklyn Doesn't Rhyme. New York, Scribner, 1994.

Nonfiction

The Heroine of the Titanic: A Tale Both True and Otherwise of the Life of Molly Brown, illustrated by Tennessee Dixon. New York, Morrow, 1991.

PUBLICATIONS FOR CHILDREN

Picture Books

Joe Finds a Way, with Betty Miles, illustrated by Lee Ames. Syracuse, L. W. Singer, 1967.
"It's Spring," She Said, illustrated by Julie Maas. New York, Knopf, 1968.
Just Think!, with Betty Miles, illustrated by Pat Grant Porter. New York, Knopf, 1971.
Martin's Hats, illustrated by Marc Simont. New York, Morrow, 1984.
Old Henry, illustrated by Stephen Gammell. New York, Morrow, 1987.
The Grandpa Days, illustrated by Emily Arnold McCully. New York, Simon & Schuster, 1989.
Lottie's Circus, illustrated by Irene Trivas. New York, Morrow, 1989.
One Very Best Valentine's Day, illustrated by Emily Arnold McCully. New York, Simon and Schuster, 1990.
A Seed, a Flower, a Minute, an Hour: A First Book of Transformations, illustrated by Hans Poppel. New York, Simon and Schuster, 1992.
Editor, *The Days Before Now,* by Margaret Wise Brown, illustrated by Thomas B. Allen. New York, Simon and Schuster, 1994.

Other

In the City (reader), illustrated by Dan Dickas. New York, Macmillan, 1964.
People Read (reader) with Betty Miles, illustrated by Dan Dickas. New York, Macmillan, 1964.

*

Media Adaptations: *Old Henry* is available on cassette from National Library Service for the Blind and Physically Handicapped, 1987; *A Gathering of Days: A New England Girl's Journal, 1830-32,* is available on unabridged cassette from Random House and was read on "Books by Radio" over a University of Michigan radio station.

Biography: Essay in *Something about the Author Autobiography Series,* Volume 11, Detroit, Gale, 1991.

Manuscript Collection: Kerlan Collection, University of Minnesota.

Critical Study: Entry in *Children's Literature Review,* Volume 18, Detroit, Gale, 1989.

Joan Blos comments:

Words, for me, have always been important. It is said that I spoke at an early age and well before I entered school my father and mother were writing down the "poems" I spoke to them. "First in town it thunders and glitters," begins one surviving example. It rises to the question: "What will you do when the storm is out, and it is beginning to rain?" Observation and question continue to be the basis of what I write.

"Writing begins in caring," I say to the children when asked to speak in schools. By that I mean that writing begins with concern for the world, the events and the people therein. I believe that this world of ours matters and that our small lives count. Writing also means caring about the words which are set down on paper. It's a struggle for me and I wouldn't call it enjoyable. Once I told an interviewer that, although I don't like writing, I *love* having written. That's what keeps me going back—back to the pads and the pens and the pencils, the typewriter, and the wastebaskets (two!) which are under my desk. I think it's important for others to know that writing isn't something you do because you find it easy. Most of the time I'm grateful if I can do it at all. Beyond the caring for words, and one's world, writing has to do with caring for those for whom you write. I suppose that's why I write for children and am happy to hear from them. I like to think of my books, my works, as ways of saying things, to children, for whom I deeply care. However hard I find this work of writing, I would not, do not, want ever to give it up! I hope I get better and better at writing; I know that there is nothing that I would rather do.

*   *   *

Joan W. Blos's first novel for older children, *A Gathering of Days: A New England Girl's Journal, 1830-32,* won numerous awards, among them the Newbery Medal and the American Book Award. It is a well-crafted book of historical fiction with a protagonist, Catherine Hall, who is as vividly alive as any of her readers. Catherine's human qualities are revealed early as she wishes "that my hair were curly, as Matty's is, and our mother's." She delights in visiting the Shipmans, their nearest neighbors, but wishes that she could reciprocate with splendid dinners on special occasions (since her mother died years before the journal begins, that is not possible). Here is a real child, loving, usually obedient, but full of fun, too. Having taken great pride in assuming many of her mother's duties, Catherine resents her new stepmother who appears with little warning about halfway through the book, constantly referring to her as "she" or "her" in the journal. On the wedding day, Catherine writes, "On this day, in Boston, they married. I will not call her Mother." Her stepbrother, Daniel, later comes up with a compromise, "Mammann," as Catherine gradually adjusts. In contrast, she dearly loves her friend Cassie, whose death is a terrible blow. Eventually matters sort themselves out as Catherine comes to terms with herself and with those around her. She accepts both Cassie's death and her stepmother; as she prepares to set off on a trip at the end of the journal, she has matured considerably from the girl who first began it.

Blos's other historical novel, *Brothers of the Heart: A Story of the Old Northwest 1837-38,* has a male protagonist. The tale, set in Michigan, is told through flashback using devices such as letters and journal and diary entries. These fictionalized accounts give the reader a strong sense of verisimilitude; the book rings true, for Blos has also captured the speech cadences and language of the period. Through friendships and relatives several of the characters are linked to Catherine Hall, from *A Gathering of Days,* so that readers can gain a sense of continuity.

The sharp characterization of the first historical fiction novel continues in *Brothers of the Heart* as Shem Perkins, born lame, attempts to make his own way after an unfortunate scene with his upset father. After running away from home, he receives gainful employment and is sent on a dangerous expedition which almost costs him his life but which ensures his maturity and builds his self-confidence, enabling him to return to his family and to the girl he will eventually marry. The reader also learns of another culture as Shem takes in the aged Ottowan Indian, Mary Goodhue, learning from her and tending to her until her death. Through her he discovers his own strengths and makes the realization that he and Mary's long-dead Indian husband were truly brothers of the heart.

The richness of the novel lies in the presentation of the growth of the Michigan region along with the development of characters and insight into the feelings of crippled Shem and the attitudes of others about him. The language, with its rhythms and lilt of earlier times, is remarkably spare, not replete with full-blown descriptions, yet giving the reader a strong sense of place and characterization. Blos has accomplished the fine feat of balancing history with universal human experience, uniting the book's past with the reader's present.

—Marilyn F. Apseloff

BLUE, Zachary. See **STINE, R(obert) L(awrence).**

BLUME, Judy (née Sussman). American. Born in Elizabeth, New Jersey, 12 February 1938. Educated at New York University, B.S. in education 1960. Married 1) John M. Blume in 1959 (divorced 1975), one daughter and one son; 2) Thomas A. Kitchens in 1976 (divorced); 3) George Cooper in 1987, one stepdaughter. Writer of juvenile and adult fiction. Founder, KIDS Fund, 1981. Recipient: *New York Times* best books for children list, 1970, Nene Award, 1975, Young Hoosier Book Award, 1976, and North Dakota Children's Choice Award, 1979, all for *Are You There God? It's Me, Margaret;* Charlie May Swann Children's Book Award, 1972, Young Readers Choice Award, Pacific Northwest Library Association, and Sequoyah Children's Book Award of Oklahoma, both 1975, Massachusetts Children's Book Award, Georgia Children's Book Award, and South Carolina Children's Book Award, all 1977, Rhode Island Library Association Award, 1978, North Dakota Children's Choice Award, and West Australian Young Readers' Book Award, both 1980, United States Army in Europe Kinderbuch Award, and Great Stone Face Award, New Hampshire Library Council, both 1981, all for *Tales of a Fourth Grade Nothing;* Arizona Young

Readers Award, and Young Readers Choice Award, Pacific Northwest Library Association, both 1977, and North Dakota Children's Choice Award, 1983, all for *Blubber;* South Carolina Children's Book Award, 1978, for *Otherwise Known as Sheila the Great;* Texas Bluebonnet List, 1980, Michigan Young Reader's Award, and International Reading Association Children's Choice Award, both 1981, First Buckeye Children's Book Award, Nene Award, Sue Hefley Book Award, Louisiana Association of School Libraries, United States Army in Europe Kinderbuch Award, West Australian Young Readers' Book Award, North Dakota Children's Choice Award, Colorado Children's Book Award, Georgia Children's Book Award, Tennessee Children's Choice Book Award, and Utah Children's Book Award, all 1982, Northern Territory Young Readers' Book Award, Young Readers Choice Award, Pacific Northwest Library Association, Garden State Children's Book Award, Iowa Children's Choice Award, Arizona Young Readers' Award, California Young Readers' Medal, and Young Hoosier Book Award, all 1983, all for *Superfudge;* American Book Award nomination, Dorothy Canfield Fisher Children's Book Award, Buckeye Children's Book Award, and California Young Readers Medal, all 1983, all for *Tiger Eyes;* Golden Archer Award, 1974; Today's Woman Award, 1981; Eleanor Roosevelt Humanitarian Award, Favorite Author—Children's Choice Award, Milner Award, and Jeremiah Ludington Memorial Award, all 1983; Carl Sandburg Freedom to Read Award, Chicago Public Library, 1984; Civil Liberties Award, Atlanta American Civil Liberties Union, and John Rock Award, Center for Population Options, Los Angeles, both 1986; D.H.L., Kean College, Union, New Jersey, 1987; South Australian Youth Media Award for Best Author, South Australian Association for Media Education, 1988. Agent: Harold Ober Associates, Inc., 425 Madison Ave., New York, NY 10017, U.S.A. Lives in New York City.

PUBLICATIONS FOR YOUNG ADULTS

Fiction

The One in the Middle Is the Green Kangaroo, illustrated by Lois Axeman. Chicago, Reilly and Lee, 1969; revised edition with new illustrations, Scarsdale, New York, Bradbury Press, 1991.

Iggie's House. Englewood Cliffs, New Jersey, Bradbury Press, 1970; London, Heinemann, 1981.

Are You There God? It's Me, Margaret. Englewood Cliffs, New Jersey, Bradbury Press, 1970; London, Gollancz, 1978.

Freckle Juice, illustrated by Sonia O. Lisker. New York, Four Winds Press, 1971; London, Heinemann, 1984.

Then Again, Maybe I Won't. Scarsdale, New York, Bradbury Press, 1971; London, Heinemann, 1979.

It's Not the End of the World. Scarsdale, New York, Bradbury Press, 1972; London, Heinemann, 1979.

Tales of a Fourth Grade Nothing, illustrated by Roy Doty. New York, Dutton, 1972; London, Bodley Head, 1979.

Otherwise Known as Sheila the Great. New York, Dutton, 1972; London, Bodley Head, 1979.

Deenie. Scarsdale, New York, Bradbury Press, 1973; London, Heinemann, 1980.

Blubber. Scarsdale, New York, Bradbury Press, 1974; London, Heinemann, 1980.

Forever. Scarsdale, New York, Bradbury Press, 1975; London, Gollancz, 1976.

Starring Sally J. Freedman As Herself. Scarsdale, New York, Bradbury Press, 1977; London, Heinemann, 1983.
Superfudge. New York, Dutton, and London, Bodley Head, 1980.
Tiger Eyes. Scarsdale, New York, Bradbury Press, 1981; London, Heinemann, 1982.
The Pain and the Great One, illustrated by Irene Trivas. Scarsdale, New York, Bradbury Press, 1984; London, Heinemann, 1985.
Just As Long As We're Together. New York, Orchard, and London, Heinemann, 1987.
Fudge-a-Mania. New York, Dutton, 1990.

Other

The Judy Blume Diary: The Place to Put Your Own Feelings. New York, Dell, 1981.

PUBLICATIONS FOR ADULTS

Novels

Wifey. New York, Putnam, 1978; London, Macmillan, 1979.
Smart Women. New York, Putnam, 1983; London, Sphere, 1984.

Other

Letters to Judy: What Your Kids Wish They Could Tell You. New York, Putnam, and London, Heinemann, 1986.
The Judy Blume Memory Book. New York, Dell, 1988.

Producer with Lawrence Blume, *Otherwise Known As Sheila the Great,* Barr Films, 1988.

*

Media Adaptations: *Forever* (television movie), CBS-TV, 1978; *Freckle Juice* (film), Barr Films, 1987; *Otherwise Known as Sheila the Great* (film), Barr Films, 1988.

Biography: Entry in *Dictionary of Literary Biography,* Volume 52, Detroit, Gale, 1986; essay in *Speaking for Ourselves: Autobiographical Sketches by Notable Authors of Books for Young Adults,* Volume 1, compiled and edited by Donald R. Gallo, National Council of Teachers of English, 1990.

Manuscript Collection: Kerlan Collection, University of Minnesota, Minneapolis.

Critical Study: Entry in *Children's Literature Review,* Detroit, Gale, Volume 2, 1976, Volume 15, 1988; entry in *Contemporary Literary Criticism,* Detroit, Gale, Volume 12, 1980, Volume 30, 1984; *The Pied Pipers* by Emma Fisher and Justin Wintle, Paddington Press, 1975; *Breakthrough: Women in Writing* by Diana Gleasner, New York, Walker, 1980; *Judy Blume's Story* by Betsey Lee, New York, Dillon Press, 1981; *Presenting Judy Blume* by Maryann Weidt, Boston, Twayne, 1989.

*   *   *

Until the mid-1960s, fiction for young people could be characterized for the most part as predictable and simplistic; very little

appeared that might disturb the reader unduly, and a tidy, happy ending was mandatory. Characters were often one-dimensional, and plots ranged from simple to silly. In 1967, however, a teen novel was published that forever destroyed the spoken and unspoken taboos defining junior fiction. S.E. Hinton's *The Outsiders,* a powerful story of class struggle in an Oklahoma high school, was iconoclastic in its gritty realism, its believable, doomed characters, and its uncompromising honesty. The book opened doors previously closed to teenage readers and, in effect, permitted a new generation of writers to tackle the real issues that concerned teenagers with honesty and realism.

It remained for another author to extend that frankness and realism into the world of literature for the younger adolescent, the eleven- and twelve-year-old on the brink, as it were, of full-blown teenage angst. By 1970 this author, Judy Blume, had published two children's books. The first was a pleasant but conventional picture book about a middle child who feels ignored by parents and siblings until he becomes a hit in a school play. The second, *Iggie's House,* was a somewhat didactic piece of junior fiction which dealt with the impact of a black family moving into a previously all-white suburban neighborhood. Reviewers were lukewarm about the book primarily because of the weakness of its characterization, its predictable plot, and some dreadful dialogue. This reception made Blume decide to write a more honest novel about the early adolescent experience based on her own vivid memories of what it was like to be an eleven-year-old girl going through this culture's rites of passage. In the process, Blume managed to ignore publishing taboos and strictures perhaps even more than Hinton had done a few years before, while at the same time penning a work that became one of the great success stories in the history of children's book publishing.

In 1970 *Are You There God? It's Me, Margaret* was published, but this time critical response was anything but lukewarm. Reviewers either loved it or hated it, but what was more important was the response of young readers to eleven-year-old Margaret's wistful longings for religion, her period, breasts, and the first bra, all dished up with large dollops of the easy, good humor that would become characteristic of many of Blume's later books. Preteen girls loved the book and wrote letters by the hundreds to tell its author just how closely they identified with Margaret and shared a sense of cozy familiarity with her dilemmas. But it was only when the book appeared in paperback in 1974 that the hundreds of letters became thousands, all of them from readers who saw themselves and their lives reflected perfectly in Margaret's story.

Response to the book clearly reveals Blume's greatest gift as a writer for young people: her ability to share her own vividly remembered childhood experiences in ways that the reader can both understand and identify with easily and completely. At the same time, Blume does not write down to her readers; she is uncompromising in the frankness of her topics and her refusal to be less than honest in her writing. As a result young people write to Blume as one twelve-year-old did: "You are writing about me. I feel like you know all my secrets."

Her confidence in her success as a writer established with *Are You There God?,* Blume entered a highly prolific period. *Then Again, Maybe I Won't* is the story of thirteen-year-old Tony Miglion's attempts to cope with his upwardly mobile family as well as his burgeoning sexuality. The effects of divorce on a bewildered preteen girl is the subject of *It's Not the End of the World,* while *Deenie* is the story of a seventh-grader plagued by a mother who is determined that Deenie will become a model until the girl's diagnosis of scoliosis interferes with her plans. Children's cruelty toward one another is the subject of *Blubber*, a story of a fat girl, a born victim, who becomes the target of her entire class's ridicule and persecution with nearly disastrous results. In *Forever*, the joys and the disappointments of first love are shown through the story of Michael and Katherine; more importantly, however, the joys and disappointments of one's first sexual experiences are described clearly and explicitly, in a way that even preteens can understand. For this reason alone, *Forever* has made Blume the most censored children's author in the United States for several years running.

In 1981 the book that many critics felt was Blume's finest appeared. *Tiger Eyes* is the story of one family's struggle to overcome the shock and horror of a father's violent, unexpected death. Davey, the young protagonist, must not only deal with the loss of her parent, but with her mother's inability to accept what has happened and the well-meant if bumbling efforts of other relatives attempting to help. *Tiger Eyes* is notable for the strength of Blume's characterizations, often faulted by critics, and its complexities of plot and theme. Blume's latest novel, *Just as Long as We're Together*, is a return to the world of adolescent girls, much like an updated version of *Are You There God?*

In her twenty years as a writer Blume has achieved a pinnacle of success that few others have. She is the most widely read author of contemporary young people's fiction in the world, and her books have sold tens of millions of copies. She still receives up to two thousand letters a month from young readers; the most poignant of these have been collected in a book called *Letters to Judy*. Anyone who has any doubt about Blume's rapport with her readers might profit from a look at this book.

Blume has achieved her success as a result of several factors. Her almost total recall of how it felt to be young makes her books speak directly to her readers. She is forthright and frank as no writer for young people had dared to be before she appeared on the scene. At the same time, her own sense of humor and her sense of what makes young readers laugh has softened some of her messages and made them palatable. Her books certainly have been controversial, but their acceptance by the young has been universal, and Blume has continued to breach old barriers and blaze new trails, an achievement of which few contemporary authors of books for any age group can boast.

—Audrey Eaglen

———

BODE, Janet. American. Born in Penn Yan, New York, 14 July 1943. Educated at University of Maryland, B.A. 1965; graduate study at Michigan State University, and Bowie State College. Writer, since 1975. Has worked in Germany, Mexico, and the United States as a personnel specialist, program director, community organizer, public relations director, and teacher. Recipient: Outstanding Social Studies Book by the National Council for Social Studies and the Children's Book Council, 1979, for *Rape*; American Library Association's Best Books for Young Adults, and a Notable Children's Trade Book in the Field of Social Studies from the National Council for Social Studies and the Children's Book Council, both 1980, for *Kids Having Kids*; *Rape* was selected one of New York Public Library's Book for the Teen Age, 1980; *Kids Having Kids*, was selected one of New York Public Library's Book for the Teen Age,

1981 and 1982. Agent: Kevin McShane, Fifi Oscard Associates, Inc., 19 West 44th St., New York, NY 10036, U.S.A.

PUBLICATIONS FOR YOUNG ADULTS

Nonfiction

Kids' School Lunch Bag. Washington, D.C., Children's Foundation, 1972.
View from Another Closet: Exploring Bisexuality in Women. New York, Hawthorn, 1976.
Fighting Back: How to Cope with the Medical, Emotional and Legal Consequences of Rape. New York, Macmillan, 1978.
Kids Having Kids: The Unwed Teenage Parent. New York, F. Watts, 1980.
Rape: Preventing It: Coping with the Legal, Medical and Emotional Aftermath. New York, F. Watts, 1980.
Different Worlds: Interracial and Cross-Cultural Dating. New York, F. Watts, 1989.
New Kids on the Block: Oral Histories of Immigrant Teens. New York, F. Watts, 1989.
Real-Life Rape. New York, F. Watts, 1990.
The Voices of Rape. New York, F. Watts, 1990.
Beating the Odds: Stories of Unexpected Achievers, drawings by Stan Mack. New York, F. Watts, 1991.
Truce: Ending the Sibling War. New York, F. Watts, 1991.
Kids Still Having Kids: People Talk about Teen Pregnancy, art by Stan Mack. New York, F. Watts, 1992.
Compiler, *Death Is Hard to Live With: Teenagers and How They Cope with Death*. New York, Delacorte, 1993.

*   *   *

Janet Bode lets young adults speak for themselves. Bode's interviews with teens are interspersed with analysis, advice, and comments from professionals; they cover issues of immediate importance to teens and topics that reflect the crises of society. Bode speaks frequently to young adults, teachers, and librarians and declares, "Students are my best resource." In her talks and in her books, Bode provides her telephone number and address encouraging teens to contact her to talk about problems and to share their stories. Bode uses the young adults' own words as much as possible and the discussions throughout Bode's books have an honest ring that create immediate connections with readers. Expert interviews which sometimes follow teen's stories are never preachy or arrogant but provide information and differing viewpoints, and offer practical suggestions for help.

Kids Having Kids: The Unwed Teenage Parent chronicles the health risks associated with teen pregnancy and birth control, describes options, and through each teen's story introduces the reader to the sudden responsibilities and difficulties of the parenting role. Kimberly says, "My life came to a screeching halt when I got pregnant and had Brandy. It's an enormous amount of responsibility that no seventeen-year-old should have."

Case histories of five interracial dating couples are recorded in *Different Worlds: Interracial and Cross-Cultural Dating*. The added pressures of society's raised eyebrows are described humorously and poignantly by teens impatient with status quos. The stories included acknowledge the transience of most teen relationships—

four of five couples interviewed end their relationship—but the hurt and sense of the injustices experienced lingers.

The anguish of being separated from familiar worlds and families ties together the interviews of teen immigrants from diverse countries in *New Kids on the Block: Oral Histories of Immigrant Teens.* Bode introduces each teen's story with an introductory paragraph about the youth's country of origin, but each teen tells his or her own story of flight, often in miserable conditions, to a land of hope for a better life. Varied cultural backgrounds, and individual personalities meld into a common goal—fitting in as an American teen. Abdul, age seventeen, escaped Afghanistan with his family and after six years as a refugee in several countries, finally made America his home. "I hated this place. l didn't have any friends.... Now I'm seventeen and the American kids don't always know that I'm a foreigner. They tease less. I found out that if you act the way they do, say the same things they say, do the things they do, they will be calm. So I try not to act strange to them. I wear t-shirts and stone-washed jeans and aviator glasses. My hair looks like their hair."

Beating the Odds: Stories of Unexpected Achievers explores the lives of eleven adolescents who are succeeding in the face of seemingly insurmountable odds. These young people tell how they deal with abusive parents, drug addiction, physical disabilities, parental suicides, and incarceration. Professional information provided by psychiatrists, probation officers, and health care workers focuses on the importance of setting goals and ways to make positive life changes. No rosy scenarios are painted, but a feeling of faith in the individual's abilities to triumph over pain is prevalent.

Bode is particularly adept at exploring many sides of the complex issues teens suggest she investigate. In *The Voices of Rape* the author interviews teens who have been raped; teens who have raped someone; and police, prosecutors, judges, defense attorneys, and hospital staff involved in rape cases, as well as rape crisis counselors and psychologists. Bode tackles date rape, stranger rape, and males who have been raped. The facts Bode presents are staggering: one out of every four women experience sexual intercourse for the first time through rape. But, as in Bode's other nonfiction works, the theme of survival and practical strategies for recovery and assistance provide hope and a sense of being in control for teen readers. Bode urges her readers to action: "Today you could make it your goal to break through what remains of the silence about sexual assault. You could choose to be the generation that deals directly and honestly with the issue, the generation that does far more than make things a little easier for rape survivors who decide to report."

Bode's abilities to communicate honestly with young adults and to provide information and help in a way that teens find palatable make her books a valuable tool for teens, parents, teachers, and librarians. Bode's works also provide snapshots and insights into some of society's most pressing issues and impart a sense of certainty that today's teens will find solutions to many of the ills they have inherited.

—Hollis Lowery-Moore

BOISSARD, Janine. French. Born in Paris, France, 18 December 1932. Married Michael Oriano in 1954; two daughters and two sons. Free-lance writer. Recipient: *A Matter of Feeling* was selected one of New York Public Library's Books for the Teen Age, 1981,

1982; Palmes Academiques, for her young adult books. Agent: Max Becker, 115 East 82nd St., New York, NY 10028. Address: 9 rue de Villersexel, Paris 75007, France.

PUBLICATIONS FOR YOUNG ADULTS

Fiction

L'esprit de famille. Paris, Fayard, 1977; as *A Matter of Feeling,* translated by Elizabeth Walter, Boston, Little, Brown, 1980.
L'Avenir de Bernadette (title means "Bernadette's Future"). Paris, Fayard, 1978.
Claire et le bonheur. Paris, Fayard, 1979; as *Christmas Lessons,* translated by Mary Feeney, Boston, Little, Brown, 1984; as *A Question of Happiness,* New York, Ballantine, 1985.
Une femme neuve. Paris, Fayard, 1980; as *A New Woman,* translated by Mary Feeney, Boston, Little, Brown, 1982.
Moi, Pauline! Paris, Fayard, 1981; as *A Time to Choose,* translated by Mary Feeney, Boston, Little, Brown, 1985.
Les miroirs de l'ombre (title means "The Looking-Glass of Shadows"). Paris, Fayard, 1982.
Cecile, la poison (also published as *Cecile et son amour*). Paris, Fayard, 1984; as *Cecile: A Novel,* translated by Mary Feeney, Boston, Little, Brown, 1988.
Un femme reconciliee. Paris, Fayard, 1986; as *A Different Woman,* translated by Mary Feeney, Boston, Little, Brown, 1988.

Other

L'esprit de famille (television series; title means "Family Spirit"). Paris, Fayard, 1977.
Rendez-vous avec mon fils (title means "A Date with My Son"). Paris, Fayard, 1981.
Vous verrez—, vous m'aimerez (title means "You'll See, You'll Love Me"). Paris, Plon, 1987.
Croisiere. Paris, Fayard, 1988.
Les pommes d'or. Paris, Fayard, 1988.

*

Janine Boissard comments:

I always knew that I would be a writer. I don't believe that I decided to be one—it was inevitable, genetic. I am a "popular" writer, meaning one who, in simple and accessible language, speaks of reading herself, of life's joys and pains. But also one which offers to her public the possibility of dreams, of escape, without which one does not live well. A popular novel reveals at one time "us" and a projection of us.

I try to make known in my books that substantive life of which Severine speaks in *Une femme reconciliee*—to help the most people possible to find themselves, to give them hope.

Style is something different from good writing, other than the simple organization of words and the choice of those words. It is an invisible thread woven by each writer, which makes the phrase vibrate, gives to it its rhythm and secret music. That thread, for me, comes directly from the soul, from its instinct, and it is that which gives life to characters, settings, and dialogue. One does not invent a style. One has it—one is it.

*   *   *

Janine Boissard writes about love—the heaving, impetuous love that sends young heroines out into winter streets barefoot, that makes them think the street lamps have been lit just for them. But her love stories are also about families—the bonds between husbands and wives, parents and children, sisters and sisters—and the self-love that results from the struggle of coming to know one's true character through first time experiences. Originally published in France, Boissard's series of novels about the Moreau family—Dr. Charles and Mathilde, portrayed as real people with desires and disappointments of their own, and their four daughters Claire ("the Princess") Bernadette (the horsewoman), Pauline (a hopeful writer and the narrator of the first three novels), and Cecile ("the Pest")— are a rich mix of spirited family conversations and descriptions of French food, changing seasons, and ordinary things made meaningful through careful observation. Readers are likely to find the French way of life as depicted by Boissard appealing: the Moreau daughters live passionately and freely, hold strong opinions, and speak frankly about politics, religion, ethics, sex and birth control, and women's roles in families and society. The narrative style is a mixture of reflective reporting and personal confession, and the novels collectively read like one long story. As with most any series, the reader who follows the family through each book is made to feel with every reference to past events like she is in on their secrets.

Like nineteenth-century novels that have at their heart great houses that become like characters, these are built around La Marette, the family house along the Oise River in a village near Paris. One of Boissard's strongest accomplishments in these novels is the sense of place she creates at La Marette that has as much to do with the family that lives there as it does the structure itself. The Moreau sisters are friends, rivals, and mentors to each other, and the comforts represented by La Marette are both help and hindrance in varying degrees to them. Each finds adventure, independence, and adversity away from La Marette; each returns to it for celebration, refuge, and comfort. Through La Marette, Boissard successfully raises home and family above their explicit, practical functions in the lives of her characters and joins them into one idea. She draws life as a series of choices, and home and family life as the process of preparation for choice making. Family members become like rooms with mirrors reflecting consequences of choices already made and windows with a view to the future.

While the life of these novels comes from the life of La Marette and the palpable energy between family members, much of their plots are devoted to romance. In fact, they contain everything one might ridiculously imagine about French affairs: moody artists and worldly doctors wooing inexperienced young women during trysts in garrets, cafes, and mountain inns—with plenty of crepes and wine thrown in for good measure. In *A Matter of Feeling,* seventeen-year-old Pauline has her first love affair with Pierre, a forty-year-old painter of troubled seascapes. In *Christmas Lessons,* Pauline spends the holiday with her lively extended family in Burgundy, where all try to come to grips with unwed Claire's pregnancy. In *A Time to Choose,* Pauline breaks the home ties to follow her own path as a writer and pursues a famous author, whom she finally snags after running away to a Brittany island. *Cecile,* narrated by the youngest Moreau as she reaches young adulthood, ties up many of the loose ends of the now grown sisters' lives and brings the series to a forward-looking close as the family deals with the death of Dr. Moreau and recognizes the foundation that a shared past gives them in developing adult relationships with one another. It is perhaps most notable of the series because Cecile is the most interesting member of the Moreau family. By bringing her out of the background and into full life, the book speaks with a fresh voice about personal and family transition. Cecile, who has spent a lonely childhood befriending imaginary saints and real juvenile delinquents who meet untimely deaths, dives into nursing school and finds first love with an angelic, "Save the Children" doctor.

Boissard takes an easy route with her romances, providing fantasy escapes rather than first love encounters that square realistically with most young readers' experiences. If not believable, these affairs do at least capture with accuracy and feeling the intense highs and lows that a person in love might experience. And all the naivete, self-importance, rebellion, and idealism of youth is here. Boissard catches these things and uses them to color the larger self-discovery process that is a familiar theme in young adult fiction, all the while bringing it home to La Marette, where the garden gate has been left open, the walnuts are ready for shelling, and where, as Pauline says in *A Matter of Feeling:* "...you are gently greeted by the scent of polished wood, baked apples, and the heavy velvet from which curtains used to be made. And there are sounds, too— the everyday sounds of a happy house."

—Tracy J. Sukraw

BOLTON, Evelyn. See **BUNTING, Eve.**

BOND, Nancy. American. Born in Bethesda, Maryland, 8 January 1945. Educated at Mount Holyoke College, B.A. 1966; College of Librarianship, Aberystwyth, Dyfed, Wales, Dip.Lib., 1972. Correspondent in sales department, Houghton Mifflin, publishers, Boston, 1966-67; head of overseas sales publicity, Tutorial Books, Oxford University Press, London, England, 1967-68; Assistant Children's Librarian, Lincoln Public Library, Massachusetts, 1969-71; Head Librarian, Levi Heywood Memorial Library, Gardner, Massachusetts, 1973-75; administrative assistant, Massachusetts Audubon Society, Lincoln, 1976-77. Since 1979, Instructor in Children's Literature, Simmons College, Boston; since 1980, salesperson, Barrow Book Store, Concord. Director, Mount Holyoke Alumnae *Quarterly,* 1979-82. Recipient: Newbery honor, *Boston Globe-Horn Book* honor, International Reading Association and the Welsh Arts Council, all 1976, for *A String in the Harp; Boston Globe-Horn Book* honor, 1981, for *The Voyage Begun.* Address: 109 Valley Rd., Concord, MA 01742, U.S.A.

PUBLICATIONS FOR YOUNG ADULTS

Fiction

Country of Broken Stone. New York, Atheneum, 1980.
The Voyage Begun. New York, Atheneum, 1981.
A Place to Come Back To. New York, Macmillan, 1984.
Another Shore. New York, Macmillan, 1988.
Truth to Tell. New York, Macmillan, 1994.

PUBLICATIONS FOR CHILDREN

Fiction

A String in the Harp. Atheneum, 1976.
The Best of Enemies. Atheneum, 1978.

*

Biography: Entry in *Fifth Book of Junior Authors & Illustrators,* New York, H.W. Wilson, 1983; essay in *Something about the Author Autobiography Series,* Volume 13, Detroit, Gale, 1992; essay in *Speaking for Ourselves, Too* compiled and edited by Donald R. Gallo, National Council of Teachers of English, 1993.

Critical Study: Entry in *Children's Literature Review,* Volume 11, Detroit, Gale, 1986.

Nancy Bond comments:

Fiction has a unique power to connect us to people we would otherwise never meet—not only the characters in stories, but the writers who create them. Stories can make us think about ourselves, the world we share, and how it looks through someone else's eyes; they can make us feel less lonely, help us to put feelings into words and identify them. When I began to write stories I discovered that writing is a way of finding out about myself—what I think about things that matter to me, like the way families and friendships work, the responsibilities involved in loving, the challenges of accepting change, the different ways people have of solving the same problem.

*   *   *

Coping with life's changing patterns is ever constant, often difficult, and frequently, for children, especially traumatic. In her six novels to date Nancy Bond explores this nebulous theme through a variety of stories, each with different settings, individualized plots, and highly distinctive characters.

In *A String in the Harp* Bond uses the change theme as scaffolding around which she builds a strong, powerful story about a family's struggles to rebuild their lives after the mother dies in a car accident. David, the father, takes his children to Wales where they gradually learn, after many false starts and tattered feelings, to be a family again. This adjustment to a life without their mother, to each other as separate identities, and to a new and foreign place is skillfully molded into an intriguing and diverting story. Adding further dimension is a carefully threaded, gripping fantasy about the Welsh bard Taliesin's harp key, lost in the sixth century and returned, under strange and fantastical circumstances, by twelve-year-old Peter. This harp key supplies a pivotal point in the family's coming together and is Bond's means of melding her story into a cohesive whole.

The Best of Enemies uses a similar theme but one handled much differently. Charlotte, who has enjoyed being the youngest child in a close, loving Massachusetts family, finds herself facing numerous changes: her mother has gone back to work, her sister has become involved with her own problems, one of her brothers has married, and her "special brother" is pursuing his own life, leaving her behind. Unwillingly she is drawn into a community scuffle, played out against the annual Patriot's Day festivity, but through this involvement Charlotte is able to face and accept the changing pat-

terns of life. Once more Bond's theme becomes the structural beam while the plot is the brick work that holds it all together.

Set along Hadrian's Wall in England, *Country of Broken Stone* describes how Valerie and Edward's marriage forces adjustment on their newly combined families. Penelope, the protagonist, comfortable in the old, quiet, and organized life, finds the large, noisy group and her responsibilities as stepsister disquieting. Into this Bond introduces another troubling element—Ran, a local boy who arouses Penelope's curiosity and interest but whose upbringing, beliefs, and background are entirely alien to her own. Local legends with foreboding undertones, continued problems at Valerie's archaeological dig, and a frightening brushfire highlight the suspense and broaden the impact of the family dynamics, eventually testing Penelope's feelings for her entire family and Ran as well.

The Voyage Begun again explores the theme of people's reaction to change, this time on several levels. Eleven-year-old Mickey, a rebellious, feisty girl, fights against change within herself as she comes to care first for a crotchety old boatbuilder and later for sixteen-year-old Paul who befriends her. Their struggle to help the old man after his home and boat are destroyed by vandals is set in a futuristic time on Cape Cod, when the world is quickly running out of energy, a crisis Bond uses to strengthen her theme as she subtly depicts the various characters reacting to their changing environment.

In *A Place to Come Back To* Bond returns to the characters and setting of *The Best of Enemies.* Charlotte, now fifteen, once more finds her inner world in turmoil as her interest in Oliver heightens, and she finds she needs to make decisions she is not sure she is ready for.

Bond's latest novel, *Another Shore,* is set in the reconstructed village of Louisbourg, Nova Scotia. Using time travel as a vehicle, Bond propels eighteen-year-old Lynn back to 1744. Time becomes the plot's antagonist as Lynn, unable to return to the twentieth century, struggles to cope in an entirely different world.

All of these books are peopled with finely etched characters whose problems, sensitivities, joys, and successes are so succinctly defined that readers easily become involved in their lives. However, such definitive portrayals, plus the author's penchant for highly detailed descriptions, create exceptionally long books for the child reader and bring Bond her greatest criticism.

At the same time this length allows the author to distinctively place her story, thoroughly probe feelings, develop intricate, multilevelled plots, and give a depth not often found in children's books. Although some paring could be accomplished without tempering the effect, the cross-generational friendship found in *The Best of Enemies* and *The Voyage Begun* and the mixing of people from different backgrounds in *A String in the Harp* and *Country of Broken Stone* are successful partly because of this slow and careful building. Readers who take the time will come away with echoes of well-turned phrases and vivid scenes and will have found rich, imaginative tales to long remember.

—Barbara Elleman

———

BONHAM, Frank. American. Born in Los Angeles, California, 25 February 1914. Educated at Glendale Junior College, California. Served in U.S. Army, 1942-43. Married Gloria Bailey in 1938;

three sons. Self-employed writer. Ghostwriter of western stories for Ed Earl Repp during the late 1930s; contributor of approximately five hundred short stories, novels, and novelettes to magazines, including *Saturday Evening Post* serials, short stories to *McCall's, American,* and to mystery and western magazines; former director, CRASH Inc. (Community Resources And Self-Help). Recipient: Mystery Writers of America Edgar Allan Poe Award runner-up, 1964, for *Honor Bound,* 1967, for *The Mystery of the Red Tide,* 1969, for *Mystery of the Fat Cat;* a notable book citation by the American Library Association, and George C. Stone Center for Children's Book Award, 1967, for *Durango Street;* Woodward Park School Annual Book Award, 1971, for *Viva Chicano;* Southern California Council on Literature for Children and Young People prize for a "notable body of work," 1980. *Died 17 December 1989.*

PUBLICATIONS FOR YOUNG ADULTS

Fiction

Burma Rifles: A Story of Merrill's Marauders. New York, Crowell, 1960.
War beneath the Sea. New York, Crowell, 1962.
Deepwater Challenge. New York, Crowell, 1963.
Honor Bound. New York, Crowell, 1963.
The Loud, Resounding Sea. New York, Crowell, 1963.
Speedway Contender. New York, Crowell, 1964.
Durango Street. New York, Dutton, 1965.
The Mystery of the Red Tide, illustrated by Brinton Turkle. New York, Dutton, 1966.
Mystery in Little Tokyo, illustrated by Kazue Mizumura. New York, Dutton, 1966.
The Ghost Front. New York, Dutton, 1968.
Mystery of the Fat Cat, illustrated by Alvin Smith. New York, Dutton, 1968.
The Nitty Gritty, illustrated by Alvin Smith. New York, Dutton, 1968.
The Vagabundos. New York, Dutton, 1969.
Viva Chicano. New York, Dutton, 1970.
Chief. New York, Dutton, 1971.
Cool Cat. New York, Dutton, 1971.
The Friends of the Loony Lake Monster. New York, Dutton, 1972.
Hey, Big Spender! New York, Dutton, 1972.
A Dream of Ghosts. New York, Dutton, 1973.
The Golden Bees of Tulami. New York, Dutton, 1974.
The Missing Persons League. New York, Dutton, 1975.
The Rascals from Haskell's Gym. New York, Dutton, 1977.
Devilhorn. New York, Dutton, 1978.
The Forever Formula. New York, Dutton, 1979.
Gimme an H, Gimme an E, Gimme an L, Gimme a P. New York, Scribner, 1980.
Premonitions. New York, Holt, Rinehart, 1984.

Plays

Television Series: *Wells Fargo, Restless Gun, Shotgun Slade,* and *Death Valley Days.*

PUBLICATIONS FOR ADULTS

Novels

Lost Stage Valley. New York, Simon and Schuster, 1948; Kingswood, Surrey, World's Work, 1950.
Bold Passage. New York, Simon and Schuster, 1950; London, Hodder and Stoughton, 1951.
Blood on the Land. New York, Ballantine, 1952; London, Muller, 1955.
Snaketrack. New York, Simon and Schuster, 1952; as *The Outcast of Crooked River,* London, Hodder and Stoughton, 1953.
The Feud at Spanish Ford. New York, Ballantine, 1954.
Night Raid. New York, Ballantine, 1954.
Rawhide Guns. New York, Popular Library, 1955; as *Border Guns,* London, Muller, 1956.
Defiance Mountain. New York, Popular Library, 1956; London, Consul, 1962.
Hardrock. New York, Ballantine, 1958; London, Muller, 1960.
Tough Country. New York, Dell, and London, Muller, 1958.
Last Stage West. New York, Dell, and London, Muller, 1959.
The Sound of Gunfire. New York, Dell, 1959; London, Consul, 1960.
One for Sleep. New York, Fawcett, 1960; London, Muller, 1961.
The Skin Game. New York, Fawcett, 1962; London, Muller, 1963.
Trago.... New York, Dell, 1962.
By Her Own Hand. Derby, Connecticut, Monarch, 1963.
Cast a Long Shadow. New York, Simon and Schuster, 1964.
Logan's Choice. New York, Fawcett, 1964.
Break for the Border. New York, Berkley, 1980.
Fort Hogan. New York, Berkley Publishing, 1980.
The Eye of the Hunter. New York, Evans, 1989.
That Bloody Bozeman Trail-Stagecoach West. New York, Tor, 1990.

Short Stories

The Wild Breed. New York, Lion, 1955.
The Best Western Stories of Frank Bonham, edited by Bill Pronzini. Athens, Swallow Press/Ohio University Press, 1989.

*

Biography: Essay in *Something about the Author Autobiography Series,* Volume 3, Detroit, Gale, 1972; entry in *Authors and Artists for Young Adults,* Volume 1, Detroit, Gale, 1989.

Manuscript Collection: Kerlan Collection, University of Minnesota, Minneapolis.

Critical Study: Entry in *Contemporary Literary Criticism,* Volume 12, Detroit, Gale, 1980.

*   *   *

In 1965, the riots in the Watts section of Los Angeles left that area of the city in blackened ruins, reminding many people of the burned-out, bombed cities of World War II Europe. That same year, *Durango Street,* a ground-breaking young adult novel by Frank Bonham, was published. Rufus Henry, the black teenage protagonist, typified many of the youths and youth gangs existing in Los Angeles at the time of the 1965 riots. Rufus is a self-assured teenager who is paroled from a juvenile detention camp and immediately gets involved in an urban ghetto gang, the Moors. As the most clever and resourceful member, he quickly becomes the gang leader. The conflicts between the Moors and a rival gang, the Gassers, results in violence. However, a young black social worker attempts to direct the gang rivalry and activities into more constructive competition.

Much like *The Outsiders* by S.E. Hinton, another landmark young adult novel published two years later, *Durango Street* was not the typical young adult novel. Writing about a black teenager growing up and living in a ghetto was not the usual setting or model character that teenagers normally read about in the young adult books available in the early '60s. Bonham was, in part, responsible for introducing social realism into young adult fiction. Prior to this, there was very little realistic fiction being written for young adults. Most young adult books depicted the family-oriented teenager dealing with a problem or self-identity crisis. Conflicts in the earlier novels revolved around dating, cars, and teenage social life. Invariably, the main character was aided and supported by understanding middle-class parents living in a middle-class setting, and the resolution of the novel usually was a positive, happy one for the main teenage character. Rufus Henry in *Durango Street* does not fit this mold at all. He has grown up in a fatherless home, with a hardworking mother overwhelmed by the demands of parenting a teenage son. He has no father figure to turn to for guidance, and as a member of an underprivileged minority, he sees little hope for a promising future.

Like many of his novels, Bonham relied on field research to write *Durango Street,* attending the meetings of street gangs and meetings between social workers and the parents of gang members. He also visited a detention camp to observe the day-to-day life of incarcerated youths. Thus, the novel accurately depicts people and their problems in an urban slum setting that most teenagers had never before encountered in their reading. Bonham deals with the subject and characters sympathetically. He does not condemn Rufus for his actions but shows a black teenager who has the potential of escaping from poverty by developing his talents as an athlete and leader. The reader sees Rufus making the decision to complete high school and to aspire to attend college.

Bonham's earlier books for young adults were adventure tales. *Burma Rifles: A Story of Merrill's Marauders* was based on a story told to him by a police sergeant in Little Tokyo, Los Angeles. Bonham pursued the story about Japanese-American men imprisoned in an internment camp who were recruited to fight behind the enemy lines in Burma. Other adventure tales followed, including *War beneath the Sea* and *Speedway Contender,* to name a few. After the publication of *Durango Street,* he began writing mysteries aimed at a young audience—*Mystery of the Red Tide, Mystery in Little Tokyo, The Ghost Front,* and *Mystery of the Fat Cat.*

In looking at the books Bonham has written for young adults, one is struck by the many different subjects and topics he has covered—gangs, teenage suicide, auto racing, missing persons, jungle warfare. He has commented that he is a do-gooder in his books for young people. In dealing with such subjects as delinquency, he hoped his books would have a positive effect on teenager readers with personal problems. His last novel, *Gimme an H, Gimme an E, Gimme an L, Gimme a P,* published in 1980, deals with teen suicide. In writing the novel, Bonham noted that suicide is the principal cause of death among young adults, and that he hoped the novel would come to the attention of young readers with emotional problems who may have contemplated or were contemplating suicide.

Although Bonham has chosen to write about subjects that are not pleasant, his social consciousness throughout his novels is evident. He writes about significant social problems and treats them with authenticity. His background research—talking with students and counselors, exploring settings, be it an urban slum or prison—makes his novels believable to his audience. While he may be didactic, he does it with such subtlety that his young adult audience can accept it.

—Donald J. Kenney

BOSTON, L(ucy) M(aria Wood). British. Born in Southport, Lancashire, England, 10 December 1892. Educated at Downs School, Seaford, Sussex; Somerville College, Oxford. Married in 1917 (marriage dissolved 1935); one son. Author of children's books. Briefly trained as a nurse before going to France to treat the wounded during the First World War; indulged herself in the cultural arts while traveling through Europe, 1935-39; began a personal restoration project of a manor house at Hemingford Grey, which later served as a background for her books; started her literary career at the age of sixty-two. Recipient: Carnegie (commended), 1954, and Lewis Carroll Shelf Award, 1969, for *The Children of Green Knowe,* which was also named an ALA Notable Book; Carnegie (commended), 1958, for *The Chimneys of Green Knowe;* Carnegie Medal, 1961, for *A Stranger at Green Knowe,* which was also named an ALA Notable Book; *The River at Green Knowe* was named an ALA Notable Book; Spring Book Festival Awards (middle honor), 1967, for *The Sea Egg. Died 25 May 1990.*

<small>PUBLICATIONS FOR YOUNG ADULTS</small>

Fiction

The Children of Green Knowe, illustrated by son, Peter Boston. London, Faber, 1954; New York, Harcourt, 1955.
The Chimneys of Green Knowe, illustrated by P. Boston. London, Faber, 1958; as *Treasure of Green Knowe,* New York, Harcourt, 1958.
The River at Green Knowe, illustrated by P. Boston. London, Faber, and New York, Harcourt, 1959.
A Stranger at Green Knowe, illustrated by P. Boston. London, Faber, and New York, Harcourt, 1961.
An Enemy at Green Knowe, illustrated by P. Boston. London, Faber, and New York, Harcourt, 1964.
The Stones of Green Knowe, illustrated by P. Boston. London, Bodley Head, and New York, Atheneum, 1976.

<small>PUBLICATIONS FOR CHILDREN</small>

Fiction

The Castle of Yew, illustrated by Margery Gill. London, Bodley Head, and New York, Harcourt, 1965.
The Sea Egg, illustrated by P. Boston. London, Faber, and New York, Harcourt, 1967.

The House that Grew, illustrated by Caroline Hemming. London, Faber, 1969.
Nothing Said, illustrated by P. Boston. London, Faber, and New York, Harcourt, 1971.
The Guardians of the House, illustrated by P. Boston. London, Bodley Head, 1974; New York, Atheneum, 1975.
The Fossil Snake, illustrated by P. Boston. London, Bodley Head, 1975; New York, Atheneum, 1976.

PUBLICATIONS FOR ADULTS

Fiction

Yew Hall. London, Faber, 1954.
Persephone. London, Collins, 1969; as *Strongholds,* New York, Harcourt, 1969.

Plays

The Horned Man; or, Whom Will You Send to Fetch Her Away? London, Faber, 1970.

Nonfiction

Memory in a House (autobiography). London, Bodley Head, 1973; New York, Macmillan, 1974.
Perverse and Foolish: A Memoir of Childhood and Youth. London, Bodley Head, and New York, Atheneum, 1979.

*

Biography: Entry in *Third Book of Junior Authors,* New York, H.W. Wilson, 1972.

Critical Study: *Lucy Boston* by Jasper A. Rose, London, Bodley Head, 1965, New York, Walck, 1966; entry in *Children's Literature Review,* Volume 3, Detroit, Gale, 1978.

*   *   *

Lucy Boston lived an exceptionally long and active life, and she was creative in many spheres. Her achievements include a dazzling collection of masterpiece patchwork quilts and a garden of great beauty and subtlety. She did not begin to write until she was sixty.

In 1937 she bought the Manor House at Hemingford Grey and restored it. Her deep and abiding attachment to the house lit a long fuse, which later turned her into a writer in whose every work (*The Sea Egg* is the sole exception) the house appears, fictionalized as "Green Knowe." Her love of the house and its setting shines clear.

According to her own account in *Memory in a House,* Faber would have published *The Children of Green Knowe* on their adult list, alongside *Yew Hall,* her first adult novel, had Boston not wished it to be illustrated. Thus as if by accident she found her true vocation, for it was as a children's writer that she attained a worldwide reputation. In addition to an adult novel and some fine poetry, she wrote twelve children's books, moving across the past and present of her house, peopling it and giving "a local habitation and a name" to the anonymous past generations who lived there. It is worth noticing that in this enterprise, love of the house is matched by love

of children; it was their company she called up to fill the void of the past.

Jasper Rose's monograph on Lucy Boston's work (Bodley Head, 1965) is at some pains to distinguish her from other children's writers, but the truth is more interesting: together with William Mayne and Philippa Pearce, who both began to publish for children at about the same time, Lucy Boston's "Green Knowe" books caught a wave. Lucy at sixty was fully in touch with the spirit of the times, and was one of a galaxy of talented writers, exploring and mapping the possibilities of children's books as fully serious literature.

Three aspects of Lucy Boston's writing made her quintessentially a children's writer. First, the limpid clarity and simplicity of her prose which made thought of subtlety and delicacy easily accessible. Second, her total lack of condescension to young readers. "I do not know how anyone can judge of what they write, unless they are writing for themselves," she has said (*Memory in a House.*) Third, it came naturally to her as a writer to take up her stand on the large ground which adults and children have in common.

Time, change, memory—the mutability of people, and the continuity of talismanic objects were among her recurring themes. Other writers have worked with those, but she has never had her equal at evoking the physical sensations of the fleeting moment—at awakening a rapt attention to the mercurial beauties of the natural world. Speaking to the Children's Book Circle in 1968, Lucy Boston said:

> I would like to remind adults of joy, now obsolete, and I would like to encourage children to use and trust their senses for themselves at first hand—their ears, eyes and noses, their fingers and soles of their feet, their skins and their breathing, their muscular joy and rhythms and heartbeats, their instinctive loves and pity and awe of the unknown....

These words illuminate clearly what it was about children which so attracted her to writing about and for them. In the startling vividness with which tactile and sensory experience is observed and set down—in the sea-rough pebble with "a drag like a kitten's tongue," the cat's eyes that "had a vertical black slit that was like the gap between curtains," or the golden goblet made from a foil sweet paper—the experiences of the fictional children display the undimmed sharpness of the author's perceptions, the reverie of a childhood lived on into late old age.

The first of the sequence, *The Children of Green Knowe,* sets the framework of all the books. Alone in winter, visiting his grandmother, Tolly plays hide-and-seek with children who have lived there in the past. They are not ghosts, but presences. Of all the crowd of children past and present who people the books, it is Susan the blind girl, heroine of *The Chimneys of Green Knowe,* who really stands out; Lucy Boston's talent is peculiarly apt for conveying the world of a child who lacking one sense has the other senses honed razor sharp, who being a girl with an insensitive and conventional mother must struggle for any independence, any life of her own.

For besides the beauty of the natural world, at its pinnacle in her beloved house and garden, one other thing fired Lucy Boston's imagination to incandescence. That was her indignant sympathy for all subordinates, for all whose personality is assailed, whom the world is trying to pressure into being other than what they are. The majority of such embattled selves are and have always been children, though the finest example in the whole of her work is the magnificent tour de force with which she identifies with Hanno, the captive gorilla in *A Stranger at Green Knowe,* the most serious and the best of the books.

Atmosphere rather than plot is Lucy Boston's forte. The plots would be conventional or whimsical if not transformed by the intensity with which everything is imagined. It would be possible to suggest that all the children in all the books are really one child, and that child is as much a projection of the author as the eccentric and kindly Mrs. Oldknowe, the owner of the fictional house and grandmother and friend to the children, past and present. But one can only be grateful for the potent and lyrical talent which has enabled Lucy Boston to make a gift to her readers of her haunted and extraordinary house, her evocative garden, and her joyful, enhanced awareness of the natural world.

—Jill Paton Walsh

BRADBURY, Ray (Douglas). Also writes as D.R. Banat, Leonard Douglas, William Elliott, Douglas Spaulding, Leonard Spaulding, Brett Sterling. American. Born in Waukegan, Illinois, 22 August 1920. Educated at Los Angeles High School, graduated 1938. Married Marguerite Susan McClure in 1947; four daughters. Newsboy in Los Angeles, California, 1940-43. Since 1943, full-time writer. President, Science-Fantasy Writers of America, 1951-53; member of the Board of Directors, Screen Writers Guild of America, 1957-61. Recipient: O. Henry prize, 1947, for short story "Homecoming," 1948, for short story "Powerhouse"; Best Author of 1949 in Science Fiction and Fantasy from the National Fantasy Fan Federation; Benjamin Franklin award for best story of 1953-54 in an American magazine, for "Sun and Shadow" in *The Reporter;* American Academy award, 1954; Commonwealth Club of California gold medal, 1954, for *Fahrenheit 451;* award from National Institute of Arts and Letters, 1954, for contribution to American literature; *New York Times* Best Illustrated Books of the Year, 1955, and Boys' Clubs of America Junior Book award, 1956, both for *Switch on the Night;* Golden Eagle award, for screenwriting, 1957; Academy award nomination, 1963, for "Icarus Montgolfier Wright"; Mrs. Ann Radcliffe award, Count Dracula Society, 1965, 1971; Aviation and Space Writers award, 1968, for "An Impatient Gulliver above Our Roots," in *Life,* and 1979, for ABC-television documentary, "Infinite Space Beyond Apollo"; "Mars Is Heaven!" was selected for the Science Fiction Hall of Fame by the Science Fiction Writers of America, 1970; Valentine Davies award from the Writers Guild of America, West (joint winner with Philip Dunne), 1974, for work in cinema; Life Achievement award from the World Fantasy Convention, 1977; Balrog award for best poet, 1979; Gandalf award, 1980; George Foster Peabody award from the University of Georgia, Emmy nomination from the Academy of Television Arts and Sciences, and American Film Festival Blue Ribbon award, all 1982, all for "The Electric Grandmother"; Jules Verne award, 1984; Body of Work award, PEN, 1985; Home Box Office Ace award for Writing a Dramatic Series, 1985, for *Ray Bradbury Theater;* Nebula Grand Master, 1988; Bram Stoker Life achievement award, 1989. The play version of "The Martian Chronicles" won five Los Angeles Drama Critics Circle awards. D.Litt.: Whittier College, California, 1979. Agent: Don Congdon, Harold Matson Company, 276 Fifth Avenue, New York, NY 10010. Address: 10265 Cheviot Drive, Los Angeles, CA 90064, U.S.A.

PUBLICATIONS

Novels

The Martian Chronicles. New York, Doubleday, 1950; as *The Silver Locusts,* London, Hart Davis, 1951.
Fahrenheit 451. New York, Ballantine, 1953; London, Hart Davis, 1954.
Dandelion Wine. New York, Doubleday, and London, Hart Davis, 1957.
Something Wicked This Way Comes. New York, Simon and Schuster, 1962; London, Hart Davis, 1963.
Death Is a Lonely Business. New York, Knopf, 1985; London, Grafton, 1986.
A Graveyard for Lunatics: Another Tale of Two Cities. New York, Knopf, and London, Grafton, 1990.
Green Shadows, White Whale, illustrated by Edward Sorel. New York, Knopf, 1992.

Short Stories

Dark Carnival. Sauk City, Wisconsin, Arkham House, 1947; abridged edition, London, Hamish Hamilton, 1948; abridged edition, as *The Small Assassin,* London, New English Library, 1962.
The Illustrated Man. New York, Doubleday, 1951; revised edition, London, Hart Davis, 1952.
The Golden Apples of the Sun. New York, Doubleday, 1953; revised edition, London, Hart Davis, 1953.
The October Country. New York, Ballantine, 1955; London, Hart Davis, 1956.
A Medicine for Melancholy. New York, Doubleday, 1959; revised edition, as *The Day It Rained Forever,* London, Hart Davis, 1959.
The Ghoul Keepers. Ontario, Canada, Pyramid Books, 1961.
The Machineries of Joy. New York, Simon and Schuster, and London, Hart Davis, 1964.
The Autumn People (comic adaptation). New York, Ballantine, 1965.
The Vintage Bradbury. New York, Random House, 1965.
Tomorrow Midnight (comic adaptation). New York, Ballantine, 1966.
Twice Twenty-Two (selection). New York, Doubleday, 1966.
Bloch and Bradbury: Ten Masterpieces of Science Fiction, with Robert Bloch. New York, Tower, 1969; as *Fever Dreams and Other Fantasies,* London, Sphere, 1970.
I Sing the Body Electric! New York, Knopf, 1969; London, Hart Davis, 1970.
Whispers from Beyond, with Robert Bloch. New York, Peacock Press, 1972.
Ray Bradbury: Selected Stories, edited by Anthony Adams. London, Harrap, 1975.
The Best of Bradbury. New York, Bantam, 1976.
Long after Midnight. New York, Knopf, 1976; London, Hart Davis MacGibbon, 1977.
The Aqueduct. Glendale, California, Squires, 1979.
To Sing Strange Songs. Exeter, Devon, Wheaton, 1979.
The Last Circus, and The Electrocution. Northridge, California, Lord John Press, 1980.
The Stories of Ray Bradbury. New York, Knopf, and London, Granada, 1980.
Dinosaur Tales. New York, Bantam, 1983.
A Memory of Murder. New York, Dell, 1984.
The Toynbee Convector. New York, Knopf, 1988; London, Grafton, 1989.

Plays

The Meadow, in *Best One-Act Plays of 1947-48,* edited by Margaret Mayorga (produced Hollywood, 1960). New York, Dodd, Mead, 1948.

Way in the Middle of the Air (produced Hollywood, 1962).

The Anthem Sprinters and Other Antics (produced Beverly Hills, 1967; Los Angeles, 1968). New York, Dial Press, 1963.

To the Chicago Abyss (produced Los Angeles, 1964). Included in *The Wonderful Ice-Cream Suit and Other Plays,* 1972.

The World of Ray Bradbury (produced Los Angeles, 1964; New York, 1965).

The Wonderful Ice-Cream Suit (produced Los Angeles, 1965; New York, 1987). Included in *The Wonderful Ice-Cream Suit and Other Plays,* 1972.

The Day It Rained Forever, music by Bill Whitefield (produced Edinburgh, 1988). New York, French, 1966.

Leviathan 99 (radio play). British Broadcasting Corporation, 1966; (produced Los Angeles, 1972).

The Pedestrian. New York, French, 1966.

Dandelion Wine, adaptation of his own story, music by Billy Goldenberg (produced New York, 1967). Woodstock, Illinois, Dramatic Publishing, 1988.

Any Friend of Nicholas Nickleby's Is a Friend of Mine (produced Hollywood, 1968).

Christus Apollo, music by Jerry Goldsmith (produced Los Angeles, 1969).

The Wonderful Ice-Cream Suit and Other Plays (includes *The Veldt* and *To the Chicago Abyss*). New York, Bantam, 1972; as *The Wonderful Ice-Cream Suit and Other Plays for Today, Tomorrow, and Beyond Tomorrow,* London, Hart Davis, 1973.

Madrigals for the Space Age, music by Lalo Schifrin (produced Los Angeles, 1976). Associated Music Publishers, 1972.

Pillar of Fire (produced Fullerton, California, 1973). Included in *Pillar of Fire and Other Plays,* 1975.

Pillar of Fire and Other Plays for Today, Tomorrow, and Beyond Tomorrow (includes *Kaleidoscope, Pillar of Fire,* and *The Foghorn*). New York, Bantam, 1975.

The Foghorn (produced New York, 1977). Included in *Pillar of Fire and Other Plays,* 1975.

That Ghost, That Bride of Time: Excerpts from a Play-in-Progress. Glendale, California, Squires, 1976.

The Martian Chronicles, adaptation of his own stories (produced Los Angeles, 1977).

Fahrenheit 451, adaptation of his own novel (produced Los Angeles, 1979).

The Veldt (produced London, 1980). Included in *The Wonderful Ice-Cream Suit and Other Plays,* 1972; Woodstock, Illinois, Dramatic Publishing, 1988.

Forever and the Earth (radio play). Athens, Ohio, Croissant, 1984.

A Device Out of Time. Woodstock, Illinois, Dramatic Publishing, 1986.

The Flying Machine. Woodstock, Illinois, Dramatic Publishing, 1986.

Falling Upward (produced Los Angeles, 1988).

Screenplays: *It Came from Outer Space,* with David Schwartz, Universal, 1952; *The Beast from 20,000 Fathoms,* Warner Bros., 1953; *Moby Dick,* with John Huston, Warner Bros., 1956; *Icarus Montgolfier Wright,* with George Clayton Johnston, Format Films, 1961; *Picasso Summer* (as Douglas Spaulding), with Edwin Booth,

Warner Bros./Seven Arts, 1972; *Something Wicked This Way Comes,* Walt Disney, 1983.

Television Plays: *Shopping for Death,* 1956, *Design for Loving,* 1958, *Special Delivery,* 1959, *The Faith of Aaron Menefee,* 1962, and *The Life Work of Juan Diaz* (all Alfred Hitchcock Presents series); *The Marked Bullet* (*Jane Wyman's Fireside Theatre* series), 1956; *The Gift* (*Steve Canyon* series), 1958; *The Tunnel to Yesterday* (Trouble Shooters series), 1960; *I Sing the Body Electric!* (*The Twilight Zone* series), 1962; *The Jail* (*Alcoa Premiere* series), 1962; *The Groom* (*Curiosity Shop* series), 1971; *Walking on Air,* 1987; *The Coffin,* from his own story, 1988 (U.K.).

Also author of forty-two scripts for *Ray Bradbury Television Theatre,* USA Cable Network, 1985-90.

Poetry

Old Ahab's Friend, and Friend to Noah, Speaks His Piece: A Celebration. Glendale, California, Squires, 1971.

When Elephants Last in the Dooryard Bloomed: Celebrations for Almost Any Day in the Year. New York, Knopf, 1973; London, Hart Davis MacGibbon, 1975.

That Son of Richard III: A Birth Announcement. Privately printed, 1974.

Man Dead? Then God Is Slain! Northridge, California State University, 1977.

Where Robot Mice and Robot Men Run Round in Robot Towns: New Poems, Both Light and Dark. New York, Knopf, 1977; London, Hart Davis MacGibbon, 1979.

The Bike Repairman. Northridge, California, Lord John Press, 1978.

Twin Hieroglyphs That Swim the River Dust. Northridge, California, Lord John Press, 1978.

The Author Considers His Resources. Northridge, California, Lord John Press, 1979.

This Attic Where the Meadow Greens. Northridge, California, Lord John Press, 1980.

The Ghosts of Forever, illustrated by Aldo Sessa. New York, Rizzoli, 1981.

The Haunted Computer and the Android Pope. New York, Knopf, and London, Granada, 1981.

Then Is All Love? It Is, It Is! Orange County Book Society, 1981.

The Complete Poems of Ray Bradbury. New York, Ballantine, 1982.

America. Northridge, California, Lord John Press, 1983.

The Love Affair. Northridge, California, Lord John Press, 1983.

To Ireland. Northridge, California, Lord John Press, 1983.

Forever and the Earth. Athens, Ohio, Croissant, 1984.

The Last Good Kiss, illustrated by Hans Burkhardt. Northridge, California State University, 1984.

Long after Ecclesiates. Goldstein Press, 1985.

Death Has Lost Its Charm for Me. Northridge, California, Lord John Press, 1987.

A Climate of Palettes. Northridge, California, Lord John Press, 1988.

Other

Editor, *Timeless Stories for Today and Tomorrow.* New York, Bantam, 1952.

Switch on the Night (for children). New York, Pantheon, and London, Hart Davis, 1955.

Editor, *The Circus of Dr. Lao and Other Improbable Stories.* New York, Bantam, 1956.

R Is for Rocket (for children). New York, Doubleday, 1962; London, Hart Davis, 1968.

S Is for Space (for children). New York, Doubleday, 1966; London, Hart Davis, 1968.

Teacher's Guide: Science Fiction, with Lewy Olfson. New York, Bantam, 1968.

Contributor, *Three to the Highest Power: Bradbury, Oliver, Sturgeon,* edited by William F. Nolan. New York, Avon, 1968.

The Halloween Tree (for children), illustrated by Joseph Mugnaini. New York, Knopf, 1972; London, Hart Davis MacGibbon, 1973.

Mars and the Mind of Man, with Bruce Murray, Arthur C. Clarke, Walter Sullivan, and Carl Sagan. New York, Harper, 1973.

Zen and the Art of Writing, and The Joy of Writing. Santa Barbara, California, Capra Press, 1973.

The Mummies of Guanajuato, photographs by Archie Lieberman. New York, Abrams, 1978.

Beyond 1984: Remembrance of Things Future. New York, Targ, 1979.

Los Angeles, photographs by West Light. Port Washington, New York, Skyline Press, 1984.

The Art of Playboy. New York, van der Marck Editions, 1985.

Orange County, photographs by Bill Ross and others. Port Washington, New York, Skyline Press, 1985.

The April Witch (for children), with Gary Kelley. Mankato, Minnesota, Creative Education, 1987.

Fever Dream (for children), illustrated by Darrel Anderson. New York, St. Martin's, 1987.

The Foghorn (for children), illustrated by Gary Kelley. Mankato, Minnesota, Creative Education, 1987.

The Other Foot (for children), with Gary Kelley. Mankato, Minnesota, Creative Education, 1987.

The Veldt (for children), with Gary Kelley. Mankato, Minnesota, Creative Education, 1987.

Zen in the Art of Writing. Santa Barbara, California, Capra Press, 1990.

The Smile. Mankato, Minnesota, Creative Education, 1991.

Yestermorrow: Obvious Answers to Impossible Futures (essays). Santa Barbara, California, Capra Press, 1991.

Editor, *A Day in the Life of Hollywood.* San Francisco, Collins, 1992.

*

Media Adaptations: *Fahrenheit 451* (film), Universal, 1966; *The Illustrated Man* (film), Warner Bros., 1969; *The Screaming Woman* (television movie), 1972; *The Foghorn* (filmstrip and cassette), Listening Library, 1975; *Frost and Fire* (filmstrip and cassette), Listening Library, 1975; *The Illustrated Man* (filmstrip and cassette), Listening Library, 1975; *A Sound of Thunder* (filmstrip and cassette), Listening Library, 1975; *There Will Come Soft Rains* (filmstrip and cassette), Listening Library, 1975; *Usher II* (filmstrip and cassette), Listening Library, 1975; *The Veldt* (filmstrip and cassette), Listening Library, 1975; *Bradbury Reads Bradbury* (recording), Listening Library, 1976; *Fahrenheit 451* (filmstrip and cassette), Listening Library, 1976; *The Illustrated Man* (cassette), Caedmon, 1976; *The Martian Chronicles* (cassette), Caedmon, 1976; *Murderer* (television movie), Boston, WGBH-TV, 1976; *The Veldt* (videocassette), Barr, 1979; *The Martian Chronicles* (television mini-series), NBC-TV, 1980; *The Small Assassin* (cassette), Caedmon, 1981; *All Summer in a Day* (videocassette), Learning Corp., 1982; *The Electric Grandmother* (television movie, based on *I Sing the Body Electric,* co-authored by Bradbury), NBC-TV, 1982; *Quest* (videocassette), Pyramid, 1983; *Forever and the Earth* (radio drama), Croissant, 1984; *Fantastic Tales of Ray Bradbury* (cassette), Listening Library, 1986; *Zukunftsmusik* (opera, by Georgia Holof and David Mettere, based on *Fahrenheit 451),* produced Fort Wayne, Indiana, 1988; *The Visitor* (videocassette), AIMS Media, 1989. Videocassettes based on short stories by Bradbury, produced by Atlantis Films and distributed by Beacon Films include: *And So Died Riabouchinska, Coffin, The Emissary, The Fruit at the Bottom of the Bowl, Gotcha, The Man Upstairs, On the Orient North, Punishment without Crime, Skeleton, The Small Assassin, There Was an Old Woman,* and *Tyrannosaurus Rex.*

Biography: *The Ray Bradbury Companion: A Life and Career History, Photolog, and Comprehensive Checklist of Writings* (includes bibliography) by William F. Nolan, Detroit, Gale, 1975; entry in *Dictionary of Literary Biography,* Detroit, Gale, Volume 2, 1978; Volume 8, 1981; *Ray Bradbury* by Wayne L. Johnson, New York, Ungar, 1980; *Ray Bradbury* by David Morgen, Boston, Massachusetts, Twayne, 1986.

Bibliography: *Ray Bradbury* (includes bibliography) edited by Joseph D. Olander and Martin H. Greenberg, New York, Taplinger, and Edinburgh, Harris, 1980.

Critical Study: introduction by Gilbert Highet to *The Vintage Bradbury,* 1965; entry in *Contemporary Literary Criticism,* Detroit, Gale, Volume 1, 1973; Volume 3, 1975; Volume 10, 1979; Volume 15, 1980; Volume 42, 1987; *The Drama of Ray Bradbury* by Ben F. Indick, Baltimore, T-K Graphics, 1977; *The Bradbury Chronicles* by George Edgar Slusser, San Bernardino, California, Borgo Press, 1977; *Ray Bradbury and the Poetics of Reverie: Fantasy, Science Fiction, and the Reader* by William F. Toupence, Ann Arbor, UMI Research Press, 1984.

*   *   *

When asked how he would liked to be remembered by future generations, Ray Bradbury once replied "as a magician of ideas and words." Indeed, Bradbury is such a magician, and he is one of the twentieth century's most important storytellers and allegorists. An author who writes from personal experience and cultural inheritance, who relies on the history of ideas and free word association, and who threw his first million words away, Bradbury has proven himself a warlock of words and a teller of universal tales that incorporate myths, beliefs, themes, rituals, and character types that define both American and world cultures.

Bradbury's short stories, novels, stage plays, screen plays, poems, and radio plays appeal to all ages, and his dexterity with issues of youth and age, and coming-of-age, make his writing significant and meaningful to a wide-ranging public. He has always drawn heavily from his personal experience, making autobiography the largest overriding thematic element of his work. Bradbury is a visionary who is sensitive to the emotions and idiosyncrasies and wonders that comprise the human experience. If at times the logic of his stories is suspect, his ability to solve the human equation makes these logistic errors insignificant.

Bradbury's first professional sale, entitled "Pendulum," was co-authored with Henry Hasse and appeared in the November 1941 issue of *Super Science Stories.* Bradbury, however, had had a variety of short stories published in science fiction and fantasy fanzines as early as January 1938. By the mid-1940s, Bradbury was regularly appearing in several "pulp" magazines.

Some of his early contributions to *Weird Tales* and other such periodicals were the beginnings of his first major story type and thematic device: these were stories of the "Dark Carnival." In these tales, Bradbury used the travelling carnival as a metaphor for life. His first published book, a collection of "Dark Carnival" stories, weird tales, and others, was published in 1947 and reappeared in 1955 as *The October Country.* By 1962, several of the themes and ideas from the "Dark Carnival" stories were adapted, synthesized, and expanded into the novel *Something Wicked This Way Comes.* Ultimately, four Bradbury short-story collections have been framed by the "Dark Carnival" mythos. Between and beyond *Dark Carnival* and *The October Country,* there were *The Illustrated Man* and *The Small Assassin.* Bradbury published a second "Dark Carnival" novel, *Death Is a Lonely Business,* in 1985.

The genres and related story types that Ray Bradbury has created and contributed to since those early "pulp" days are numerous. A representative list includes the "Dark Carnival" stories, gothic tales, weird tales, dark fantasy, weird menace, detective fiction, and science fiction. Bradbury not only writes genre fiction, he crosses between genres, and even ignores such categorization all together. For example, *Fahrenheit 451* and *Dandelion Wine* fall neatly into no specific genres. *Fahrenheit 451* is a futuristic novel dependent neither on science fiction, fact, nor horror fiction for its ultimate message. It is influenced by George Orwell's *1984* but is uniquely Bradbury. Its author claims that like Orwell's novel, *Fahrenheit 451* was designed to prevent a potential future, not predict one. *Dandelion Wine* likewise is a beautiful, brilliant novel, but really does not fit any one specific genre classification.

The subjects and social issues addressed in the fiction of Ray Bradbury are some of the most poignant and profound of the human experience. Here are found detailed discussions of religions of various sorts, youth, age, death and dying, nature and the environment, life and living, family and friends, race, gender, love, sex, eros, the rural community, a variety of geographical locales, and much more. The episodic novel *The Martian Chronicles* among other things, is best appreciated as an environmental allegory. In the 1940s and early 1950s, Bradbury was writing intelligent, insightful stories about ethnicity and race relations and about issues of gender long before such stories became fashionable. Stories like "The Big Black and White Game" and "The Other Foot" told more about racial harmony than many things before or since; stories like "I'll Not Look for Wine" and "Cora and the Great Wide World" featured women with great stamina and independence and individual identity.

This only begins to survey Bradbury's prose. It should be noted that Bradbury's best novels are episodic (i.e. they are a carefully woven series of short stories). In terms of poetry, Bradbury has published four major volumes. These include: *When Elephants Last in the Dooryard Bloomed, Where Robot Mice and Robot Men Run Round in Robot Towns, The Haunted Computer and the Android Pope,* and *The Complete Poems of Ray Bradbury.* In addition, Bradbury has written stage plays and motion picture screenplays. In the 1950s, Bradbury stories were adapted for several comic-

book series. From the late 1980s through 1990, Bradbury himself adapted his stories for "The Ray Bradbury Theater" television series.

Ray Bradbury's most recent short-story collection, *The Toynbee Convector,* is as fine a collection as he has ever done and his most recent novel (again episodic in organization), the fictionalized autobiography *Green Shadows, White Whale,* is considered one of his finest. The novel recounts Bradbury's experiences with famed movie director and mogul John Huston, and the making of the movie *Moby Dick* (which Bradbury scripted), in the mid-1950s. Like Mark Twain, Ray Bradbury's appeal is universal; it transcends all generations and is timeless. Many young adults will not only find the author's works quite realistic, but will rank him as among the best storytellers of science fiction and fantasy.

—Garyn G. Roberts

———

BRADLEY, Marion Zimmer. Has also written as Lee Chapman, John Dexter, Miriam Gardner, Valerie Graves, Morgan Ives, and Elfrida Rivers. American. Born in Albany, New York, 3 June 1930. Educated at New York State College for Teachers, 1946-48; Hardin-Simmons University, Abilene, Texas. B.A. in English, Spanish, Psychology 1964; University of California, Berkeley. Married 1) Robert A. Bradley in 1949 (divorced 1964); one son; 2) Walter Henry Breen in 1964 (divorced 1990); one son and one daughter. Editor, *Marion Zimmer Bradley's Fantasy Magazine,* since 1988. Singer and writer. Recipient: Invisible Little Man award, 1977; Leigh Brackett Memorial Sense of Wonder award, 1978, for *The Forbidden Tower; Locus* award, 1984, for best fantasy novel, for *The Mists of Avalon.* Agent: Scovil Chichak Galen Literary Agency, 381 Park Avenue South, New York, NY 10016, U.S.A.

PUBLICATIONS FOR YOUNG ADULTS

Fiction

The Door Through Space. New York, Ace, 1961; London, Arrow, 1979.
Seven from the Stars. New York, Ace, 1962.
Falcons of Narabedla. New York, Ace, 1964.
The Brass Dragon. New York, Ace, 1969; London, Methuen, 1978.
Hunters of the Red Moon. New York, DAW, 1973; London, Arrow, 1979.
Endless Voyage. New York, Ace, 1975; revised edition, as *Endless Universe,* 1979.
The Ruins of Isis. Norfolk, Virginia, Donning, 1978; London, Arrow, 1980.
The Survivors, with Paul Edwin Zimmer. New York, DAW, 1979; London, Arrow, 1985.
The House between the Worlds. New York, Doubleday, 1980.
Survey Ship. New York, Ace, 1980.
Web of Light. Norfolk, Virginia, Donning, 1982.
The Mists of Avalon. New York, Knopf, and London, Joseph, 1983.
The Inheritor. New York, Tor, 1984.
Web of Darkness. New York, Pocket Books, 1984; Glasgow, Drew, 1985.

Night's Daughter. New York, Ballantine, and London, Inner Circle, 1985.

Warrior Woman. New York, DAW, 1985; London, Arrow, 1987.

The Fall of Atlantis (contains *Web of Light* and *Web of Darkness*). Riverdale, New York, Baen Books, 1987.

"Darkover" series:

The Sword of Aldones [and] *The Planet Savers.* New York, Ace, 1962; London, Arrow, 2 vols., 1979.

The Bloody Sun. New York, Ace, 1964; London, Arrow, 1978.

Star of Danger. New York, Ace, 1965; London, Arrow, 1978.

The Winds of Darkover. New York, Ace, 1970; London, Arrow, 1978.

The World Wreckers. New York, Ace, 1971; London, Arrow, 1979.

Darkover Landfall. New York, DAW, 1972; London, Arrow, 1978.

The Spell Sword. New York, DAW, 1974; London, Arrow, 1978.

The Heritage of Hastur. New York, DAW, 1975; London, Arrow, 1979.

The Shattered Chain. New York, DAW, 1976; London, Arrow, 1978.

The Forbidden Tower. New York, DAW, 1977; London, Prior, 1979.

Stormqueen. New York, DAW, 1978; London, Arrow, 1980.

Two to Conquer. New York, DAW, 1980; London, Arrow, 1982.

Sharra's Exile. New York, DAW, 1981; London, Arrow, 1983.

Children of Hastur (includes *The Heritage of Hastur* and *Sharra's Exile*). New York, Doubleday, 1981.

Hawkmistress. New York, DAW, 1982; London, Arrow, 1985.

Oath of the Renunciates (includes *The Shattered Chain* and *Thendara House*). New York, Doubleday, 1983.

Thendara House. New York, DAW, 1983; London, Arrow, 1985.

City of Sorcery. New York, DAW, 1984; London, Arrow, 1986.

The Heirs of Hammerfell. New York, DAW, 1989.

Rediscovery, with Mercedes Lackey. New York, DAW, 1993.

Short Stories

The Dark Intruder and Other Stories. New York, Ace, 1964.

The Jewel of Arwen. Baltimore, T-K Graphics, 1974.

The Parting of Arwen. Baltimore, T-K Graphics, 1974.

Lythande, with Vonda McIntyre. New York, DAW, 1986.

The Best of Marion Zimmer Bradley, edited by Martin H. Greenberg. New York, DAW, 1988.

Jamie & Other Stories: The Best of Marion Zimmer Bradley. Illinois, Academy Chicago Publishers, 1993.

PUBLICATIONS FOR CHILDREN

Fiction

The Colors of Space. Derby, Connecticut, Monarch, 1963.

PUBLICATIONS FOR ADULTS

Novels

Castle Terror. New York, Lancer, 1965.

Souvenir of Monique. New York, Ace, 1967.

Bluebeard's Daughter. New York, Lancer, 1968.

Dark Satanic. New York, Berkley, 1972.

In the Steps of the Master (novelization of TV play). New York, Grosset and Dunlap, 1973.

Can Ellen Be Saved? (novelization of TV play). New York, Grosset & Dunlap, 1975.

Drums of Darkness. New York, Ballantine, 1976.

The Catch Trap. New York, Ballantine, 1979; London, Sphere, 1986.

The Firebrand. New York, Simon & Schuster, 1987; London, Joseph, 1988.

Black Trillium, with Julian May and Andre Norton. New York, Doubleday, 1990; London, Grafton, 1991.

Other

The Rivendell Suite. Privately printed, 1969.

A Complete Cumulative Checklist of Lesbian, Variant, and Homosexual Fiction. Privately printed, 1960.

Translator, *El Villano en su Ricon,* by Lope de Vega. Privately printed, 1971.

Men, Halflings, and Hero-Worship. Baltimore, T-K Graphics, 1973.

The Necessity for Beauty: Robert W. Chambers and the Romantic Tradition. Baltimore, T-K Graphics, 1974.

Contributor, *Essays Lovecraftian,* edited by Darrell Schweitzer. Baltimore, T-K Graphics, 1976.

Experiment Perilous: Three Essays in Science Fiction, with Alfred Bester and Norman Spinrad. Brooklyn, New York, Algol Press, 1976.

Editor and contributor, *Legends of Hastur and Cassilda.* Thendara House Publications, 1979.

Editor, *The Keeper's Price.* New York, DAW, 1980.

Editor and contributor, *Tales of the Free Amazons.* Thendara House Publications, 1980.

Editor, *Sword of Chaos.* New York, DAW, 1982.

Editor, *Greyhaven.* New York, DAW, 1983.

Editor, *Sword and Sorceress 1-10.* New York, DAW, 1984-93; vols. 1-5 published London, Headline, 1988-93.

Editor, *Free Amazons of Darkover.* New York, DAW, 1985.

Editor, *Other Side of the Mirror.* New York, DAW, 1987.

Editor, *Red Sun of Darkover.* New York, DAW, 1987.

Editor, *Four Moons of Darkover.* New York, DAW, 1988.

Editor, *Domains of Darkover.* New York, DAW, 1990.

Editor, *Leroni of Darkover.* New York, DAW, 1991.

Editor, *Renunciates of Darkover.* New York, DAW, 1991.

Editor, *Towers of Darkover.* New York, DAW, 1993.

*

Bibliography: *Leigh Brackett, Marion Zimmer Bradley, Anne McCaffrey: A Primary and Secondary Bibliography* by Rosemarie Arbur, Boston, Hall, 1982.

Biography: Entry in *Dictionary of Literary Biograpy,* Volume 8: *Twentieth-Century American Science Fiction Writers,* Detroit, Gale, 1981.

Manuscript Collection: Boston University.

Critical Study: *The Gemini Problem: A Study in Darkover* by Walter Breen, Baltimore, T-K Graphics, 1975; *The Darkover Dilemma: Problems of the Darkover Series* by S. Wise, Baltimore, T-K Graphics, 1976.

As long as inheritance is both desirable and frightful, and adolescence is a terrifying time of crisis and loss of control, the work of Marion Zimmer Bradley will have appeal for young adults. This prolific author often deals with these themes in her novels, particularly the "Darkover" series. Although her work is uneven, it is frequently powerful. The treatment of feminist themes makes her science fiction especially appealing to young women, but strong male characters make it universally accessible.

The "Darkover" novels have proven so popular that other writers, some former fans, have been eager to carry on the series while Bradley has moved on. Part of the appeal has surely been the creation of a world in which the most frightening aspects of the teen years are embodied in such a graphic style. The Darkovians are both blessed and cursed by "laran," a talent which bestows psychic gifts. At adolescence, the onset of power is accompanied by horrifying, uncontrolled manifestations of the talented child's future abilities. Fires, storms, and death are the result of this psychic mayhem before older members of society teach the newly talented to control their talents and emotions. Those without "laran" may feel themselves to be outcast by society, lacking in some essential element of a complete person, or simply at the mercy of those who manifest talent. Terran visitors to the planet create other tensions— should Darkovian society embrace the technology of the outsiders? Will they be at the mercy of their guests if they do so, or will the Terrans deny them technological advantages in order to control the balance of power? In addition, the inheritance of the gift of laran, which is a genetic trait, adds other complications. Breeding for laran has led to both undesirable mutations and a society which is harshly repressive to women. Questions of both feminine independence and male-female relationships are explored against this background.

Most recently, Bradley has become interested in the reinterpretation of myth and legend from the female or even feminist point of view. Her first work in this vein, *The Mists of Avalon* is undoubtedly her masterpiece. It is a brilliantly reimagined treatment of the Arthurian legend told from the perspectives of the various women involved, notably Arthur's sister Morgaine. Seen from this vantage, the Matter of Britain becomes the conflict between the old religion of the Goddess and the new Christian belief—a conflict that is mirrored in the land and the people, most especially in the relationships between men and women. Both the prose style and the character development are sustained to a degree rarely reached in her other work. Her descriptions of the British landscape, both as lovingly and reverently seen by Morgaine and as fearfully perceived by Gwenhyfar, are powerful evocations. She effectively captures individual and recognizable voices for Igraine, Viviane, Morgaine, and Gwenhyfar, and uses them to skillfully portray the changing philosophical and emotional climate. The male characters, although not the focus of this retelling, have believable and complex motivations. Perhaps the most triumphant success of the novel is the remarkable degree to which these stock characters, trapped in their foreordained fates, have been given independent spirit and free will. Despite these virtues, *The Mists of Avalon* is a less successful book for young adults. This is at least due in part to the fact that the narrative voice is largely given over to adult characters. Their concerns are the concerns of adulthood: aging and self-realization, relationships with children, preservation of culture and society. These are notoriously unimportant concerns to the teenaged audience. However, the novel will be a valuable reading experience for the mature reader and is likely to be one that can be returned to in later years with pleasure.

The Firebrand attempts the same kind of reimagining with the Trojan War. Again, the female characters are the focus of attention, with Kassandra providing the major viewpoint. For whatever reason, whether a failure of the modern reader to find this myth as compelling as the Arthurian legend, or the author's lack of conviction, this novel fails to create the vital tension that made *Mists* so compelling. Both the characters and the plot fail to take on the spark of life.

Most recently, Bradley has published *Black Trillium,* a collaboration with Andre Norton and Julian May. Although the premise is promising—three heroines undertake a quest, each according to her abilities—the novel fails to come together satisfactorily. The characters never find their own voices, and somehow the plot threads do not converge smoothly. Despite these flaws, the presence of the names of three of science fiction's grande dames on the cover (all with a strong appeal to young adults) is sure to make this a viable title for years.

—Cathy Chauvette

———

BRANCATO, Robin F(idler). American. Born in Reading, Pennsylvania, 19 March 1936. Educated at University of Pennsylvania, B.A. 1958; City College of the City University of New York, M.A. 1976. Married John J. Brancato in 1960; two sons. Copy editor, John Wiley & Sons, New York City, 1959-61; teacher of English, journalism, and creative writing, Hackensack High School, Hackensack, New Jersey, 1967-79, 1985, part-time teacher, 1979-84; currently teaching in Teaneck, New Jersey. Writer in residence, Kean College of New Jersey, about 1985. Recipient: American Library Association Best Book award, 1977, for *Winning,* 1980, for *Come Alive at 505,* and 1982, for *Sweet Bells Jangled out of Tune.* Lives in Teaneck, New Jersey.

PUBLICATIONS FOR YOUNG ADULTS

Fiction

Don't Sit under the Apple Tree. New York, Knopf, 1975.
Something Left to Lose. New York, Knopf, 1976.
Winning. New York, Knopf, 1977.
Blinded by the Light. New York, Knopf, 1978.
Come Alive at 505. New York, Knopf, 1980.
Sweet Bells Jangled out of Tune. New York, Knopf, 1980.
Facing Up. New York, Knopf, 1984.
Uneasy Money. New York, Knopf, 1986.

Also contributor of short stories to *Sixteen,* edited by Donald Gallo, Dell, 1984, and *Connections,* edited by Gallo, Dell, 1989; contributor of one-act play to *Centerstage,* edited by Gallo, HarperCollins, 1990.

*

Media Adaptations: *Blinded by the Light* was made into a television "Movie of the Week" for the Columbia Broadcasting System (CBS), December 1980.

Biography: Entry in *Speaking for Ourselves: Autobiographical Sketches by Notable Authors of Books for Young Adults* edited and compiled by Donald R. Gallo, National Council of Teachers of English, 1990; essay in *Something about the Author Autobiography Series,* Volume 9, Detroit, Gale, 1990; essay in *Authors and Artists for Young Adults,* Volume 9, Detroit, Gale, 1992.

Critical Study: *Contemporary Literary Criticism,* Volume 35, Detroit, Gale, 1985.

*   *   *

Brancato's first two novels, which are set in Pennsylvania where the author grew up, have young female protagonists and explore some of her remembered childhood experiences. In *Don't Sit under the Apple Tree,* twelve-year-old tomboy Mary Ellis Carpenter faces a changing relationship with her closest friend, a boy named Jules, and suffers pangs of an unrelenting conscience. Set in 1945, the war permeates this novel, particularly when the friends hear that Jules' brother has been killed. Mary Ellis also learns an important lesson from her grandmother: that it is okay to enjoy life after a loved one passes away. Reviewers praised the novel for its humor and sensitivity.

Something Left to Lose fictionalizes the events leading up to Brancato's move away from her childhood home. The novel explores the bonds between Jane Ann, Rebbie, and Lydia—three ninth-grade friends with distinct personalities and problems. Overweight Rebbie resents her mother's alcoholism and strikes out by taking risks and pulling pranks. However, she also relies on her horoscope, an indication that she is looking for outside guidance. Jane Ann, the main character, is torn between following Rebbie's adventurous leadership or holding to the standards of her more stable family. Lydia seems to be the perfect daughter. Their friendship is tested several times—when Rebbie's father dies of a heart attack, and when Jane Ann must move away after her father is promoted—but the girls vow to remain friends. Critics praised the novel for showing that every adolescent faces difficult problems in his or her own way.

Other Brancato novels deal with hard-hitting, contemporary issues and are based on the author's observations and research. In *Winning,* Gary Madden, a high school senior and former football star, learns to cope with paralysis after an injury. He moves from contemplating suicide to accepting his condition through the help of his English teacher, who is grieving over the recent loss of her husband. Brancato was inspired to write the novel when her sons began playing football. It involved meticulous research into medical rehabilitation. Reviewers praised the novel for raising a difficult issue without becoming overly sentimental.

Facing Up details the overwhelming guilt junior Dave Jacoby feels over the death of Jep, his best friend. After Jep discovers that Dave has dated Jep's girl behind his back, Dave unintentionally wrecks the car they are in and Jep dies. Though he is ruled blameless in the accident, Dave cannot forgive himself. He withdraws, flees, and briefly contemplates suicide, but finally realizes, with the help of friends, that the memories will haunt him but that he can cope. This effort was less favorably received than other Brancato novels.

Sweet Bells Jangled out of Tune builds young readers' empathy for the plight of the homeless. Fifteen-year-old Ellen Dohrmann learns to accept responsibility for her once beautiful, wealthy grandmother Eva, who gave her pleasant childhood memories. Now se-nile, Eva wears an old fur cape in the summer; collects items from garbage and tips left on restaurant tables; and lives in a dilapidated fire hazard. Ellen realizes that her grandmother suffers from a treatable psychological problem and intervenes, but later feels guilty over her difficult decision—tricking Eva to sign herself into a psychiatric ward. The novel was widely praised by critics for its honest portrayal of the problems faced by street people.

Based on extensive research including a first-hand visit to a religious cult, *Blinded by the Light* reveals Brancato's concern about the brainwashing of cult followers. Gail Brower, a college freshman, tries to rescue her brother Jim from the Light of the World (L.O.W.) cult. When she visits him, however, she is never left alone, is caught up in the chants, and is almost sucked into the cult. Her friend Doug rescues her just in time, but her brother remains a member. Readers can gain insight into cults, their leaders, and techniques used to recruit and retain followers. Brancato's work gained much attention because of its timely subject matter and was adapted for television.

Two later Brancato novels deal with less traumatic problems. *Come Alive at 505* reflects Brancato's interest in radio and the idea that boys, as well as girls, fall in love. Denny, the protagonist, explores his interest in being a disc jockey and must decide whether to work or go to college. Critics predicted the book would particularly appeal to media-crazed teens. In *Uneasy Money,* eighteen-year-old Mike Bronti does what others only dream about: he wins two million dollars in a lottery. Mike spends recklessly until his allotment for the first year is almost gone. At that point he and a friend go through all the letters asking for money and decide to help a woman needing a wheelchair. Though relatively lighthearted, the book places an adolescent into a situation where he must learn to handle a difficult challenge.

Brancato is also the author of short fiction dealing with adolescents and their problems. Her short story "Fourth of July" provides a test of values as Chuck, whose friend has stolen money from him, resists a strong impulse to get full revenge. In her short story "White Chocolate," Wally, the son of mixed races, feels anger and clashes with his English teacher. "The War of Words," a one-act play, pits two groups, the Notes and the Grunts, against each other. The Notes use rhyming language and look down on the Grunts. As a test, the two groups have a poetry contest; the audience serves as a judge. This work reflects Brancato's background as a teacher and seems designed for a class.

Brancato's works offer young adults a chance to gain vicarious experiences while identifying with real problems. Rather than protecting young readers from adversity, Brancato teaches them about their own capacity for dealing with difficult issues. Her works often raise questions—but intentionally do not always provide answers—in order to encourage readers to think for themselves. However, her fiction also offers hope and shows the value of friendship.

—Edna Earl Edwards

———

BRANSCUM, Robbie. American. Born in Big Flat, Arkansas, 17 June 1937. Married 1) Duane Branscum in 1952 (divorced 1969); 2) Lesli J. Carrico in 1975 (divorced), one daughter. Recipient: Friends of American Writers Award, 1977, for *Toby, Granny and George;* outstanding book of the year citations, *New York Times,*

1977, for *The Saving of P.S.,* 1978, for *To the Tune of a Hickory Stick,* and 1982, for *The Murder of Hound Dog Bates: A Novel;* "Best of the Best 1966-1978," *School Library Journal* in 1979, for *Johnny May;* Edgar Allan Poe Award, 1983, for *The Murder of Hound Dog Bates: A Novel.* Address: PO Box 629, Lucerne, CA 95458, U.S.A.

PUBLICATIONS FOR YOUNG ADULTS

Fiction

Me and Jim Luke. Garden City, Doubleday, 1971.
Johnny May. Garden City, Doubleday, 1975.
The Three Wars of Billy Joe Treat. New York, McGraw, 1975.
Toby, Granny, and George, illustrated by Glen Rounds. Garden City, Doubleday, 1976.
The Saving of P.S. Garden City, Doubleday, 1977.
Three Buckets of Daylight. New York, Lothrop, 1978.
To the Tune of a Hickory Stick. Garden City, Doubleday, 1978.
The Ugliest Boy, illustrated by Michael Eagle. New York, Lothrop, 1978.
For Love of Jody, illustrated by Allen Davis. New York, Lothrop, 1979.
Toby Alone. Garden City, Doubleday, 1979.
Toby and Johnny Joe. Garden City, Doubleday, 1979.
The Murder of Hound Dog Bates: A Novel. New York, Viking, 1982.
Cheater and Flitter Dick: A Novel. New York, Viking, 1983.
Spud Tackett and the Angel of Doom. New York, Viking, 1983.
The Adventures of Johnny May, illustrated by Deborah Howland. New York, Harper, 1984.
The Girl. New York, Harper, 1986.
Johnny May Grows Up, illustrated by Bob Marstall. New York, Harper, 1987.
Cameo Rose. Cambridge, Massachusetts, Harper, 1989.
Old Blue Tilley. New York, Macmillan, 1991.

*

Biography: Essay in *Speaking for Ourselves: Autobiographical Sketches by Notable Authors of Books for Young Adults,* Volume 1, compiled and edited by Donald R. Gallo, National Council of Teachers of English, 1990; essay in *Something about the Author Autobiographical Series,* Volume 17, Detroit, Gale, 1994.

Robbie Branscum comments:

I think like a lot of writers, I write about young adults for adults to read also.

I know about the world of young adults because I live in it and understand them, I know where they are coming from and they know I know it, even though I write about a way of life that's no longer here.

Maybe the world I write about is gone, but young adults and children are the same. I don't write or talk down to them, I give them credit for knowing a lot of things I don't. I think my love for them shows in my books and I also have many adult fans—my oldest one is ninety-eight and is a school teacher from Arkansas.

I write laying flat on the floor with my dog Toby for company. I write about how things were when I was growing up and hope my young friends enjoy reading it as much as I do writing it. The hardest book I have ever written is *The Girl,* about child abuse and from the letters I received from young fans, I found I was far from alone, it's very sad but true.

I hope to bring a moment of joy to my young friends. God bless them all.

*   *   *

Robbie Branscum is a prolific author whose novels weave intricate patterns of love and hope, good and evil, pain and poverty, and faith and fellowship deep in the Arkansas hills where she grew up. Her success as an author is rooted in her fascination with words, her love of books and people, and her ability to translate the experiences of her youth into stories that speak vividly and candidly to her readers. She cannot recall a time when she could not read, and she remembers reading voraciously from the three crates of books that were in the one-room school she attended for seven years. Through her writing, she strives to give her readers the pleasures she found in books as she was growing up.

Branscum was four when her father died, and her mother left Robbie and her siblings with their grandparents on their small farm while she went to the city to earn a living. Both the joys and the adversities of Branscum's early years resonate in the inherent drama of her protagonists in such books as *Johnny May, Toby, Granny, and George, Three Buckets of Daylight, The Murder of Hound Dog Bates,* and *The Girl* who, left with other relatives by an absent mother, struggle to survive and to find confirmation and identity. The relatives may be grandparents, aunts, or uncles, and the circumstances can vary widely. For example, both Johnny May and Toby (her granny had named her October, her birth month) find love and happiness as they mature in the sequels to those initial novels. In stark contrast is the plight of "the girl" who, by never being named, becomes a symbolic victim of greed and abuse.

Child abuse is a significant plot element in *Toby, Granny, and George,* but its impact in *The Girl* makes this study of physical and psychological intimidation one of Branscum's strongest examples of realistic fiction. The girl's great-grandmother, Granny, nurtures the children as they dream of escaping their oppressive environment as soon as their mother returns. After Granny dies, the girl's brother Gene rescues her from their lecherous uncle's assault and forces him to leave the farm. When their mother does return, it is not to take the children away but to announce that she has married again and that they have a new half sister and brother. When their mother leaves, Gene reassures the distraught girl that, as Granny had said, it won't be long before they are grown up and free. Mystery and intrigue are familiar ingredients in Branscum's fiction. In her first novel, *Me and Jim Luke,* Sammy John and Jim Luke discover a body in a hollow tree one night while possum hunting, which leads them on an adventure that involves the Ku Klux Klan. While this opening is based on her grandfather's account of finding a dead revenuer, the fast-paced adventure that follows is the product of Branscum's rich imagination. Branscum's mysteries are often laced with a measure of humor, as in *The Murder of Hound Dog Bates* wherein Sassafras Bates is convinced that one of his guardian aunts has poisoned his dog and sets out to prove it, unaware of where his detective work will take him. In *Toby, Granny, and George* the mysterious drownings of Minnie Lou Jackson and Deacon Treat in the church's baptizing hole give Toby great concern for Preacher Davis, who is suspect in both cases. With Granny's help, Toby not only discovers the truth about these deaths but also learns who her mother is.

A baptizing hole figures also in *Three Buckets of Daylight,* but here it is the ghostly old house in a dark hollow that commands the attention of Jackie Lee and Jimmy Jay as they discover a link between a local moonshining operation and the three witchy Blackgrove sisters, one of whom puts a curse on the boys. Jackie Lee pines for his mother, but his grandparents remind him that times are hard and that his mother is a long way off. His insecurity dissipates when he is liberated from the curse and freed of unknown fear. In *The Adventures of Johnny May* Johnny May, who is convinced she has witnessed a murder in the woods, learns that things are not always what they seem and that she and her grandparents are free to experience a joyous Christmas. In *Cameo Rose* Branscum's protagonist lives with her grandfather who is the local sheriff (her parents were killed in a car wreck), and when a man is murdered Cameo sets out to find the murderer, not realizing that she and her grandpa would be threatened also. Cameo Rose, like Johnny May and Toby, is resourceful and independent as she unravels the mysterious events.

Ministers play significant roles in many of Branscum's novels. Preacher Davis in the Toby series is a special ally to Granny in the neighborhood controversies, and his moral leadership is especially important to Toby. In a rare plot switch in *The Saving of P.S.,* Priscilla Sue lives with her widowed minister father who courts and marries a widow who has recently moved to town. Loyal to her mother's memory, P.S. runs away with their smelly old dog Brimstone. Her odyssey helps her put things into perspective so she can return home and accept her father's newfound happiness. Branscum portrays a negative side of religion in *Spud Tackett and the Angel of Doom* when during World War II a strange preacher comes to town with a scheme of salvation that Spud's grandma knows is pure fraud and declares it openly to thwart this false angel's plan. However, in *Old Blue Tilley,* set on the eve of World War II, young Hambone paints an engaging portrait of the circuit rider he has lived with since his parents died. Reminiscent of Preacher Davis in the Toby series, Blue Tilley is a strong man who lives his faith and is willing to fight for values important to his flock and to a teenage boy struggling to put his own life into perspective.

Branscum's novels of rural life in Arkansas are rich in the language, customs, and lore of the hill country Branscum knows so well. The dialect of her characters and their patterns of behavior frame a way of life that is unique for most of today's young adult readers who would benefit from reading of varying lifestyles. In her rural settings, animals such as Toby's hound dog George, Priscilla Sue's old dog Brimstone in *The Saving of P.S.,* and Cheater's pet rooster Flitter Dick in *Cheater and Flitter Dick,* add a special dimension to Branscum's stories.

Without question Robbie Branscum is a gifted storyteller whose narratives present authentic characters in unique settings. Her protagonists move toward independence and fulfillment in an atmosphere where individualism is strong but so are families and community. It is not surprising that Branscum's novels are beginning to draw the attention of filmmakers and that she is gaining a new audience in Great Britain where her books are now beginning to be published.

—Hugh Agee

BRIDGERS, Sue Ellen. American. Born in Greenville, North Carolina, 20 September 1942. Educated at East Carolina University, Greenville, 1960-63; Western Carolina University, Cullowhee, North Carolina, 1974-76, B.A. (summa cum laude) 1976. Married Ben Oshel Bridgers in 1963; two daughters and one son. Since 1970, writer. Member of board of directors for the North Carolina Center for Public TV, Chapel Hill, North Carolina, since 1984; the Jackson County Library, Sylva, North Carolina, since 1985; and the North Carolina Humanities Council, since 1990. Recipient: Breadloaf Writers' Conference fellowship, 1976; *Boston Globe-Horn Book* award for fiction, Christopher award, named to American Library Association list of best books for young adults, all 1979, and American Book award nomination, 1981, all for *All Together Now;* American Book award nomination, 1983, for *Notes for Another Life;* ALAN award, Assembly on Literature for Adolescents of the National Council of Teachers of English, 1985, for her outstanding contributions to young adult literature; Ragin-Rubin award, 1992. Address: 64 Savannah Dr., Sylva, NC 28779, U.S.A.

PUBLICATIONS FOR YOUNG ADULTS

Fiction

Home before Dark (originally appeared in *Redbook*). New York, Knopf, 1976.
All Together Now. New York, Knopf, 1979.
Notes for Another Life. New York, Knopf, 1981.
Permanent Connections. New York, Harper, 1987.
Keeping Christina. New York, HarperCollins, 1993.

PUBLICATIONS FOR ADULTS

Novels

Sara Will. New York, Harper, 1985.

*

Biography: *Presenting Sue Ellen Bridgers* by Ted Hipple, Boston, Twayne, 1990; essay in *Speaking for Ourselves: Autobiographical Sketches by Notable Authors of Books for Young Adults,* Volume 1, compiled and edited by Donald R. Gallo, National Council of Teachers of English, 1990.

Manuscript Collection: Hunter Library, Western Carolina University, Cullowhee, North Carolina.

Critical Study: *Sue Ellen Bridgers' Southern Literature for Young Adults* by Pamela Sissi Carroll, Auburn, Alabama, Auburn University Press, 1989.

Sue Ellen Bridgers comments:

I grew up in a world defined by story. The belief that connections are made and history revealed on dark summer porches and beside winter fires made me want to be a writer. Writing stories that are of interest to young people is both a challenge and a pleasure because I recall my own teenage reading more clearly than last week's adult novel.

*   *   *

Sue Ellen Bridgers has published four novels for young adults: *Home Before Dark, All Together Now, Notes for Another Life,* and *Permanent Connections.* Her latest novel, *Keeping Christina,* is being published this summer (1993). All of these novels are about adolescents facing problems and obstacles that confront most youth in their day-to-day lives. And each of these novels has a southern setting and/or a southern tradition. As Ms. Bridgers has noted, "Memory must lie at the root of fiction, even when we do not intend it or recognize it." Bridgers does indeed draw upon her memories of growing up in North Carolina. She writes about family and people who care, though they sometimes hurt one another along the way.

In *Home Before Dark,* fourteen-year-old Stella Mae Willis, the youthful protagonist of Bridgers's first novel, is the oldest child of a family of migrant workers. The family has moved around all of Stella Mae's life; it is the only life she has ever known. In her own words, "Everything we ever had went into the car, and all we had was each other." Now her father, James Earl, wants to come home and, after a long absence, has returned to the family tobacco farm in North Carolina where the family attempts to establish roots for the first time. This has profound—albeit different—effects on Stella Mae and her family.

Declaring "I'm never leaving," Stella is excited about her new home, but her mother Mae is fearful and depressed. Later, when Mae is struck by lightning in a freak accident, Stella imagines she was waiting to be struck down because she didn't like it there.

Besides the sadness that her mother's death brings, Stella also experiences the happiness of her first real friend, a boy named Toby whose family lives and works on the same farm as the Willises. However, it is Rodney Biggers who becomes Stella's first boyfriend. Toby and Rodney compete for Stella's attention but Rodney's selfish temperament culminates in a violent climax. Through the course of the novel, Stella Mae learns that home is not a place but a feeling, a give and take with the people you love.

All Together Now describes the stories of several different characters from the point of view of each. Set in a small, southern town, this novel focuses on twelve-year-old Casey, who has come against her will to spend the summer with her grandparents while her mother works two jobs and her father fights in Korea. While staying with her grandparents, Casey meets Dwayne Pickens, a retarded man who had once been a childhood friend of her father. Casey tries to dress and look like a boy because Dwayne doesn't like girls. By the end of the summer, Dwayne learns that Casey is a girl, but he still looks forward to seeing her again the next summer.

Although *Notes for Another Life* is not autobiographical, Bridgers does draw on personal experience as she notes in her autobiographical essay:

> When I was eleven my father suffered his first debilitating bout with mental depression. The treatment of mental illness was too modern a science for our rural area, and Mother's desperation to find him help led her to a psychiatrist in Raleigh. Periodically over the next fifteen years he was hospitalized, treated with medication and shock treatments until he was able to function, then sent home for a period of time during which he farmed and carried on some semblance of normality before slipping back into a catatonic, depressed state that once again required hospitalization. The effects of his illness on each of us children were individual and private."

Thirteen-year-old Wren and her sixteen-year-old brother Kevin, in *Notes for Another Life,* live with their grandparents because their father, Tom, is mentally ill and their mother cannot cope with the situation. The mother, Karen, a career woman who only occasionally visits her children, lives and works in Atlanta. Wren and Kevin have lived with their paternal grandparents, Bliss and Bill, for six years and share genuine concern for each other. This concern grows as mental illness, divorce, and attempted suicide all become problems with which this family must cope.

In Bridgers's fourth young adult novel, *Permanent Connections,* seventeen-year-old Rob Dickson must live with his senile grandfather and his agoraphobic aunt while his uncle recovers from hip surgery. At the beginning of the novel, Rob and his parents are living in New Jersey. Rob is a restless teenager, and his parents suspect that he is on drugs and do not know what to do with him. When his Uncle Farley has to have hip surgery, Rob's father decides that it is time for Rob to make a visit to the country, which, of course, is the North Carolina that Bridgers knows so well and describes so adeptly.

In North Carolina, Rob is angry and withdrawn. One evening, during a thunderstorm, Rob has a heated argument with his grandfather and storms out of the house. Later, Rob and his grandfather are out looking for one another. After they look for one another all night long, Rob begins to realize how much his family means to him and how much he means to each member of his family. As in most young adult novels, there is no "and they lived happily ever after" ending. Bridgers realistically tells a story of three generations—a son, a father, and a grandfather—who are indeed permanently connected.

In describing her writing process, Bridgers indicates that the idea for each novel begins with a character, usually a vision of the main character. In "Stories My Grandmother Told Me," she writes, "Technically the characters always come first and then the kind of people they are dictates what they do, just as you and I are the products of heredity and environment." And in a recent speech she said, "While I'm writing the story, it is mine. But when you're reading it, it's yours. You bring your own experiences to the story."

—Robbie W. Strickland

———

BROOKS, Bruce. American. Born in Richmond, Virginia, 23 September 1950. Educated at University of North Carolina, Chapel Hill, B.A. 1972; University of Iowa, M.F.A. 1980. Married Penelope Winslow in 1978; two sons. Writer. Also worked as a letterpress printer, a newspaper reporter, a magazine reporter, and a teacher. Recipient: *The Moves Make the Man* was named a best book of 1984 by *School Library Journal,* a notable children's book by the American Library Association (ALA), and a notable book of the year by the *New York Times,* 1984, and received a *Boston Globe-Horn Book* Award and Newbery Honor from the ALA, both 1985; *Midnight Hour Encores* was named a best book of 1986 by *School Library Journal,* a best book for young adults in 1986 by the ALA, a *Horn Book* Fanfare Honor List book in 1987, a teacher's choice by the National Council of Teachers of English in 1987, a young adult choice by the International Reading Association in 1988, and an ALA/*Booklist* best of the 1980s book for young adults; *No*

Kidding was named a best book for young adults by the ALA, an ALA/*Booklist* young adult editor's choice, a best book by *School Library Journal,* and a notable children's trade book in social studies; *Everywhere* was named a notable children's book by the ALA and a best book by *School Library Journal; On the Wing* was an ALA Best Book for Young Adults, 1990; *Predator!* was an ALA Best Book for Young Adults, 1992; John Burroughs award, 1992, for *Nature By Design; What Hearts* was a Newbery Honor Book, an ALA Notable Children's Book, an ALA Best Book for Young Adults, and a Horn Book Fanfare book, all 1993. Address: 11208 Legato Way, Silver Spring, MD 20901, U.S.A.

PUBLICATIONS FOR YOUNG ADULTS

Fiction

The Moves Make the Man. New York, Harper, 1984.
Midnight Hour Encores. New York, Harper, 1986.
No Kidding. New York, Harper, 1989.
What Hearts. New York, HarperCollins, 1992.

Nonfiction

On the Wing: The Life of Birds from Feathers to Flight. New York, Scribner, 1989.
Predator! New York, Farrar, Straus, 1991.
Nature by Design. New York. Farrar, Straus, 1991.
Making Sense: Animal Perception and Communication. New York, Farrar, Straus, 1993.

PUBLICATIONS FOR CHILDREN

Fiction

Everywhere. New York, Harper, 1990.

Nonfiction

Boys Will Be. New York, Holt, 1993.
Those Who Love the Game, with Glenn Rivers. New York, Holt, 1994.

*

Biography: Essay in *Speaking for Ourselves: Autobiographical Sketches by Notable Authors of Books for Young Adults,* Volume 1, compiled and edited by Donald R. Gallo, National Council of Teachers of English, 1990.

*   *   *

The publication of his much-acclaimed first novel, the 1985 Newbery Honor book *The Moves Make the Man,* established Bruce Brooks as a commanding new presence in the world of books for young readers. As one critic put it, "Armed with talent and technique [he] strode into the world of children's and young adult fiction as if on stilts."

Yet, as one of his own characters observes, "Talent and technique [alone] could not create power." What makes Brooks such a power-

ful writer are not only his talent and technique, but his matchless ability to create highly intelligent, complex characters invested with strong, idiosyncratic voices and his success in developing his ambitious, yet subtly stated themes. Three themes are typical: a fascination with process—analyzing and understanding how things work, whether sports, music, or the human heart in order to capture their essential truth; the characters' need to manipulate that truth and other people; and a closely reasoned examination—without violating the works' fictional form—of the sometimes symbiotic, occasionally dialectical relationship of lies and truth, of emotion and thought, of intellect and love.

These themes are ambitious considerations for the sometimes fragile framework of young-adult literature, and with these, Brooks, more than most writers of his generation, has tested and expanded the parameters of the genre, perhaps because he respects the intelligence of his "hardworking readers who are ready to be inspired," perhaps because in his writing he refuses to be confined by traditional limitations, perhaps because he recognizes the potential power of literature to enrich and expand lives.

Brooks also loves a challenge. In his first two books, *The Moves Make the Man* and *Midnight Hour,* he wrote, respectively, in the first-person voices of Jerome Foxworth, a thirteen-year-old African-American living in the recently desegregated South, and of Sibilance Spooner, a sixteen-year-old white musical prodigy, one of the finest cellists in the world. At the same time, he integrated considerable expository material about basketball and music into his narratives. That the narrators' voices are authentic in their believable verisimilitude and that the integration of exposition and fiction is seamless speak for Brooks's skill as a writer.

In his third book, *No Kidding,* he dared to distance his challenging material from the reader by writing in the more remote third person and setting the story in a bleakly dystopian future world where 69 percent of the adults are alcoholics. His fourth book, *Everywhere,* a novella, is a marvel of subtle economy, which, though marketed for a mid-range audience, reveals large and haunting truths for all ages about the healing power of love.

What Hearts, another Newbery Honor title, is a departure in form, a collection of four interrelated short stories in which the reader follows the maturation of a boy named Asa. Like Jerome and Sibilance, Asa is preternaturally intelligent. He has been forced into an unnatural adult maturity by the circumstances of a mother's illness and has, at best, an uneasy relationship with a domineering, unsympathetic stepfather.

In these characters, Brooks shows his great sympathy for young people who are outsiders, whether by virtue of their intelligence or domestic or societal circumstances. Almost all of his characters come from broken homes, and many of them are further challenged by a parent's mental illness or alcoholism. Given this context, it is no wonder that control or manipulation of the truth and other people is a consistent theme—from Brooks's first book, in which Bix Rivers resolutely refuses to learn the fake-out, duplicitous moves of basketball, to the last, in which Asa invents a reality of dramatic baseball games. To lie may be to control the truth or other people's perception of it, to bring some order to a chaotic personal world, or simply to survive, but in extreme cases it is also, as Bix understands, to invite the alternate reality of madness, which is an exercise in ultimate solitude.

For Brooks and his characters, redemption sometimes can be found in the giving up of control, as in the case of Sam, perhaps Brooks's most controlling character. In his self-imposed maturity, Sam betrays his essential adolescent self but finally finds that self when his mother practices her own deception, and Sam is released to say poignantly to her, "Can I be myself...can I just be your boy?" More often, though, redemption is found in a character's discovery of love, which, in its sweet simplicity, is the perfect complement to the complex intellectuality that defines so many of Brooks's characters. To give expression to words of love is, for Brooks, not only an exercise in honesty, but an act of completion, a rejection of isolation, which is most obviously manifested in Asa, but also in Sibilance and her discovery of her love for her father, and certainly in the case of the healing love of the young narrator for his grandfather in *Everywhere*.

Bruce Brooks is that rarity in the world of books for young readers—a novelist of ideas. But he is also a rare stylist whose writer's razzle always dazzles thanks to his uncanny ear for voice and his gift for powerful imagery and unforgettable simile and metaphor. Ultimately, though, it is his own luminous intelligence which brings light to the sometimes dark complexities of who we humans are and why we behave as we do. He understands the workings of the human heart and demonstrates in his memorable works of fiction how it can challenge the intellect to develop subtle and inventive strategies for survival.

—Michael Cart

BROOKS, Terry. American. Born in Sterling, Illinois, 8 January 1944. Educated at Hamilton College, Clinton, New York, B.A. 1966; Washington and Lee University, Lexington, Virginia, LL.B. 1969. Married Judine Elaine Alba in 1987; one daughter and one son from a previous marriage. Partner, Besse, Frye, Arnold, Brooks and Miller, Attorneys at Law, Sterling Illinois, 1969-86; writer, 1977—. Recipient: *The Elfstones of Shannara* was selected one of American Library Association's Best Young Adult Books, and one of *School Library Journal*'s Best Books for Young Adults, both 1982; *Magic Kingdom for Sale—Sold* was selected one of *School Library Journal*'s Best Books for Young Adults, 1986. Address: c/o Ballantine/Del Rey, 201 East 50th Street, New York, NY 10022, U.S.A.

PUBLICATIONS

Novels

The Sword of Shannara, illustrated by the Brothers Hildebrandt. New York, Ballantine, 1977.
The Elfstones of Shannara, illustrated by Darrell K. Sweet. New York, Ballantine, 1982.
The Wishsong of Shannara, illustrated by Darrell K. Sweet. New York, Ballantine, 1985.
Magic Kingdom for Sale—Sold. New York, Ballantine, 1986.
The Black Unicorn. New York, Ballantine, 1987.
Wizard at Large. New York, Ballantine, 1988.
The Scions of Shannara. New York, Ballantine, 1990.
The Druid of Shannara. New York, Ballantine, 1991.
The Elf Queen of Shannara. New York, Ballantine, 1992.
Hook (based on screenplay by Jim V. Hart and Malia Scotch Marmo). New York, Fawcett, 1992.
The Talismans of Shannara. New York, Ballantine, 1993.

The Tangle Box. New York, Ballantine, 1994.

*

Media Adaptations: *The Sword of Shannara* (cassette), Caedmon, 1986; plus several others of his work were adapted to cassette, Dove.

*   *   *

The publication of Terry Brooks's first novel *The Sword of Shannara* in 1977 brought fantasy novels into the literary mainstream. Until *Shannara* no fantasy writer except J. R. R. Tolkien had made such an impression on the general public. Brooks's novel opened up the market for fantasy writers. The author creates a fascinating picture of a post-nuclear world where magic has succeeded science as the operational force. Brooks's "Shannara" series portrays a land under the influence of spells and sorceries. In some cases humanity has mutated into new races, called after the ancient legends: dwarves, trolls, and gnomes. Some of these new races are well-intentioned, and some are not. Humankind exists in the shadow of evil.

However there is hope. The last of the magic-working druids stalks the land, combatting evil wherever he finds it. Allanon constantly seeks out the young people of a single family, the Ohmsfords, and deviously attempts to use them to fulfill the needs of the country as he perceives them. The family is distantly related to the elven royal house of Shannara, and some of its members possess innate powers beyond those of their fellows. The druid works to bring out those latent talents, and in doing so brings the young people to a new maturity. The druid also encourages respect for the land and environmental concerns.

The first three books, *The Sword of Shannara, The Elfstones of Shannara,* and *The Wishsong of Shannara,* are all individual adventures. The concluding four volumes, *The Scions of Shannara, The Druid of Shannara, The Elf Queen of Shannara,* and *The Talismans of Shannara,* make up a single quest involving several members of the Ohmsford family.

Brooks's writing is strongest when dealing with problems that relate to present concerns. The first novel, with its chapters on warring elves and wraiths contrasted with one young man's search for a talisman to use against the evil, is very reminiscent of Tolkien's work. With the second book, *The Elfstones of Shannara,* Brooks moves away from the established pattern and breaks new ground. *Elfstones* is a very environmental novel, the focus of concern being the magical tree, the Ellcrys, which protects the lands from the ancient demons. The tree is old and dying and a complex ritual is required to restore it. The protagonist, Wil Ohmsford, is recruited by the druid Allanon to keep Amberle, the elven maiden responsible for the ritual, safe until she has completed her mission. Amberle is unsure of herself, and Wil needs to keeps assuring both himself and the girl of the importance of their quest.

The druid Allanon is both a strength and a weakness in Brooks's works. His reticence keeps the plots moving along smoothly, but one feels, along with the heroes, that the druid could have been more forthcoming with his knowledge. The constant revelation that Allanon knew everything all the time grows wearisome. The character is so shrouded in mystery that the occasional glimpses of humanity he shows are almost out of place. Most of the other major characters are extremely well done, giving the reader friends to agonize over and cry for. The women are generally portrayed more sympathetically; the witches in *Elfstones* are both menacing and pathetic, and Amberle is an exceptionally endearing character.

Brooks's third novel, *The Wishsong of Shannara,* was the first to have a female protagonist. Brin Ohmsford shares the limelight with her brother Jair, but it is her power that is ultimately tested and her decision that affects the outcome of the plot. Brin is the focus of the story in a way that no female character had been in fantasy literature before. Brooks does not use another woman in a leading role until the third book of the most current Shannara saga.

Wren Ohmsford is a highly intriguing character. Raised by the Gypsy-like Rovers of the Westland, she is highly skeptical of the druid's claims that she alone can bring back the elves from their self-imposed exile. Her journey to the volcanic island where the elves are hiding has the potential to be one of the best in the series. Unfortunately it fails. Wren's journey is riddled with gloom. Almost every one of the companions she attracts meets a hideous doom. She is deceived by her most constant companion and forced to face unpleasant truths about everything she believes. This does not make her a better person, only more resigned to the will of fate.

Terry Brooks has set the standard for contemporary fantasy writing. His "Shannara" series has opened up new vistas for the reader to enjoy.

—Louise J. Winters

BUNTING, (Anne) Eve(lyn). Also writes as Evelyn Bolton; A.E. Bunting. American. Born in Maghera, County Derry, Ireland, 19 December 1928; emigrated to the United States, 1958; became citizen, 1967. Educated at Methodist College, Belfast, 1936-45; Queen's University, Belfast, 1945-47; Pasadena City College, c. 1959. Married Edward Bunting in 1951; one daughter and two sons. Freelance writer, mainly for young people, 1969—. Teacher of writing, University of California, Los Angeles, 1978, 1979, and at writer's conferences. Recipient: Society of Children's Book Writers Golden Kite award, Outstanding Science Trade Book for Children from the National Science Teachers Association and the Children's Book Council, Notable Children's Trade Book in the Field of Social Studies from the National Council for Social Studies and the Children's Book Council, and Child Study Association of America's Children's Books of the Year, all 1976, all for *One More Flight; The Big Red Barn,* 1979, *Goose Dinner* and *The Waiting Game,* 1981, *The Valentine Bears,* 1986, and *The Mother's Day Mice* and *Sixth Grade Sleepover,* 1987, were all named Child Study Association of America's Children's Books of the Year; *Winter's Coming* was named one of the *New York Times* Top Ten Books, 1977; Notable Work of Fiction from the Southern California Council on Literature for Children and Young People, 1977, for *Ghost of Summer;* Classroom Choice from Scholastic Paperbacks, 1978, for *Skateboards: How to Make Them, How to Ride Them; If I Asked You, Would You Stay?* was selected one of American Library Association's Best Books for Young Adults, 1984; PEN Special Achievement award, 1984, for her contribution to children's literature; Nene award from the Hawaii Association of School Librarians and the Hawaii Library Association, 1987, for *Karen Kepplewhite Is the World's Best Kisser; The Mother's Day Mice,* 1986, and *The Wednesday Surprise,* 1989, were selected as *School Library Journal*'s Best Books of the Year;

Southern California Council on Literature for Children and Young People award for Excellence in a Series, 1986, for "Lippincott Page Turners" series; Parents' Choice from the Parents' Choice Foundation, and one of *School Library Journal*'s Best Books of the year, both 1987, both for *Ghost's Hour, Spook's Hour;* Parents' Choice award from the Parents' Choice Foundation, 1988, for *The Mother's Day Mice;* Virginia Young Readers award, 1988-89, California Young Readers Medal, 1989, and South Carolina Young Adult Book award, 1988-89, all for *Face at the Edge of the World;* Surrey School Book of the Year award, 1989, for *Sixth Grade Sleepover;* Notable Children's Trade Book, Southern California Council on Literature for Children and Young People award for Outstanding Work of Fiction for Young Adults, 1989, Sequoyah Children's Book award from the Oklahoma Library Association, 1990, and California Young Reader's Medal, 1992, all for *A Sudden Silence;* Children's Book Council Children's Choice award, 1989, for *Seaworld Book of Sharks;* Sequoyah Children's Book award from the Oklahoma Library Association, Mark Twain award from the State of Missouri, and Sunshine State Young Readers award, all 1989, all for *Sixth Grade Sleepover;* Southern California Council on Literature for Children and Young People award for Outstanding Work of Fiction for Young Adults, 1990, for *The Wall;* Soaring Eagle award, 1990, for *Someone Is Hiding on Alcatraz Island;* South Carolina Book award, Mystery Writers of America Edgar Allan Poe nomination, 1991, and Nebraska Golden Sower award, 1992, all for *Is Anybody There?;* Jane Addams Honor award, 1990, for *The Wednesday Surprise.* Address: 1512 Rose Villa Street, Pasadena, CA 91106, U.S.A.

PUBLICATIONS FOR YOUNG ADULTS

Fiction

A Gift for Lonny, illustrated by Robert Quackenbush. Lexington, Massachusetts, Ginn, 1973.
Box, Fox, Ox and the Peacock, illustrated by Leslie Morrill. Lexington, Massachusetts, Ginn, 1974.
The Once-a-Year Day, illustrated by W.T. Mars. Chicago, Children's Press, 1974.
We Need a Bigger Zoo!, illustrated by Bob Barner. Lexington, Massachusetts, Ginn, 1974.
The Wild One. New York, Scholastic, 1974.
Barney the Beard, illustrated by Imero Gobbato. New York, Parents Magazine Press, 1975; London, Warne, 1978.
The Dinosaur Machines (The Day of the Dinosaurs, Death of a Dinosaur, The Dinosaur Trap, Escape from Tyrannosaurus), illustrated by Judith Leo. St. Paul, Minnesota, EMC Corp., 4 vols., 1975.
No Such Things...? (The Creature of Cranberry Cove, The Demon, The Ghost, The Tongue of the Ocean), illustrated by Scott Earle. St. Paul, Minnesota, EMC Corp., 4 vols., 1976.
Josefina Finds the Prince, illustrated by Jan Palmer. Champaign, Illinois, Garrard, 1976.
Blacksmith at Blueridge, photographs by Peter Fine. New York, Scholastic, 1976.
Skateboard Saturday, photographs by Richard Hutchings. New York, Scholastic, 1976.
One More Flight, illustrated by Diane de Groat. New York and London, Warne, 1976.
The Skateboard Four, illustrated by Phil Kantz. Chicago, Whitman, 1976.

Winter's Coming, illustrated by Howard Knotts. New York, Harcourt Brace, 1977.

The Big Cheese, illustrated by Sal Murdocca. New York, Macmillan, 1977; London, Macmillan, 1980.

Cop Camp, photographs by Richard Hutchings. New York, Scholastic, 1977.

Ghost of Summer. New York, Warne, 1977.

Creative Science Fiction (The Day of the Earthlings, The Followers, The Island of One, The Mask, The Mirror Planet, The Robot People, The Space People, The Undersea People), illustrated by Don Hendricks. Mankato, Minnesota, Creative Education, 8 vols., 1978.

Creative Romance (Fifteen, For Always, The Girl in the Painting, Just Like Everyone Else, Maggie the Freak, Nobody Knows But Me, Oh, Rick!, A Part of the Dream, Survival Camp!, Two Different Girls), illustrated by Robert Gadbois. Mankato, Minnesota, Creative Education, 10 vols., 1978.

The Big Find, photographs by Richard Hutchings. Mankato, Minnesota, Creative Education, 1978.

Magic and the Night River, illustrated by Allen Say. New York, Harper, 1978.

Going Against Cool Calvin, illustrated by Don Brautigan. New York, Scholastic, 1978.

The Haunting of Kildoran Abbey. New York, Warne, 1978; London, Warne, 1979.

The Big Red Barn, illustrated by Howard Knotts. New York, Harcourt Brace, 1979.

The Cloverdale Switch. New York, Lippincott, 1979; as *Strange Things Happen in the Woods,* New York, Archway, 1984.

Yesterday's Island, illustrated by Stephen Gammell. New York, Warne, 1979.

Mr. Pride's Umbrella, illustrated by Maggie Ling. London, Warne, 1980.

The Robot Birthday, illustrated by Marie DeJohn. New York, Dutton, 1980.

Demetrius and the Golden Goblet, illustrated by Michael Hague. New York, Harcourt Brace, 1980.

Terrible Things, illustrated by Stephen Gammell. New York, Harper, 1980; as *Terrible Things: An Allegory of the Holocaust,* Jewish Publication Society, 1989.

St. Patrick's Day in the Morning, illustrated by Jan Brett. Boston, Houghton Mifflin, 1980.

Blackbird Singing, illustrated by Stephen Gammell. New York, Macmillan, 1980.

The Empty Window, illustrated by Judy Clifford. New York, Warne, 1980.

The Skate Patrol, illustrated by Don Madden. Chicago, Whitman, 1980.

Goose Dinner, illustrated by Hoawrd Knotts. New York, Harcourt Brace, 1981.

Jane Martin and the Case of the Ice Cream Dog. Champaign, Illinois, Garrard, 1981.

Rosie and Mr. William Star. Boston, Houghton Mifflin, 1981.

The Skate Patrol Rides Again, illustrated by Don Madden. Chicago, Whitman, 1981.

The Spook Birds, illustrated by Blanche Sims. Chicago, Whitman, 1981.

The Waiting Game. New York, Lippincott, 1981.

The Ghosts of Departure Point. New York, Lippincott, 1982.

The Happy Funeral, illustrated by Vo-Dinh Mai. New York, Harper, 1982.

The Skate Patrol and the Mystery Writer, illustrated by Don Madden. Chicago, Whitman, 1982.

The Traveling Men of Ballycoo, illustrated by Kaethe Zemach. New York, Harcourt Brace, 1983.

The Valentine Bears, illustrated by Jan Brett. New York, Clarion, 1983.

Karen Kepplewhite Is the World's Best Kisser. New York, Clarion, 1983.

Clancy's Coat, illustrated by Lorinda Bryan Cauley. New York, Warne, 1984.

The Ghost Behind Me. New York, Archway, 1984.

If I Asked You, Would You Stay? New York, Lippincott, 1984.

Jane Martin, Dog Detective, illustrated by Amy Schwartz. New York, Harcourt Brace, 1984.

The Man Who Could Call Down Owls, illustrated by Charles Mikolaycak. New York, Macmillan, 1984.

Monkey in the Middle, illustrated by Lynn Munsinger. New York, Harcourt Brace, 1984.

Someone Is Hiding on Alcatraz Island. New York, Clarion, 1984; London, Fontana, 1986.

Surrogate Sister. New York, Lippincott, 1984; London, Hodder and Stoughton, 1985; as *Mother, How Could You!,* New York, Simon and Schuster, 1986.

Face at the Edge of the World. New York, Clarion, 1985; London, Fontana, 1987.

The Haunting of Safekeep. New York, Lippincott, 1985.

Janet Hamm Needs a Date for the Dance. New York, Clarion, 1986.

The Mother's Day Mice, illustrated by Jan Brett. New York, Clarion, 1986.

Sixth-Grade Sleepover. San Diego, Harcourt Brace, 1986.

Ghost's Hour, Spook's Hour, illustrated by Donald Carrick. New York, Clarion, 1987.

Will You Be My POSSLQ? San Diego, Harcourt Brace, 1987.

Happy Birthday, Dear Duck, illustrated by Jan Brett. New York, Clarion, 1988.

How Many Days to America? A Thanksgiving Story, illustrated by Beth Peck. New York, Clarion, 1988.

Is Anybody There? New York, Lippincott, 1988.

A Sudden Silence. San Diego, Harcourt Brace, 1988.

The Ghost Children. New York, Clarion, 1989.

No Nap, illustrated by Susan Meddaugh. New York, Clarion, 1989.

The Wednesday Surprise, illustrated by Donald Carrick. New York, Clarion, 1989.

The Wall, illustrated by Ronald Himler. Boston, Houghton Mifflin, 1990.

Such Nice Kids. Boston, Houghton Mifflin, 1990.

Our Sixth-Grade Sugar Babies. New York, Harper, 1990.

In the Haunted House, illustrated by Susan Meddaugh. Boston, Houghton Mifflin, 1990.

Fly Away Home, illustrated by Ronald Himler. Boston, Houghton Mifflin, 1991.

The Hideout. San Diego, Harcourt Brace, 1991.

Jumping the Nail. San Diego, Harcourt Brace, 1991.

Night Tree, illustrated by Ted Rand. San Diego, Harcourt Brace, 1991.

A Perfect Father's Day, illustrated by Susan Meddaugh. Boston, Houghton Mifflin, 1991.

Sharing Susan. New York, Harper, 1991.

A Turkey for Thanksgiving, illustrated by Diane de Groat. Boston, Houghton Mifflin, 1991.

The Bicycle Man, illustrated by Thomas B. Allen. San Diego, Harcourt Brace, 1992.

Coffin on a Case. New York, Harper, 1992.

Day Before Christmas. Boston, Houghton Mifflin, 1992.

Our Teacher's Having a Baby. Boston, Houghton Mifflin, 1992.

Summer Wheels, illustrated by Thomas B. Allen. San Diego, Harcourt Brace, 1992.

Red Fox Running, illustrated by Wendell Minor. New York, Clarion, 1993.

Someday a Tree, illustrated by Ronald Himler. Boston, Houghton Mifflin, 1993.

Flower Garden, illustrated by Kathryn Hewitt. San Diego, Harcourt Brace, 1994.

Fiction as Evelyn Bolton (illustrated by John Keely)

Stable of Fear. Mankato, Minnesota, Creative Education, 1974.

Lady's Girl. Mankato, Minnesota, Creative Education, 1974.

Goodbye Charlie. Mankato, Minnesota, Creative Education, 1974.

Ride When You're Ready. Mankato, Minnesota, Creative Education, 1974.

The Wild Horses. Mankato, Minnesota, Creative Education, 1974.

Dream Dancer. Mankato, Minnesota, Creative Education, 1974.

Fiction as A.E. Bunting

Pitcher to Center Field, illustrated by Len Freas. Chicago, Children's Press, 1974.

Surfing Country, illustrated by Dale King. Chicago, Children's Press, 1974.

High Tide for Labrador, illustrated by Bernard Garbutt. Chicago, Children's Press, 1975.

Springboard to Summer, illustrated by Rob Sprattler. Chicago, Children's Press, 1975.

Poetry

Scary, Scary Halloween, illustrated by Jan Brett. New York, Clarion, 1986.

Other

The Two Giants (Irish folktale), illustrated by Eric von Schmidt. Lexington, Massachusetts, Ginn, 1972.

Say It Fast (tongue twisters), illustrated by True Kelley. Lexington, Massachusetts, Ginn, 1974.

Skateboards: How to Make Them, How to Ride Them, with Glenn Bunting. New York, Harvey House, 1977.

The Sea World Book of Sharks, photographs by Flip Nicklin. San Diego, Sea World, 1979.

The Sea World Book of Whales. New York, Harcourt Brace, 1980.

The Giant Squid. New York, Messner, 1981.

The Great White Shark. New York, Messner, 1982.

Also author of stories for basal readers published by several educational houses, including Heath, Laidlaw Brothers, Lyons and Carnahan, Scott, Foresman, Bowmar Educational, Scholastic, and Rand McNally. Contributor to anthologies, including *Cricket's Choice,* 1975, and *Scribner's Anthology for Young People.* Contributor of adult and juvenile stories to periodicals, including *Jack and Jill* and *Cricket.*

Media Adaptations: *How Many Days to America?* (film), Coronet/MTI Film and Video, 1991; *A Desperate Exit* (television movie adaptation of *A Face at the Edge of the World); The Wall* (segment on *Reading Rainbow).*

Biography: Entry in *Authors and Artists for Young Adults,* Volume 5, Detroit, Gale, 1990; essay in *Speaking for Ourselves: Autobiographical Sketches by Notable Authors of Books for Young Adults,* Volume 1, compiled and edited by Donald R. Gallo, National Council of Teachers of English, 1990.

Manuscript Collection: Kerlan Collection, University of Minnesota, Minneapolis.

Critical Study: Entry in *Children's Literature Review,* Volume 28, Detroit, Gale, 1992.

*   *   *

Eve Bunting is one of a few talented authors who can produce everything from picture books to sensitive, suspenseful books for young adults. She is an accomplished mystery writer, as evidenced by her "Lippincott Page Turners" series and mysteries set in her native Ireland. Combining an innate gift for storytelling with a keen eye for spotting trends, Bunting is often at the forefront of the young-adult genre with topical books exploring themes like alcoholism, racism, teenage prostitution, and sexual abuse. Bunting claims to gather 90 percent of her story ideas from current events; shrewd assessment of her audience has made Bunting a very popular and marketable author.

Believing it is "dishonest to write a novel about characters free from any problems of a serious nature," Bunting explores the ways in which her characters are affected by crises both within themselves and in others. She has had varying degrees of success integrating the problem aspect of her novels within the context of the story.

A Sudden Silence is a moving portrayal of the destruction caused by alcohol abuse. When Jesse's brother is killed by a hit-and-run driver, Jesse struggles with grief coupled with guilt over his helplessness at preventing the accident. He also experiences conflicting emotions about his feelings for his brother's girlfriend, Chloe. As the two teens join forces to find the person responsible for Bry's death, a tentative friendship forms. The relationship between Chloe and Jesse is well drawn; it stands alone on its own merits while exposing the universality of alcohol abuse by depicting the social and economic differences between the two families. When Jesse discovers that Chloe's mother was responsible for his brother's death, there is no easy resolution. Bunting resists the convenience of a happy ending.

Surrogate Sister offers an interesting slant on a very modern issue, surrogate motherhood. By presenting the matter from a sibling's point of view, Bunting poses thought-provoking questions regarding this sensitive topic. When Cassie's widowed mother, despite Cassie's objections, agrees to become a surrogate mother for a childless couple, Cassie is faced with the insensitivity of her classmates and her own confusion about the morality of her mother's decision. While the issue is presented in a straightforward and compassionate manner, Bunting tries too hard to link together disparate elements of the story, namely, Cassie's concern over her blossoming sexual relationship with a college student and her friend's pregnancy. Cassie experiences an understandable curiosity about the childless couple, but the ease with which she locates them diminishes the effect of her feelings. Most importantly, in terms of characterization, one wonders if Cassie's warm and affectionate mother would have persisted with the surrogate pregnancy in light of Cassie's extreme hostility and strong opposition.

Certain themes run throughout Bunting's books; one suspects that these issues are of fundamental concern to her. There is a self-consciousness that is, at times, disconcerting. The parents in Bunting's books are often nonconformists, yet there is always a prevailing sense of morality. In *Surrogate Sister*, Cassie decides against a sexual relationship with her boyfriend. In *Would You Be My POSSLQ?*, the heroine is a spunky college freshman who embarks on an alternative living arrangement with a Person Of The Opposite Sex Sharing Living Quarters. Although Jamie has been raised in a strict Catholic family and has witnessed the heartache caused by her sister's decision to bear a child out of wedlock, she agrees to share her apartment with Kyle on a purely platonic level. Jamie, attracted to Kyle, does not rely on her innate good sense and bases her decision on rather flimsy financial reasons. Therefore, her subsequent decision to separate so that a romantic relationship can develop is not believable. Jamie's emotional recovery from cancer, however, adds a special element to the story. Her relationships with terminal cancer patients are honest, straightforward, and extremely touching. There is also a nice thematic juxtaposition among Jamie's and her sisters' situations: Phoebe, pregnant again, is marrying her boyfriend; Tig, at fourteen, is being pressured for a more physical relationship with her boyfriend; Jamie is trying to sort out her complicated feelings about Kyle and her own mortality.

Bunting portrays the negative consequences of peer pressure in *Jumping the Nail*. The "Nail" is a dangerous cliff, off limits even to anyone brave enough to attempt a jump into the deep water below. Scooter, the class bad boy, decides to make the leap. He convinces his unstable girlfriend, Elisa, to join him, leading her into a downward spiral that ends in suicide. Dru and Mike are the couple who try, unsuccessfully, to stop the madness that follows. The story is somewhat superficial, especially in its treatment of the serious topics of teen depression and suicide. Elisa's illness is treated far too frivolously for it to be the motivation for the chain of events that occurs.

Perhaps one of Bunting's most successful books is *If I Asked You, Would You Stay?*, an unusual story about two runaways who forge an uneasy alliance that leads to love. While Crow and Valentine are fully realized characters, Crow lacks the intensity that is crucial to the story's success. With notable exceptions—Crow and Jesse—Bunting experiences a problem with realistic characterization in her male heroes. They are idealized, invariably sensitive, and understanding, not prone to typical teen attitudes and behavior.

In an evaluation of Eve Bunting, Eric Kimmel states, "She writes too often from her head rather than her gut, raising sensitive issues but pulling away from the risks that go along with them." If Bunting were less concerned with conveying her message, loosened the restraints, took some risks, and allowed her characters the freedom to tell their own stories, she would achieve the level of high-quality writing of which she is surely capable.

—Maryclare O'Donnell Himmel

BURCH, Robert J(oseph). American. Born in Inman, Georgia, 26 June 1925. Educated at University of Georgia, Athens, B.A. in agriculture 1949; Hunter College, New York, 1955. Served in the United States Army, in New Guinea and Australia, 1943-46. Worked in a commercial greenhouse, 1950; civil servant, United States Army Ordinance Depot, Atlanta, 1951-53, and in Japan, 1953-55; office worker, 1953-55; Muir & Company Advertising, New York, 1956-59, and Walter E. Heller & Company, New York, 1959-62; writer, since 1959. Recipient: Fellowship in juvenile literature, Bread Loaf Writers' Conference, 1960; children's book award from Child Study Association of America and Jane Addams Children's Book award, both 1967, for *Queenie Peavy;* Georgia Children's Book award, 1969, for *Skinny,* 1971, for *Queenie Peavy,* and 1974, for *Doodle and the Go-Cart;* George S. Stone Center for Children's Books award, 1974; Phoenix award from the Children's Literature Association, 1986, for *Queenie Peavy.* Address: 2021 Forest Dr., Fayetteville, GA 30214, U.S.A.

PUBLICATIONS FOR YOUNG ADULTS

Fiction

Tyler, Wilkin, and Skee, illustrated by Don Sibley. New York, Viking, 1963.
Skinny, illustrated by Don Sibley. New York, Viking, 1964; illustrated by Ian Ribbons, London, Methuen, 1965.
D. J.'s Worst Enemy, illustrated by Emil Weiss. New York, Viking, 1965.
Queenie Peavy, illustrated by Jerry Lazare. New York, Viking, 1966.
Simon and the Game of Chance, illustrated by Fermin Rocker. New York, Viking, 1970.
Doodle and the Go-Cart, illustrated by Alan Tiegreen. New York, Viking, 1972.
Hut School and the Wartime Home-Front Heroes, illustrated by Ronald Himler. New York, Viking, 1974; as *Home-Front,* New York, Viking, 1992.
Two That Were Tough, illustrated by Richard Cuffari. New York, Viking, 1976.
The Whitman Kick. New York, Dutton, 1977.
Wilkin's Ghost, illustrated by Lloyd Bloom. New York, Viking, 1978.
Ida Early Comes over the Mountain. New York, Viking, 1980.
Christmas with Ida Early, illustrated by Gail Owens. New York, Viking, 1983.
King Kong and Other Poets. New York, Viking, 1986.

PUBLICATIONS FOR CHILDREN

Fiction

The Traveling Bird, illustrated by Susanne Suba. New York, McDowell, Obolensky, 1959.
A Funny Place to Live, illustrated by W. R. Lohse. New York, Viking, 1962.
Renfroe's Christmas, illustrated by Rocco Negri. New York, Viking, 1968.
Joey's Cat, illustrated by Don Freeman. New York, Viking, 1969.
The Hunting Trip, illustrated by Susanne Suba. New York, Scribners, 1971.

The Jolly Witch, illustrated by Leigh Grant. New York, Dutton, 1975.

PUBLICATIONS FOR ADULTS

Other

Translator, *A Jungle in the Wheat Field,* by Egon Mathieson. New York, McDowell, Obolensky, 1960.
A Peircean Reduction Thesis: The Foundations of Topological Logic. Lubbock, Texas Tech University Press, 1991.

*

Media Adaptations: *Ida Early Comes over the Mountain* (as "The Incredible Ida Early," television movie), National Broadcasting Corporation (NBC), 1987.

Biography: Entry in *Dictionary of Literary Biography,* Volume 52: *American Writers for Children since 1960: Fiction,* Detroit, Gale, 1986.

Manuscript Collection: University of Georgia, Athens.

*   *   *

As the author of nineteen books for children and young adults, Robert Burch writes with sensitivity and compassion about the rural Georgia landscape and people he knows so well. Despite traveling widely before becoming interested in writing at the age of thirty while living in New York, Burch has been content to draw on the experiences of his childhood and youth for the substance of his narratives. He has mastered his craft well, and his strong sense of place and his ability to develop strong characters enrich his fiction. Growth and change permeate his stories, whether it is Alan Ponder's coming to terms with the personal upheavals of his senior year in high school in *The Whitman Kick* or the elderly Mr. Hilton's coping with the perceived loss of freedom and independence he faces in *Two That Were Tough* as his daughter presses him to leave his home and the old grist mill he has operated for years to move to Atlanta to live with her.

While Burch has written four picture books, his novels have been his most effective vehicle for speaking to his readers. As a boy in a rural community during the Depression, Burch learned that being happy and enjoying life were not dependent upon material possessions, and this is a strong theme in many of his books, most notably in *Tyler, Wilkin, and Skee* and *Doodle and the Go-Cart*. In *Skinny,* readers meet a boy who longs to be adopted by Miss Bessie who operates the local hotel and who has taken him in after his father dies. Even though Skinny is not adopted and must go to an orphanage, readers come away feeling that Skinny's good qualities and resourcefulness will carry him far, and that he will come back to visit Miss Bessie at the hotel.

Queenie Peavy, a character study of a thirteen-year-old girl whose father is in prison, was Burch's first female protagonist and his first venture into contemporary realistic fiction. Queenie, a tomboy who chews tobacco and throws rocks with deadly accuracy, is frequently in trouble as she struggles with a negative self-image. She wants to believe that when her father is released from prison, he will be a changed person. This is not the case, and Burch avoids a sentimen-

tal ending as Queenie accepts the fact that her father is not a good person and that she can lead a rewarding life by building on her strengths.

Whether set in the Depression or in more contemporary times, Burch's novels remain faithful to small town life. *Tyler, Wilkin, and Skee,* the story of a year in the life of three brothers living on a farm during the Depression, offers a touching picture of family life and underscores the importance of school and church in the social fabric of a community. *Hut School and the Wartime Home-Front Heroes* and *The Whitman Kick* reflect the impact of World War II on the people in small towns. A more familiar form of change is evident for contemporary readers of *King Kong and Other Poets,* where the transformation of a community through encroaching urbanization serves as a backdrop to the changes going on in the lives of young people in this story of the power of friendship in healing the pain of loneliness and loss. Through a poetry contest, Marilyn, a shy newcomer from California whose mother has died, learns that she, too, can fit in and be accepted by her peers. The unusual title comes from the fact that the students want the security of pseudonyms before they engage in class poetry writing and sharing. Poetry also plays a significant role in *The Whitman Kick*.

Burch's most memorable character may be Ida Early who, in *Ida Early Comes over the Mountain,* arrives unexpectedly to care for the four Sutton children after their mother dies. With her tall tales and antics, she helps the children overcome their grief and find joy in life again. Ida Early's appeal—one reviewer calls Ida "a mountain Mary Poppins" while another extends the image by saying that "she makes Mary Poppins look like Elsie Dinsmore"—lies in her raucous humor which results in an unconventional and unforgettable Christmas tableau. Before his second Ida Early book, Burch had never given much thought to sequels, although he had used the middle brother of *Tyler, Wilkin, and Skee* in *Wilkin's Ghost* and Renfroe, the younger brother in *D. J.'s Worst Enemy,* as the central character of *Renfroe's Christmas*. Burch admits he had Ida as a babysitter in an early draft of *Simon and the Game of Chance,* a story that deals with a large family in which the mother suffers from mental illness, but he removed her because her strong personality was a distraction. Ida has been featured in *The Incredible Ida Early,* a television film.

To think of Burch as a regional writer would be misleading as his universal themes and unique characters have earned him an international readership with Danish editions of *Skinny, Tyler, Wilkin, and Skee,* and *D. J.'s Worst Enemy*; German editions of *Queenie Peavy* and *Ida Early Comes Over the Mountain*; and a Japanese edition of *Queenie Peavy*. Burch's work has won numerous awards, including in 1986 the Children's Literature Association's Phoenix Award which honored *Queenie Peavy* as a work of enduring literary merit.

Burch is confortably settled in his Georgia home on land that once belonged to his grandfather, watching new businesses and new people arrive in his childhood community. Yet his childhood memories of adults telling stories on the front porch continue to feed his fertile imagination as he works on a new Ida Early story and processes thoughts of other narratives still to be written.

—William Agee

────────

BURGESS, Anthony. Pseudonym for John Anthony Burgess Wilson; also writes as Joseph Kell. British. Born in Manchester,

Lancashire, 25 February 1917. Educated at Xaverian College, Manchester; Manchester University, B.A. (honours) in English 1940. Served in the British Army Education Corps, 1940-46; sergeant-major. Married 1) Llewela Isherwood Jones in 1942 (died 1968); 2) Liliana Macellari in 1968, one son. Lecturer, Extra-Mural Department, Birmingham University, 1946-48; education officer and lecturer, Central Advisory Council for Adult Education in the Forces, 1946-48; lecturer in phonetics, Ministry of Education, 1948-50; English master, Banbury Grammar School, Oxfordshire, 1950-54; senior lecturer in English, Malayan Teachers Training College, Khata Baru, 1954-57; English language specialist, Department of Education, Brunei, Borneo, 1958-59; writer-in-residence, University of North Carolina, Chapel Hill, 1969-70; professor, Columbia University, New York, 1970-71; visiting fellow, Princeton University, New Jersey, 1970-71; distinguished professor, City University of New York, 1972-73; literary adviser, Guthrie Theatre, Minneapolis, 1972-75. Also composer. Recipient: Fellow, Royal Society of Literature, 1969; National Arts Club award, 1973; Prix du Meilleur Livre Etranger, 1981, for *Earthly Powers;* D.Litt., Manchester University, 1982; Commandeur de Mérite Cultural (Monaco), 1986; Commandeur des Arts et des Lettres (France), 1986; *Sunday Times* Mont Blanc award, 1987. Address: 44 rue Grimaldi, MC 98000, Monaco.

PUBLICATIONS

Novels

A Time for a Tiger. London, Heinemann, 1956.
The Enemy in the Blanket. London, Heinemann, 1958.
Beds in the East. London, Heinemann, 1959.
The Doctor Is Sick. London, Heinemann, and New York, Norton, 1960.
The Right to an Answer. London, Heinemann, 1960; New York, Norton, 1961.
Devil of a State. London, Heinemann, 1961; New York, Norton, 1962.
The Worm and the Ring. London, Heinemann, 1961; revised edition, 1970.
A Clockwork Orange. London, Heinemann, 1962; New York, Norton, 1963.
The Wanting Seed. London, Heinemann, 1962; New York, Norton, 1963.
Honey for the Bears. London, Heinemann, 1963; New York, Norton, 1964.
The Eve of Saint Venus. London, Sidgwick and Jackson, 1964; New York, Norton, 1967.
The Malayan Trilogy (includes *Time for a Tiger, The Enemy in the Blanket, Beds in the East*). London, Heinemann, 1964; as *The Long Day Wanes,* New York, Norton, 1965.
Nothing Like the Sun: A Story of Shakespeare's Love-Life. London, Heinemann, and New York, Norton, 1964.
A Vision of Battlements, illustrated by Edward Pagram. London, Sidgwick and Jackson, 1965; New York, Norton, 1966.
Tremor of Intent. London, Heinemann, and New York, Norton, 1966.
Enderby (includes *Inside Mr. Enderby* and *Enderby Outside;* also see below). New York, Norton, 1968.

Enderby Outside. London, Heinemann, 1968.
MF. London, Cape, and New York, Knopf, 1971.
The Clockwork Testament: or, Enderby's End. London, Hart Davis MacGibbon, 1974; New York, Knopf, 1975.
Napoleon Symphony. London, Cape, and New York, Knopf, 1974.
Beard's Roman Women, photos by David Robinson. New York, McGraw Hill, 1976; London, Hutchinson, 1977.
Abba Abba. London, Faber, and Boston, Little Brown, 1977.
1985. London, Hutchinson, and Boston, Little Brown, 1978.
Man of Nazareth. New York, McGraw Hill, 1979; London, Magnum, 1980.
Earthly Powers. London, Hutchinson, and New York, Simon and Schuster, 1980.
The End of the World News. London, Hutchinson, 1982; New York, McGraw Hill, 1983.
Enderby (includes *Inside Mr. Enderby, Enderby Outside, The Clockwork Testament*). London, Penguin, 1982.
Enderby's Dark Lady; or, No End to Enderby. London, Hutchinson, and New York, McGraw Hill, 1984.
The Kingdom of the Wicked. London, Hutchinson, and New York, Arbor House, 1985.
The Pianoplayers. London, Hutchinson, and New York, Arbor House, 1986.
Any Old Iron. London, Hutchinson, and New York, Random House, 1989.

Novels as Joseph Kell

One Hand Clapping. London, Davies, 1961; as Anthony Burgess, New York, Knopf, 1972.
Inside Mr. Enderby. London, Heinemann, 1963.

Short Stories

Will and Testament: A Fragment of Biography, illustrated by Joe Tilson. Verona, Italy, Plain Wrapper Press, 1977.
The Devil's Mode and Other Stories. London, Hutchinson, and New York, Random House, 1989.

Plays

Cyrano de Bergerac, adaptation of the play by Rostand (produced Minneapolis, 1971). New York, Knopf, 1971; musical version, as *Cyrano,* music by Michael Lewis, lyrics by Burgess (produced New York, 1972).
Oedipus the King, adaptation of play by Sophocles (produced Minneapolis, 1972; Southampton, Hampshire, 1979). Minneapolis, University of Minnesota Press, 1972; London, Oxford University Press, 1973.
The Cavalier of the Rose (story adaptation), in *Deer Rosenkavalier,* libretto by Hofmannsthal, music by Richard Strauss. Boston, Little Brown, 1982; London, Joseph, 1983.
Blooms of Dublin, music by Burgess, adaptation of the novel *Ulysses* by James Joyce (broadcast 1983). London, Hutchinson, 1986.
Cyrano de Bergerac (not same as 1971 version), adaptation of the play by Rostand (produced London, 1983). London, Hutchinson, 1985.
Oberon Old and New (includes original libretto by James Robinson Planché), music by Carl Maria von Weber. London, Hutchinson, 1985.

Carmen, adaptation of the libretto by Henri Meilhac and Ludovic Halévy, music by George Bizet (produced London, 1986). London, Hutchinson, 1986.

A Clockwork Orange, music by Burgess, adaptation of his own novel. London, Hutchinson, 1987.

A Clockwork Orange 2004 (produced London, 1990).

Screenplay: Special languages for *Quest for Fire,* 1981.

Radio Plays: *Blooms of Dublin,* music by Burgess, 2 February 1982; *A Meeting in Valladolid,* 1991.

Television Plays: *Moses—The Lawgiver,* with others, 1975; *Jesus of Nazareth,* with others, 1977; *A Kind of Failure* (documentary; *Writers and Places* series), 1981; *The Childhood of Christ,* music by Berlioz, 1985; *A.D.,* 1985.

Poetry

Moses: A Narrative. London, Dempsey and Squires, and New York, Stonehill, 1976.

A Christmas Recipe, illustrated by Fulvio Testa. Verona, Italy, Plain Wrapper Press, 1977.

Other

Translator, with Llewela Burgess, *The New Aristocrats,* by Michel de Saint-Pierre. London, Gollancz, 1962; Boston, Houghton Mifflin, 1963.

Translator, with Llewela Burgess, *The Olive Trees of Justice,* by Jean Pelegri. London, Sidgwick and Jackson, 1962.

The Novel Today. London, Longman, 1963.

Here Comes Everybody: An Introduction to James Joyce for the Ordinary Reader. London, Faber, 1965; revised edition, London, Hamlyn, 1982; as *Re Joyce,* New York, Norton, 1965.

Translator, *The Man Who Robbed Poor Boxes,* by Jean Servin. London, Gollancz, 1965.

Editor, *The Coaching Days of England 1750-1850.* London, Elek, and New York, Time-Life, 1966.

Editor, *A Journal of the Plague Year,* by Daniel Defoe. London, Penguin, 1966.

Editor, *A Shorter Finnegans Wake* by James Joyce. London, Faber, and New York, Viking Press, 1966.

Editor, with Francis Haskell, *The Age of the Grand Tour.* London, Elek, and New York, Crown, 1967.

The Novel Now: A Student's Guide to Contemporary Fiction. London, Faber, and New York, Norton, 1967; revised edition, Faber, 1971.

Urgent Copy: Literary Studies. London, Cape, and New York, Norton, 1968.

Editor, *Malaysian Stories,* by W. Somerset Maugham. Singapore, Heinemann, 1969.

Shakespeare. London, Cape, and New York, Knopf, 1970.

Joysprick: An Introduction to the Language of James Joyce. London, Deutsch, 1973; New York, Harcourt Brace, 1975.

Obscenity and the Arts (lecture). Valletta, Malta Library Association, 1973.

New York, with editors of Time-Life books, photos by Dan Budnik. New York, Time-Life, 1976.

Ernest Hemingway and His World. London, Thames and Hudson, and New York, Scribner, 1978.

On Going to Bed. London, Deutsch, and New York, Abbeville, 1982.

This Man and Music. London, Hutchinson, 1982; New York, McGraw Hill, 1983.

Ninety-Nine Novels: The Best in English since 1939: A Personal Choice. London, Allison and Busby, and New York, Summit, 1984.

Flame into Being: The Life and Work of D.H. Lawrence. London, Heinemann, and New York, Arbor House, 1985.

Homage to QWERT YUIOP: Selected Journalism 1978-1985. London, Hutchinson, 1986; as *But Do Blondes Prefer Gentlemen?,* New York, McGraw Hill, 1986.

Little Wilson and Big God, Being the First Part of the Confessions of Anthony Burgess. New York, Weidenfeld and Nicolson, 1986; London, Heinemann, 1987.

They Wrote in English. London, Hutchinson, 1988.

You've Had Your Time: Being the Second Part of the Confessions of Anthony Burgess. London, Heinemann, and New York, Weidenfeld, 1990.

On Mozart: A Paean for Wolfgang. Boston, Houghton Mifflin, 1991.

Other as John Burgess Wilson

English Literature: A Survey for Students. London, Longman, 1958.

Language Made Plain. London, English Universities Press, 1964; New York, Crowell, 1965; revised edition, London, Fontana, 1975.

PUBLICATIONS FOR CHILDREN

Fiction

A Long Trip to Teatime, illustrated by Fulvio Testa. London, Dempsey and Squires, and New York, Stonehill, 1976.

The Land Where Ice Cream Grows, illustrated by Fulvio Testa. London, Benn, and New York, Doubleday, 1979.

*

Media Adaptations: *A Clockwork Orange* (film, directed by Stanley Kubrick), Warner Brothers, 1971; *A Clockwork Orange* (cassette), Caedmon, 1973; *Anthony Burgess Reads from "The Eve of Saint Venus" and "Nothing Like the Sun"* (cassette), Caedmon, 1974; *Anthony Burgess Reads from "A Clockwork Orange" and "Enderby"* (cassette), Spoken Arts, 1974.

Biography: *Anthony Burgess* by A.A. DeVitis, New York, Twayne, 1972; entry in *Dictionary of Literary Biography,* Volume 14, Detroit, Gale, 1983.

Bibliography: *Anthony Burgess: A Bibliography* by Jeutonne Brewer, Metuchen, New Jersey, Scarecrow Press, 1980; *Anthony Burgess: An Annotated Bibliography and Reference Guide* by Paul Boytinck, New York, Garland, 1985.

Manuscript Collection: Mills Memorial Library, Hamilton, Ontario.

Critical Study: in *The Red Hot Vacuum* by Theodore Solotaroff,

New York, Atheneum, 1970; *Shakespeare's Lives* by Samuel Schoenbaum, Oxford, Clarendon Press, 1970; *Anthony Burgess* by Carol M. Dix, London, Longman, 1971; *The Consolations of Ambiguity: An Essay on the Novels of Anthony Burgess* by Robert K. Morris, Columbia, University of Missouri Press, 1971; entry in *Contemporary Literary Criticism,* Volume 1, Detroit, Gale, 1973; Volume 2, 1974; Volume 4, 1975; Volume 5, 1976; Volume 8, 1978; Volume 10, 1979; Volume 13, 1980; Volume 15, 1980; Volume 22, 1982; Volume 40, 1986; *The Clockwork Universe of Anthony Burgess* by Richard Mathews, San Bernardino, California, Borgo Press, 1978; *Anthony Burgess: The Artist as Novelist* by Geoffrey Aggeler, Tuscaloosa, University of Alabama Press, 1979, and *Critical Essays on Anthony Burgess* edited by Aggeler, Boston, Hall, 1986; *Anthony Burgess* by Samuel Coale, New York, Ungar, 1981; *Anthony Burgess: A Study in Character* by Martina Ghosh-Schellhorn, Frankfurt, Germany, Lang, 1986.

*   *   *

Anthony Burgess has written prolifically since the 1950s. His output includes a novel trilogy set in Malay; another group of three novels featuring Enderby, an off-beat poet; two critical examinations of James Joyce; and a biography of Shakespeare. Another novel, *Earthly Powers,* provides an eccentric, comprehensive view of twentieth-century culture. He has composed numerous orchestral works, screenplays, television scripts and reviews, and continues to produce acerbic commentary on current events in London and Dublin newspapers. Yet, for many, Burgess's reputation stands on the notoriety of one novel, *A Clockwork Orange,* and its 1971 film version produced and directed by Stanley Kubrick. Certainly, *A Clockwork Orange* is the work by which young adults know Anthony Burgess best.

If there ever was a literary work that demands thorough, open discussion, *A Clockwork Orange* is that work. Typically it rivets the attention of its readers even as it repels them by its violence, iconoclasm, and neologistic "slanguage." Like many of Burgess's works, *A Clockwork Orange* bears the marks of his private fixations: a love of music; a fascination with languages; an approach-avoidance attitude toward the doctrines of Roman Catholicism; the painful memory of a violent assault on his wife by thieves that caused her to miscarry while he was away serving in the military during World War II.

Aside from these personal preoccupations, the novel addresses some deeply troubling social phenomena of the mid-twentieth century including the epidemic growth of teenage gangs throughout the Western world and the universal application of B. F. Skinner's behavior modification techniques in prisons, asylums, and psychiatric clinics. In 1961, Burgess had directly observed the *stilyaqi,* gangs of young thugs, in Leningrad. Throughout the late '50s and early '60s, he had followed in the press the horrifying antics of their London counterparts, "The Teddy Boys." As for Skinner, his influential studies, *The Behavior of Organisms* and *Verbal Behavior,* as well as his novel *Walden II* all suggest remedies for antisocial behavior (such as that of teenage gangs), but make little attempt to understand the cognitive functions and complex learning patterns underlying such behaviors. More troubling for Burgess was the failure of Skinner's behavior modification strategies to recognize

the importance of free will (a primary tenet of Catholic theology) in a properly functioning human being. *A Clockwork Orange* registers Burgess's deeply felt conflict about the need to control violence while at the same time respecting the freedom of the individual to choose goodness over evil.

The medium for carrying Burgess's message is Alex, a teenaged gang leader whose very name implies his function. "Alex" might be translated as either "without law" or "without word." In some sense, Alex is without either. He recognizes no law beyond his personal pleasure in inflicting pain on innocent victims and experiencing the high that drugs and classical music alike provide him. Not even the consensus will of his gang of thugs merits his loyalty, nor does he respect or speak the legal language or "word" of his society. What he does speak is *Nadsat,* the Russian equivalent of "teen." *Nadsat,* Burgess's own creation, intermingles Russian words (transliterated into English) with British and American slang, sometimes combining terms in the two languages and placing them in a syntactic arrangement uncommon in either language. The effect is startling, a violation of our received idea of communication:

> Our pockets were full of deng, so there was no real need from the point of view of crasting any more pretty polly to tolchock some old veck in an alley and viddy him swim in his blood while we counted the takings and divided by four, nor to do the ultra violent on some shivering starry grey-haired ptitsa in a shop and go smecking off with the till's guts. But, as they say, money isn't everything.

Besides his inspired use of *Nadsat,* Burgess also employs more traditional literary techniques to make his problematic argument about the necessity for allowing fully realized human beings to choose from an unlimited range of behaviors. In several cases he overlaps or superimposes an evil element on an apparently good one so that we are led to conclude that the two extremes are aspects of a single human nature. For example, Alex's foil is F. Alexander, an author whose wife Alex unmercifully beats and rapes. F. Alexander's book, titled *A Clockwork Orange,* concerns the immorality of turning a juicy, sensuous organic being (an orange) into a machine (a clockwork). After Alex has been imprisoned for two years and transformed by behavior modification techniques (which are as psychologically violent as the physical brutality Alex had perpetrated on his innocent victims) into a "good" boy, he finds his way, as if by instinct, back to F. Alexander's cottage (which, significantly, bears the name HOME). Not recognizing Alex as his wife's assailant, F. Alexander invites Alex (who has just been brutally beaten himself by his former gangmate now turned policeman) into his home. There Alex discovers a copy of *A Clockwork Orange* on the spine of which is printed his host's name: "F. Alexander. Good Boy, I thought, he is another Alex. Then I leafed through, standing in his pyjamas and bare nogas...and I could not viddy what the book was about."

The conflation of Alex with F. Alexander and F. Alexander with Anthony Burgess works to impress on the reader the notion that we all share a common fallen nature as well as the potential to overcome that nature with good. This theme is reinforced by other coincidences of contraries and recurring symbols in the novel. For example, Ludwig van Beethoven, whose music incites Alex in his unreformed state to violent fantasies, seems related, in more than name only, to the "Ludivico technique" that is used to cure Alex of his brutal tendencies. Furthermore, Alex's frequent address to his readers, "Oh, my brothers," implies the readers' collusion in Alex's violent projects; and the recurring milk imagery in the novel suggests a common source of nourishment, one that carries both good and evil tendencies for all of humankind.

Although the original London edition of *A Clockwork Orange* includes a final chapter that anticipates a future for Alex wherein he *chooses* a law-abiding (if not truly good) life, the American version ends with Alex reverting to his natural, evil self. The reader is left to wrestle with the implications of such evil for society. While the American edition does not provide the hopeful ending that some readers might long for, it does provide a helpful afterword and (unauthorized) glossary by critic Stanley Edgar Hyman. It is particularly appropriate that this novel have an afterword for it is too disturbing, too provoking to be left unanswered.

—Mary Lowe-Evans

———

BURNS, Olive Ann. Also writes as Amy Larkin. American. Born in Banks County, Georgia, 17 July 1924. Educated at Mercer University, 1942-44; University of North Carolina at Chapel Hill, A.B. 1946. Married Andrew H. Sparks in 1956; one daughter and one son. Writer and free-lance journalist. Staff writer for the *Coca-Cola Bottler* and the *Laundryman's Guide,* in Atlanta, Georgia, 1946-47; *Atlanta Journal and Constitution,* Georgia, staff writer for the Sunday magazine, 1947-57; author of local newspaper advice column "Ask Amy," under pseudonym Amy Larkin, 1960-67; contributor of articles to *Atlanta Weekly.* Recipient: *Cold Sassy Tree* was included in the annual lists of recommended selections for young adults by the New York Public Library, American Library Association, *School Library Journal,* and *Booklist,* all 1985. *Died 4 July 1990.*

PUBLICATIONS

Fiction

Cold Sassy Tree. New York, Ticknor and Fields, 1984.
Leaving Cold Sassy: The Unfinished Sequel to Cold Sassy Tree. New York, Ticknor and Fields, 1992.

Nonfiction

Down Home Southern Cooking. New York, Doubleday, 1987.

*

Media Adaptations: *Cold Sassy Tree* (cassette), Books on Tape; abridged version, Bantam Audio; *Cold Sassy Tree* (television movie), Turner Broadcasting, 1989.

*   *   *

It took Olive Ann Burns ten years to write *Cold Sassy Tree,* and it took only a few months more for it to become one of the most talked about and highly-acclaimed books in the country. Will Tweedy, the fourteen-year-old narrator of the book, has been compared to Huck Finn and Holden Caulfield. Burns herself has been compared to Southern writers Eudora Welty and Alice Walker. Burns has a wonderful ear for dialogue, which makes Will, Grandpa Blakeslee, and Grandpa Blakeslee's second wife, Miss Love, so alive and so likable.

While this book was written as an adult novel—the central character is Grandpa Blakeslee, fifty-nine years old, three weeks a widower—it has proven to be widely popular with young adults. The story begins with Grandpa Blakeslee's sudden elopement with Miss Love, and chronicles family happenings of the next year. The time is 1906 and the place is Cold Sassy, Georgia. It is filled with marvelous and funny stories of Cold Sassy, a small, pious town, which after Grandpa's death—"over his dead body"—is renamed Progressive City. The book recounts, with humor and compassion, birth and death, ordinary daily chores and extraordinary family and community celebrations. Most of all, the book celebrates life.

Focused on adult behaviors, the book shows and accepts human nature, warts and all. It is never didactic, as are many young adult novels dealing with social problems that must be resolved in present-day socially acceptable ways. The book offers a perspective on life that is time and place specific; but as we laugh about these specifics, we must smile at the specifics of our own time and place.

Before writing *Cold Sassy Tree,* Burns had collected family stories from her own parents, taking the stories down in their own words, exactly as they were told, and adding her own recollections as well as those of other family members. She wanted to preserve their voices for her own two children and she ended up with two typewritten volumes, along with letters, photographs, and other memorabilia. "Details matter," she told her editor, and she paid attention to details. Grandpa Blakeslee is modeled after her own grandfather, and Will Tweedy after her father, who was also fourteen years old in 1906.

Following the great reception of *Cold Sassy Tree,* Burns began a sequel, which she titled "Time, Dirt, and Money." She worked on this book for almost five years, while battling recurrences of cancer, but she died before it was finished. Her publisher combined this unfinished sequel with a remembrance of the author by her editor, Katrina Kenison, and titled it *Leaving Cold Sassy.* The sequel begins ten years later; Will Tweedy is twenty-five years old, about to fall in love with his wife-to-be and trying to adjust to changes in Progressive City. The story was to be a portrait of this marriage. The unfinished sequel ends though before the marriage takes place; it is less than a fourth of the length of *Cold Sassy Tree.* It has some of the same sparkling dialogue, but the central characters—Will and his beloved Sanna—are less compelling than whiskey-snorting, outspoken, cantankerous Grandpa Blakeslee.

Leaving Cold Sassy is worthwhile reading for several reasons. It shows an author's work in progress. Burns rewrote and rewrote *Cold Sassy Tree* and the difference between it and the sequel clearly shows the difference between finished and unfinished writing. Kenison provides in her reminiscence valuable details on how Burns practiced her craft, which is fascinating to those who enjoy good literature as well as to those who wish to write good literature. Kenison's discussion of Burns' methods of collecting family history is also useful to those who wish to embark on their own family history but don't know how to begin. After reading *Leaving Cold Sassy* though, the reader is likely to leave Progressive City and return to Cold Sassy itself. For the scandalous turns in Cold Sassy, Georgia, are so exuberant and so touching and so funny that you will wish you could have lived there yourself.

—Mary Lystad

BURROUGHS, Edgar Rice. Also wrote as Normal Bean; John Tyler McCulloch. American. Born in Chicago, Illinois, 1 September 1875. Educated at Harvard School, Chicago, 1888-91; Phillips Academy, Andover, Massachusetts, 1891-92; Michigan Military Academy, Orchard Lake, 1892-95. Served in the United States 7th Cavalry, 1896-97; Illinois Reserve Militia, 1918-19. Married 1) Emma Centennia Hulbert in 1900 (divorced 1934), two sons and one daughter; 2) Florence Dearholt in 1935 (divorced 1942). Writer, 1912-50. Instructor and assistant commandant, Michigan Military Academy, Orchard Lake, Michigan, 1895-96; owner of a stationery store, Pocatello, Idaho, 1898; associated with American Battery Company, Chicago, Illinois, 1899-1903; associated with Sweetser-Burroughs Mining Company in Idaho, 1903-04; railroad policeman, Oregon Short Line Railroad Company, Salt Lake City, Utah, 1904; manager of stenographic department, Sears, Roebuck and Company, Chicago, 1906-08; partner, Burroughs and Dentzer (advertising agency), Chicago, 1908-09; office manager, Physicians Co-Operative Association, Chicago, 1909; partner, State-Burroughs Company (sales firm), Chicago, 1910-11; worked for Champlain Yardley Company, stationers, Chicago, 1910-11; manager, System Service Bureau, Chicago, 1912-13; mayor, Malibu Beach, California, 1933; United Press war correspondent in the Pacific during Second World War. Founder of Edgar Rice Burroughs, Inc. (publishing house), 1913, Burroughs-Tarzan Enterprises, 1934-39, and Burroughs-Tarzan Pictures, 1934-37; columnist ("Laugh It Off"), *Honolulu Advertiser,* 1941-42, 1945. *Died 19 March 1950.*

PUBLICATIONS

Novels

Tarzan of the Apes. Chicago, McClurg, 1914; London, Methuen, 1917.
The Return of Tarzan. Chicago, McClurg, 1915; London, Methuen, 1918.
The Beasts of Tarzan. Chicago, McClurg, 1916; London, Methuen, 1918.
A Princess of Mars. Chicago, McClurg, 1917; London, Methuen, 1919.
The Son of Tarzan. Chicago, McClurg, 1917; London, Methuen, 1919.
The Gods of Mars. Chicago, McClurg, 1918; London, Methuen, 1920.
Out of Time's Abyss. London, Tandem, 1918.
Tarzan and the Jewels of Opar. Chicago, McClurg, 1918; London, Methuen, 1919.
The Warlord of Mars. Chicago, McClurg, 1919; London, Methuen, 1920.
Thuvia, Maid of Mars. Chicago, McClurg, 1920; London, Methuen, 1921.
Tarzan the Terrible. Chicago, McClurg, and London, Methuen, 1921.
The Chessmen of Mars. Chicago, McClurg, 1922; London, Methuen, 1923.
At the Earth's Core. Chicago, McClurg, 1922; London, Methuen, 1923.
The Girl from Hollywood. New York, Macaulay, 1923; London, Methuen, 1924.
Pellucidar. Chicago, McClurg, 1923; London, Methuen, 1924.

Tarzan and the Golden Lion. Chicago, McClurg, 1923; London, Methuen, 1924.
Tarzan and the Ant Men. Chicago, McClurg, 1924; London, Methuen, 1925.
The Bandit of Hell's Bend. Chicago, McClurg, 1925; London, Methuen, 1926.
The Tarzan Twins (for children). Joliet, Illinois, Volland, 1927; London, Collins, 1930.
The Outlaw of Torn. Chicago, McClurg, and London, Methuen, 1927.
The War Chief. Chicago, McClurg, 1927.
The Master Mind of Mars. Chicago, McClurg, 1928; London, Methuen, 1939.
Tarzan, Lord of the Jungle. Chicago, McClurg, and London, Cassell, 1928.
The Monster Men. Chicago, McClurg, 1929.
Tarzan and the Lost Empire. New York, Metropolitan, 1929; London, Cassell, 1931.
Tanar of Pellucidar. New York, Metropolitan, 1930; London, Methuen, 1939.
Tarzan at the Earth's Core. New York, Metropolitan, 1930; London, Methuen, 1938.
A Fighting Man of Mars. New York, Metropolitan, 1931; London, Lane, 1932.
Tarzan the Invincible. Tarzana, California, Burroughs, 1931; London, Lane, 1933.
Tarzan the Triumphant. Tarzana, California, Burroughs, 1931; London, Lane, 1933.
Jungle Girl. Tarzana, California, Burroughs, 1932; London, Odhams Press; as *The Land of Hidden Men,* New York, Ace Books, 1963.
Apache Devil. Tarzana, California, Burroughs, 1933.
Tarzan and the City of Gold. Tarzana, California, Burroughs, 1933; London, Lane, 1936.
Pirates of Venus. Tarzana, California, Burroughs, 1934; London, Lane, 1935.
Tarzan and the Lion-Men. Tarzana, California, Burroughs, 1934; London, W.H. Allen, 1950.
Lost on Venus. Tarzana, California, Burroughs, 1935; London, Methuen, 1937.
Tarzan and the Leopard Men. Tarzana, California, Burroughs, 1935; London, Lane, 1936.
Swords of Mars. Tarzana, California, Burroughs, 1936; London, New English Library, 1966.
Tarzan's Quest. Tarzana, California, Burroughs, 1936; London, Methuen, 1938.
Tarzan and the Tarzan Twins, with Jad-Bal-Ja, the Golden Lion (for children). Racine, Wisconsin, Whitman Publishing, 1936.
Back to the Stone Age. Tarzana, California, Burroughs, 1937.
The Oakdale Affair: The Rider. Tarzana, California, Burroughs, 1937.
The Lad and the Lion. Tarzana, California, Burroughs, 1938.
Tarzan and the Forbidden City, illustrated by John Coleman Burroughs. Tarzana, California, Burroughs, 1938; London, W.H. Allen, 1950.
Carson of Venus. Tarzana, California, Burroughs, 1939; London, Goulden, 1950.
The Deputy Sheriff of Comanche County. Tarzana, California, Burroughs, 1940.
Synthetic Men of Mars. Tarzana, California, Burroughs, 1940; London, Methuen, 1941.
Land of Terror. Tarzana, California, Burroughs, 1944.

Escape on Venus. Tarzana, California, Burroughs, 1946; London, New English Library, 1966.

Tarzan and the Foreign Legion. Tarzana, California, Burroughs, 1947; London, W.H. Allen, 1949.

The People That Time Forgot. New York, Ace Books, 1963.

Beyond the Farthest Star. New York, Ace Books, 1964.

Tarzan and the Madman. New York, Canaveral Press, 1964; London, New English Library, 1966.

The Girl from Farris's. Kansas City, Missouri, House of Greystoke, 1965.

The Efficiency Expert. Kansas City, Missouri, House of Greystoke, 1966.

I Am a Barbarian. Tarzana, California, Burroughs, 1967.

Pirate Blood (as John Tyler McCulloch). New York, Ace Books, 1970.

Short Stories

Jungle Tales of Tarzan. Chicago, McClurg, and London, Methuen, 1919.

Tarzan the Untamed. Chicago, McClurg, and London, Methuen, 1920.

The Mucker. Chicago, McClurg, 1921; as *The Mucker* and *The Man without a Soul,* London, Methuen, 2 vols., 1921-22.

The Land That Time Forgot. Chicago, McClurg, 1924; London, Methuen, 1925.

The Cave Girl. Chicago, McClurg, 1925; London, Methuen, 1927.

The Eternal Lover. Chicago, McClurg, 1925; London, Methuen, 1927; as *The Eternal Savage,* New York, Ace Books, 1963.

The Mad King. Chicago, McClurg, 1926.

The Moon Maid. Chicago, McClurg, 1926; London, Stacey, 1972; abridged edition, as *The Moon Men,* New York, Canaveral Press, 1962; augmented edition, London, Tandem, 1975.

Tarzan the Magnificent. Tarzana, California, Burroughs, 1939; London, Methuen, 1940.

Llana of Gathol. Tarzana, California, Burroughs, 1948; London, New English Library, 1967.

Beyond Thirty. Privately printed, 1955; as *The Lost Continent,* New York, Ace Books, 1963.

The Man-Eater. Privately printed, 1955.

Savage Pellucidar. New York, Canaveral Press, 1963.

John Carter of Mars. New York, Canaveral Press, 1964.

Tales of Three Planets. New York, Canaveral Press, 1964.

Tarzan and the Castaways. New York, Canaveral Press, 1964; London, New English Library, 1966.

The Wizard of Venus. New York, Ace Books, 1970.

Other

Official Guide of the Tarzan Clans of America. Privately printed, 1939.

*

Biography: Entry in *Dictionary of Literary Biography,* Volume 8: *Twentieth Century American Science Fiction Writers,* Detroit, Gale, 1981.

Critical Studies: *Edgar Rice Burroughs: Master of Adventure* by Richard A. Lupoff, New York, Canaveral Press, 1965, revised edition, New York, Ace, 1968; *Tarzan Alive: A Definitive Biography of*

Lord Greystoke by Philip José Farmer, New York, Doubleday, 1972, London, Panther, 1974; *Burroughs' Science Fiction* by Robert R. Kudlay and Joan Leiby, Geneseo, New York, School of Library and Information Science, 1973; *Edgar Rice Burroughs: The Man Who Created Tarzan* (includes bibliography) by Irwin Porges, Provo, Utah, Brigham Young University Press, 1975, London, New English Library, 1976; *A Guide to Barsoom* by John Flint Roy, New York, Ballantine, 1976; *The Burroughs Bestiary: An Encyclopaedia of Monsters and Imaginary Beings Created by Edgar Rice Burroughs* by David Day, London, New English Library, 1978; *Tarzan and Tradition: Classical Myth in Popular Literature* by Erling B. Holtsmark, Westport, Connecticut, Greenwood Press, 1981.

*   *   *

Edgar Rice Burroughs, best known as the creator of Tarzan, was a prolific author of vigorous adventure novels set in primitive lands, on other planets, and in the interior of the earth. His fiction often contains surprisingly deft satire and unexpected speculation about evolutionary mutations. As a result, his work, though frequently dismissed as immature, has been credited with stimulating the popularity of science fiction and adventure fantasy in the first half of the twentieth century.

Despite the worldwide appeal of his Tarzan character, Burroughs's Tarzan books, though often read by many young people, were for many years less familiar to the public than the long series of Tarzan films. As a result, misconceptions about Burroughs's work persist. Yet these novels, while carelessly written, are usually superior to the films. Indeed, the first Johnny Weissmuller Tarzan movie (1932) was well acted, but only the recent *Greystoke: The Legend of Tarzan, Lord of the Apes* (1983) comes close to capturing the essence of Burroughs's vision. But his science fiction series have always enjoyed a loyal following; they remain primarily appealing to those who enjoy adolescent adventure. Nevertheless, despite hasty writing and slapdash plotting, the prolific Burroughs should be recognized as a myth-making, popular novelist with a natural talent for storytelling.

Somewhat like L. Frank Baum, the creator of Oz, and later science fiction master Robert Heinlein, Burroughs turned to writing in middle age after a mediocre business career during which he had traveled widely around the United States, especially in the raw territory of the West. Yet after a tentative beginning, he enjoyed a quick success and a long career notable for a sensible professionalism during which he continued several popular series and wrote a number of interesting individual works such as *The Moon Maid* (1926).

His first professional sale was *Under the Moons of Mars,* serialized in 1912 and introducing Burroughs's popular invincible hero John Carter, who is transported to Mars apparently by astral projection, following a battle with Apaches in Arizona. This novel, published in book form as *A Princess of Mars,* described Carter's period of captivity with green warriors, his meeting with the beautiful princess Dejah Thoris of the empire of Helium, and their subsequent escape and return to her home. Two sequels, *The Gods of Mars* and *The Warlord of Mars,* continued the saga of John Carter and established this Virginia gentleman as the "greatest swordsman of two worlds." Although Burroughs's conception of a modern Mars dominated by unending wars and haunted by memories of an ancient civilized past has been traced to the influence of forgotten authors like the English adventure novelist Edwin L.

Arnold, Burroughs showed originality in exploiting this setting for a series of heroic adventures.

In later years, Burroughs continued the saga of his romanticized Mars, with the descendants of John Carter and Dejah Thoris experiencing adventures among the sandy wastes and ruined cities of this imagined planet of adventure. In *The Master Mind of Mars,* Burroughs introduced a secondary hero, Ulysses Paxton, while developing satire on repressive institutional religions—always a favorite target of the author in the Tarzan novels and other books. In one of the most fast-paced and vigorous action adventures of the series, *A Fighting Man of Mars,* the hero's role is given to Hadron of Hastor, a protégé of John Carter. Plucky young princesses are permitted to star in *Thuvia, Maid of Mars* and *Llana of Gathol* which features the granddaughter of Carter. The "Martian" series eventually reached eleven books, and its popularity remains second only to the Tarzan books.

Burroughs's famous series was the Tarzan saga, describing the fortunes of John Clayton, Lord Greystoke, whose aristocratic parents are abandoned on the west coast of Africa and who, after being orphaned and raised as an ape, grows into a leader of the simian tribe and a superhuman hero. The story of Tarzan's progress to manhood in *Tarzan of the Apes* remains a compelling one despite Burroughs's extremely limited understanding of science. In essence, Burroughs's tale is a myth of the victory of heredity and talent over the constraints of a hostile environment. The narrative of Tarzan's emerging intelligence, mastery of his environment, and his discovery of his true identity—an event resulting from his involvement with the victims set ashore from another mutiny—contains a fascinating appeal for readers interested in the development of human intelligence. Although Burroughs was obviously indebted to Rudyard Kipling's story of Mowgli in his "Jungle Books," Burroughs produced a distinctly American variation on Kipling's theme.

Burroughs followed *Tarzan of the Apes* with many other Tarzan novels; the series eventually reached twenty-four entries. In *The Return of Tarzan,* Tarzan leaves civilization to return to Africa, where he becomes the chieftain of a tribe of black warriors and discovers a source of wealth in Opar, a colony established by survivors of the fall of Atlantis. However, Tarzan does not succumb to the love of La, the white-skinned queen of Opar; instead, the establishment of his identity as the true Lord Greystoke and the death of his cousin Cecil Clayton, the fiance of Jane Porter, free him to marry Jane, the American woman who is his first love.

Most of Burroughs's adventure novels depict the importance of a primitive environment to act as a stimulus and a challenge for his heroes and heroines. This return to primitivism provides the theme of *The Son of Tarzan,* one of the best novels in the Tarzan series wherein Tarzan's son gains heroic stature after being kidnapped and abandoned in Africa. Another imaginative novel in the series is *Tarzan the Terrible,* in which Burroughs draws on his inventiveness to imagine an entire lost continent or land mass in the central African jungle, complete with a dehumanizing religion which is as usual the subject of Burroughs's satire. A satirical tone also underlies *Tarzan and the Ant Men,* which Richard Lupoff, one of Burroughs's better critics, regards as one of the best Tarzan novels.

However, too many of the later Tarzan books become involved with the lost race motif of H. Rider Haggard's novels, a theme usually embodied in pairs of lost and feuding cities which have flourished in hidden valleys cut off from civilization. Late in the series, Tarzan gains immortality through an African shaman's secret formula, and his enduring quest for heroic adventure finally takes him into the jungles of Indonesia during World War II in *Tarzan and the Foreign Legion.* But in his waning years, Burroughs tended to grow tired of his invincible hero.

Early in his career, Burroughs also began an adventure saga set in a primitive world called Pellucidar located inside the earth (an idea which had been used by Jules Verne and other authors). However, after a couple of vigorous early books involving the explorer David Innes, this series quickly lost momentum (except for *Tarzan at the Earth's Core,* when the indomitable lord of the jungle is taken to Pellucidar in an effort to breathe fresh life into the series).

A fourth adventure series set on Venus was inaugurated in the thirties. Unlike Burroughs's more famous adventure series, this group of stories employs a hero, Carson Napier, who though resourceful and athletic has many limitations. Although the Venus novels blend romance and comedy and contain some of Burroughs's most imaginative depictions of alien societies, only five books in the series were completed and the final two were connected groups of pulp novelettes. Though the Venus saga continues to entertain readers, it never gained the popularity of the Tarzan and Martian series.

In addition to his four major adventure series, Burroughs also wrote a number of other imaginative novels, mostly composed in the period 1912-1932, which have interested readers of science fiction and outdoors. Generally, these books celebrate Burroughs's fascination with primitivism as an influence that produces heroic qualities. In *The Cave Girl,* a weak and sheltered Boston aristocrat develops into a manly warrior after being abandoned on a rugged Pacific island and falling in love with the lovely island princess. A similar process of rediscovering primitive strengths and emotions takes place for Victoria Custer, a proper American woman in *The Eternal Savage,* when she falls in love with a warrior from a stone age milieu.

The thematic interest in some of the other novels is more speculative. *The Moon Maid* and its sequel *The Moon Men* satirize a world dominated by a communist horde called the Kalkars, but their oppressive forces are finally routed by the Red Hawk, a nomadic war leader who is the final descendant of a line of heroes who have battled the Kalkars. *The Land That Time Forgot* and its sequels offer adventure on a primitive "lost continent" (probably suggested by Arthur Conan Doyle's *The Lost World*), but the violent action is supplemented by evolutionary speculation. Another unusual novel, *The Monster Men,* apparently influenced by H. G. Wells's *The Island of Dr. Morearn,* features a mad scientist defeated by a primitive warrior who is one of his creations. Finally, a late novella, *Beyond the Farthest Star,* is unusual in the Burroughs canon because it uses a science-fiction setting to depict the brutality and futility of war.

Burroughs's worlds of primitive adventure contain several elements which are "politically correct" by the standards of the nineties. The magnificent bond of Waziri warriors who often aid Tarzan are an admirable tribute to African blacks. Moreover, Burroughs published two Western novels about a white Apache, *The War Chief* and *Apache Devil* by drawing on his experiences in the Seventh Cavalry. These two novels are similar to Zane Grey's *The Vanishing American* and Max Brand's "Cheyenne" novels in showing a surprising sympathy for Native Americans. As for Burroughs's depiction of women, only the most extreme feminists might find fault with the courage and resourcefulness of the last of Burroughs's heroines, such as Nadara the cave girl, and Dejah Thoris, the princess of Mars.

To be sure, Burroughs's fiction is often crudely written and seldom offers a complex view of human character. But Burroughs remains a widely read author of durable adventure fiction set in a variety of primitive worlds.

—Edgar L. Chapman

————

BURTON, Hester (Wood-Hill). British. Born in Beccles, Suffolk, England, 6 December 1913. Educated at Headington School, Oxford University, 1932-36, B.A. (honours) in English 1936. Married Reginald W.B. Burton in 1937; three daughters. Writer of historical novels for children and biographer. Part-time grammar school teacher; assistant editor, Oxford Junior Encyclopedia, London, 1956-61; examiner in public examination. Recipient: Carnegie Medal, 1963, and Honorable Mention in the New York *Herald Tribune* Children's Spring Book Festival, 1964, for *Time of Trial;* runner up for Carnegie Medal, c. 1962, for *Castors Away!;* Boston *Globe-Horn Book* award, 1971. Address: Mill House, Kidlington, Oxford, England.

PUBLICATIONS FOR YOUNG ADULTS

Fiction

The Great Gale, illustrated by Joan Kiddell-Monroe. London, Oxford University Press, 1960; as *The Flood at Reedsmere,* illustrated by Robin Jacques, Cleveland, World, 1968.
Castors Away!, illustrated by Victor Ambrus. London, Oxford University Press, 1962; Cleveland, World, 1963.
Time of Trial, illustrated by Victor Ambrus. London, Oxford University Press, 1963: Cleveland, World, 1964.
No Beat of Drum, illustrated by Victor Ambrus. London, Oxford University Press, 1966; Cleveland, World, 1967.
In Spite of All Terror, illustrated by Victor Ambrus. London, Oxford University Press, 1968; New York, World, 1969.
Otmoor for Ever!, illustrated by Gareth Floyd. London, Hamish Hamilton, 1968.
Thomas, illustrated by Victor Ambrus. London, Oxford University Press, 1969; as *Beyond the Weir Bridge,* New York, Crowell, 1970.
Through the Fire, illustrated by Gareth Floyd. London, Hamish Hamilton, 1969.
The Henchmans at Home, illustrated by Victor Ambrus. London, Oxford University Press, 1970; New York, Crowell, 1972.
The Rebel, illustrated by Victor Ambrus. London, Oxford University Press, 1971; New York, Crowell, 1972.
Riders of the Storm, illustrated by Victor Ambrus. London, Oxford University Press, 1972; New York, Crowell, 1973.
Kate Rider, illustrated by Victor Ambrus. London, Oxford University Press, 1974; as *Kate Ryder,* New York, Crowell, 1975.
To Ravensrigg, illustrated by Victor Ambrus. London, Oxford University Press, 1976; New York, Crowell, 1977.
A Grenville Goes to Sea, illustrated by Colin McNaughton. London, Heinemann, 1977.
Tim at the Fur Fort, illustrated by Victor Ambrus. London, Hamish Hamilton, 1977.
When the Beacons Blazed, illustrated by Victor Ambrus. London, Hamish Hamilton, 1978.

Five August Days, illustrated by Trevor Ridley. London, Oxford University Press, 1981.

Radio Play: *The Great Gale,* from her own story, 1961.

Television Play: *Castors Away!,* from her own story, 1968.

Other

Editor, *A Book of Modern Stories.* London, Oxford University Press, 1959.
Editor, *Her First Ball: Short Stories,* illustrated by Susan Einzig. London, Oxford University Press, 1959.
A Seaman at the Time of Trafalgar, illustrated by Victor Ambrus. London, Oxford University Press, 1963.

PUBLICATIONS FOR ADULTS

Other

Barbara Bodichon, 1827-1891. London, Murray, 1949.
Editor, *Coleridge and the Wordsworths.* London, Oxford University Press, 1953.
Editor, *Tennyson.* London, Oxford University Press, 1954.

*

Biography: Essay in *Something about the Author Autobiography Series,* Volume 8, Detroit, Gale, 1989, pp. 51-64.

Critical Study: Entry in *Children's Literature Review,* Volume 1, Detroit, Gale, 1976.

*   *   *

Towards the end of *The Great Gale* when the flooded East Anglian village of Reedsmere has been visited both by the Queen and by the Minister of Housing, Mr. Macmillan, Mary whispers to her friend Myrtle: "I shall never forget today.... Today we were part of history." Later after hearing on the radio the full extent of the havoc wrought by the gale she has a different thought. "Perhaps, after all, it was not an exciting, but a solemn and dreadful thing to be part of history." This duality of response on the part of individuals caught up in a national crisis is very characteristic of Hester Burton's novels, whether they are set in the 17th, 18th, 19th, or 20th centuries; it is not for nothing that one of her most highly praised books is called *Time of Trial* (though in this case the "time" is 1801, and the "trial" is in one sense that of the heroine's radical book-seller father accused of sedition). Burton has modestly acknowledged a tendency to "find refuge" in history because the present age is becoming increasingly difficult to understand, whereas the past, in so far as historians have selected and interpreted the evidence, is easier to see in perspective. Moreover she has confessed that she is inclined to choose an historical event or theme because it echoes something she has experienced in her own life. One can see, for instance, that *Castors Away!,* with its vivid and at times harrowing account of the autumn of the Battle of Trafalgar has its parallel in some events of the Second World War, while *No Beat of Drum,* with its portrayal of the harsh poverty of the English farm-labourers in

1829 to 1831, mirrors to a certain extent the divisive class-conflicts of the 1930s. Yet in fact her most successful novel of all is the one which is derived most directly from lived experience. *In Spite of All Terror* evokes for us with a wonderful visual concreteness the outbreak of war in 1939, the evacuation of an East London school to the remoteness of the Oxfordshire countryside, the trauma of Dunkirk, the excitement of the Battle of Britain, and the anguish of the bombing of London in the autumn of 1940. It is moreover the most compulsively readable of her novels, its characterisation remains convincing while covering an extremely varied range of social classes, and it has in Liz Hawtin a protagonist who is at the same time the most believable and the most engaging of all Burton's heroines.

Even in this novel Burton supplemented her own recollections with the use of books, as well as other people's memories. Her more strictly historical novels have all been thoroughly and intelligently researched, using contemporary documents and diaries as well as modern scholarship, so that they recreate for us with powerful authenticity both the atmosphere and the detailed ways of life of her chosen period. (In keeping with the spirit of her self-acknowledged selectivity she has made herself particularly at home in the period of the French Revolution and the Napoleonic Wars— *The Rebel, Riders of the Storm, Time of Trial,* and *Castors Away!*— and also in the period of the English Civil War—*Thomas* and *Kate Rider.*) In general her stories move at a brisk pace and are well supplied with incident; for the young adolescent reader their appeal is probably enhanced by a disposition to include, and even to work for, moments of strong feeling and uninhibited emotional release. An attractive example of her historical work at its best is *No Beat of Drum* in which the action moves from the impoverished countryside of southern England to the penal settlements of Van Diemen's Land. One cannot fault the generosity of the author's sympathy with the exploited and starving labourers, and she shows understanding of the "Captain Swing" riots even though she does not condone them. The portrayal of life in Tasmania is as vividly detailed as that of life in Hampshire, and one's only reservation about the latter part of the book is that the plot relies rather too much on coincidence.

The "excitement" of "being part of history" has always been strongly present in Burton's fiction, but in some of her later work the "solemn and dreadful" aspects have come more to the fore. Thus even in the relatively early *Castors Away!* the more barbarous features of the naval warfare of the time were rendered with an unflinching realism which makes some parts of the book strong meat for juvenile stomachs. A few years later in *Thomas* Burton seemed to have lost contact temporarily with her young readership by a too remorseless insistence on the hardships, miseries, and frustrations of her three protagonists; indeed her description of the Great Plague of London makes harrowing reading for an adult. Unfortunately, her next two novels, *The Rebel* and *Riders of the Storm,* were weakened by uncharacteristic elements of contrivance. However, in *Kate Rider* she returned fully to form, with a story about a girl growing up in the early years of the Civil War. *To Ravensrigg,* set in the late 18th century, recounts how an adolescent girl confronts the discovery of her own unsuspected illegitimacy and is helped to trace her true origins by a group of Quaker anti-slave-trade campaigners, one of whom falls in love with her; more than usually romantic in its story-line, it makes an absorbing and moving tale. Burton's most recent novel, *Five August Days,* is her sole venture into the strictly contemporary. The local East Anglian detail is as vivid as ever, and though plot and characterisation show

rather less of her own individual distinction, they still make compulsive reading for eleven- to twelve-year-olds of either sex.

In addition to her full-length novels Burton has also published in *The Henchmans at Home* a collection of six related stories about a country doctor's family in Victorian England which contains some of her most appealing work.

—Frank Whitehead

———

BUTLER, Octavia E(stelle). American. Born in Pasadena, California, 22 June 1947. Educated at Pasadena City College, 1965-68, A.A. 1968; California State University, 1969. Since 1970, freelance writer. Recipient: Hugo award, World Science Fiction Convention, 1984, for short story "Speech Sounds"; Hugo award, Nebula award, Science Fiction Writers of America, Locus award from *Locus* magazine, and award for best novelette from *Science Fiction Chronicle Reader,* all 1985, all for novelette "Bloodchild"; Nebula award nomination, 1987, for novelette "The Evening and the Morning and the Night." Address: P.O. Box 40671, Pasadena, CA 91114, U.S.A.

PUBLICATIONS

Science Fiction

Kindred. New York, Doubleday, 1979; London, Women's Press, 1988; Boston, Beacon Press, 1988.
The Evening and the Morning and the Night. Eugene, Oregon, Pulphouse, 1991.
Parable of the Sower. New York, Four Walls Eight Windows, 1993.

"Patternmaster" series:

Patternmaster. New York, Doubleday, 1976; London, Sphere, 1978.
Mind of My Mind. New York, Doubleday, 1977; London, Sidgwick & Jackson, 1978.
Survivor. New York, Doubleday, and London, Sidgwick & Jackson, 1978.
Wild Seed. New York, Doubleday, and London, Sidgwick & Jackson, 1980; New York, Warner, 1988.
Clay's Ark. New York, St. Martin's, 1984.

"Xenogenesis" series:

Dawn. New York, Warner, and London, Gollancz, 1987.
Adulthood Rites. New York, Warner, and London, Gollancz, 1988.
Imago. New York, Warner, and London, Gollancz, 1989.

*

Biography: Entry in *Dictionary of Literary Biography,* Volume 33: *Afro-American Fiction Writers after 1955,* Detroit, Gale, 1984.

Critical Study: Entry in *Contemporary Literary Criticism,* Volume 38, Detroit, Gale, 1986; *Suzy Charnas, Joan Vinge, and Octavia Butler* by Richard Law, with others, San Bernardino, California, Borgo Press, 1986.

Octavia Butler, winner of both the Hugo and Nebula awards, writes about power, its use and abuse and how it affects those who wield it. As a science fiction writer, she creates alternate worlds where people are bred for their psionic powers as in the Patternist series or, as in the "Xenogenesis" trilogy, a post-holocaust Earth where survivors must deal with alien visitors who are genetic "traders." Her situations pit characters against racial, gender, and sexual conflicts and the violence—personal and global—that often results. Murder, child abuse, rape, suicide, ecological disasters, and war reveal the horrific elements wrought by the misapplication of political and technological power. Butler's works are widely popular with young adult readers of science fiction.

Patternmaster, Butler's first novel, begins her exploration of these themes that run through four more books: *Wildseed, Mind of My Mind, Clay's Ark,* and *Survivor.* The psionic Patternists can, through a Patternmaster, link their minds and control mutes, humans without psionic powers, and battle Clayarks, humans mutated by an extraterrestrial disease who prey on mutes and Patternists. *Clay's Ark,* Butler's darkest, most violent novel, reveals how a surviving astronaut unwillingly spreads an extraterrestrial virus that causes the mutation the Patternists and mutes call Clayarks.

Butler, the only African-American woman publishing in science fiction, pointedly develops slave-master relationships to show how the Patternists' power allows them to "program" and often abuse mutes. In *Patternmaster*'s world of the distant future, psionic power, not race or gender, determines superiority, but the often coercive selective breeding practiced to produce superior powers harks back to the treatment of slaves on American plantations. Although such programs clearly dehumanize the people involved, ethical questions are implied rather than directly addressed in the series. Here, though, as in other of Butler's work, she makes clear that coercive relationships warp the powerful even as they debilitate the powerless.

Mind of My Mind, set in contemporary California, develops a bit of "Patternmaster" history to show how Doro, the four-thousand-year-old Founder, sees Mary, the daughter of one of his many bodies, as the culmination of one of his breeding programs. A greater success than he had counted on, she becomes the first Patternmaster by killing her father, an act with mythic resonances that establishes the violent means of succession to the position of Patternmaster. If Mary had turned out to be yet another failed experiment, Doro would simply have killed her, as he has killed untold numbers of other failures. His disregard for human life disturbs Emma, the shape-shifting healer who is his female counterpart. Their story is told in *Wildseed,* where Doro, wandering Africa as a slave trader in the 1600s, is drawn to a power he does not recognize as one his projects. He finds Anyanwu, the Emma in *Patternmaster.* Anyanwu/Emma as the life-giving, life-protecting earthmother contrasts and conflicts with the manipulative, destructive Doro. Their struggle to co-exist results in an uneasy, often violent balance of their attributes.

Survivor picks up the saga some years after *Clay's Ark.* A group of mute Missionaries, a religious sect dedicated to preserving and spreading the unmutated "God-image of humankind" by colonizing other planets, demonstrates exactly the kind of prejudice and closemindedness that undermines relationships between individuals and cultures. Only the protagonist, Alanna, comes to respect the planet's native Tehkohn and love their leader. Otherwise, the colonists embrace segregation and effectively cut themselves off from cultural growth and enrichment. Butler extends the use of alien contact as a metaphor for change through *Dawn, Adulthood Rites,* and *Imago,* the trilogy gathered in "Xenogenesis."

The "Xenogenesis" trilogy shows humans having committed the ultimate global violence of nuclear war. The alien Oankali, a species which procures new genetic material by crossbreeding with other species, enter the picture in time to rescue several hundred survivors from the ruined planet. Among the rescued is the remarkable Lilith Iyapo who becomes both midwife and mother to the race the Oankali would create. Humans, the communal Oankali learn, are plagued by the combined drives of intelligence and hierarchy which forestall peaceful co-existence. Violence will always underlie and define the human condition, unless the hierarchical element is bred out. This process presents a challenge even for the ooloi, the third sex of the Oankali who are responsible for mixing the genetic materials of parents to produce desired characteristics in the offspring. As in the "Patternmaster" series, the technique involves no technology—the ooloi manipulate DNA and RNA within their own bodies. Nor are ethical questions directly addressed, though many humans reject the Oankali "gift" because, like the Missionaries, they believe change will destroy rather than improve the human race.

Bloodchild (Isaac Asimov's Science Fiction Magazine, June 1984), the novelette for which Butler won the Hugo and Nebula awards, fits the patterns of violence and metamorphosis evident in her other work. Here, though, Terrans are kept and bred in preserves by the Tlic, aliens who must incubate their eggs in host bodies and find that initial implantation in human bodies produces the strongest offspring. The twist is that love of a sort exists between the Tlic and their selected humans, which seems an ironic commentary on the complexities of the paternalistic master-slave relationship. Butler's earlier novel *Kindred* opened up some of these master/slave connections, but in a different vein. Butler uses the convention of time travel to show how Dana, a twentieth-century African-American woman, finds herself enslaved to Rufus, her white nineteenth-century great-great-grandfather. Dana must rescue him from life-threatening situations so he can live to father her great-grandmother. The physical and mental brutality Dana experiences as she is literally whipped into servitude provides a unique and clear lesson on how both the powerful and the powerless are ill-served in such unbalanced situations.

Although Butler's strongest, most positive characters are females, she rarely focuses on gender or race as issues except as an historical point, as when Dana finds being a black woman hampers her in the nineteenth-century South. On the whole, her outlook seems dark—humankind is incapable of the communal effort demanded for the survival of the species. The possibility of the necessary qualities glimmers only in the kindness of individual characters. In *Patternmaster,* Teray's power is tempered with compassion for mutes and even Clayarks. Anyanwu/Emma in *Mind of My Mind* and *Wild Seed* eases the lives of as many of Doro's offspring as she possibly can. Rye, the protagonist of the Nebula Award-winning short story "Speech Sounds" (*Isaac Asimov's Science Fiction Magazine,* December 1983), witnesses horror after horror in a world sundered by a virus that destroys the language center in the brains of most humans. Rye and others who can still read or talk are not only suspect but often killed. Even so, the kindness and compassion of a stranger who saves her from a crowd regenerates those qualities in Rye. Such individual kindness provides the basis for the hope offered by Octavia Butler's powerful work.

—Linda G. Benson

BYARS, Betsy (née Cromer). American. Born in Charlotte, North Carolina, 7 August 1928. Educated at Furman University, Greenville, South Carolina, 1946-48; Queens College, Charlotte, 1948-50, B.A. in English 1950. Married Edward Ford Byars in 1950; three daughters and one son. Recipient: America's Book of the Year selection, Child Study Association, 1968, for *The Midnight Fox,* 1969, for *Trouble River,* 1970, for *The Summer of the Swans,* 1972, for *The House of Wings,* 1973, for *The Winged Colt of Casa Mia* and *The 18th Emergency,* 1974, for *After the Goat Man,* 1975, for *The Lace Snail,* 1976, for *The TV Kid,* and 1980, for *The Night Swimmers;* Lewis Carroll Shelf award, 1970, for *The Midnight Fox;* Newbery Medal, 1971, for *The Summer of the Swans;* Best Books for Spring selection, *School Library Journal,* 1971, for *Go and Hush the Baby;* Book List, *Library Journal,* 1972, for *House of Wings;* National Book award finalist, 1973, for *House of Wings; New York Times* Outstanding Book of the Year, 1973, for *The Winged Colt of Casa Mia* and *The 18th Emergency,* 1979, for *Good-bye Chicken Little,* and 1982, for *The Two-Thousand-Pound Goldfish;* Book List, *School Library Journal,* 1974, for *After the Goat Man;* Dorothy Canfield Fisher Memorial Book award, Vermont Congress of Parents and Teachers, 1975, for *The 18th Emergency;* Woodward Park School Annual Book award, 1977, Child Study Children's Book award, Child Study Children's Book Committee at Bank Street College of Education, 1977, Hans Christian Andersen Honor List for Promoting Concern for the Disadvantaged and Handicapped, 1979, Georgia Children's Book award, 1979, Charlie May Simon Book award, Arkansas Elementary School Council, 1980, Surrey School Book of the Year award, Surrey School Librarians of Surrey, British Columbia, 1980, Mark Twain award, Missouri Association of School Librarians, 1980, William Allen White Children's Book award, Emporia State University, 1980, Young Reader Medal, California Reading Association, 1980, Nene award runner up, 1981 and 1983, and Golden Archer award, Department of Library Science of the University of Wisconsin—Oskosh, 1982, all for *The Pinballs;* Best Book of the Year, *School Library Journal,* 1980, and American Book award for Children's Fiction (hardcover), 1981, both for *The Night Swimmers;* Notable Children's Book, *School Library Journal,* 1981, Children's Choice, International Reading Association, 1982, Tennessee Children's Choice Book award, Tennessee Library Association, 1983, Sequoyah Children's Book award, 1984, all for *The Cybil War;* Parents' Choice award for literature, Parents' Choice Foundation, 1982, Best Children's Books, *School Library Journal,* 1982, CRABbery award, Oxon Hill Branch of Prince George's County Library, 1983, Mark Twain award, 1985, all for *The Animal, the Vegetable, and John D. Jones;* Notable Book of the Year, *New York Times,* 1982, for *The Two-Thousand-Pound Goldfish;* Regina Medal, Catholic Library Association, 1987; Carlie May Simon award, 1987, for *The Computer Nut;* South Carolina Children's Book award, and Maryland Children's Book award, both 1988, both for *Cracker Jackson.* Address: 4 Riverpoint, Clemson, SC 29631, U.S.A.

PUBLICATIONS FOR YOUNG ADULTS

Fiction

The Midnight Fox, illustrated by Ann Grifalconi. New York, Viking, 1968; London, Faber, 1970.
Trouble River, illustrated by Rocco Negri. New York, Viking, 1969.

The Summer of the Swans, illustrated by Ted CoConis. New York, Viking, 1970; London, Hippo, 1980.
The House of Wings, illustrated by Daniel Schwartz. New York, Viking, 1972; London, Bodley Head, 1973.
The 18th Emergency, illustrated by Robert Grossman. New York, Viking, 1973; London, Bodley Head, 1974.
The Winged Colt of Casa Mia, illustrated by Richard Cuffari. New York, Viking, 1973; London, Bodley Head, 1974.
After the Goat Man, illustrated by Ronald Himler. New York, Viking, 1974; London, Bodley Head, 1975.
The TV Kid, illustrated by Richard Cuffari. New York, Viking, and London, Bodley Head, 1976.
The Pinballs. New York, Harper, and London, Bodley Head, 1977.
The Cartoonist, illustrated by Richard Cuffari. New York, Viking, and London, Bodley Head, 1978.
Good-bye Chicken Little. New York, Harper, and London, Bodley Head, 1979.
The Night Swimmers, illustrated by Troy Howell. New York, Delacorte, and London, Bodley Head, 1980.
The Cybil War, illustrated by Gail Owens. New York, Viking, and London, Bodley Head, 1981.
The Animal, the Vegetable, and John D. Jones, illustrated by Ruth Sanderson. New York, Delacorte, and London, Bodley Head, 1982.
The Two-Thousand-Pound Goldfish. New York, Harper, and London, Bodley Head, 1982.
The Glory Girl. New York, Viking, and London, Bodley Head, 1983.
The Computer Nut, illustrated with computer graphics by Guy Byars. New York, Viking, and London, Bodley Head, 1984.
Cracker Jackson. New York, Viking, and London, Bodley Head, 1985.
The Blossoms Meet the Vulture Lady, illustrated by Jacqueline Rogers. New York, Delacorte, and London, Bodley Head, 1986.
The Not-Just-Anybody Family, illustrated by Jacqueline Rogers. New York, Delacorte, and London, Bodley Head, 1986.
A Blossom Promise, illustrated by Jacqueline Rogers. New York, Delacorte, 1987.
The Blossoms and the Green Phantom, illustrated by Jacqueline Rogers. New York, Delacorte, and London, Bodley Head, 1987.
The Burning Questions of Bingo Brown, illustrated by Cathy Bobak. New York, Viking, and London, Bodley Head, 1988.
Bingo Brown and the Language of Love, illustrated by Cathy Bobak. New York, Viking, 1989.
Bingo Brown, Gypsy Lover. New York, Viking, 1990.
The Moon and I (autobiography). Englewood Cliffs, New Jersey, Messner, 1991.
The Seven Treasure Hunts. New York, Harper, 1991.
Wanted...Mud Blossom. New York, Delacorte, 1991.
Bingo Brown's Guide to Romance. New York, Viking, 1992.
Coast to Coast. New York, Delacorte, 1992.

PUBLICATIONS FOR CHILDREN

Fiction

Clementine, illustrated by Charles Wilton. Boston, Houghton, 1962.
The Dancing Camel, illustrated by Harold Berson. New York, Viking, 1965.

Rama, the Gypsy Cat, illustrated by Peggy Bacon. New York, Viking, 1966.

The Groober, illustrated by the author. New York, Harper, 1967.

Go and Hush the Baby, illustrated by Emily A. McCully. New York, Viking, 1971; London, Bodley Head, 1980.

The Lace Snail, illustrated by the author. New York, Viking, 1975.

The Golly Sisters Go West, illustrated by Sue Truesdell. New York, Harper, 1986.

Beans on the Roof, illustrated by Melodye Rosales. New York, Delacorte, and London, Bodley Head, 1988.

Hooray for the Golly Sisters, illustrated by Sue Truesdell. New York, Harper, 1990.

The Golly Sisters Ride Again, pictures by Sue Truesdell. New York, HarperCollins, 1994.

*

Media Adaptations: The following were adapted for ABC-TV as episodes of the *ABC Afterschool Special*: "Pssst! Hammerman's After You," adapted from *The 18th Emergency,* 1973; "Sara's Summer of the Swans," adapted from *The Summer of the Swans,* 1974; "Trouble River," 1975; "The Winged Colt," adapted from *The Winged Colt of Casa Mia,* 1976; "The Pinballs," 1977; "Daddy, I'm Their Mamma Now," adapted from *The Night Swimmers,* 1981.

Biography: Entry in *Dictionary of Literary Biography,* Volume 52: *American Writers for Children since 1960: Fiction,* Detroit, Gale, 1986.

Manuscript Collection: Clemson University, South Carolina.

Critical Studies: Entry in *Children's Literature Review,* Volume 16, Detroit, Gale, 1989; entry in *Contemporary Literary Criticism,* Volume 35, Detroit, Gale, 1985.

*   *   *

Betsy Byars has written many highly acclaimed books for young people. Her teenage characters are carefully drawn, their concerns in growing up clearly and sympathetically presented.

The Summer of the Swans is about one day in Sara's fourteenth summer. Sara lives in a coal mining area of West Virginia. Since her mother's death she and her siblings have been cared for by their aunt; her father works in Ohio and visits infrequently. This summer is a confusing one for Sara. Until now her life has flowed smoothly. Now she has to worry abut her enormous feet, her impossible body, her vivacious, beautiful older sister Wanda, and her burdensome mentally impaired younger brother Charlie. Sara's moods are as sudden as the appearance of the swans on the lake near their home. Sara takes Charlie to see the swans, and he delights in watching them glide silently about. That night Charlie disappears to look for the swans. Sara searches frantically for Charlie all the next day. Charlie, who cannot speak, is lost and helpless. During that long day Sara leaves her own miseries behind and concentrates on the needs of someone else. This strong, compassionate book, which won the Newbery award in 1971, addresses mental disability with honesty and courage.

The Night Swimmers is a story of three children whose mother is dead and whose father leaves them alone while he performs as a country-western singer. The father is set on becoming a star, and places his oldest child, Retta, in charge of feeding, clothing and entertaining her two younger brothers. It is Retta who finds the swimming pool belonging to a colonel who goes to bed early. She and her brothers sneak into his yard in the night, and with new bathing suits and inner tubes do the things that rich people do. Retta seems to have everything under control in their lives until the brothers struggle for their own independence, and one almost drowns while swimming alone in the pool. The crisis brings family members back together again to rethink their needs and relationships. This book, rich in family frustrations and affections, won the American Book Award for Juvenile Fiction in 1980.

The Cybil War is a lighthearted view of young love. Simon and Tony's friendship was sealed in second grade, when the class was asked to write essays on their fathers. Neither had a father. Simon falls in love with their red-haired classmate, Cybil, the first time he sees her cross her eyes. But Tony succeeds, with outrageous lies, in keeping them apart. Finally Simon finds out the truth, wins Cybil, and confronts Tony. The course of true love is simple, direct, and wonderful.

The Blossom Family stories recount the adventures of an atypical, spirited family. The father was a rodeo star; he is now dead. The mother and older daughter are on the rodeo circuit. In *Blossom Promise,* mother and daughter are at the Tucson Rodeo. Grandfather, Pap, remains on the farm with the two young sons. Junior is going for an overnight with his friend Mad Mary, who lives in a cave in the woods. Vern and his friend Michael have built a raft and are about to ride downstream on the Snake River. But when Pap has a sudden heart attack, all family members put their own pursuits on hold to address his needs. With love and determination, they see Pap and themselves through this emergency, becoming stronger individually and closer as a family.

Byar's Bingo Brown stories are rollicking good fun. Bingo is a young man learning about mixed-sex conversations, romance, and love. He is an intelligent young man who learns that young ladies require tact, understanding, and appropriate Christmas presents. In *Bingo Brown, Gypsy Lover,* Bingo must deal with Melissa, who finds him more romantic than a gypsy-lover, and his mother, whose major concern is his soon-to-be-born brother. The effect of a new sibling on a twelve-year-old is artfully and delightfully presented. First Bingo has to deal with his mother's own preoccupation with her body. Then he has to worry about her probable comparison of him, imperfect and clumsy, with arms that are too long, with a perfect younger child. He is certain that his mother will do all the great, loving things with his brother that she has not done with him. The baby arrives, premature, and Bingo makes several trips to the hospital to look at Jamie in the nursery window. He worries over Jamie's health and he develops pride in Jamie. He wants to be a wonderful older brother, although he feels like a helpless young grandfather.

Byars presents well both the inner lives and outward behaviors of her characters. She shows them in a variety of settings, mostly rural and close to home. But she also shows their needs for adventure and exploration, as they move towards leaving home and taking on adult roles.

—Mary Lystad

C

CALVERT, Patricia. American. Born in Great Falls, Montana, 22 July 1931. Educated at Winona State University, Minnesota, B.A. 1976, graduate study, since 1976. Married George J. Calvert in 1951; two daughters. Laboratory clerk, St. Mary's Hospital, 1948-49; clerk typist, General Motors Acceptance Corp., 1950-51. Cardiac laboratory technician, Mayo Clinic, 1961-64; enzyme laboratory technician, 1964-70. Senior editorial assistant in publications, since 1970; instructor, Institute of Children's Literature, since 1987. Recipient: Best book award from American Library Association, juvenile fiction award from Society of Midland Authors, and juvenile award from Friends of American Writers, all 1980, all for *The Snowbird;* award for outstanding achievement in the arts from Young Women's Christian Association (YWCA), 1981, for *The Snowbird;* Mark Twain Award nomination from Missouri Association of School Libraries, 1985, for *The Money Creek Mare;* Maude Hart Lovelace Award nomination, 1985, for *The Stone Pony;* Junior Library Guild selection and ALA Best Book for Young Adults, both 1986, both for *Yesterday's Daughter;* ALA Young Adult Best Book award, 1987; William Allan White Award, 1987, for *Hadder MacColl;* "Best of 1990," Society of School Librarians International, 1991, for *When Morning Comes;* Junior Library Guild selection, 1993, for *Picking up the Pieces.* Address: Foxwood Farm, 6130 County Road, #7 S.E., Chatfield, MN 55923, U.S.A.

PUBLICATIONS FOR YOUNG ADULTS

Fiction

The Snowbird. New York, Scribner, 1980.
The Money Creek Mare. New York, Scribner, 1981.
The Stone Pony. New York, Scribner, 1982.
The Hour of the Wolf. New York, Scribner, 1983.
Hadder MacColl. New York, Scribner, 1985.
Yesterday's Daughter. New York, Scribner, 1986.
Stranger, You and I. New York, Scribner, 1987.
When Morning Comes. New York, Macmillan, 1989.
The Person I Used to Be. New York, Macmillan, 1993.
Picking Up the Pieces. New York, Scribner, 1993.
Bigger. New York, Scribner, 1994.

Other

Contributor, *Developing Reading Efficiency,* 4th edition, edited by Lyle L. Miller. Edina, Burgess, 1980.
Editor, *The Communicator's Handbook: Techniques and Technology.* Gainesville, Maupin House Publishing, 1990.

*

Biography: Essay in *Speaking for Ourselves, Too* compiled and edited by Donald R. Gallo, National Council of Teachers of English, 1993; essay in *Something about the Author Autobiography Series,* Volume 17, Detroit, Gale, 1994.

Patricia Calvert comments:

If I have entertained readers with my novels, that's what I in-tended to do. If I have informed their hearts, that's what I hoped might happen. One of the best letters I ever received was from a boy in a state far from mine who wrote: "I never thought much about my own life until I read your book." The truth is, of course, that in the process of creating a story I have entertained and informed myself as well, a fact that continually astonishes and delights me. During the creation of fiction, I have been able to live so many other lives—to have been a variety of girls and boys, their parents, friends and enemies—even to have been a dog, a horse, a forest, a creek! At the moment, I am working on a book entitled *Writing to Ritchie,* about two young brothers, David and Ritchie, who are in foster care. I discovered that I shared their experiences as keenly as the experiences I share day to day with my co-workers, my husband, my children. I have occasionally referred to my career as an author as "my other life," but when I am in a mood to be honest I admit the truth: It is my *real* life.

*   *   *

The main characters in Patricia Calvert's novels for young adults struggle with loss and change. Some, like JoBeth Cunningham in *The Stone Pony,* must deal with the death of a family member or friend. Others, Like *Hadder MacColl,* must embark on an entirely new way of life.

In *The Snowbird,* her first book, Calvert employs many of the themes and situations she explores in subsequent novels. Thirteen-year-old Willie (Willanna) Bannerman and her younger brother TJ are sent to live with their uncle Randall and his wife Belle in Dakota Territory in 1883 after their parents die in a fire. Willie tries to deal with her loss by nurturing her hatred for the men who had started the fire and makes up private stories to help her cope with her situation. She also tries to shield herself from additional pain by remaining emotionally distant.

However, in spite of herself, Willie comes to love the eccentric Belle, whose dreams will never materialize on the impoverished prairie. Willie also raises a silvery white filly, the Snowbird, that seems a dream personified. Both Belle and the Snowbird suffer horribly when Willie is forced to ride the young horse too far seeking help for Belle during childbirth. The loss of another baby pushes Belle beyond her endurance, and she abandons Randall and the children. Willie frees the Snowbird after she has nursed the mare to health. In rage and pain, she yells at TJ, "Did it ever occur to you...that everybody I ever loved got up and left me?" But Willie ultimately demonstrates her resilience.

Calvert's other historical novel, *Hadder MacColl,* deals with the loss of an entire way of life. Set in Scotland during Bonnie Prince Charlie's war to reclaim the throne, events move inexorably to the destruction of the Highlanders at the Battle of Culloden in 1746. Hadder, the fierce and independent daughter of Chieftain Big Archibald, is appalled that her older brother Leofwin's Edinburgh education has convinced him that rebellion will bring disaster. Hadder despises his softness and insists that Highland traditions need never change.

Yet seeing hundreds of Highlanders, including Leofwin, dead on the battlefield makes Hadder question her assumptions Big Archibald's death, hastened by despair, severs her remaining tie to

Scotland, and to survive she indentures herself and sails to Boston. Although parts of the Highlanders' way of life may seem strange to modern readers, Hadder's grief, particularly when she discovers Leofwin's body, cuts across time and place.

Like Hadder, JoBeth in *The Stone Pony* must work through the death of a sibling, in this case her talented older sister Ashleigh, who had suffered from cancer. Calvert effectively portrays the anger and guilt experienced by survivors. Images of Ashleigh's beauty and success haunt JoBeth, who feels she can never replace her sister and thinks she should have died instead. Learning to ride her sister's horse and developing a friendship with Luke, who exercises horses at the stable, draw JoBeth outside herself.

Jake Mathiessen in *The Hour of the Wolf* must deal not only with the death of his friend Danny Yumiat but also with memories of his own suicide attempt. After Danny drowns while running his sled dogs for the Iditarod race, Jake trains to enter the grueling competition himself. Danny's sister, Kamina, a staunch defender of native tradition, scoffs at Jake's chances and runs her own team. Facing hardships on the trail, Jake acknowledges that even someone as talented as Danny could be overtaken by fear and depression powerful enough to cause him to kill himself.

Sometimes loss can drive people to the kinds of behavior exhibited by Cat Kincaid in *When Morning Comes*. Her promiscuity stems from an endless search to experience the love she had never received from her father who died in Vietnam and her mother who had never recovered from her own grief.

Fifteen-year-old Ella Rae Carmody must adjust to a series of changes after her mother leaves her family in *The Money Creek Mare*. Leenie O'Brien in *Yesterday's Daughter* has to deal with the return of the mother who had left town sixteen years earlier after Leenie's birth. Raised by her grandparents, Leenie is unwilling to forgive her mother's long absence. *Stranger, You and I* presents the other side of the picture as Zee Crofton realizes she is too young to bring up a child alone and gives up her son for adoption.

In Calvert's worlds, adults are often weak and ineffective. Mothers, in particular, frequently abandon their children physically or psychologically. Jake's mother is more concerned about preserving an impeccable house than in helping her son cope with feelings of failure. Cat's mother, who has spent most of her life with cigarettes, alcohol, and men, tells Cat she no longer has a place for her daughter because she wants to remarry and move to California. Tired of dealing with poverty and family stress, Hugh McBride's mother rents a small apartment and leaves her family temporarily in *Stranger, You and I*.

Again and again, adult responsibilities fall on Calvert's young protagonists. Hugh plans a vacation for his parents in hopes of saving their marriage. Ella Rae schemes to help her father breed a successful race horse. Hadder maps her own future for herself and the woman who had raised her. Calvert portrays characters such as Leenie, JoBeth, and Hugh as more dependable, serious, and mature than the average adolescent. Just as Belle tells Willie that the girl has been "older, my girl, than I'll ever be!" so Cat's mother claims that she is not as strong as Cat. Hugh's mother describes him as the glue that holds the family together, and Ella Rae's mother entrusts the diner and younger siblings to her.

Often the adolescents maintain their self-control by rejecting emotional, especially romantic, involvement. Leenie denies her sexuality from fear that she will become pregnant as her mother had. JoBeth considers involvement with museum artifacts safer than emotional entanglements with people. In fact, JoBeth's declining interest in the stone pony whose inscription she had tried to deci-

pher to impress her father corresponds to her increasing ease in riding Ashleigh's horse.

Animals play an important role in many of Calvert's plots. They can connect their owners with the past as Sionnach, the horse from Leofwin, ties Hadder to her brother. They can help a person care for another living creature as Cat discovers in her fondness for the old dog Peaches. Jake's survival depends on his care of his sled dogs, and he considers them closer friends than most humans he knows. Animals can represent dreams like the Snowbird and the unborn horse in *The Money Creek Mare*. Nature provides a refuge for Leenie when she enters the swamp to avoid her mother.

Many young adults in rural and small town settings exhibit remarkable innocence. Wholesome Hooter Lewis resists Cat's attempts at seduction which she had perfected in the city. Ella Rae's down-home speech and manners set her apart from the wealthy girls at the finishing school where she has been sent by adults who hope to adopt her. Hugh McBride offers to forfeit his plans in order to marry his best friend Zee even though he is not her baby's father.

Yet, Calvert makes clear that the future for both Hugh and Zee lies beyond small town Vandalia. In fact, the confines of that town had trapped Hugh's parents into early marriage. With its complex plot and well-realized characters, *Stranger, You and I* demonstrates Calvert's growth as a writer. Although certain themes and plot elements have remained constant in her novels, she has not exhausted the possible variations.

—Kathy Piehl

———

CAMERON, Eleanor (Frances). American. Born in Winnipeg, Manitoba, Canada, 23 March 1912. Educated at University of California, Los Angeles, 1931-33; Art Center School, Los Angeles, one-year. Married Ian Stuart Cameron in 1934; one son. Library clerk, Los Angeles Public Library, 1930-36, and Los Angeles Schools Library, 1936-42; research librarian, Foote, Cone & Belding Advertising, Los Angeles, 1943-44; research assistant, Honing, Cooper & Harrington, Los Angeles, 1956-58; librarian, Dan B. Miner Co., advertising, Los Angeles, 1958-59; writer. Member of the editorial board, *Cricket* magazine, La Salle, Illinois, since 1973, and *Children's Literature in Education,* New York, since 1982; since 1977 member of the advisory board, Center for the Study of Children's Literature, Simmons College, Boston. Children's Literature judge, National Book awards, 1980. Gertrude Clarke Whittall Lecturer, Library of Congress, Washington, D.C., 1977. Recipient: Hawaiian Children's Choice Nene award, 1960, for *The Wonderful Flight to the Mushroom Planet;* Mystery Writers of America Scroll award, 1964, for *A Spell Is Cast;* California Literature Silver Medal award from Commonwealth Club of California, 1965, for *A Spell Is Cast,* and 1970, for *The Green and Burning Tree: On the Writing and Enjoyment of Children's Books;* Southern California Council on Literature for Children and Young People award, 1965, for distinguished contribution to the field of children's literature; *Boston Globe-Horn Book* award, 1971, for *A Room Made of Windows;* National Book award for children's literature, 1974, for *The Court of the Stone Children;* National Book award runner-up, 1976, for *To the Green Mountains;* FOCAL award, 1985, for *Julia and the Hand of God;* Kerlan award, 1985, for body of work; FOCAL award,

1990, for *A Room Made of Windows.* Agent: E. P. Dutton, 375 Hudson St., New York, NY 10014, U.S.A.

PUBLICATIONS FOR YOUNG ADULTS

Fiction

The Wonderful Flight to the Mushroom Planet, illustrated by Robert Henneberger. Boston, Little, Brown, 1954.
Stowaway to the Mushroom Planet, illustrated by Robert Henneberger. Boston, Little, Brown, 1956.
Mr. Bass's Planetoid, illustrated by Louis Darling. Boston, Little, Brown, 1958.
The Terrible Churnadryne, illustrated by Beth and Joe Krush. Boston, Little, Brown, 1959.
A Mystery for Mr. Bass, illustrated by Leonard Shortall. Boston, Little, Brown, 1960.
A Spell Is Cast, illustrated by Beth and Joe Krush. Boston, Little, Brown, 1964.
Time and Mr. Bass, illustrated by Fred Meise. Boston, Little, Brown, 1967.
A Room Made of Windows, illustrated by Trina Schart Hyman. Boston, Little, Brown, 1971; London, Gollancz, 1972.
The Court of the Stone Children. New York, Dutton, 1973.
To the Green Mountains. New York, Dutton, 1975.
Julia and the Hand of God, illustrated by Gail Owens. New York, Dutton, 1977.
Beyond Silence. New York, Dutton, 1980.
That Julia Redfern, illustrated by Gail Owens. New York, Dutton, 1982.
Julia's Magic, illustrated by Gail Owens. New York, Dutton, 1984.
The Private Worlds of Julia Redfern. New York, Dutton, 1988.

PUBLICATIONS FOR CHILDREN

Fiction

The Mysterious Christmas Shell, illustrated by Beth and Joe Krush. Boston, Little, Brown, 1961.
The Beast with the Magical Horn, illustrated by Beth and Joe Krush. Boston, Little, Brown, 1963.

PUBLICATIONS FOR ADULTS

Novel

The Unheard Music. Boston, Little, Brown, 1950.

Other

The Green and Burning Tree: On the Writing and Enjoyment of Children's Books. Boston, Little, Brown, 1969.
The Seed and the Vision: On the Writing and Appreciation of Children's Books. New York, Dutton, 1993.

*

Media Adaptations: *The Court of the Stone Children* has been adapted into a play.

Biography: Essay in *Something about the Author Autobiography Series,* Volume 10, Detroit, Gale, 1990, pp. 37-55; entry in *Dictionary of Literary Biography,* Volume 52: *American Writers for Children since 1960: Fiction,* Detroit, Gale, 1986, pp. 66-74.

Manuscript Collection: Kerlan Collection, University of Minnesota, Minneapolis.

Critical Study: Entry in *Children's Literature Review,* Volume 1, Detroit, Gale, 1976.

*   *   *

Eleanor Cameron has written books for younger and older adolescents and for adults. Though she denies writing for any specific age level, her strong, realistic characters make her books particularly appropriate for bridging the gap between children's and adult literature. She has a good sense of how the world is perceived differently by young and old, how remarks of adults can be misunderstood by adolescents, and how behaviors of adolescents can be misinterpreted by adults. Her plots are well-paced and absorbing; she makes readers care about her characters and want to see how they make out.

Her series of books about Julia—*Julia's Magic, That Julia Redfern, Julia and the Hand of God, A Room Made of Windows,* and *The Private Worlds of Julia Redfern*—tell Julia's story from age six to age fifteen, showing changes in Julia herself and in her family constellation as she grows older. Julia is a forthright and determined young lady who reacts to life's challenges with strength and vigor. Throughout the series, she encounters a number of interesting characters and gradually develops her ambition to be a writer. The tone of the books is generally optimistic, although Cameron is often praised for her ability to mix in serious themes and real emotions. It should also be noted that Julia's age in the various books does not necessarily correspond to their publication dates; she is older in some of the earlier books.

In *A Room Made of Windows,* Julia is twelve and well along in her efforts to become a writer. She keeps a Book of Strangeness, which begins with a list of her most beautiful and most detested words. This is followed by another list of Dogs Alive and Dogs Dead and then a list of Cats Alive and Cats Dead, which give the names of all the dogs and cats she's ever known. A somewhat traumatic situation arises for Julia when her mother announces her intention to marry "Uncle Phil." On that same day Julia sees her story "The Mask"—about her deceased father being a writer and handing on his mask to her—in print. Julia must balance her desire to continue her father's legacy with the necessity of accepting her new stepfather.

In *The Private World of Julia Redfern,* Julia is fifteen years old, and her relationship with her stepfather continues to be rocky. But Julia becomes more successful with her writing, which allows her to express the loss she feels over the death of her father. Her first beau, John, encourages joyous and hopeful feelings. The impetuous younger Julia gradually becomes a more aware, a more tolerant, and a more secure human being. In some ways, Julia's development mirrors Cameron's own growth following her parents' divorce and her mother's remarriage.

Cameron's son inspired her to write a series of science-fiction fantasies with boy characters for younger adolescents, the Mushroom Planet books. Reviewers praised Cameron's skillful combination of fantasy with scientific fact, and predicted that the stories would appeal to young readers' need for a private place. The books describe the remarkable adventures of Chuck and David, the spaceships they build, and the friendships they develop with two scientists and the small green people who live on the planet Basidium. Chuck and David lead the sort of life most people only dream about, for they can reach Basidium in their spaceship in two hours. The planet is called Basidium partly because it is covered with mushrooms—some taller than five feet—and partly because the people who live there are spore, or Mushroom People.

In the first book of the series, *The Wonderful Flight to the Mushroom Planet,* the boys take their first trip, accompanied by the learned astronomer Mr. Tyco Bass. In the second book, *Stowaway to the Mushroom Planet,* they return to Basidium in an even better spaceship with Tyco's cousin, Mr. Theodosius Bass, also a gifted individual. This time they are joined by a stowaway who ridicules the idea of space travel yet wishes to obtain its secrets for his own glory. The trip is a huge success, for good triumphs over evil and the stowaway's plans are thwarted. Chuck and David, along with the Basses, remain the sole keepers of certain scientific verities.

Cameron has written other distinguished novels of adolescent adventure, such as her National Book Award-winner *The Court of the Stone Children.* In this book and *The Terrible Churnadryne,* in which a young girl meets a ghost from Napolean's era while visiting a French museum, Cameron moves toward pure fantasy. Her more realistic *A Spell Is Cast* involves Cory Winterslow taking a cross-country journey from her New York City home to California in order to spend Easter vacation with her uncle and grandmother, who live in a great old house on cliffs beside the Pacific Ocean. During her stay Cory finds out several troubling things about her family, but she also finds more love and friendship than she has ever known and learns to accept other people's needs and limitations.

Eleanor Cameron is a gifted storyteller. She cares about her characters and describes them skillfully, warts and all. She is cognizant of the difficulties in growing up, but is also aware of the joys and challenges and absurdities life holds for everyone. She exposes the magic in the everyday world and captures the essence of her young readers' existence.

—Mary Lystad

CAPUTO, Philip. American. Born in Chicago, Illinois, 10 June 1941. Educated at Purdue University, West Lafayette, Indiana; Loyola University, Chicago, Illinois, B.A. 1964. Served in the United States Marine Corps, 1964-67. Married Jill Esther Ongemach in 1969; two sons. Promotional writer and member of staff of a house paper, 3-M Corp., Chicago, Illinois, 1968-69; local correspondent, *Chicago Tribune,* Chicago, 1969-72; correspondent in Rome, Beirut, Saigon, and Moscow, 1972-77; writer and lecturer. Notable assignments include coverage of violence in Beirut, Yom Kippur War, Ethiopian Civil War, Turkish invasion of Cyprus, fall of Saigon, 1975. Recipient: Pulitzer Prize, with William Hugh Jones, 1972, for coverage of primary election fraud; George Polk award, 1973,

for coverage of captivity by Palestinian guerrillas; also received Illinois Associated Press award, Illinois United Press award, and Green Gael award from American Bar Association.

PUBLICATIONS

Fiction

A Rumor of War. New York, Holt, 1977.
Horn of Africa. New York, Holt, 1980.
DelCorso's Gallery. New York, Holt, 1983.
Indian Country. New York, Bantam, 1987.
Means of Escape. New York, HarperCollins, 1991.

*   *   *

Philip Caputo's five book-length works are divided into two categories, memoirs and novels. The former, *A Rumor of War* and *A Means of Escape* deal respectively with his career as a U.S. Marines officer in Vietnam in the 1960s and his subsequent activity as a journalist covering tumultuous military events in Lebanon, Israel, Vietnam, Eritrea, and Afghanistan. The latter, *Horn of Africa, DelCorso's Gallery,* and *Indian Country,* tend to derive from his experiences as a reporter, although *Indian Country* features a Vietnam Veteran's efforts to rebuild his life in the forests of northern Michigan following a traumatic betrayal.

All of Caputo's works graphically explore the evil human beings inflict on each other. Like two of his literary models, Joseph Conrad and Ernest Hemingway, Caputo describes and analyzes the hearts of darkness that turn ostensibly good people into casual murderers and torturers. His world is filled with purposeful and accidental mayhem as armed men shoot and eviscerate children, women, and the elderly as well as their enemies. His depiction of war erases any romance about what it does to participants, including himself.

Thus, Caputo's work is not for the fainthearted. Those offended by verbal and visual obscenities, sexual exploitation, and graphic descriptions of mutilated corpses should avoid his work, especially his novels. Those mature enough for unflinching depiction of the human condition will find him rewarding.

Ironically, his memoirs should prove the least objectionable to the fastidious. *A Rumor of War* contains horrifying passages as Caputo recounts his experiences as a Marine officer in Vietnam. Caputo mercilessly analyzes his motives for joining the military. His response to guerilla warfare and his participation in bureaucratic cover-ups makes for powerful, informative reading and redeems the horrors he recounts. *Means of Escape,* written a decade later, is less intense but equally valuable. Based on his career as a reporter covering "bang bang" in Lebanon, Vietnam, Israel, Eritrea, and Afghanistan, this memoir explores his motives for undertaking a series of risky assignments that led to his being held as a spy and later wounded by Palestinian guerilas, his reporting the North Vietnamese capture of Saigon and his escape by helicopter, and his trekking across the Afghan border with mujahadin as Soviet gunships hover overhead. Increasingly bothersome to Caputo is the realization that his marriage and fatherhood, plus his aging body, make these assignments irresponsible if not foolhardy. Ultimately *Means of Escape* is a vehicle for Caputo to determine why he became the adult he is.

A Rumor of War and *Means of Escape* are valuable also in terms of their less violent parts. Caputo in both writes lengthy segments in which he recounts growing up in an Italian-American community in Chicago and its suburbs. His search for his Italian roots eventually leads to an idyllic section of *Means of Escape* in which he recounts a joyful visit to a Calabrian village where his distant cousins still live. Thus extracts from each memoir can prove quite informative on subjects besides war and allow readers to avoid the more shocking segments.

Caputo's novels intensify the author's experiences as he creates a series of memorable male characters who in restlessness, ruthlessness, and madness challenge the envelope of human possibility. *Horn of Africa,* based loosely on his reporting of the Eritrean war of independence against Ethiopia, follows three men purportedly on a CIA-sponsored mission from Sudan into Eritrea. The point of view character, Charles Gage, is a down-at-the-heels American reporter looking for a job. He is joined on the mission by a sacked British military officer Patrick Moody, and an American soldier of fortune, Jeremy Norstrad. Their undercover mission develops into a nightmare as Moody and Norstrad battle each other, and the three face the dangers of the desert, tribal enmities, and the Ethiopian military. In many ways comparable to Conrad's *Heart of Darkness, Horn of Africa* explores the impact on westerners who are being removed from their cultural moorings in a lawless land where force is the only guarantee of survival.

DelCorso's Gallery is a thinly disguised autobiography in which the main character, Nick DelCorso, a news photographer, grapples with the conflicting claims of marriage, parenthood, and photojournalism. DelCorso, like Caputo, has major assignments in Vietnam and Lebanon that bring him face-to-face with death. His acceptance of such assignments endangers his marriage. *DelCorso's Gallery,* while full of the violence of war, offers insights into the motives and ethics of journalists as they weigh the dangers of getting stories, pictures, and professional fame in wartime.

Indian Country by contrast is the least autobiographical of Caputo's novels. Set in the Upper Peninsula of Michigan, it follows a Vietnam Veteran's efforts to build a normal life. Christian Starkman, the son of a minister, initially did not want to join the military but did so when his Ojibwa friend Bonny George St. George was drafted. Starkman returns from Vietnam, but his friend does not because of a mistake Starkman made during a battle. Something of a recluse, Starkman works as an estimator for a timber company and eventually marries June, a divorcee, and sets up housekeeping with her and their children. However, Starkman is not at peace and his descent into illusion and paranoia creates a crisis in his career and marriage. Not until he comes to grips with his guilt does he find a way out of his predicament.

Like all of Caputo's writing, *Indian Country* strongly depicts the violence humans can commit. However, in this novel Caputo also develops in June his only strong female character, a woman whose tenacious will to help her husband and save their marriage is equally memorable. Caputo also provides insight into Native American customs as Starkman tries to gain peace of mind through contact with Bonnie George's elderly grandfather.

In conclusion, Caputo's memoirs and novels are aimed at mature readers who are willing to face the potential evil and madness in themselves and other humans. Those willing to understand the turmoil of the late twentieth century will gain humbling insight into what people can do. Caputo seeks to shed light on the evil he has observed in himself and humankind, and by facing it, lessen its power. In the process he spins some engrossing stories.

—Lawrence B. Fuller

CARD, Orson Scott. Has also written as Brian Green. Born in Richland, Washington, 24 August 1951. Educated at Brigham Young University, B.A. (with distinction) 1975; University of Utah, M.A. 1981. Married Kristine Allen in 1977; three sons and one daughter. Worked as a volunteer Mormon missionary in Brazil, 1971-73; operated repertory theatre in Provo, Utah, 1974-75; Brigham Young University Press, Provo, editor, 1974-76; *Ensign,* Salt Lake City, Utah, assistant editor, 1976-78; free-lance writer and editor, 1978—. Senior editor, Compute! Books, Greensboro, N.C., 1983. Teacher at various universities and writers workshops. Local Democratic precinct election judge and Utah State Democratic Convention delegate. Recipient: John W. Campbell Award for best new writer of 1977, World Science Fiction Convention, 1978; Hugo Award nominations, World Science Fiction Convention, 1978, 1979, 1980, for short stories, and 1986, for novelette, "Hatrack River"; Nebula Award nominations, Science Fiction Writers of America, 1979, 1980, for short stories; Utah State Institute of Fine Arts prize, 1980, for epic poem "Prentice Alvin and the No-Good Plow"; Hamilton/Brackett Award, 1981, for *Songmaster;* Nebula Award, 1985, Hugo Award, 1986, and Hamilton/Brackett Award, 1986, all for novel *Ender's Game;* Nebula Award, 1986, Hugo Award, 1987, and *Locus* Award, 1987, all for novel *Speaker for the Dead;* World Fantasy Award, 1987, for novelette, "Hatrack River"; Hugo Award, and Locus Award nomination, both 1988, both for novella "Eye for Eye"; Locus Award for best fantasy, Hugo Award nomination, and World Fantasy Award nomination, all 1988, all for novel *Seventh Son.* Agent: Barbara Bova, 207 Sedgwick Rd., West Hartford, CT 06107. Address: 546 Lindley Rd., Greensboro, NC 27410, U.S.A.

PUBLICATIONS

Fiction

Hot Sleep. New York, Baronet, 1978; London, Futura, 1980.
A Planet Called Treason. New York, St. Martin's, 1979; London, Pan, 1981; revised edition, Dell, 1980; new revised edition published as *Treason,* St. Martin's, 1988.
Songmaster. New York, Dial, 1980; London, Futura, 1981.
Hart's Hope. New York, Berkley, 1982; London, Unwin, 1986.
The Worthing Chronicle. New York, Ace, 1983.
Wyrms. New York, Arbor House, 1987.
A Woman of Destiny (historical novel). New York, Berkley, 1983; published as *Saints,* New York, Tor, 1988.
The Abyss (screenplay novelization). New York, Pocket, and London, Century, 1989.
Worthing Saga. New York, Tor, 1990; London, Legend, 1991.
The Changed Man. New York, Tor, 1992.
Lost Boys. New York, HarperCollins, 1992.

"Ender Wiggins" series:

Ender's Game. New York, Tor, 1985; London, Unwin, 1985.
Speaker for the Dead. New York, Tor, 1986; London, Century, 1987.
Xenocide. New York, Tor, 1991.

"Tales of Alvin Maker" series:

Seventh Son. New York, Tor, 1987; London, Century, 1988.
Red Prophet. New York, Tor, and London, Century, 1988.

Prentice Alvin. New York, Tor, and London, Century, 1989.

"Homecoming Saga" series:

The Memory of Earth. New York, Tor, 1993.
The Call of Earth. New York, Tor, 1993

Short Stories

Capitol. New York, Ace, 1978.
Unaccompanied Sonata and Other Stories. New York, Dial, 1981.
Folk of the Fringe. West Bloomfield, Michigan, Phantasia Press, 1989; London, Century, 1990.

"Maps in a Mirror" series:

Maps in a Mirror. New York, Tor, 1990; London, Century, 1991.
Flux. New York, Tor, 1992.
Cruel Miracles. New York, Tor, 1992.
Monkey Sonatas. New York, Tor, 1993.

Plays

The Apostate (produced Provo, Utah, 1970).
In Flight (produced Provo, 1970).
Across Five Summers (produced Provo, 1971).
Of Gideon (produced Provo, 1971).
Stone Tables (produced Brigham Young University, Provo,, 1973).
A Christmas Carol (adapted from the story by Charles Dickens; produced Provo, 1974).
Father, Mother, Mother, and Mom (produced Provo, 1974; published in *Sunstone,* 1978).
Liberty Jail (produced in Provo, 1975).
Rag Mission (as Brian Green); published in *Ensign,* July, 1977.

Other

Listen, Mom and Dad. Salt Lake City, Bookcraft, 1978.
Saintspeak: The Mormon Dictionary. Midvale, Utah, Signature, 1981.
Ainge. Midvale, Utah, Signature, 1982.
Compute's Guide to IBM PCjr Sound and Graphics. Greensboro, North Carolina, Compute, 1984.
Cardography. Eugene, Oregon, Hypatia Press, 1987.
Characters and Viewpoint. Cincinnati, Ohio, Writers Digest, 1988; London, Robinson, 1989.
How to Write Science Fiction and Fantasy. Cincinnati, Ohio, Writers Digest, 1990.
Editor, *Dragons of Darkness*. New York, Ace, 1981.
Editor, *Dragons of Light*. New York, Ace, 1983.
Editor, *Future on Fire*. New York, Ace, 1991.

*

Biography: Entry in *Contemporary Literary Criticism,* Detroit, Gale, Volume 44, 1987, Volume 47, 1988, Volume 50, 1988.

* * *

Orson Scott Card is a Mormon writer of fantasy and science fiction, most of which is suitable for and interesting to young adult readers. While Card's Mormon beliefs inform all of his works, his most popular fiction is not overtly religious or moralistic. His stories are usually highly engaging adventures, in which young people of extraordinary ability must deal with moral, political, intellectual, and social problems that test them and require personal growth that is often painful.

The most broadly appealing of his works are the novels in the "Tales of Alvin Maker" series: *Seventh Son, Red Prophet,* and *Prentice Alvin*. These books tell the story of Alvin Miller, the seventh son of a seventh son. He is born in 1800 in an alternative America, geographically recognizable as the frontier Midwest, but historically different. The main difference is that some people are born with magical gifts, the abilities to mentally control the basic elements of earth, air, fire, and water. Alvin's special birth means he is a "maker," a possessor of the ability to master all forms of magic, not only controlling all the elements, but also able to learn the particular cultural forms of magic possessed by Native Americans and brought from Africa by the slaves. The three novels currently comprising the series tell Alvin's adventures growing up with his family, being caught up in the Indian wars that involved the historical figures of Tecumseh and his brother, the Prophet, and learning the trade of blacksmith while simultaneously learning how to use his magical powers in the service of making. Though cast as adventures, each of these novels focuses on Alvin's personal problems as a gifted young person, such as learning to get along with his family and his various teachers, to live in his society, to use his gifts for good ends, and discovering what he should ultimately do with his life. He learns that his mission in life is to defeat the "unmaker," an entropic force that wants all motion or making to cease. Card gives depth and reality to Alvin's struggles in part by presenting vivid, deep, and sympathetic portraits of a variety of characters, even those who are evil. These stories also explore major American themes such as race and slavery, gender roles, religious fanaticism, and humanity's relationship with nature. Of special interest in the series are the appearances of historical and mythical characters, such as William Blake, Napoleon, and Mike Fink. Card's narratives are fast-paced and gripping, but spiced with vivid descriptions and humorous episodes. Card has announced his intention of publishing two or three more books to complete this series.

While the *Alvin Maker* books and those in the science fiction series, *Homecoming,* are suitable for all young adult readers, educators should be aware that these books contain violent events and that Card's presentation of adult sexuality is frank, though morally serious. There is no gratuitous violence or sex in these books, but Card does deal realistically with both themes when it is appropriate to his stories. Among Card's novels that would be of interest to young adults, two are especially violent and, therefore, likely to offend less-sophisticated or sensitive readers: *Hart's Hope* and *Wyrms*.

Card's most successful science fiction series—winner of Hugo and Nebula awards—is aimed at older readers, but is appropriate to and widely admired by high school and college students. These are the three novels about Ender Wiggins: *Ender's Game, Speaker for the Dead,* and *Xenocide*. *Ender's Game* is the tale of a child genius who is trained to lead Earth's space fleet against a greatly feared and possibly overwhelming alien enemy. In the last phase of his training, when he thinks he is playing strategic games, he is actually leading the fleet by remote control, and he successfully wipes out the entire alien species. Because of the time distortions of light-speed space travel, Ender is still a young man thousands of years after the events of *Ender's Game,* when humans have realized that they were in error to think of the destroyed aliens as enemies. Ender himself is led to this realization because he has come into contact with a cocoon that contains the seeds of the rebirth of that race and he has become a speaker for the dead. In *Speaker for the Dead*, he is caught up in finding a new planet on which that species can start again, and this turns out to be a planet on which humanity has accidentally encountered another intelligent species. In *Xenocide*, a middle-aged Ender works with three non-human intelligent species, all of whom might be destroyed by a fearful and ignorant humanity. These books are also highly engaging adventures, characterized by social, political, spiritual, and intellectual puzzles and conflicts. One especially important central theme is the complex of problems posed by colonialism and imperialism in the modern world and how radically different cultures can relate to each other in mutually beneficial ways.

While Card is best known for his novels, his short stories are also excellent. *Maps in a Mirror: The Short Fiction of Orson Scott Card* collects most of his stories, and sections of this large collection have been published in separate paperbacks. The hardcover collection is a good resource since it contains introductions and afterwords in which Card talks about his life, career, and some of the ideas behind his stories. The best of these stories for young adults and classroom use are probably those in the sections "Maps in a Mirror" and "Cruel Miracles," such as "Unaccompanied Sonata," "The Porcelain Salamander," "Middle Woman," "St. Amy's Tale," "Kingsmeat," and "Holy." Like the novels, these stories are sometimes quite violent but always have at least one challenging moral or intellectual dilemma at their center that can provoke serious thought and discussion.

—Terry Heller

———

CARTER, Alden R(ichardson). American. Born in Eau Claire, Wisconsin, 7 April 1947. Educated at University of Kansas, B.A. 1969; Montana State University, teaching certificate, 1976. Served in U.S. Navy, 1969-74; became lieutenant senior grade; nominated for Navy Achievement Medal. Married Carol Ann Shadis in 1974; one son and one daughter. Writer. Taught high school English and journalism for four years in Marshfield, Wisconsin. Speaker at workshops, including ALAN Workshop on Young Adult Literature and National Council of Teachers of English. Recipient: Best Book for Young Adults citation, American Library Association, 1984, for *Growing Season*; Best Book for Young Adults citations, ALA, New York Public Library, Los Angeles Public Library, and the Child Study Association, Best Book for Reluctant Readers citation, ALA Young Adult Services Committee, all 1985, all for *Wart, Son of Toad*; Best Book for Young Adults citations, ALA and Los Angeles Public Library, and Best Book for the Teenage citation, New York Public Library, all 1987, all for *Sheila's Dying*; Children's Book COuncil/National Science Teacher's Association Outstanding Science Trade Book for Children citation, 1988, for *Radio: From Marconi to the Space Age*; Best Book citation, ALA, and Best Book for the Teenage citation, New York Public Library, both 1989, both for *Up Country*; Best Book for the Teenage citation and Best Children's Fiction Book of the Year citation, Society of Midland Authors, both 1990, both for *Robodad*. Address: 1113 West Onstad Drive, Marshfield, WI 54449, U.S.A.

PUBLICATIONS FOR YOUNG ADULTS

Fiction

Growing Season. New York, Coward McCann, 1984.
Wart, Son of Toad. New York, Putnam, 1985.
Sheila's Dying. New York, Putnam, 1987.
Up Country. New York, Putnam, 1989.
Robodad. New York, Putnam, 1990; as *Dancing on Dark Water*, New York, Scholastic, 1993.
Dogwolf. New York, Scholastic, 1994.

Nonfiction

Supercomputers, with Wayne Jerome LeBlanc. New York, F. Watts, 1985.
Modern China, with photographs by Carol S. Carter and Alden R. Carter. New York, F. Watts, 1986.
Modern Electronics, with Wayne Jerome LeBlanc. New York, F. Watts, 1986.
Illinois. New York, F. Watts, 1987.
Radio: From Marconi to the Space Age. New York, F. Watts, 1987.
The Shoshoni. New York, F. Watts, 1989.
The Battle of Gettysburg. New York, F. Watts, 1990.
Last Stand at the Alamo. New York, F. Watts, 1990.
The Colonial Wars: Clashes in the Wilderness. New York, F. Watts, 1992.
The American Revolution: War for Independence. New York, F. Watts, 1992.
The War of 1812: Second Fight for Independence. New York, F. Watts, 1992.
The Civil War: American Tragedy. New York, F. Watts, 1992.
The Mexican War: Manifest Destiny. New York, F. Watts, 1992.
The Spanish-American War: Imperial Ambitions. New York, F. Watts, 1992.
The Monitor and the Merrimack: Battle of the Ironclads. New York, F. Watts, 1993.
China Past—China Future. New York, F. Watts, 1994.

"The American Revolution" series:

Colonies in Revolt. New York, F. Watts, 1988.
Darkest Hours. New York, F. Watts, 1988.
At the Forge of Liberty. New York, F. Watts, 1988.
Birth of the Republic. New York, F. Watts, 1988.

*

Biography: Essay in *Speaking for Ourselves, Too: More Autobiographical Sketches by Notable Authors for Young Adults* compiled and edited by Donald R. Gallo, National Council of Teachers of English, 1993.

Critical Study: Entry in *Children's Literature Review,* Volume 22, Detroit, Gale, 1991.

Alden R. Carter comments:

I am always astonished by the courage of people, and young people in particular. I find the coming-of-age process endlessly intriguing, and if readers of my books come to share my fascination, then I have done my work well. I concentrate on characterization because the human soul matters more to me—and I think to serious readers whatever their age—than elaborate plots. Like people in real life, my characters do not survive their problems unscathed; all of us collect our store of disappointments, scars, and sad wisdom in the teenage years. Yet through their struggles, my characters grow and—like the vast majority of young people in real life—reach the threshold of adulthood triumphant in the realization of their own grit, resilience, and courage.

My nonfiction books also reflect my interest in the struggles of individuals and nations to overcome what often seem unscalable obstacles. History teaches the hard lesson that we fail more than we succeed. Yet we are a remarkably persistent and ingenious species, and ultimately we find the fingernail crack in the slippery surface, gain a toehold on the rock, and—inch by inch—work upward toward the summit and the open sky beyond.

*　　*　　*

The ability of young adults to adjust to difficult situations with the help of family and friends is a theme Alden R. Carter explores in each of his five young adult novels. In *Growing Season,* seventeen-year-old Rick Simons reluctantly moves with his family from Milwaukee to a dairy farm in rural Wisconsin during his senior year. Rick only intends to stay for six months, to help get things going, and then return to Milwaukee to study architecture in college. But life on the farm is filled with daily chores, broken machinery, livestock problems, and family squabbles which demand his time and energy and Rick is unable to leave. Eventually, his resentment recedes and Rick comes to enjoy farm life. His family's determined acceptance of adversity and understanding of his feelings and mistakes, along with his friendship with Lorie, enable him to remain on the farm indefinitely. He may even find a way to use his architectural inclinations to improve their family farm and others like it. In this heart-warming novel, filled with familial love, supportive friendships, and the frustrations inherent in change and growth, Carter shows the advantages of life in the country, even for a city-bred teenager like Rick.

The question of the city vs. the country also figures in *Up Country.* Like Rick, sixteen-year-old Carl Staggers leaves Milwaukee to live in rural Wisconsin, but his situation is more severe than Rick's. Carl's stay up country is court-mandated when his mother is arrested for a hit-and-run accident and ordered into a recovery program for alcoholics. Carl does not want to leave his lucrative, but illegal electronics repair business and live with his aunt, uncle, and cousin whom he has not seen for eight years. His relatives are kind to him, but Carl is annoyed by their countrified ways. His cousin Bob encourages him to date Signa, who becomes a loyal friend. When Carl's illegal activities are discovered, Signa and his country family stand by him throughout the legal proceedings. Even though his mother is now a recovering alcoholic and Carl can return to the city and live with her, he chooses to remain in the country where his friend Signa and a family he can count on will help him as he continues to learn how being the child of an alcoholic has affected his life.

Fourteen-year-old Shar's life has also been affected by an inadequate parent. Her father is a victim of brain damage caused by an aneurysm which has destroyed the part of his brain that controls higher emotions, like love. *RoboDad* is the story of how Shar learns to cope with a father who has no emotional connection to his family, a father who used to be her best buddy but now makes uncaring remarks about her physical appearance, a father who

chooses to look for a lost ski rather than save her brother after a water-skiing accident, a father who makes people so uncomfortable that her best friend won't come to her home and her boyfriend breaks up with her, a father who has to be tranquilized so he doesn't hurt himself or anyone else. Shar and her family come to understand how each of them deals with their father's emotional detachment: Shar cries, Sid fights, Alex remains cheerful, and their mother works hard to pay the bills and keep things as calm as possible. Her mother's honesty helps Shar accept the fact that the father she loved so much is dead, but she can still go on caring for the man he has become even though he will never be able to love her back.

Steve Michaels in *Wart, Son of Toad* is also faced with a difficult situation involving his father. Steve and his father have lived alone since his mother and sister Roxy were killed in an automobile accident three years earlier. Steve attends the high school where his father is a very unpopular biology teacher. The students call his father the "Toad," and refer to Steve as "Wart." Unhappy students threaten his father and tease Steve. Mr. Michaels refuses to be intimidated, even when students vandalize his car. Steve, on the other hand, fights with one of the chiding jocks. Life is not easy for Steve and his father at home either; they argue constantly over Steve's grades and lack of desire to go to college. The shadow of Steve's mother and Roxy hovers over them as they both deal with their grief. Steve and his father eventually come to understand one another, and help each other put the past behind them and move on in new directions—Steve to pursue a course in auto mechanics and a relationship with his girlfriend Trish and Mr. Michaels to leave teaching and work as a guide for a wildlife foundation.

Dealing with death is also emphasized in *Sheila's Dying.* Jerry Kincaid has been dating Sheila Porter, but plans to break up with her. Before he tells her, however, she becomes ill, and he learns she is suffering from terminal cancer. Sheila's grandmother, her legal guardian, is alcoholic and unable to help Sheila, so Jerry supports Sheila through her medical ordeal. Bonnie Harper, Sheila's only other friend, wants to share in Sheila's care. Up to this point Jerry and Bonnie have had an adversarial relationship, but they manage to work together to meet Sheila's ever increasing needs. After a while they develop a friendship which sustains them through this trying time. Sheila knows she is dying and tells Jerry she hopes Bonnie will take her place as his steady girlfriend. By the end of the story, Jerry and Bonnie have fallen in love. Their mutual concern for Sheila has minimized any disagreements they may have had and made them appreciate the good in each other. They have not only helped Sheila through a difficult time, but themselves as well.

As Carter's characters struggle and adapt in various situations, they grow toward adulthood. The support of friends and family helps them in this process. Young adult readers find these characters real, their problems compelling, their feelings familiar, and their decisions satisfying. Such responses to his skillfully written stories consequently make Carter's young adult novels excellent fare for young adult readers.

—Elizabeth A. Poe

———

CASSEDY, Sylvia. American. Born in Brooklyn, New York, 29 January 1930. Educated at Brooklyn College, 1946-51, B.A. 1951; Johns Hopkins University, Baltimore, 1959-60. Married 1) Leslie

Verwiebe in 1949 (died 1950); 2) Edward Cassedy in 1952, three daughters and one son. Teacher of creative writing to children, Queens College, City University of New York, Flushing, 1973-74, Great Neck Public Library, New York, 1975-79, and Manhasset Public Schools, New York, 1977-84. Instructor in teaching creative writing to children, Nassau County Board of Cooperative Education, New York, 1978-79. *Died 6 April 1989.*

PUBLICATIONS FOR YOUNG ADULTS

Fiction

Behind the Attic Wall. New York, Crowell, 1983; London, Bodley Head, 1984.
M.E. and Morton. New York, Crowell, and London, Bodley Head, 1987.
Lucie Babbidge's House. New York, Crowell, 1989.

PUBLICATIONS FOR CHILDREN

Fiction

Little Chameleon, illustrated by Rainey Bennett. Cleveland, World, 1966.
Pierino and the Bell, illustrated by Evaline Ness. New York, Doubleday, 1966.
Marzipan Day on Bridget Lane, illustrated by Margot Tomes. New York, Doubleday, 1967.
The Best Cat Suit of All, pictures by Rosekranz Hoffman. New York, Dial, 1991.

Poetry

Roomrimes, illustrated by Michele Chessare. New York, Crowell, 1987.
Zoomrimes, illustrated by Michele Chessare. New York, Crowell, 1993.

Other

In Your Own Words: A Beginner's Guide to Writing. New York, Doubleday, 1979.
Editor, and Translator with Kunihiro Suetake, *Birds, Frogs, and Moonlight,* illustrated by Vo-Dinh. New York, Doubleday, 1967.
Editor, and Translator with Parvathi Thampi, *Moon-Uncle, Moon-Uncle: Rhymes from India,* illustrated by Susanne Suba. New York, Doubleday, 1973.
Translator with Kunihiro Suetake, *Red Dragonfly on my Shoulder: Haiku,* illustrated by Molly Bang. New York, HarperCollins, 1992.

*   *   *

Sylvia Cassedy wrote with a young eye. In her fiction the boundary between young people and adults—a boundary often blurred or absent in literature for this age group—is firmly present. On one side are the fantasies and helplessness of being young, on the other

the rigidity and dreariness of being grown-up. Her preadolescent characters haven't yet developed the armour to shield themselves from the world's harsh realities nor have they lost their unique enjoyment of its physical details; they revel in odd, messy minutiae, such as smeary pink nail polish or soft corners of paper.

All of Cassedy's characters cope with reality through the transforming power of imagination. In her first book, *Behind the Attic Wall,* orphaned Maggie is stripped of love and security. Appropriately, she invents a game of domineering the imaginary "Backwoods Girls," who have even less than she. The talking dolls that Maggie discovers spring naturally out of this needy game; now instead of just pretending to, she can really give. The line between how much the dolls are Maggie's own creation and how much they are "real" is very fine, which makes their existence all the more haunting. The result is a remarkably powerful novel about caring and continuity.

In *M.E. and Morton,* Mary Ella—or M.E., as she prefers to call herself—also uses fantasy as a solace, in pretending that her bottles of paint are orphans. As well, she fantasizes that she is more popular and loved than she is. Her neighbour Polly pretends, too—she imagines that the bugs on her ceiling are dancing and that she can shrink herself to fit into a toy train. Unlike the unhealthy fantasies of M.E., however, Polly's inventions enable her to transform her dull, poverty-stricken life into joy. M.E.'s slow older brother, Morton, is a perfect companion for Polly. He doesn't suffer from his sister's guilty confusion and can engage with Polly in simple play. It is easier to label this book realism than it is to call *Behind the Attic Wall* fantasy. The use of imagination, however, results in a similar "magic" in both: make-believe comes true through the healing power of love.

The author's final novel, *Lucie Babbidge's House,* digs deeper into the themes she has developed in her first two works, resulting in a more complex and cynical story. The utterly bleak orphanage where Lucie lives and goes to school is a symbol of both adult and child cruelty: Lucie's teacher verbally abuses her, and her classmates ape that bullying. Like Maggie, Lucie creates a fantasy around some dolls that she finds in a dollhouse in a hidden room where she escapes to whenever possible. She makes the dolls play all the roles she has known—her over-literate teacher and beloved deceased parents, as well as herself as a child who was once happy. The dollhouse fantasy is gradually made obvious as the story proceeds, then a third level of reality is added as Lucie receives letters from Delia, a girl her own age in England. These three levels of reality—Lucie's school life, her made-up dollhouse life, and Delia's life, which may or may not be fantasy—begin to get mixed up, which threaten Lucie's sanity. The way she saves herself, by standing up to her teacher with words, provides a slender but strong thread of hope. This novel lacks the promise of love present at the end of Cassedy's first two novels, but its sadness is balanced by the black humour of the ridiculous restrictions in Lucie's daily life. The result is a brilliant comment on the gap between adults' and children's perceptions of reality.

Desperately lonely Maggie, posturing M.E., resilient Polly, stolid Morton, and pathetic but determined Lucie, all emerge as unforgettable personalities. While the leisurely pace of Cassedy's fiction may discourage readers looking for continuous action, each novel builds suspense in delicate layers to reach a surprise ending. The author's precise, measured language—the language of the poet she was—results in impeccable prose. Sylvia Cassedy was a compelling and original writer for young people.

—Kit Pearson

CAUDILL, Rebecca. American. Born in Poor Fork (now Cumberland), Kentucky, 2 February 1899. Educated at Sumner County High School, Portland, Tennessee, graduated 1916; Wesleyan College, Macon, Georgia, 1916-20, B.A. in English 1920; Vanderbilt University, Nashville, 1921-22, M.A. 1922. Married James Sterling Ayars in 1931; one son (died 1956) and one daughter. English and history teacher, Sumner County High School, Portland, Tennessee, 1920-21; English teacher, Collegio Benet, Rio de Janeiro, 1922-24; editor, *Torchbearer* magazine, Nashville, 1924-30; author of books for children and young people, since 1943. Originator of hospitality program for international students, University of Illinois; former alumni trustee, Wesleyan College; secretary of board of trustees, Urbana Free Library; Member of the Board of Trustees, Pine Mountain Settlement School, Kentucky, 1967-85. Teacher at writing workshops. Rebecca Caudill Public Library, Cumberland, Kentucky, named in 1965. Recipient: Newbery award runner-up, 1949, for *Tree of Freedom;* "honor book" citations, *New York Herald-Tribune*, 1949, for *Tree of Freedom,* and 1954, for *House of the Fifers;* Wesleyan College Alumnae award for Distinguished Achievement, 1954; Nancy Bloch Memorial award for best juvenile book dealing with inter cultural relations, 1956, for *Susan Cornish;* Friends of American Writers award, 1965, for *The Far-Off Land;* author of Caldecott Honor Book, 1965, *A Pocketful of Cricket;* citation for most representative American book recommended for translation into other languages, Hans Christian Andersen award Committee, 1966, for *A Pocketful of Cricket;* Clara Ingram Judson award, Society of Midland Authors, 1966, for *A Certain Small Shepherd;* award for distinguished service in the field of children's reading (with husband, James Ayars), Chicago Children's Reading Round Table, 1969; "Author of the Year" citation, Illinois Association of Teachers of English, 1972. *Died 2 October 1985.*

PUBLICATIONS FOR YOUNG ADULTS

Fiction

Barrie and Daughter, illustrated by Berkeley Williams. New York, Viking, 1943.
Tree of Freedom, illustrated by Dorothy Bayley Morse. New York, Viking, 1949.
House of the Fifers, illustrated by Genia. New York, Longmans, 1954.
Susan Cornish, illustrated by E. Harper Johnson. New York, Viking, 1955.
The Far-Off Land, illustrated by Brinton Turkle. New York, Viking, 1964; London, Hart Davis, 1965.
Contrary Jenkins with husband, James Ayars, illustrated by Glen Rounds. New York, Holt, 1969.

Poetry

Come Along!, illustrated by Ellen Raskin. New York, Holt, 1969.
Wind, Sand, and Sky, illustrated by Donald Carrick. New York, Dutton, 1976.

Other

Florence Nightingale, illustrated by William Neebe. Evanston, Illinois, Row Peterson, 1953.

PUBLICATIONS FOR CHILDREN

Fiction

Happy Little Family, illustrated by Decie Merwin. Philadelphia, Winston, 1947.
Schoolhouse in the Woods, illustrated by Decie Merwin. Philadelphia, Winston, 1949.
Up and Down the River, illustrated by Decie Merwin. Philadelphia, Winston, 1951.
Saturday Cousins, illustrated by Nancy Woltemate. Philadelphia, Winston, 1953.
Schoolroom in the Parlor, illustrated by Decie Merwin. Philadelphia, Winston, 1959.
Time for Lissa, illustrated by Velma Ilsley. New York, Thomas Nelson, 1959.
Higgins and the Great Big Scare, illustrated by Beth Krush. New York, Holt, 1960.
The Best-Loved Doll, illustrated by Elliott Gilbert. New York, Holt, 1962.
A Pocketful of Cricket, illustrated by Evaline Ness. New York, Holt, 1964; London, Harrap, 1966.
A Certain Small Shepherd, illustrated by William Pène du Bois. New York, Holt, 1965; Edinburgh, Oliver and Boyd, 1966.
Did You Carry the Flag Today, Charley?, illustrated by Nancy Grossman. New York, Holt, 1966.
Somebody Go and Bang a Drum, illustrated by Jack Hearne. New York, Dutton, 1974.

PUBLICATIONS FOR ADULTS

Other

The High Cost of Writing. Cumberland, Kentucky, Southeast Community College, 1965.
My Appalachia: A Reminiscence, photographs by Edward Wallowtich. New York, Holt, 1966.

*

Manuscript Collection: University of Kentucky, Lexington; Kerlan Collection, University of Minnesota, Minneapolis; de Grummond Collection, University of Southern Mississippi, Hattiesburg; and May Massee Collection, Emporia State College, Kansas.

Media Adaptations: *A Pocketful of Cricket* (filmstrip and record), Miller-Brody, 1976.

Biography: Entry in *More Junior Authors,* edited by Muriel Fuller, New York, H.W. Wilson, 1963.

*   *   *

Rebecca Caudill has written books for elementary school, junior high school, and senior high school readers. Set in the Kentucky mountain country of her birth, these books bespeak former times in our country and of seldom-heralded rural areas. Caudill's characters are at one with their family, their animals, and their land.

The Tree of Freedom takes place in Kentucky in the spring of 1780, when homesteading is in full swing. Thirteen-year-old

Stephanie Venable and her family make the long, hard journey from Carolina to Kentucky to take up their land grant claim of four hundred acres; they aim to build a house and start a farm. Stephanie brings with her an apple seed; her Grandmother Linney had carried an apple seed from France to Charleston, and planted it next to the house that her family built years before. Stephanie wanted to do the same at the family's new home in Kentucky, to plant a "tree of freedom," a link with her past and a symbol of her future. Kentucky in 1780 was full of promise, and full of hardship. Before winter the seven Venables would have to clear the land, build a cabin, and plant a crop. Talk of hostile Indians in the area, the call for Revolutionary Army volunteers to fight the British, and the threat of a Britisher's claim to the Venable's land, make the tasks more hazardous and difficult. But Stephanie goes ahead and plants her seed, and the Venables build a cabin and start their crops. Noel, the oldest child, goes off to join the Revolutionary Army. When he leaves, Stephanie shoulders more of the burden of family work. When Noel returns, he announces that he has been given the opportunity to read law in Williamsburg. He urges his family to allow Stephanie to study to be a teacher in Williamsburg. The book, which is well researched, ends with the hope of freedom and of opportunity for young people.

Barrie and Daughter is a fine story of understanding and affection between father and daughter. Fern's mother insists that a girl has one calling: to marry and run a household. She could also teach school, but that was the extent of a girl's options. This is not Fern's view of her future. The Barries live at Poor Fork, in the mountains of Kentucky, at the turn of the century. It is against the background of rigid mores of the mountain country that the novel is set. When Fern's father opens a store, Fern discovers that she enjoys the ordering and selling of goods. Fern and her father are similar in their imagination, their caring for others, and their courage. Their store is a new kind of store to the valley, one that is honest and one that puts the good of the neighbors first. Around the keeping of the store comes romance, and the strength to fight against hate and violence.

Caudill's "Happy Little Family" series includes *Happy Little Family, Schoolhouse in the Woods, Schoolhouse in Parlor, Saturday Cousins,* and *Up and Down the River.* In them Caudill writes to entertain and to provide readers with information on how life was led in an earlier time in a rural part of the country. Her books are not about community leaders, but about community members. They move at a slow, deliberate pace. Important in the activity is the change of seasons, for seasons direct to a large degree what one does in a life without central heat and air, without complex machines and public transportation. Relationships between family members in the books are positive and involve strong sets of reciprocal obligations. There are few social problems found in the books, and views of self, people, and the world are positive. Hostile forces appear, and the spectre of death is always there on the farm, but life itself is celebrated. If the pictures seem a little too perfect, they are still vibrant and plausible.

In *Up and Down the River,* summertime has finally arrived and the Fairchild family is ready for adventure. The family, consisting of two parents, three adolescents, and two younger children, has lots of work to do on the farm—there are animals to feed, eggs to gather, newborns to watch, stove wood to chop and carry. But Bonnie and Debbie have time to start a business venture, like their big sister who receives ten cents for every organ lesson she gives. Bonnie and Debbie decide to sell products ordered through their mother's magazines. They sell sensational new bluing at ten cents a package, and beautiful colored pictures at ten cents each. They are

successful in selling their products up and down the river to their distant neighbors, who are not only pleased to buy thir wares, but who also give them presents—a newborn lamb, decorated dinner plates. The everyday activities of the two girls, while not climactic, are nonetheless good fun.

Caudill provides strong descriptions of a geographic region and its distinctive cultures that are not often seen in books for young adults. She reminds us of the diversity of our country, and also of its developmental history from a harsh, agricultural beginning.

—Mary Lystad

———

CAVANNA, Betty (Elizabeth Cavanna). Also writes as Betsy Allen; Elizabeth Headley. American. Born in Camden, New Jersey, 24 June 1909. Educated at local schools, Haddenfield, New Jersey; Douglass College (now part of Rutgers University), New Brunswick, New Jersey, 1925-29, Litt.B. in journalism 1929 (Phi Beta Kappa). Married 1) Edward Talman Headley in 1940 (died 1952), one son; 2) George Russell Harrison in 1957 (died 1979). Reporter, Bayonne *Times,* New Jersey, 1929-31; advertising manager and then art director, Westminster Press, Philadelphia, Pennsylvania, 1931-41; full-time writer, since 1941. Recipient: Honor book, Spring Book Festival, 1946, for *Going on Sixteen,* and 1947, for *Secret Passage;* citation from New Jersey Institute of Technology and English Teachers Association of New Jersey, 1966, for *Mystery at Love's Creek;* runner-up, Edgar Allan Poe award, 1970, for *Spice Island Mystery,* and 1972, for *The Ghost of Ballyhooly;* citation from New Jersey Institute of Technology, 1976, for *Catchpenny Street.* Address: 45 Pasture Lane, Bryn Mawr, PA 19010, U.S.A.

PUBLICATIONS FOR YOUNG ADULTS

Fiction

Puppy Stakes. Philadelphia, Westminster, 1943.
The Black Spaniel Mystery. Philadelphia, Westminster, 1945.
Going on Sixteen. Philadelphia, Westminster, 1946, revised edition, Morrow, 1985.
Spurs for Suzanna, illustrated by Virginia Mann. Philadelphia, Westminster, 1947; London, Lutterworth, 1948.
A Girl Can Dream, illustrated by Harold Minton. Philadelphia, Westminster, 1948.
Paintbox Summer, illustrated by Peter Hunt. Philadelphia, Westminster, 1949.
Spring Comes Riding. Philadelphia, Westminster, 1950; London, Lutterworth, 1952.
Two's Company, illustrated by Edward J. Smith. Philadelphia, Westminster, 1951.
Lasso Your Heart. Philadelphia, Westminster, 1952.
Love, Laurie. Philadelphia, Westminster, 1953.
Six on Easy Street. Philadelphia, Westminster, 1954.
Passport to Romance. New York, Morrow, 1955.
The Boy Next Door. New York, Morrow, 1956.
Angel on Skis, illustrated by Isabel Dawson. New York, Morrow, 1957.
Stars in Her Eyes. New York, Morrow, 1958.

The Scarlet Sail. New York, Morrow, 1959; Leicester, Brockhampton, 1962.
Accent on April. New York, Morrow, 1960.
Fancy Free. New York, Morrow, 1961.
A Touch of Magic, illustrated by John Gretzer. Philadelphia, Westminster, 1961.
A Time for Tenderness. New York, Morrow, 1962.
Almost Like Sisters. New York, Morrow, 1963.
Jenny Kimura. New York, Morrow, 1964; Leicester, Brockhampton, 1966.
Mystery at Love's Creek. New York, Morrow, 1965.
A Breath of Fresh Air. New York, Morrow, 1966.
The Country Cousin. New York, Morrow, 1967.
Mystery in Marrakech. New York, Morrow, 1968.
Spice Island Mystery. New York, Morrow, 1969.
Mystery on Safari, illustrated by Joseph Cellini. New York, Morrow, 1970.
The Ghost of Ballyhooly. New York, Morrow, 1971.
Mystery in the Museum. New York, Morrow, 1972.
Petey, illustrated by Joe and Beth Krush. Philadelphia, Westminster, 1973.
Joyride. New York, Morrow, 1974.
Ruffles and Drums, illustrated by Richard Cuffari. New York, Morrow, 1975.
Mystery of the Emerald Buddha. New York, Morrow, 1976.
Runaway Voyage. New York, Morrow, 1978.
Stamp Twice for Murder. New York, Morrow, 1981.
The Surfer and the City Girl. Philadelphia, Westminster, 1981.
Storm in Her Heart. Philadelphia, Westminster, 1983.
Romance on Trial. Philadelphia, Westminster, 1984.
Wanted: A Girl for the Horses. New York, Morrow, 1984.
Banner Year. New York, Morrow, 1987.

Fiction as Elizabeth Headley

A Date for Diane, illustrated by Janet Smalley. Philadelphia, Macrae Smith, 1946.
Take a Call, Topsy!, illustrated by Janet Smalley. Philadelphia, Macrae Smith, 1947; revised edition, as *Ballet Fever* (as Betty Cavanna), Philadelphia, Westminster, 1978.
She's My Girl! Philadelphia, Macrae Smith, 1949; as *You Can't Take Twenty Dogs on a Date* (as Betty Cavanna), Philadelphia, Westminster, 1977.
Catchpenny Street. Philadelphia, Macrae Smith, 1951; reprinted under name Betty Cavanna, Philadelphia, Westminster, 1975.
Diane's New Love. Philadelphia, Macrae Smith, 1955.
Tourjours Diane. Philadelphia, Macrae Smith, 1957.
The Diane Stories: All about America's Favorite Girl Next Door (contains *A Date for Diane, Diane's New Love,* and *Toujours Diane*). Philadelphia, Macrae Smith, 1964.

Fiction as Betsy Allen

The Clue in Blue. New York, Grosset, 1948.
Puzzle in Purple. New York, Grosset, 1948.
The Riddle in Red. New York, Grosset, 1948.
The Secret of Black Cat Gulch. New York, Grosset, 1948.
The Green Island Mystery. New York, Grosset, 1949.
The Ghost Wore White. New York, Grosset, 1950.
The Yellow Warning. New York, Grosset, 1951.
The Gray Menace. New York, Grosset, 1953.

The Brown Satchel Mystery. New York, Grosset, 1954.
Peril in Pink. New York, Grosset, 1955.
The Silver Secret. New York, Grosset, 1956.
The Mystery of the Ruby Queens. New York, Grosset, 1958.

Other

Compiler and Editor, *Pick of the Litter: Favorite Dog Stories.* Philadelphia, Westminster, 1952.
The First Book of Seashells, illustrated by Marguerite Scott. New York, Watts, 1955; London, Edmund Ward, 1965.
Arne of Norway, photographs by husband, George Russell Harrison. New York, Watts, and London, Chatto & Windus, 1960.
The First Book of Wildflowers, illustrated by Page Cary. New York, Watts, 1961.
Lucho of Peru, photographs by George Russell Harrison. New York, Watts, 1961; London, Chatto & Windus, 1962.
Paulo of Brazil, photographs by George Russell Harrison. New York, Watts, 1962; London, Chatto & Windus, 1963.
Pepe of Argentina, photographs by George Russell Harrison. New York, Watts, 1962; London, Chatto & Windus, 1963.
Lo Chau of Hong Kong, photographs by George Russell Harrison. New York, Watts, and London, Chatto & Windus, 1963.
Chico of Guatemala, photographs by George Russell Harrison. New York, Watts, and London, Chatto & Windus, 1963.
Carlos of Mexico, photographs by George Russell Harrison. New York, Watts, and London, Chatto & Windus, 1964.
Noko of Japan, photographs by George Russell Harrison. New York, Watts, 1964.
Doug of Australia, photographs by George Russell Harrison. New York, Watts, and London, Chatto & Windus, 1965.
Tavi of the South Seas, photographs by George Russell Harrison. New York, Watts, 1965; London, Chatto & Windus, 1967.
Ali of Egypt, photographs by George Russell Harrison. New York, Watts, and London, Chatto & Windus, 1966.
Demetrios of Greece, photographs by George Russell Harrison. New York, Watts, 1966, and London, Chatto & Windus.
The First Book of Wool, photographs by George Russell Harrison. New York, Watts, 1966; as *Wool,* London, Watts, 1972.
The First Book of Fiji, photographs by George Russell Harrison. New York, Watts, 1968; as *Fiji,* London, Watts, 1972.
Morocco, photographs by George Russell Harrison. New York, Watts, 1970; London, Watts, 1972.

*

Manuscript Collection: de Grummond Collection, University of Southern Mississippi, Hattiesburg.

Biography: Essay in *Something about the Author Autobiography Series,* Volume 4, Detroit, Gale, 1987; entry in *More Junior Authors,* Bronx, New York, H.W. Wilson, 1963.

Critical Study: Entry in *Contemporary Literary Criticism,* Volume 12, Detroit, Gale, 1980.

*   *   *

Betty Cavanna, also known as Betsy Allen and Elizabeth Headley, is a prolific writer of books for children and young adults, having written more than seventy books. Though she began writing more than fifty years ago, many of her books are still among the favorites of today's young people—fond remembrances they share with their parents. An early love of reading was fostered when others read to her as a young child with infantile paralysis. Though she was captivated by fairy tales, she yearned for stories about "real" people. A journalism major in college, she honed her writing skills while aspiring to her ambition of working on a newspaper and writing children's books. She was able to achieve the first goal by being hired by the *Bayonne Times* within months of her graduation. She began writing short stories soon after that and within a few years, she had most ably achieved her second goal, becoming a popular author of books for children and young adults. Recalling her childhood penchant for characters to whom she could relate, her books always seem to be about "real" people.

Cavanna uses much from her youthful memories in the detailed portrayals of both the characters and locales of her novels. Her book *Catchpenny Street* is set in Camden, New Jersey, the place of her birth and her earliest recollections. Another popular book, *Boy Next Door*, took its background from Haddonfield, a suburban town which was to serve as the Cavannas' home for the remainder of Betty's youth. Other books featured locales in New Jersey, Pennsylvania, Cape Cod, and Martha's Vineyard, where the author resided in later years. One of her historical novels, *Ruffles and Drums*, takes place in Concord, Massachusetts, where she lived in close proximity to the bridge and the battlefield which initiated the events in her book.

The circumstances of Cavanna's illness and its impact upon the experiences of her youth is generalized into the feeling of "not belonging" so common to many teenagers. As a young girl, she always wanted to conform and be a part of the crowd. As in the case of many of her characters, including Julie in *Going On Sixteen*, success in this task was not always achieved. A childhood acquaintance fostered an interest in horses and riding which later became the basis for the plots of *Banner Year*, *Wanted: A Girl for the Horses*, *Spring Comes Riding*, and *Spurs for Suzanna*. Many books highlight the author's love of the many dogs in her life, including *Going On Sixteen*, *Puppy Stakes*, *She's My Girl* (later revised as *You Can't Take Twenty Dogs on a Date*), *The Black Spaniel Mystery*, and *Pick of the Litter*. Keeping her characters close to her own knowledge and experience, Cavanna learned to fly in order to write *A Girl Can Dream*. She also tried skiing to write *Angel on Skis* and attempted sailing to add to the reality of *The Scarlet Sail*. Many of her books touch on other aspects and experiences of growing up such as loneliness, shyness, jealousy, mother-daughter rivalry and social maladjustment. Some books sensitively handle such tough topics as alcoholism, divorce, race, and prejudice.

Under the name of Betsy Allen, Cavanna wrote a series of mysteries, including *The Clue in Blue*, *The Riddle in Red*, *The Secret of Black Cat Gulch*, *The Green Island Mystery*, and *The Ghost Wore White*. Using the pseudonym Elizabeth Headley, the "Diane" stories were penned as well as several other titles. Cavanna employed her husband as photographer to author the "Around the World Today" series. These stories are about young people in several countries and include such titles as *Arne of Norway*, *Pepe of Argentina*, *Carlos of Mexico*, *Ali of Egypt*, and *Demetrios of Greece*. In later years, Cavanna's background research during her extensive travels empowered her to write novels of "pure escape fiction in authentic settings" such as *A Time for Tenderness* based in Brazil; *Jenny Kimura*, an acclaimed book about a Japanese-American girl; *Mystery at Love's Creek* in Australia; *Spice Island Mystery*, which takes place in Grenada; *Mystery on Safari*, based in East Africa; *The*

Ghost of Ballyhooly, an Irish story; and *Mystery of the Emerald Buddha*, set in Bangkok, Thailand.

Cavanna's thirst for knowledge led her to write several nonfiction titles: *First Book of Seashells*, *First Book of Wildflowers*, *First Book of Wool*, *First Book of Fiji*, and *First Book of Morocco*. She has also contributed stories to several teenage magazines.

The author believes the longevity of her books is based on the universality and timelessness of the emotions she depicts in the lives of her characters. The popularity of her stories is evidenced by the sale of nearly a million copies of *Going on Sixteen* alone. Her books have been translated into twelve languages and have been incorporated into several school curriculums. She offers girls the chance to "slip away from the accelerated pace of school work, as I did once-upon-a-time, and read a book just for fun." Ms. Cavanna has amply succeeded in this endeavor. We all enjoy escaping into her adventures and look forward to passing this pleasure on to our daughters.

—Laurie Schwartz Guttenberg

———

CHAMBERS, Aidan. Also writes as Malcolm Blacklin. British. Born in Chester-le-Street, County Durham, 27 December 1934. Educated at Queen Elizabeth I Grammar School, Darlington, County Durham, 1948-53; Borough Road College, London, 1955-57. Served in the Royal Navy, 1953-55. Married Nancy Harris Lockwood in 1968. Teacher of English and drama in English schools, 1957-68. Since 1969 proprietor and publisher, Thimble Press, and publisher, *Signal: Approaches to Children's Books*, and *Young Drama: The Magazine about Child and Youth Drama*, South Woodchester, Gloucestershire; tutor, Further Professional Studies Department, University of Bristol, 1970-82. Columnist ("Young Reading"), *Times Educational Supplement*, London, 1970-72; columnist ("Letter from England"), *Horn Book*, Boston, 1972-84; writer and presenter, with Nancy Chambers, *Bookbox* programme, Radio Bristol, 1973-75; writer and presenter, *Children and Books* programme, BBC Radio, 1976; *Ghosts*, Thames-TV, 1980; and *Long, Short, and Tall Stories*, BBC-TV, 1981. General editor, Topliners, Club 75, and Rockets series, 1967-81, and 1977-1990 M Books series, Macmillan, publishers, London; since 1982 visiting lecturer for Westminster College, Oxford; cofounder and since 1989 editorial publisher of Turton & Chambers. Recipient: Children's Literature Association award, 1978, for article "The Reader in the Book"; Eleanor Farjeon award, 1982; Silver Pencil award (Netherlands), 1985, 1986. Address: Lockwood, Station Rd., South Woodchester, Stroud, Gloucestershire GL5 5EQ, England.

Publications for Young Adults

Fiction

Ghost Carnival: Stories of Ghosts in Their Haunts, illustrated by Peter Wingham. London, Heinemann, 1977.

Novels

Breaktime. London, Bodley Head, 1978; New York, Harper, 1979.

Seal Secret. London, Bodley Head, 1980; New York, Harper, 1981.

Dance on My Grave. London, Bodley Head, 1982; New York, Harper, 1983.

The Present Takers. London, Bodley Head, 1983; New York, Harper, 1984.

Now I Know. London, Harper, 1987; as *NIK: Now I Know,* New York, Harper, 1988.

The Toll Bridge. London, Bodley Head, 1992; New York, Harper, 1994.

Plays

Johnny Salter (produced Stroud, Gloucestershire, 1965). London, Heinemann, 1966.

The Car (produced Stroud, Gloucestershire, 1966). London, Heinemann, 1967.

The Chicken Run (produced Stroud, Gloucestershire, 1967). London, Heinemann, 1968.

The Dream Cage: A Comic Drama in Nine Dreams (produced Stroud, Gloucestershire, 1981). London, Heinemann, 1982.

Television Series: *Ghosts,* 1980; *Long, Short and Tall Stories,* 1980-81. Contributor to *Winter's Tales for Children Four,* Macmillan. General editor, Macmillan "Topliners" series. Author of column, "Letter from England," *Horn Book.* Contributor to numerous periodicals, including *Times Educational Supplement.* Reviewer for *Children's Book News.*

Other

Haunted Houses, illustrated by John Cameron Jarvies. London, Pan, 1971.

More Haunted Houses, illustrated by Chris Bradbury. London, Pan, 1973.

Great British Ghosts, illustrated by Barry Wilkinson. London, Pan, 1974.

Great Ghosts of the World, illustrated by Peter Edwards. London, Pan, 1974.

Book of Flyers and Flying, illustrated by Trevor Stubley. London, Kestrel, 1976.

Book of Cops and Robbers, illustrated by Allan Manham. London, Kestrel, 1977.

Editor, with Nancy Chambers, *Ghosts.* London, Macmillan, 1969.

Editor, *I Want to Get Out: Stories and Poems By Young Writers.* London, Macmillan, 1971.

Editor, with Nancy Chambers, *Hi-Ran-Ho: A Picture Book of Verse,* illustrated by Barbara Swiderska. London, Longman, 1971.

Editor, with Nancy Chambers, *World Minus Zero: An SF Anthology.* London, Macmillan, 1971.

Editor, with Nancy Chambers, *In Time to Come: An SF Anthology.* London, Macmillan, 1973.

Editor, *The Tenth [and Eleventh] Ghost Book.* London, Barrie and Jenkins, 2 vols., 1975-76; published together as *The Bumper Book of Ghost Stories,* London, Pan, 1976.

Editor, *Fighters in the Sky.* London, Macmillan, 1976.

Editor, *Funny Folk: A Body of Comic Tales,* illustrated by Trevor Stubley. London, Heinemann, 1976.

Editor, *Men at War.* London, Macmillan, 1977.

Editor, *Escapers.* London, Macmillan, 1978.

Editor, *War at Sea.* London, Macmillan, 1978.

Editor (as Malcolm Blacklin), *Ghosts 4.* London, Macmillan, 1978.

Editor, *Animal Fair,* illustrated by Anthony Colbert. London, Heinemann, 1979.

Editor, *Aidan Chambers' Book of Ghosts and Hauntings,* illustrated by Antony Maitland. London, Kestrel, 1980.

Editor, *Ghosts That Haunt You,* illustrated by Gareth Floyd. London, Kestrel, 1980.

Editor, *Loving You, Loving Me.* London, Kestrel, 1980.

Editor, *Ghost after Ghost,* illustrated by Bert Kitchen. London, Kestrel, 1982.

Editor, *Out of Time: Stories of the Future.* London, Bodley Head, 1984; New York, Harper, 1985.

Editor, *A Sporting Chance: Stories of Winning and Losing.* London, Bodley Head, 1985.

Editor, *Shades of Dark: Ghost Stories.* London, Hardy, 1984; New York, Harper, 1986.

Editor, *A Haunt of Ghosts.* New York, Harper, 1987.

Editor, *A Quiver of Ghosts.* London, Bodley Head, 1987.

Editor, *Love All.* London, Bodley Head, 1988.

Editor, *On the Edge.* London, Macmillan, 1990.

PUBLICATIONS FOR CHILDREN

Fiction

Cycle Smash. London, Heinemann, 1968.

Marle. London, Heinemann, 1968.

Don't Forget Charlie and the Vase, illustrated by Clyde Pearson. London, Macmillan, 1971.

Mac and Lugs, illustrated by Barbara Swiderska. London, Macmillan, 1971.

Ghosts 2 (short stories). London, Macmillan, 1972.

Snake River, illustrated by Peter Morgan. Stockholm, Almqvist och Wiksell, 1975; London, Macmillan, 1977.

Fox Tricks (short stories), illustrated by Robin and Jocelyn Wild. London, Heinemann, 1980.

PUBLICATIONS FOR ADULTS

Play

Everyman's Everybody (produced London, 1957).

Other

The Reluctant Reader. Oxford, Pergamon Press, 1969.

Introducing Books to Children. London, Heinemann, 1973; revised edition, Boston, Horn Book, 1983; London, Heinemann, 1984.

Axes for Frozen Seas (lecture). Huddersfield, Yorkshire, Woodfield and Stanley, 1981.

Editor, *Plays for Young People to Read and Perform.* Stroud, Gloucestershire, Thimble Press, 1982.

Editor, with Jill Bennett, *Poetry for Children: A Signal Bookguide.* Stroud, Gloucestershire, Thimble Press, 1984.

Editor, *Booktalk: Occasional Writing on Literature and Children.* London, Bodley Head, and New York, Harper, 1985.

The Reading Environment. Stroud, Gloucestershire, Thimble Press, 1990.

Tell Me: Children, Reading and Talk. Stroud, Gloucestershire, Thimble Press, 1993.

Biography: Essay in *Something about the Author Autobiography Series,* Volume 12, Detroit, Gale, 1991; essay in *Speaking for Ourselves, Too* compiled and edited by Donald R. Gallo, National Council of Teachers of English, 1993.

Critical Study: Entry in *Contemporary Literary Criticism,* Volume 35, Detroit, Gale, 1985.

*   *   *

Aidan Chambers significantly combines the roles of critic and theorist with those of writer and anthologist for young adults. He has followed his early studies (*The Reluctant Reader* and *Introducing Books to Children*) with numerous papers and lectures, reflecting on the nature and values of adolescent fiction from the reader's, the writer's, and the teacher's standpoint. Although he may not be one of the top sellers, he is certainly one of the most challenging and influential authors for young people. His work implicitly denies any firm distinction between adult and juvenile fiction. He is prepared to write frankly about anything that his adolescent characters might experience, including Ditto's sexual encounter with Helen, Hal's homosexuality, or Nik's religious scepticism, and this openness has not been welcomed by all reviewers. Chambers has always emphasised the significance of stories as a way of discovering meaning, of changing lives. His awareness of Iser and other reader-response theorists has helped to shape what he knew instinctively from the act of composing: that readers must construct the meaning of stories for themselves, that authors do not always know what is to be found in the stories they have written. The technique of his novels suggests the influence of major experimental novelists, particularly B. S. Johnson, whose book *The Unfortunates* has been glowingly praised by Chambers, though *Albert Angelo* would also seem to have been a model.

After a number of books for younger readers, Chambers produced *Breaktime,* his first important novel for young adults. The story is itself about storying, about ways of telling. It centres on Ditto, a sixth-former who is challenged by the claims of Morgan, a contemporary and a rationalist, that fiction is simply a form of lying, a game rather than life. In one sense the book is Ditto's response: the story of his holiday break, camping, disturbing a political meeting, being involved in a burglary, losing his virginity. Like Morgan at the end, readers have to make their own sense of the narrative, to decide how much of it is true. The story is told in a mixture of external narrator and internal stream-of-consciousness styles, including a montage of headlines, typescript and handwriting, play text, cartoons, lists, and quotations. The effect is rather like Joyce or Vonnegut for adolescents. Chambers presents the literal and metaphorical climax with Helen in three-part counterpoint: the events, Ditto's thoughts, and—in a separate column—sections from a textbook describing the act of intercourse. Such framing devices and the way in which Ditto's story also incorporates the stories of others means that the reader feels simultaneously involved in and detached from the events described.

Published four years later, *Dance on My Grave* is also narrated in a cinematic montage of different documents, presenting Hal's account of his life as given to a social worker but involving the reader in evaluating the validity of what is being told. Hal capsizes a dinghy on the Thames and is rescued by the rather older Barry Gorman. The two are brought together as friends and lovers, but after Barry has casually slept with a Norwegian au pair girl, Hal is filled with anger and jealousy. After their quarrel, Barry goes off on his motorbike and is killed. Hal finally keeps the promise that they made each other, that the survivor would dance on the other's grave, and this bizarre episode was apparently drawn from an actual incident.

Now I Know, again told in a complex mixture of modes and parallel texts, is thematically even more demanding in its exploration of religious belief and other modes of knowing. A history teacher persuades Nik, a bright, inquisitive but uncommitted young man of seventeen, to undertake research for an amateur film about the Second Coming. He falls in love with a Christian feminist called Julie, but on the morning after her rejection of his sexual advances she is injured by a terrorist bomb and loses her sight. His ensuing attempts at induced mystical experiences end in organising his own crucifixion in a scrap-yard. The text is assembled out of passages of third-person narration, extracts from Nik's notes, poems and doodles, tapes made by Julie from her hospital bed, and the report of an ambitious young policeman investigating the events. It is heavily intertextual, with quotations or echoes from the Bible, Joyce, Jung, Simone Weil, and others.

The repeated theme of these books is the painful passage from adolescence through greater understanding to maturity. Like Hal, Nik ends changed though not converted. The more recent novel *The Toll Bridge* similarly describes a young man's escape from the conformist pressures of parents, school, and girlfriend to become toll-keeper on a bridge far from home. There is a violent triangular relationship between three young people with names they give one another: Jan, Tess, and Adam. The form is again highly sophisticated and open to different ways of reading. It is impossible for bald outlines of plot to convey either the subtlety of the narration or the conviction with which adolescent dilemmas are presented. There is an element of truth in the criticisms advanced by some who find Chambers's themes unsuitable, the style self-conscious, the plots contrived, or the minor characters two-dimensional. Nevertheless, the originality and driving power of the novels are undeniable. Even the simpler stories for young people, like *Seal Secret* and *The Present Takers,* can be read at deeper and more metaphorical levels; beneath the exciting surface narrative run other stories about moral choice, motivation, and self-understanding. Everything that Chambers has written can be seen as demonstrating the power of language and of active reading where "the reader plays the text."

—Robert Protherough

———

CHERRYH, C.J. (Carolyn Janice Cherry). American. Born in St. Louis, Missouri, 1 September 1942. Educated at the University of Oklahoma, Norman, 1960-64, B.A. in Latin 1964 (Phi Beta Kappa); John Hopkins University, Baltimore (Woodrow Wilson Fellow, 1965-66), M.A. in classics 1965. Taught Latin and ancient history in Oklahoma City public schools, 1965-76; free-lance writer, since 1977. Artist-in-residence and teacher, Central State University, 1980-81. Recipient: Woodrow Wilson fellow, 1965-66; John W. Campbell award, 1977, for Best New Writer in Science Fiction; Hugo award, World Science Fiction Convention, 1978, for short story "Cassandra," 1982, for novel *Downbelow Station,* and in 1988; Balrog award, for short story "A Thief in Korianth." Address: 1901 Bella Vista, Edmond, OK 73034, U.S.A.

PUBLICATIONS

Science Fiction

The Book of Morgaine. New York, Doubleday, 1979; as *The Chronicles of Morgaine,* London, Methuen, 1985.

Gate of Ivrel. New York, DAW, 1976; London, Futura, 1977.

Well of Shiuan. New York, DAW, 1978; London, Magnum, 1981.

Fires of Azeroth. New York, DAW, 1979; London, Methuen, 1982.

Brothers of Earth. New York, DAW, 1976; London, Futura, 1977.

Hunter of Worlds. New York, DAW, 1976; London, Futura, 1977.

The Faded Sun: Kesrith. New York, DAW, 1978.

The Faded Sun: Shon'Jir. New York, DAW, 1979.

Hestia. New York, DAW, 1979; London, VGSF, 1988.

The Faded Sun: Kutath. New York, DAW, 1980.

Serpent's Reach. New York, DAW, 1980; London, Macdonald, 1981.

Downbelow Station. New York, DAW, 1981; London, Methuen, 1983.

Wave without a Shore. New York, DAW, 1981; London, VGSF, 1988.

Merchanter's Luck. New York, DAW, 1982; London, Methuen, 1984.

Port Eternity. New York, DAW, 1982; London, Gollancz, 1989.

The Pride of Chanur. New York, DAW, 1982; London, Methuen, 1983.

The Dreamstone. New York, DAW, 1983; London, VGSF, 1987.

40000 in Gehenna. Huntington Woods, Michigan, Phantasia Press, 1983; London, Methuen, 1986.

The Tree of Swords and Jewels. New York, DAW, 1983; London, VGSF, 1988.

Chanur's Venture. Huntington Woods, Michigan, Phantasia Press, 1984; London, Methuen, 1986.

Voyager in Night. New York, DAW, 1984; London, Methuen, 1985.

Angel with the Sword. New York, DAW, 1985; London, Methuen, 1987.

Cuckoo's Egg. Huntington Woods, Michigan, Phantasia Press, 1985; London, Methuen, 1987.

The Kif Strike Back (Chanur). Huntington Woods, Michigan, Phantasia Press, 1985; London, Methuen, 1987.

The Gates of Hell, with Janet Morris. New York, Baen, 1986.

Soul of the City, with Janet Morris and Lynn Abbey. New York, Ace, 1986.

Visible Light. West Bloomfield, Michigan, Phantasia Press, 1986; London, Methuen, 1988.

The Faded Sun Trilogy. London, Methuen, 1987.

Glass and Amber. Cambridge, Massachusetts, NESFA Press, 1987.

Kings in Hell, with Janet Morris. New York, Baen, 1987.

Legions of Hell. New York, Baen, 1987.

Chanur's Homecoming. New York, DAW, 1986; London, Methuen, 1988.

Cyteen. New York, Warner, 1988; London, New English Library, 1989.

The Betrayal. New York, Popular Library, 1989.

The Rebirth. New York, Popular Library, 1989.

The Vindication. New York, Popular Library, 1989.

Exile's Gate. New York, DAW, 1988; London, Methuen, 1989.

The Paladin. New York, Baen, 1988; London, Mandarin, 1990.

Smuggler's Gold. New York, DAW, 1988.

A Dirge for Sabis, with Leslie Fish. New York, Baen, 1989.

Ealdwood (includes *The Dreamstone* and *The Tree of Swords and Jewels*). London, Gollancz, 1989.

Reap the Whirlwind (Sword of Knowledge), with Mercedes Lackey. New York, Baen, 1989.

Rimrunners. New York, Warner, 1989; London, New English Library, 1990.

Rusalka. New York, Ballantine, 1989; London, Mandarin, 1990.

Wizard Spawn (Sword of Knowledge), with Nancy Asire. New York, Baen, 1989.

Chernevog. New York, Ballantine, 1990; London, Mandarin, 1991.

Heavy Time. New York, Warner, 1991; London, New English Library, 1991.

Yvgenie. New York, Ballantine, 1991.

Chanur's Legacy. New York, DAW, 1992.

The Goblin Mirror. New York, Ballantine, 1992.

Hellburner. New York, Warner, 1992.

Short Stories

Festival Moon. New York, DAW, 1987.

Troubled Waters. New York, DAW, 1988.

Other

Translator, *The Green Gods,* by Charles and Nathalie Henneberg. New York, DAW, 1980.

Translator, *Star Crusade,* by Pierre Barbet. New York, DAW, 1980.

Translator, *The Book of Shai,* by Daniel Walther. New York, DAW, 1984.

Editor, *Sunfall.* New York, DAW, 1981; London, Mandarin, 1990.

Editor, *Fever Season.* New York, DAW, 1987.

Editor, *Merovingen Nights.* New York, DAW, 1987.

Editor, *Divine Right.* New York, DAW, 1989.

Editor, *Flood Tide.* New York, DAW, 1990.

*   *   *

The talent that sets C.J. Cherryh apart from other authors is her ability to create, and make comprehensible, cultures and societies very different from our own—sometimes alien, sometimes human, always intriguing. It is a measure of her talent that she communicates these complex cultural structures within the context of fast-paced action/adventure stories. No ink is wasted on expository material; it often seems that the cultures were fully formed before her pen touched the paper.

Cherryh writes of universes, each with its own set of cultures and history. Most of her stories are set in the Alliance-Union universe, which includes the Chanur, Faded Sun, and Merovingen cultures. However, her body of work also includes multiple stories set in the Morgaine, the Ealdwood, and the Rusalka universes, plus a few single, unrelated stories.

Vivid characters populate Cherryh's universes, and it is the interactions of these characters that illuminate the cultures. This is not to say that the characters exist only to display the culture; generally, both the characters and the cultures exist to serve the story.

Young adults are most likely to be interested in Cherryh's portrayals of coming-of-age within the cultures she creates. While this is rarely the main theme—and is never the only theme—several of her stories focus on a young adult in the process of finding his or (more often) her place in the society Cherryh has created for the story.

Cyteen, set in the Alliance-Union universe, is one such book. It is the story of Ariane Emory, a powerful woman of the Union government, who dies unexpectedly. Her allies arrange to have her "replicated"—not just genetically cloned, but mentally duplicated—by subjecting the clone Ari to the same experiences and events that shaped the original Ari. The axiom that children inherit the world their parents create finds its ultimate expression in Ari, who at sixteen must wield the power her predecessor amassed over a lifetime to fight inherited enemies and to complete inherited schemes.

In the "Faded Sun" trilogy, *Kesrith, Shon'Jir,* and *Kutath,* the coming of age of Melein and her brother Niun is precipitated by the near annihilation of their species. As the last two Mri in known space, Melein and Niun must find their place in a society which no longer exists anywhere but within themselves and perhaps on the legendary Mri home world—if it exists, if it can be found, and if Mri still live on it.

One of Cherryh's most fascinating stories of coming-of-age occurs in the "Rusalka" trilogy, *Rusalka, Chernevog,* and *Yvgenie.* The trilogy begins with Pyetr and the wizard Sasha fleeing the results of their adolescent mischief and growing into an adult view of life in the haunted forests of ancient Russia. The trilogy ends with Pyetr's daughter Illyana struggling against the rules her parents impose on her—rules which have their roots in her parents' own harsh coming-of-age experiences, rules which the reader fully understands. Young adult readers will, no doubt, be amazed to find themselves siding with the parents in this contention.

Merchanter's Luck, Angel with the Sword, and *The Paladin* are also primarily young adult stories. The family-crewed spaceships of the Alliance-Union universe are the setting for *Merchanter's Luck.* Young Sandy Kreja has to crew his small ship alone when pirates kill his family. Young Allison Reilly despairs of ever getting posted as crew on her family's huge multigenerational ship. A perfect match, if Sandy can overcome his distrust and Allison can overcome her big-ship arrogance. In *Angel with the Sword,* Altair Jones finds that caring for others is worthwhile, even in Merovingen, a harsh and unforgiving city designed to make fish bait out of unwary young orphans. In *The Paladin,* young Taizu is savagely catapulted out of childhood by the murder of her family and finds both the hazards and rewards of adulthood in her single-minded determination for revenge.

In all of these books, the characters' growth is the main story, and any other themes serve to support it. Usually, however, coming-of-age is too limited a theme for Cherryh's cultural creations. Young adults' stories are more often embedded within much larger stories. For example, in the "Chanur" series, young Hilfy Chanur is on her first voyage with her legendary Aunt Pyanfar to learn the family business, interstellar trade. In the adventures that follow, Hilfy learns what it takes to justify the swagger she affects as a daughter of the wealthy and powerful Chanur clan.

But the "Chanur" series is much more than Hilfy's story: it is Cherryh's tour de force of alien sociology. Pyanfar and her crew are Hani—a feline species very much like lions. (A male is only expected to fight for territory and stay out of the way while his sisters and daughters earn wealth and prestige for the clan.) In the course of the series, the Hani deal with eight different species, each with its own culture, and Chanur's fate rests on Pyanfar's understanding of those cultures.

Cherryh's talents for vivid characterization, insightful explorations of human nature and relationships, and absorbing storytelling are shared by many writers in many genres, but her ability to create and communicate comprehensible cultures stands, if not alone, then certainly in rare company. It is this ability that may ultimately hold the greatest attraction for young adult readers. In comprehending

that there is an underlying structure and coherence to even the most bizarre Cherryh culture, young adults may see that their own culture also has some kind of underlying structure; that their world is not just a jumble of unreasonable rules; that although the structure isn't as clear as Cherryh would make it, in some way, the world makes sense.

—Karen J. Gould

CHETWIN, Grace. British. Born in Nottingham; immigrated to the United States in 1964. Educated at University of Southampton, Highfield, B.A. (with honors) in philosophy. Married Arthur G. Roberts; two daughters. High school English and French teacher, Auckland, New Zealand, 1958-62; high school English teacher and department head, Devon, England, 1962-63; director, Group '72-'76 (drama group), Auckland, 1972-76; ran her own dance company in New Zealand for four years; produced operas at the amateur level; author of fantasy books since 1983. Agent: Jean V. Naggar, Jean V. Naggar Literary Agency, 216 East 75rd St., New York, NY 10021. Address: 37 Hitching Post Lane, Glen Cove, NY 11542, U.S.A.

PUBLICATIONS FOR YOUNG ADULTS

Fiction

On All Hallows' Eve. New York, Lothrop, 1984.
Out of the Dark World. New York, Lothrop, 1985.
Gom on Windy Mountain. New York, Lothrop, 1986.
The Riddle and the Rune. New York, Lothrop, 1987.
The Crystal Stair. New York, Bradbury, 1988.
The Starstone. New York, Bradbury, 1989.
Collidescope. New York, Bradbury, 1990.
Child of the Air. New York, Bradbury, 1991.
Friends in Time. New York, Bradbury, 1992.
The Chimes of Alyafaleyn. New York, Bradbury, 1993.
Jason's Seven Magnificent Night Rides. New York, Bradbury, 1994.

PUBLICATIONS FOR CHILDREN

Fiction

Mr. Meredith and the Truly Remarkable Stone, illustrated by Catherine Stock. New York, Bradbury, 1989.
Box and Cox, illustrated by David Small. New York, Bradbury Press, 1990.

PUBLICATIONS FOR ADULTS

Fiction

The Atheling. New York, Bluejay, 1987.

*   *   *

In the ten years since Grace Chetwin started writing for children and young adults, she has produced two picture books and ten books for older readers. Her young adult books all fall into the categories of either fantasy or science fiction. A competent writer with many enthusiasms, Chetwin has yet to hit a smooth stride in her writing style. She has a tendency to start writing a novel before she has completely assimilated her research and, as a result, the research calls undue attention to itself. Chetwin is at her best when she writes fantasies that are influenced by European folktales, such as the four books in her series about the wizard Gom.

The "Gom" books, which are all subtitled *From Tales of Gom in the Legends of Ulm,* are *Gom on Windy Mountain, The Riddle and the Rune, The Crystal Stair,* and *The Starstone. Gom on Windy Mountain* recounts Gom's boyhood as a woodcutter's youngest child. This first volume of the series owes much to nineteenth-century folktales and literary fairy tales, particularly to the German tales collected by the Grimms and the fairy tales of George MacDonald. As in a German fairy tale, the story contains a forest, a cottage, and a woodcutter, as well as a youngest son who must set out to seek his fortune. From MacDonald, Chetwin borrows labyrinthine caves and personified winds. Chetwin skillfully weaves these sources into an irresistible original fairy tale. The sequels maintain the atmosphere of "long ago and far away" as Gom seeks his destiny beyond the tiny village of his childhood. Unlike Chetwin's contemporary science fiction, these fantasies are based on a wide knowledge of traditional literature rather than on one or two areas of research grafted onto a story. The "Gom" tetralogy represents Chetwin's best work to date and has been well received by reviewers and critics.

Child of the Air is an ambitious fantasy novel set in a completely original secondary world with overtones of Dickens and Greek mythology. An orphaned brother and sister forced to live in a workhouse discover that they can fly, so they escape to seek others like themselves. Chetwin has created an intriguing geography for her world. The book suffers however, from an excess of invented words. Although there is a pronunciation guide at the end of the book and Chetwin attempts to define the words in context, there are simply too many neologisms for the reader to keep track of their meanings.

Two earlier books contain recurring characters. *On All Hallows' Eve* is a fantasy set in contemporary America. A preadolescent girl transplanted unwillingly from England stumbles into a menacing Otherworld on Halloween, and she must overcome a witch queen in order to rescue her sister and two local boys from the witch's evil power. The book is handicapped by an unlikable heroine who accepts her task grudgingly and ungraciously. In the sequel, *Out of the Dark World,* the heroine's temperament has improved a bit. Although she remains reluctant to take on heroic tasks, her reluctance is based on understandable fear and insecurity. *Out of the Dark World* adds science fiction to the fantasy of the earlier book. The heroine again must rescue someone from an evil power, but in this instance the victim is a male cousin who has been trapped inside a computer in the future. Chetwin's research into computers, New Age psychology, and Welsh mythology is a bit too obvious in the second book.

Another science fiction novel, *Collidescope,* contains touches of humor in the interaction between a pre-Colonial Native American and a twentieth-century teenager, brought together accidentally by an alien scout who works for an intergalactic environmental protection agency. The action is lively and fast-paced, especially in the latter half of the book when the three main characters and one villain are chasing one another through time. In this book Chetwin's research into karate, robotics, and the history of Manhattan seems to be attached onto the story in large chunks instead of being a seamless part of the narrative. However, these awkward grafts do not diminish the story itself, and Chetwin proves adept at juggling three story lines at once.

There is a certain sameness about a number of Chetwin's books. Her heroines share a similar personality and learn the same lesson from their adventures. They are all whiney brats who have to overcome their self-absorption in order to rescue fellow beings from grave danger. Although real adolescents are sometimes unduly concerned with petty personal issues, characters who exhibit such a tendency quickly grow tiresome. Readers may weary of seeing an exciting fantasy adventure interrupted by a character's complaints about her mother. This is a further argument for the superiority of the "Gom" books. Gom, too, learns lessons in life, but he is a much more likeable character than Chetwin's female protagonists. He suffers from feelings of failure, overconfidence, shame, anger, guilt, and loneliness, but his concerns never seem petty.

—Donna R. White

CHILDRESS, Alice. American. Born in Charleston, South Carolina, 12 October 1920. Educated at schools in Harlem, New York; Radcliffe Institute for Independent Study (scholar), 1966-68, graduated 1968. Married the musician Nathan Woodard in 1957; one daughter. Playwright, novelist. Actress and director, American Negro Theatre, New York, 1941-52; columnist ("Here's Mildred"), Baltimore *Afro-American,* 1956-58. Artist-in-residence, University of Massachusetts, Amherst, 1984. Also performed on radio and television. Lecturer at universities and schools; member of panel discussions and conferences on Black American theater at numerous institutions, including New School for Social Research, New York, 1965, and Fisk University, Nashville, Tennessee, 1966; visiting scholar at Radcliffe Institute for Independent Study (now Mary Ingraham Bunting Institute), Cambridge, Massachusetts, 1966-68. Member of governing board of France Delafield Hospital. Recipient: Obie award for best original Off-Broadway play, *Village Voice,* 1956, for *Trouble in Mind;* John Golden Fund for Playwrights grant, 1957; Rockefeller grant, 1967; "Outstanding Book of the Year" citation, *New York Times Book Review,* 1973, Woodward School Book award, 1974, Jane Addams Children's Book Honor award, 1974, National Book award nomination, 1974, Lewis Carroll Shelf award, 1975, and "Best Young Adult Book" citation, American Library Association, 1975, all for *A Hero Ain't Nothin' but a Sandwich;* named honorary citizen of Atlanta, Georgia, 1975, for opening of *Wedding Band;* Sojourner Truth award, National Association of Negro Business and Professional Women's Clubs, 1975; Virgin Islands Film Festival award, 1977, for *A Hero Ain't Nothin' but a Sandwich;* Paul Robeson award, 1977, for *A Hero Ain't Nothin' but a Sandwich;* "Alice Childress Week" officially observed in Charleston and Columbia, South Carolina, 1977, to celebrate opening of *Sea Island Song;* "Best Book" citation, *School Library Journal,* 1981, "Outstanding Books of the Year" citation, *New York Times,* 1982, "Notable Children's Trade Book in Social Studies" citation, National Council for the Social Studies and Children's Book Council, 1982, and Coretta Scott King Award honorable mention, 1982, all for *Rainbow Jordan.* Radcliffe Graduate Society medal, 1984; African Poets Theatre award, 1985; Audelco award, 1986; Harlem School of the Arts Humanitarian award, 1987. Agent: Flora Roberts Inc., 157 West 57th Street, Penthouse A, New York, NY 10019.

PUBLICATIONS FOR YOUNG ADULTS

Fiction

A Hero Ain't Nothin' But a Sandwich. New York, Coward McCann, 1973.
Rainbow Jordan. New York, Coward McCann, 1981.
Those Other People. New York, Putnam, 1989.

Plays

When the Rattlesnake Sounds, illustrated by Charles Lilly. New York, Coward McCann, 1975.
Let's Hear It for the Queen, illustrated by Loring Eutemey. New York, Coward McCann, 1976.

Screenplay: *A Hero Ain't Nothin' But a Sandwich,* 1977.

PUBLICATION FOR ADULTS

Novel

A Short Walk. New York, Coward McCann, 1979.

Plays

Florence (also director: produced New York, 1949). Published in *Masses and Mainstream* (New York), October 1950.
Just a Little Simple, adaptation of Langston Hughes's short story collection, *Simple Speaks His Mind,* (produced in New York, 1950).
Gold through the Trees (produced New York, 1952).
Trouble in Mind (also director: produced New York, 1955). Published in *Black Theatre: A Twentieth-Century Collection of the Work of Its Best Playwrights,* edited by Lindsay Patterson, New York, Dodd Mead, 1971.
Wedding Band: A Love/Hate Story in Black and White (produced Ann Arbor, Michigan, 1966; New York, 1972). New York, French, 1973.
String, adaptation of Maupassant's story "A Piece of String" (produced New York, 1969). With *Mojo,* New York, Dramatists Play Service, 1971.
Young Martin Luther King (produced on tour, 1969; originally entitled *The Freedom Drum*).
Wine in the Wilderness: A Comedy-Drama (televised 1969; produced New York, 1976). New York, Dramatists Play Service, 1970.
Mojo: A Black Love Story (produced New York. 1970). With *String,* New York, Dramatists Play Service, 1971.
Sea Island Song (produced Charleston, South Carolina, 1977).
Gullah (produced Amherst, Massachusetts, 1984).
Moms: A Praise Play for a Black Comedienne, music and lyrics by Childress and Nathan Woodard (produced New York, 1987).

Television Plays: *Wine in the Wilderness: A Comedy-Drama,* (WGBH-TV), 1969; *Wedding Band,* American Broadcasting Companies (ABC-TV), 1973; *String,* Public Broadcasting Service (PBS-TV), 1979.

Other

Like One of the Family: Conversations from a Domestic's Life. New York, Independence, 1956.
Many Closets. New York, Coward McCann, 1987.
Editor, *Black Scenes.* New York, Zenith, 1971.

*

Biography: Entry in *Dictionary of Literary Biography,* Volume 7: *Twentieth-Century American Dramatists* by Rosemary Curb, Detroit, Gale, 1981; entry in *Dictionary of Literary Biography,* Volume 38: *Afro-American Writers after 1955: Dramatists and Prose Writers* by Trudier Harris, Detroit, Gale, 1985; entry in *Fifth Book of Junior Authors and Illustrators* edited by Sally Holmes Holtze, Bronx, New York, Wilson, 1983.

Critical Studies: Entry in *Children's Literature Review,* Volume 14, Detroit, Gale, 1988; entry in *Contemporary Literary Criticism,* Volume 12, Detroit, Gale, 1980; Volume 15, Detroit, Gale, 1980.

Theatrical Activities: Director: **Play**—*Florence,* New York, 1949. Actress: **Plays**—Dolly in *On Strivers Row* by Abram Hill, New York, 1940; Polly Ann in *Natural Man* by Theodore Browne, 1941; Blanche in *Anna Lucasta* by Philip Yordan, New York, 1944.

*   *   *

When the social agitation of the 1960s brought about the development of a new genre of hard-hitting problem novels aimed specifically at teenage readers, editor F.N. Monjo challenged dramatist Alice Childress to devote her writing skills to a book for young readers. The result was *A Hero Ain't Nothin' But a Sandwich,* which is such a powerful book that it helped shape the new genre as well as bring it respect.

The story circles around thirteen-year-old Benjie, a heroin addict, who may or may not make it out of the vicious cycle in which he finds himself. The twenty-three chapters consist of monologues from a dozen characters—Benjie, his mother, his stepfather, his teachers, his pusher, his grandmother, his friend. On the first page Benjie compares his life where "You best get over being seven or eight right soon" because "My block ain't no place to be a chile in peace," to that of a "rich chile like in some movin picture or like on TV—where everybody is livin it up and their room is perfect-lookin and their swimmin pool and their block and their house..." Benjie's comparison aptly illustrates the differences between the new realistic problem novel and the old romanticized fiction commonly offered to young readers. In the new books it was acceptable to have characters from lower-class families who lived in harsh and difficult settings rather than in idyllic and pleasant suburbia. These characters faced major problems and used colloquial and sometimes vulgar language. Many of the books had unhappy endings.

Some adults were shocked at this new realism, and *A Hero Ain't Nothin' But a Sandwich* was widely censored, eventually coming before the Supreme Court in a case against eight other books as well. But as movies, television, rock music, videos, magazines, and even the daily news made commonplace much that used to be considered obscene or at least inappropriate for young readers, critics began paying less attention to the controversial language in Childress's writing and more to its substance.

Childress uses the same dramatic technique of switching first-person viewpoints from chapter to chapter in *Rainbow Jordan* and *Those Other People*. The technique lets readers get into the minds of characters in ways that are more credible than if an omniscient narrator were describing the events. Since there's no narrator to tie together all the pieces, readers have to draw their own conclusions—a responsibility that censors fear teenage readers may not be prepared for.

Childress's greatest strength is in developing characters that make readers see such social issues as racism, sexism, drugs, and child abuse in personal terms. Few readers will forget the heroic Butler Craig, Benjie's unconventional stepfather, or fourteen-year-old Rainbow Jordan and fifty-seven-year-old Josephine who suffer together when Rainbow's childlike mother leaves for an out-of-town gig.

Childress has also written two one-act plays. *Let's Hear It for the Queen* is a humorous play for children that parodies the "Queen of Hearts" nursery rhyme. *When the Rattlesnake Sounds*, written for young adults, has a more serious intent. It takes viewers and performers beyond the stereotype of Harriet Tubman leading slaves through wilderness swamps to freedom. The setting is a hotel in Cape May, New Jersey, where Tubman is scrubbing, with two other young women, the hotel's linens and the guests' clothing to earn money for the support of the underground railway.

—Alleen Pace Nilsen

CHRISTIE, (Dame) Agatha (Mary Clarissa née Miller). Also wrote as Agatha Christie Mallowan; Mary Westmacott. British. Born in Torquay, Devon, 15 September 1890. Educated privately at home; studied singing and piano in Paris. Married 1) Colonel Archibald Christie in 1914 (divorced, 1928, died, 1962), one daughter; 2) the archaeologist Max Edgar Lucien Mallowan in 1930 (died, 1978). Writer. During World War I, served as Voluntary Aid Detachment (V.A.D.) nurse in a Red Cross Hospital, Torquay, South Devon, England, and worked in the dispensary of University College Hospital, London, during World War II; also assisted her husband (Max Mallowan) on excavations in Iraq and Syria and on the Assyrian cities; worked in dispensary for University College Hospital, London, England. President, Detection Club. Recipient: Fellow, Royal Society of Literature, 1950; Grand Master award, Mystery Writers of America, 1954; New York Drama Critics' Circle award, 1955, for *Witness for the Prosecution;* Commander of the British Empire, 1956; D.Litt., University of Exeter, 1961; Dame Commander, Order of the British Empire, 1971. *Died 12 January 1976.*

PUBLICATIONS

Novels

The Mysterious Affair at Styles. London, Lane, 1920, New York, Dodd, 1927.

The Secret Adversary. London, Lane, 1920; New York, Dodd, 1922.

The Murder on the Links. London, Lane, and New York, Dodd, 1923.

The Man in the Brown Suit. London, Lane, and New York, Dodd, 1924.

The Secret of Chimneys. London, Lane, and New York, Dodd, 1925.

The Murder of Roger Ackroyd. London, Collins, and New York, Dodd, 1926.

The Big Four. London, Collins, and New York, Dodd, 1927.

The Mystery of the Blue Train. London, Collins, and New York, Dodd, 1928.

The Seven Dials Mystery. London, Collins, and New York, Dodd, 1929.

The Murder at the Vicarage. London, Collins, and New York, Dodd, 1930.

The Floating Admiral, with others. London, Hodder & Stoughton, 1931; New York, Doubleday, 1932.

The Sittaford Mystery. London, Collins, 1931; as *The Murder at Hazelmoor,* New York, Dodd, 1931.

Peril at End House. London, Collins, and New York, Dodd, 1932.

Lord Edgware Dies. London, Collins, 1933; as *Thirteen at Dinner,* New York, Dodd, 1933.

Murder in Three Acts. New York, Dodd, 1934; as *Three Act Tragedy,* London, Collins, 1935.

Murder on the Orient Express. London, Collins, 1934; as *Murder in the Calais Coach,* New York, Dodd, 1934.

Why Didn't They Ask Evans?. London, Collins, 1934; as *The Boomerang Clue,* New York, Dodd, 1935.

Death in the Clouds. London, Collins, 1935; as *Death in the Air,* New York, Dodd, 1935.

The A.B.C. Murders: A New Poirot Mystery. London, Collins, and New York, Dodd, 1936; as *The Alphabet Murders,* New York, Pocket Books, 1966.

Cards on the Table. London, Collins, 1936; New York, Dodd, 1937.

Murder in Mesopotamia. London, Collins, and New York, Dodd, 1936.

Death on the Nile. London, Collins, 1937; New York, Dodd, 1938.

Dumb Witness. London, Collins, 1937; as *Poirot Loses a Client,* New York, Dodd, 1937.

Appointment with Death: A Poirot Mystery. London, Collins, and New York, Dodd, 1938.

Hercule Poirot's Christmas. London, Collins, 1938; as *Murder for Christmas,* New York, Dodd, 1939; as *A Holiday for Murder,* New York, Avon, 1947.

Murder Is Easy. London, Collins, 1939; as *Easy to Kill,* New York, Dodd, 1939.

One, Two, Buckle My Shoe. London, Collins, 1940; as *The Patriotic Murders,* New York, Dodd, 1941; as *An Overdose of Death,* New York, Dell, 1953.

Sad Cypress. London, Collins, and New York, Dodd, 1940.

Ten Little Niggers. London, Collins, 1939; as *And Then There Were None,* New York, Dodd, 1940; as *Ten Little Indians,* New York, Pocket Books, 1965.

Evil Under the Sun. London, Collins, and New York, Dodd, 1941.

N or M?: A New Mystery. London, Collins, and New York, Dodd, 1941.

The Body in the Library. London, Collins, and New York, Dodd, 1942.

Five Little Pigs. London, Collins, 1942; as *Murder in Retrospect,* New York, Dodd, 1942.

The Moving Finger. New York, Dodd, 1942; London, Collins, 1943.

Death Comes as the End. New York, Dodd, 1944; London, Collins, 1945.

Towards Zero. London, Collins, and New York, Dodd, 1944.

Sparkling Cyanide. London, Collins, 1945; as *Remembered Death,* New York, Dodd, 1945.

The Hollow: A Hercule Poirot Mystery. London, Collins, and New York, Dodd, 1946; as *Murder After Hours,* New York, Dell, 1954.

Taken at the Flood. London, Collins, 1948; as *There Is a Tide...,* New York, Dodd, 1948.

The Crooked House. London, Collins, and New York, Dodd, 1949.

A Murder Is Announced. London, Collins, and New York, Dodd, 1950.

They Came to Baghdad. London, Collins, and New York, Dodd, 1951.

Mrs. McGinty's Dead. London, Collins, and New York, Dodd, 1952; as *Blood Will Tell,* New York, Detective Book Club, 1952.

They Do It with Mirrors. London, Collins, 1952; as *Murder with Mirrors,* New York, Dodd, 1952.

After the Funeral. London, Collins, 1953; as *Funerals Are Fatal,* New York, Dodd, 1953; as *Murder at the Gallop,* London, Fontana, 1963.

A Pocket Full of Rye. London, Collins, 1953; New York, Dodd, 1954.

Destination Unknown. London, Collins, 1954; *So Many Steps to Death,* New York, Dodd, 1955.

Hickory, Dickory, Dock. London, Collins, 1955; as *Hickory, Dickory, Death,* New York, Dodd, 1955.

Dead Man's Folly. London, Collins, and New York, Dodd, 1956.

4:50 from Paddington. London, Collins, 1957; as *What Mrs. McGillicuddy Saw!,* New York, Dodd, 1957; as *Murder She Said,* New York, Pocket Books, 1961.

Ordeal by Innocence. London, Collins, 1958; New York, Dodd, 1959.

Cat Among the Pigeons. London, Collins, 1959; New York, Dodd, 1960.

The Pale Horse. London, Collins, 1961; New York, Dodd, 1962.

The Mirror Crack'd from Side to Side. London, Collins, 1962; as *The Mirror Crack'd,* New York, Dodd, 1963.

The Clocks. London, Collins, 1963; New York, Dodd, 1964.

A Caribbean Mystery. London, Collins, 1964; New York, Dodd, 1965.

At Bertram's Hotel. London, Collins, 1965; New York, Dodd, 1966.

Third Girl. London, Collins, 1966; New York, Dodd, 1967.

Endless Night. London, Collins, 1967; New York, Dodd, 1968.

By the Pricking of My Thumbs. London, Collins, and New York, Dodd, 1968.

Hallowe'en Party. London, Collins, and New York, Dodd, 1969.

Passenger to Frankfurt. London, Collins, and New York, Dodd, 1970.

Nemesis. London, Collins, and New York, Dodd, 1971.

Elephants Can Remember. London, Collins, and New York, Dodd, 1972.

Postern of Fate. London, Collins, and New York, Dodd, 1973.

Murder on Board. New York, Dodd, 1974.

Curtain: Hercule Poirot's Last Case. London, Collins, and New York, Dodd, 1975.

Sleeping Murder. London, Collins, and New York, Dodd, 1976.

The Scoop, and Behind the Screen, with others. London, Gollancz, and New York, Harper, 1983.

Short Stories

Poirot Investigates. London, Lane, 1924; New York, Dodd, 1925.

Partners in Crime. London, Collins, and New York, Dodd, 1929; as *The Sunningdale Mystery,* London, Collins, 1933.

The Under Dog, and Other Stories. London, Readers Library, 1929, New York, Dodd, 1951.

The Mysterious Mr. Quin. London, Collins, and New York, Dodd, 1930; as *The Passing of Mr. Quin.*

The Thirteen Problems. London, Collins, 1932; as *The Tuesday Club Murders,* New York, Dodd, 1933; selection, as *The Mystery of the Blue Geraniums, and Other Tuesday Club Murders,* New York, Bantam, 1940.

The Hound of Death, and Other Stories. London, Odhams Press, 1933.

The Listerdale Mystery, and Other Stories. London, Collins, 1934.

Parker Pyne Investigates. London, Collins, 1934; as *Mr. Parker Pyne, Detective,* New York, Dodd, 1934.

Murder in the News, and Other Stories. London, Collins, 1937; *Dead Man's Mirror, and Other Stories,* New York, Dodd, 1937.

The Regatta Mystery, and Other Stories. New York, Dodd, 1939.

The Mystery of the Baghdad Chest. Los Angeles, Bantam, 1943.

The Mystery of the Crime in Cabin 66. Los Angeles, Bantam, 1943; as *The Crime in Cabin 66,* London, Vallencey, 1944.

Poirot and the Regatta Mystery. Los Angeles, Bantam, 1943.

Poirot on Holiday. London, Todd, 1943.

Problem at Pollensa Bay [and] *Christmas Adventure.* London, Todd, 1943.

The Veiled Lady [and] *The Mystery of the Baghdad Chest.* London, Todd, 1944.

Poirot Knows the Murderer. London, Todd, 1946.

Poirot Lends a Hand. London, Todd, 1946.

Labours of Hercules: Short Stories. London, Collins, 1947; as *The Labours of Hercules: New Adventures in Crime by Hercule Poirot,* New York, Dodd, 1947.

Witness for the Prosecution, and Other Stories. New York, Dodd, 1948.

The Mousetrap and Other Stories. New York, Dell, 1949; as *Three Blind Mice, and Other Stories,* New York, Dodd, 1950.

The Adventure of the Christmas Pudding, and Selection of Entrees. London, Collins, 1960.

Double Sin, and Other Stories. New York, Dodd, 1961.

13 for Luck!: A Selection of Mystery Stories for Young Readers. New York, Dodd, 1961; London, Collins, 1966.

Star Over Bethlehem, and Other Stories (as Agatha Christie Mallowan). London, Collins, and New York, Dodd, 1965.

Surprise! Surprise!: A Collection of Mystery Stories with Unexpected Endings, edited by Raymond T. Bond. New York, Dodd, 1965.

13 Clues for Miss Marple. New York, Dodd, 1966.

Selected Stories. Moscow, Progress Publishers, 1969.

The Golden Ball, and Other Stories. New York, Dodd, 1971.

Poirot's Early Cases. London, Collins, 1974; as *Hercule Poirot's Early Cases,* New York, Dodd, 1974.

Miss Marple's Final Cases, and Two Other Stories. London, Collins, 1979.
The Agatha Christie Hour. London, Collins, 1982.
Hercule Poirot's Casebook: Fifty Stories. New York, Putnam, 1984.
Miss Marple, the Complete Short Stories. New York, Putnam, 1985.
English Country House Murders: Tales of Perfidious Albion, and others, edited by Thomas Godfrey. New York, Mysterious Press, 1989.

Plays

Black Coffee (produced London, 1930). London, Ashley, and Boston, Baker, 1934.
Ten Little Niggers, adaptation of her own novel (produced Wimbledon and London, 1943). London, French, 1944; as *Ten Little Indians* (produced New York, 1944), New York, French, 1946.
Appointment with Death, adaptation of her own novel (produced Glasgow and London, 1945). London, French, 1956; in *The Mousetrap and Other Plays,* 1978.
Murder on the Nile, adaptation of her novel *Death on the Nile* (as *Little Horizon,* produced Wimbledon, 1945; as *Murder on the Nile,* produced London and New York, 1946). London and New York, French, 1948.
The Hollow, adaptation of her own novel (produced Cambridge and London, 1951; Princeton, New Jersey, 1952; New York, 1978). London and New York, French, 1952.
The Mousetrap, adaptation of her story "Three Blind Mice" (broadcast 1952; produced Nottingham and London, 1952; New York, 1960). London and New York, French, 1954.
Witness for the Prosecution, adaptation of her own story (produced Nottingham and London, 1953; New York, 1954). London and New York, French, 1954.
Spider's Web (produced Nottingham and London, 1954; New York, 1974). London and New York, French, 1957.
Towards Zero, with Gerald Verner, adaptation of the novel by Christie (produced Nottingham and London, 1956). New York, Dramatists Play Service, 1957; London, French, 1958.
The Unexpected Guest (produced Bristol and London, 1958). London, French, 1958; in *The Mousetrap and Other Plays,* 1978.
Verdict (produced Wolverhampton and London, 1958). London, French, 1958; in *The Mousetrap and Other Plays,* 1978.
Go Back for Murder, adaptation of her novel *Five Little Pigs* (produced Edinburgh and London, 1960) London, French, 1960; in *The Mousetrap and Other Plays,* 1978.
Rule of Three: Afternoon at the Seaside, The Patient, The Rats (produced Aberdeen and London, 1962; *The Rats* produced New York, 1974; *The Patient* produced New York, 1978). London, French, 3 vols., 1963.
Fiddlers Three. (produced Southsea, 1971; London, 1972).
Akhnaton (as *Akhnaton and Nefertiti,* produced New York, 1979; as *Akhnaton,* produced London, 1980). London, Collins, and New York, Dodd, 1973.
The Mousetrap, and Other Plays (includes *Witness for the Prosecution, Ten Little Indians, Appointment with Death, The Hollow, Towards Zero, Verdict, Go Back for Murder*). New York, Dodd, 1978.

Radio Plays: *The Mousetrap,* 1952; *Personal Call,* 1960.

Novels as Mary Westmacott

Giant's Bread. London, Collins, and New York, Doubleday, 1930.

Unfinished Portrait. London, Collins, and New York, Doubleday, 1934.
Absent in the Spring. London, Collins, and New York, Farrar & Rinehart, 1944.
The Rose and the Yew Tree. London, Heinemann, and New York, Rinehart, 1948.
A Daughter's a Daughter. London, Heinemann, 1952; New York, Dell, 1963.
The Burden. London, Heinemann, 1956; New York, Dell, 1963.

Poetry

The Road of Dreams. London, Bles, 1925.
Poems. London, Collins, and New York, Dodd, 1973.

Other

Come, Tell Me How You Live (travel). London, Collins, and New York, Dodd, 1946; revised edition, 1975.
Editor, with others, *The Times of London Anthology of Detective Stories.* New York, John Day, 1973.
An Autobiography. London, Collins, and New York, Dodd, 1977.

*

Media Adaptations: *The Murder of Roger Ackroyd* (play by Michael Morton and first produced under the title *Alibi* on the West End at Prince of Wales Theatre), 1928; *Philomel Cottage* (play by Frank Vosper and first produced under the title *Love from a Stranger* on the West End at Wyndham's Theatre), in 1936; *Peril at End House* (play by Arnold Ridley and first produced on the West End at the Vaudeville Theatre), 1940; *Murder at the Vicarage* (play by Moie Charles and Barbara Toy and first produced in London at the Playhouse Theatre), 1949; *Towards Zero* (play by Gerald Verner and first produced on Broadway at the St. James Theatre), 1956; *Philomel Cottage* (filmed as *Love from a Stranger*), United Artists, 1937, and Eagle Lion, 1947; *And Then There Were None* (film), Twentieth Century-Fox, 1945; *Witness for the Prosecution* (film), United Artists, 1957; *Witness for the Prosecution* (television), Columbia Broadcasting System, 1982; *The Spider's Web* (film), United Artists, 1960; *Murder She Said* (film), Metro-Goldwyn-Mayer, 1962; *Murder at the Gallop* (film), Metro-Goldwyn-Mayer, 1963; *Mrs. McGinty's Dead* (filmed as *Murder Most Foul*), Metro-Goldwyn-Mayer, 1965; *Ten Little Indians* (film), Associated British & Pathe Film, 1965; *The Alphabet Murders* (film), Metro-Goldwyn-Mayer, 1967; *Endless Night* (film), British Lion Films, 1971; *Murder on the Orient Express* (film), EMI, 1974; *Death on the Nile* (film), Paramount, 1978; *The Mirror Crack'd* (film), EMI, 1980; *The Seven Dials Mystery* and *Why Didn't They Ask Evans?* (films), London Weekend Television, 1980; *Evil Under the Sun* (film), Universal, 1982; *Murder Ahoy,* (film, features the character Miss Jane Marple in a story not written by Christie), Metro-Goldwyn-Mayer, 1964.

Critical Studies: *Studies in Agatha Christie's Writings* by Frank Behre, Gothenburg, Universitetet, 1967; *Agatha Christie: Mistress of Mystery* by Gordon C. Ramsey, New York, Dodd, 1967, revised edition, London, Collins, 1968; entry in *Contemporary Literary Criticism,* Detroit, Gale, Volume 1, 1973, Volume 6, 1976, Volume 8, 1978, Volume 12, 1980, Volume 39, 1986, Volume 48, 1988; *The Mysterious World of Agatha Christie* by Jeffrey Feinman, New York, Award Books, 1975; *An Agatha Christie Chronology* by Nancy

Blue Wynne, New York, Ace Books, 1976; *The Mystery of Agatha Christie* by Derrick Murdoch, Toronto, Pagurian Press, 1976; *Agatha Christie: First Lady of Crime* edited by H.R.F. Keating, London, Weidenfeld & Nicolson, and New York, Holt, 1977; *The Mystery of Agatha Christie* by Gwyn Robyns, New York, Doubleday, 1978; *The Bedside, Bathtub, and Armchair Companion to Agatha Christie* edited by Dick Riley and Pam McAllister, New York, Ungar, 1979, London, Angus & Robertson, 1983, revised edition, Ungar, 1986; *A Talent to Deceive: An Appreciation of Agatha Christie* (includes bibliography by Louise Barnard) by Robert Barnard, London, Collins, and New York, Dodd, 1980; *The Agatha Christie Who's Who* by Randall Toye, New York, Holt, and London, Muller, 1980; *The Gentle Art of Murder: The Detective Fiction of Agatha Christie* by Earl F. Bargainnier, Bowling Green, Ohio, Bowling Green University Press, 1981; entry in *Dictionary of Literary Biography,* Detroit, Gale, Volume 13: *British Dramatists Since World War II,* Detroit, Gale, 1982, Volume 77: *British Mystery Writers, 1920-1939,* 1989; *Murder She Wrote: A Study of Agatha Christie's Detective Fiction* by Patricia D. Maida and Nicholas B. Spornick, Bowling Green, Ohio, Bowling Green University, 1982; *The Life and Crimes of Agatha Christie* by Charles Osborne, London, Collins, 1982, New York, Holt, 1983; *The Agatha Christie Companion: The Complete Guide to Agatha Christie's Life and Work* by Dennis Sanders and Len Lovalio, New York, Delacorte, 1984, London, W.H. Allen, 1985; *Agatha Christie: A Biography* by Janet Morgan, London, Cape, 1984, New York, Knopf, 1985; *The Life and Times of Miss Jane Marple: An Entertaining and Definitive Study of Agatha Christie's Famous Amateur Sleuth,* New York, Dodd, 1985, and *The Life and Times of Hercule Poirot,* New York, Putnam, and London, Pavilion, 1990, both by Anne Hart; *An A to Z of the Novels and Short Stories of Agatha Christie* by Ben Morselt, Phoenix, Arizona, Phoenix, 1986.

*   *   *

Judged by most conventional criteria, Agatha Christie is, at best, a mediocre writer. Her characterization is almost always two-dimensional, and in novel after novel she deploys the same troupe of pasteboard stereotypes (the peppery-but-gallant colonel, the poor little rich girl, the well-brought-up young man with half-baked radical notions, and so on). She seems convinced that all foreigners have funny and instantly recognizable national mannerisms (Italians are always excitable, and Germans are mostly stolid), and her sense of place is rudimentary. Her prose can be tersely economical but she lapses into cliche on the least provocation and tends, when trying to sound sophisticated, to stultify her sentences with French tags.

On the other hand, Christie's world sales have topped four hundred million (she is, after Shakespeare and the Bible, history's best-selling writer), so the relevance of conventional criteria to a discussion of her work seems questionable. There is little purpose in berating oranges for not being bananas, and complaints that Christie is not George Eliot (or even, for that matter, Margery Allingham) seem so obviously true and so obviously beside the point as to be hardly worth making. It could, indeed, be plausibly argued that the very characteristics that deny her a place in the Great Tradition contribute largely to her phenomenal success in other areas and among young adult readers. For Christie's paramount concern is with the creation of plot, and anything which might tend to obscure the stark linear sequence of problematically related events (complex motivation, for example, or the pressure of social circumstance) is ruthlessly excised. The end towards which her narratives progress is not the private (and often provisional) closure of the conventional novel (the making and breaking of relationships), but the public revelation of factual truth (the identity of a murderer and the means by which the crime was committed). Moreover, although her fictional detectives undoubtedly share some common ground with the protagonists of other genres (the hero of the quest-romance, for example), they (and in Christie's case this mostly means the moustachioed Belgian Hercule Poirot or the prim, spinsterly Jane Marple) remain essentially unaffected, even by their most gruesome adventures. Christie's sleuths, that is, enter the narrative fully formed; their function is not to develop in response to events but only to analyse those events in order to distill apparent chaos into logical order. And as with the detectives so, mutatis mutandis with the other characters. The colonels, vicars, bright young things, and embittered old maids are of interest not for themselves but only in relation to the crimes for which each may turn out to be responsible. Even the hapless victims are seldom sufficiently distinctive to become objects of sympathy; indeed, the reader learns to look forward eagerly to their demise as a trigger for the progression of clues and deductions which it is the book's primary purpose to retail.

It is apparent that Christie's fiction (and indeed the classic English detective story in general) is founded upon a set of clearly established conventions. This, of course, is more or less true of all literary genres, but in Christie's novels the conventions operate primarily as rules in a game played between author (or narrator) and reader: the latter is provided by the former with all of the evidence necessary to solve a criminal mystery and is challenged to anticipate the detective's final revelation of the truth. And it is in the playing of this game that Christie is supremely successful. Unlike many of her contemporaries (Dorothy Sayers, for example), she never premises her solutions on the reader's possession of recondite knowledge but bases them on clearly visible and apparently commonplace clues (the state of the murdered girl's fingernails in *The Body in the Library,* for example). She is, in addition, extremely inventive in her manipulation (even, occasionally, transgression) of generic conventions. In *The Murder of Roger Ackroyd* the murderer is also the narrator; in *Murder on the Orient Express* all of the possible suspects turn out to be equally guilty; in *Hercule Poirot's Christmas* it is the investigating policeman who blurts out a confession in the penultimate chapter. No character can ever be safely exempted from suspicion and Christie, indeed, is adept at playing on and against the generically conditioned reflexes of even her most hardened readers. In *Death on the Nile,* for example, the solution to Linnet Doyle's murder is impossible to guess not only because the method of its commission is so diabolically original, but also because the killers are the two people whom our previous experience of Christie's writing would lead us to exclude as possibilities—the prime suspect and a clean-cut English gentleman.

At the height of her powers in the 1930s and 1940s (her later work shows some decline in ingenuity) Christie, then, is more sensibly regarded as a superb game-player than as a fourth-rate novelist. Her characters resemble chess pieces which she shifts about the board in dazzling variations on familiar strategies, and her objective—to frustrate the predictions of her reader while still providing a fully satisfying closure—is almost always realized. Hers, in the end, is a comfortingly orderly world, where all loose ends can be tied into neat bows and in which, once the murderer has been identified, no further or larger problems remain to be resolved.

—Robert Dingley

CHRISTOPHER, John. Pseudonym for Christopher Samuel Youd; has also written as Hilary Ford, William Godfrey, Peter Graaf, Peter Nichols, and Anthony Rye. British. Born in Knowsley, Lancashire, 16 April 1922. Educated at Peter Symonds' School, Winchester. Served in the Royal Signals, 1941-46. Married twice; four daughters and one son from first marriage. Since 1958 full-time writer. Recipient: Rockefeller-Atlantic award, 1946; Christopher award, 1971; *Guardian* award, 1971; Children's Literature prize (Germany), 1976; George G. Stone Center for Children's Books award, 1977. Agent: La Rochelle, Rye, East Sussex TN31 7JY, England.

PUBLICATIONS FOR YOUNG ADULTS

Fiction

The Caves of Night. London, Eyre and Spottiswoode, and New York, Simon and Schuster, 1958.
The Long Voyage. London, Eyre and Spottiswoode, 1960; as *The White Voyage,* New York, Simon and Schuster, 1961.
The Tripods Trilogy. New York, Macmillan, 1980.
The White Mountains. London, Hamish Hamilton, and New York, Macmillan, 1967.
The City of Gold and Lead. London, Hamish Hamilton, and New York, Macmillan, 1967.
The Pool of Fire. London, Hamish Hamilton, and New York, Macmillan, 1968.
The Lotus Caves. London, Hamish Hamilton, and New York, Macmillan, 1969.
The Guardians. London, Hamish Hamilton, and New York, Macmillan, 1970.
The Sword of the Spirits Trilogy. New York, Macmillan, 1980; as *The Prince in Waiting Trilogy,* London, Penguin, 1983.
The Prince in Waiting. London, Hamish Hamilton, and New York, Macmillan, 1970.
Beyond the Burning Lands. London, Hamish Hamilton, and New York, Macmillan, 1971.
The Sword of the Spirits. London, Hamish Hamilton, and New York, Macmillan, 1972.
In the Beginning (reader for adults). London, Longman, 1972; revised edition (for children), as *Dom and Va,* London, Hamish Hamilton, and New York, Macmillan, 1973.
A Figure in Grey (as Hilary Ford). Kingswood, Surrey, World's Work, 1973.
Wild Jack. London, Hamish Hamilton, and New York, Macmillan, 1974; original version (reader for adults), London, Longman, 1974.
Empty World. London, Hamish Hamilton, 1977; New York, Dutton, 1978.
Fireball. London, Gollancz, and New York, Dutton, 1981.
New Found Land. London, Gollancz, and New York, Dutton, 1983.
Dragon Dance. London, Viking Kestrel, and New York, Dutton, 1986.
When the Tripods Came. New York, Dutton, 1988.

PUBLICATIONS FOR ADULTS

Novels

The Year of the Comet. London, Joseph, 1955; as *Planet in Peril,* New York, Avon, 1959.

The Death of Grass. London, Joseph, 1956; as *No Blade of Grass,* New York, Simon and Schuster, 1957.
Giant's Arrow (as Anthony Rye). London, Gollancz, 1956; as Samuel Youd, New York, Simon and Schuster, 1960.
Malleson at Melbourne (as William Godfrey). London, Museum Press, 1956.
The Friendly Game (as William Godfrey). London, Joseph, 1957.
A Scent of White Poppies. London, Eyre and Spottiswoode, and New York, Simon and Schuster, 1959.
The World in Winter. London, Eyre and Spottiswoode, 1962; as *The Long Winter,* New York, Simon and Schuster, 1962.
Sweeney's Island. New York, Simon and Schuster, 1964; as *Cloud on Silver,* London, Hodder and Stoughton, 1964.
The Possessors. London, Hodder and Stoughton, and New York, Simon and Schuster, 1965.
A Wrinkle in the Skin. London, Hodder and Stoughton, 1965; as *The Ragged Edge,* New York, Simon and Schuster, 1966.
Patchwork of Death (as Peter Nichols). New York, Holt Rinehart, 1965; London, Hale, 1967.
The Little People. London, Hodder and Stoughton, and New York, Simon and Schuster, 1967.
Pendulum. London, Hodder and Stoughton, and New York, Simon and Schuster, 1968.

Novels as Samuel Youd

The Winter Swan. London, Dobson, 1949.
Babel Itself. London, Cassell, 1951.
Brave Conquerors. London, Cassell, 1952.
Crown and Anchor. London, Cassell, 1953.
A Palace of Strangers. London, Cassell, 1954.
Holly Ash. London, Cassell, 1955; as *The Opportunist,* New York, Harper, 1957.
The Choice. New York, Simon and Schuster, 1961; as *The Burning Bird,* London, Longman, 1964.
Messages of Love. New York, Simon and Schuster, 1961; London, Longman, 1962.
The Summers at Accorn. London, Longman, 1963.

Novels as Peter Graaf

Dust and the Curious Boy. London, Joseph, 1957; as *Give the Devil His Due,* New York, Mill, 1957.
Daughter Fair. London, Joseph, and New York, Washburn, 1958.
Sapphire Conference. London, Joseph, and New York, Washburn, 1959.
The Gull's Kiss. London, Davies, 1962.

Novels as Hilary Ford

Felix Walking. London, Eyre and Spottiswoode, and New York, Simon and Schuster, 1958.
Felix Running. London, Eyre and Spottiswoode, 1959.
Bella on the Roof. London, Longman, 1965.
Sarnia. London, Hamish Hamilton, and New York, Doubleday, 1974.
Castle Malindine. London, Hamish Hamilton, and New York, Harper, 1975.
A Bride for Bedivere. London, Hamish Hamilton, 1976; New York, Harper, 1977.

Short Stories

The Twenty-Second Century. London, Grayson, 1954; New York, Lancer, 1962.

*

Biography: Essay in *Speaking for Ourselves, Too* compiled and edited by Donald R. Gallo, National Council of Teachers of English, 1993.

*   *   *

As the first important English writer of science fiction specifically for young adults, John Christopher is—like H.G. Wells before him—a skilled writer with a strong social conscience who uses the genre of science fiction to explore concerns about the direction of social and technological change, and the dangers presented by the fallibility of human nature. Looking to the past to help him envision the future, Christopher characteristically sees a regression, whereby in the England of the future most people live without machines, and technological power is controlled by a small elite. Christopher writes fluently and prolifically; not all of his novels meet the standards set by his best works, but his first two trilogies and *The Lotus Caves* and *The Guardians,* particularly, present memorable and troubling images of the future which stir the reader to question aspects of contemporary society and his or her role therein.

The subject of mind control, whether through indoctrination or by physical means, preoccupies Christopher throughout his work, and his central characters virtually always find themselves in rebellion against powerful figures who seek to impose or to maintain their control over human minds. In the "Tripods" trilogy, Christopher's first major work for young people, almost all human beings on Earth have come under the control of an alien race, the "Masters," who affix a metal cap to the skull of every adolescent boy and girl which enables their thoughts to be entirely subdued to the Masters's will throughout the rest of their lives. Capped humans live contentedly in quasi-medieval agrarian communities, avoiding the ruins of their cities and any sophisticated machinery, and willingly sending their most promising young people to spend short and painful lives as slaves in the Masters's domed cities. The young uncapped protagonists of *The White Mountains* are enlisted by a secret resistance movement, and in two subsequent novels they infiltrate the Masters's cities and destroy them. The great conclave held at the end of the trilogy, which hopes to establish a new world order, proves however that these leaders are in some ways their own worst enemies, as representatives of different races and factions begin quarrelling among themselves. Only in his young heroes' final determination to work together to heal these rifts among the nations does Christopher offer a slight hope that freed human beings can do anything other than squabble and seek to enslave each other anew.

Variations on this theme of mind control and rebellion are found in *The Lotus Caves,* set on a colonized Moon, and *The Guardians* and *Wild Jack,* both set in an England of the future. The tranquilizing and euphoric state induced in its human worshippers by the Plant, a vast, beautiful, and beneficent organism which has found a refuge in the Moon caves, is resisted by thirteen-year-old Marty because it will destroy his independent will and prevent him from returning to his family. He escapes from the Plant, however, with a certain sense of regret, and hopes to keeps its whereabouts secret from the other Moon colonists lest they interfere with it and destroy it. As this novel makes imaginative use of the Homeric story of the Lotus Eaters, so *Wild Jack* displaces the legend of Robin Hood into a futuristic England where the outlaw and his band have set up an active resistance to the complacent and privileged city-dwellers, who deploy Earth's seriously-depleted energy resources to benefit the ruling class, and condemn other humans to struggle for survival as best they can. A strong physical barrier also separates the classes in *The Guardians,* one of Christopher's bleakest and most powerful visions of the future. Rob runs away from the Conurbs, where industrial workers are crowded together in a passive society whose athletic spectacles and meaningless riots arising out of them provide the chief distractions from a numbing routine existence; in the County, however, Rob experiences the idyllic life of the privileged Edwardian country-house dweller, where all is serene, orderly, and beautiful. Accepted into this privileged class and world, Rob is utterly content, until his shattering discovery that social division is maintained by a ruling elite, the Guardians, who perform a sort of lobotomy on any members of the County set who question the status quo, thus ensuring their tranquillity and conformity. Rob is invited to become a Guardian, at the cost of betraying his friend; he chooses, instead, to join a band of rebels in their apparently hopeless task of unseating the Guardians and changing the social system.

The second of Christopher's trilogies, the "Winchester" trilogy which begins with *The Prince in Waiting,* also offers a bleak vision of the future of England and the part which scientific knowledge and technological power will play in it. At the outset, as in the beginning of the first trilogy, English society has returned to a medieval way of life: technology is feared and shunned, a priestly class shares power with a military elite, and city states such as Winchester wage sporadic warfare amongst themselves, led by knights on horseback. Luke, who finds himself unexpectedly in line to become his city's Prince, also learns that the scientific knowledge of the past is secretly preserved by the priests or Seers, who use it to keep the populace in awe of their apparent powers until they are able to find a strong ruler who will unite England once more and restore technology. Luke is to be this ruler, prepared to break the bonds of tradition and bring England enlightenment. Like the Arthurian story, which it partially recalls, Luke's venture turns to tragedy as love is betrayed, Luke cuts himself off from his friends, and eventually uses his technological power for brutal military purposes. Christopher seems to imply that history repeats itself in cycles, and this destructive use of technology will again eventually lead to disaster, and the rejection of all scientific knowledge.

Luke's inclination and training in the fields of masculine and military leadership lead to his failure, in his inability to understand and communicate with women. The need of men and women for each other, and for a greater understanding of each other, is directly addressed in two of Christopher's novels from the 1970s—*Dom and Va,* and *Empty World.* The setting of the first of these is not the future but the past, as a youth aggressively trained as a hunter and a girl from a gentle agrarian tribe come to recognize their need not only for each other as individuals but also for the contrasting qualities and strengths which each of them represents. The same recognition is experienced by the young couple in *Empty World,* who find themselves almost the sole survivors of a plague which has swept over the world. In this novel, however, it is not enough that they should find each other and begin the human race anew; the novel ends with them making a gesture of compassion to someone else, a desperate and hostile woman who had previously tried to kill the boy. While their decision to let her rejoin them is a dangerous one, it offers hope that the new society which may arise will be one founded on compassion and forgiveness rather than jealousy and revenge.

Christopher's plots are skillfully constructed, and his spare direct story-telling keeps his novels consistently gripping. Characterization is not his strong point, although the central character in each of the first two trilogies does undergo significant development and change. Many of his young heroes, however, seem the same, and secondary characters are sketched in with a few attributes suiting their roles in the plot. Young women are generally confined to being decorative and sympathetic, although in his "Fireball" trilogy Christopher responds to the feminist awareness of the 1980s by creating at least two interesting females—one a Viking girl who retains her courage and aplomb when she is (rather improbably) transported to an Aztec kingdom and sets up court in a pyramid as chief bride of the gods, and the other an ancient Chinese mystic whose psychic powers enable her to appear as a seductive young woman. As these details might suggest, the geographical focus which gave intensity to many of Christopher's earlier novels is exchanged in this third trilogy for a fantastical exploration of how the twentieth century might look if history had developed differently: if, for example, the Romans had remained rulers of Britain, the Aztecs extended their empire far northwards, and the Industrial Revolution never occurred. The speculation is intriguing, but the trilogy does not carry the conviction of Christopher's earlier work.

Christopher's novels, while they often explore the responses to technology possible in some future society, do not make detailed use of scientific knowledge or devices; they are concerned, rather, with human nature and society, and the ways in which one individual or group may attempt to impose and maintain its control over other people. Although they have no assurance of being able to establish a more just and truly free society themselves, Christopher's heroes inevitably choose to reject and actively rebel against the forces which seek to deprive their fellow humans of the right to choose and the spirit to rebel. This lack of any easy assurance or simple solution to the problems posed by human social organization has made Christopher's fiction seem pessimistic to some; on the other hand, their realistic, open-ended conclusions, which recognize human problems as ongoing and not to be resolved by one victory, give his novels a maturity of vision which makes them of continuing interest and relevance.

—Gwyneth Evans

———

CHUTE, Marchette (Gaylord). American. Born in Wayzata, Minnesota, 16 August 1909. Educated at Central High School, Minneapolis, 1921-25; Minneapolis School of Art, 1925-26; University of Minnesota, Minneapolis, 1926-30, B.A. 1930 (Phi Beta Kappa). Writer, mainly of biography and history. Member of executive board, National Book Committee, since 1954; judge for National Book awards, 1952, 1959. President, American PEN, 1955-57. Recipient: American Library Association notable book award for *Geoffrey Chaucer of England;* Author Meets the Critics award for best nonfiction of 1950, American Library Association notable book award, and New York Shakespeare Club award, 1954, all for *Shakespeare of London;* Poetry Society of American Chap-Book

award, Secondary Education Board award, American Library Association notable book award, and New York Shakespeare Club award, all 1954, for *Ben Jonson of Westminster;* Outstanding Achievement award of University of Minnesota, 1957; co-winner of Women's National Book Association Constance Lindsay Skinner award, 1959. Litt.D.: Western College, Oxford, Ohio, 1952; Carleton College, Northfield, Minnesota, 1957; Dickinson College, Carlisle, Pennsylvania, 1964. Vice-President, 1961, and Secretary, 1962, National Institute of Arts and Letters; Member, American Academy; Benjamin Franklin Fellow, Royal Society of Arts. Address: c/o Elizabeth M. Roach, 66 Glenbrook Road, Morris Plains, NJ 07950, U.S.A.

PUBLICATIONS FOR YOUNG ADULTS

Fiction

The Innocent Wayfaring, illustrated by the author. New York, Scribner, 1943; London, Phoenix House, 1956.
The Wonderful Winter, illustrated by Grace Golden. New York, Dutton, 1954; London, Phoenix House, 1956.

Poetry (illustrated by the author)

Rhymes about Ourselves. New York, Macmillan, 1932.
Rhymes about the Country. New York, Macmillan, 1941.
Rhymes about the City. New York, Macmillan, 1946.
Around and About. New York, Dutton, 1957.
Rhymes about Us, illustrated by the author. New York, Dutton, 1974.

Other

An Introduction to Shakespeare. New York, Dutton, 1951; as *Shakespeare and His Stage,* London, University of London Press, 1953.
Jesus of Israel, with Ernestine Perrie. New York, Dutton, 1961; London, Gollancz, 1962.
The Green Tree of Democracy. New York, Dutton, 1971.

PUBLICATIONS FOR ADULTS

Plays

Sweet Genevieve, with M.G. Chute (produced New York, 1945).
The Worlds of Shakespeare, with Ernestine Perrie (produced New York, 1963). New York, Dutton, 1963.

Other

The Search for God. New York, Dutton, 1941; London, Benn, 1946.
Geoffrey Chaucer of England. New York, Dutton, 1946; London, Hale, 1951.
The End of the Search. New York, North River Press, 1947.
Shakespeare of London. New York, Dutton, 1950; London, Secker & Warburg, 1951.
Ben Jonson of Westminster. New York, Dutton, 1953; London, Hale, 1954.

Stories from Shakespeare. Cleveland, World, 1956.
Two Gentle Men: The Lives of George Herbert and Robert Herrick. New York, Dutton, 1959; London, Secker & Warburg, 1960.
The First Liberty: A History of the Right to Vote in America 1619-1850. New York, Dutton, 1969; London, Dent, 1970.
P.E.N. American Center: A History of the First Fifty Years. New York, P.E.N. American Center, 1972.

*

Manuscript Collections: New York Public Library; Kerlan Collection, University of Minnesota, Minneapolis.

* * *

Chute is a scholarly writer who is well known for her meticulously researched adult biographies on such literary greats as Shakespeare, Chaucer, Herbert, and Ben Jonson. She has also drawn on this background of an earlier England for lively books for young people.

The Wonderful Winter is set for the most part in Elizabethan London. The major character, a young nobleman, runs away from home accompanied by his pet dog. After a few misadventures, he is taken on by Shakespeare's company of players. He helps behind the scenes and becomes a boy actor. In the process the reader becomes well acquainted with the business of theatre in this period. Descriptions of the Globe Theatre and of personalities of the time make the book excellent, easy-reading background for a study of the Shakespearian plays. As the young hero matures, he feels guilt at having run away from home. He admits his true identity and returns home.

The Innocent Wayfaring is set in the fourteenth-century countryside of Chaucer's England. To be precise, the story takes place during three days in June 1370 in Surrey. The scene opens on Midsummer Eve in the Manor of Rotheby where the Lord, Sir Hugh Richmond, and wife, Lady Emily, are engaged in an amusing discussion of redecorating. Lady Emily manages very neatly to have her husband select exactly the colors and styles upon which she has already decided. The conversation turns to their fifteen-year-old daughter, Anne, who for the past month has been residing in the convent headed by the Prioress, Dame Agatha, who is Sir Hugh's intimidating older sister. There Anne is to learn sewing, spinning, embroidery, and maidenly behavior. Both Anne and her father prefer hawking.

Anne, unhappy with the only career alternatives available to her—to be either a wife or a nun—runs away to London to become a traveling entertainer. To this end she takes the Prioress's pet monkey with her. Action follows rapidly as Anne finds her way to a country fair, loses her monkey, accuses a young man of stealing it, engages in a farcical and hilarious trial over the matter, and is rescued from the affair by the young man who literally carries her off. They travel on together and as they become acquainted discover that they are both running away. The young man, Nicholas Ware, seeks knowledge and wishes to be a poet rather than go into his father's business. Anne is attempting to escape a constrained existence as a wife. They increasingly feel that they have a great deal in common, and young adult readers will also feel they have a great deal in common with these lively and likeable teenagers.

They spend the night in an ale house, have an encounter with a highwayman, survive a violent summer storm, and arrive at the kitchen of the Castle Waring where they become acquainted, as does the reader, with the various residents of a medieval manor—the cook, reeve, miller, blacksmith, steward, plasterer, and peasants. The Lady of the Castle sees Anne as a prospective daughter-in-law and treats her well—the description of the Lady's bedroom and her toilet articles gives an excellent picture of the personal life of a wealthy woman of the period. Anne escapes from the castle and rejoins Nick who persuades her both to agree to marry him and to return home. At the end of the book after being welcomed home, Anne announces that she is returning with Aunt Agatha to the convent to learn to be a good wife while Nick returns to London to enter his father's business.

Chute has also written of Biblical and early American times and for both children and adults. Besides being a historian and biographer, Chute is a published poet, playwright, and sometime illustrator of her own books.

—Reba Pinney

———

CISNEROS, Sandra. American. Born in Chicago, Illinois, 20 December 1954. Educated at Loyola University of Chicago, Illinois, B.A. 1976; University of Iowa, Iowa City, M.F.A. 1978. Writer. Has taught at universities, including University of California, Berkeley, and University of Michigan. Worked previously as a high school teacher, counselor, college recruiter, and arts administrator. Recipient: National Endowment for the Arts fellow, 1982 and 1987; Before Columbus Foundation award, 1985, for *The House on Mango Street;* Dobie-Paisano fellow, 1986; PEN/West Fiction award, and Lannan Foundation award, both 1991, for *Woman Hollering Creek and Other Stories.* Agent: Susan Bergholz, 340 West 72nd St., New York, NY 10023, U.S.A.

PUBLICATIONS

Poetry

Bad Boys. Mango Publications, 1980.
The Rodrigo Poems. Bloomington, Indiana, Third Women Press, 1985.
My Wicked, Wicked Ways. Bloomington, Indiana, Third Women Press, 1987.

Short Stories

The House on Mango Street. Arte Publico, 1983.
Woman Hollering Creek and Other Stories. Random House, 1991.

Other

Contributor, *Emergency Tacos: Seven Poets con Picante.* March/Abrazo Press, 1989.

*

Biography: Essay in *Authors & Artists for Young Adults,* Volume 9, Detroit, Gale, 1992.

Sandra Cisneros writes about life in the Latino communities of Mexican-American border towns, focusing particularly on the struggles of Latina women. In her short-story collections *The House on Mango Street* and *Woman Hollering Creek,* Cisneros creates female characters who seek identity and affirmation in the face of poverty and oppression. The subject matter is often harsh—many of the women in these stories suffer physical and emotional abuse within their male-dominated communities and beyond those borders, in the racist, classist mainstream society—but Cisneros' characters usually dream of and fight their way to independence and self-fulfillment. The language in all of the stories is vibrant and poetic, the narrators, speaking in a mixture of English and Spanish, evoke the tastes, smells, and colors of their environment.

The nameless girl narrating the stories in *The House on Mango Street* offers a clear-eyed, unsentimental account of life in and around her impoverished, Latino neighborhood. In the title story, the narrator's own desire for a "real house" reflects her need to be considered a "real" person in mainstream society, to be treated with dignity, and to live freely and creatively. Her observations and hopes shape the tone and theme of all the stories in the collection. To the narrator and her family ("Mama, Papa, Carlos, Kiki, my sister Nenny, and me"), having a "real house" means achieving a stereotypical white, upper-middle class standard of life. The narrator wants a house that is "white with trees around it, a great big yard and grass growing without a fence," but what she has on Mango Street is a house that is "small and red with tight steps in front and windows so small you'd think they were holding their breath." The poverty imposed on the narrator by race and class threatens to smother her, as it suffocates her friend Sally, a victim of child abuse and the central character in "What Sally Said."

The final story in *The House on Mango Street* suggests that the narrator finds a way out of this life through her imagination and writing. The collection ends on a very brief (two-paragraph) story of hope, entitled "A House of My Own." In this story, the narrator, focused and determined, visualizes her own place, her own identity as a female and a writer: "Not a flat. Not an apartment in back. Not a man's house. Not a daddy's. A house all my own. With my porch and my pillow, my pretty purple petunias.... Only a house quiet as snow, a space for myself to go, clean as paper before the poem."

The characters in *Woman Hollering Creek* also seek escape from the stigma of their race and class, at the same time, however, they celebrate the customs and language that bring them together as a unique community. The opening story, "My Lucy Friend Who Smells Like Corn," is a joyous description of the friendship between two young Latina girls. This story is a first-person, stream-of-consciousness appreciation of innocence and girlhood in a Texas border community. An example would be the narrator's proclamation: "I'm going to scratch your mosquito bites, Lucy, so they'll itch you, then put Mercurochrome smiley faces on them. We're going to trade shoes and wear them on our hands.... I'm going to peel a scab from my knee and eat it, sneeze on the cat, give you three M & M's I've been saving for you since yesterday, comb your hair with my fingers and braid it into teeny-tiny braids real pretty."

As the stories in the collection progress, however, the narrators grow more self-aware, more experienced, more exposed to the difficulties of coming-of-age as a female Latina in a white, male-dominated society. Bittersweet stories of childhood, such as "Eleven," "Barbie-Q," and "Mericans" give way to darker tales of adulthood, such as the title story, "Woman Hollering Creek." In this story a young bride, Cleofilas, dreams of romantic love and marriage as it is portrayed in the "telenovelas" she watches religiously. She imagines a life like that of the telenovela heroine, Lucia Mendez, who suffers "all kinds of hardships of the heart, separation and betrayal" for the sake of love, and is "always loving, no matter what, because *that* is the most important thing..." Instead Cleofilas finds herself in a physically abusive marriage, legally bound to "this husband whose whiskers she finds each morning in the sink, whose shoes she must air each evening on the porch...this man, this father, this rival, this keeper, this lord, this master, this husband till kingdom come." By the end of the story Cleofilas learns to distinguish romance from reality and, through the help of other women, finds the courage to start a new life for herself and her children.

Cisneros's stories are lively and bold, exposing young readers to the tales and voices of Latino culture, but also demonstrating the range of form and style possible in storytelling. Cisneros's experiments with language and content serve as models to young readers who may not see their experience reflected in "traditional" culture stories, and to young writers who wish to express their own experience in "alternative" narrative forms.

—Mary D. Esselman

CLAPP, Patricia. American. Born in Boston, Massachusetts, 9 June 1912. Educated at Kimberley School, Montclair, New Jersey; Columbia University School of Journalism, 1932. Married Edward della Torre Cone in 1933; one son and two daughters. Writer of adult and children's books and plays; since 1940 member of the Board of Managers, Studio Players, Upper Montclair, New Jersey. Recipient: National Book Award runner-up, and Lewis Carroll Shelf Award, both 1969, both for *Constance: A Story of Early Plymouth;* American Library Association Best Young Adult Book citation, 1982, for *Witches' Children: A Story of Salem.* Address: 83 Beverley Rd., Upper Montclair, NJ 07043, U.S.A.

<small>PUBLICATIONS FOR YOUNG ADULTS</small>

Fiction

Constance: A Story of Early Plymouth. New York, Lothrop, 1968.
Jane-Emily. New York, Lothrop, 1969.
I'm Deborah Sampson: A Soldier in the War of the Revolution. New York, Lothrop, 1977.
Witches' Children: A Story of Salem. New York, Lothrop, 1982.
The Tamarack Tree. New York, Lothrop, 1986.

Plays

Peggy's on the Phone. Chicago, Dramatic Publishing, 1956.
Smart Enough to Be Dumb. Chicago, Dramatic Publishing, 1956.
The Incompleted Pass. Chicago, Dramatic Publishing, 1957.
Her Kissin' Cousin. Cedar Rapids, Iowa, Heuer Publishing, 1957.
The Girl out Front. Chicago, Dramatic Publishing, 1958.
The Ghost of a Chance. Cedar Rapids, Iowa, Heuer Publishing, 1958.
The Curley Tale. Cedar Rapids, Iowa, Art Craft, 1958.
Inquire Within. Evanston, Illinois, Row Peterson, 1959.

The Girl Whose Fortune Sought Her (published in *Children's Plays from Favorite Stories,* edited by S. E. Kamerman, Boston, Plays Inc., 1959).
Edie-across-the-Street. Boston, Baker, 1960.
The Honeysuckle Hedge. Franklin, Ohio, Eldridge, 1960.
Never Keep Him Waiting. Chicago, Dramatic Publishing, 1961.
Red Heels and Roses. New York, McKay, 1961.
If a Body Meet a Body. Cedar Rapids, Ohio, Heuer Publishing, 1963.
Now Hear This. Franklin, Ohio, Eldridge, 1963.
The Magic Bookshelf (published in *Fifty Plays for Junior Actors,* edited by S.E. Kamerman, Boston, Plays Inc., 1966).
The Other Side of the Wall (published in *Fifty Plays for Holidays,* edited by S.E. Kamerman, Boston, Plays Inc., 1969).
The Do-Nothing Frog (published in *100 Plays for Children,* edited by A.S. Burack. Boston, Plays Inc., 1970).
The Invisible Dragon. Chicago, Dramatic Publishing, 1971.
A Specially Wonderful Day. Chicago, Encyclopedia Britannica Educational Corp., 1972.
The Toys Take over Christmas. Chicago, Dramatic Publishing, 1977.
Mudcake Princess. Chicago, Dramatic Publishing, 1979.
The Truly Remarkable Puss in Boots. Chicago, Dramatic Publishing, 1979.

Also author of several other plays, including *A Feather in His Cap, The Wonderful Door, A Wish Is for Keeping, Susan and Aladdin's Lamp, The Signpost, The Friendship Bracelet, Christmas in Old New England, The Straight Line from Somewhere, Yankee Doodle Came to Cranetown,* and *When Ecstasy Cost a Nickel,* published in *Instructor Magazine, Plays Magazine, Grade Teacher Magazine,* and *Yankee Magazine,* 1958-81.

Nonfiction

Dr. Elizabeth: The Story of the First Woman Doctor. New York, Lothrop, 1974.

PUBLICATIONS FOR CHILDREN

Fiction

King of the Dollhouse, illustrated by Judith Gwyn Brown. New York, Lothrop, 1974.

Poetry

Popsical Song. Chicago, Encyclopedia Britannica Education Corp., 1972.

PUBLICATIONS FOR ADULTS

Plays

A Candle on the Table. Boston, Baker, 1972.
The Retirement. Franklin, Ohio, Eldridge, 1972.

Other

Contributor, *Through the Eyes of a Child,* edited by Donna E. Norton. Merrill, 1983.

Media Adaptations: *I'm Deborah Sampson: A Soldier in the War of the Revolution* has been optioned for filming by Walt Disney Studios.

Biography: Entry in *Fifth Book of Junior Authors and Illustrators,* New York, H.W. Wilson, 1983; essay in *Something about the Author Autobiography Series,* Volume 4, Detroit, Gale, 1987; essay in *Speaking for Ourselves, Too* compiled and edited by Donald R. Gallo, National Council of Teachers of English, 1993.

Manuscript Collection: Kerlan Collection, University of Minnesota, Minneapolis; De Grummond Collection, University of Southern Mississippi, Hattiesburg.

*   *   *

Much of Patricia Clapp's work in adolescent literature was preceded by years of writing plays for children. Active in theatre herself, in her play writing she developed an ear for dialogue, speech, and allowing a character to tell his own story. This was training which was essential when Clapp turned to writing novels, for as she considered the stories of her characters, she heard them speaking. The result is a series of novels which avoided the obtrusive narrator and focused instead on the interior life of the character.

In combining this approach with meticulous historical research, Clapp used a form of historical fiction that had the advantage of being both immediate and dramatic—a throwback to writing for the theatre. It also provided Clapp with a unique point of reference in her historical stories; she could tell of the madness of the Salem witch trials from inside, expressing all the ambiguity, misunderstanding, and fear that her protagonist must have felt in the real event. She can allow the reader to experience almost simultaneously the bombardment of Vicksburg with Rosemary Leigh by having her character record the events as they happen. In short, such a technique moves a reader to the inside of the action.

The result is a novel that is not objective; it is not meant to be. It is instead a highly subjective recording of historical events, a recording which recounts some of the reactions and perceptions of other characters but which always keeps the filtering, subjective vision of the protagonist at the forefront. In Constance, the young girl may first view Plymouth Colony with disdain, but it is clear that others do not share her perceptions. Even the reader sees that some of her observations are colored and her perceptions incorrect—or deliberately misleading. At times, Clapp allows the reader to see things that the writer is not aware of, such as the malice and manipulation of Abigail Williams that Mary Warren seems to dismiss or ignore before the witch craze swept through Salem.

For three of her works—*Constance, The Tamarack Tree,* and *Dr. Elizabeth: The Story of the First Woman Doctor*—Clapp used a journal or diary as the means of recording her character's thoughts. *Constance* began as a question after Clapp found the name of the fourteen-year-old girl in a chart of her husband's genealogy: What must it have been like for a young adolescent to be ripped from her comfortable home in London and set on a bleak, wintry, desolate shore in a new world? The conventional understanding is that the first settlers arrived with spirited enthusiasm, but Clapp posits another perspective. By allowing Constance to speak to the reader from the privacy of her journal, Clapp allows her character to speak with an honesty and forthrightness which may not have had another vent in the context of Plymouth; she allows readers to see a very different vision of the Plymouth colony.

In *The Tamarack Tree,* Rosemary keeps a journal during the siege of Vicksburg; she begins it as a kind of therapy: it will take her mind off the constant bombardment and the horrendous exigencies of a siege. But here again Clapp, in letting Rosemary speak in the privacy of the diary, allows for a freedom of thought and expression which Rosemary might not have found in besieged Vicksburg: she is able to oppose slavery with a vehemence and force which would have isolated her in the city. The result is a more ambiguous, mixed vision of life in the South during the 1860s.

In two novels—*I'm Deborah Sampson: A Soldier in the War of the Revolution* and *Witches' Children*—Clapp abandons the journal device and has her characters speak in the first person. There is a different kind of immediacy here. In *Constance* and *The Tamarack Tree,* the journal stands between the reader and writer; the primary audience of Constance and Rosemary is the journal itself, with the suggestion that this is not only a record of events but a way of coming to understand them. In *I'm Deborah Sampson* and *Witches' Children,* the characters speak without that barrier, and at times it lends them an urgency which is vivid and convincing. The confusion and ambiguity which Marry Warren feels, for example, lends a complexity to the action of the "possessed" girls which conventional historical accounts may not include. Years after the trials, in a voice still filled with the pain, terror, and guilt for her role in the deaths of neighbors and even one she loved, Mary speaks as one still trying to make sense of what happened, still trying to understand how a game became an obsession. The complexities that she feels suggest the complexities of history, which is not a neat bundle of dates and events in Clapp's vision, but instead a messy jumble of people who feel and act out of those feelings. Mary does not assign blame, though it is tempting for the reader to blame the other girls, or the insensitive and terrorized townspeople, or the stern and unyielding judges. But Clapp does not allow Mary to do this, with the result that the book ends in an ambiguity that Mary too must have felt.

I'm Deborah Sampson has a similarly strong voice, and it too is told from the perspective of years. Here there is less ambiguity, however. The book's tittle suggests the strength and assertiveness of Deborah, a woman who could pry a musket ball out of her own wound. The concluding line of the novel—"I'm Deborah Sampson. I'm strong and I'm free."—is stated by the sixty-year-old character and attests to the union of the first person narrator with the thematic issue of freedom.

That affirmation of Deborah Sampson is linked to another large consideration in Clapp's first-person narratives: the growth of the young woman to adulthood. In each of these novels, and most especially in *Constance,* Clapp combines the story of a young woman in a familiar historical setting with the story of a young woman coming to understand and celebrate her femininity. Constance moves from flirtatious crushes to deep and abiding love, overcoming even the strong strictures of her society to find that love. Rosemary Leigh comes to accept, though perhaps reluctantly, the need that others feel to accept and fulfill certain roles, a need which she too feels. The characters' speculation about their time and their world are mixed together with their musings of what it is like to be an adolescent in this remarkable setting, and it is that combination more than anything else which makes Clapp's characters vivid and real. (Clapp's protagonists are in fact real historical persons, with the exception of Rosemary Leigh, whom Clapp invented and put into Vicksburg so that she might be able to articulate an outside perspective on slavery.)

Dr Elizabeth: The Story of the First Woman Doctor is Clapp's biography of Elizabeth Blackwell, who was the first woman to graduate in the United States with a medical degree. Here, too, she is concerned with letting her character speak for herself, and so she turns to the journal form once again. The device again yields new perspectives; Clapp could have written a straightforward biography of a woman fighting for women's rights against a monolithic medical structure, but in using the journal form one sees not just the women's rights champion but the real woman, who had doubts and fears and frustrations.

Clapp's two fantasies—*Jane-Emily* and *King of the Dollhouse*—are less interesting works, lacking the strong historical context which gives so much power to the works of historical fiction. *Jane-Emily* focuses on the young Jane, who becomes possessed by the evil spirit of her dead Aunt Emily; *King of the Dollhouse* is an episodic novel of a miniature kind which watches over eleven babies in a young girl's dollhouse. Neither shows a protagonist in a moment of growth; neither is completely convincing in its narrative voice.

Clapp's strength comes from the voices that dominate her books. They may be voices that are at times petulant, loving, argumentative, resolved, angry, or fearful. But in crafting those voices, Clapp produces vivid characters who work out of their historical context and who make that historical context clear and dramatic for the reader.

—Gary D. Schmidt

CLARK, Mary Higgins. American. Born in New York City, 24 December 1929. Educated at Villa Maria Academy; Ward Secretarial School; New York University; Fordham University, Bronx, New York, B.A. (summa cum laude) 1979. Married 1) Warren F. Clark in 1949 (died 1964); three daughters and two sons; 2) Raymond Charles Ploetz in 1978 (marriage annulled). Writer. Advertising assistant, Remington Rand, New York, 1946; stewardess, Pan American Airlines, 1949-50; radio scriptwriter and producer for Robert G. Jennings, 1965-70; vice-president, partner, creative director, and producer of radio programming, Aerial Communications, New York City, 1970-80; chairman of the board and creative director, David J. Clark Enterprises, New York City, since 1980. Chairman, International Crime Writers Congress, 1988; president, Mystery Writers of America. Recipient: New Jersey Author award, 1969, for *Aspire to the Heavens,* 1977, for *Where Are the Children?,* and 1978, for *A Stranger Is Watching;* Grand Prix de Litterature Policiere (France), 1980; honorary doctorate, Villanova University, 1983. Agent: Eugene H. Winick, McIntosh & Otis, Inc., 475 Fifth Ave., New York, NY 10017. Address: 2508 Cleveland Ave., Washington Township, NJ 07675, U.S.A.

PUBLICATIONS

Novels

Where Are the Children? New York, Simon & Schuster, and London, Talmy Franklin, 1975.

A Stranger Is Watching. New York, Simon & Schuster, and London, Collins, 1978.

The Cradle Will Fall. New York, Simon & Schuster, and London, Collins, 1980.

A Cry in the Night. New York, Simon & Schuster, 1982; London, Collins, 1983.

Stillwatch. New York, Simon & Schuster, and London, Collins, 1984.

Missing in Manhattan, with Thomas Chastain and others. New York, Morrow, 1986.

Weep No More, My Lady. New York, Simon & Schuster, and London, Collins, 1987.

Caribbean Blues, with others. South Yarmouth, Massachusetts, J. Curley, 1988.

While My Pretty One Sleeps. New York, Simon & Schuster, and London, Century, 1989.

Loves Music, Loves to Dance. New York, Simon & Schuster, 1991.

All around the Town. New York, Simon & Schuster, 1992.

I'll Be Seeing You. New York, Simon & Schuster, 1993.

Short Stories

The Anastasia Syndrome and Other Stories. New York, Simon & Schuster, 1989; London, Century, 1990.

Other

Aspire to the Heavens: A Biography of George Washington (for children). New York, Meredith Press, 1969.

Contributor, *I, Witness.* New York, Times Books, 1978.

Editor, *Murder on the Aisle: The 1987 Mystery Writers of America Anthology.* New York, Simon & Schuster, 1987.

*

Media Adaptations: *A Stranger Is Watching* (film), Metro-Goldwyn-Mayer, 1982; *The Cradle Will Fall* ("Movie of the Week"), CBS, 1984; *A Cry in the Night* (film), Rosten Productions, 1985; *Where Are the Children?* (film), Columbia, 1986; *Stillwatch* (broadcast), CBS, 1987; *Weep No More My Lady,* Ellipse; *A Cry in the Night* (which will star Clark's daughter Carol), Ellipse; two stories from *The Anastasia Syndrome,* Ellipse.

*   *   *

A masterful and popular storyteller, Mary Higgins Clark intricately laces suspense through tightly woven storylines to pull readers into her stories. Her novels deal with ordinary people who are suddenly catapulted into terrifying circumstances. One moment they are changing bedclothes, or standing near the street as a funeral procession passes; the next they seem to be living their worst nightmares.

The plots Clark creates are complex, providing many twists and turns, barricading the solution to the mystery from both reader and characters. Clues in the form of subtle details are placed along the way. The reader becomes involved in figuring out who the adversary is and cheering the characters on when they head for the same conclusions. When dramatic irony is employed, the reader agonizes that the characters are led away from the malefactor. The reader's involvement in the story is intense and the storyline extraordinarily entertaining.

In Clark's first and one of her best-known novels, *Where Are the Children?,* Nancy twice falls victim to the same crime committed by the same man: her two children are abducted and abused. Clark depicts the kind of man who would keep his wife so drugged up that she must be cared for as if she were a helpless little girl. She shows us what type of man would kidnap and kill his own children and then haunt their mother with the same crime seven years later. Many of Clark's themes deal with mental disorders. Her research is apparent in the facts she weaves into her novels. The reader learns about multiple-personality disorders and manipulative criminals.

Clark's victims often have a friend or relative dedicated to seeing their adversary punished. This character is usually a very strong woman who puts a great deal of pressure on herself to help her loved one. At several points in the plot the reader will seize a clue that this character has overlooked.

Darcy is the strong friend in *Loves Music, Loves to Dance.* When her dear friend Erin is killed, possibly by someone who placed a personal ad she had answered, Darcy is determined to find the killer. To ease her pain, Darcy has donated some of Erin's belongings to a sixteen-year-old, bedridden girl. As she places one of Erin's posters on the girl's bedroom wall, Darcy can't help feeling she's missing a clue. "Darcy stepped back to be sure the poster was hanging straight. It was. Then what was gnawing at her? *The personal ads.* But why now? Shrugging, she closed her toolbox." The reader knows what Darcy is overlooking and longs to point this out to her.

The extensive research Clark executes for her novels is evident. She succeeds in getting into the heads of the criminals in her novels. In *Loves Music, Loves to Dance* it is clear to the reader that Charley is the murderer and a sort of alter personality. "A long time had passed. Charley had become a blurred memory, a shadowy figure lurking somewhere in the recesses of his mind, until two years ago...." The reader also knows that Charley is posing as a friend. "The look he'd been waiting for came into Erin's eyes. That tiny first flicker of awareness that something wasn't quite right. She recognized the subtle change in his tone and manner." But the reader does not know which of the men Erin and Darcy date harbors the alter personality named Charley. Though the reader doesn't know who killed Erin, many different suspects are presented and the reader is involved in trying to determine who is guilty before the FBI does.

In *All around the Town,* the reader knows who is guilty. The suspense builds as the strong character uncovers clues to identify the guilty party and the reader fervently hopes she will find out in time to save the victim. *All around the Town* is about a girl named Laurie who is abducted at the age of four and returned to her family after two years. Years later, she is arrested for killing one of her college professors, but has no memory of this crime. Her older sister Sarah, a prosecuting attorney, begins to build a case to defend her. Sarah is the strong character determined to avenge her loved one's injury. The amount of pressure she places on herself is intense. During the time Laurie is missing, Sarah makes pacts with God that if Laurie is returned she will forever take care of her. Now, years later she must hold up her end of the bargain and defend her sister's innocence. "That night when Sarah settled in bed, she had the nagging feeling that something she should have noticed had escaped her attention."

The reader worries both about Sarah and about Laurie's innocence, the key to which lies in her memory of those years she had been abducted. Again suspense is built because the reader knows what the key is, but cannot jump into the story to rescue Laurie and Sarah.

Clark keeps the reader guessing as to her novels' resolutions and a surprise twist always occurs at the end of each. The reader never feels cheated by Clark's economical but informative and entertaining prose. The intensity of the suspense and the intricate weavings of the plot keep the reader turning the pages.

—Lisa A. Wroble

* * *

CLARKE, Arthur C(harles). Also writes as E. G. O'Brien; Charles Willis. British. Born in Minehead, Somerset, 16 December 1917. Educated at Huish's Grammar School, Taunton, Somerset, 1927-36; King's College, London, 1946-48, B.Sc. (honours) in physics and mathematics 1948. Flight Lieutenant in the Royal Air Force, 1941-46; served as Radar Instructor, and Technical Officer on the first Ground Controlled Approach radar; originated proposal for use of satellites for communications, 1945. Married Marilyn Mayfield in 1954 (divorced 1964). Assistant auditor, Exchequer and Audit Department, London, 1936-41; assistant editor, *Physics Abstracts*, London, 1949-50; from 1954, engaged in underwater exploration and photography of the Great Barrier Reef of Australia and the coast of Sri Lanka. Director, Rocket Publishing, London, Underwater Safaris, Colombo, and the Spaceward Corporation, New York. Has made numerous radio and television appearances (most recently as presenter of the television series *Arthur C. Clarke's Mysterious World,* 1980, and *World of Strange Powers,* 1985), and has lectured widely in Britain and the United States; commentator, for CBS-TV, on lunar flights of Apollo 11, 12 and 15; Vikram Sarabhai Professor, Physical Research Laboratory, Ahmedabad, India, 1980; acted role of Leonard Woolf in the film *Beddagama* ("The Village in the Jungle"), 1979. Recipient: International Fantasy award, 1952, for *The Exploration of Space;* Hugo award, 1956, for "The Star"; Kalinga prize, 1961; Junior Book award, Boy's Club of America, 1961, for *The Challenge of the Sea;* Franklin Institute Ballantine Medal, 1963, for originating concept of communications satellites; Aviation-Space Writers Association Ball award, 1965, for best aerospace reporting of the year in any medium; American Association for the Advancement of Science-Westinghouse Science Writing award, 1969; Hugo award, Second International Film Festival special award, and Academy of Motion Picture Arts and Sciences award nomination, 1969, all for *2001: A Space Odyssey; Playboy* editorial award, 1971, 1982; Nebula award, 1972, for "A Meeting with Medusa"; Nebula award, 1973, Jupiter award, 1973, John W. Campbell Memorial award, 1974, and Hugo award, 1974, all for *Rendezvous with Rama;* American Institute of Aeronautics and Astronautics award, 1974; Boston Museum of Science Washburn award, 1977, for "contributions to the public understanding of science"; GALAXY award, 1979; Nebula and Hugo awards, 1980, both for *The Fountains of Paradise;* National Academy of Television Arts and Sciences Emmy award, 1981, for contributions to satellite broadcasting; "Lensman" award, 1982; Marconi International Fellowship, 1982; Institute of Electrical and Electronics Engineers Centennial medal, 1984; American Astronautical Society E. M. Emme Astronautical Literature award, 1984; Science Fiction Writers of America Grand Master award, 1986; Vidya Jyothi

medal, 1986; Charles A. Lindbergh award, 1987; named to Society of Satellite Professionals Hall of Fame, 1987; named to Aerospace Hall of Fame, 1988; Association of Space Explorers (Riyadh) Special Acievement award, 1989. D.Sc., Beaver College, Glenside, Pennsylvania, 1971; D.Litt., University of Bath, 1988. Chairman, British Interplanetary Society, 1946-47, 1950-53. Guest of Honor, World Science Fiction Convention, 1956. Fellow, Royal Astronomical Society; Fellow, King's College, London, 1977; Chancellor, University of Moratuwa, Sri Lanka, since 1979. C.B.E. (Commander, Order of the British Empire), 1989. Agent: David Higham Associates, 5-8 Lower John St., Golden Square, London W1R 4HA. Address: "Leslie's House," 25 Barnes Place, Colombo 7, Sri Lanka.

PUBLICATIONS

Novels

Prelude to Space. New York, Galaxy, 1951; London, Sidgwick and Jackson, 1953; as *Master of Space,* New York, Lancer, 1961; as *The Space Dreamers,* New York, Lancer, 1969.

The Sands of Mars. London, Sidgwick and Jackson, 1951; New York, Gnome Press, 1952.

Against the Fall of Night. New York, Gnome Press, 1953; revised edition, as *The City and the Stars,* London, Muller, and New York, Harcourt Brace, 1956.

Childhood's End. New York, Ballantine, 1953; London, Sidgwick and Jackson, 1954.

Earthlight. London, Muller, and New York, Ballantine, 1955.

The Deep Range. New York, Harcourt Brace, and London, Muller, 1957.

A Fall of Moondust. London, Gollancz, and New York, Harcourt Brace, 1961.

Glide Path. New York, Harcourt Brace, 1963; London, Sidgwick and Jackson, 1969.

2001: A Space Odyssey (novelization of screenplay). New York, New American Library, and London, Hutchinson, 1968.

Rendezvous with Rama. London, Gollancz, and New York, Harcourt Brace, 1973.

Imperial Earth: A Fantasy of Love and Discord. London, Gollancz, 1975; New York, Harcourt Brace, 1976.

The Fountains of Paradise. London, Gollancz, and New York, Harcourt Brace, 1979.

2010: Odyssey Two. New York, Ballantine, and London, Granada, 1982.

The Songs of Distant Earth. London, Grafton, and New York, Ballantine, 1986.

Cradle, with Gentry Lee. London, Gollancz, and New York, Warner, 1988.

2061: Odyssey Three. New York, Ballantine, and London, Grafton, 1988.

Rama II, with Gentry Lee. London, Gollancz, and New York, Bantam, 1989.

Beyond the Fall of Night, with Gregory Benford. New York, Putnam, 1990; with *Against the Fall of Night,* London, Gollancz, 1991.

The Ghost from the Grand Banks. New York, Bantam, and London, Gollancz, 1990.

The Garden of Rama, with Gentry Lee. London, Gollancz, and New York, Bantam, 1991.

Rama Revealed, with Gentry Lee. London, Gollancz, and New York, Bantam, 1993.

Short Stories

Expedition to Earth. New York, Ballantine, 1953; London, Sidgwick and Jackson, 1954.

Reach for Tomorrow. New York, Ballantine, 1956; London, Gollancz, 1962.

Tales from the White Hart. New York, Ballantine, 1957; London, Sidgwick and Jackson, 1972.

The Other Side of the Sky. New York, Harcourt Brace, 1958; London, Gollancz, 1961.

Tales of Ten Worlds. New York, Harcourt Brace, 1962; London, Gollancz, 1963.

The Nine Billion Names of God: The Best Short Stories of Arthur C. Clarke. New York, Harcourt Brace, 1967.

Of Time and Stars: The Worlds of Arthur C. Clarke. London, Gollancz, 1972.

The Wind from the Sun: Stories of the Space Age. New York, Harcourt Brace, and London, Gollancz, 1972.

The Best of Arthur C. Clarke 1937-1971, edited by Angus Wells. London, Sidgwick and Jackson, 1973.

The Sentinel: Masterworks of Science Fiction and Fantasy. New York, Berkley, 1983; London, Panther, 1985.

A Meeting with Medusa, with *Green Mars,* by Kim Stanley Robinson. New York, Tor, 1988.

Dilemmas: The Secret, with *Flowers for Algernon,* by Daniel Keyes, New York, Houghton Mifflin, 1989.

Tales from Planet Earth. London, Century, 1989; New York, Bantam, 1990.

I Remember Babylon and Other Stories. Mattituck, New York, Amereon, n.d.

The Possessed and Other Stories. Mattituck, New York, Amereon, n.d.

Plays

Arthur C. Clarke's Mysterious World (television series). Yorkshire Television, 1980; with Simon Welfare and John Fairley, A and W Publishers, 1980.

Arthur C. Clarke's World of Strange Powers (television series). ITV, 1984; with Simon Welfare and John Fairley, New York, Putnam, 1984.

Screenplay: *2001: A Space Odyssey,* with Stanley Kubrick, 1968.

Nonfiction

Interplanetary Flight: An Introduction to Astronautics. London, Temple Press, 1950; New York, Harper, 1951; revised edition, 1960.

The Exploration of Space. London, Temple Press, and New York, Harper, 1951; revised edition, 1959; revised edition, New York, Pocket Books, 1979.

The Exploration of the Moon, illustrated by R.A. Smith. London, Muller, 1954; New York, Harper, 1955.

The Young Traveller in Space (for children). London, Phoenix House, 1954; as *Going into Space,* New York, Harper, 1954; as *The Scottie Book of Space Travel,* London, Transworld, 1957; revised edition, with Robert Silverberg, as *Into Space: A Young Person's Guide to Space,* New York, Harper, 1971.

The Coast of Coral. London, Muller, and New York, Harper, 1956.

The Making of a Moon: The Story of the Earth Satellite Program. London, Muller, and New York, Harper, 1957; revised edition, New York, Harper, 1958.

The Reefs of Taprobane: Underwater Adventures Around Ceylon. London, Muller, and New York, Harper, 1957.

Boy Beneath the Sea (for children), with Mike Wilson. New York, Harper, 1958.

Voice across the Sea. London, Muller, 1958; New York, Harper, 1959; revised edition, London, Mitchell Beazley, and Harper, 1974.

The Challenge of the Spaceship: Previews of Tomorrow's World. New York, Harper, 1959; London, Muller, 1960.

The Challenge of the Sea. New York, Holt Rinehart, 1960; London, Muller, 1961.

The First Five Fathoms: A Guide to Underwater Adventure, with Mike Wilson. New York, Harper, 1960.

Indian Ocean Adventure, with Mike Wilson. New York, Harper, 1961; London, Barker, 1962.

Profiles of the Future: An Inquiry into the Limits of the Possible. London, Gollancz, 1962; New York, Harper, 1963; revised edition, New York, Harper, 1973; London, Gollancz, 1974, 1982; New York, Holt Rinehart, 1984.

Indian Ocean Treasure, with Mike Wilson. New York, Harper, 1964; London, Sidgwick and Jackson, 1972.

Man and Space, with the editors of *Life.* New York, Time, 1964.

The Treasure of the Great Reef. London, Barker, and New York, Harper, 1964; revised edition, New York, Ballantine, 1974.

Voices from the Sky: Previews of the Coming Space Age. New York, Harper, 1965; London, Gollancz, 1966.

The Promise of Space. New York, Harper, and London, Hodder and Stoughton, 1968.

First on the Moon, with Neil Armstrong, Michael Collins, Edwin E. Aldrin, Jr., Gene Farmer, and Dora Jane Hamblin. London, Joseph, and Boston, Little Brown, 1970.

Beyond Jupiter: The Worlds of Tomorrow, with Chesley Bonestell. Boston, Little Brown, 1972.

The Lost Worlds of 2001. New York, New American Library, and London, Sidgwick and Jackson, 1972.

Report on Planet Three and Other Speculations. London, Gollancz, and New York, Harper, 1972.

The View from Serendip (on Sri Lanka). New York, Random House, 1977; London, Gollancz, 1978.

Ascent to Orbit: A Scientific Autobiography: The Technical Writings of Arthur C. Clarke. New York and Chichester, Sussex, Wiley, 1984.

1984: Spring: A Choice of Futures. New York, Ballantine, and London, Granada, 1984.

The Odyssey File, with Peter Hyams. New York, Ballantine, and London, Granada, 1985.

Astounding Days: A Science Fictional Autobiography. London, Gollancz, 1989; New York, Bantam, 1990.

Other

Islands in the Sky (for children). London, Sidgwick and Jackson, and Philadelphia, Winston, 1952; revised edition, Penguin, 1972.

Across the Sea of Stars. New York, Harcourt Brace, 1959.

From the Oceans, From the Stars. New York, Harcourt Brace, 1962.

Dolphin Island: A Story of the People of the Sea (for children). New York, Holt Rinehart, and London, Gollancz, 1963.

An Arthur C. Clarke Omnibus. London, Sidgwick and Jackson, 1965.

Prelude to Mars. New York, Harcourt Brace, 1965.

Editor, *Time Probe: The Science in Science Fiction.* New York, Delacorte Press, 1966; London, Gollancz, 1967.

Editor, *The Coming of the Space Age: Famous Accounts of Man's Probing of the Universe.* London, Gollancz, and New York, Meredith, 1967.

The Lion of Comarre, and Against the Fall of Night. New York, Harcourt Brace, 1968; London, Gollancz, 1970.

A Second Arthur C. Clarke Omnibus. London, Sidgwick and Jackson, 1968.

Editor, *Three for Tomorrow.* Sphere, 1972.

Contributor, *Mars and the Mind of Man.* New York, Harper, 1973.

Technology and the Frontiers of Knowledge (lectures), with other. New York, Doubleday, 1973.

Four Great Science Fiction Novels. London, Gollancz, 1978.

Editor, with George Proctor, *The Science Fiction Hall of Fame 3: The Nebula Winners 1965-1969.* New York, Avon, 1982.

Selected Works. Heinemann, 1985.

Editor, *July 20, 2019: A Day in the Life of the 21st Century.* New York, Macmillan, 1986; London, Grafton, 1987.

Arthur C. Clarke's Chronicles of the Strange and Mysterious, edited by Simon Welfare and John Fairley. San Francisco, Collins, 1987.

Editor, *Project Solar Sail.* New York, Penguin, 1990.

How the World Was One: Towards the Tele-family of Man. New York, Bantam, and London, Gollancz, 1992.

The Hammer of God. New York, Bantam, 1993.

Also author of introduction to *No Place Too Far;* of afterwords to Paul Preuss's *Venus Prime,* Volumes 1-6, Avon, 1988-91; of a movie treatment based on *Cradle;* contributor of over six hundred articles and short stories, occasionally under pseudonyms E. G. O'Brien and Charles Willis, to numerous magazines, including *Harper's, Playboy, New York Times Magazine, Vogue, Holiday,* and *Horizon.*

*

Media Adaptations: *A Fall of Moondust* (recording), Harcourt, 1976; *Arthur C. Clarke Reads from his 2001: A Space Odyssey* (recording), Caedmon, 1976; *The Nine Billion Names of God* (recording), Caedmon, 1978; *The Star* (recording), Caedmon, 1978; *Transit of Earth* (recording), Caedmon, 1978; *Childhood's End* (recording), 1979; *The Fountains of Paradise* (recording), Caedmon, 1979; *2010: Odyssey Two* (recording), Caedmon, 1983; *2010* (film, directed by Peter Hyams), MGM, 1984; *The Star* (television movie), CBS-TV, 1985. *Childhood's End, The Songs of Distant Earth, The Fountains of Paradise,* and *Cradle* have all been optioned for films.

Biography: Essay in *Authors and Artists for Young Adults,* Volume 4, Detroit, Gale, 1990.

Bibliography: *Arthur C. Clarke: A Primary and Secondary Bibliography* by David N. Samuelson. Boston, Hall, 1984.

Manuscript Collection: Mugar Memorial Library, Boston University.

Critical Study: Entry in *Contemporary Literary Criticism,* Volume 1, Detroit, Gale, 1973; Volume 4, 1975; Volume 13, 1980; Volume 16, 1981; Volume 18, 1981; Volume 35, 1985; *Arthur C. Clarke* edited by Joseph D. Olander and Martin H. Greenberg, New York, Taplinger, and Edinburgh, Harris, 1977; *The Space Odysseys of Arthur C. Clarke* by George Edgar Slusser, San Bernardino, California, Borgo Press, 1978; *Arthur C. Clarke* (includes bibliography) by Eric S. Rabkin, West Linn, Oregon, Starmont House, 1979, revised edition, 1980; *Against the Night, The Stars: The Science Fiction of Arthur C. Clarke* by John Hollow, New York, Harcourt Brace, 1983, revised edition, Athens, Ohio University Press-Swallow Press, 1987.

*   *   *

As the only novelist to win science fiction's coveted quartet—the Hugo, Nebula, Campbell, and Jupiter awards—for one work, *Rendezvous with Rama,* and as the co-creator of one of the more widely influential films of the twentieth century, *2001: A Space Odyssey,* Arthur C. Clarke is one of the most prophetic and significant writers in his chosen genre. Apart from his literary endeavors, however, Clarke may best be remembered as the inventor of the communication satellite, an idea he first expounded in a 1945 article entitled "Extraterrestrial Relays." Although Clarke writes mostly fiction, he has written several nonfiction books, including the book that first brought him national attention, *The Exploration of Space.* It is Clarke's emphasis on science fiction, however, that allows his writing to transcend conventional age barriers. It is easy to note that he focuses within his vast body of work on two simple themes: spiritualism and technology. A study of these aspects and their relationship with each other reveals the traits and methods which make up Clarke's writing.

The aspect of "spiritualism" is an important one to Clarke as he feels that the search for man's place in the universe is humankind's fundamental quest. This quest takes many forms throughout Clarke's prose but the most prevalent is the Phoenix-like rebirth of childhood. This "spiritual" rebirth may appear as either a physical or a psychological entity but, regardless of the manifestation, Clarke commonly conceives it with the aid of technology.

Since his background is in science and mathematics, Clarke's infatuation with technology is considerable. The scientific details of his writing are lavishly illustrated, and at times Clarke may even seem preoccupied with the science of his fiction. But Clarke's description of technology is flawless; he pays particular attention to minute aspects and in doing so promotes realism. The "tech-speak" Clarke uses allows the fictional worlds he creates to function not as mere settings but almost as characters unto themselves. This literal-minded utilization of technology coupled with the "spiritual" quest is the crux on which Clarke's writing is based.

Clarke's greatest literary success, *Rendezvous with Rama,* also functions as an excellent example of his blend of spiritualism and technology. The novel chronicles the attempts of a research team sent to investigate a cylindrical object hurtling through the solar system. The UFO is given the name "Rama" and is eventually discovered to be an alien ship, although its crew has long since vanished. As the research team searches for clues to Rama's purpose and origin, they function as an allegory for the human need to question the meaning of life, bringing into play Clarke's spiritual quest. The depiction of Rama is beautifully achieved, making the mystery and elusiveness of the ship's purpose all the more alluring.

In both its effect and scope, Clarke's cinematic collaboration with Stanley Kubrick, *2001: A Space Odyssey,* often considered the greatest modern science fiction film, stands as his masterpiece. Although novels such as *Childhood's End* and *Rendezvous with Rama* have garnered more literary praise than *2001,* it remains the title most associated with Clarke. With its heavy reliance on technology and the inclusion of a healthy dose of Clarke's spiritual quest, *2001* is also emblematic of his writing overall. The plot and structure are similarly indicative of Clarke's other novels, thus providing a glimpse of Clarke's intent in the whole of his work.

Both the film and novel versions of *2001: A Space Odyssey* began when Kubrick contacted Clarke and proposed the idea of making the "proverbial good science fiction movie." Intrigued by the concept, Clarke began proposing possible plots; the pair eventually agreed on Clarke's 1951 short story "The Sentinel" as the basis for the film. The process of writing *2001* was a unique one, whereas the novelization was written in lieu of a script thus binding the two works inexplicably together. A short while after the film came out, the novelization was released; despite being written in tandem, the two works differ in certain respects, most notably in the film's negation of explanatory dialogue which is replaced by Kubrick's stunning visuals, whereas in the novel Clarke's "tech-speak" is ever-present. Throughout the writing process the original story changed dramatically, and although the film bears little resemblance to "The Sentinel," the gist of Clarke's "spiritual" message is still intact.

Episodic in construction, *2001* is the chronicle of man's first contact with sentient life, other than that found on earth. In the first section of the film, appropriately titled "The Dawn of Man," the concept of the monolith is introduced. Apes, arduously beginning the process of evolution, are hungrily grazing about a barren wasteland, they have not yet learned to hunt and are merely foragers, when they come across a giant black slab from which an ear-piercing sound is emanating. One of the apes is taught, presumably by the monolith, to use an elongated piece of bone as a tool, and later as a weapon. Thus the apes are forcefully nudged into evolution. The film then progresses to the next stage in man's development in the year 2001, when another monolith is found, this time buried beneath the surface of the moon. When it is touched, it produces the same sound the apes had heard, except that the sound is now being directed towards Jupiter (another discrepancy between novel and film encroaches here, as the book substitutes Saturn for Jupiter). The next section of the film, "Jupiter Mission: 18 Months Later," chronicles two astronauts, Frank Poole and David Bowman, as they pilot their ship with the help of the super-computer HAL 9000 towards Jupiter, where the remaining members of the crew will be taken out of suspended animation and they will all be told the mission's objective. Subsequent malfunctions and accidents leave Bowman alone as the ship reaches Jupiter and he embarks on the final step in humankind's next developmental stage.

Through the monolith and Bowman's physical transformation, a tangible voice is given to Clarke's notion of the "spiritual" nature of humanity, and the quest for a metaphysical section of the universe to call humanity's own is the essence of Clarke's writing. The constant questioning of the bounds of the known is what makes Clarke's written journeys enthralling. In *2001,* although co-writing credit must be given to Kubrick, mainly for the visual impact of the film version and not the novelization, Clarke deftly conveys his fascination of "tech-speak" and his obsession with "spiritualism," making it the finest example of his literary genius.

—Michael J. Tyrkus

CLEAVER, (Leroy) Eldridge. American. Born in Wabbaseka, Arkansas, 31 August 1935. Educated at junior college; also educated in Soledad Prison. Married Kathleen Neal in 1967; one daughter and one son. Prisoner at Soledad Prison, 1954-57, 1958-66; assistant editor and contributing writer, *Ramparts,* San Francisco, California, 1966-68; minister of information, Black Panther Party, Oakland, California, 1967-71; presidential candidate, Peace and Freedom Party, 1968; in exile in Cuba, Algeria, and France, 1968-75; owner of boutique in Hollywood, California, 1978-79; founder of Eldridge Cleaver Crusades, 1979; independent candidate for Congress in 8th Congressional District, California, 1984; contributor to *Commonweal, National Review,* and other periodicals. Lecturer at universities. Recipient: Martin Luther King Memorial Prize, 1970, for *Soul on Ice.*

PUBLICATIONS

Nonfiction

Soul on Ice, introduction by Maxwell Geismar. New York, McGraw, 1968.
Eldridge Cleaver: Post-Prison Writings and Speeches, edited by Robert Scheer. New York, Random House, 1969.
Eldridge Cleaver's Black Papers. McGraw, 1969.
Author of introduction, *Do It!,* by Jerry Rubin. New York, Simon and Schuster, 1970.
Revolution in the Congo, with others. London, Revolutionary People's Communications Network, 1971.
Contributor, *The Black Panther Leaders Speak: Huey P. Newton, Bobby Seale, Eldridge Cleaver, and Company Speak Out through the Black Panther Party's Official Newspaper,* edited by G. Louis Heath. Metuchen, New Jersey, Scarecrow, 1976.
Soul on Fire. Waco, Texas, Word, 1978.

Also author, with others, of *War Within: Violence or Non-violence in Black Revolution,* 1971, of *Education and Revolution,* Center for Educational Reform, and of pamphlets for the Black Panther Party and People's Communication Network. Work appears in anthologies, including *Prize Stories, 1971: The O. Henry Awards.*

*

Critical Study: Entry in *Contemporary Literary Criticism,* Volume 30, Detroit, Gale, 1984.

*   *   *

Anger, outrage, the raw energy of the 1960s: these are the forces that burst from the pages of Eldridge Cleaver's *Soul on Ice,* a work widely popular among young adults during this time of social upheaval and civil-rights awareness. Published in 1968, this is not a series of somber disquisitions by a man in academic regalia. Quite the contrary. Here is a street-wise black, a man who has spent most of his adult life in California prisons, shouting into the faces of white Americans and telling them that a social revolution is at hand. No one doubts Cleaver's conviction, even if his literary credentials are unconventional.

Perhaps as much as anything, *Soul on Ice* has an odor—an odor of sweat, mean streets, sex, darkness, and blood. These are the qualities that triumph over Cleaver's uneven style. At times he is too learned, pedantic even, as if in compensation for his lack of formal education. In this mode he comments on the "man whose soul or emotional apparatus had lain dormant in a deadening limbo of desuetude...." At the other extreme, he errs in using the sassy harangue, as when he calls the public opinion makers "a lot of coffee-drinking, cigarette-smoking, sly, suck-assing, status-seeking, cheating, nervous, dry-balled, tranquillizer-gulched, countdown-minded, out-of-style, slithering snakes." At its best, though, Cleaver's style is stark, indisputable. "I became a rapist," he matter-of-factly states in his first section. And later, "...I started to write. To save myself."

Loosely divided into four sections, *Soul on Ice* begins with "Letters from Prison," an account of Cleaver's life behind bars, his conversion to the Muslim religion, and his devotion to Malcolm X. Throughout this section, one experiences the routine, the boredom, the hopes, and the politics of prison life. The second section, "Blood of the Beast," argues that dissatisfaction among American Negroes is part of a worldwide revolutionary spirit. Cleaver insists that black Americans should not participate in the Vietnam War; only "fools...go to another country to fight for something they don't have for themselves." The third section houses a series of poignant letters between Cleaver and his attorney, Beverly Axelrod, who ultimately rallies enough public support to gain the writer parole. "White Woman, Black Man," the book's final section, may be its least convincing intellectually, but its most powerful emotionally. What Cleaver grapples with is the enigma of myth itself, in this case the myth of the Black Man as all body, White Man as all mind; Black Woman as fecund domestic, White Woman as dream maiden. Cleaver ends with an endorsement of love—whether generalized in the form of brotherhood or particularized in the form of miscegenation—as the only solution to class conflict, the same conclusion that has been argued for Malcolm X.

Eldridge Cleaver: Post-Prison Writings and Speeches, edited by Robert Scheer and published in 1969, is less satisfying than *Soul on Ice*. From a literary perspective the essays show little craftsmanship, much anger, and a penchant for obscene grandstanding, as in the writer's famous four-letter response to then-governor of California Ronald Reagan. The reader should realize, however, that following Cleaver's release from prison in 1966, he fell under the influence of Huey P. Newton and joined the Black Panther Party, an organization which operated free lunch programs for some inner-city children but which also advocated "total liberty for black people or total destruction for America." Cleaver became the Panthers' Minister of Information and frequently found himself embroiled in disputes with the police and FBI, even as he was giving lectures on college campuses. Then in 1968, he was wounded in a gunfight between the Panthers and the Oakland, California, police. A curious charge of assault and attempted murder was followed by an outpouring of support from around the world. During this same period, the Peace and Freedom Party nominated Eldridge Cleaver to be their candidate for President of the United States. But Cleaver feared for his life. He had a solid defense against the Oakland indictments, but given the hostility and paranoia of the times, he doubted that he would survive another confinement. Someone would arrange to have him killed. He decided to jump bail and leave the country, a man on the run.

For the next seven years, Eldridge Cleaver visited such communist countries as Cuba, North Vietnam, China, and the Soviet Union, and lived more permanently in Algeria and France. Initially, he was regarded as a revolutionary hero, a spokesman for the disenfranchised blacks of the world. As the years passed, however, he became increasingly disillusioned with the communism he saw actually being practiced. Suicide was never far from his mind. Then he had a Christian mystical experience. *Soul on Fire,* published in 1978, is Cleaver's autobiography of his exile. The book concludes with his return to the United States, where a possible prison sentence is reduced to twelve hundred hours of community service.

Since 1975 Eldridge Cleaver has been an active lecturer at universities and churches, telling the story of his life. His message is that secular zeal is not incompatible with religious zeal. *Soul on Fire* is neither as incendiary nor as immediate as *Soul on Ice,* and yet to those who would charge him with selling out his earlier principles, Cleaver writes that "communism had nothing to offer me but another chapter in tyranny." His more careful followers remember that love is an essential focal point in *Soul on Ice.* Cleaver the Muslim and Cleaver the Christian meet at that point.

—Walker Rutledge

CLEAVER, Vera and Bill. Americans. **Vera Cleaver (née Allen):** Born in Virgil, South Dakota, 6 January 1919. Educated at schools in Kennebec, South Dakota, and Perry and Tallahassee, Florida. Married Bill Cleaver in 1945. Free-lance accountant, 1945-54; accountant (civilian), United States Air Force, Tachikawa, Japan, 1954-56, and Chaumont, France, 1956-58. *Died 11 August 1992.* **Bill Cleaver (William Joseph Cleaver):** Born in Hugo, Ohio, 24 March 1920. Educated at schools in Vancouver, British Columbia, and Seattle, WA. Served in the United States Army Air Corps, in Italy, 1942-45; United States Air Force, in Japan, 1954-56, and in France, 1956-58. Jeweler and watchmaker, 1950-54. *Died 20 August 1981.* Recipients: (Vera Cleaver) Children's Choice Award, 1986, for *Sweetly Sings the Donkey;.* (Vera and Bill Cleaver) Recipients: *Horn Book* Honor List, 1967, for *Ellen Grae; Horn Book* Honor List, 1969, American Library Association (ALA) notable book, 1970, Newbery Honor Book, and National Book award nomination, all for *Where the Lilies Bloom;* National Book award nomination, 1971, for *Grover; New York Times* outstanding book, ALA notable book, 1973, for *Me Too;* National Book award nomination, 1974, all for *The Whys and Wherefores of Littabelle Lee;* Golden Spur award, Western Writers of America, and Lewis Carroll Bookshelf award, and *New York Times* outstanding book citation, all 1975, all for *Dust of the Earth;* Western Writers of America Spur award, 1976. National Book award nomination, 1979, for *Queen of Hearts.*

PUBLICATIONS FOR YOUNG ADULTS

Fiction

Ellen Grae, illustrated by Ellen Raskin. Philadelphia, Lippincott, 1967; with *Lady Ellen Grae,* London, Hamish Hamilton, 1973.
Lady Ellen Grae, illustrated by E. Raskin, Philadelphia, Lippincott, 1968; with *Ellen Grae,* London, Hamish Hamilton, 1973.
Where the Lilies Bloom, illustrated by Jim Spanfeller. Philadelphia, Lippincott, 1969; London, Hamish Hamilton, 1970.
Grover, illustrated by Frederic Marvin. Philadelphia, Lippincott, 1970; London, Hamish Hamilton, 1971.

The Mimosa Tree. Philadelphia, Lippincott, 1970; London, Oxford University Press, 1977.

I Would Rather Be a Turnip. Philadelphia, Lippincott, 1971; London, Hamish Hamilton, 1972.

The Mock Revolt. Philadelphia, Lippincott, 1971; London, Hamish Hamilton, 1972.

Delpha Green and Company. Philadelphia, Lippincott, 1972; London, Collins, 1975.

Me Too. Philadelphia, Lippincott, 1973; London, Collins, 1975.

The Whys and Wherefores of Littabelle Lee. New York, Atheneum, 1973; Hamish Hamilton, 1974.

Dust of the Earth. Philadelphia, Lippincott, 1975; London, Oxford University Press, 1977.

Trial Valley. Philadelphia, Lippincott, and London, Oxford University Press, 1977.

Queen of Hearts. Philadelphia, Lippincott, 1978.

A Little Destiny. New York, Lothrop, 1979.

The Kissimmee Kid. New York, Lothrop, 1981.

Hazel Rye. New York, Lippincott, 1983.

Fiction by Vera Cleaver

Sugar Blue, illustrated by Eric Nones. New York, Lothrop, 1984.

Sweetly Sings the Donkey. New York, Lippincott, 1985.

Moon Lake Angel. New York, Lothrop, 1987.

Belle Pruitt. New York, Lippincott, 1988.

PUBLICATIONS FOR ADULTS

Novel by Vera Cleaver

The Nurse's Dilemma. New York, Bouregy, 1966.

*

Media Adaptations: *Where the Lilies Bloom* (film), United Artists, 1974.

Manuscript Collections: Kerlan Collection, University of Minnesota, Minneapolis; University of North Carolina, Chapel Hill.

Illustrator (Bill Cleaver): *Follow the Zookeeper* by Patricia Relf, 1984; *The Case of the Missing Mother* by James Howe, 1983.

Biography: Entry in *Dictionary of Literary Biography,* Detroit, Gale, Volume 52: *American Writers for Children since 1960: Fiction* by Jane Harper Yarbrough. Detroit, Gale, 1986, pp. 91-97.

Critical Study: Entry in *Children's Literature Review,* Volume 6. Detroit, Gale, 1984.

*   *   *

Together Vera and Bill Cleaver were known for their novels for young adult readers on contemporary themes that are full of humor, imagination, and a zest for life. After Bill Cleaver's death, Vera Cleaver continued to write these books that have strong characters, rural and largely poverty-stricken settings, and real family groups.

The Cleavers' first book, *Ellen Grae,* was an immediate success. Eleven-year-old Ellen Grae is the sort of girl who takes off her starched petticoat after she gets to school and stuffs it in her desk because she doesn't like scratchy things. She lives with Mr. and Mrs. McGruder outside the village of Thicket because her mother and father are divorced. Ellen Grae has a special friend in Ira, a gentle person who lives with his pet goat Missouri in a tin shack by the river. Ira sells boiled and parched peanuts for a living and cannot seem to talk to anyone but Ellen Grae. When Ira tells Ellen Grae a violent secret of his childhood, she is faced with a real dilemma. Telling that secret will get Ira in terrible trouble. The young girl's sense of compassion and her sense of justice are beautifully described, and the outcome in a small compassionate community is a just one.

A courageous and strong fourteen-year-old girl struggles to preserve the dignity and independence of her family after the death of her parents, in *Where the Lilies Bloom.* Set in the Great Smoky Mountains of North Carolina—land described in an old hymn as "Where the Lilies Bloom So Fair"—it tells the story of human resourcefulness against the harshness of poverty and isolation. Mary Call, after burying her second parent in a tender, homemade service, must conceal his death from those who would send the four children to the county home. She also cares for a developmentally disabled older sister, goes to school, and supports the family. She does the latter by "wildcrafting," gathering medicinal plants and herbs on the slopes of the Great Smokies and selling them to pharmaceutical companies. The difficult and exhausting work provides a fair living and a unique education for a family. This gentle tale of adversity and love celebrates life.

The Mock Revolt is set in the town of Medina, Florida, and features thirteen-year old Ussy Mock, whose ambition in life is to get away from the deadly dullness of his town and family. He aims to earn enough money to buy a motorcycle so that he may travel to Pensacola, New Orleans, San Antonio, and San Francisco. When he gets to San Francisco, things do not work out the way he plans. Ussy meets up with a migrant labor family and the harsh realities of poverty. His own dreams of independence take second place to his sense of fairness and his need to help this family.

Belle Pruitt, written by Vera Cleaver, is about an eleven-year-old who is a gold-star student as long as she isn't asked to do anything creative. To create is not a part of her nature; she thinks that when she grows up she may become a reporter of facts. Belle's ordinary world turns upside down when her little brother dies of pneumonia and her spirited mother withdraws into a silent world. No one seems able to help her mother or pull the family back together. Belle realizes that she alone must take on the task, and she does so by transforming a weedlot into a beautiful garden. The wonderful new life which is emerging she hopes will help her mother recover.

In their books, the Cleavers juxtaposed the world of the prosperous and the less-fortunate, yet both possessed dignity. A number of their characters have deficits—they can't learn arithmetic, they are no good at English composition, they are unable to reason adequately—but these people are not pitiable because they find they do have some strengths and often others come forward to support them. It is not an idealized world, but one that by and large is compassionate and just.

—Mary Lystad

CLEMENTS, Bruce. American. Born in New York City, 25 November 1931. Educated at Columbia University, New York, A.B. 1954; Union Theological Seminary, New York, B.D. 1956; State University of New York, Albany, M.A. 1962. Married Hanna Charlotte Margarete Kiep in 1954; one son and three daughters. Ordained Minister of the United Church of Christ: pastor in Schenectady, New York, 1957-64; instructor, Union College, Schenectady, New York, 1964-67. Recipient: Nominated for the National Book Award, 1974, for *I Tell a Lie Every So Often.* Address: Department of English, Eastern Connecticut State College, Willimantic, CT 06226, U.S.A.

PUBLICATIONS FOR YOUNG ADULTS

Fiction

Two against the Tide. New York, Farrar Straus, 1967.
The Face of Abraham Candle. New York, Farrar Straus, 1969.
I Tell a Lie Every So Often. New York, Farrar Straus, 1974.
Prison Window, Jerusalem Blue. New York, Farrar Straus, 1977.
Anywhere Else But Here. New York, Farrar Straus, 1980.
Coming About. New York, Farrar Straus, 1984.
The Treasure of Plunderell Manor. New York, Farrar Straus, 1987.
Tom Loves Anna Loves Tom. New York, Farrar Straus, 1990.

Other

From Ice Set Free: The Story of Otto Kiep. New York, Farrar Straus, 1972.
Coming Home to a Place You've Never Been Before, with Hanna Clements. New York, Farrar Straus, 1975.

*

Biography: Essay in *Speaking for Ourselves, Too* compiled and edited by Donald R. Gallo, National Council of Teachers of English, 1993.

Bruce Clements comments:

More than anything else, I am interested in the courage of ordinary young people, in the things they do to make their lives work and have meaning. The most important question I ask about any character, first and last, is: *What does he or she want?* If I can keep that clear to myself, and if I know the world in which that character has to act—its limitations, its possibilities—the story will come.

*   *   *

Bruce Clements's concern with moral order and his interest in teaching come through very clearly in his writings for young persons. Both his fiction and nonfiction strongly emphasize man's responsibility to his fellow man and society's need to support other societies. His writing style is crisp and clear; in a few words and phrases Clements conjures up vivid images of people, places, and times in conflict.

His novel *Two against the Tide* is a fantasy, set on an island near the coast of Maine. A community of middle-aged and elderly persons have stopped aging physically through a life-preserving drug discovered one hundred years before by a physician. Into this "utopia" come a brother and sister. The children must decide, after a

summer on the island, whether or not to remain there and accept perpetual youth. The characters are sharply drawn; the plot is well paced, wise, and witty.

The Face of Abraham Candle is set in the Colorado of silver-mining days and focuses upon a young adolescent, suddenly orphaned and restless for adventure, who explores the caves of Mesa Verde in search of Indian relics. *Prison Window, Jerusalem Blue* focuses on a ninth-century English girl and her brother who are captured by Viking sailors and carried away to Denmark to become slaves. *Coming About,* set in the present, is a story of a young adolescent who is a loner and a mechanical genius, who thinks a lot about war and peace. To most of his peers he is "weird," but to one who becomes his friend, he is a complex individual trying to find, amidst good and evil, a meaningful place in his world.

The Treasure of Plunderell Manor is a fast-paced adventure tale, set in nineteenth-century England. A fourteen-year-old orphan girl begins a new job as maid to a seventeen-year-old orphan heiress, whose aunt and uncle keep her imprisoned in a tower room. The wicked aunt and uncle order the servant girl to spy on her mistress so as to discover the whereabouts of her family's hidden treasures. When instead, the servant and mistress become friends, the aunt and uncle plot to murder them both. Servant and mistress work together to prevent the aunt and uncle's evil schemes. It is the servant girl who finds the family treasures, secures her mistress's future, and in so doing secures her own as well. This book abounds with good and evil characterizations, chases and hair-raising escapes. Its ending is surprising and sensitive.

Tom Loves Anna Loves Tom is an honest and direct, modern-day love affair. It deals with aspects of adolescent affairs which are of great concern to teenagers: love and friendship, acquaintance rape, abortion. The book celebrates a love-at-first-sight relationship—tender and giving—between two sixteen-year-olds. All boy-girl relationships Tom and Anna know about, though, are not that successful. Acquaintance rape, as seen by both the victim and the victimizer, in its short and long-term effects, is poignantly presented. Abortion, as it affects a teenage mother and father, as well as adult relatives, is shown candidly and without rancor. There are other parts of this book that are moving and meaningful—adolescent relationships to pesky siblings, to parents, to elderly relatives. Of all Clements's books, this one may most closely touch young adult readers about to enter the twenty-first century.

Among the works of nonfiction, *From Ice Set Free* is a biography of Clements's father-in-law, a German raised in Scotland who was hanged by the Nazis in Berlin in 1944 as a resister to their regime. *Coming Home to a Place You've Never Been Before* is a documentary account of twenty-four hours in a halfway house for ex-junkies and ex-drug pushers.

Each of Clements's books shows considerable research; the historical and geographical backgrounds are detailed and complex. But more, the books show an understanding of persons living out their lives within the boundaries of special cultures, with their own needs and goals placed in juxtaposition to group demands and limitations. Clements is not easy reading, but he is worth the effort. His stories are powerful, with strong characters facing basic human choices.

—Mary Lystad

COATSWORTH, Elizabeth (Jane). American. Born in Buffalo, New York, 31 May 1893. Educated at Park Street School, 1899-1907; Los Robles School, Pasadena, California, 1907-09; Buffalo Seminary, 1909-11; Vassar College, Poughkeepsie, New York, B.A. 1915 (Phi Beta Kappa); Columbia University, New York, M.A. 1916; Radcliffe College, Cambridge, Massachusetts. Married Henry Beston in 1929 (died 1968); two daughters. Author and poet. Recipient: Newbery Medal, American Library Association, 1931, for *The Cat Who Went to Heaven;* Children's Spring Book Festival Honor award, 1940, for *The Littlest House,* and 1971, for *Under the Green Willow;* New England Poetry Club Golden Rose, 1967; Child Study Association of America Children's Books of the Year, 1968, for *Bob Bodden and the Good Ship Rover* and *The Lucky Ones: Five Journeys toward a Home,* 1971, for *The Snow Parlor and Other Bedtime Stories,* 1972, for *Good Night,* 1973, for *The Wanderers,* 1974, for *All-of-a-Sudden Susan,* and 1975, for *Marra's World;* Hans Christian Andersen award Highly Commended Author (U.S.), 1968; Kerlan award, University of Minnesota, 1975, for "recognition of singular attainments in the creation of children's literature." *Door to the North: A Saga of Fourteenth Century America, The Princess and the Lion,* and *The Sparrow Bush: Rhymes* were selected for the *Horn Book* honor list. Litt.D., University of Maine, Orono, 1955; L.H.D., New England College, Henniker, New Hampshire, 1958. *Died 31 August 1986.*

PUBLICATIONS FOR YOUNG ADULTS

Fiction

Toutou in Bondage, illustrated by Thomas Handforth. New York, Macmillan, 1929.
The Boy with the Parrot: A Story of Guatemala, illustrated by Wilfred Bronson. New York, Macmillan, 1930.
Knock at the Door, illustrated by Francis D. Bedford. New York, Macmillan, 1931.
Cricket and the Emperor's Son, illustrated by Weda Yap. New York, Macmillan, 1932; revised edition, illustrated by Juliette Palmer, Surrey, World's Work, 1962.
Away Goes Sally, illustrated by Helen Sewell. New York, Macmillan, 1934; London, Woodfield, 1955; revised edition, illustrated by Caroline Sharpe, London, Blackie, 1970.
The Golden Horseshoe, illustrated by Robert Lawson. New York, Macmillan, 1935; revised edition, as *Tamar's Wager,* illustrated by R. Payne, London, Blackie, 1971.
Sword of the Wilderness, illustrated by Harve Stein. New York, Macmillan, 1936; London, Blackie, 1972.
Alice-All-by-Herself, illustrated by Marguerite de Angeli. New York, Macmillan, 1937; London, Harrap, 1938.
Dancing Tom, illustrated by Grace Paull. New York, Macmillan, 1938; London, Combridge, 1939.
Five Bushel Farm, illustrated by Helen Sewell. New York, Macmillan, 1939; London, Woodfield, 1958.
The Fair American, illustrated by Helen Sewell. New York, Macmillan, 1940; revised edition, illustrated by Caroline Sharpe, London, Blackie, 1970.
The Littlest House, illustrated by Marguerite Davis. New York, Macmillan, 1940; Kingswood, Surrey, World's Work, 1958.
A Toast to the King, illustrated by Forrest Orr. New York, Coward, 1940; London, Dent, 1941.
Tonio and the Stranger: A Mexican Adventure, illustrated by Wilfred Bronson. New York, Grosset, 1941.

You Shall Have a Carriage, illustrated by Henry Pitz. New York, Macmillan, 1941.
Forgotten Island, illustrated by Grace Paull. New York, Grosset, 1942.
Houseboat Summer, illustrated by Marguerite Davis. New York, Macmillan, 1942.
The White Horse, illustrated by Helen Sewell. New York, Macmillan, 1942; as *The White Horse of Morocco,* illustrated by Caroline Sharpe, London, Blackie, 1973.
Thief Island, illustrated by John Wonsetler. New York, Macmillan, 1943.
Twelve Months Makes a Year (stories), illustrated by Marguerite Davis. New York, Macmillan, 1943.
The Big Green Umbrella, illustrated by Helen Sewell. New York, Grosset, 1944.
Trudy and the Tree House, illustrated by Marguerite Davis. New York, Macmillan, 1944.
The Kitten Stand, illustrated by Kathleen Keeler. New York, Grosset, 1945.
The Wonderful Day, illustrated by Helen Sewell. New York, Macmillan, 1946; illustrated by Caroline Sharpe, London, Blackie, 1973.
Plum Daffy Adventure, illustrated by Marguerite Davis. New York, Macmillan, 1947; Kingswood, Surrey, World's Work, 1965.
Up Hill and Down: Stories, illustrated by James Davis. New York, Knopf, 1947.
The House of the Swan, illustrated by Kathleen Voute. New York, Macmillan, 1948; Kingswood, Surrey, World's Work, 1959.
The Little Haymakers, illustrated by Grace Paull. New York, Macmillan, 1949.
The Captain's Daughter, illustrated by Ralph Ray. New York, Macmillan, 1950; London, Collier Macmillan, 1963.
American Adventures 1620-1945, illustrated by Robert Frankenburg. New York, Macmillan, 1968.
First Adventure, illustrated by Ralph Ray. New York, Macmillan, 1950.
The Wishing Pear, illustrated by Ralph Ray. New York, Macmillan, 1951.
Boston Belles, illustrated by Manning Lee. New York, Macmillan, 1952.
Aunt Flora, illustrated by Manning Lee. New York, Macmillan, 1953.
Old Whirlwind: A Story of Davy Crockett, illustrated by Manning Lee. New York, Macmillan, 1953.
The Sod House, illustrated by Manning Lee. New York, Macmillan, 1954.
Cherry Ann and the Dragon Horse, illustrated by Manning Lee. New York, Macmillan, 1955.
Door to the North: A Saga of Fourteenth Century America, illustrated by Frederick T. Chapman. Philadelphia, Winston, 1950; Kingswood, Surrey, World's Work, 1960.
Dollar for Luck, illustrated by George Hauman and Doris Hauman. New York, Macmillan, 1951; as *The Sailing Hatrack,* illustrated by Gavin Rowe, London, Blackie, 1972.
The Last Fort: A Story of the French Voyageurs, illustrated by Edward Shenton. Philadelphia, Winston, 1952; London, Hamish Hamilton, 1953.
The Giant Golden Book of Cat Stories with Kate Barnes, illustrated by Feodor Rojankovsky. New York, Simon & Schuster, 1953; London, Publicity Products, 1955.

The Giant Golden Book of Dog Stories, illustrated by Feodor Rojankovsky. New York, Simon & Schuster, 1953; London, Publicity Products, 1954.

Horse Stories with Kate Barnes, illustrated by Feodor Rojankovsky. New York, Simon & Schuster, 1954.

Hide and Seek, illustrated by Genevieve Vaughan-Jackson. New York, Pantheon, 1956.

The Peddler's Cart, illustrated by Zhenya Gay. New York, Macmillan, 1956; as *The Pedlar's Cart,* illustrated by Margery Gill, London, Blackie, 1971.

The Giant Golden Books of Dogs, Cats, and Horses (contains *Horse Stories, The Giant Golden Book of Cat Stories,* and *The Giant Golden Book of Dog Stories*), with Kate Barnes. New York, Simon & Schuster, 1957.

The Cave, illustrated by Allen Houser. New York, Viking, 1958; as *Cave of Ghosts,* London, Hamish Hamilton, 1971.

The Dog from Nowhere, illustrated by Don Sibley. Evanston, Illinois, Row, Peterson, 1958.

Down Tumbledown Mountain, illustrated by Aldren Watson. Evanston, Illinois, Row, Peterson, 1958.

You Say You Saw a Camel!, illustrated by Brinton Turkle. Evanston, Illinois, Row, Peterson, 1958.

Desert Dan, illustrated by Harper Johnson. New York, Viking, 1960; London, Harrap, 1963.

Lonely Maria, illustrated by Evaline Ness. New York, Pantheon, 1960; London, Hamish Hamilton, 1967.

Ronnie and the Chief's Son, illustrated by Stefan Martin. New York, and London, Macmillan, 1962.

Jon the Unlucky, illustrated by Esta Nesbitt. New York, Holt, 1964; Chalfont St. Giles, Buckinghamshire, Sadler, 1968.

The Hand of Apollo, illustrated by Robin Jacques. New York, Viking, 1965; Kingswood, Surrey, World's Work, 1967.

The Fox Friend, illustrated by John Hamberger. New York, Macmillan, 1966.

The Place, illustrated by Marjorie Auerbach. New York, Holt, 1966.

The Ox-Team, illustrated by Peter Warner. London, Hamish Hamilton, 1967.

Troll Weather, illustrated by Ursula Arndt. New York, Macmillan, 1967; Kingswood, Surrey, World's Work, 1968.

Lighthouse Island, illustrated by Symeon Shimin. New York, Norton, 1968.

George and Red, illustrated by Paul Giovanopoulos. New York, Macmillan, 1969.

They Walk in the Night, illustrated by Stefan Martin. New York, Norton, 1969.

The Wanderers, illustrated by Trina Schart Hyman. New York, Four Winds, 1972.

Daisy, illustrated by Judith Gwyn Brown. New York, Macmillan, 1973.

All-of-a-Sudden Susan, illustrated by Richard Cuffair. New York, Macmillan, 1974.

Marra's World, illustrated by Krystyna Truska. New York, Greenwillow, 1975.

Other

Runaway Home, with Mabel O'Donnell, illustrated by Gustaf Tenggren. Evanston, Illinois, Row, Peterson, 1942.

Editor, *Tales of the Gauchos,* by William Henry Hudson, illustrated by Henry C. Pitz. New York, Knopf, 1946.

Editor, *Indian Encounters: An Anthology of Stories and Poems,* illustrated by Frederick T. Chapman. New York, Macmillan, 1960.

The Princess and the Lion, illustrated by Evaline Ness. New York, Pantheon, 1963; illustrated by Tessa Jordan, Philadelphia, Pennsylvania, Hamilton, 1971.

Daniel Webster's Horses, illustrated by Cary. Champaign, Illinois, Garrard, 1971.

PUBLICATIONS FOR CHILDREN

Fiction

The Cat and the Captain, illustrated by Gertrude Kaye. New York, Macmillan, 1927; revised edition, illustrated by Berniece Loewenstein, 1974.

The Cat Who Went to Heaven, illustrated by Lynd Ward. New York, Macmillan, 1930; London, Dent, 1949.

Pika and the Roses, illustrated by Kurt Wiese. New York, Pantheon, 1959.

The Noble Doll, illustrated by Leo Politi. New York, Viking, 1961.

Jock's Island, illustrated by Lilian Obligado. New York, Viking, 1963; London, Angus & Robertson, 1965.

The Secret, illustrated by Don Bolognese. New York, Macmillan, 1965; Kingswood, Surrey, World's Work, 1967.

Chimney Farm Bedtime Stories, with husband, Henry Beston, illustrated by Maurice Day. New York, Holt, 1966.

Bess and the Sphinx (includes verse), illustrated by Bernice Loewenstein. New York, Macmillan, 1967; London, Blackie, 1974.

Bob Bodden and the Good Ship "Rover," illustrated by Ted Schroeder. Champaign, Illinois, Garrard, 1968; London, Watts, 1972.

The Lucky Ones: Five Journeys toward a Home, illustrated by Janet Doyle. New York, Macmillan, 1968.

Indian Mound Farm, illustrated by Fermin Rocker. New York, Macmillan, and London, Collier, Macmillan, 1969.

Bob Bodden and the Seagoing Farm, illustrated by Frank Aloise. Champaign, Illinois, Garrard, 1970; London, Watts, 1972.

Grandmother Cat and the Hermit, illustrated by Irving Boker. New York, Macmillan, 1970; as *Grandmother Cat,* London, Bodley Head, 1971.

The Snow Parlor and Other Bedtime Stories, illustrated by Charles Robinson. New York, Grosset, 1971.

Under the Green Willow, illustrated by Janina Domanska. New York, Macmillan, 1971.

Good Night, illustrated by Jose Aruego. New York, Macmillan, 1972.

Pure Magic, illustrated by Ingrid Fetz. New York, Macmillan 1973; as *The Werefox,* New York, Collier, 1975; as *The Fox Boy,* London, Blackie, 1975.

Poetry

Night and the Cat, illustrated by Fougita. New York, Macmillan, 1950.

Mouse Chores, illustrated by Genevieve Vaughan-Jackson. New York, Pantheon, 1955.

The Peaceable Kingdom and Other Poems, illustrated by Fritz Eichenberg. New York, Pantheon, 1958.

The Children Come Running, illustrated by Roger Duvoisin and others. New York, Golden Press, 1960.
The Sparrow Bush: Rhymes, illustrated by Stefan Martin. New York, Norton, 1966.
Down Half the World, illustrated by Zena Bernstein. New York, Macmillan, 1968.

Other

UNICEF Christmas Book. Huntsville, Alabama, UNICEF, 1960.
Reading Round Table, Blue Book: Stories by Elizabeth Coatsworth. edited by George Manolakes. Brooklyn, New York, American Book, 1965.
Reading Round Table, Green Book. Brooklyn, New York, American Book, 1965.

PUBLICATIONS FOR ADULTS

Novels

Here I Stay, illustrated by Edwin Earle. New York, Coward, 1938; London, Harrap, 1939.
The Trunk. New York, Macmillan, 1941.
The Enchanted: An Incredible Tale, illustrated by Robert Winthrop. New York, Pantheon, 1951; London, Dent, 1952.
Silky: An Incredible Tale, illustrated by John Carroll. New York, Pantheon, and London, Gollancz, 1953.
Mountain Bride: An Incredible Tale. New York, Pantheon, 1954.
The White Room, illustrated by George W. Thompson. New York, Pantheon, 1958; London, Dent, 1959.

Poetry

Fox Footprints. New York, Knopf, 1923.
Atlas and Beyond: A Book of Poems, illustrated by Harry Cimino. New York, Harper, 1924.
Compass Rose. New York, Coward, 1929.
Country Poems. New York, Macmillan, 1942.
Summer Green, illustrated by Nora S. Unwin. New York, Macmillan, 1948.
The Creaking Stair, illustrated by William A. Dwiggins. New York, Coward, 1949.
Poems, illustrated by Vee Guthrie. New York, Macmillan, 1957.

Other

The Sun's Diary: A Book of Days for Any Year. New York, Macmillan, 1929.
Mary's Song. Nash, 1938.
Country Neighborhood, illustrated by Hildegard Woodward. New York, Macmillan, 1944.
Maine Ways, illustrated by Mildred Coughlin. New York, Macmillan, 1947.
South Shore Town. New York, Macmillan, 1948.
Maine Memories. Brattleboro, Vermont, Stephen Greene, 1968.
Editor, *Especially Maine: The Natural World of Henry Beston from Cape Cod to the St. Lawrence.* Brattleboro, Vermont, Stephen Greene, 1970.
Personal Geography: Almost an Autobiography. Brattleboro, Vermont, Stephen Greene, 1976; London, Prior, 1979.

Media Adaptations: *The Cat Who Went to Heaven* (record or cassette), Newbery Award Records, 1969; *The Cat Who Went to Heaven* (filmstrip with cassette), Miller/Brody, 1970; *Bob Bodden and the Good Ship "Rover"* (filmstrip with cassette), Taylor Associates, 1970. *Away Goes Sally, The Cat Who Went to Heaven, The Enchanted, Here I Stay, Lonely Maria, Personal Geography, Princess and the Lion, Pure Magic,* and *Ronnie and the Chief's Son* have been adapted as talking books; *The Cat Who Went to Heaven, Country Neighborhood, The Enchanted, Good Night, Houseboat Summer, Last Fort, Mountain Bride, Old Whirlwind, Poems, Ronnie and the Chief's Son, Silky, Toast to the King, White Room, Wishing Pear,* and *Trunk* have been adapted as Braille books.

Manuscript Collections: Kerlan Collection, University of Minnesota, Minneapolis; Bowdoin College Library, Brunswick, Maine.

*   *   *

Elizabeth Coatsworth's imagination was as boundless as her pen was prolific. The author of some ninety books for children, Coatsworth wrote on such diverse subjects as Viking-raided Ireland (*The Wanderers*), the ancient inhabitants of the fjords and mountains in Norway (*Troll Weather*), and a city boy's summer in *Lighthouse Island.* Her vision encompassed lonely children and their search for independence, magic dolls, refugees, forests where animals can turn into people, and, above all, nature.

Although she travelled widely, the bulk of her work concerns America in all its phases. History books aside, she wrote of the desert, the plains, the mountains, Indians, pioneers, immigrants. But it is from Maine that her finest books have come, and in Maine that she found for decades the resources to create one lapidary tale after another.

Although born in 1893, the author continued to understand the perceptions of the young throughout her long writing career. One of her most successful themes is that of the lonely and different child learning to cope in an adverse world. *Lonely Maria* and *Grandmother Cat and the Hermit* both deal with this idea, as does *Marra's World* which combines the theme with Coatsworth's favorite setting—an island off the Maine Coast. With the subtle use of magic and fantasy, it conveys the mood of a legend. Marra is regarded as hopeless by her teacher and schoolmates and even by her father and grandmother: "Everything about her life bewildered her." But when it comes to nature, Marra excels. She knows everything about the island. Gradually, with the help of a friend, she accepts herself as different, and the enchantment begins. Marra's mother is Nerea, a seal who was human for a time and who returned to the sea. Here, and in *The Enchanted,* Coatsworth touches on the ancient mythic theme where one being is able to work extraordinary changes for love of another.

Coatsworth reached her apogee in her nature writing, notably "The Incredible Tales" tetralogy about New England originally written for adults. As critic Edmund Fuller observes: "As with all Miss Coatsworth's work, *Silky* is a poet's book, mystic, delicate, lovely. With these 'Incredible Tales' she has created a rich, fresh medium that is at once original and yet the revival of a tradition neglected or distorted in this material age." *The Enchanted,* the best of the four, begins: "There is in northern Maine a township or, as they say here, a 'plantation,' called the Enchanted. It lies in the heart of the forest country and is seldom entered except by lumbermen bound for some winter logging camp from which they return with curious stories." A young man, David Ross, decides to try farming and buys a place right next to the Enchanted. His neighbors are a warm, closely knit family named Perdry, and he falls in love with one of the daughters and marries her. For their honeymoon they camp in the forest: "The stream seemed to sing its continual braided song especially for them, and the big pine sheltered them as though it liked them. They sat for many hours between its curving roots, their backs to its wide trunk, looking out at the water flowing by, always new water, and new ripples of light, yet always essentially the same stream catching the sunlight in the same net of motion." The magic in this tale and in Coatsworth's others is not arbitrary. It is all planned, provided for. Her special gift was the weaving together of a local story and her own vivid characters. The events that conclude *The Enchanted,* the metamorphosis of the Perdrys, are at once anticipated and surprising.

It was Coatsworth's intention to instruct through her stories, but she was never pedantic. The works do not come together with quite the ease of a folktale that has been repeated from generation to generation, but are a combination of good New England common sense and modern legend. In *All-of-a-Sudden Susan,* building a feeling of danger, Coatsworth writes: "Everything was uneasy, except people, who are always the last to notice what's happening around them." A weakened dam bursts in a storm and Susan is carried away on the flood with her magic doll, Emelida, who talks to her. Susan sees uprooted houses, bloated animals, even a dead woman. "You can't keep people from dying," Emelida comforts her. "They do it all the time and we may be doing it, too, for all we know. But meantime, enjoy yourself."

The Sod House follows immigrants from their arrival in Boston to the settling of a community in Kansas. The New England Emigrant Aid Society helps the Traubels buy land on the Osage River. They are not welcome as Northerners at a time when North and South are angling for control of the territory. Political reasons are carefully explained. The Indians the Traubels meet are portrayed solemnly and informatively (Coatsworth was always interested in their way of life), and Ilse, the child in the story, is allowed to fulfill her possibilities, as are most of Coatsworth's fictive children.

The Lucky Ones, a collection of five stories about the homeless and the stateless from different parts of the world—Tibet, Algeria, Rwanda, Hungary, and Hong Kong—explains why they are refugees, and describes the adversity they meet in trying to adjust to another way of life. Each story is preceded by a poem, and while in some cases the political background is not given enough detail, the children in the stories, and the children who read them, are treated with the respect that marks all Coatsworth's work.

Using her considerable creativeness and knowledge, her love of the natural world, and her regard for children, Coatsworth was responsible for consistently fine literature for readers whose imaginations are as young and fresh as her own was.

—Angela Wigan

COBALT, Martin. See **MAYNE, William (James Carter).**

COFFEY, Brian. See **KOONTZ, Dean R.**

COLE, Brock. American. Born in Charlotte, Michigan, 29 May 1938. Educated at Kenyon College, Gambier, Ohio, B.A. University of Minnesota, Minneapolis, Ph.D. Married; two sons. Instructor in English composition, University of Minnesota; instructor in philosophy, University of Wisconsin until 1975. Since 1975 writer and illustrator. Recipient: Juvenile award, Friends of American Writers, 1980, for *The King at the Door;* California Young Reader Medal, California Reading Association, 1985, and Young Readers' Choice award, Pacific Northwest Library Association, both for *The Indian in the Cupboard,* which was also named a *New York Times* outstanding book, 1981; Smarties "Grand Prix" for children's books, Book Trust, 1985, for *Gaffer Samson's Luck;* Parent's Choice award, Parent's Choice Foundation, 1986, for *The Giant's Toe;* Carl Sandburg award, Friends of Chicago Public Library, 1988, for *The Goats,* which was also named a *New York Times* notable book, an American Library Association (ALA) best book for young adults, and an ALA notable book, all 1987. Address: 309 Highland Ave., Buffalo, NY 14222-1750, U.S.A.

PUBLICATIONS FOR YOUNG ADULTS

Fiction

The King at the Door, self-illustrated. Garden City, New York, Doubleday, 1979.
The Winter Wren, self-illustrated. New York, Farrar, Straus, 1984.

Novels

The Goats. New York, Farrar, Straus, 1987.
Celine. New York, Farrar, Straus, 1989.

PUBLICATIONS FOR CHILDREN

Fiction

No More Baths, self-illustrated. Garden City, New York, Doubleday, 1980.
Nothing but a Pig, self-illustrated. Garden City, New York, Doubleday, 1981.
The Giant's Toe, self-illustrated. New York, Farrar, Straus, 1986.
Alpha and the Dirty Baby. New York, Farrar, Straus, 1991.

*

Biography: Essay in *Speaking for Ourselves, Too* compiled and edited by Donald R. Gallo, National Council of Teachers of English, 1993.

Critical Study: Entry in *Children's Literature Review,* Volume 18, Detroit, Gale, 1989, pp. 81-85.

Illustrator: *The Indian in the Cupboard* by Lynne Reid Banks, New

York, Doubleday, 1980; *Gaffer Samson's Luck* by Jill Paton Walsh, New York, Farrar, Straus, 1984.

*   *   *

An accomplished artist and writer of picture books, Brock Cole turns to an older audience in his two young adult novels, *The Goats* and *Celine*. His watercolor illustrations on the books' hardcover jackets immediately wed the visual and the verbal, a combination that influences all of Cole's work.

In *Celine,* an artist opens her story by discussing her painting "Test Patterns" and struggles throughout the novel to create an apt, insightful self-portrait. Her brief infatuation with her next-door neighbor stems largely from the fact that he, too, is an artist who understands the powerful language of color and line. Cole masterfully uses the persona of a young adult artist to contrast the conflicting images of fine art and pop culture. When given the assignment to paint a portrait, Celine admires the realism achieved by a classmate. Ironically, the classmate mimics with remarkable success faces from photographs and magazine covers while Celine always pursues original artistic expression. Through the character of Celine, Cole presents the artist operating within her world and outside of it. Television and media images barrage Celine from all sides but she never allows them to overwhelm her. Rather, she asserts her individuality by controlling them. She "call[s] the remote control my zapper" and sprinkles her television viewing with social commentary and philosophical musings. A true artist, Celine sees her world, in all its discomfort, and chooses to affect it.

Cole realizes the young adult arena with veracity. A high school junior, Celine attends confusing parties, wonders about her so-called relationship with her self-identified boyfriend, rebels against her parents (even as she turns to them for assistance), and finds surprising comfort in her friendship with Jake, the neighbor's child. Cole renders Jake's juvenile concerns with equal authenticity; he turns to Celine for the stability and honesty he lacks at home.

Like Jake, the nameless protagonists in *The Goats* gain realistic dimension from their age-appropriate concerns. Their desire to be included by friends means they cannot comprehend their outcast standing. Once abandoned, they think of parents as their rescuers. They enter a summer camp for less privileged children and see the co-existence of comradery and conflict. As they grow toward understanding, Cole names the characters (Laura and Howie) and slowly empowers them with independence.

Like Celine, Laura and Howie rebel against the injustices they suffer without anger. Together they find the individual strength which will fortify. Celine and Jake undergo similar, though less dramatic, abandonment. Celine's parents are divorced and remarried; Jake's are on the verge of divorce. They feel disconnected until they risk connecting to each other. Jake becomes Celine's superhero, she his wise champion—like Laura and Howie, they hold on.

These two novels depict a disturbing reality in which children endure abandonment. The adults leave them behind to forage alone in the woods. Like Hansel and Gretel, they unite to succeed and return home. Though Celine's father demands her to "show a little maturity," Cole exposes adults as unreliable and immature. At the end of the novel, Celine nurtures not only Jake, but also prepares a homecoming for the adults—and her maturity surpasses theirs.

Brock Cole's array of commanding characters triumph over their problems by reaching out to each other. They hold on and bridge adversity with the strength of human relationships.

—Cathryn M. Mercier

COLLIER, Christopher and James Lincoln. Americans. **Christopher Collier:** Born in New York, New York, 29 January 1930. Educated at Clark University, Worcester, Massachusetts, B.A. 1951; Columbia University, New York, New York, M.A. 1955, Ph.D. 1964. Served in United States Army, 1952-54. Married 1) Virginia Wright in 1954, one son and one daughter; 2) Bonnie Bromberger in 1969, one son. Teacher, Julian Curtiss School, Greenwich, Connecticut, 1955-58; teacher of social studies, New Canaan High School, Connecticut, 1959-61; instructor in history, Columbia University, Teachers College, New York City, 1958-59; instructor, University of Bridgeport, Connecticut, 1961-64, assistant professor, 1964-67, associate professor, 1967-71, professor of history, 1971-78, David S. Day Professor of History, 1978-84, chairman of department, 1978-81. Since 1984 professor of history, University of Connecticut, Storrs. Visiting professor, New York University, 1974; visiting lecturer, Yale University, 1977 and 1981; chairman, Columbia University Seminar on Early American History, 1978-79. Director, National Endowment for the Humanities Summer Institute for College Teachers, 1989. Consultant to numerous public and private organizations, including museums, historical societies, law firms, public utilities, and text, trade, and scholarly publishers. Since 1985 Connecticut State Historian; member of various historical commissions. Address: 876 Orange Center Rd., Orange, CT 06477, U.S.A. **James Lincoln Collier:** Also writes as Charles Williams. Born in New York, New York, 27 June 1928. Educated at Hamilton College, Clinton, New York, A.B. 1950. Served in the United States Army, 1950-51. Married 1) Carol Burrows in 1952 (divorced), two sons; 2) Ida Karen Potash in 1983. Writer; magazine editor, 1952-58. Address: 71 Barrow St., New York, NY 10014, U.S.A.

Recipients (Christopher Collier and James Lincoln Collier): Newbery Honor Book, a Jane Addams Honor Book, and a finalist for a National Book award, all 1975, for *My Brother Sam Is Dead;* Notable Children's Trade Book in the Field of Social Studies by the National Council for Social Studies and the Children's Book Council, 1981 and 1982 respectively, for *Jump Ship to Freedom* and *War Comes to Willy Freeman;* Phoenix award, 1994, for *My Brother Sam Is Dead.*

Recipient (Christopher Collier): Institute for Studies in American Music fellowship, 1985; Christopher award, 1987, for *Decision in Philadelphia: The Constitutional Convention of 1787.*

Recipient (James Lincoln Collier): Child's Study Association Book award, 1971, for *Rock Star;* London *Observer* Book of the Year award and American Book award nomination, both for *The Making of Jazz: A Comprehensive History.*

PUBLICATIONS FOR YOUNG ADULTS

Historical Novels (Christopher Collier and James Lincoln Collier)

My Brother Sam Is Dead. New York, Four Winds, 1974.
The Bloody Country. New York, Four Winds, 1976.
The Winter Hero. New York, Four Winds, 1978.
Jump Ship to Freedom. New York, Delacorte, 1981.
War Comes to Willy Freeman. New York, Delacorte, 1983.
Who Is Carrie?. New York, Delacorte, 1984.

The Clock, illustrated by Kelly Maddox. New York, Delacorte, 1992.

Other (Christopher Collier)

Editor, *The Public Records of the State of Connecticut, 1802-03,* Volume 11, State Library of Connecticut, 1967.

Roger Sherman's Connecticut: Yankee Politics and the American Revolution. Middletown, Connecticut, Wesleyan University Press, 1971.

Connecticut in the Continental Congress. Chester, Connecticut, Pequot Press, 1973.

Roger Sherman: Puritan Politician. New Haven Colony Historical Society, 1976.

The Pride of Bridgeport: Men and Machines in the Nineteenth Century. Bridgeport Museum of Art, Science, and Industry, 1979.

The Literature of Connecticut History, with Bonnie B. Collier. Hartford, Connecticut Humanities Council, 1983.

Decision in Philadelphia: The Constitutional Convention of 1787, with James Lincoln Collier. New York, Random House, 1986.

Contributor to *Lyme Miscellany,* edited by George Willauer, Middletown, Connecticut, Wesleyan University Press, 1977; and *Long Island Sound: The People and the Environment,* Oceanic Society, 1978. Author of foreword to *Connecticut: A Bibliography of Its History,* edited by Roger Parks, Hanover, University Press of New England, 1986. Contributor to history and legal journals. Editor, *Monographs in British History and Culture,* 1967-72, and *Connecticut History Newsletter,* 1967-73.

Fiction (James Lincoln Collier)

The Teddy Bear Habit; or, How I Became a Winner, illustrated by Lee Lorenz. New York, Norton, 1967.

Rock Star. New York, Four Winds Press, 1970.

Why Does Everybody Think I'm Nutty?. New York, Grosset and Dunlap, 1971.

It's Murder at St. Basket's. New York, Grosset and Dunlap, 1972.

Rich and Famous: The Further Adventures of George Stable. New York, Four Winds Press, 1975.

Give Dad My Best. New York, Four Winds Press, 1976.

Planet Out of the Past. New York, Macmillan, 1983.

When the Stars Begin to Fall. New York, Delacorte, 1986.

Outside Looking In. New York, Macmillan, 1987.

The Winchesters. New York, Macmillan, 1988.

My Crooked Family. New York, Simon & Schuster, 1991.

The Clock, illustrated by Kelly Maddox. New York, Delacorte, 1992.

Nonfiction (James Lincoln Collier)

Cheers. New York, Avon, 1960.

Battleground: The United States Army in World War II. New York, Norton, 1965.

A Visit to the Fire House, photographs by Yale Joel. New York, Norton, 1967.

Which Musical Instrument Shall I Play?, photographs by Yale Joel. New York, Norton, 1969.

Danny Goes to the Hospital, photographs by Yale Joel. New York, Norton, 1970.

Practical Music Theory: How Music Is Put Together from Bach to Rock. New York, Norton, 1970.

The Hard Life of the Teenager. New York, Four Winds Press, 1972.

Inside Jazz. New York, Four Winds Press, 1973.

Jug Bands and Hand Made Music. New York, Grosset and Dunlap, 1973.

The Making of Man: The Story of Our Ancient Ancestors. New York, Four Winds Press, 1974.

Making Music for Money. New York, Watts, 1976.

CB. New York, Watts, 1977.

The Great Jazz Artists, illustrated by Robert Andrew Parker. New York, Four Winds Press, 1977.

Louis Armstrong: An American Success Story. New York, Macmillan, 1985.

Duke Ellington. New York, Macmillan, 1991.

PUBLICATIONS FOR ADULTS

Novels (James Lincoln Collier)

Somebody up There Hates Me. New York, Macfadden 1962.

Fires of Youth (as Charles Williams). London, Penguin, 1968.

Nonfiction (James Lincoln Collier)

The Hypocritical American: An Essay on Sex Attitudes in America. Indianapolis, Bobbs-Merrill, 1964.

The Fine Art of Swindling, with others, edited by Walter Brown Gibson. New York, Grosset and Dunlap, 1966.

Sex Education U.S.A.: A Community Approach, with others. New York, Sex Information and Education Council of the United States, 1968.

The Making of Jazz: A Comprehensive History. Boston, Houghton Mifflin, and London, Hart Davis MacGibbon, 1978.

Louis Armstrong: An American Genius. New York, Oxford University Press, 1983, as *Louis Armstrong: A Biography,* London, Joseph, 1984.

Decision in Philadelphia: The Constitutional Convention of 1787, with Christopher Collier. New York, Random House, 1986.

Duke Ellington. New York, Oxford University Press, and London, Joseph, 1987.

The Reception of Jazz in America; A New View. Brooklyn, Institute for Studies in American Music, Conservatory of Music, Brooklyn College of the City University of New York, 1988.

Benny Goodman and the Swing Era. New York, Oxford University Press, 1989.

The Rise of Selfishness in the United States. New York, Oxford University Press, 1991.

Jazz; the American Theme Song. New York, Oxford University Press, 1993.

*

Media Adaptations: *My Brother Sam Is Dead* has been adapted as a record, a cassette, and a filmstrip with cassette.

Biography: Entry in *Fifth Book of Junior Authors and Illustrators,* edited by Sally Holmes Holtze, New York, H.W. Wilson, 1983; essays in *Speaking for Ourselves: Autobiographical Sketches by Notable Authors of Books for Young Adults,* Volume 1, compiled and edited by Donald R. Gallo, National Council of Teachers of English, 1990.

Critical Studies: Entry in *Children's Literature Review,* Volume 3, Detroit, Gale, 1978, p. 44; entry in *Contemporary Literary Criticism,* Volume 30, Detroit, Gale, 1984, p. 70.

Manuscript Collection: Kerlan Collection, University of Minnesota, Minneapolis.

Christopher Collier comments:

The young adult books I write with my brother are intended to teach about important aspects of American history. They are as carefully researched as are the books I write for other historians. My brother, James, works just as hard to make our stories exciting and believable. It is our hope that young people will have a good time learning history so that they will remember it for the rest of their lives.

James Lincoln Collier comments:

It seems to me that the best audience for fiction in the United States is young people. Unimpressed by prizes and reviews, they read what they like, and to a surprising extent they like the best. That this is so is crucially important for American literature, for if these, the young, do not come to appreciate the best writing, there will a generation hence be no audience for literature; and soon after the great tradition of Melville, Hawthorne, James, Faulkner, Hemingway, and so many others will be dead.

*   *   *

Christopher Collier and James Lincoln Collier are a brother team of writers who are best known for two historical fiction trilogies about adolescents growing up in New England during the American Revolution and the early days of the Republic. Christopher (Kit), an American historian and professor, provides the historical theme and framework for the novels, while James (Jim), a musician, editor, and writer gives life to the characters and plot.

The Colliers have a clear purpose for writing their historical fiction: to teach history to potential learners by flinging "them into a living past." They believe that writers of historical fiction for young readers must perform "an act of creation that vivifies on paper scenes no longer replicable in concrete fact" (*ALAN Review,* Winter 1987, p. 5).

This combination of historian and writer has produced some of the most accurate, enjoyable-to-read, teachable historical fiction novels written for young adults. The first book of the Brother Sam trilogy, *My Brother Sam Is Dead,* won a Newbery honor for its hard recreation of fact and empathetic understanding of human relationships. Because many historians view the American War for Independence as much a civil war as a revolution, the Colliers selection of Redding, Connecticut, as the setting is appropriate not only because Christopher knows it well but also because the known number of Loyalists and Patriots there was about equal. Timmy, the twelve-year-old protagonist, reflects this division in his own thinking. He mentally switches sides numerous times in the novel, favoring at one time the Patriotism of his brother Sam who has run off to serve in the Continental army, and then the Loyalism to the Crown of his Tory father, and then switching back again. The novel makes it clear that the decision of which side to support was not an easy one. Timmy is caught up between the idealistic hero worship of Sam and his father Eliphalet's disapproval of a rebellion over no more than "a few pence in taxes." The novel shows a realistic relationship between a father and his sons. And, when Tim must become a man and take on the responsibility of caring for his mother and the family business, he finds his own private war to be no easier. The ironic conclusion of the novel may make some young readers wonder if any war is ever noble. Sam is arrested on a trumped-up charge of stealing cattle and shot by the Continental army he served so loyally and idealistically.

The next two books in this trilogy, *The Bloody Country* and *The Winter Hero,* also deal with the question of war as a solution to human problems. *Bloody Country* follows pioneers from Connecticut to the Wyoming Valley of Pennsylvania in a dispute that the two states eventually go to war over. The valley was awarded to Pennsylvania by Congress in 1782. Ben Buck, the young protagonist of the novel, his parents, his sister Annie and her husband, and the family slave Joe Mountain, half Indian and half black, are a part of the group of Connecticut settlers whom the Pennsylvanians are trying to dispossess. The Bucks have worked hard to make a life for themselves, building a flour mill on the banks of the Susquehanna near Wilkes Barre. If they are driven back to Connecticut they will lose all they own and their sacrifice will count for nought. Ben begins to realize that his only future is as a servant with no chance for a family or land. This causes him to reflect on the plight of Joe, attempting to look at him for the first time as a person rather than chattel. The book's theme is the balance between property values and the value of human life. It is full of action which leads from an Indian raid that kills Ben's mother to the flooding of the Susquehanna and the destruction of the mill. However, through all the action and the eventual positive outcome for the family, the difficult questions still remain unanswered.

The Winter Hero, the third book in the trilogy, is set in Massachusetts in 1878 during another rarely studied historical event—Shays' Rebellion. The Revolution is over, but laws passed in far-away Boston are making western Massachusetts farmers, who have no representatives, poorer while the rich are getting richer. The story is told through the eyes of twelve-year-old Justin Conkey and is filled with lessons in basic political economics that can be understood by young readers. Likewise, the concept of the importance of representation rather than conflict is a major theme. Although not as rich in interesting relationships as the first two novels, Justin's desire to be a hero is typical of an adolescent boy. Throughout the novel, even after he is forced to become a serving boy for a wealthy creditor, Major Mattoon, Justin continues to attempt to understand why some people can rule over others and why the power structure makes a few people rich at the expense of everyone else. As in the two earlier novels, the questions are left to the readers to answer.

The Arabus family trilogy is the second by the Collier brothers. It relates the story of blacks during the Revolution; the focus of these three novels is on the relationship of the Constitution to black Americans. *Jump Ship to Freedom,* the middle book of the trilogy which was written first, attempts to show how the sectional division over the slavery question affected the writing of the Constitution. The book introduces readers to Daniel, the son of Jack Arabus, whose story is told in book one, *War Comes to Willy Freeman.* Daniel is the slave of a cruel Stratford, Connecticut, couple who confiscate government bonds belonging to Dan's mother and hide them in a family Bible. Throughout the narrative Dan fights against his self-concept as a stupid "nigger," beginning to realize as the book progresses that his worth is not measured by his sale price and that he is as honest and honorable as anyone. Dan bravely follows his neighbor William Samuel Johnson to Philadelphia and the Constitutional Convention in an attempt to get his help in gaining some cash from U.S. notes given Dan's father for fighting in the Revolution. He meets up with Fatherscreft who has been charged with carrying a message from the Congress in New York to the Philadelphia Congress. Just before Fatherscreft dies he entrusts Dan with the message. Dan has learned from Fatherscreft that if the Convention fails the U.S. will probably fall apart and Dan's bonds will be worthless and he will be unable to purchase his or his mother's freedom. Ironically, however, he also learns that the message he is carrying includes a plan to continue slavery in all the states and unsettled wilderness south of the Ohio River.

Dan's story is continued in book three of the trilogy *Who is Carrie?* Carrie, who doesn't know where she came from, lives the life of a slave in New York City. During the story she thinks she learns who her parents were and, if she is right, she should not be a slave. Although she is powerless, she is never without hope. The importance of this book and the other five is that each asks some of the difficult questions of U.S. history in a way that adolescents cannot only grasp them, but come to understand the human importance of them.

—Arthea J.S. Reed

———————

COLMAN, Hila. Also writes as Teresa Crayder. American. Born in New York City. Educated at Radcliffe College, Cambridge, Massachusetts. Married Louis Colman in 1945; two sons. Publicity/promotion officer, Russian War Relief, New York, 1940-45; executive director, Labor Book Club, New York, 1945-47. Since 1949 free-lance writer. Member of Democratic Town Committee, Bridgewater, Connecticut; former member of Bridgewater Board of Education, Connecticut; chairperson of Zoning Board of Appeals, Bridgewater, Connecticut. Recipient: Child Study Committee award, 1962, for *The Girl from Puerto Rico*; Garden State Children's Book award, New Jersey Library Association, 1979, for *Nobody Has to Be a Kid Forever*. Address: 76 Hemlock Rd., Box 95, Bridgewater, CT 06752, U.S.A.

PUBLICATIONS FOR YOUNG ADULTS

Fiction

The Big Step. New York, Morrow, 1957.
A Crown for Gina. New York, Morrow, 1958.
Julie Builds Her Castle. New York, Morrow, 1959.
Best Wedding Dress. New York, Morrow, 1960.
The Girl from Puerto Rico. New York, Morrow, 1961.
Mrs. Darling's Daughter. New York, Morrow, 1962.
Watch That Watch. New York, Morrow, 1962; Kingswood, Surrey, World's Work, 1963.
Peter's Brownstone House, illustrated by Leonard Weisgard. New York, Morrow, 1963.
Phoebe's First Campaign. New York, Morrow, 1963.
Cathy and Lisette (as Teresa Crayder), illustrated by Evelyn Copelman. New York, Doubleday, 1964.
Classmates by Request. New York, Morrow, 1964.
Christmas Cruise. New York, Morrow, 1965.
The Boy Who Couldn't Make up His Mind. New York, Macmillan, 1965.
Bride at Eighteen. New York, Morrow, 1966.

Dangerous Summer. New York, Bantam, 1966.
Sudden Fame (as Teresa Crayder). New York, Macmillan, 1966.
Thoroughly Modern Millie (novelization of screenplay). Bantam, 1966.
Car-Crazy Girl. New York, Morrow, 1967.
Mixed-Marriage Daughter. New York, Morrow, 1968.
Something out of Nothing, illustrated by Sally Trinkle. New York, Weybright and Talley, 1968.
Andy's Landmark House, illustrated by Fermin Rocker. New York, Parents' Magazine Press, 1969.
Claudia, Where Are You?. New York, Morrow, 1969.
The Happenings at North End School. New York, Morrow, 1970.
Daughter of Discontent. New York, Morrow, 1971.
End of the Game, photographs by Milton Charles. Cleveland, World, 1971.
The Family and the Fugitive. New York, Morrow, 1972.
Benny the Misfit, illustrated by Elaine Raphael. New York, Crowell, 1973.
Chicano Girl. New York, Morrow, 1973.
Diary of a Frantic Kid Sister. New York, Crown, 1973.
Friends and Strangers on Location. New York, Morrow, 1974.
After the Wedding. New York, Morrow, 1975.
Ethan's Favorite Teacher, illustrated by John Wallner. New York, Crown, 1975.
That's the Way It Is, Amigo, illustrated by Glo Coalson, New York, Crowell, 1975.
The Amazing Miss Laura. New York, Morrow, 1976.
Nobody Has to Be a Kid Forever. New York, Crown, 1976.
The Case of the Stolen Bagels, illustrated by Pat Grant Porter. New York, Crown, 1977.
Sometimes I Don't Love My Mother. New York, Morrow, 1977.
Rachel's Legacy. New York, Morrow, 1978.
The Secret Life of Harold the Bird Watcher, illustrated by Charles Robinson. New York, Harper, 1978.
Tell Me No Lies. New York, Crown, 1978.
Ellie's Inheritance. New York, Morrow, 1979.
Accident. New York, Morrow, 1980.
What's the Matter with the Dobsons?. New York, Crown, 1980.
Confessions of a Storyteller. New York, Crown, 1981.
The Family Trap. New York, Morrow, 1982.
Girl Meets Boy. New York, Scholastic, 1982.
Don't Tell Me That You Love Me. New York, Archway, 1983.
My Friend, My Love. New York, Archway, 1983.
Not for Love. New York, Morrow, 1983.
Just the Two of Us. New York, Scholastic, 1984.
Nobody Told Me What I Need to Know. New York, Morrow, 1984.
Weekend Sisters. New York, Morrow, 1985.
A Fragile Love. New York, Pocket Books, 1985.
Triangle of Love. New York, Pocket Books, 1985.
Happily Ever After. New York, Scholastic, 1986.
Suddenly. New York, Morrow. 1987.
The Double Life of Angela Jones. New York, Morrow, 1988.
Rich and Famous Like My Mom. New York, Crown, 1988.
Forgotten Girl. New York, Crown, 1990.

Nonfiction

Beauty, Brains, and Glamour: A Career in Magazine Publishing, illustrated by Jacqueline Tomes. Cleveland, World, 1968.
A Career in Medical Research, illustrated by Edna Mason Kaula. Cleveland, World, 1968.

Making Movies: Student Films to Features, illustrated by George
  Guzzi. Cleveland, World, 1969.
City Planning: What It's All About—In the Planners' Own Words.
  Cleveland, World, 1971.

PUBLICATIONS FOR ADULTS

Nonfiction

The Country Weekend Cookbook, with Louis Colman. New York,
  Barrows, 1961.
Cleopatra (as Teresa Crayder). New York, Coward McCann, 1969.
Hanging On. New York, Atheneum, 1977.

*

Media Adaptations: *Tell Me No Lies* (Afterschool Specials, "Un-
forgivable Secrets" and "Sometimes I Don't Love My Mother")
ABC-TV, 1982.

Biography: Essay in *Authors and Artists for Young Adults,* Volume
1, by Hila Colman. Detroit, Gale, 1989; essay in *Speaking for
Ourselves: Autobiographical Sketches by Notable Authors of Books
for Young Adults,* Volume 1, compiled and edited by Donald R.
Gallo, National Council of Teachers of English, 1990; essay in
Something about the Author Autobiography Series, Volume 14, Detroit, Gale, 1992.

Hila Colman comments:

I love writing for adolescents because I find it an exciting age—
something new is always happening. It is a dramatic time of life, a
point when leaving childhood and becoming an adult are meeting
head-on with all the accompanying conflicts of emotions, choices
to be made, and new experiences to be enjoyed or feared. The
number of stories to be written are endless, and as a writer I feel
lucky to have so much rich material to choose from.

*   *   *

Hila Colman writes books about interpersonal problems young
adolescents have at home and with peers. She does this with clarity
and directness, dealing with intergenerational and intragenerational
concerns of grandparents, parents, and children. Her grandmothers
are usually strong people, some with conventional and some with
unconventional views of social behavior. Her parents are shown
with strengths, frailties, and self-doubts. Teenagers wrestle with
the multiple social and personal crises of growing up.

Mixed-Marriage Daughter concerns the child of a Jewish mother
and a Protestant father. Her Jewish grandmother desperately wants
the child to believe in and to practice the orthodox Jewish faith. The
child questions, rebels, and makes peace with her extended family.
She manages in the end to be a friend of, but not bound to, her
grandmother.

At some point many young people begin a secret diary. Sara
begins *Diary of a Frantic Kid Sister* the week of her eleventh birthday and ends it as her twelfth birthday approaches. She vows that
she will tell only the real truth here, because everyone she knows
lies—her parents, her teachers, the principal of her school. The
person who lies the most and thinks she gets away with it is Sara's
sister Deirdre, four years her elder. Deirdre, Sara perceives, is more

loved by their parents, more popular in school, and more accomplished in life. Sara's grief over Deirdre is all the more intense
because of her own feelings of inadequacy and aimlessness. Her
anger over her sister gives way in time to some understanding of her
sister's complications in life. Only then are they able to coexist,
almost peacefully. One particularly welcome aspect of the story is
the serious professional interests of the three main characters—
first mother and Deirdre, and then Sara. The former two are committed to music, the latter to literature. The needs of women for
creativity and independence, as well as family connectedness, are
clearly presented. And Sara herself, for all the daily hassles she
must contend with, remains full of zest. This is a warm and very
witty book.

Rachel's Legacy, set in the Jewish East Side of New York City in
the early 1900s, is about the immigrant experience. The Ginsbergs
arrive at Ellis Island from their Russian village with great hopes and
expectations for the future. Their story, spanning three generations
of family life, is full of strong and complex emotions, successes and
failures, and support and betrayal as family members reach out in
diverse ways to make their place in the new world.

Tell Me No Lies focuses upon a teenager who has never known
her real father. She has been told by her mother that her father left
for Saudi Arabia right after her birth. When her mother finally tells
her the truth, she seeks to meet her father, who is now married with
three more children and doesn't know she exists. The meeting is a
painful one, and the teenager realizes that the settled stranger does
not acknowledge her as his daughter. Once she gets to know her
father, the daughter is more able to forgive her mother, accept her
mother's affection for her, and accept her mother's new husband's
desire to adopt her.

What's the Matter with the Dobsons? looks at a well-educated,
well-to-do family that seemingly has everything. But look again—
thirteen-year-old Amanda feels that her father favors her younger
sister Lisa, and Lisa feels that her mother favors older sister Amanda.
The parents quarrel over the children, and the quarrels become so
intense that the parents separate. Amanda and Lisa want their
parents back again; they want a whole family. But as mother explains, it isn't so simple when people get into situations they don't
know how to get out of. The parents do reunite, but no great
changes come about. Parents and children are the same people, with
the same faults and virtues as before. Only now they know they
have to make accommodations if their family life is to work; they
can't each have their own way. The book travels outside of the
immediate family as well, presenting with compassion and restraint
the problems of teenage dating and the issue of a widowed grandmother dating.

Colman's families and family members have real feelings and real
problems. They do not all live happily ever after. But they are able
to deal with adversity, alter courses in their lives, and provide
comfort to those close to them. Colman's works reflect more accurately than most American books for adolescents changing family
structures and functions, and the meaning of these changes to family members. As such they are possible sources of comfort for
some readers in personal and family crises, who will glean from
these books identification, understanding, and support.

—Mary Lystad

CONFORD, Ellen. Born in New York, New York, 20 March 1942. Educated at Hofstra University, Hempstead, New York, 1959-62. Married David H. Conford in 1960; one son. Writer of books for children and young adults. Recipient: One of the best books of the year from *School Library Journal*, 1971, for *Impossible, Possum*; one of the Children's Books of International Interest, 1974, for *Just the Thing for Geraldine*; one of the Library of Congress Children's Books of the Year, 1974, for *Me and the Terrible Two*; listed in Child Study Association of America Books of the Year, 1975, both *The Luck of Pokey Bloom* and *Dear Lovey Hart, I Am Desperate*; one of the Best Books for Young Adults by the American Library Association, 1976, for *The Alfred G. Graebner Memorial High School Handbook of Rules and Regulations*; Surrey School award, 1981, Pacific Northwest Young Reader's Choice Award, 1981, and California Young Reader's Medal, 1982, all for *Hail, Hail, Camp Timberwood*; One of *School Library Journal's* Best Books of the Year, 1983, and received a Parents' Choice award, 1983, for *Lenny Kandell, Smart Aleck*; Parents' Choice award, 1985, for *Why Me?*, 1986, for *A Royal Pain*; South Carolina Young Adult Book award, 1986-87, and South Dakota Prairie Pasque award, 1989, both for *If This is Love, I'll Take Spaghetti*. Agent: McIntosh and Otis Inc., 310 Madison Ave., New York, NY 10017. Address: 26 Strathmore Rd., Great Neck, NY 11023, U.S.A.

PUBLICATIONS FOR YOUNG ADULTS

Fiction

Dreams of Victory, illustrated by Gail Rockwell. Boston, Little, Brown, 1973.
Felicia, the Critic, illustrated by Arvis Stewart. Boston, Little, Brown, 1973; London, Hamish Hamilton, 1975.
Me and the Terrible Two, illustrated by Charles Carroll. Boston, Little, Brown, 1974.
The Luck of Pokey Bloom, illustrated by Bernice Lowenstein. Boston, Little, Brown, 1975.
Dear Lovey Hart, I Am Desperate. Boston, Little, Brown, 1975.
The Alfred G. Graebner Memorial High School Handbook of Rules and Regulations. Boston, Little, Brown, 1976.
And This Is Laura. Boston, Little, Brown, 1977.
Hail, Hail, Camp Timberwood, illustrated by Gail Owens. Boston, Little, Brown, 1978.
Anything for a Friend. Boston, Little, Brown, 1979.
We Interrupt This Semester for an Important Bulletin. Boston, Little, Brown, 1979.
The Revenge of the Incredible Dr. Rancid and His Youthful Assistant, Jeffrey. Boston, Little, Brown, 1980.
Seven Days to a Brand New Me. Boston, Little, Brown, 1982.
To All My Fans, with Love, from Sylvie. Boston, Little, Brown, 1982.
If This Is Love, I'll Take Spaghetti. New York, Four Winds Press, 1983; London, Fontana, 1984.
Lenny Kandell, Smart Aleck, illustrated by Walter Gaffney-Kessell. Boston, Little, Brown, 1983.
You Never Can Tell. Boston, Little, Brown, 1984.
Strictly for Laughs. New York, Putnam, 1985.
Why Me?. Boston, Little, Brown, 1985.
A Royal Pain. New York, Scholastic, 1986.
The Things I Did for Love. New York, Bantam, 1987.
Genie with the Light Blue Hair. New York, Bantam, 1989.

Loving Someone Else. New York, Bantam, 1991.
Dear Mom, Get Me Out of Here! Boston, Little, Brown, 1992.
I Love You, I Hate You, Get Lost. New York, Scholastic, 1994.

PUBLICATIONS FOR CHILDREN

Fiction

Impossible, Possum, illustrated by Rosemary Wells. Boston, Little, Brown, 1971.
Why Can't I Be William?, illustrated by Philip Wende. Boston, Little, Brown, 1972.
Just the Thing for Geraldine, illustrated by John Larrecq. Boston, Little, Brown, 1974.
Eugene the Brave, illustrated by Larrecq. Boston, Little, Brown, 1978.
A Case for Jenny Archer, illustrated by Diane Palmisciano. Boston, Little, Brown, 1988.
A Job for Jenny Archer, illustrated by Diane Palmisciano. Boston, Little, Brown, 1988.
Jenny Archer, Author, illustrated by Diane Palmisciano. Boston, Little, Brown, 1989.
What's Cooking, Jenny Archer?, illustrated by Diane Palmisciano. Little Brown, 1989.
Jenny Archer to the Rescue. Boston, Little, Brown, 1990.
Can Do, Jenny Archer, illustrated by Diane Palmisciano. Boston, Springboard Books, 1991.
Nibble, Nibble, Jenny Archer, illustrated by Diane Palmisciano. Boston, Little, Brown, 1993.

*

Media Adaptations: *And This Is Laura* and *The Alfred G. Graebner Memorial High School Handbook of Rules and Regulations* (television movie); "Getting Even: A Wimp's Revenge" (based on *The Revenge of the Incredible Dr. Rancid and His Youthful Assistant, Jeffrey*) (an "ABC Afterschool Special"), 1986. *Dear Lovey Hart, I Am Desperate* (an "ABC After School Special," also film), Walt Disney's Educational Media Co.; *Dreams of Victory* (sound recording disc); *If This Is Love, I'll Take Spaghetti, Lenny Kandell, Smart Aleck, The Luck of Pokey Bloom*, and *The Revenge of the Incredible Dr. Rancid and His Youthful Assistant, Jeffrey*, (sound recording cassettes.)

Biography: Essay in *Speaking for Ourselves: Autobiographical Sketches by Notable Authors of Books for Young Adults*, Volume 1, compiled and edited by Donald R. Gallo, National Council of Teachers of English, 1990.

Manuscript Collection: Kerlan Collection, University of Minnesota, Minneapolis.

Critical Study: Entry in *Children's Literature Review*, Volume 10, Detroit, Gale, 1986.

* * *

Ellen Conford has explained that she writes books she hopes will lure readers away from television for a few hours, and her books are designed to do just that—compete with the streamlined world of videos and TV. Fast-paced and optimistic, Conford's stories offer engaging, sometimes quirky characters, uncomplicated plots, and simple solutions, complete with a generous dose of humor. Written in a style best described as comic realism, the majority of the books deal with the lighter problems of adolescence—especially romance—as seen through the eyes of teenagers.

Conford's works can be grouped into two categories, each with a slightly different approach. Her earlier works, embracing most of the publications from *Dear Lovey Hart, I Am Desperate* to *Hail, Hail, Camp Timberwood,* employ thirteen and fourteen-year-old girls as protagonists and treat the transition from childhood to adolescence, often incorporating romance as a plot complication. Several of these also include a change in the heroine's surroundings and use her gradual adjustment as a way of illustrating emotional growth. Conford returns to this strategy, but with a male protagonist, in a recent title, *Dear Mom, Get Me Out of Here.*

Love and the attendant complications become progressively more important in the works published after 1978, such as *The Things I Did for Love,* which humorously explores why people fall in love. The books from this period frequently feature girls aged fifteen to seventeen and are a logical continuation of Conford's previous stories. It is as if her earlier heroines have grown older and now confront a new set of problems; indeed, *We Interrupt This Semester for an Important Bulletin* actually continues the adventures of Carrie Wasserman, the protagonist from *Dear Lovey Hart.*

A number of the later publications also experiment with more improbable plots or settings, resulting in some of Conford's weakest works. Her recent fantasy novel, *Genie with the Light Blue Hair,* tries to blend romance and humor with a magic lamp, Aladdin-style; *A Royal Pain,* a strained variation of Mark Twain's *The Prince and the Pauper,* takes place in a fictitious European country.

Conford's protagonists narrate their own stories, with the cast of characters remaining much the same from book to book. The typical heroine is an average girl, mildly pretty, reasonably intelligent, and possessed of a wry sense of humor. Her biggest problem is unrequited love and/or a lack of self-confidence. Usually she has one or more close girlfriends. Practical and passive, they serve as a sounding board for her woes but rarely emerge as strong characters. In addition, the heroine often begins the story with a male as a platonic friend or convenient companion; he provides rides to school and casual conversation, then steps (or is shunted) aside once her love interest appears. As for the love interest, in many stories he is virtually faceless—attractive, but with little personality. Most protagonists come from happy, healthy families, complete with father, mother, and one or two siblings. Firmly ensconced in the middle class, they live in comfortable houses in suburbia, spending their time at school and shopping malls.

Conford deals with surfaces and the visible rather than complex psychological studies. Accordingly, her heroines usually have fairly straightforward goals: they want to be popular or they want a particular boy's affection. The actions taken to achieve this also affect exteriors—buying new clothes, trying new makeup, or learning to make small talk. Social success and physical attractiveness are important to them and are even sometimes equated. This is ironic since an underlying theme in many of the books is developing self-confidence by recognizing inner qualities. Occasionally Conford tries to invert the message: *Why Me?* and *You Never Can Tell* touch on the perils of loving someone for appearance rather than self. Unfortunately, neither story has the impact it should, perhaps because, like the protagonists themselves, Conford settles for surface rather than substance and neither develops the characters nor

delves into the issues; indeed, in the latter, she undercuts her own point by ending with the protagonist still loving someone for his appearance.

Conford's plots have become progressively more streamlined, with fewer scenes devoted to developing characters or setting and greater emphasis on the heroine's internal monologues detailing her obsession with a particular boy. Accordingly, the early novels, most notably *The Alfred G. Graebner Memorial High School Handbook of Rules and Regulations* and *Dear Lovey Hart, I Am Desperate,* contain some of Conford's best writing. In the former, the story advances thorough a series of well-chosen vignettes; with the latter, strong secondary characters and subplots provide the necessary depth. Her approach occasionally backfires in later works where the subject matter could benefit from more complex plots, stronger characterizations, and/or less self-absorbed protagonists.

Conford's greatest asset is her humor, whether it be the wry commentary of her narrators, the one-liners in the dialogue, or the cleverly constructed incidents that leave the protagonist bewildered and the reader delighted. One of Conford's favorite and most effective techniques for treating a subject is to juxtapose the real and the imaginary. For example, *Seven Days to a Brand New Me* rests on the humorous contrast between the effervescent advice given in a self-help book, the exotic adventures described in a paperback romance, and the everyday life and frustrations of the narrator, a high school girl struggling to overcome shyness and gain the attention and affection of the boy at the next locker.

At her worst, Conford produces readable but forgettable fiction; at her best, warm and witty tales portraying the pitfalls of adolescence—well worth missing a few television shows to enjoy.

—Deidre Johnson

CONLY, Jane Leslie. American. Born in Virginia. Educated at Smith Hopkins University; attended the Writing Seminars Program at Johns Hopkins University. Married, one daughter. Lives in Baltimore, Maryland.

PUBLICATIONS FOR YOUNG ADULTS

Fiction

Racso and the Rats of NIMH. New York, Harper, 1986.
RT, Margaret and the Rats of NIMH. New York, Harper, 1990.
Crazy Lady! New York, Harper, 1993.

*   *   *

Jane Leslie Conly's emerging career as a writer for young adults includes two titles, *Racso and the Rats of NIMH* and *RT, Margaret and the Rats of NIMH.* These titles are sequels to her father's (Robert C. O'Brien, pseudonym used by Robert Conly) highly acclaimed work *Mrs. Frisby and the Rats of NIMH.* All three books are a combination of animal fantasy and science fiction and focus on a group of rats who have become a super intelligent life form through experimentation with their DNA at a laboratory named NIMH, standing for the National Institute of Mental Health. Although these new life forms still look like rats physically, they are capable of reading and learning so successfully that they deliberately keep their knowledge from all humans, including the scientists at NIMH. As the rats become conscious of their continuing dependency on humans they courageously and secretly form their own civilization by growing their own food independent of man in a remote forest preserve named Thorn Valley. The direction in which their society evolves and their ultimate confrontation with man is the central focus of the Conly novels.

Jane Leslie Conly explores the struggles of the new NIMH civilization at Thorn Valley by introducing a new generation of young adult characters who are the offspring of the original group at NIMH. These characters, including Racso, Timothy and Christopher, frequently find themselves in humorous predicaments typically springing from their peccadilloes. Spunky and outspoken Racso is a recognizable young adult with his cravings for candy bars, potato chips, and pop rock and his dislike for being told what to do, especially by adults. More importantly these young adults become aware of their social responsibility within the formation of their new utopian civilization "where work and pleasure are a part of everyone's life." Racso's contributions in saving the NIMH culture are notable because of the knowledge he brings about human use of computer science technology that the rats of NIMH would be unaware of in their isolation at Thorn Valley.

Conly departs significantly from her father's fantasy and other traditionally male-dominated animal fantasies such as *The Wind in the Willows* and *Watership Down* by emphasizing the importance of female contributions in the Thorn Valley utopia. Young adult females such as Beatrice lead a reconnaissance group which locates the dam backing up the river thereby threatening to flood all of Thorn Valley along with the NIMH community. Eventually she is part of a sabotage group that reprograms the computer controlling the dam to malfunction and ultimately self-destruct. The rats of NIMH demonstrate they can master computer technology relatively quickly thereby encouraging readers to embrace new modes of learning in their futures too.

Conly's second book *RT, Margaret, and the Rats of NIMH* returns to the issue of human reaction to the rats as a new, intelligent life form. Their initial discovery by humans comes through two children when ten-year-old Margaret and her younger, asthmatic brother RT (which stands for the name Artie or Arthur) become separated and lost from their parents while camping in Thorn Valley. Christopher, a young rat from NIMH, secretly takes food from the NIMH community and gives it to RT. When Margaret discovers Christopher and his capabilities as a new life form, she ineffectually holds him for ransom for guidance out of the wilderness. Ultimately the rats help the children return to their home and human civilization in exchange for helping with chores and tasks in the rat community. A sense of self-esteem and experience in cooperative learning between the human children and the new life form at NIMH suggests positive potential between the two intelligent civilizations. Although the children's response to the rats is one of growing friendship and love, adult response from the outside world toward the rats is one of fear and intolerance giving way to an innuendo of exploitation and this atmosphere lingers in the closing pages of the novel. A few adults demonstrate sensitivity toward the possibility of a new life form, but Conly implies the human world is unprepared for such an event.

Overall, Conly appeals to a young adult audience through her ability to inject humor and lively action into the adventures and challenges of the younger generation in Thorn Valley while making all of us aware that gender and physical bias are a remote part of the past in her provocative view of the future.

—Richard D. Seiter

———

CONRAD, Pam. Born in New York, New York, 18 June 1947. Educated at Hofstra University, Hempstead, New York, 1977-79; New School for Social Research, New York, B.A. 1984. Married Robert R. Conrad in 1967 (divorced, 1982); two daughters. Since 1979 writer; teacher of writing courses at Queens College, New York. Recipient: Society of Children's Book Writers grant, 1982; Western Writers of America Spur award, American Library Association (ALA) notable book and best book for young adults citations, Society of Children's Book Writers Golden Kite award honor book citation, National Council for Social Studies and the Children's Book Council notable trade book in the field of social sciences citation, *Horn Book* honor list citation, National Cowboy Hall of Fame Western Heritage award, and Child Study Association of America's children's books of the year citation, all 1985, International Reading Association Children's Book award, *Boston Globe-Horn Book* award honor book, Women's National Book Association Judy Lopez Memorial award, and Society of Midland Authors' outstanding books about the Midwest or by midwestern authors citation, all 1986, and ALA *Booklist* "Best of the '80s" books for children citation, all for *Prairie Songs*. ALA recommended book for the reluctant young adult reader citation, 1987, and International Reading Association young adult choices citation, 1988, both for *Holding Me Here;* ALA best book for young adults citation, 1987, for *What I Did for Roman;* ALA *Booklist* children's editors' choices citation, 1988, for *Staying Nine;* ALA best books for young adults citation, ALA *Booklist* Children's Editors' Choices citation, Western Writers of America Spur award for best western juvenile, and National Council for the Social Studies and Children's Book Council notable children's trade book in social studies citation, all 1989, and International Reading Association teachers' choices citation, 1990, all for *My Daniel;* ALA notable children's book citation, and *New York Times* notable book citation, both 1989, *Horn Book* fanfare honor list, and International Reading Association and Children's Book Council children's choice citation, both 1990, all for *The Tub People; Boston Globe-Horn Book* award honor book, 1990, Notable Trade Books for Language Arts, National Council of Teachers of English, 1990, and Mystery Writers of America Edgar award, 1991, both for *Stonewords: A Ghost Story;* Orbis Pictus award honor book, National Council of Teachers of English, 1991, and Notable Children's Trade Books in Social Studies, National Council for Social Studies/Children's Book Council, 1991, for *Prairie Visions*. Agent: Maria Carvainis, Maria Carvainis Agency, Inc., 235 West End Ave., New York, NY 10023, U.S.A.

PUBLICATIONS FOR YOUNG ADULTS

Fiction

Prairie Songs, illustrated by Darryl S. Zudeck. New York, Harper, 1985.
Holding Me Here. New York, Harper, 1986.

What I Did for Roman. New York, Harper, 1987; as *A Seal upon My Heart,* London, Oxford University Press, 1988.
Taking the Ferry Home. New York, Harper, 1988.
My Daniel. New York, Harper, 1989.
Stonewords: A Ghost Story. New York, Harper, 1990.
Pedro's Journal, illustrated by Peter Koeppen. Honesdale, Pennsylvania, Boyds Mills Press, 1991.
Prairie Visions: The Life and Times of Solomon Butcher, illustrated by Zudeck. New York, HarperCollins, 1991.

PUBLICATIONS FOR CHILDREN

Fiction

I Don't Live Here!, illustrated by Diane de Groat. New York, Dutton, 1983.
Seven Silly Circles, illustrated by Mike Wimmer. New York, Harper, 1987.
Staying Nine, illustrated by Mike Wimmer. New York, Harper, 1988.
The Tub People (picture book), illustrated by Richard Egielski. New York, Harper, 1988.
The Lost Sailor (picture book), illustrated by Richard Egielski. New York, HarperCollins, 1992.
Molly and the Strawberry Day (picture book), illustrated by Mary Szilagyi. New York, Harper, 1993.
The Tub Grandfather (picture book), illustrated by Richard Egielski. New York, HarperCollins, 1993.
Kitchen Poem: Waiting for You (picture book). New York, Harper, forthcoming.
This Mess (picture book). New York, Harper, forthcoming.
Pumpkin Moon. New York, Harcourt, forthcoming.

*

Biography: Entry in *Sixth Book of Junior Authors and Illustrators,* New York, H.W. Wilson, 1989; essay in *Speaking for Ourselves, Too* compiled and edited by Donald R. Gallo, National Council of Teachers of English, 1993.

Critical Study: Entry in *Children's Literature Review,* Volume 18, Detroit, Gale, 1989.

*   *   *

Pam Conrad has written a wide variety of stories in the past decade. She has created picture books, stories for young readers, and middle and young adult novels concerning a number of themes, settings, and situations.

Her first book, *I Don't Live Here!,* is for younger readers. While she was sending it to publishers she began developing her second book, *Prairie Songs.* Published in 1985, this historical novel has received numerous awards, including the 1986 International Reading Association Children's Book award.

A turn of the century novel, *Prairie Songs* takes place in Nebraska. The Downing family lives in a sod home, miles from any neighbors. To the narrator, Louisa, it is a beautiful place but lonely and desolate to the newcomer Emmeline Berryman. Through Louisa's

eyes, we watch Emmeline change from a beautiful, hopeful lady expecting her first child to a miserable and pathetic figure. Tragically, she loses the baby and eventually succumbs to madness. This would be a profoundly sad story except the Downings are pioneer people of courage, strength, determination, loyalty, and resourcefulness. Their ability to endure provides a balance between the tragic experience of Emmeline and the heroic efforts of many prairie families.

In 1991, she wrote *Prairie Visions: The Life and Times of Solomon Butcher.* We were introduced to Butcher in *Prairie Songs* when he photographed the Downing family. This nonfiction exploration of prairie life includes stories and photos collected by Butcher in the late 1800s. Taken together, *Prairie Visions* and *Prairie Songs* provide an important historical description of life in the sod houses. The excellent writing deserves to be read aloud and is especially appealing to younger adolescents.

Nebraska is also the setting for *My Daniel.* Julia Creath Summerwaite, eighty years old, has come east to see her grandchildren and take them to the Natural History Museum. The narration is alternated chapter by chapter between Julia and the author. Julia chronicles the adventures she shared with her brother during the prairie years, and Conrad describes the modern-day visit to the museum. This is an extraordinary story about sixteen-year-old Daniel who finds the remains of an enormous dinosaur in the creek bed of his farm. He tries to keep the knowledge from the fortune hunters but in the process loses his life when struck by lightening. Julia is eventually able to contact a reputable paleontologist who takes the bones to the museum and reconstructs them into an enormous brontosaurus. Her story, her memories, her love for Nebraska and her family make Julia a remarkable and memorable character.

For the younger adolescent reader, Conrad has written *Stonewords: A Ghost Story.* Winner of the 1991 Edgar Award given by the Mystery Writers of America, the story is a complex, intricate plot of two girls who can travel back and forth through time. Zoe and Zoe Louise lived in the same house, separated by a staircase and one hundred years of time. Zoe lives with her grandparents because her mother is a shadowy person who periodically slips in and quickly out of her daughter's life. The reader will recognize the psychological undercurrents in what on the surface appears to be a time travel ghost story. Loneliness and the need for an imaginary playmate coupled with the need for a nurturing mother are critical pieces of Zoe's circumstances. These needs provide the motivation necessary for her to continue to seek out such a dangerous adventure. Suspenseful and strange, scary enough to hold interest, this mysterious ghost story proves how versatile Conrad can be as a writer.

Learning the truth about people is a theme that runs through each of Conrad's three young adult novels. In *Holding Me Here,* Robin Lewis snoops to learn about a boarder in her home. Believing she can bring about a reconciliation between the woman and an estranged husband, Robin interferes and almost creates a disaster. Robin is so well defined that readers will ache for her when she realizes that good intentions aren't enough, and a little knowledge is a dangerous thing.

In *What I Did for Roman,* sixteen-year-old Darcie wants to discover the truth about her real father and discovers a very painful family secret. She also believes she has fallen in love with a man, Roman, who works in a zoo. Feeling desperate for affection and security she follows him around all summer and almost dies as he "tests death." In coming to terms with the loss of Roman, she realizes that she only knew one truth about him.

Ali Mintz learns the truth about the life of rich and beautiful Simone Silver in *Taking the Ferry Home*. Vacationing on a resort island, Ali meets the wealthy Simone and they attempt to become friends. This plot is based on the old themes and stereotypes about rich girls, and neither character has the qualities or depth found in Conrad's other works. The story includes adults who struggle with substance abuse, adding to the overall tone of heaviness and despair. Conrad once again effectively uses the narrative technique of alternating chapters between Simone and Ali. They take turns telling their story which provides each of them the opportunity to express their own point of view.

Taken together, Pam Conrad has produced a notable collection of works for young readers and young adults. Her words are imbued with meaning. She understands the worries, concerns, and desires of young people and provides realistic portraits of them. Her descriptions are fresh and wise, leaving the reader satisfied and perhaps inspired. She writes phrases that are memorable for their touching and simple truth.

—Caroline S. McKinney

COOPER, Susan (Mary). British. Born in Burnham, Buckinghamshire, England, 23 May 1935. Educated at Somerville College, Oxford, M.A. 1956. Married Nicholas J. Grant in 1963 (divorced, 1983), one son, one daughter, three stepchildren. Writer. Reporter and feature writer, *Sunday Times,* London, England, 1956-63. Recipient: *Horn Book* Honor List citation for *Over Sea, Under Stone; Horn Book* Honor List and American Library Association Notable Book citations, both 1970, both for *Dawn of Fear; Boston Globe-Horn Book* award, American Library Association Notable Book citation, Carnegie Medal runner-up, all 1973, and Newbery Award Honor Book, 1974, all for *The Dark Is Rising;* American Library Notable Book citation, for *Greenwitch; Horn Book* Honor List and American Library Association Notable Book citation, Newbery Medal, Tir na N'og Award (Wales), and commendation for Carnegie Medal, all 1976, for *The Grey King;* Tir na N'og Award for *Silver on the Tree;* Christopher Award, Humanitas Prize, Writers Guild of America Award, and Emmy Award nomination from Academy of Television Arts and Sciences, all 1984, all for *The Dollmaker;* Emmy Award nomination, 1987, and Writers Guild of America Award, 1988, for teleplay *Foxfire; Horn Book* Honor List citation, 1987, for *The Selkie Girl;* B'nai B'rith Janusz Korczak Award, 1989, for *Seaward.*

PUBLICATIONS FOR YOUNG ADULTS

Fiction

Dawn of Fear, illustrated by Margery Gill. New York, Harcourt, 1970; London, Chatto and Windus, 1972.
Jethro and the Jumbie, illustrated by Ashley Bryan. New York, Atheneum, 1979; London, Bodley Head, 1987.
Seaward. New York, Atheneum, and London, Bodley Head, 1983.
The Boggart. New York, McElderry/Macmillan, 1993.

"The Dark Is Rising" series:

Over Sea, Under Stone, illustrated by Margery Gill. London, Cape, 1965; New York, Harcourt, 1966.
The Dark Is Rising, illustrated by Alan E. Cober. London, Chatto and Windus, and New York, Atheneum, 1973.
Greenwitch. London, Chatto and Windus, and New York, Atheneum, 1974.
The Grey King, illustrated by Michael Heslop. London, Chatto and Windus, and New York, Atheneum, 1975.
Silver on the Tree. London, Chatto and Windus, and New York, Atheneum, 1977.

Other

Reteller, *The Silver Cow: A Welsh Tale,* illustrated by Warwick Hutton. New York, Atheneum, 1983.
Reteller, *The Selkie Girl,* illustrated by W. Hutton. New York, McElderry/Macmillan, 1986.

PUBLICATIONS FOR ADULTS

Fiction

Mandrake (science-fiction novel). London, Hodder, 1964.

Plays

Foxfire (with Hume Cronyn; first produced at Stratford, Ontario, 1980; Minneapolis and New York, 1982). New York and London, Samuel French, 1983.

Television Plays: author of *Dark Encounter,* 1976; author of teleplay version of Anne Tyler's novel *Dinner at the Homesick Restaurant.* (With Cronyn) *The Dollmaker* (adaptation of novel of the same title by Harriette Arnow), produced by American Broadcasting Companies, Inc., 1984. *Foxfire* (teleplay), produced by Columbia Broadcasting System, Inc., 1987.

Other

Behind the Golden Curtain: A View of the U.S.A. London, Hodder, 1965, New York, Scribner, 1966.
J. B. Priestley: Portrait of an Author. London, Heinemann, 1970; New York, Harper, 1971.
Contributor, Michael Sissons and Philip French, editors, *The Age of Austerity: 1945-51.* London, Hodder, 1963.
Editor and author of preface, J. B. Priestley, *Essays of Five Decades.* Boston, Little, Brown, 1968.
Author of introduction, John and Nancy Langstaff, editors, *The Christmas Revels Songbook: In Celebration of the Winter Solstice.* Boston, David R. Godine, 1985.

PUBLICATIONS FOR CHILDREN

Fiction

Tam Lin, illustrated by Warwick Hutton. New York, McElderry/Macmillan, 1991.

Matthew's Dragon, illustrated by J.A. Smith. New York, McElderry/
Macmillan, 1991.
Danny and the Kings, illustrated by J.A. Smith. New York,
McElderry/Macmillan, 1993.

*

Media Adaptations: "The Dark Is Rising" (two-cassette recording), Miller-Brody, 1979; "The Silver Cow" (filmstrip), Weston
Woods, 1985; "The Silver Cow" (recording), Weston Woods, 1986.

Biography: Entry in *Fourth Book of Junior Authors,* New York,
H.W. Wilson, 1978; essay in *Something about the Author Autobiog-
raphy Series* Volume 6, Detroit, Gale, 1988; essay in *Speaking for
Ourselves: Autobiographical Sketches by Notable Authors of Books
for Young Adults,* Volume 1, compiled and edited by Donald R.
Gallo, National Council of Teachers of English, 1990.

Manuscript Collection: Osborne Collection, Toronto Public Library.

Critical Study: Entry in *Children's Literature Review,* Volume 4,
Detroit, Gale, 1982.

*   *   *

Susan Cooper has come to be recognized as a major author of
books for children and young adults. Her first work for children,
Over Sea, Under Stone, came as a response to a contest designed to
honor the memory of E. Nesbit. Set in Cornwall, this is a family
adventure story concerning Simon, Barnabus, and Jane's search for
a mysterious grail. The magic and myth, so much a part of the
subsequent books of the "Dark Is Rising" series, is only hinted at
here. The story draws upon the King Arthur legend and suggests
connections to a world outside that of the contemporary environment.

Dawn of Fear calls upon the actual experiences of English childhood during World War II, but recasts them in the form of the
fictional story of Derek and his friends Peter and Geoffrey. One of
the strengths of this work lies in its ability to contrast the world of
childhood play with the horrors of war without either losing the
sense of innocent play or minimizing the atrocities of the world
conflict.

Cooper's major contribution to date has been "The Dark Is
Rising" series, which greatly expands the mythical theme suggested
in *Over Sea, Under Stone* and reveals Cooper's extraordinary prow-
ess as an author of fantasy. *The Dark Is Rising,* set in
Buckinghamshire, is the second work in the sequence. Here the
battle lines between good and evil are formally established as the
forces of Light and Dark are drawn into conflict. The Light, aided
by Will Stanton, youngest of the Old Ones, seeks to gather together
the Six Signs of the Light that will enable Light to overcome Dark.
Yet the drawing of lines between good and evil, Light and Dark,
rather than completely clarifying the conflict, serves as a mecha-
nism to cast doubt upon the nature of good and evil as concepts.
The shadowy aspect of the conflict and the inability to "read"
clearly the motivations of some of the characters are areas in which
Cooper has been criticized. However, I feel that the ambiguity of
protagonists and antagonists is a deliberate literary device. Rather
than succumbing to artistic flaw, Cooper goes beyond the conven-

tional expectations of her readers by inviting them to glimpse the
complex, the unexplainable, and often the threatening aspects of
mankind's nature. By offering the thesis that the human psyche
may manifest itself in explicit actions or present itself in a mysterious and often frustrating manner, Cooper exceeds the traditional
presentations of good versus evil often found in fantasy literature.

Greenwitch, the third book in the series, is quite different in
mood from the earlier books. In this dreamlike novel set in Cornwall,
magic often occurs during the hours of darkness and yet readers are
not left with the feeling that experiences have been merely imagined. The Greenwitch, a figure created by village women, comes
into possession of a great secret coveted by the powers of Light and
Dark. Young Jane's innocence moves the creature to release the
secret. Jane is an interesting figure because at first she appears to be
a rather flat character who reacts according to convention. Yet as
the story progresses, we learn that even those who are skilled and
knowledgeable in fighting the powers of the Dark are powerless in
this instance. Ironically it is Jane who is successful, not through
dramatic means, but rather through communicating her compassion
for the Greenwitch.

Will Stanton is the central figure in the suspense-filled *The Grey
King,* fourth part of the sequence, set in Wales. Will is assisted in
his quest for a golden harp by several people, including Bran, son of
King Arthur, brought forward in time. Cooper continues her explo-
ration of the many guises of evil and reiterates the theme that the
Dark is a wily foe, capable of taking many forms.

Silver on the Tree rivals *The Dark Is Rising* in complexity. Set in
Buckinghamshire, the book functions as the grand final conclusion
of the series, combining intricate themes borrowed from previous
books. The five children—Simon, Jane, Barnabus, Will, and Bran—
are called together to assist in resolving the dramatic conflict between Light and Dark. In this book, Cooper is at her most powerful, drawing upon the full range of her creative genius. Characterizations are complex and there are surprises in store for both the reader
and the characters.

Cooper's subsequent works are major departures from the preceding series. *Jethro and the Jumbie, The Silver Cow: A Welsh Tale,
The Selkie Girl, Tam Lin,* and *Matthew's Dragon* are compact, imaginative works intended for a younger audience. In the first book set
on a Caribbean island, Cooper introduces a black protagonist who
must deal with the mischievous spirit called the Jumbie. *The Silver
Cow, The Selkie Girl,* and *Tam Lin* form a picture book trilogy and
return to the Celtic material used in Cooper's earlier works. In *The
Silver Cow* a fairy cow given as a gift is misused by a young boy's
father, with consequences to follow. *The Selkie Girl* is the tragic
love story of the marriage of a mortal man and a Selkie girl. This is
a story of transformation, a theme that intrigues Cooper and appears in many of her works. In *Tam Lin,* Cooper modifies the old
story of Tam Lin, the enchanted knight, for a contemporary audience. Margaret is the adventurous king's daughter who finds sitting
and waiting for someone to marry her, dull business and would
rather seek adventure. She finds more than she bargained for (but
not more than what she can cope with) when she meets Tam Lin in
the off-limits Carterhays wood. On being informed of the manner in
which she can save his enchanted soul from the fairies, Margaret
holds fast (literally as well as figuratively), despite the dangerous
transformations which he undergoes, ultimately winning the hand
of the fair knight. *Matthew's Dragon* is a delightful picture book
which stands alone in its subject matter. It is the story of a little boy
who has a night adventure with a story book dragon. Matthew has
an opportunity to meet all of the dragons who ever existed in story.

The description of the celestial flying scene vaguely echoes some of the material to be found in Cooper's fantasy novels.

The novel *Seaward* is perhaps the most complex and least clearcut of all of Cooper's works for young people. Here she appears purposely to avoid explanations and instead chooses to offer the reader a world of possibilities, so many in fact that they create an extremely ambiguous text. This is a challenging novel, with subtleties which may perhaps be best appreciated by an adult audience. The protagonists, Cally and West, are adolescents caught up in the drama of having to cope with the deaths of their parents, events around which swirl mystery and innuendo. At the height of their personal tragedy they are transported to a Celtic world ruled by the old gods who would use the children should they be unable to resist the temptations placed before them. This is an allegorical tale about coming of age in a hostile world.

Vestiges of ancient Celtic "Wild Magic" haunt a Canadian family in the form of a Boggart in Cooper's most recent work *The Boggart*. Having inherited the old Castle Keep in Scotland, the Volnik family also inherits an ancient prank-loving creature, the Boggart, who comes back to Canada with them via the conveyance of an old desk once housed in Castle Keep. Cooper exhibits a rare sense of humor in this story as protagonists Emily and Jessup cope with the often amusing but sometimes dark consequences of the Boggart's pranks. Cooper deftly interweaves folklore with new technology as the children must enter a computer game in order to rescue the Boggart and enable him to return to his homeland. She offers readers an amazingly clear-cut writing style free of the symbolic subtleties found in the *Dark Is Rising* sequence and, particularly, in *Seaward*.

Susan Cooper's work is fully illustrative of a richly creative imagination. Throughout her books major themes resurface, allowing the reader to experience and internalize the depth of her commitment to her social ideals as well as to her art. While she freely acknowledges her debt to the past, her fantasy writing for children and young people offers readers original perspectives in an area which continues to maintain a firm grasp upon the hearts of readers and authors alike.

—Karen Patricia Smith

———

CORMIER, Robert (Edmund). Also writes as John Fitch IV. American. Born in Leominster, Massachusetts, 17 January 1925. Educated at St. Cecilia's Parochial School, Leominster; Leominster High School, graduated 1942; Fitchburg State College, Massachusetts, 1943-44. Married Constance B. Senay in 1948; three daughters and one son. Scriptwriter, WTAG Radio, Worcester, Massachusetts, 1946-48; reporter and columnist ("And So On"), Worcester *Telegram and Gazette,* 1948-55; reporter, columnist (as John Fitch IV), and associate editor, Fitchburg *Sentinel and Enterprise,* 1955-78; free-lance writer, 1978—. Recipient: Best human interest story of the year award, Associated Press in New England, 1959 and 1973; Bread Loaf Writers Conference fellowship, 1968; best newspaper column award, K.R. Thomson Newspapers, Inc., 1974; outstanding book of the year awards, *New York Times,* 1974, for *The Chocolate War,* 1977, for *I Am the Cheese,* and 1979, for *After the First Death;* "Best Book for Young Adults" citations, American Library Association, 1974, for *The Chocolate War,* 1977, for *I Am the Cheese,* 1979, for *After the First Death,* and 1983, for *The Bumblebee Flies Anyway;* Maxi Award, *Media and Methods,* 1976;

Woodward School Annual Book Award, 1978, for *I Am the Cheese;* Lewis Carroll Shelf Award, 1979, for *The Chocolate War;* "Notable Chidren's Trade Book in the Field of Social Studies" citation, National Council for Social Studies and Children's Book Council, 1980, for *Eight Plus One;* Assembly on Literature for Adolescents (ALAN) Award, National Council of Teachers of English, 1982; "Best of the Best Books, 1970-1983" citations, American Library Association, for *The Chocolate War, I Am the Cheese,* and *After the First Death;* "Best Books of 1983" citation, *School Library Journal,* for *The Bumblebee Flies Anyway;* Carnegie Medal nomination, 1983, for *The Bumblebee Flies Anyway;* Reader's Choice Award, 1983, for the *Eight Plus One* short story "President Cleveland, Where Are You?"; "Honor List" citation from *Horn Book,* 1986, for *Beyond the Chocolate War;* Young Adult Services Division "Best Book for Young Adults" citation, American Library Association, 1988, for *Fade;* World Fantasy Award nomination, 1989, for *Fade;* Margaret A. Edwards Award, American Library Association, 1991, for *The Chocolate War, I Am the Cheese,* and *After the First Death.* D.Litt.: Fitchburg State College, 1977. Agent: Curtis Brown, 10 Astor Place, New York, NY 10003. Address: 1177 Main Street, Leominster, MA 01453, U.S.A.

PUBLICATIONS FOR YOUNG ADULTS

Fiction

The Chocolate War. New York, Pantheon, 1974; London, Gollancz, 1975.
I Am the Cheese. New York, Pantheon, and London, Gollancz, 1977.
After the First Death. New York, Pantheon, and London, Gollancz, 1979.
The Bumblebee Flies Anyway. New York, Pantheon, and London, Gollancz, 1983.
Beyond the Chocolate War. New York, Knopf, and London, Gollancz, 1985.
Fade. New York, Delacorte Press, and London, Gollancz, 1988.
Other Bells for Us to Ring, illustrated by Deborah K. Ray. New York, Delacorte Press, 1990; as *Darcy,* London, Gollancz, 1990.
We All Fall Down. New York, Delacorte Press, and London, Gollancz, 1991.
Tunes for Bears to Dance To. New York, Delacorte Press, and London, Gollancz, 1992.

Short Stories

Eight Plus One. New York, Pantheon, 1980.
Contributor, *Sixteen: Short Stories by Outstanding Writers for Young Adults.* New York, Delacorte Press, 1984.

Other

I Have Words to Spend: Reflections of a Small Town Editor (autobiography). New York, Doubleday, 1991.

PUBLICATIONS FOR ADULTS

Novels

Now and at the Hour. New York, Coward McCann, 1960.

A Little Raw on Monday Mornings. New York, Sheed and Ward, 1963.
Take Me Where the Good Times Are. New York, Macmillan, 1965.

Nonfiction

Contributor, *Celebrating Children's Books: Essays in Honor of Zena Sutherland,* edited by Betsy Hearne and Marilyn Kay. New York, Lothrop, 1981.
Contributor, *Trust Your Children: Voices against Censorship in Children's Literature,* edited by Mark I. West. New York, Neal-Schuman, 1987.

*

Media Adaptations: *The Chocolate War, I Am the Cheese,* and *After the First Death* (recordings), Random House/Miller Brody, 1982; *I Am the Cheese* (film), Almi, 1983; *The Chocolate War* (film), Management Company Entertainment Group, 1989.

Biography: Entry in *Dictionary of Literary Biography* by Joe Stines, Volume 52, Detroit, Gale, 1986; entry in *Concise Dictionary of American Literary Biography: Broadening Views, 1968-1988* by Sylvia Patterson Iskander, Detroit, Gale, 1989; essay in *Authors and Artists for Young Adults,* by Dieter Miller, Volume 3, Detroit, Gale, 1990; essay in *Speaking for Ourselves: Autobiographical Sketches by Notable Authors of Books for Young Adults,* Volume 1, compiled and edited by Donald R. Gallo, National Council of Teachers of English, 1990.

Manuscript Collection: Fitchburg State College, Massachusetts.

Critical Studies: *Presenting Robert Cormier* by Patricia J. Campbell, Boston, Twayne, 1985; "An Interview with Robert Cormier," by Anita Silvey, in *Horn Book,* March-April, May-June, 1985; entry in *Children's Literature Review,* Volume 12, Detroit, Gale, 1987; "The Bland Face of Evil in the Novels of Robert Cormier" by Nancy Vaglahn, in *The Lion and the Unicorn: A Critical Journal of Children's Literature,* June 1988, pp. 12-18; "Kind of a Funny Dichotomy: A Conversation with Robert Cormier" by Roger Sutton, in *School Library Journal,* June 1991, pp. 28-33.

Robert Cormier comments:

My books have been accepted by young readers for which I am grateful because young readers are a marvelous audience, open and responsive. I do not, however, write books for young people but about them. I write for the intelligent reader and this intelligent reader is often twelve or fourteen or sixteen years old. A work of fiction, if true to itself, written honestly, will set off shocks of recognition in the sensitive reader no matter what age that reader is. And I write for that reader.

*   *   *

The novels of Robert Cormier have added a new dimension to young adult literature. Dealing with evil, abuse of power, and corruption, they present a dark view of humanity, but one tempered by an underlying morality. All set in fictional Monument, Massachusetts, except for *We All Fall Down* and *Tunes for Bears to Dance To,* Cormier peoples his town with a variety of characters who breathe and experience life to the fullest. A first-rate stylist, Cormier commands and controls language through his fast-paced sentence structure, his vivid verbs, and his sparkling metaphors and similes. His award-winning books grab their readers' attention and compel them to think about the issues raised, long after the final pages have been turned.

After completing three adult novels (*Now and at the Hour, A Little Raw on Monday Mornings,* and *Take Me Where the Good Times Are*), Cormier began writing for the young adult audience with *The Chocolate War,* which recounts Jerry Renault's courageous stand—he refuses to participate in his school's annual fund-raising chocolate sale—against a gang called the Vigils headed by manipulative Archie Costello, and against the corrupt headmaster of Trinity High School, Brother Leon. Jerry's crushing defeat at the novel's close made many adults question the role of the hero, note the absence of effective adult role models, and reject the novel as too pessimistic; yet teen readers accepted it, recognizing the pressures of peer conformity and the abuses of power, and begged for a sequel, which Cormier wrote eleven years later. The high school represents a microcosm of the world, a world teens face daily. The book makes an unforgettable impact; the reader questions whether Jerry will even survive.

In *I Am the Cheese,* the corruption and abuse of power become even more explicit and violent with the death of Anthony and Louise Delmonte (David and Louise Farmer) after Mr. Delmonte testifies against organized crime and the family is supposedly secure in the government's Witness Re-establishment Program. Their son, Adam, is trapped between two apparently equal evils: organized crime and corrupt government. No way out exists for Adam who continues to circle the grounds of the sanatorium when he is not drugged, to look for the father he believes to be still alive. He is the cheese left to stand alone at the end of the nursery song "The Farmer in the Dell." Alternating points of view and narrative voices add to the complexity and mystery of this powerful novel's outcome, which defies the reader's expectations. Again Cormier leaves unanswered questions, such as what, if any role, did Amy Hertz, Adam's girlfriend, play in the discovery and consequent demise of the Farmers.

The narrative style of *After the First Death* also alternates chapters and point of view from those centering on the Marchands—father and son—to those focusing on a hijacking of a busload of first graders. Cormier sensitively treats the dilemma of eighteen-year-old Kate Forrester, who chances to be driving the bus the day of the hijacking, and that of the youngest member of the terrorists, Miro Shantas. *After the First Death,* the title taken from Dylan Thomas's poem "A Refusal to Mourn the Death, by Fire, of a Child in London," recounts a suspenseful story of betrayal and maturation, in which Cormier forces his readers to question father and son relationships, patriotism, and even the novel itself. Does the father narrate the son's chapters, or does General Marchand go insane only after his son's suicide? Is the General a patriot or a fool for sending his son as an intermediary with the terrorists? These unsettling questions contribute to making the novel unforgettable.

In contrast to the first three novels, *Eight Plus One,* a short-story collection, presents an entirely different side of Cormier. Written between 1965 and 1975 and set earlier—some during the Great Depression—these stories, although entertaining, are more family-oriented, occasionally sentimental, and very human. Introducing each story is a chapter discussing an aspect of writing which Cormier wished he had known when he was beginning to write seriously; for example, where ideas for stories originate and the value of figurative language. This book and *I Have Words to Spend: Reflections of a Small Town Editor,* also written prior to the novels, present the same side of Robert Cormier: a gentle man whose loving relations with his family often contribute to his narrative voice. *I Have Words to Spend,* not published until 1991, was not intended for a young adult audience and probably is not as enjoyable to them as are the novels. To adult readers, however, *I Have Words to Spend*—a collection of Cormier's human interest newspaper columns, carefully selected and most capably edited by his wife, Constance Senay Cormier—presents an entertaining, sometimes humorous, always revealing glimpse of small-town life and the philosophy and attitudes of a loving father and family-oriented man.

The gentle Cormier recedes in *The Bumblebee Flies Anyway,* another powerful novel. This one deals with teens in a hospital for the terminally ill where sixteen-year-old Barney Snow tries to make dreams come true, especially for Mazzio who is plugged into a machine and wants to be set free. Barney, who believes he loves Mazzio's twin sister, constructs a life-size model car nicknamed the Bumblebee after the heavy-bodied, short-winged bee who, according to the laws of aerodynamics, should not be able to fly but who flies anyway. The idea is to allow Mazzio to drive the car off the hospital roof, fly for one glorious moment, and thus leave this life in style. This extremely poignant novel, like *I Am the Cheese* and *After the First Death,* presents the reader with courageous characters but also with provocative problems, such as the reliability of the narrator who does not realize why he is hospitalized and who creates his own vocabulary to cover up unpleasantries in this sometimes brutal but always mesmerizing novel.

Cormier then turned his attention to a sequel. Although aware of the difficulties involved in writing sequels, he nevertheless acceded to multiple requests and produced *Beyond the Chocolate War,* a book not as shattering as *The Chocolate War* but still taut and suspenseful. Cormier does not just flesh out his characters from the earlier novel more; he creates new ones, such as Ray Bannister who has just moved to Monument, a talented magician whose act involves a guillotine. Set a few months after the close of its predecessor, *Beyond the Chocolate War* reveals Archie, who as a senior must choose his successor as leader of the Vigils. However, the book centers on Obie, who, revolted by Archie's evil, plans revenge against him with that guillotine and must confront evil himself. Again the abuses of power, evil, resentment, and hatred play a part but so does love as Cormier creates a tender first experience with love for Obie, reminiscent of Adam's love for Amy in *I Am the Cheese.* The novel does not seem as relentlessly honest as Cormier's others—almost as if the author is answering some of the criticism of the earlier book—but the violence and psychological suspense are as heavy, and the book is a compelling read.

In *Fade,* Cormier grips the reader once again, destroying myths. Into a completely realistic setting, Cormier injects an element of fantasy—the fade or the ability to become invisible that is passed down from uncle to nephew through the generations. In this his most autobiographical novel according to the author, Cormier portrays Paul Moreaux who inherits the fade but soon recognizes the painful responsibility that goes hand in hand with it, leaving Paul and the reader to question whether the fade is a gift or a curse. Never certain when an episode of the fade will overtake him, Paul becomes isolated from family and friends. He becomes a writer but must always be on the lookout for the next generation's fader. In the five-part structure, Cormier addresses issues of bigotry, evil, revenge, and murder, as well as the desire to be a writer and issues relevant to writers. *Fade* is a powerful book for both teen and adult

readers—so powerful that readers may find themselves, along with the other characters, questioning whether faders can possibly exist.

Cormier's next novel, *We All Fall Down,* evokes the death and destruction of the plague which inspired the nursery rhyme, "Ring Around the Rosy," from which the novel's title is derived. Cormier depicts the far-reaching effects of evil in the lives of the innocent Jerome family, victims of a senseless house trashing. This novel, not one for the fainthearted, centers on Buddy Walker, a teenage alcoholic facing his parents' impending divorce. Grief-stricken by his role in the trashing, Buddy seeks out one of his victims and begins a relationship with her that proves to be both touching and tragic. Multiple points of view are presented from Jane Jerome, whose sister Karen is hospitalized in a coma after accidentally confronting the trashers; to Buddy; to the Avenger, the primary character in the subplot, whose identity is not revealed until the novel's close when Cormier once again tricks his readers. The presentation of Buddy's and the Avenger's points of view, echoing that of terrorist Miro's in *After the First Death,* endows even the most evil characters with humanity and the readers of this electrifying novel with a broader perspective on life itself.

In *Tunes for Bears to Dance To* Cormier explores collective evil in the revelation of the horrors of the Holocaust on a Jewish survivor, Mr. Levine, and individual evil in the form of a bigoted, abusive grocer named Hairston. Eleven-year-old Henry Cassavant, whose family is still reeling from the death of Henry's brother Eddie, has left Monument and moved to Wickburg. Henry considers himself lucky to get a job at the grocery until the grocer forces Henry to commit a purely evil act of destruction. This book unites themes of previous novels, such as ineffectual parents, corruption of innocence, child abuse, death, and power. Although most of the characters are not well developed, the main themes of this novelette, which might almost be considered a parable, are forcefully delivered, particularly to a teenage audience.

Cormier in his only novel for younger children *Other Bells for Us to Ring* (entitled *Darcy* in England) presents a vivid account of life during World War II. He writes in the genteel manner that characterizes his short stories and newspaper columns but still depicts the achingly accurate feelings of the protagonist, eleven-year-old Darcy Webster. The title is drawn from Kenneth Patchen's moving poem "At the New Year," which serves as the novel's preface and deserves rereading at the novel's close. Set in Frenchtown, a part of Monument (in contrast to the two preceding novels which were set in Burnside and Wickburg (*We All Fall Down*) and Wickburg (*Tunes for Bears*), *Other Bells* is written from the perspective of Darcy, an outsider to Frenchtown. Darcy's new and adventuresome friend Kathleen Mary O'Hara, an Irish Catholic, introduces her to Catholicism and precipitates a painful spiritual crisis. Both girls must deal with alcoholic fathers, though the girls and their fathers differ considerably in their actions. In addition to questioning religion, Darcy must learn about wartime sacrifice, experience the absence of a father missing in action and a mother often depressed and withdrawn, and ultimately deal not only with death but also with miracles. After reading this poignant and revealing novel about adolescent insecurities, which in true Cormier fashion, raises issues and questions but leaves them unanswered, adult readers will recognize feelings they may have been out of touch with for years.

Cormier has written some powerful works—some suspenseful, thrilling novels and some quietly realistic, gentle stories and newspaper columns—all revealing his understanding of how evil and goodness work in the world. Although his outstanding reputation is based upon the former group of novels, the latter deserve praise too. His skill as a craftsman is undisputed. His impact on the field of young adult literature is immense and comparable only with the pleasure his readers derive from discovering another Cormier novel has been published.

—Sylvia Patterson Iskander

————

CRAYDER, Teresa. See **COLMAN, Hila**

————

CREW, Gary. Australian. Born in Brisbane, Australia, 23 September 1947. Educated at Queensland Institute of Technology; University of Queensland, Diploma of Civil Engineering Drafting, 1970, B.A. 1979, M.A. 1984. Married Christine Joy Willis in 1970; two daughters and one son. Senior draftsman and drafting consultant, McDonald, Wapner, and Priddle, Brisbane, Queensland, Australia, 1962-72; English teacher, Everton Park State High School, Brisbane, 1974-78; Mitchelton State High School, Brisbane, 1978-81; Subject master in English, Aspley High School, Brisbane, 1982; Subject master in English and head of English department, Albany Creek High School, Brisbane, 1983-88; Creative writing lecturer, Queensland University of Technology, 1989—; series editor, Heinemann Octopus, 1990—. Recipient: Book of the Year award, Children's Book Council of Australia, and Alan Marshall Prize for Children's Literature, both 1991, both for *Strange Objects; Lucy's Bay* was short listed for the Children's Book Council of Australia's picture book of the year, 1993. Agent: c/o Reed Australia, P.O. Box 460, Port Melbourne, Victoria 3027. Address: Green Mansions, 66 Picnic Street, Enoggera, Queensland 4051, Australia.

PUBLICATIONS FOR YOUNG ADULTS

Novels

The Inner Circle. Melbourne, Heinemann, 1985.
The House of Tomorrow. Melbourne, Heinemann, 1988.
Strange Objects. Melbourne, Heinemann, 1990; Simon and Schuster, 1993.
No Such Country: A Book of Antipodean Hours. Melbourne, Heinemann, 1991.
Angel's Gate. Melbourne, Heinemann, 1993.

PUBLICATIONS FOR CHILDREN

Fiction

Tracks, illustrated by Gregory Rogers. Lothian, 1992.
Lucy's Bay, illustrated by Gregory Rogers. Jam Roll Press, 1992.
The Figures of Julian Ashcroft, illustrated by Hans DeHaas. Jam Roll Press, 1993.
First Light, illustrated by Peter Gouldthorpe. Lothian, 1993.

Gulliver in the South Seas, illustrated by John Burge. Lothian, in press.

Other

Contributor, *At Least They're Reading! Proceedings of the First National Conference of the Children's Book Council of Australia.* Thorpe, 1992.
Contributor, *The Blue Dress,* edited by Libby Hathorne. Melbourne, Heinemann, 1992.
Contributor, *Hair Raising,* edited by Penny Matthews. Omnibus, 1992.
Contributor, *The Second Authors and Illustrators Scrapbook.* Omnibus, 1992.

*

Media Adaptations: *Sleeping over at Lola's* (radio play), Australian Broadcasting Commission; *Strange Objects* (film), Zoic Films.

Biography: Essay in *The Second Authors and Illustrators Scrapbook* by Gary Crew, Omnibus, 1992.

Gary Crew comments:

From my earliest memories I recall that the happiest times for me were being curled up with a book or scraps of paper and coloured pencils—I suppose, when I look back that I was always escaping into, or creating, other worlds. I think that my ideas for the novels that I create today come from some of these earliest childhood times.

More than anything else I would like to be known as a writer of wonderful books, a writer who has enriched and opened up the imagination of young people so that now, in the present, they may see the world as a better place—and carry the phenomenal possibilities of youth into the future.

*   *   *

Even in his two picture books Gary Crew uses symbolism to make a universal statement relevant to young adults. *Tracks,* a seemingly simple illustrated poem, suggests, by tracing the slimy silver trail of a slug, that something mundane can create a great beauty. *Lucy's Bay* is a rites-of-passage picture story, in textured prose, about facing one's pains and fears, especially those that stem from the past, and moving forward. The image of regeneration here is a tuft of gossamer containing seeds from a reed pool.

Crew's first two novels are deliberate attempts to confront contemporary personal and societal problems through well-crafted literary models accessible to young people. Both *The Inner Circle* and *The House of Tomorrow* develop themes of personal and cultural identity, displacement and regeneration, through strong and thought-provoking plots which gain rich linguistic and literary texture by the conscious use of imagery and symbolism. His third book, *Strange Objects,* which was named Australian Book of the Year for older readers, is an archetypal post-modernist young adult novel using a variety of structures: a scrapbook diary, newspaper reports, extracts from library books, psychological studies, historical data and footnotes. *No Such Country: A Book of Antipodean Hours* is even more ambitious; a "big" contemporary novel of calculated literary intent. Here Crew elaborates past themes but in a very different context: Australia's search for identity by coming to terms with the Aboriginal presence. In a much more complex way it develops the theme of guilt and its consequences, embedded in *Lucy's Bay*.

The Inner Circle confronts Aboriginality in contemporary urban Australia and suggests that white Australians must not only co-exist with Aborigines but be prepared to take up the spiritual values that permeate Aboriginal culture. The novel focuses equally on two displaced urban teenagers, one white, one black, who come together when they each seek refuge in a disused powerhouse near a city park. Their stories are told through alternating and interlocking first-person narratives. Tony, the white boy, is calculatingly and cynically ambitious and has adopted a tough facade to hide the hurt he is suffering from his parents' fractured relationship and their separate buying of his favours. Joe, the Aborigine, is from a loving and supportive country family whom he keeps in ignorance of his impecunious finances and the racism that has driven him from his job. Despite a series of frustrations the boys' relationship is ultimately a healing one. The possibility of racial harmony is suggested by the recurring image of the wheel of the bicycle which Tony wants Joe to have, and by Joe's planting of an indigenous palm to replace an exotic rosebush growing in a circular bed in the park. Black and white Australia can and must share the same soil.

The House of Tomorrow is the case-study, journal-like narrative of Mr. Mac, an aging English master, in which he includes the personal folio of a deeply disturbed pupil, Danny Coley. The boy's complex problems are ultimately revealed to stem from his being half Asian, born of his dead father's liaison, formed while fighting in Vietnam. The book's title comes from the words of the Prophet of Khalil Gibran, and its theme is expressed in that seer's quotation, "your children...are the sons and daughters of Life's longing for itself." The mysticism (Danny's ancestral voices and those of his senile Pentecostal grandfather); the death images, including two suicides; the Christian symbolism (baptism); and the implied regeneration through the child of Liz Murray—a colleague of Mr. Mac—are pointers to the richness of Crew's next two novels.

Both *The Inner Circle* and *The House of Tomorrow* are complex but not daunting, and already have a devoted young readership. *Strange Objects* and *No Such Country* are even more ambitious and challenging, in that both are multilayered, explore intricate philosophical concepts and weave their way through the natural and the supernatural. The "strange objects" of the former are present-day rediscoveries in Australia by a disturbed teenage boy, significantly called Steven Messenger, of a seventeenth-century "cannibal pot," a mummified hand wearing a ring which has strange psychological powers, and a leather journal. By appropriating and wearing the cursed ring Steven becomes identified with Pelgrom, a cabin boy from the *Batavia,* wrecked off Western Australia in 1629. Because Pelgrom and Steven have no real regard for Aboriginal life, art or spirituality, and scant interest in nature or the environment, both eventually vanish into the landscape.

Crime against Aborigines and the guilt engendered in a community by the cover-up of a tribal massacre trigger the action of Crew's *tour de force, No Such Country*. New Canaan is in bondage to an unscrupulous, manipulative Messianic figure, the Father. Only two white girls and the aptly named resurrected black, Sam Shadows, have the perception and courage to combat the pervasive evil of the Father. Together they bring about an Armageddon that cleanses and regenerates the Antipodean land, so that the earth breathes "warm and strong, as it had done since the beginning." Its biblical echoes,

its recurring imagery—a foreboding fishing net to catch sinners, the Lamb's book of life, a white heron, an hour glass—its literary allusions, its intriguing mysticism and, above all, its lucid but evocative prose make *No Such Country* a highly significant contribution to young adult literature internationally.

—Maurice Saxby

———

CREW, Linda. American. Born in Corvallis, Oregon, 8 April 1951. Educated at Lewis and Clark College, Portland, Oregon, 1969-70; University of Oregon, Eugene, B.A. 1973. Married Herb Crew in 1974; two sons, one daughter. Writer. Recipient: *Children of the River* was chosen as a Golden Kite Honor Book, 1989, a Michigan Library Association Young Adult Honor Book, and an American Library Association Best Book for Young Adults, and received the International Reading Association Children's Book Award in the older readers category; *Nekomah Creek* was chosen as an ALA Notable Book for Children. Agent: Robin Rue, Anita Diamant Agency, 310 Madison Ave., New York, NY 10017.

PUBLICATIONS FOR YOUNG ADULTS

Fiction

Children of the River. New York, Delacorte, 1989.
Someday I'll Laugh about This. New York, Delacorte, 1990.
Nekomah Creek, illustrated by Charles Robinson. New York, Delacorte, 1991.

PUBLICATIONS FOR ADULTS

Fiction

Ordinary Miracles. New York, Morrow, 1993.

*

Biography: Essay in *Speaking for Ourselves, Too* compiled and edited by Donald R. Gallo, National Council of Teachers of English, 1993.

Linda Crew comments:

I think of my writing process as the creating of a tapestry—the rough draft being the warp, the subsequent versions the weft, and finally, the finishing touches are the fancy French knots. My raw material is real life, which I weave with fictional threads into a story that I hope will express my feelings better than a strict recounting of the facts ever could. Because I've used so many incidents from my family's life in my books, we've all become confused over which details really happened and which were added in my embroidered version. That's why, when a reader asks me if one of my stories is true, the only honest answer is often that none of it really happened, but yes, it's all completely true!

*　　*　　*

Linda Crew entered the young adult literature scene with the publication in 1989 of her first book, *Children of the River*. With this novel, Crew gives young adults a glimpse into the experiences of Cambodian refugees and the struggles many faced when forced to flee their native land for the United States in search of a life free of tyranny and uncertainty. This is a thought-provoking, impressive novel that portrays believable characters and situations readers can identify and sympathize with.

The story of Sundara, the protagonist of *Children of the River*, begins in April 1975, with Sundara, age thirteen, fleeing her native Cambodia after the dreaded Khmer Rouge gain control of the country. Sundara heads for the United States with her aunt, uncle and infant cousin, enduring a difficult ocean journey on a ship crowded with several hundred refugees. The story fast-forwards to September 1979. Sundara, now seventeen, is amazed at how different Americans are; after four years, she does not understand her American peers or their typically American teenage interests, hopes, and concerns. A class writing assignment illustrates the distance between the two cultures; Sundara's life centers on her struggles to deal with the circumstances of the life she left behind in Cambodia, with trying to find her place in a culture alien to her, while her classmates are concerned with video games, dress codes, and cafeteria food. Sundara fears her classmates will ridicule her because she is so different from them; but, in fact, they come to understand her, and even admire her courage. The story is subtle in showing that, despite cultural differences, young adult fears and concerns about fitting in, love, and family relationships are experiences common to young people everywhere. It also shows how the struggle for power often results in the senseless destruction of a people, and how we, as Americans, have learned to take freedom for granted, allowing many of the values we once held dear to disappear.

Crew's second book, *Someday I'll Laugh about This*, is a lighter story about a coming-of-age summer vacation. Twelve-year-old Shelby wants this summer to be like the summers before; she wants nothing to change. But this summer everything will change. Her thirteen-year-old cousin, Kirsten, has a boyfriend she's moping about leaving for two weeks. Kirsten has also befriended the new girl whose father is ruining their ocean view with the new condominiums he is building. And, much to Shelby's regret, the uncle she is fond of is bringing someone new to meet the family. Like everything and everyone around her, Shelby is changing—growing into a young woman. She learns to accept these changes occurring within herself and others, and learns several lessons along the way about the importance of being yourself, and that standing up for what you believe in can make a difference.

—Suzanne M. Valentic

CRICHTON, (John) Michael. Also writes as Jeffery Hudson; John Lange; Michael Douglas, a joint pseudonym. American. Born in Chicago, Illinois, 23 October 1942. Educated at Harvard University, Cambridge, Massachusetts, A.B. (summa cum laude) 1964 (Phi Beta Kappa); Harvard Medical School, M.D. 1969; Salk Institute, La Jolla, California, 1969-70. Married 1) Joan Radam in 1965 (divorced 1971); 2) Kathleen St. Johns in 1978 (divorced 1980); 3) Suzanne Childs (divorced); 4) Anne-Marie Martin in 1987; one daughter. Full-time writer of books and films; director of films and teleplays. Recipient: Mystery Writers of America Edgar Allan Poe award, 1968, for *A Case of Need*, and 1980, for *The Great Train Robbery*; Association of American Medical Writers award, 1970, for *Five Patients: The Hospital Explained*. Agent: International Creative Management, 40 West 57th Street, New York, NY 10019, U.S.A.

PUBLICATIONS

Fiction

The Andromeda Strain. New York, Knopf, and London, Cape, 1969.
The Terminal Man. New York, Knopf, and London, Cape, 1972.
Westworld. New York, Bantam, 1974.
The Great Train Robbery. New York, Knopf, and London, Cape, 1975.
Eaters of the Dead: The Manuscript of Ibn Fadlan, Relating His Experiences with the Northmen in A.D. 922. New York, Knopf, and London, Cape, 1976.
Congo. New York, Knopf, 1980; London, Allen Lane, 1981.
Sphere. New York, Knopf, and London, Macmillan, 1987.
Jurassic Park. New York, Knopf, 1990; London, Century, 1991.
Rising Sun. New York, Knopf, 1992.
Three Complete Novels, (contains *The Andromeda Strain, The Terminal Man*, and *The Great Train Robbery*). New York, Wing Books, 1993.

Plays

Screenplays: *Westworld*, MGM, 1973; *Coma*, based on a novel by Robin Cook, United Artists, 1977; *The Great Train Robbery*, United Artists, 1978; *Looker*, Warner Bros., 1981; *Runaway*, Tri-Star Pictures, 1984; *Jurassic Park*, with John Koepp, Universal, 1993; *Rising Sun*, with Philip Kaufman and Michael Backes, Twentieth Century Fox, 1993.

Fiction as John Lange

Odds On. New York, New American Library, 1966.
Scratch One. New York, New American Library, 1967.
Easy Go. New York, New American Library, 1968; London, Sphere, 1972; as *The Last Tomb*, as Michael Crichton, New York, Bantam, 1974.
The Venom Business. Cleveland, World, 1969.
Zero Cool. New York, New American Library, 1969; London, Sphere, 1972.
Drug of Choice. New York, New American Library, 1970; as *Overkill*, New York, Centesis, 1970.
Grave Descend. New York, New American Library, 1970.
Binary. New York, Knopf, and London, Heinemann, 1972.

Fiction as Jeffery Hudson

A Case of Need. Cleveland, World, and London, Heinemann, 1968.

Fiction as Michael Douglas

Dealing; or, the Berkeley-to-Boston Forty-Brick Lost-Bag Blues, with Douglas Crichton. New York, Knopf, 1971.

Nonfiction

Five Patients: The Hospital Explained. New York, Knopf, 1970; London, Cape, 1971.
Jasper Johns. New York, Abrams, and London, Thames and Hudson, 1977.
Electronic Life: How to Think about Computers. New York, Knopf, and London, Heinemann, 1983.
Travels. New York, Knopf, and London, Macmillan, 1988.

Theatrical Activities

Director: All films, *Westworld,* 1973; *Coma,* 1978; *The Great Train Robbery,* 1978; *Looker,* 1981; *Runaway,* 1984; *Pursuit* (television movie), 1972.

*

Media Adaptations: *The Andromeda Strain* (film), Universal in 1971; *Binary* (television movie entitled *Pursuit*), for ABC-TV, 1972; *A Case of Need* (film, *The Carey Treatment*), MGM, 1973; *The Terminal Man* (film), MGM, 1974; *Jurassic Park* (film, directed by Steven Spielberg), Universal, 1993; *Rising Sun* (film), Twentieth Century Fox, 1993; *Congo* has also been optioned for filming.

Biography: Entry in *Dictionary of Literary Biography Yearbook: 1981,* Detroit, Gale, 1982.

Critical Study: Entry in *Contemporary Literary Criticism,* Volume 2, Detroit, Gale, 1974; Volume 6, 1976; Volume 54, 1989; *The Making of Jurassic Park* by Don Shay and Jody Duncan, New York, Ballantine, 1993.

*   *   *

As the founder of a distinct literary genre (the techno-thriller) and the author of several blockbuster novels, coupled with the immense popularity of the 1993 film version of *Jurassic Park,* Michael Crichton has ascended to an extremely high level of public popularity. When Crichton began his writing career in the mid-sixties he was producing mysteries under the names of John Lange and Jeffery Hudson to pay his way through medical school. These early novels *(Zero Cool, Overkill, Binary, A Case of Need,* etc.) are all demonstrative of Crichton's writing style; he combines the ability to write with cinematic fluidity and a critically technical way of describing (courtesy of his medical school training) to produce engaging and realistic novels. During this period, Crichton debated whether to continue with medicine or pursue writing full-time. Then, in 1969, he wrote what would become his greatest literary achievement—*The Andromeda Strain,* the success of which made his decision to quit medicine respectable.

Until this time Crichton's writing had been that of formulaic thrillers, almost pulp fiction. In *The Andromeda Strain* Crichton blended his scientific background and knowledge with his gift for writing tight, suspenseful, and entertaining plots to produce his trademark—the techno-thriller. Although the techno-thriller is based primarily on science fiction, it is still, in terms of construction, the thriller and typically functions as such. Subsequent novels such as *The Terminal Man, Sphere, Congo,* and *Eaters of the Dead* follow the patterns and methods Crichton established in *The Andromeda Strain* but fail to live up to the standards of this predecessor. Even

Crichton's return to classic thrillers with such novels as *The Great Train Robbery* and *Rising Sun* display the techno-thriller's reliance on science. Since Crichton's novels exhibit similar characteristics, it is possible to explore the aspects of one novel to examine his writing style.

The Andromeda Strain is the account of a group of scientists desperately trying to keep an extraterrestrial micro-organism from wreaking ecological Armageddon on an unsuspecting Earth. The book is filled with scientific details, like glossaries, transcripts, charts, graphs, printouts, etc., which make *The Andromeda Strain* read more like science fact than science fiction. Furthermore, the book is structured like a "Classified Government Document," making its premise more immediate. Consequently, Crichton's fictional world is not one of far-off future-distant worlds, exotic aliens, and fantastic machinery, it is rather a tale of man's survival and his present state of affairs.

Crichton fills his novels with the dangers, horrors, and wonders of what he feels is possible in the present day and the human ability to cope with them. This blending of reality and fantasy make these novels frightening not only in possibility but probability as well. The journalistic stance Crichton commonly assumes is relatively unbiased, although his sentiments ultimately underlie his works as a whole. In this way Crichton transforms his novels into "wake-up" calls in which he attempts to alert his readers to any scientific discoveries or social processes he sees as potentially dangerous (e.g. *The Andromeda Strain* proposes the notion of the abuse of science in the guise of germ warfare). That blend of reality and fiction is why Crichton's books are so popular (virtually all of his novels have been best-sellers); they suspend disbelief, allow total immersion in a fictional world, and, as a bonus, don't take too much time to read.

The cinematic flow of Crichton's works is due to their lack of text-bogging characterization, and this absence is the main criticism that has been levied against him. His characters have been described as one-dimensional and mere plot puppets. But his use of stereotypes stems from his desire to tell the story at hand and not slow down for superfluous description. Crichton expects the reader to bring into the novel a preconceived notion of any character they might encounter (in *The Andromeda Strain,* a scientist or politician), thus allowing the creation of a reader-identity for the character, rather than being force-fed an author's personal and rigid conception. By allowing reader identification with characters in this manner Crichton ensures the fluidity of the story since action is quicker than characterization.

Crichton's novels also display remarkable clarity and actuality in the portrayal of the cultures in which they are set. This trait is demonstrated prominently in the novels *The Great Train Robbery* and *Rising Sun.* These two novels are set respectively in Victorian England and the Japanese society of Los Angeles. Crichton's description of these cultures is not done through a sporadic introduction of ideas but rather by totally immersing the reader in these societies. Although Crichton refrains from distinct characterization of individuals, he does describe his subjects with some detail. He frequently interrupts the story with historically descriptive asides to clarify episodes (a device he also uses to explain scientific processes).

Although Crichton wrote prolifically after the publication of *The Andromeda Strain,* it was not until 1990 that he finally wrote a novel that rivals its intensity. *Jurassic Park* is the story of an amusement park run amuck. Crichton's park is not populated with rides, clowns, and a midway however, but rather with live dinosaurs. Like *The Andromeda Strain,* the novel tells of a group of scientists who desperately try to save themselves and society, but these characters are escaping from the jaws of hungry, biogenetically engineered dinosaurs, not a mutating germ. All of Crichton's conventions are intact, including a subtle warning against the misuse of science (biogenetics), making *Jurassic Park* his best work since *The Andromeda Strain.*

The traits of the techno-thriller combined with Crichton's scriptlike writing style make his novels easily transferrable to film. Many of his novels have in fact been made into motion pictures *(The Andromeda Strain, The Terminal Man, Jurassic Park,* etc.) and some even by Crichton himself *(Westworld, The Great Train Robbery).* These almost verbatim celluloid representations of his novels all display the stylistic fluidity of Crichton's writing. Although the films may come under the same attacks levied against his novels, they are nevertheless entertaining and serve as testaments to Crichton's desire to tell a good story, and if a message (or warning) happens to slip in, so be it.

—Michael J. Tyrkus

———

CROSS, Gillian (Clare). British. Born in London, 24 December 1945. Educated at North London Collegiate School, 1957-64; Somerville College, Oxford, 1965-69, B.A. 1969, M.A. 1972; University of Sussex, Brighton, 1970-73, D.Phil. in English, 1974. Married Martin Cross in 1967; two sons and two daughters. Author of juvenile and young adult books. Also worked as teacher, assistant to old-style village baker, office clerical assistant, and assistant to Parliament member. Recipient: Carnegie highly commended book, 1982, and Guardian award runnerup, 1983, for *The Dark behind the Curtain;* an American Library Association's (ALA) best book for young adults, 1984, a Whitbread award runnerup, 1984, among ALA's notable books of the year, 1985, and an Edgar award runnerup, 1986, for *On the Edge;* a Carnegie commended book, 1986, and listed among ALA's best books for young adults, 1987, for *Chartbreak;* listed among ALA's notable books of the year, 1987, for *Roscoe's Leap;* Carnegie medal, 1991, for *Wolf.* Address: 41 Essex Rd., Gravesend, Kent DA11 0SL, England.

PUBLICATIONS FOR YOUNG ADULTS

Fiction

Revolt at Ratcliffe's Rags, illustrated by Tony Morris. Oxford and New York, Oxford University Press, 1980.
Born of the Sun, illustrated by Mark Edwards. Oxford, Oxford University Press, 1983; New York, Holiday House, 1984.
On the Edge. Oxford, Oxford University Press, 1984; New York, Holiday House, 1985.
Chartbreak. Oxford, Oxford University Press, 1986, as *Chartbreaker,* New York, Holiday House, 1987.
Roscoe's Leap. Oxford, Oxford University Press, and New York, Holiday House, 1987.
The Dark behind the Curtain, illustrated by David Parkins. Oxford, Oxford University Press, 1982, New York, Oxford University Press, 1984.

A Map of Nowhere. Oxford, Oxford University Press, 1988, New York, Holiday House, 1989.
Twin and Super-Twin, illustrated by Maureen Bradley. Oxford, Oxford University Press, and New York, Holiday House, 1990.
The Demon Headmaster. Oxford, Oxford University Press, 1990.
Wolf. Oxford, Oxford University Press, 1990, and New York, Holiday House, 1991.
The Great American Elephant Chase. New York, Holiday House, 1992.

PUBLICATIONS FOR CHILDREN

Fiction

The Runaway, illustrated by Reginald Gray. London, Methuen, 1979.
The Iron Way, illustrated by Tony Morris. London and New York, Oxford University Press, 1979.
Save Our School, illustrated by Gareth Floyd. London, Methuen, 1981.
A Whisper of Lace. Oxford and New York, Oxford University Press, 1981.
The Demon Headmaster, illustrated by Gary Rees. Oxford and New York, Oxford University Press, 1982.
The Mintyglo Kid, illustrated by G. Floyd. London, Methuen, 1983.
The Prime Minister's Brain, illustrated by Sally Burgess. Oxford, Oxford University Press, 1985.
Swimathon!, illustrated by Gareth Floyd. London, Methuen, 1986.
Gobbo the Great. London, Methuen, 1991.
The Monster from Underground. London, Heinemann, 1991.

*

Biography: Entry in *Sixth Book of Junior Authors and Illustrators,* New York, H.W. Wilson, 1989; essay in *Speaking for Ourselves, Too* compiled and edited by Donald R. Gallo, National Council of Teachers of English, 1993.

*   *   *

Gillian Cross offers varying blends of history, suspense, and social concern in her young adult novels designed to capture and hold readers' attention. Whether writing about Victorian times or contemporary problems, she appeals to adolescents who may be less than enthusiastic about reading.

Although initially her first novel, *The Iron Way,* appears to be a straightforward historical narrative, the book contains themes that clearly relate to contemporary problems. Set in Victorian England, the novel deals with the coming of the railway to a rural society mistrustful of change and suspicious of the Irish railway workers. When sixteen-year-old Kate Penfold agrees to board laborer Conor O'Flynn, she does so out of a desperate need for funds to support herself and younger siblings. However, the Penfolds and Con find themselves caught between villagers and navvies as violent incidents escalate and eventually result in Con's death. Astute readers can easily recognize the application of the theme of the destructive power generated by fear of those who are different.

The mixture of history and suspense is more complex in *A Whisper of Lace,* which involves the nineteenth-century smuggling of lace to England from Europe. Francis Merrowby and his sister are caught in an increasingly dangerous enterprise masterminded by a shadowy figure who turns out to be their long-absent, older brother. Secret messages, nocturnal coach rides, and daring schemes to outwit the authorities supply plenty of intrigue. But Cross does not ignore the devastating economic consequences of such smuggling on the impoverished English lace workers.

Exploitation serves as a powerful theme in *The Dark behind the Curtain,* in which the ghosts of children from Victorian times seek revenge through contemporary children acting in a school production of *Sweeney Todd.* Marshall, who portrays the evil Todd, bullies cast members and threatens his former friend Jackus, just as the stage character destroyed the lives of people in his day. Tension heightens as past and present, stage and school grow ever closer in a web of evil.

Exposing secrets of the past forms the basis of *Roscoe's Leap,* in which a family is literally divided and lives in separate wings of a huge mansion spanning a river. Only the arrival of an architecture student engaged in research about Samuel Roscoe, the ancestor who had constructed the house, starts a process of discovery for Stephen, who cannot understand memories of events from his early childhood. Mechanical toys, including a model of the French Terror, provide an explanation of how cruelty can affect one generation to the next.

Questions about repression and the family fill *On the Edge,* one of Cross's most powerful novels. Tug, the son of a journalist who reports extensively on terrorist activities, is kidnapped by members of a group devoted to exposing the repressive power of families. Subject to brainwashing techniques at the country house where his captors have taken him, Tug grows increasingly uncertain about the identity of his "real" mother. Authorities are reluctant to interfere in what they perceive as a family unit. A parallel story of Jinny, a local girl convinced that Tug is held captive, points out the control exercised by many parents. Her own authoritative father dominates his children and provides little more freedom than Tug experiences in his prison. Even readers who overlook such comparisons will be enthralled by the mounting tension over what will happen to Tug.

Even more suspense permeates *Wolf,* which won the Carnegie medal. In this novel the terrorist is Cassy's own father, a member of the IRA, who is willing to sacrifice anyone's life to advance his cause. Sent by her grandmother, with whom she usually stays, to Goldie, her beautiful but irresponsible mother, Cassy unknowingly carries with her the plastic explosive her father had brought to his mother's home. Goldie lives with a West African artist in an abandoned London house. As Lyall and his son do research on myths and facts about wolves for a school presentation they are preparing, the reader is increasingly aware that a human wolf is stalking Cassy. Cross intersperses fragments from the tale of Red Riding Hood to heighten the tension, and Cassy's fear affects the reader as well.

Cross incorporates other social issues besides terrorism into her young adult novels. *Revolt at Ratcliffe's Rags* documents what happens when three students bent on completing a school report investigate a local factory and get involved in labor unrest. The resulting strike tears apart the community and families and reveals that economic problems do not always have simple solutions.

In *Chartbreak* Cross uses the world of rock music to explore the search for identity of recording star Finch. Interspersing newspaper articles and magazine interviews with Finch's own account of her rise to fame, Cross contrasts public perceptions with personal reality.

Map of Nowhere combines adolescents' fascination with adventure games with the necessity for making moral decisions in real life. Nick Miller, who wants to join the gang of which his older brother is a member, becomes their spy to help set up a robbery. However, his growing friendship for Joseph and Ruth Fisher makes him reluctant to betray the hardworking but poor family that refuses financial gain if it involves betraying moral principles.

Almost all of Cross's books are set in England. However, *Born of the Sun* takes a family to South America in quest of an ancient city long sought by Paula Staszic's archeologist father. His growing irrationality on the journey reveals symptoms of his physical illness that receives an unexpected cure deep in the jungle. Cross's most recent book, another historical novel, is set in the frontier days of the United States. In *The Great American Elephant Chase* Cissie Keenan and Tad Hawkins must take an elephant cross country to Nebraska after the animal's owner, Cissie's father, dies.

Young adults will be a drawn to Cross's works because her realistic representations of characters and settings are appealing to them, and because she shows she is attuned to the interests and experiences of her young readers.

—Kathy Piehl

CROSSLEY-HOLLAND, Kevin (John William). British. Born in Mursley, Buckinghamshire, 7 February 1941. Educated at Bryanston School; St. Edmund Hall, Oxford, M.A. (honours) in English language and literature 1962. Married 1) Caroline Fendall Thompson in 1963, two sons; 2) Ruth Marris in 1972; 3) Gillian Cook in 1982, two daughters. Editor, Macmillan, publishers, London, 1962-71; Gregory Fellow, University of Leeds, 1969-71; talks producer, BBC, London, 1972; editorial director, Victor Gollancz Ltd., publishers, London, 1972-77; English Lecturer, University of Regensburg, 1978-80. Since 1975 general editor, Mirror of Britain series, Andr Deutsch Ltd., publishers, London; since 1983 editorial consultant, Boydell and Brewer, publishers, Woodbridge, Suffolk. Lecturer in English, Tufts in London programme, 1967-78; Arts Council Fellow in English, Winchester School of Art, 1983, 1984; Visiting Fulbright Professor of English, St. Olaf College, Northfield, Minnesota, 1987-88. Chairman of the Literature Panel, Eastern Arts Association, 1986-89. Since 1991 Endowed Chair in the Humanities and Fine Arts, University of St. Thomas, St. Paul, Minnesota. Recipient: Arts Council award, 1968, for *The Green Children;* poetry award, 1972, for *The Rain-Giver;* Poetry Book Society Choice, 1976, for *The Dream-House;* Francis Williams award, 1977, for *The Wildman;* Carnegie Medal, 1986, for *Storm.* Agent: Rogers Coleridge and White, 20 Powis Mews, London W11 1JN. Address: The Old Vicarage, Walsham-le-Willows, Bury St. Edmunds, Suffolk 1P31 3B2, England; 288 Laurel Avenue, St. Paul, MN 55102, U.S.A.

PUBLICATIONS FOR YOUNG ADULTS

Fiction

Havelok the Dane, illustrated by Brian Wildsmith. London, Macmillan, 1964; New York, Dutton, 1965.
King Horn, illustrated by Charles Keeping. London, Macmillan, 1965; New York, Dutton, 1966.

The Green Children, illustrated by Margaret Gordon. London, Macmillan, 1966; New York, Seabury Press, 1968; new edition, illustrated by Alan Marks, London, Oxford University Press, 1994.

Editor, *Winter's Tales for Children 3.* London, Macmillan, 1967.

The Callow Pit Coffer, illustrated by Margaret Gordon. London, Macmillan, 1968; New York, Seabury Press, 1969.

Wordhoard: Anglo-Saxon Stories, with Jill Paton Walsh. London, Macmillan, and New York, Farrar Straus, 1969.

Translator, *Storm and Other Old English Riddles,* illustrated by Miles Thistlethwaite. London, Macmillan, and New York, Farrar Straus, 1970.

The Pedlar of Swaffham, illustrated by Margaret Gordon. London, Macmillan, 1971; New York, Seabury Press, 1972.

The Sea-Stranger, illustrated by Joanna Troughton. London, Heinemann, 1973; New York, Seabury Press, 1974.

The Fire-Brother, illustrated by Joanna Troughton. London, Heinemann, and New York, Seabury Press, 1975.

Green Blades Rising: The Anglo-Saxons. London, Deutsch, 1975; New York, Seabury Press, 1976.

The Earth-Father, illustrated by Joanna Troughton. London, Heinemann, 1976.

The Wildman, illustrated by Charles Keeping. London, Deutsch, 1976.

Editor, *The Faber Book of Northern Legends [Northern Folktales],* illustrated by Alan Howard. London, Faber, 2 vols., 1977-80.

Translator, *Beowulf,* illustrated by Charles Keeping. London, Oxford University Press, 1982.

The Dead Moon and Other Tales from East Anglia and the Fen Country, illustrated by Shirley Felts. London, Deutsch, 1982.

Editor, *The Riddle Book,* illustrated by Bernard Handelsman. London, Macmillan, 1982.

Tales from the Mabinogion, with Gwyn Thomas, illustrated by Margaret Jones. London, Gollancz, 1984; Woodstock, New York, Overlook Press, 1985.

Axe-Age, Wolf-Age: A Selection from the Norse Myths, illustrated by Hannah Firmin. London, Deutsch, 1985.

The Fox and the Cat: Animal Tales from Grimm, with Susan Varley, illustrated by Varley. London, Andersen Press, 1985; New York, Lothrop, 1986.

Storm, illustrated by Alan Marks. London, Heinemann, 1985.

British Folk Tales: New Versions. London and New York, Orchard, 1987; selections as *Boo!, Dathera Dad, Piper and Pooka,* and *Small-Tooth Dog,* illustrated by Peter Melnyczuk, London, Orchard, 4 vols., 1988.

Northern Lights: Legends, Sagas and Folk-Tales, illustrated by Alan Howard. London, Faber, 1987.

The Quest for Olwen, with Gwyn Thomas, illustrated by Margaret Jones. Cambridge, Lutterworth Press, 1988.

Wulf. London, Faber, 1988.

Under the Sun and Over the Moon, illustrated by Ian Penney. London, Orchard, and New York, Putnam, 1989.

Sleeping Nanna, illustrated by Peter Melnyczuk. London, Orchard, 1989; New York, Ideal, 1990.

Sea Tongue, illustrated by Clare Chaurce. London, BBC/Longman, 1991.

Tales from Europe. London, BBC, 1991.

The Tale of Taliesin, with Gwyn Thomas. London, Gollancz, 1992.

Long Tom and the Dead Hand, illustrated by Shirley Felts. London, Deutsch, 1992.

The Labours of Herekles, illustrated by Peter Utton. London, Orion, 1993.

The Green Children, illustrated by Alan Marks. London, Oxford University Press, 1994.

PUBLICATIONS FOR ADULTS

Poetry

On Approval. London, Outposts, 1961.

My Son. London, Turret, 1966.

Alderney: The Nunnery. London, Turret, 1968.

Confessional. Frensham, Surrey, Sceptre Press, 1969.

Norfolk Poems. London, Academy, 1970.

A Dream of a Meeting. Frensham, Surrey, Sceptre Press, 1970.

More Than I Am. London, Steam Press, 1971.

The Wake. Richmond, Surrey, Keepsake Press, 1972.

The Rain-Giver. London, Deutsch, 1972.

Petal and Stone. Knotting, Bedfordshire, Sceptre Press, 1975.

The Dream-House. London, Deutsch, 1976.

Between My Father and My Son. Minneapolis, Black Willow Press, 1982.

Time's Oriel. London, Hutchinson, 1983.

Waterslain and Other Poems. London, Hutchinson, 1986.

The Painting-Room and Other Poems. London, Century Hutchinson, 1988.

East Anglian Poems. Colchester, Jardine, 1988.

Oenone in January. Llandogo, Old Stile Press, 1988.

New and Selected Poems: 1965-1990. London, Hutchinson, 1991.

Eleanor's Advent. Llandogo, Old Stile Press, 1992.

Other

Translator, *The Battle of Maldon and Other Old English Poems,* edited by Bruce Mitchell. London, Macmillan, and New York, St. Martin's Press, 1965.

Editor, *Running to Paradise: An Introductory Selection of the Poems of W.B. Yeats.* London, Macmillan, 1967; New York, Macmillan, 1968.

Translator, *Beowulf.* London, Macmillan, and New York, Farrar Straus, 1968.

Editor, *Winter's Tales 14.* London, Macmillan, 1968.

Pieces of Land: Journeys to Eight Islands. London, Gollancz, 1972.

Editor, with Patricia Beer, *New Poetry 2.* London, Arts Council, 1976.

Translator, *The Exeter Riddle Book.* London, Folio Society, 1978; as *The Exeter Book of Riddles,* London, Penguin, 1979; revised edition, 1993.

The Norse Myths: A Retelling. London, Deutsch, and New York, Pantheon, 1980.

Translator, *The Anglo-Saxon World.* Woodbridge, Suffolk, Boydell Press, 1982; New York, Barnes and Noble, 1983.

Editor, *Folk-Tales of the British Isles.* London, Folio Society, 1985; New York, Pantheon, 1988.

Editor, *The Oxford Book of Travel Verse.* Oxford and New York, Oxford University Press, 1986.

Translator, *The Wanderer.* Colchester, Jardine, 1986.

Editor, *Medieval Lovers: A Book of Days.* London, Century Hutchinson, and New York, Weidenfeld and Nicolson, 1988.

Translator, *The Old English Elegies.* London. Folio Society, 1988.

The Stones Remain: Megalithic Sites of Britain, photographs by
Andrew Rafferty. London, Rider, 1989.
Editor, *Medieval Gardens: A Book of Days.* New York, Rizzoli,
1990.

*

Manuscript Collection: Brotherton Collection, University of Leeds;
Lillian H. Smith and Osborne Collections, Toronto Public Library.

Biography: Entry in *Fourth Book of Junior Authors,* New York,
H.W. Wilson, 1978; entry in *Dictionary of Literary Biography,*
Volume 40, Detroit, Gale, 1985.

*   *   *

Kevin Crossley-Holland is a British author who writes across
the spectrum of literature. He has written picture books, junior
novels, poetry, and nonfiction; he has translated Norse and Old
English myths, legends, folktales, and poetry; he has retold English
folktales; he has collaborated on modern retellings of Welsh legends. With such a wide variety of interests, it is not surprising that
his audience ranges widely too: from children and young adults to
Anglo-Saxon scholars. If there is one theme that unites Crossley-
Holland's work, it is his fascination with Britain's ancient past,
particularly with the Anglo-Saxon period. Another consistent thread
running throughout his work is his love of words. In all his writing,
he attempts to render his stories into what he calls "lapidary English," referring to the smooth, polished facets of a gemstone. Since
he is a poet, his poetic grasp of the sounds and nuances of words
enables him to meet this goal more often than not.

Although Crossley-Holland's picture books are intended for
younger readers, young adults will find much to interest them in
books like *Beowulf* and *The Wildman.* Some critics feel that *Beowulf,*
a masterly retelling of the Old English poem, is Crossley-Holland's
best work. *The Wildman* is almost a prose poem, told in first person
by a captured merman. Readers with an appreciation of art will
enjoy Charles Keeping's evocative illustrations in both of these
books. Similarly, the three Welsh legends retold in picture-book
format by Crossley-Holland and Gwyn Thomas—*Tales from the
Mabinogion, The Quest for Olwen,* and *The Tale of Taliesin*—have
much to offer older readers. These tales were originally intended for
adults, and the authors do not patronize their supposed audience of
young readers by removing any of the adult motivations and actions. The illustrations by Margaret Jones provide a sophisticated
and explicit accompaniment to the text.

Crossley-Holland's junior novels, such as *King Horn* and *Wulf,*
are also historical. Although they generally deal with young adult
protagonists, these books are written at a level more suited to
younger readers: simple, direct sentences and little detail or description. More likely to appeal to teens is *Wordhoard: Anglo-
Saxon Stories,* co-written by Jill Paton Walsh. A collection of original stories rather than a novel, this book successfully recreates an
era so ancient as to be almost inaccessible. Using numerous Old
English poems and histories as the basis of these stories, Crossley-
Holland and Paton Walsh draw a sympathetic picture of Anglo-
Saxon life, ending with the death of King Harold, the last Saxon
king. Each story is independent, yet the consistent tone of the tales
creates a unified volume.

Crossley-Holland's true genius lies in retelling ancient myths,
legends, and tales. In *British Folk Tales* he retells fifty-five stories

and ballads, mostly English (with one or two Scottish or Welsh
tales). Some of the stories are familiar, such as "Jack and the
Beanstalk" and "Goldilocks and the Three Bears"; others are more
obscure: "The Last of the Picts" and "The Pedlar of Swaffham," for
example. Although all the tales are well told, the collection is somewhat uneven because of the author's varied approaches to the material. This collection also includes "The Wildman," later reprinted
as a picture book. Another book of British tales, *The Dead Moon
and Other Tales from East Anglia and the Fen Country,* is a more
unified collection. These are mostly scary or sad tales, beautifully
told with a mere hint of the East Anglian dialect. Several of the
stories in this volume have also been reprinted as picture books.

Britain's Viking heritage appears in several of Crossley-Holland's
collections of tales. *Northern Lights: Legends, Sagas, and Folk-
Tales* is his largest collection of Norse myths. Selections from *Northern Lights* were also printed as *Axe-Age, Wolf-Age.* Crossley-Holland does not have as strong a feel for these myths as he has for his
native English folktales, but he successfully captures the tone of
his medieval Icelandic sources.

Young adult readers who have an interest in ancient Britain may
enjoy some of Crossley-Holland's adult works, such as his translations of Old English literature and his nonfiction books about Anglo-
Saxon England. *Green Blades Rising,* for instance, introduces the
Anglo-Saxon lifestyle in a direct manner that is easily accessible to
older children, using many photographs and quotations from Old
English literature.

All of Crossley-Holland's best work combines his storytelling
skills with his mastery of the poetic elements of language. The most
memorable tales in *The Dead Moon* and *British Folk Tales* benefit
from this marriage of prose and poetry. *Beowulf,* originally a poem,
retains the Anglo-Saxon poetic phrasing while fleshing out the characters and the story. Combining these skills creates and maintains
an appropriate tone for each story, whether it is the rough and
ready action of *Beowulf* or the sad, haunting lament of *The Wildman.*

—Donna R. White

———

CRUTCHER, Chris(topher C.). Born in Cascade, Idaho, 17 July
1946. Educated at Eastern Washington State University, Cheney,
B.A. 1968. Teacher, Kennewick Dropout School, Kennewick, Washington, 1970-73; teacher, Lakeside School, Oakland, California,
1973-76, director of school, 1976-80; child protection team specialist, Community Mental Health, Spokane, Washington, 1980-
82; since 1982 child and family therapist. Recipient: Named to
American Library Association's list of best books for young adults,
1983, for *Running Loose,* 1986, for *Stotan!,* and 1989, for *Chinese
Handcuffs;* named to *School Library Journal*'s best books for young
adults list, and to American Library Association's list of best books
for young adults, both 1988, for *The Crazy Horse Electric Game;*
Michigan Library Association Best Young Adult Book of 1992, for
Athletic Shorts; ALAN award for Significant Contribution to Adolescent Literature. Agent: Liz Darhansoff, 1220 Park Ave., New
York, NY 10028. Address: East 3405 Marion Ct., Spokane, WA
99223, U.S.A.

PUBLICATIONS FOR YOUNG ADULTS

Fiction

Running Loose. New York, Greenwillow, 1983.
Stotan!. New York, Greenwillow, 1986.
The Crazy Horse Electric Game. New York, Greenwillow, 1987.
Chinese Handcuffs. New York, Greenwillow, 1989.
Staying Fat for Sarah Byrnes. New York, Greenwillow, 1993.

Other

Athletic Shorts: Six Short Stories. New York, Greenwillow, 1991.
The Deep End. New York, Morrow, 1992.

*

Media Adaptations: Screenplay for *Running Loose* and *The Crazy Horse Electric Game* is forthcoming. Options for the following: *The Deep End,* Interscope Pictures; *Staying Fat for Sarah Byrnes,* Columbia Pictures; "A Brief Moment in the Life of Angus Bethune" from *Athletic Shorts,* Disney Pictures.

Biography: Essay in *Speaking for Ourselves: Autobiographical Sketches by Notable Authors of Books for Young Adults,* Volume 1, compiled and edited by Donald R. Gallo, National Council of Teachers of English, 1990.

Chris Crutcher comments:

Though most of my books are considered young adult, that is never my consideration in writing them. My storytelling style does not change from a novel about so-called young adults to one about adults. I choose the story, tell it, and let the marketing people decide what it is. My mission is to write truths as I see them; reflect the world as it appears to me, rather than as others would have it. I would like to tell stories so "right on" that they punch a hole in the wall between young adult and adult literature.

*   *   *

Many authors have used sports as a metaphor for the ups and downs of life, but very few with the combined humor and poignancy of Chris Crutcher. In his four young adult novels and the related book of short stories, Crutcher's characters engage in a wide variety of athletic activities while facing the typical and not so typical—yet sometimes very real—problems of adolescence. These are complex, sometimes irreverent, and deeply compelling works, in large part because the young male protagonists are portrayed so distinctly and with such realism. While the sporting events lend excitement and action, they are not really the central focus. Rather, these stories achieve their satisfaction and success from the characters' struggles to make sense of life and the depiction of friendship's power to aid in the struggle.

In Crutcher's first young adult novel, *Running Loose,* senior Louis Banks earns a starting position on the football team after a summer of hard training. But during the second game he takes a very public stand against the coach, who had ordered his team to injure the opponent's star player. Louis is disappointed that he won't be playing football, and only his girlfriend Becky seems to agree with his actions. When Becky is killed in an automobile accident, Louis finds coping with each day becomes a monumental challenge. With help from friends, adult and adolescent, Louis proves he's more than up to dealing with Becky's loss.

The power of friendship is also strongly evident in *Stotan!* Walker, Lion, Nortie, and Jeff are four friends brought even closer by their shared experiences as swimmers, including Stotan week. (A stotan is a cross between a stoic and a spartan, and the swimming coach devises a week of training worthy of the name.) Walker, the narrator, has a drug addicted older brother who can make his life complicated, if not dangerous. Lion lives alone above a bar, a talented artist who lost his parents in a boating accident. Nortie attempts to break the pattern of an abusive father by working at a day care center, and Jeff develops leukemia. In the closing scenes at the state swim meet Walker, Lion, and Nortie defy a judge's ruling and swim three legs of the four-man relay without Jeff, leaving their lane eerily quiet while the other teams finish the race.

Willie Weaver's friends in *The Crazy Horse Electric Game* are an unlikely bunch: a principal at a high school in Oakland known as "Last Chance," students there called Telephone Man and Hawk, and a bus driver and part-time pimp named Lacey. Left with slurred speech and a physical handicap after a waterskiing accident, baseball hero Willie can't cope with the suffocating memories of his small hometown or the pity of his family and friends. He runs away, only to be beaten up by an Asian American gang when he arrives in Oakland. Willie does heal, both emotionally and physically, but returning home brings unpleasant revelations still to be faced.

Dillon Hemingway of *Chinese Handcuffs* has a shattering experience to understand: he witnessed his brother Preston's suicide. Preston's loss is especially difficult because of Dillon's attraction to his brother's girlfriend Stacey and further complicated when he discovers she is pregnant with his brother's baby. He also learns that Jennifer, a good friend and star basketball player, is being sexually abused by her stepfather, a talented lawyer. Dillon begins to find his own way as he helps Jennifer and Stacey, and his confidence returns as he trains for the triathalon.

Athletic Shorts is a book of six short stories, five of which focus on characters from the earlier works. These short works stand on their own but will be particularly appreciated with knowledge of the novels. Readers get Telephone Man's warped view of other racial groups, handed to him from his father, along with his perspective of events from a crucial day in *The Crazy Horse Electric Game.* In two other stories, readers gain insights into Willie Weaver's hometown friends Johnny and Petey, as Johnny wrestles his dad and Petey wrestles a girl. And in the final story, Louis Banks from *Running Loose* befriends his boss' nephew who is ill with acquired immuno-deficiency syndrome (AIDS). In so doing, Louis is forced to choose what he knows is right over his friendship with Carter.

These brief descriptions of Crutcher's works can only begin to capture their spirit. The humor, for example, ranges from outrageous (picture the results of eating a box of biscuit mix and drinking a bottle of strawberry shampoo) to wacky (Lion has a seatbelt on the toilet in his apartment) and from subtle (the English teacher's comments about the characters in a class novel apply directly to the characters of *The Crazy Horse Electric Game*) to groanable (Johnny composes intricate puns, among them the one based on *Bless the Beasts and Children* which results in "Bless the beets and the chilled wren"). But the humor is offset in Crutcher's stories by very serious and real issues: suicide, sexual abuse, racial prejudice, and alcoholism, among others.

Girls who read these books will respond to the humor and the serious issues. Teachers who read them will appreciate their "literacy"—as in Johnny's atrociously delightful puns and the letters that Dillon writes to his brother after reading the letters in Alice Walker's *The Color Purple.* Of course it's neither teachers or even girls who are the main target of these books. Most directly, Crutcher writes for boys, who all too often choose not to read because there aren't as many books that appeal to them—books with "real" characters in "real world" situations. In this goal, writing books that will hook young male readers, Crutcher is entirely successful. At the same time, he's created rich and complex works for all readers, adult and adolescent, male and female.

—Bonnie O. Ericson

CUSICK, Richie Tankersley. American. Born in New Orleans, Los Angeles, 1 April 1952. Educated at University of Southwestern Louisiana, Lafayette, B.A. 1975. Married Rick Cusick in 1980. Ward clerk, Ochsner Foundation Hospital, New Orleans, Los Angeles, summers, 1970-72; writer, Hallmark Cards, Inc., Kansas City, Montana, 1975-84; free-lance writer. Recipient: Children's Choice award, IRA, 1989, for *The Lifeguard;* Book for the Teen Age, New York Public Library, 1990, for *Trick or Treat.* Agent: Mary Jack Wald Associates, Inc., Literary Representatives, 111 East 14th St., New York, NY 10003. Address: 7501 Westgate, Lenexa, KS 66216, U.S.A.

PUBLICATIONS FOR YOUNG ADULTS

Horror Novels

Evil on the Bayou. New York, Dell, 1984.
The Lifeguard. New York, Scholastic, 1988.
Trick or Treat. New York, Scholastic, 1989.
April Fools. New York, Scholastic, 1990.
Scarecrow. New York, Pocket Books, 1990.
Teacher's Pet. New York, Scholastic, 1990.
Vampire. New York, Pocket Books, 1991.
Blood Roots. New York, Pocket Books, 1992.
Buffy the Vampire Slayer. New York, Pocket Books, 1992.
Fatal Secrets. New York, Pocket Books, 1992.
The Mall. New York, Pocket Books, 1992.
Silent Stalker. New York, Pocket Books, 1993.

*   *   *

Throughout her writing career, Richie Tankersley Cusick has shown her appreciation for the gothic literary tradition. From her very first book in 1984, *Evil on the Bayou* (number twenty-one in the Dell Twilight Series and later reissued as a separate), Cusick has illustrated her love for the gothic style with dramatic plots, endangered heroines, weird mysteries, and hints of the supernatural. Most of Cusick's work can be roughly classified as young adult thrillers, and even those horror novels written for adults, *Scarecrow* and *Blood Roots,* are read by young people too. These novels incorporate gothic details, adding an atmospheric flavor not present in all thrillers.

Her first book, the aforementioned *Evil on the Bayou,* was published before the current popularity of young adult thrillers most notably exemplified by the works of Cusick, Christopher Pike, and R. L. Stine. However, Cusick published her next book *The Lifeguard* in 1988, and this book was evidently a greater success in the marketplace than her first book. From 1988 to 1993 she has published over ten titles.

There are certain characteristics in Cusick's books which separate them from those by other young adult thriller authors. One is the persistent sense of gothic details—both from the English gothic tradition and the decadent, brooding feeling of the Southern gothic. In fact, her second novel for adults, *Blood Roots* (1993), shows strong influence from the writings of V. C. Andrews due to the setting (a decaying old southern plantation house), use of the first person narrative (her only use of this literary device to date), and the extremely hateful, dysfunctional family described in the story.

Interestingly enough, one of the weaker features of Cusick's writing revolves around her use of the occult. Cusick claims to believe in the supernatural, but she has not been able to incorporate it successfully into her books thus far. This is due in part to the lack of accurate descriptions about the occult practice in question; the plentiful presence of snakes in *Evil on the Bayou* may have been intended to be symbolic of voodoo rituals and African snake gods, but they slithered around in her book as sinister, nasty, poisonous reality. In other titles, the supernatural is dangled as a possible rationale for what is going on, but usually turns out not to be the solution to the mystery. For example, in *Trick or Treat* there's a spooky old house where a murder was committed, but in the end it turns out that ghosts aren't guilty of the present-day crimes, living people are. In *Vampire* there are no supernatural vampires at all, just a disturbed, human murderer. When Cusick does use the supernatural for its own sake, the results are not particularly effective. In her adult horror book, *Scarecrow,* we are given a weird, stereotypical hillbilly family in the Ozarks, complete with a psychic child. There are menacing scarecrows around, somewhat reminiscent of Robert Westall's *The Scarecrows,* but not nearly as frightening. In *Buffy the Vampire Slayer* Cusick novelizes a film from a story by Joss Wheldon. This book lacks the enthusiasm of some of Cusick's other works, perhaps because she did not make up the original tale herself or because she is not as successful in writing a horror genre spoof.

In spite of the above criticisms, Cusick is deservedly popular with teen readers. Her writing skills have sharpened so that she now produces fast-action, quickly paced stories. The thrillers include a mystery with many false leads, with the perpetrator of the crimes often turning out to be one of the more sympathetic—and least suspected—characters. The stories are told from the point of view of a teenage female protagonist, making the books appealing to young women who enjoy scary reads. There is a basic identification for many teens with the central characters who often come from broken homes. The characters deal with difficult relationships, some familial and some romantic. They often learn self-reliance in their struggles with the unknown evil and start to understand the importance of not taking people at face value. These are themes that Lois Duncan has used very successfully in her young adult thrillers, and Cusick is able to take these ideas and given them freshness.

In many of her books, Cusick uses the literary device of a prologue to set the stage and grab the reader. Also early in many of the titles, the central character is placed in a situation which describes tension, often with family members. For example, in *Silent Stalker*

(1993) the heroine is unhappy on the very first page because of being forced to spend the summer with an unloved and virtually unknown father. Immediately the reader can guess that the young woman will be thrust into danger and may not be able to count on her only family member in the immediate vicinity. In *Vampire* the heroine is sent to stay with an unknown uncle who runs a "haunted house of horror." When people start getting killed, Darcy doesn't know if she can trust this strange relative or not. The heroines must learn quickly to make important judgments which may well determine if they will live or die.

Overall, Cusick has produced a number of exciting, popular young adult thrillers. Her books are probably read by teens more for the fun of the terrifying plot than the adolescent developmental concepts that are included. Yet these concepts are important for making three-dimensional, believable characters. It's not enough to create a terrifying story, a writer of young adult books must create people that readers care about and identify with as they devour the books.

—Cosette Kies

————

D

DAHL, Roald. British. Born in Llandaff, Glamorgan, Wales, 13 September 1916. Educated at Repton School, Yorkshire. Served in the Royal Air Force, 1939-45: in Nairobi and Habbanyah, 1939-40; with a fighter squadron in the Western Desert, 1940 (wounded); in Greece and Syria, 1941; assistant air attaché, Washington, D.C., 1942-43; wing commander, 1943; with British Security Co-ordination, North America, 1943-45. Married 1) the actress Patricia Neal in 1953 (divorced 1983), one son and four daughters (one deceased); 2) Felicity Ann Crosland in 1983. Member of the Public Schools Exploring Society expedition to Newfoundland, 1934; member of the Eastern staff, Shell Company, London, 1933-37, and Shell Company of East Africa, Dar-es-Salaam, 1937-39. Recipient: Mystery Writers of America Edgar Allan Poe award, 1954, 1959, and 1980; New England Round Table of Children's Librarians award, 1972, and Surrey School award, 1973, both for *Charlie and the Chocolate Factory;* Surrey School award, 1975, and Nene award, 1978, both for *Charlie and the Great Glass Elevator;* Surrey School award, 1978, and California Young Reader Medal, 1979, both for *Danny: The Champion of the World;* Federation of Children's Book Groups award, 1982, for *The BFG;* Massachusetts Children's award, 1982, for *James and the Giant Peach; New York Times* Outstanding Books award, 1983, Whitbread award, 1983, and West Australian award, 1986, all for *The Witches;* World Fantasy Convention Lifetime Achievement award, and Federation of Children's Book Groups award, both 1983; Maschler award runner-up, 1985, for *The Giraffe and the Pelly and Me; Boston Globe/Horn Book* nonfiction honor citation, 1985, for *Boy: Tales of Childhood;* International Board on Books for Young People awards for Norwegian and German translations of *The BFG,* both 1986; Smarties award, 1990, for *Esio Trot.* D.Litt.: University of Keele, Staffordshire, 1988. *Died 23 November 1990.*

PUBLICATIONS FOR CHILDREN AND YOUNG ADULTS

Fiction

The Gremlins, illustrated by Walt Disney Studio. New York, Random House, 1943; London, Collins, 1944.
James and the Giant Peach, illustrated by Nancy Ekholm Burkert. New York, Knopf, 1961; London, Allen and Unwin, 1967.
Charlie and the Chocolate Factory, illustrated by Joseph Schindelman. New York, Knopf, 1964; London, Allen and Unwin, 1967.
The Magic Finger, illustrated by William Pène du Bois. New York, Harper, 1966; London, Allen and Unwin, 1968.
Fantastic Mr. Fox, illustrated by Donald Chaffin. New York, Knopf, and London, Allen and Unwin, 1970.
Charlie and the Great Glass Elevator, illustrated by Joseph Schindelman. New York, Knopf, 1972; London, Allen and Unwin, 1973.
Danny: The Champion of the World, illustrated by Jill Bennett. London, Cape, and New York, Knopf, 1975.
The Wonderful Story of Henry Sugar and Six More. London, Cape, 1977; as *The Wonderful World of Henry Sugar,* New York, Knopf, 1977.

The Complete Adventures of Charlie and Mr. Willy Wonka, illustrated by Faith Jaques. London, Allen and Unwin, 1978.
The Enormous Crocodile, illustrated by Quentin Blake. London, Cape, and New York, Knopf, 1978.
The Twits, illustrated by Quentin Blake. London, Cape, 1980; New York, Knopf, 1981.
George's Marvellous Medicine, illustrated by Quentin Blake. London, Cape, 1981; New York, Knopf, 1982.
The BFG, illustrated by Quentin Blake. London, Cape, and New York, Farrar Straus, 1982.
The Witches, illustrated by Quentin Blake. London, Cape, and New York, Farrar Straus, 1983.
The Giraffe and the Pelly and Me, illustrated by Quentin Blake. London, Cape, and New York, Farrar Straus, 1985.
Matilda, illustrated by Quentin Blake. London, Cape, and New York, Viking Kestrel, 1988.
Roald Dahl: Charlie and the Chocolate Factory, Charlie and the Great Glass Elevator, The BFG. New York, Viking, 1989.
Esio Trot, illustrated by Quentin Blake. New York, Viking, 1990.
The Minpins. New York, Viking, 1991.
The Vicar of Nibbleswickle, illustrated by Quentin Blake. New York, Viking, 1992.

Recordings: *Charlie and the Chocolate Factory,* Caedmon, 1975; *James and the Giant Peach,* Caedmon, 1977; *Fantastic Mr. Fox,* Caedmon, 1978; *Roald Dahl Reads His "The Enormous Crocodile" and "The Magic Finger,"* Caedmon, 1980; *Bedtime Stories to Children's Books,* Center for Cassette Studies, 1973.

Poetry

Revolting Rhymes, illustrated by Quentin Blake. London, Cape, 1982; New York, Knopf, 1983.
Dirty Beasts, illustrated by Rosemary Fawcett. London, Cape, 1983; New York, Farrar Straus, 1984.
Rhyme Stew, illustrated by Quentin Blake. New York, Viking, 1990.

Other

Boy: Tales of Childhood. London, Cape, and New York, Farrar Straus, 1984.
Going Solo. London, Cape, and New York, Farrar Straus, 1986.
The Dahl Diary, 1992, illustrated by Quentin Blake. New York, Puffin, 1991.

PUBLICATIONS FOR ADULTS

Novels

Sometime Never: A Fable for Supermen. New York, Scribner, 1948; London, Collins, 1949.
My Uncle Oswald. London, Joseph, 1979; New York, Knopf, 1980.

Short Stories

Over to You: Ten Stories of Flyers and Flying. New York, Reynal, 1946; London, Hamish Hamilton, 1947.

Someone Like You. New York, Knopf, 1953; London, Secker and
    Warburg, 1954; revised edition, London, Joseph, 1961.
Kiss, Kiss. New York, Knopf, and London, Joseph, 1960.
Twenty-Nine Kisses. London, Joseph, 1969.
Selected Stories. New York, Random House, 1970.
Penguin Modern Stories 12, with others. London, Penguin, 1972.
Switch Bitch. New York, Knopf, and London, Joseph, 1974.
The Best of Roald Dahl. New York, Random House, 1978; London,
    Joseph, 1983.
Tales of the Unexpected. London, Joseph, and New York, Vintage,
    1979.
More Tales of the Unexpected. London, Joseph, 1980; as *Further
    Tales of the Unexpected,* Bath, Chivers, 1981.
A Roald Dahl Selection: Nine Short Stories, edited by Roy
    Blatchford. London, Longman, 1980.
Two Fables. London, Viking, 1986; New York, Farrar Straus, 1987.
A Second Roald Dahl Selection: Eight Short Stories, edited by Hélène
    Fawcett. London, Longman, 1987.
Ah, Sweet Mystery of Life, illustrated by John Lawrence. London,
    Cape, 1988; New York, Knopf, 1989.

Plays

The Honeys (produced New York, 1955).

Screenplays: *You Only Live Twice,* with Harry Jack Bloom, 1967;
Chitty-Chitty-Bang-Bang, with Ken Hughes, 1968; *The Night-Dig-
ger,* 1970; *The Lightning Bug,* 1971; *Willy Wonka and the Chocolate
Factory,* 1971.

Television Play: *Lamb to the Slaughter* (*Alfred Hitchcock Presents*
series), 1955.

Other

Editor, *Roald Dahl's Book of Ghost Stories.* London, Cape, and
    New York, Farrar Straus, 1983.

*

Media Adaptations: *36 Hours* (film, adaptation of "Beware of the
Dog"), MGM, 1964; *Delicious Inventions* (film, excerpted from
Willie Wonka and the Chocolate Factory, Paramount, 1971), Films,
Inc., 1976; *Roald Dahl's Charlie and the Chocolate Factory: A Play*
(play by Richard George), New York, Knopf, 1976; *Willie Wonka
and the Chocolate Factory—Storytime* (filmstrip, excerpted from
the 1971 Paramount film), Films, Inc., 1976; *Willie Wonka and the
Chocolate Factory—Learning Kit* (filmstrip, excerpted from the
1971 Paramount film), Films, Inc., 1976; *The Great Switcheroo*
(recording), Caedmon, 1977; *Tales of the Unexpected* (television
movie), WNEW-TV, 1979; *Roald Dahl's James and the Giant Peach:
A Play* (play by Richard George), Penguin, 1982; *The Witches* (film),
Lorimar, 1990.

Critical Study: Entry in *Contemporary Literary Criticism,* Volume
1, Detroit, Gale, 1973; Volume 6, 1976; Volume 18, 1981; Entry in
Children's Literature Review, Volume 1, Detroit, Gale, 1976; Volume 7, 1984; *Roald Dahl* by Chris Powling, London, Hamish
Hamilton, 1983.

*   *   *

Clues to the origin of Roald Dahl's fictional world may be found
in *Boy,* the first volume of his autobiography, where the author
discusses his life at public schools in Wales and England. "I was
appalled by the fact that masters and senior boys were allowed
literally to wound other boys, and sometimes quite severely. I
couldn't get over it. I never have got over it," he insists. Indeed, in
story after story he administers sure and swift punishment to wan-
tonly cruel adults, such as the horrible aunties in *James and the
Giant Peach* or the evil headmistress in *Matilda.*

A second revealing description in *Boy* has young Roald being
upbraided for not liking the rules. And why should he? What he
sees is a sadistic, bandy-legged, sanctimonious headmaster whom
the system rewards with England's highest Christian post: that of
Archbishop of Canterbury. Early on, the six-foot, six-inch Dahl
begins to see himself as an outsider, as one whose literary mission
is to expose the mistakes of God and man and to present an order in
which things operate as every young person knows they are supposed to operate.

To appreciate the Dahl outsider, one must recognize that he is
someone who intuitively understands the controlling system. The
difference is that he refuses to subscribe to it. At his best, he is the
conman with a conscience, the individual who can skillfully defeat
his adversaries at their own game. Willie Wonka in *Charlie and the
Chocolate Factory* is this kind of person, becoming wonderfully
wealthy by outwitting his unscrupulous competitors. A better example is the benign pickpocket in his story "The Hitchhiker," a
man who can undo that most obvious of authority figures—a coarse,
belligerent motorcycle cop.

The abiding principle in Dahl's work is one of schoolboy justice—poetic or otherwise. If, for example, the conman is neither an
inspiring child nor worthy adult, Dahl takes great pleasure in having
him generate his own comeuppance. This is the case with Uncle
Oswald, a legendary seducer who gets seduced in "The Visitor."
Similarly, in "Parson's Pleasure," an antique dealer who poses as an
honest churchman and then dupes rural people out of their price-
less furniture ends up collecting a pile of kindling instead of a rare
Chippendale.

Too easily is Dahl's fiction segregated into adult and children's
categories. In actual fact, both worlds are enormously similar, even
though a certain sexual mischievousness is reserved for older readers. Elementary fair play is ever the issue at hand. So what if
bizarre, improbable events are necessary in order to settle the score!
Wild ducks train shotguns upon a family of hunters in *The Magic
Finger.* And in "Lamb to the Slaughter," which became an *Alfred
Hitchcock Presents* teleplay, a loving wife deftly decks her callous
husband with a frozen leg of lamb. She and the unwitting officers
then eat the evidence.

To insist that Dahl's world is too violent for young readers is to
miss the point. All of his fiction is governed by an innocent, grand-
scale reasoning: virtue is hyperbolically rewarded, while vice is
rigorously punished. Of course Willie Wonka will freely give his
fabulous chocolate factory to a kind, impoverished boy named
Charlie Bucket. Charlie deserves it. Unsophisticated logic demands
no less. And of course the evil women in *The Witches* will be turned
into mice. They deserve to be caught in traps and beheaded. After
all, they have laid plans to kill every child in England.

Dahl's stories are distinguished by imaginative, free-wheeling
plots, not by intense character development. Verbal ingenuity, however, is more evident in works for younger readers. Here, rhymes
and alliterations are accompanied by outrageous puns and word
coinages. Some of the cleverest neologisms appear in *The BFG,*

where a gentle giant eats disgusting *snozzcumbers* while longing for something more *scrumdillyumptious*.

Another difference is that in the children's stories, magic is often needed to save the day. The heroine of *Matilda* discovers that she has psycho-kinetic powers, and the little girl in *The Magic Finger* can cast a spell by pointing with her index finger. In "The Swan," perhaps the most chilling piece that Dahl ever wrote, bullies tie young Peter Watson between two rails. Peter scrunches as low as he can and somehow survives being run over by a train. Still he is not set free. The bullies now kill a beautiful swan, cut off its wings, attach them to Peter, and make him climb a tall tree. They then start shooting at him with a .22-caliber rifle, taunting him to fly. And fly he does! He soars gracefully through the heavens to the safety of his own back garden.

"The Swan" is particularly interesting in that it corrects the notion that Dahl's natural adversaries are always children and adults. Here the enemies are Peter's schoolmates. Conversely, there are remarkably loving child-adult relationships depicted in *Danny: The Champion of the World, Matilda, The BFG,* and *Charlie and the Chocolate Factory.* One of the best involves a child hero and his cigar-smoking, Norwegian grandmother in *Witches.* When the lad is turned into a mouse, Dahl avoids the expected, sentimental trap of reversing the fate. The boy philosophically accepts his condition, telling his adoring grandmother, "It doesn't matter who you are or what you look like so long as somebody loves you." Such fundamental wisdom marks the timeless appeal of Roald Dahl's fiction for readers of all ages.

—Walker Rutledge

DALY, Maureen. American. Born in Castlecaufield, County Tyrone, Ireland, 15 March 1921. Educated at St. Mary Springs Academy, Fond du Lac, Wisconsin; Rosary College, River Forest, Illinois, B.A. 1942. Married the writer William P. McGivern in 1946 (died 1983); one daughter (deceased) and one son. Since 1938 writer. Police reporter and columnist, Chicago *Tribune,* 1941-44; reporter, Chicago City News Bureau, 1941-43; associate editor, *Ladies' Home Journal,* Philadelphia, 1944-49; editorial consultant, *Saturday Evening Post,* Philadelphia, 1960-69; since 1987 reporter and columnist, *Desert Sun,* Palm Desert. Screenwriter for Twentieth Century-Fox. Lecturer on foreign lands and emerging nations. Recipient: *Scholastic* magazine's short story contest, 1936, third prize for "Fifteen," 1937, first prize for "Sixteen"; O. Henry Memorial Award, 1938, for short story "Sixteen"; Dodd, Mead Intercollegiate Literary Fellowship Novel Award, 1942, and Lewis Carroll Shelf Award, 1969, both for *Seventeenth Summer;* Freedoms Foundation Award, 1952, for "humanity in reporting"; Gimbel Fashion Award, 1962, for contribution to U.S. fashion industry through *Saturday Evening Post* articles; one of *Redbook*'s ten great books for teens, 1987, for *Acts of Love.* Agent: Eleanor Wood, Blassingame, McCauley, and Wood, 432 Park Ave. S., Suite 1205, New York, NY 10016. Address: 73-305 Ironwood St., Palm Desert, CA 92260, U.S.A.

PUBLICATIONS FOR YOUNG ADULTS

Fiction

Seventeenth Summer. New York, Dodd Mead, 1942; London, Hollis and Carter, 1947, illustrated edition, New York, Dodd Mead, 1948.
Sixteen and Other Stories, illustrated by Kendall Rossi. New York, Dodd Mead, 1961.
Acts of Love. New York, Scholastic, 1986; London, Gollancz, 1987.
First a Dream. New York, Scholastic, 1990.

Nonfiction

Smarter and Smoother: A Handbook on How to Be That Way, illustrated by Marguerite Bryan. New York, Dodd Mead, 1944.
What's Your P.Q. (Personality Quotient)?, illustrated by Ellie Simmons. New York, Dodd Mead, 1952; revised edition, 1966.
Twelve around the World, illustrated by Frank Kramer. New York, Dodd Mead, 1957.
Spanish Roundabout. New York, Dodd Mead, 1960.
Moroccan Roundabout. New York, Dodd Mead, 1961.

Other

Editor, *My Favorite Stories.* New York, Dodd Mead, 1948.
Editor, *My Favorite Mystery [Suspense] Stories.* New York, Dodd Mead, 2 vols., 1966-68.

PUBLICATIONS FOR CHILDREN

Fiction

Patrick Visits the Farm, illustrated by Ellie Simmons. New York, Dodd Mead, 1959.
Patrick Takes a Trip, illustrated by Ellie Simmons. New York, Dodd Mead, 1960.
Patrick Visits the Library, illustrated by Paul Lantz. New York, Dodd Mead, 1961.
Patrick Visits the Zoo, illustrated by Sam Savitt. New York, Dodd Mead, 1963.
The Ginger Horse, illustrated by Wesley Dennis. New York, Dodd Mead, 1964.
Spain: Wonderland of Contrasts. New York, Dodd Mead, 1965.
The Small War of Sergeant Donkey, illustrated by Wesley Dennis. New York, Dodd Mead, 1966.
Rosie, the Dancing Elephant, illustrated by Lorence Bjorklund. New York, Dodd Mead, 1967.

PUBLICATIONS FOR ADULTS

Nonfiction

The Perfect Hostess: Complete Etiquette and Entertainment for the Home. New York, Dodd Mead, 1950.
Mention My Name in Mombasa: The Unscheduled Adventures of an American Family Abroad (as Maureen Daly McGivern), with William P. McGivern, illustrated by Frank Kramer. New York, Dodd Mead, 1958.

A Matter of Honor, with William P. McGivern. New York, Arbor House, 1984.

Other

Editor, *Profile of Youth.* Philadelphia, Lippincott, 1951.

Also author of "High School Career Series," Curtis Publishing Co., 1942-49. Writer with husband of scripts for television series, including "Kojak," and of screenplay, *Brannigan.* Work represented in several textbooks and anthologies. Contributor of over two hundred articles to numerous periodicals, including *Vogue, Mademoiselle, Cosmopolitan, Woman's Day, Scholastic, Woman's Home Companion,* and *Redbook.*

*

Media Adaptations: *Seventeenth Summer* (film), Warner Bros., 1949; *The Ginger Horse* (film), Walt Disney Studios; Daly's short story, "You Can't Kiss Caroline," has also been dramatized.

Manuscript Collection: University of Oregon Library, Eugene.

Biography: Essay in *Something about the Author Autobiography Series,* Volume 1, Detroit, Gale, 1986; essay in *Speaking for Ourselves: Autobiographical Sketches by Notable Authors of Books for Young Adults,* Volume 1, compiled and edited by Donald R. Gallo, National Council of Teachers of English, 1990.

Critical Study: Entry in *Contemporary Literary Criticism,* Volume 17, Detroit, Gale, 1981.

Maureen Daly comments:

My first novel, *Seventeenth Summer,* which was written when I was a teenager and published during my last year of college, has long been considered a "break through" book which established the Young Adult Literary category in the publishing business in the United States as that mammoth segment of publishing exists today.

I would like, at this late date, to explain that *Seventeenth Summer,* in my intention and at the time of publication, was considered a full adult novel and published and reviewed as such. It was given particular praise in *New York,* as well as hundreds of other publications, and was lauded by Sinclair Lewis in a lead review in the *New York Times Book Review.*

Recently, on a lecture/visit with Dr. Ray Crisp of the Lincoln Nebraska school system, I gleaned that *Seventeenth Summer* was considered a revolutionary up-start in the "young literature" field because it depicted drinking, smoking, heterosexual and homosexual activities as events in the lives of American teenagers, unusual—I guess—in the prudish silences of my book's historic time slot.

*   *   *

Maureen Daly's major contribution to adolescent literature has been *Seventeenth Summer,* which helped to establish the romance novel among adolescent readers in the early 1940s. Although much of contemporary adolescent fiction has expanded to focus more heavily on the problem novel and its realism, many adolescent readers still prefer the romance.

Adolescent readers of romance novels identify readily with the protagonists, many of whom are the same age as the readers. The common themes in such novels, especially the possibility of leaving home and embarking on a new way of life as well as the seeking and securing of "true love," which always forms a major part of the plot, speak strongly to adolescents. Although some older readers may view such novels as exaggerated and larger than life, adolescence is a period of intense feelings and the emphasis upon emotion in the romance is an important ingredient for success with adolescent readers.

Unlike the old pattern of this genre—boy meets girl, boy loses girl, boy finally wins girl—the pattern in *Seventeenth Summer* focuses upon the role of the girl in the quest. This pattern is revealed through the actions of Angie, the main character in Daly's novel, during Angie's seventeenth summer. Little actually happens in the novel: Angie falls in love, she dates a boy named Jack from her home town, and she eventually leaves him at the end of summer to go away to college. Significantly, however, the story is told from her point of view and she is the one to terminate the relationship.

The plot is not what holds the interest of readers. Instead, the sensitivity toward adolescent feelings which pervades the story leads readers to remember the book long after finishing it. The story is definitely female oriented and consequently has more appeal for female readers. Angie has no brothers, but her three sisters, two older, and one younger, serve as foils for Angie. One older sister, Margaret, has a steady boyfriend and is planning her wedding; Lorraine, the other older sister, has difficulty sustaining any relationships with men and sees herself as a failure. On the other side of Angie is Kitty, still young enough to wonder how butterflies fly and still wanting to play catch with her father. Angie's relationship with her mother is a warm and supportive one while her father is a more shadowy character for whom she has respect but no particular closeness. The family unit, however, provides a safe environment for Angie in which she can sort out her feelings.

The main focus of Angie's summer is her growing awareness of her feelings about boys and all the attendant misunderstandings and frustrations which accompany first love. Daly's treatment of every girl's daydream of having a boy "fall" for her might be compared to the fairy tale in which a wish for a new identity is granted. As Angie points out:

> It's funny what a boy can do. One day you're nobody and the next day you're the girl that some fellow goes with and the other fellows look at you harder and wonder what you've got and wish that they had been the one to take you out first. And the girls say hello and want you to walk down to the drugstore to have Cokes with them because the boy who likes you might come along and he might have other boys with him. Going with a boy gives you a new identity—especially going with a fellow like Jack Daly.

Accompanying the love story, however, are elements which distinguish *Seventeenth Summer* from the usual romance. Although Daly's portrayal of society may seem tame by today's standards, she pushed the limits of what was socially acceptable in the 1940s. Jack smokes a pipe and drinks beer. During one of their dates, Jack takes Angie to a roadhouse where she asks him to explain why the male pianist has painted fingernails. He looks embarrassed, tries to respond, but offers no answer. Lorraine, Angie's older sister, depends upon traveling salesmen for dates and ends up being left behind each time the salesman moves on. The world created in the novel suggests that drinking, smoking and even dating do not necessarily lead to sin and damnation, a view quite avant garde for the time, and which was further enhanced by the fact that Daly was only seventeen herself when she wrote the major portion of the novel.

Daly also broke with the usual tradition of the omniscient author and chose to have Angie present her own story. Although the first person point of view today is an accepted form of narration, it was not used with great frequency in the writings of the 1940s. As a result of Daly's choice, however, readers experience a story that has a stronger and more believable sense of personal emotion and sensitivity than might otherwise have occurred. This sensitivity is heightened by Daly's prose, such as in Angie's description of her first kiss:

> In the movies they always shut their eyes but I didn't. I didn't think of anything like that, though I do remember a quick thought passing through my mind again about how much he smelled like Ivory soap when his face was so close to mine. In the loveliness of the next moment I think I grew up. I remember that behind him was the thin, yellow arc of moon, turned over on its back, and I remember feeling my hands slowly relax on the rough lapels of his coat. Sitting on the cool grass in my sprigged dimity with the little blue and white bachelor's buttons pinned in my hair, Jack kissed me and his lips were as smooth and baby-soft as a new raspberry.

Some critics find Angie's innocence offensive and unbelievable. But the strength of the book and its staying power—over a million and a half copies have been sold since its publication—lie in readers remembering Angie as an individual, not as a representative of the 1940s. Readers many years after their first experience with *Seventeenth Summer* have written to Daly to tell her how well her portrayal of first love matched their own experiences. It is little surprise, therefore, that the book remains in print and is used so often by teachers of adolescent literature to represent the beginning of the American adolescent romance.

—Charles R. Duke

DANIEL, Colin. See **WINDSOR, Patricia (Frances).**

DANZIGER, Paula. American. Born in Washington, D.C., 18 August 1944. Educated at Montclair State College, New Jersey, B.A. 1967, M.A. Substitute teacher, Edison, New Jersey, 1967; Title I teacher, Highland Park, New Jersey, 1967-68; junior-high school English teacher, Edison, New Jersey, 1968-70; English teacher, Lincoln Junior High School, West Orange, New Jersey, 1977-78; since 1978 full-time writer. Worked for the Educational Opportunity Program, Montclair State College, until 1977. Recipient: New Jersey Institute of Technology award, and Young Reader Medal Nomination, California Reading Association, both 1976, Massachusetts Children's Book award, first runner-up, 1977, winner, 1979, and Nene award, Hawaii Association of School Librarians and the Ha-

waii Library Association, 1980, all for *The Cat Ate My Gymsuit;* Child Study Association of America's Children's Books of the Year citation, 1978, Massachusetts Children's Book award, Education Department of Salem State College, 1979, Nene award, 1980, California Young Reader Medal Nomination, 1981, and Arizona Young Reader award, 1983, all for *The Pistachio Prescription;* Children's Choice award, International Reading Association and the Children's Book Council, 1979, for *The Pistachio Prescription,* 1980, for *The Cat Ate My Gymsuit* and *Can You Sue Your Parents for Malpractice?,* 1981, for *There's a Bat in Bunk Five,* and 1983, for *The Divorce Express.* New Jersey Institute of Technology award, and New York Public Library's Books for the Teen Age citation, both 1980, and Land of Enchantment Book award, New Mexico Library Association, 1982, all for *Can You Sue Your Parents for Malpractice?;* Read-a-Thon Author of the Year award, Multiple Sclerosis Society, and Parents' Choice award for Literature, Parents' Choice Foundation, both 1982, Woodward Park School Annual Book award, 1983, and South Carolina Young Adult Book award, South Carolina Association of School Librarians, 1985, all for *The Divorce Express;* CRABbery award, Prince George's County Memorial Library System (MD), 1982, and Young Readers Medal, 1984, both for *There's a Bat in Bunk Five;* Parents' Choice award for Literature, Bologna International Children's Book Fair exhibitor, and Child Study Association of America's Children's Books of the Year citation, all 1985, all for *It's an Aardvark-Eat-Turtle World.*

PUBLICATIONS FOR YOUNG ADULTS

Fiction

The Cat Ate My Gymsuit. New York, Delacorte, 1974.
The Pistachio Prescription. New York, Delacorte, 1978.
Can You Sue Your Parents for Malpractice?. New York, Delacorte, 1979.
There's a Bat in Bunk Five. New York, Delacorte, 1980.
The Divorce Express. New York, Delacorte, 1982.
It's an Aardvark-Eat-Turtle World. New York, Delacorte, 1985.
This Place Has No Atmosphere. New York, Delacorte, 1986.
Remember Me to Harold Square. New York, Delacorte, 1987.
Everyone Else's Parents Said Yes. New York, Delacorte, 1989.
Make Like a Tree and Leave. New York, Delacorte, 1990.
Earth to Matthew. New York, Delacorte, 1991.
Not for a Billion Gazillion Dollars. New York, Delacorte, 1992.
Amber Brown Is Not a Crayon. Putnam, New York, forthcoming.

*

Media Adaptations: *The Cat Ate My Gymsuit* (film, cassette), Cheshire, 1985; *The Cat Ate My Gymsuit* (cassette), *The Pistachio Prescription* (cassette), *There's a Bat in Bunk Five* (cassette), *Can You Sue Your Parents for Malpractice?* (cassette), and *The Divorce Express* (cassette), Listening Library, 1985-86.

Biography: Essay in *Authors and Artists for Young Adults,* Volume 4, Detroit, Gale, 1990; essay in *Speaking for Ourselves: Autobiographical Sketches by Notable Authors of Books for Young Adults,* Volume 1, compiled and edited by Donald R. Gallo, National Council of Teachers of English, 1990.

Critical Studies: Entry in *Children's Literature Review,* Volume 20,

Detroit, Gale, 1990; entry in *Contemporary Literary Criticism,* Volume 21, Detroit, Gale, 1982.

*   *   *

Because Paula Danziger's books are fast-paced, easy reading, and filled with realistic situations that young adults recognize and with dialogue that they would love to deliver, critics of young adult literature often dismiss them as light entertainment. Even Danziger herself through such characters as Marcy Lewis, the protagonist of her first novel, *The Cat Ate My Gymsuit* (1974), is faintly apologetic of the fact that her novels may lack the depth of a heavyweight young adult offering. Marcy demurs, "My life is not easy. I know I'm not poor. Nobody beats me. I have clothes to wear, my own room, a stereo, a TV, and a push button phone. Sometimes I feel guilty being so miserable, but middle class kids have problems too." Marcy sets the stage for the rest of Danziger's protagonists—the middle class kids of today, whose experiences include the modern restructuring of the family, the complications of changing role models, fears of personal ineffectualness in a demanding world, and the universal challenges of adolescence.

The Cat Ate My Gymsuit is Paula Danziger's most representative work in terms of its comprehensive use of these important young adult themes. Furthermore, Danziger has revealed that her first novel was also her most angry and autobiographical since it was written in conjunction with events in her own life that forced her to deal with the leftover frustrations and fears of her youth. The author's personal success in facing up to those personal issues can be deduced from her method of resolving her characters' problems at the end of the novel. Marcy begins counseling with a psychiatrist while Ms. Finney, Marcy's teacher, decides to specialize in bibliotherapy.

Marcy's family life is classically and overbearingly patriarchal; her father is a bitter and unhappy man. Slowly we realize that the abuse Marcy receives from him, while not overtly physical, is the worst kind of verbal and emotional abuse. Mr. Lewis's favorite topics are Marcy's weight, her clumsiness, and eventually her support of her freethinking English teacher, Barbara Finney. Equally as subjugated by Mr. Lewis are Marcy's younger brother Stuart, who becomes practically invisible since Marcy is her father's favorite verbal target, and Marcy's mother. Mrs. Lewis's goal is to keep peace in the family, which she attempts to do by acting as the family's mediator; after each confrontation, she privately placates both her husband and Marcy. Mrs. Lewis maintains the family's delicate balance of artificial normality by prescribing tranquilizers for herself and huge bowls of ice cream for her children. The ice cream, of course, only exacerbates Marcy's weight problem and gives her father more ammunition for future confrontations. More ominously, Mrs. Lewis's dependence on prescription tranquilizers helps her convince herself that she has no other personal options than to endure the abusive situation in which she and her children suffer. The tranquilizers also serve as a form of emotional blackmail as Mrs. Lewis attempts to convince Marcy to follow her lead and accept the status quo.

Then, in the middle of the school year, Barbara Finney takes over Marcy's English class at school and begins a support group for her students which they name Smedley. From her involvement with Smedley, Marcy learns that her family is not functioning as it should. Her attempts to call this fact to the attention of her father meet with additional rebuffs and increased abuse. Marcy's mother, however, is more receptive—although hesitatingly so—to suggestions

for improving family communication. Finally, Ms. Finney's refusal to pledge allegiance to the American flag and her consequent dismissal from the school system forces everyone to take a stand. Marcy's family is split between her father's "follow the rules" philosophy and Marcy's newfound courage to assert fledgling convictions. Mrs. Lewis, in the face of a family rift she cannot mediate, supports Marcy's efforts to reinstate Ms. Finney, and everyone's definitions of individual roles within the family are challenged. Mr. Lewis learns that his economic responsibility to his family, which he grudgingly fulfills, does not grant him the power to make them perform as he thinks they should. Marcy, and eventually her mother, challenge their dependence on that economic power—Marcy by refusing to be placated by binge-shopping with her mother after each argument with her father, and Mrs. Lewis by deciding to break from the homemaker mold and return to the workforce. Marcy and her friends learn through their banding together to save Ms. Finney's job that no one is too young to recognize injustice and wage effective battle against it. At the end of the novel and in keeping with its overall humorous tone, Marcy gets her first pimple, symbolic of her entrance into the world of adolescence. She welcomes this previously dreaded status now that she knows how to seek support and encouragement from her friends in Smedley.

Danziger's later novels rework one or all of her major themes. In *The Pistachio Prescription* (1978), for example, Cassie Stephens must face the disintegration of her parents' marriage while coping with her own insecurity as the self-proclaimed ugly duckling asthmatic of her family. Along the way, she and her friends unite to insure that the newly elected officers of the "freshperson" class will be people who are truly representative of their group and not the school snobs.

Lauren Allen asks *Can You Sue Your Parents for Malpractice?* (1979) when she takes a course entitled "Law for Children and Young People." Her teacher encourages his students to publish a newsletter about students' rights, teaching them that they can have some control over their own lives. Lauren's father, like Marcy's father from *The Cat Ate My Gymsuit,* feels his traditional patriarchal control over his family is threatened when his oldest daughter Melissa moves in with her boyfriend. As Lauren watches her sister struggle to create a relationship unlike their parents' tense marriage, Lauren herself challenges the socially acceptable by dating a boy younger than herself.

Marcy Lewis returns in *There's a Bat in Bunk Five* (1980). Her relationship with her father has progressed, although it's far from perfect. Spending the summer as a counselor-in-training at a creative arts camp directed by her former teacher Ms. Barbara Finney gives Marcy a chance to be on her own and practice some of the self-confidence she's learned since the ninth grade. Troubled campers and an attentive fellow counselor show her that she's got more to learn. Additionally, *There's a Bat in Bunk Five* is set near Woodstock, New York, a locale with which Danziger is personally familiar and which is used as the setting for her next two novels.

The Divorce Express (1982) and *It's an Aardvark-Eat-Turtle World* (1985) are about best friends who become "steps" when their parents decide to live together. Phoebe Brooks, the first-person narrator of *The Divorce Express,* must adjust to shuttling back and forth between her New York City mother and her Woodstock-based father. Her new friend Rosie Wilson shares Phoebe's divorce woes although Phoebe is still working through the many difficulties of her situation, and Rosie has adopted a more accepting and philosophical point of view. Rosie, a departure from Danziger's early protagonists, has more than mere adolescence to cope with: through her, Danziger deals not only with children of divorce but also with children of biracial marriage. When, in *It's an Aardvark-Eat-Turtle World*, Phoebe's father Jim and Rosie's mother Mindy decide to join their two households, Danziger switches the point of view to Rosie's first-person narration. Jim and Mindy are a warm and nurturing adult couple—Danziger's first—and the conflict in this novel is generated not by inflexible, tradition-minded grown-ups but by Phoebe's childish rejection of the new family structure. Phoebe's anger and rebelliousness are traits she shares with Danziger's early protagonists as she sorts through her confused feelings to achieve a final acceptance of the loving, cohesive family unit that Jim, Mindy, and Rosie offer her. Interestingly, Danziger has admitted that Phoebe's anger had been difficult to write about and that she had identified more with stable, self-knowledgeable Rosie during the writing of *It's an Aardvark-Eat-Turtle World*. Indeed, in identifying with Rosie, Danziger shows a dramatic progression—both personally and creatively—from the early, angry, autobiographical *The Cat Ate My Gymsuit*.

As if to demonstrate that progression, anger and autobiography have been all but discarded in Danziger's latest novels, which focus on sixth-grader Matthew Martin. Matthew, whose adventures are related in evenhanded and reflective third person, is a distinct departure from Danziger's feminine protagonists, whose stories are narrated in energetic, if self-absorbed, first person. Matthew's most serious problems are loving-but-quirky parents who diverge philosophically on the topics of health food and junk food, an older sister who is charting an unsteady course through her own adolescence, and the disgruntled female members of his sixth-grade class who find him grossly immature.

As engaging a protagonist as Matthew is, however, Paula Danziger's earlier novels remain her best. Sometimes angry, but always honest and unfailingly humorous, characters like Marcy Lewis, Phoebe Brooks, and Rosie Wilson walk modern teenagers through situations similar to those in which they will sooner or later find themselves. In the process, Paula Danziger's characters give her readers cheerful permission to be themselves and to look confidently into the future.

—Patricia L. Bradley

DAVIS, Jenny. American. Born in Louisville, Kentucky, 29 June 1953. Educated at Allegheny Community College, Pittsburgh, Pennsylvania, A.A. 1973; University of Kentucky, Lexington, B.A. 1976, M.A. 1983. Married Dee Davis in 1975 (divorced 1981); two sons. Child advocate, Appalachian Regional Hospitals, Hazard, Kentucky, 1973-75; sex educator, Fayette County Health Department, Lexington, Kentucky, 1983-85; teacher, The Lexington School, Lexington, since 1985. Address: 723 Melrose, Lexington, KY 40502, U.S.A.

Publications for Young Adults

Novels

Goodbye and Keep Cold. New York, Orchard Books, 1987.
Sex Education. New York, Orchard Books, 1988.

Checking on the Moon. New York, Orchard Books, 1991.

*

Biography: Essay in *Speaking for Ourselves, Too* compiled and edited by Donald R. Gallo, National Council of Teachers of English, 1993.

*   *   *

Jenny Davis is not afraid to write about controversial subjects such as venereal disease, death, sex education, wife abuse, mental illness, and rape. Her books are not "simple problem" novels, but rather are complex creations where characters live realistic lives facing an assortment of difficulties which are not always solved but are dealt with satisfactorily.

Goodbye and Keep Cold is told by Edda Combs who has been out of college a year and is living in a beach house. Edda knows she will soon have to enter the adult world, but for now she sits and thinks about her life since the day her father was killed at a Kentucky strip mine. Edda's childhood world is full of complications: her mother (Frances) is romantically involved with the man (Henry John) who accidentally kills her husband (Edda's father); Edda learns that her father acquired herpes from her mother's best friend; her mother divorces her dead husband; a move to Lexington, Kentucky, and to schools where violence is the norm; her mother adopts Henry John's infant daughter; and her mother and Henry John marry.

The failings of adults are presented in a realistic fashion that young people will be able to accept, though Davis's characters do not face easy solutions to their problems. There is generally an older person, usually a relative, there to listen and to give advice when needed. Edda's family has Banker, a distant relative who has lived with them since Edda was two.

Sex Education, Davis's second novel, is told by sixteen-year-old Olivia Sinclair, who is in a psychiatric hospital. She writes about her past as a sort of therapy. (Davis herself spent her fifteenth year in a psychiatric hospital and, incidentally, once taught sex education classes.) Drawing from her own experiences Davis tells the story of two young people who get caught up in an outside class project of caring for someone else. They are assigned a pregnant woman who, as they later find out, has a husband who beats her. As the two young people try to help Maggie, her husband pushes David who falls down icy steps and breaks his neck. Livvy is so upset by David's death that she is institutionalized where she retreats into sleep for seven months. Livvy's psychiatrist suggests that she write down everything that led to her admittance to the hospital and, as she is finishing, the teacher who had guided the class project comes to visit and asks Livvy's forgiveness for not realizing what might happen. Through this encounter Livvy is able to make peace with herself and accept that no one was really to blame for David's death. She realizes that she has not lost him completely, that a part of David will always be with her in her mind.

Again in *Checking on the Moon* the narrator is a young woman who is trying to make sense of a recent period in her life. Cab (who was born in one) and her brother Bill live with their grandmother in one of the ethnic areas of Pittsburgh while their mother travels through Europe with her new husband. Cab and Bill become involved with setting up a neighborhood crime-watch group after Bill's girlfriend Jessica is raped. Both Bill and Jessica's reactions are very true-to-life. Davis does not sugarcoat the situation by pretending the rape makes no difference to their relationship; it does, but both learn to deal with it.

Davis's subject matter and style of writing have strong appeal to teenage readers. All are told by young adults who are trying to understand themselves and their worlds. The problems they face are those common to many young adults, such as the search for identity, coping with parents, and dealing with friends. Accidents, illness, death, and disease are a part of the adult world young people must also come to terms with. Davis's characters do so with varying degrees of success.

—Hazel K. Davis

DAVIS, Terry. American.

PUBLICATIONS FOR YOUNG ADULTS

Fiction

Vision Quest. New York, Delacorte, 1979.
If Rock and Roll Were a Machine. New York, Delacorte, 1992.

*   *   *

With his first two novels, Terry Davis has carved a definite niche in the field of young adult literature. His works explore the lives of young men who confront seemingly insurmountable challenges and obstacles successfully. His protagonists are not perfect young men; they are adolescents who have seen their share of grief and failure. Yet, somehow, they manage to rise above what is lacking in their lives. They "gut it out" to utilize a phrase which would be in the vocabulary of both of Davis's young male protagonists, Louden and Bert. Each realizes victory in two arenas: the playing fields of his particular sport and in his quest for his own identity.

Vision Quest, Davis's first novel for young adult readers, relates the story of Louden Swain, a wrestler. Louden is attempting to drop two weight classes so that he can challenge the reportedly unbeatable Gordon Shute in their last year of high school competition. This feat requires tremendous physical discipline. Louden's mental discipline is also an integral part of the training. In his "vision quest," Louden must find his balance. Balance in life is a recurring theme in *Vision Quest.* Davis's characters must achieve the proper balance in their lives in order to find happiness and fulfillment. Louden cannot simply obsess about his sport. He has concerns in his personal life which require his attention as well: his relationship with his father, his teammates and friends, and his girlfriend Carla all have their place in Louden's life and in his quest to be the best he can be.

Bert Bowden, the protagonist of Davis's second novel, *If Rock and Roll Were a Machine,* is a fairly typical adolescent. He envisions himself as the star of the football team when, in reality he is too small for the sport. Sports are important in Bert's high school; it is the same high school attended by one Louden Swain some twenty years earlier. At one time Bert fancied himself a good student but the work of a rather sadistic teacher has all but destroyed

Bert's self-image. The purchase of a motorcycle seems to signal Bert's separation from his childhood and the painful memories it holds for him. He discovers a freedom on the bike and an acceptance by other bikers which is important to his psyche. The motorcycle dealer becomes a friend and confidante; the other important influence in Bert's life is his English teacher who encourages Bert to continue working on his writing. Davis uses Bert's essays and other writing to provide insight into Bert's thoughts and feelings.

Both of Davis's novels focus on the important role which sports can play in an adolescent's life. Each person must find his (or her) own sport and work hard to become a skilled athlete. Not everyone wins every match, either. Davis ends *Vision Quest* with Louden and Shute taking the wrestling mat. It is not until *If Rock and Roll Were a Machine* that the reader learns what happened in that fateful match. In this novel, set twenty years after *Vision Quest,* Davis, in a move of wonderful irony, has Bert walk by the trophy case near the gym. There is a display case dedicated to the epitome of self-discipline, Louden Swain. Swain went on to become an Olympic wrestler. He later joined the Air Force and became an astronaut. He was killed in a shuttle explosion at the age of thirty-one. Bert does not always win his matches either. He has the opportunity to play against his nemesis, his former fifth-grade teacher Mr. Lawler. Bert is beating Lawler handily when Lawler simply refuses to continue the game. Bert's victory is a Pyrrhic one at best.

Davis is quick to puncture stereotypes as well. His characters are honest and lifelike, not simply cardboard cutouts or archetypes. There are few "dumb jocks" on the team. Both Louden and Bert are avid readers. Motorcyclists are not all tattooed, long-haired outlaws. Bert is certainly not the typical Harley rider; he is, however, confronted with the stereotypical response a motorcyclist receives when he goes off riding in unfamiliar territory. Finally, teachers are not always wonderful and supporting people. Certainly Bert has a caring teacher in Mr. Tanneran, but not all of Bert's teachers have been nurturing. The same is true for Louden Swain.

Perhaps the overriding theme of Davis's work deals with growth and change. Louden and Bert each are growing up and growing away from some of the things they held as precious when they were children. They are each a man-child, on the brink of adulthood. They waver between childhood and adulthood, reacting childishly in some circumstances then acting well beyond their years in others. Davis has captured that stage of growing up portrayed in other authors' works like Chris Crutcher and Judy Blume. His protagonists learn to face the truths, the tough truths. Davis has his "heroes" tell their truths to the reader. These truths are complex; they are frequently hurtful. Yet, by revealing these truths Davis's characters achieve that measure of growth which is not possible without pain: they are the truths which allow the characters to like themselves. Ultimately, then, Davis's message to readers is that one must be able to like oneself in order to be truly happy.

—Teri S. Lesesne

DEAVER, Julie Reece. American. Born in Geneva, Illinois, 13 March 1953. Teacher's aide in special education in Pacific Grove, California, 1978-88. Illustrator for *Reader's Digest, New Yorker, Chicago Tribune,* and *McCall's Working Mother.* Recipient: Best Book for Young Adults citation, 1988, for *Say Goodnight, Gracie;*

Books for the Teenage recommendation, New York Public Library, *Book List* Young Adult Editors' Choice citation, and Books for Children recommendation, Library of Congress, all 1988; Virginia State Reading Association Young Readers Award, 1991, for *Say Goodnight, Gracie.* Agent: c/o Harper and Row Publishers, Inc., 10 East 53rd Street, New York, NY 10022. Lives in Pacific Grove, California.

PUBLICATIONS FOR YOUNG ADULTS

Fiction

Say Goodnight, Gracie. New York, Harper, 1988.
First Wedding, Once Removed. New York, Harper, 1990.
You Bet Your Life. New York, Harper, 1993.

Also author of a screenplay based on *Say Goodnight, Gracie.* Writer for television series *Adam's Rib,* 1973.

Julie Reece Deaver comments:

I love writing about young adults, but I never set out to write for that particular age group. As a teenager, I won a short story contest with *Seventeen Magazine,* and it was natural for me to write about characters my own age. But as I grew older, I found that my characters stayed teenagers, and that I really loved writing about that time of life when people are on the brink of adulthood.

In writing, I work without an outline, but just go where my characters want me to go. This means a lot of rewriting when the book is done, but I've found it hard to create and stick to any kind of structure or outline. The joy is in seeing what will happen to my characters.

I get a lot of fan mail asking me how to be a writer, and I like to tell my readers not to get too serious about their work, to find fun in it, and to take their inspiration not only from the classics but from all kinds of entertainment: picture books, comic strips, movies, television, songs. It all ends up adding spice to your writing.

When I was working in television, a screenwriter gave me some wonderful advice about writing. "Aim for the high," she told me, and I've found it to be true. If you write something that truly delights you, chances are your readers will be pleased, too.

*   *   *

Julie Reece Deaver's novels for young adults chronicle the pain and adjustments inherent in coping with change and loss. Set in Glen Ellyn, Illinois, the Chicago suburb where Deaver grew up, the books focus on the relationships of middle-class teenagers with their friends and families.

Say Goodnight, Gracie represents an impressive writing debut. Morgan Hackett and Jimmy Woolf have been neighbors and best friends since babyhood. In fact, their mothers have maintained a close friendship since their own high school days. Now seventeen, Jimmy and Morgan share aspirations for stage careers and regularly travel to Chicago after school, he to dance class, she to an acting workshop. Jimmy's bid for a major stage part appears more imminent than Morgan's, especially when he lands an audition for a touring production of *Oklahoma.* But when he blows his chance, he lashes out at Morgan, and their friendship suffers a major test. The greatest challenge is one Morgan must overcome without Jimmy. After dropping her off for class, Jimmy is killed by a drunken

driver. Deaver's depiction of Morgan's denial, anger, and depression is telling and accurate. Parents and a school friend offer some help, but Morgan's healing begins only after she breaks down and acknowledges the pain to her aunt, a psychiatrist.

The novel's strength lies not only in the handling of loss and grief but in the creation of a genuine boy-girl friendship based on humor, shared interests, and deep affection. The dialogue between Morgan and Jimmy is casual, witty, and believable. Even though there are hints that romance might develop some day, the two have a strong relationship without that component. As Jimmy says, "Lovers come and go, but friends go on and on." When he dies, readers join Morgan in missing him.

In contrast, *First Wedding, Once Removed* appears lightweight. As in her first novel, Deaver chooses first-person narration, this time revealing the events through the eyes of fourteen-year-old Alwilda (Pokie). She and her older brother, Gib, share an intense interest in airplanes and spend hours together at Mitchell Field, where they watch planes and dream of the time when they can begin flying lessons. However, the summer following Gib's high school graduation is bittersweet as Pokie realizes that his departure for college will signal a significant change in their daily camaraderie. When he assures her that he'll come home from college for holidays and summers, she protests that such visits won't be the same as having him around all the time.

Her fears prove correct. Gib soon meets and falls in love with Nell, and his holidays are cut short to visit her. Pokie resents the intrusion, especially the following summer when Nell arrives after a fight with her parents. Pokie's second-place status is made apparent in Gib's declining interest in airplanes. When he takes the money he had saved for flying lessons to buy an engagement ring, Pokie's devastation is complete. During the same year Gib leaves for college, however, Pokie herself abandons her long-time friend Junior. She begins high school and finds little time for an eighth grader she suddenly considers immature. But Gib's impending wedding makes Pokie realize her thoughtlessness toward Junior. "I forgot what it feels like to have someone leave you behind," she explains.

Although there are no indications that the book is set in the past, certain aspects of the story give the novel a nostalgic air. The idealized brother-sister relationship fails to ring true. The refusal of Nell's parents to attend their daughter's wedding or even meet her future in-laws simply because they think she is too young to marry seems implausible. Equally unconvincing is the emphasis on the physical distance between Gib and his family, when the University of Missouri is only a day's drive away and everyone in the book flies between Chicago and Columbia, anyway. The largest strain on readers' credulity, however, is the immaturity of Pokie and Junior. They seem more like fifth and sixth graders than people in junior high and high school. For example, Junior insists on dressing like a giant mouse for Halloween, and Pokie's disbelief in Gib's developing romance seems unlikely in a high-school student.

Perhaps in future novels Deaver will regain the firm footing in plot and character development she demonstrated in *Say Goodnight, Gracie.* One can only speculate what her next portrayal of suburban life might include.

—Kathy Piehl

DHONDY, Farrukh. Indian. Born in Poona, Bombay, in 1944. Educated at Wadia College, Poona, B.Sc.; Cambridge University, 1964-67, B.A. in English 1967; University of Leicester, M.A. in English. English teacher, Henry Thornton Comprehensive School, Clapham, London; teacher, later head of English, Archbishop Temple School, Lambeth, London, 1974-80. Since 1985 commissioning editor for multicultural television programs, Channel Four Television, London. Writer of television scripts, plays, and fiction for adults and children. Recipient: Children's Rights Workshop Other awards, 1977, for *East End at Your Feet,* and 1979, for *Come to Mecca, and Other Stories;* Collins/Fontana award for books for multi-ethnic Britain, for *Come to Mecca, and Other Stories;* Beckett prize, for television play, 1984; Dhondy's works were represented in "Children's Fiction in Britain, 1900-1990," an exhibition sponsored by the British Council's Literature Department, 1990. Address: c/o Jonathan Cape Ltd., 32 Bedford Sq., London WC1B 3SG, England.

PUBLICATIONS FOR YOUNG ADULTS

Fiction

East End at Your Feet. London, Macmillan, 1976.
Come to Mecca, and Other Stories. London, Collins, 1978.
The Siege of Babylon. London, Macmillan, 1978.
Poona Company. London, Gollancz, 1980.
Trip Trap. London, Gollancz, 1982.
Bombay Duck. London, Cape, 1990.
Black Swan. Boston, Houghton, 1992.

PUBLICATIONS FOR ADULTS

Plays

Mama Dragon (produced London, 1980).
Shapesters (produced London, 1981).
Kipling Sahib (produced London, 1982).
Trojans, adaptation of a play by Euripedes (produced London, 1982).
Romance, Romance; and The Bride. London, Faber, 1985.
Vigilantes (produced London, 1985). London, Hobo Press, 1988.
All the Fun of the Fair, with John McGrath and others (produced London, 1986).
Film, Film, Film (produced London, 1986).

Television Plays: *Maids in the Mad Shadow,* 1981; *No Problem* series, with Mustapha Matura, 1983; *Good at Art,* 1983; *Dear Manju,* 1983; *The Bride,* 1983; *Salt on a Snake's Tail,* 1983; *Come to Mecca,* 1983; *Romance, Romance,* 1983; *The Empress of the Munshi,* 1984; *Tandoori Nights* series, 1985; *King of the Ghetto,* 1986; *To Turn a Blind Eye,* 1986.

Other

The Black Explosion in British Schools, with Barbara Beese and Leila Hassan. London, Race Today, 1982.

*   *   *

Farrukh Dhondy's major works for young people appeared at a time when the United Kingdom market was crying out for quality, indigenous, multicultural writing, and he quickly became one of the leaders in this field.

Dhondy established himself with two short-story collections, *East End at Your Feet* and *Come to Mecca,* both characterized by snappy and realistic dialogue, as if the reader is overhearing a street conversation, and careful construction. The first book undoubtedly produced an impact as it was the subject of a notorious and largely racially motivated attack in a London school. Readers objected to the language used in the stories, although this was stoutly defended by local journalists and the series editor.

In *Come to Mecca* Dhondy shows a greater grasp of skill. There is a welcome variety in the style of each story: the defiance of the heroine of "Free Dinners" is as memorable as the character of Esther, who learns to grow up after taking part in a carnival, in "Go Play Butterfly"; the bitterness following racial attacks in "Salt on a Snake's Tail" is contrasted with the ironic title story, in which Dhondy ably demonstrates his dismay at "multiculturalism," a concept against which he often fulminates. In this story, Shahid, a naive Bengali teenager, becomes involved with a radical white girl, Betty, who has come to help in the strike at the clothing sweatshop where he works. When he asks her to "come to Mecca," meaning the local ballroom, Betty believes he wants to make a romantic pilgrimage to his roots, and Shahid's eyes are opened as he discovers that Betty sees him only as an issue and not as a person.

Dhondy followed these collections with a sharp and bitter novel, *The Siege of Babylon,* about a group of black adolescents who hold four hostages after a failed robbery. Although this is an angry and sometimes violent work, it loses none of the tight construction which is a hallmark of much of Dhondy's writing.

Poona Company is a much gentler book with serious undertones. Partly autobiographical, it offers fascinating vignettes of post-colonial India. Dhondy ably explores the curious mixture of class and caste and memorably portrays this eccentric, English-modelled public school. So clever is his use of words that the reader can almost feel and touch the atmosphere of the Poona bazaar. Memories that Dhondy evokes provide insight into this unfamiliar world for both black and white adolescent readers.

After an indifferent collection of stories, *Trip Trap,* in which he attempted to experiment with form, Dhondy turned his attention to other forms of media. Since then he has produced mainly scripts, although his adult novel, *Bombay Duck,* was nominated for a Whitbread Literary Award for a first novel. It is unlikely that he will write again for young adults, which is unfortunate, because voices like his need to be heard in the often insular world of children's publishing.

—Keith Barker

———

DICKINSON, Peter (Malcolm de Brissac). British. Born in Livingstone, Northern Rhodesia (now Zambia), 16 December 1927. Educated at Eton College (King's scholar), 1941-46; King's College, Cambridge (exhibitioner), B.A. 1951. Served in the British Army, 1946-48. Married 1) Mary Rose Barnard in 1953 (died 1988), two daughters and two sons; 2) Robin McKinley in 1992. Assistant editor and reviewer, *Punch,* London, 1952-69. Chairman, Society of Authors Management Committee, 1978-80. Recipient: Crime Writers Association Gold Dagger award for best mystery of the year, 1968, for *The Glass-sided Ants' Nest,* and 1969, for *The Old English Peep Show;* American Library Association Notable Book Award, 1971, for *Emma Tupper's Diary; Guardian* Award, 1977, for *The Blue Hawk; Boston Globe-Horn Book* award for nonfiction, 1977; Whitbread Award and Carnegie Medal, both 1979, both for *Tulku; The Flight of Dragons* and *Tulku* were named to the American Library Association's "Best Books for Young Adults 1979" list; Carnegie Medal, 1982, for "City of Gold"; *Horn Book* nonfiction award for *Chance, Luck, and Destiny; Boston Globe-Horn Book* award, 1989, for *Eva;* Whitbred Award, 1990, for *AK.* Agent: A.P. Watt Ltd., 20 John Street, London WC1N 2DL. Address: 61A Ormiston Grove, London W12 0JP, England.

PUBLICATIONS FOR YOUNG ADULTS

Fiction

The Weathermonger. London, Gollancz, 1968; Boston, Little Brown, 1969.
Heartsease, illustrated by Robert Hales. London, Gollancz, and Boston, Little Brown, 1969.
The Devil's Children, illustrated by Robert Hales. London, Gollancz, and Boston, Little Brown, 1970.
Emma Tupper's Diary. London, Gollancz, and Boston, Little Brown, 1971.
The Dancing Bear, illustrated by David Smee. London, Gollancz, 1972; Boston, Little Brown, 1973.
The Gift, illustrated by Gareth Floyd. London, Gollancz, 1973; Boston, Little Brown, 1974.
The Changes: A Trilogy (includes *The Weathermonger, Heartsease,* and *The Devil's Children*). London, Gollancz, 1975.
The Blue Hawk, illustrated by David Smee. London, Gollancz, and Boston, Little Brown, 1976.
Annerton Pit. London, Gollancz, and Boston, Little Brown, 1977.
Tulku. London, Gollancz, and New York, Dutton, 1979.
The Seventh Raven. London, Gollancz, and New York, Dutton, 1981.
Healer. London, Gollancz, 1983; New York, Delacorte Press, 1985.
Eva. London, Gollancz, 1988; New York, Delacorte Press, 1989.
Merlin Dreams, illustrated by Alan Lee. London, Gollancz, and New York, Delacorte Press, 1988.
AK. London, Gollancz, 1990.
A Bone from a Dry Sea. New York, Delacorte Press, 1993.

Other

Chance, Luck and Destiny, illustrated by David Smee and Victor Ambrus. London, Gollancz, 1975; Boston, Little Brown, 1976.
City of Gold and Other Stories from the Old Testament, illustrated by Michael Foreman. London, Gollancz, and New York, Pantheon, 1980.
Editor, *Presto! Humorous Bits and Pieces.* London, Hutchinson, 1975.
Editor, *Hundreds and Hundreds.* London, Penguin, 1984.

Television Series: *Mandog.* BBC-TV, 1972.

PUBLICATIONS FOR ADULTS

Novels

Skin Deep. London, Hodder and Stoughton, 1968; as *The Glass-sided Ants' Nest,* New York, Harper, 1968.
A Pride of Heroes. London, Hodder and Stoughton, 1969; as *The Old English Peep Show,* New York, Harper, 1969.
The Seals. London, Hodder and Stoughton, 1970; as *The Sinful Stones,* New York, Harper, 1970,
Sleep and His Brother. London, Hodder and Stoughton, and New York, Harper, 1971.
The Iron Lion, illustrated by Marc Brown. Boston, Little Brown, 1972; London, Allen and Unwin, 1973.
The Lizard in the Cup. London, Hodder and Stoughton, and New York, Harper, 1972.
The Green Gene. London, Hodder and Stoughton, and New York, Pantheon, 1973.
The Poison Oracle. London, Hodder and Stoughton, and New York, Pantheon, 1974.
The Lively Dead. London, Hodder and Stoughton, and New York, Pantheon, 1975.
King and Joker. London, Hodder and Stoughton, and New York, Pantheon, 1976.
Hepzibah, illustrated by Sue Porter. Twickenham, Middlesex, Eel Pie, 1978; Boston, Godine, 1980.
Walking Dead. London, Hodder and Stoughton, 1977; New York, Pantheon, 1978.
One Foot in the Grave. London, Hodder and Stoughton, 1979; New York, Pantheon, 1980.
A Summer in the Twenties. London, Hodder and Stoughton, and New York, Pantheon, 1981.
The Last House-Party. London, Bodley Head, and New York, Pantheon, 1982.
Hindsight. London, Bodley Head, and New York, Pantheon, 1983.
Death of a Unicorn. London, Bodley Head, and New York, Pantheon, 1984.
Giant Cold, illustrated by Alan E. Cober. London, Gollancz, and New York, Dutton, 1984.
A Box of Nothing, illustrated by Ian Newsham. London, Gollancz, 1985; New York, Delacorte Press, 1987.
Tefuga: A Novel of Suspense. London, Bodley Head, and New York, Pantheon, 1986.
Mole Hole, illustrated by Jean Claverie. London, Blackie, and New York, Bedrick, 1987.
Perfect Gallows: A Novel of Suspense. London, Bodley Head, and New York, Pantheon, 1987.
Skeleton-in-Waiting. London, Bodley Head, 1989; New York, Pantheon, 1990.
Play Dead. London, Bodley Head, 1991; Mysterious Press, New York, 1992.
Time and the Clock-mice, etcetera. Doubleday, London, 1993; Dell, New York, 1994.
The Yellow Room Conspiracy. Little Brown, London, 1994; Mysterious Press, New York, 1994.

Other

The Flight of Dragons, illustrated by Wayne Anderson. New York, Harper, 1979.

Contributor, *The Great Detectives,* edited by Otto Penzler. Boston, Little Brown, 1978.

Contributor, *Verdict of Thirteen,* edited by Julian Symons. New York, Harper, 1979.

*

Media Adaptations: *A Box of Nothing* (cassette), G.K. Hall, 1988; *Changes* (television serial), BBC-TV, 1975; *The Flight of Dragons* (television movie), ABC-TV, 1982.

Biography: Entry in *Dictionary of Literary Biography,* Volume 87, Detroit, Gale, 1989.

Critical Study: Entry in *Contemporary Literary Criticism,* Volume 12, Detroit, Gale, 1980, Volume 35, 1985.

Peter Dickinson comments:

I don't have much to say about my books, as I am a fairly instinctive writer, tending to go wherever the story leads me, without much by way of plan or theory. All successful books have their own voice, which establishes itself in the writer's head and keeps him on track. I like to tell stories, but any story involves more than itself. It involves its own society, and the ideas on which that is based, and a host of other complexities, all of which have to be dealt with and made to work as part of the story. I simply do the best I can to be honest about it all.

*   *   *

Peter Dickinson is one of those authors who has written almost equally for adults and for children. The boundaries between the two groups of novels are hazy, and young people may turn as readily to the contemporary adult tales (often variations on classical detective stories) as to the fantasies that are more remotely set. These adventures for young people can occur in the distant past or in a future postindustrial world of the "Changes" trilogy. Because of the immediacy with which both are realised, it is sometimes difficult to be sure (as in *The Blue Hawk*) whether the setting is in a vanished kingdom, like ancient Egypt, or in some future state.

Dickinson has a highly original, powerful imagination, which enables him to suggest the extraordinary with vivid conviction. We accept the possibility of a New Guinea tribe living in the attics of a London terrace or a chimpanzee being taught grammar in the palace of an oil sheikh. He is equally capable of capturing sixth-century Byzantium, China at the time of the Boxer rising, or contemporary Africa. He has a rare ability to get inside the thinking of, and to catch the speech styles of, women as well as men, young and old. He is also an excellent writer of prose, with a wide vocabulary and a graphic style. Despite (or perhaps because of) his own sharp intelligence, his novels show repeated concern for the instinctual, for the hidden powers, and against the coldly intellectual. Dickinson has said that young people have so much forced at them, both directly and through the media, that they need to sort out these bewildering perceptions and to fit them into some kind of structure. He believes that good fantasy novels can provide such "maps of coherence," and this is true of his own work.

The Seventh Raven, for example, is narrated convincingly in the voice of an articulate seventeen-year-old girl involved in the excitement of an annual children's opera being presented in St. Andrew's Church, Kensington. The first half of the book suggests that this will be a lively account of theatre, music, and family life built around the chaotic preparations for performing a work based on Elijah. At the dress rehearsal the novel shifts into another mode: violence intrudes into the civilised operatic world. A man is shot, and terrorists burst in seeking the nephew of the future president of their country. The unexpected arrival of the police forces them to take the children hostage, and the novel speeds towards climax in the threats of a show trial. It is not a simple thriller with good guys and bad guys, but a more complex exploration of the power of belief for good or ill, of divided sympathies, and of human change.

Dickinson has always been interested in people with special powers (like Davy's ability to "see" the thoughts of others in *The Gift*) and in cult religions (as in *The Seals*). These two concerns come together in *Healer.* The powers of healing are discovered in Pinkie Proudfoot, a girl of ten, but her story is seen through the eyes of Barry, a taciturn, unhappy boy of sixteen. Pinkie is exploited by her stepfather in the service of a dubious cult, the Foundation of Harmony, which charges the afflicted large sums for cures. Barry, whom Pinkie once cured of migraines, plans to rescue her. However, he is awkwardly uncertain of the nature of his relationship with her and very aware of another, violent side in his own nature that is liable to break out of control. As so often in Dickinson, the story plunges towards a scene of confused violence. The novel poses questions about the nature of different, interlocking responsibilities for other people, and, in a positive ending, Pinkie succeeds in helping with the integration of Barry's personality.

Dickinson's experiences of Africa underlie a number of books. *Tefuga* is a multilayered story in which a successful television journalist, Nigel Jackland, is making a film in the 1980s about colonial life in northern Nigeria in the twenties, using his mother's journal as one of his sources. Cultural juxtapositions suggest that the rituals and fetishes of the British tribe are as strange as those of the Africans. Five years later, *AK* gives what one reviewer called a "flawlessly authentic" and "dreadfully real" picture of the imagined African country of Nagala at a time of continual revolution and tribal warfare. Paul, a young war orphan, becomes a kind of adoptive son to a soldier politician, Michael Kagomi, who is by turns flung into and out of power. The greater part of the book describes the long journey of Paul and two young friends to free Michael from imprisonment in the capital, Dangoum.

Eva is a provocative and witty study of the self-destructive and the life-affirming sides of human nature. In a future world where people have become effete and listless, Eva is the thirteen-year-old daughter of a scientist responsible for a group of chimpanzees representing almost the last link with the animal world. Paralysed after a terrible car accident, Eva recovers after operations to discover that her "neurone memory" has been duplicated in the body of a chimpanzee. She assimilates the two sides of her nature and in an allusive conclusion leads the chimpanzees out of Egypt to begin the first cautious stages of creating a new culture. In a similar vein, the more recent *A Bone from a Dry Sea* relates present and past. It is based on two alternating narratives—the contemporary one in which young Vinny joins her father on an expedition to Africa, digging for evidence of early life, and the other where the author takes the reader back millions of years to suggest a hypothetical version of evolution. Dickinson continues to push out the boundaries of young people's fiction both literally, in time and space, and metaphorically in the concerns he explores and in the methods he employs.

—Robert Protherough

DILLON, Eilis. Irish. Born in Galway, 7 March 1920. Educated at Ursuline Convent, Sligo. Married 1) Cormac O Cuilleanain in 1940 (died 1970), one son and two daughters; 2) the writer Vivian Mercier in 1974. Lecturer in Creative Writing, Trinity College, Dublin, 1971-72, and University College Dublin, 1988; lecturer at American universities and colleges on three tours, speaking on writing for children and Anglo-Irish literature, especially poetry. Fellow, Royal Society of Literature. Recipient: *New York Herald Tribune* Children's Spring Book Festival Honorable Mention citations, 1960, for *The Singing Cave,* 1964, for *The Coriander,* and 1970, for *A Herd of Deer;* German Juvenile Book Prize Honor List citation, 1968, for *A Family of Foxes;* Notable Book citation, American Library Association, and Lewis Carroll Shelf Award, both 1970, for *A Herd of Deer;* Irish Book of the Year award, 1991, for *The Island of Ghosts.* D.Litt.: National University of Ireland, 1992. Agent: David Bolt Associates, 12 Heath Drive, Send, Surrey GU23 7EP, England. Address: 7 Templemore Avenue, Rathgar, Dublin 6, Ireland.

PUBLICATIONS FOR CHILDREN AND YOUNG ADULTS

Fiction

An Choill Bheo (The Live Forest). Dublin, Government Publication Sale Office, 1948.
Midsummer Magic, illustrated by Stuart Tresilian. London, Macmillan, 1950.
Oscar agus an Cóiste Sé nEasóg (Oscar and the Six-Weasel Coach). Dublin, Government Publication Sale Office, 1952.
The Lost Island, illustrated by Richard Kennedy. London, Faber, 1952; New York, Funk and Wagnalls, 1954.
The San Sebastian, illustrated by Richard Kennedy. London, Faber, 1953; New York, Funk and Wagnalls, 1954.
Ceol na Coille (The Song of the Forest). Dublin, Government Publication Sale Office, 1955.
The House on the Shore, illustrated by Richard Kennedy. London, Faber, 1955; New York, Funk and Wagnalls, 1956.
The Wild Little House, illustrated by V.H. Drummond. London, Faber, 1955; New York, Criterion, 1957.
The Island of Horses, illustrated by Richard Kennedy. London, Faber, 1956; New York, Funk and Wagnalls, 1957.
Plover Hill, illustrated by Prudence Seward. London, Hamish Hamilton, 1957.
Aunt Bedelia's Cats, illustrated by Christopher Brooker. London, Hamish Hamilton, 1958.
The Singing Cave, illustrated by Richard Kennedy. London, Faber, 1959; New York, Funk and Wagnalls, 1960.
The Fort of Gold, illustrated by Richard Kennedy. London, Faber, and New York, Funk and Wagnalls, 1961.
King Big-Ears, illustrated by Kveta Vanecek. London, Faber, 1961; New York, Norton, 1963.
A Pony and a Trap, illustrated by Monica Brasier-Creagh. London, Hamish Hamilton, 1962.
The Cats' Opera, illustrated Kveta Vanecek. London, Faber, 1962; Indianapolis, Bobbs Merrill, 1963.
The Coriander, illustrated by Richard Kennedy. London, Faber, 1963; New York, Funk and Wagnalls, 1964.
A Family of Foxes, illustrated by Richard Kennedy. London, Faber, 1964; New York, Funk and Wagnalls, 1965.
The Sea Wall, illustrated by Richard Kennedy. London, Faber, and New York, Farrar Straus, 1965.

The Lion Cub, illustrated by Richard Kennedy. London, Hamish Hamilton, 1966; New York, Duell, 1967.
The Road to Dunmore, illustrated by Richard Kennedy. London, Faber, 1966.
The Cruise of the Santa Maria, illustrated by Richard Kennedy. London, Faber, and New York, Funk and Wagnalls, 1967.
The Key, illustrated by Richard Kennedy. London, Faber, 1967.
Two Stories: The Road to Dunmore and The Key, illustrated by Richard Kennedy. New York, Meredith Press, 1968.
The Seals, illustrated by Richard Kennedy. London, Faber, 1968; New York, Funk and Wagnalls, 1969.
Under the Orange Grove, illustrated by Richard Kennedy. London, Faber, 1968; New York, Meredith Press, 1969.
A Herd of Deer, illustrated by Richard Kennedy. London, Faber, 1969; New York, Funk and Wagnalls, 1970.
The Wise Man on the Mountain, illustrated by Gaynor Chapman. London, Hamish Hamilton, 1969; New York, Atheneum, 1970.
The Voyage of Mael Duin, illustrated by Alan Howard. London, Faber, 1969.
The King's Room, illustrated by Richard Kennedy. London, Hamish Hamilton, 1970.
The Five Hundred, illustrated by Gareth Floyd. London, Hamish Hamilton, 1972.
The Shadow of Vesuvius. New York, Nelson, 1977; London, Faber, 1978.
Down in the World, illustrated by Richard Kennedy. London, Hodder and Stoughton, 1983.
The Horse-Fancier. London, Macmillan, 1985.
The Seekers. New York, Scribner, 1986.
The Island of Ghosts. London, Macmillan, 1989.
Children of Bach. London, Macmillan, 1992.

Play

The Cats' Opera, adaptation of her own story (produced Dublin, 1981).

Other

Editor, *The Hamish Hamilton Book of Wise Animals,* illustrated by Bernard Brett. London, Hamish Hamilton, 1975.
Living in Imperial Rome, illustrated by Richard Kennedy. London, Faber, 1974; as *Rome under the Emperors,* Nashville, Nelson, 1975.
Editor, with others, *The Lucky Bag: Classic Irish Children's Stories,* illustrated by Martin Gale. Dublin, O'Brien Press, 1985.

PUBLICATIONS FOR ADULTS

Novels

Death at Crane's Court. London, Faber, 1953; New York, Walker, 1963.
Sent to His Account. London, Faber, 1954; New York, Walker, 1969.
Death in the Quadrangle. London, Faber, 1956; New York, Walker, 1968.
The Bitter Glass. London, Faber, 1958; New York, Appleton Century Crofts, 1959.
The Head of the Family. London, Faber, 1960.
Bold John Henebry. London, Faber, 1965.

Across the Bitter Sea. New York, Simon and Schuster, 1973; London, Hodder and Stoughton, 1974.

Blood Relations. London, Hodder and Stoughton, and New York, Simon and Schuster, 1978.

Wild Geese. New York, Simon and Schuster, 1980; London, Hodder and Stoughton, 1981.

Citizen Burke. London, Hodder and Stoughton, 1984.

The Interloper. London, Hodder and Stoughton, 1987.

Plays

A Page of History (produced Dublin, 1966).

Radio Play: *Manna,* 1960.

Other

Inside Ireland, photographs by Tom Kennedy. London, Hodder and Stoughton, 1982; New York, Beaufort, 1984.

*

Biography: Essay in *Contemporary Authors Autobiography Series* by Eilis Dillon. Volume 3, Detroit, Gale, 1986.

Critical Study: Entry in *Contemporary Literary Criticism,* Volume 17, Detroit, Gale, 1981.

*   *   *

Eilis (pronounced El-eesh) Dillon, one of the most respected authors for young adults in Ireland, has produced over forty novels and plays since the early 1950s. Her young adult works typically take the form of adventure tales set on or near the Aran Islands off the west coast of Ireland. Besides their settings, these novels have a number of other elements and themes in common, including: kidnappings, community loyalty, the treachery and beauty of the sea, superstition juxtaposed with religious belief, historical verisimilitude, resourceful young people who overcome great trials, and a writing style that is at once elegant and straightforward.

The salvaging of a drifting brig and the kidnapping of the protagonist, Pat Harmon, are featured events in *The San Sebastion.* In *The Lost Island,* belief in the supernatural (thought by many to be typically Irish) is an important element. *The House on the Island* finds the hero Jim D'Malley searching an Irish coastal village for his villainous uncle. *The Bitter Glass,* which takes its title from a poem by Irish poet William Butler Yeats, concerns the civil strife in 1922 Ireland. *The Singing Cave* relates the eccentric exploits of an egotistical recluse. In *The Fort of Gold* the boy heroes are forced to work for the villains Kelly and Crann. In a twist on the kidnapping theme, *The Coriander* tells of how two boys hold captive a doctor who is desperately needed by the islanders. In *The Cruise of the Santa Maria,* the young male protagonists are believed to be lost at sea on a boat classed as a "hooker." More recently, in *The Seekers,* Dillon relinquishes the Irish setting and sends her Pilgrim hero and heroine on a voyage from Yorkshire, England, to Plymouth colony in Massachusetts.

Dillon's *The Island of Ghosts* once again takes us to an Irish island village in the recent past and incorporates many of the same themes and conflicts highlighted in her earlier works. The story is narrated in part by Dara, one of the island boys, and in part by his sister Barbara. This shared narration carries out one of the obvious themes of the novel—that young women can be as capable, resourceful, and fearless as young men. In spite of the equal time granted the sexes, however, the story makes clear that there remains a tendency in these island communities to neglect the education and training of daughters in favor of sons.

Dara and his friend Brendan, who have been tutored in preparation for school on the mainland by Mr. Webb, an eccentric latecomer to the island, are subsequently kidnapped by that same Mr. Webb. Tricked into sailing with him to the nearby "island of ghosts," which is said to be inhabited by the spirits of a long-deceased shipwrecked family, the boys are forced to become Mr. Webb's slaves. In the process, however, they learn what it means to become virtually self-sufficient, generating power and sustenance from what appears to be a sterile environment.

When, days after their secret departure, their sailing vessel is sighted empty and wrecked, the villagers are convinced that Mr. Webb and the boys have drowned. This belief, an example of a kind of islander fatalism about the fickleness of the sea, is exactly what Mr. Webb had sought to encourage. Left alone with his two protégés, he indulges in his reclusive tendencies while the boys maintain his minifarm. But not everyone believes the boys have drowned. Barbara and Cait, sisters to Dara and Brendan respectively, find that Mr. Lennon, the schoolmaster, shares their confidence that the boys—although perhaps victims of some strange plot—are alive and well and living on the island of ghosts. These three embark on a rescue mission and eventually the boys are found, and all, even Mr. Webb, live happily ever after.

Dillon manages to weave some rather complex issues into this spare plot. For example, her subtle indictment of unequal educational policies for boys and girls is quite effective. Her treatment of Mr. Webb and the varying responses of the two boys to his eccentricities reveal a man who is more disenchanted with the world than he is evil. The self-sufficiency Mr. Webb fosters turns out to be tremendously satisfying for Dara though Brendan resents every moment of his entrapment.

Besides such subtle revelations about the varieties of human response, *The Island of Ghosts* exposes young readers to certain Irish customs (for example "keening," a type of loud wailing lamentation for the dead), words, and attitudes that will expand their consciousness about a culture that has had deep and wide influences on our own. The cumulative effect of reading Dillon's works is a true feel for the Irish islanders and their mores. Dillon accomplishes this cultural transference in lucid accessible prose that never condescends or moralizes. If there is anything lacking in *The Island of Ghosts,* it is a convincing incorporation of the ghosts into the story. On balance, however, the effect of the novel is to reinforce confidence in the good instincts and competence of young people.

—Mary Lowe-Evans

———

DOHERTY, Berlie. British. Born in Liverpool, Lancashire, 6 November 6, 1943. Educated at Durham University, 1961-64, B.A. (honours) in English; Liverpool University, 1964-65, postgraduate certificate in social science; Sheffield University, 1977-78, postgraduate certificate in education. Married Gerard Adrian Doherty in 1966; two daughters and one son. Child care officer, Leicestershire

County Council, 1966-67; homemaker, 1967-78; English teacher, schools in Sheffield, 1978-80; teacher with British Broadcasting Corp. (BBC) Radio, Sheffield, 1980-82; since 1983 full-time writer. Writer in residence at Calderdale Libraries, 1985, and Hall Cross Comprehensive School, Doncaster, England, 1986; since 1989 chair of Arvon Foundation at Lumb Bank; member of Yorkshire Arts Literature Panel, 1988-90. Recipient: Library Association Carnegie Medal, 1986, Burnley/National Provincial Children's Book of the Year award, 1987, and *Boston Globe-Horn Book* Honor award, 1988, all for *Granny Was a Buffer Girl*; Television and Film award, New York, 1988, for *White Peak Farm*. Agent: Gina Pollinger, 222 Old Brompton Rd., London. Address: Crowden Cottage, Upper Booth, Edale, Derbyshire S30 2ZJ, England.

PUBLICATIONS FOR YOUNG ADULTS

Fiction

How Green You Are!, illustrated by Elaine McGregor Turney. London, Methuen, 1982.
The Making of Fingers Finnigan, illustrated by John Haysom. London, Methuen, 1983.
White Peak Farm. London, Methuen, 1984; New York, Orchard, 1990.
Granny Was a Buffer Girl. London, Methuen, 1986; New York, Orchard, 1988.
Tough Luck. London, Hamish Hamilton, 1988.
Spellhorn. London, Hamish Hamilton, 1989.
Dear Nobody. London, Hamish Hamilton, 1991; New York, Orchard, 1992.
Streetchild. London, Hamish Hamilton, 1993; New York, Orchard, 1994.

Poetry

Walking on Air. London, HarperCollins, 1993.

Plays

Howard's Field (first produced at Crucible Theatre, 1980).
Smells and Spells (first produced Sheffield Experimental Theatre, 1980.)
A Growing Girl's Story (first produced at Yorkshire Art Circus, Hartlepool, 1982).
A Case for Probation, in *Studio Scripts,* edited by David Self. Broadcast by BBC-Radio 4, 1983; London, Hutchingson, 1986.
The Amazing Journey of Jazz O'Neill (produced Hull, 1984).
Rock 'n' Roll Is Here to Stay, (first produced at Graves Art Gallery, Sheffield, 1984).
Return to the Ebro (first produced in Manchester Library Theatre, 1985).
Tilly Mint and the Dodo, adaption of her own story (produced Doncaster, 1986).
How Green You Are!, adaption of her own story, in *Drama 1,* edited by John Foster. London, Macmillan, 1987.
Matthew, Come Home, in *Drama 2,* edited by John Foster. London, Macmillan, 1987.
Home, in *Stage Write,* edited by Gervase Phinn. London, Unwin Hyman, 1988.

Tribute to Tom, in *Drama 3,* edited by John Foster. London, Macmillan, 1988.
Dear Nobody, based on her novel of the same name (produced Sheffield, 1993; first produced at Crucible Theatre, 1993).

Radio Plays: *The White Bird of Peace,* broadcast by BBC-Radio 4, 1983; *The Mouse and His Child,* broadcast by BBC-Radio 4, 1986; from the story by Russell Hoban, 1987; *Children of Winter,* broadcast by BBC-Radio 4, 1990; *Granny Was a Buffer Girl,* broadcast by BBC-Radio 4, 1990; *Spellhorn,* broadcast by BBC-Radio 4, 1991; *There's a Valley in Spain,* broadcast by BBC-Radio 4, 1990; *Dear Nobody,* broadcast by BBC-Radio 5, 1993

Television Plays: *Fuzzball,* BBC-TV 4, 1985; *White Peak Farm* (serial), BBC-TV 1, 1988; *Children of Winter,* BBC-TV 4, 1991.

PUBLICATIONS FOR CHILDREN

Fiction

Tilly Mint Tales, illustrated by Thelma Lambert. London, Methuen, 1984.
Children of Winter, illustrated by Ian Newsham. London, Methuen, 1985.
Paddiwak and Cosy, illustrated by Teresa O'Brien. London, Methuen, and New York, Dial Press, 1989.
Tilly Mint and the Dodo, illustrated by Janna Doherty. London, Methuen, 1989.
Snowy, illustrated by Keith Bowen. London, HarperCollins, 1992.
Old Father Christmas. London, HarperCollins, and New York, Dial, 1993.
Willa and Old Miss Annie. London, Walker Books, forthcoming.

PUBLICATION FOR ADULTS

Novel

Requiem, M. Joseph, 1991.
The Vinegar Jar. London, Hamish Hamilton, forthcoming.

*

Biography: Essay in *Something about the Author Autobiography Series,* Volume 16, Detroit, Gale, 1993; essay in *Speaking for Ourselves, Too* compiled and edited by Donald R. Gallo, National Council of Teachers of English, 1993.

Critical Study: Entry in *Children's Literature Review,* Volume 21, Detroit, Gale, 1990.

*   *   *

The intricacies of families—their joys, sorrows, secrets, dreams, expectations, rifts, and bonds—are at the heart of Berlie Doherty's three contemporary realistic novels (*Granny Was a Buffer Girl, White Peak Farm,* and *Dear Nobody*). Doherty's graceful, imagistic prose vividly evokes specific places, families, and individuals, but each description transcends time and place to make the particular universal. The drama in the novels, two of which were originally written for BBC radio, springs from character rather than plot; crystalline characterization resonates with lyrical emotion and keen observation. Interwoven through the novels, and hallmarking the lives of the characters, are the themes of independence and change.

The evening before her departure for a year of school in France, three generations of Jess's close-knit English family gather together in *Granny Was a Buffer Girl.* Jess, the story's narrator, feels like "a snake, shedding its skin." Both thrilled and scared, Jess looks forward to her approaching independence, but the accompanying, inevitable change causes her some anxiety. As her parents and grandparents share the family's "secrets, all its love stories, and all its ghost stories," Jess begins to understand the myriad complexions of love, and the strength of the bonds that connect and sustain family members. Even as she prepares to leave her family, she finds herself drawn closer to them. As her train departs, Jess, strengthened by the past and confident about her future, knows that "the snake had shed its skin." Deftly interwoven with the richly textured stories of her family, Jess's personal story of maturation is a celebration of the life-affirming power of familial ties.

White Peak Farm also explores the complexity of family relationships. Jeannie Tanner recounts how her family, headed by her sullen, hot-tempered father, is nearly shattered by dramatic change and lack of communication. Shattering their father's expectations, oldest daughter Kathleen elopes with the son of a neighboring enemy; Martin, the only son and heir to the farm, chooses art school over sheep farming; a tractor accident ultimately leaves Mr. Tanner crippled. Jeannie, too, faces painful decisions as she struggles with thoughts of her own future. Always independent, she decides to fulfill her long-time dream by going off to the university, but she knows that whatever she does with her life, she'll always make her way back to White Peak Farm. Ultimately it is the Tanners' attachment to the isolated Derbyshire farm—their lifeblood for generations—that heals rifts and binds them together as much as their unspoken love for each other. While the novel's structure is episodic, Doherty's remarkable evocation of place and its influence on the Tanners solidly links the chapters.

In *Dear Nobody,* Helen and Chris are in their last year of high school and anticipating college when Helen discovers that she is pregnant. As the pair face impending parenthood, individual family complications are revealed: Chris works to reestablish a relationship with his mother, who deserted him years earlier; Helen discovers that her own mother was an illegitimate child. Helen refuses to have an abortion or give the baby up for adoption, choosing instead to break up with Chris, excluding him from her life even though she loves him. Initially angry and confused, Chris comes to share Helen's mature realization that "I'm not ready for forever. I'm not ready for him, and he's not ready for me." Alternating Chris's first-person perspective with the letters Helen writes to the unborn child she calls "Nobody," this emotionally charged novel, like Doherty's other works, probes the Byzantine nature of love and family relationships.

Doherty's atmospheric, finely crafted novels weave individual stories into a single cohesive tapestry of bittersweet experience. In memorable stories that linger long after the reader has closed the book, Doherty explores and acknowledges the myriad gifts of the family, while exposing their inherent liabilities.

—Carolyn Shute

DONOVAN, John. American. Born in 1928. Educated at University of Virginia, Charlottesville. Writer. Executive director, Children's Book Council, New York, 1967-92; English teacher; examiner in U.S. Copyright Office; affiliated with St. Martin's Press. Recipient: *Horn Book* honor list citation, Children's Book of the Year citation, Child Study Association of America, and *Book World*'s Children's Spring Book Festival honor book citation, 1969, all for *I'll Get There, It Better Be Worth the Trip; School Library Journal*'s Best Book citation, and *New York Times* Outstanding Book of the Year citation, both 1971, and National Book award, Children's Book category, 1972, all for *Wild in the World;* Children's Book of the Year citation, Child Study Association of America, 1976, for *Family;* Children's Reading Roundtable award, Children's Reading Roundtable of Chicago, 1983. *Died in 1992.*

PUBLICATIONS FOR YOUNG ADULTS

Fiction

The Little Orange Book, illustrated by Mauro Caputo. New York, Morrow, 1961.
I'll Get There, It Better Be Worth the Trip. New York, Harper, 1969; London, Macdonald, 1970.
Wild in the World. New York, Harper, 1971.
Remove Protective Coating a Little at a Time. New York, Harper, 1973.
Good Old James, illustrated by James Stevenson. New York, Harper, 1974.
Family: A Novel. New York, Harper, 1976.
Bittersweet Temptation. New York, Zebra Books, 1979.
Translator, *Paul and Virginia.* Chester Springs, Dufour, 1983.

PUBLICATIONS FOR ADULTS

Other

The Businessman's International Travel Guide (nonfiction). New York, Stein and Day, 1971.
Editor, *U.S. & Soviet Policy in the Middle East.* New York, Facts on File, 1972.
Riverside Drive (play; produced New York, 1964).

*

Media Adaptations: *I'll Get There, It Better Be Worth the Trip* (film), 1973.

Critical Study: Entry in *Children's Literature Review,* Volume 3. Detroit, Gale, 1978, pp. 139-143; entry in *Contemporary Literary Criticism,* Volume 35. Detroit, Gale, 1985, pp. 51-56.

*   *   *

The late John Donovan was a poet of loneliness and alienation. Each of his five books, whether set on a remote mountain in New Hampshire or in the steel and glass canyons of Manhattan, features characters who are painfully isolated by circumstance or by their family's failures of communication.

In developing these themes, Donovan earned a reputation, as the British critic John Rowe Townsend put it, for being a "taboo buster." Donovan cheerfully employed expletives which had previously been deleted from books for young adults and dealt frankly with such subjects as sexual experimentation, parental alcoholism, death, and, in his first book, *I'll Get There, It Better Be Worth the Trip,* an (arguably) homosexual encounter between the thirteen-year-old protagonist Davy and his best friend, Douglas.

Since his parents' divorce, Davy has been living with his grandmother in a small Massachusetts town. When she dies, he is sent to live with his mother, a borderline alcoholic, in her Manhattan apartment. He is also reunited, during weekend visits, with his father, who has remarried. Davy's assessment of his parents' lack of enthusiasm for him is expressed in what he says of his much-loved dog, Fred: "...when you make a dog like Fred part of your family, he is a full-time member, not just someone who will be around when you want him to." Unfortunately Fred is killed by a hit-and-run driver soon after Davy and his new friend Douglas give physical expression to their friendship (they kiss each other and, spending the night together, do what is described as "it.") Davy is emotionally devastated and is consumed by guilt: "Nothing would have happened if I hadn't been messing around with (Douglas) Altschuler," he thinks bitterly. Eventually, in part through his father's support and in part through sharing his feelings with Douglas, Davy comes to terms with his guilt. "Life should be beautiful," Altschuler says, but most readers will realize that if that goal represents the "there" of the book's title, getting to it for these two emotionally vulnerable kids from fractured families will be a very difficult trip, indeed.

The family of John Gridley, the protagonist of Donovan's second novel, *Wild in the World,* is beyond fractured: its twelve members are dead. Indeed, the first six pages of the book are a laconic record of the deaths, by suicide, fire, fever, and accident, of John's parents and his six brothers and four sisters. John, the youngest, is left alone to manage the family farm on a remote mountain in New Hampshire. Emotionally he is a burnt-out case going through the motions of living but, in fact, simply waiting to die. This changes when a stray dog (or is it a wolf?) appears on the farm and John "adopts" it as a pet and calls it "Son." The name is symbolic of the emotions which Son awakens in John. These ripen as John nurses Son back to health after he is bitten by a rattlesnake. Reflecting on his newfound capacity for expressing emotion, John thinks, "Son taught me a lot. Human critters hold back." Ultimately it is John, not Son, who dies first. His untimely death, though it has tragic elements, is at least partially redeemed by his earlier discovery of his life-affirming love for Son. That the wolf/dog lives on gives tangible expression to the survival of that love. *Wild in the World*'s powerful themes are expressed in an understated, almost laconic style which lends the story the timeless power of folklore or parable.

Donovan returns to the breezy, wry style and urban setting of *I'll Get There, It Better Be Worth the Trip* in his third novel, *Remove Protective Coating a Little At a Time.* Unlike Davy Ross, fourteen-year-old Harry Knight is not the product of a broken home, but his parents, Bud and Toots, are more like uncaring older siblings than father and mother. Though rich in material matters, Harry is obviously impoverished in terms of family love, support, and attention. He finds these, almost by accident, in the person of Amelia Myers, a seventy-two-year-old self-sufficient street person whom he meets in Central Park. Learning to care for Amelia and to feel responsible for her enables Harry to end his emotional isolation.

Donovan's fourth book, *Good Old James,* conveys a large message for all ages: in James, the retired protagonist, readers will discover that adolescents have no monopoly on loneliness—it is a regular and troubling visitor to the lives of the elderly, as well.

Donovan's consistent thematic concerns reach an apotheosis in his fifth and final book, *Family,* the story of the escape from a college lab of four apes who were to have been part of a scientific experiment. Three of the apes—Sasha, the narrator; Dilys, a mature female; and Lollipop, an infant, have been born in captivity. The fourth—the largest and most powerful, a male named Moses—is a "natural," born in the wild. From Moses the other three acquire not only the more sophisticated language of the wild apes but also a learned past consisting of stories, legend, and traditions. This establishes, for them, a context of connectedness and further nourishes the spirit of family which the apes increasingly experience, a spirit which few of Donovan's earlier human characters have known. Choosing to tell the apes' story in Sasha's first person voice gives Donovan the ironic distance he needs to comment on the failings of human society, especially its persistent equation of change with progress. Sasha is a brilliant creation—grave, compassionate and—despite his disingenuous denials—reflective. When winter arrives and Moses and Lollipop are killed by hunters, Sasha and Dilys have no choice but to return to the lab and their human captors, sustained by their memories and their hope, as Sasha states, "that Man is not lost." Donovan's sensitive handling of this theme in all of his books and his groundbreaking courage and candor in writing about important but formerly "taboo" subjects establishes his as a creative presence of enduring importance in the world of young adult literature.

—Michael Cart

————

DORRIS, Michael Anthony. American. Born in Louisville, Kentucky, 30 January 1945. Educated at Georgetown University, Washington, D.C., B.A. 1967; Yale University, New Haven, Connecticut, M.Phil. 1970. Married Louise Erdrich in 1981; two sons and four daughters. Assistant Professor, Johnston College, University of Redlands, California, 1970; and Franconia College, New Hampshire, 1971-72. Instructor, 1972-76, Assistant Professor, 1976-79, Associate Professor, 1979, Professor of anthropology, 1979-88, since 1979 Chair of Native American Studies Department, and since 1988 Adjunct Professor, Dartmouth College, Hanover, New Hampshire. Visiting Assistant Professor, University of New Hampshire, 1973-74, and University of Auckland, 1980. Director of urban bus program, summer, 1967, 1968, 1969. Native American Council member, since 1972, chairman, 1973-76, since 1979. Consultant to National Endowment for the Humanities, since 1976; consultant to television stations, including Los Angeles Educational Television stations, including Los Angeles Educational Television, 1976, and Toledo Public Broadcast Center, 1978. Editor, *Viewspoint,* 1967; since 1974 member of editorial board, *American Indian Culture and Research Journal;* member of editorial advisory board, MELUS, 1977-79. Recipient: Woodrow Wilson fellowship, 1967, 1980; National Institute of Mental Health research grant, 1971; Spaulding-Potter Program grant, 1973; Dartmouth College faculty fellowship, 1977; Guggenheim fellowship, 1978; Rockefeller fellowship, 1985; Indian Achievement award, 1985; National Endowment for the Arts fellowship, 1988; National Book Critics Circle

award, for nonfiction, 1989; Scott O'Dell, 1993, for *Morning Girl.*
Address: Erdrich/Dorris, Box 70, Cornish Flat, NH 03746, U.S.A.

PUBLICATIONS

Novels

A Yellow Raft in Blue Water. New York, Holt, 1987; London,
   Hamilton, 1988.
Crown of Columbus, with Louise Erdrich. New York, and London,
   Harper Collins, 1991.
Morning Girl. New York, Hyperion, 1992.
Rooms in the House of Stone. Minneapolis, Minnesota, Milkweed,
   1993.

Other

Native Americans: Five Hundred Years After. New York, Crowell,
   1975.
Contributor, *Racism in the Textbook.* New York, Council on Inter-
   racial Books for Children, 1976.
Contributor, *Separatist Movements,* edited by Ray Hill. Elmsford,
   New York, Pergamon, 1979.
Guide to Research on North American Indians, with Arlene B.
   Hirschfelder and Mary Gloyne Byler. Chicago, American Li-
   brary Association, 1983.
The Broken Cord. New York, Harper, 1987; London, Harper Collins,
   1990.
Route Two. Northridge, California, Lord John Press, 1990.

*   *   *

An author of both fiction and nonfiction, Michael Dorris writes
with intelligence, humor, and affection. He is an author who asks
such questions as: What makes each person unique? What binds us
together? What keeps us apart? What shapes our values, customs,
traditions and defines our ethnicity?

Although the themes about which he writes are universal, Dorris,
a member of the Modoc tribe, often uses Native Americans as the
principal protagonists in his works of fiction. His three major nonfiction books deal in part or entirely with Native American subjects.

In 1975, Michael Dorris wrote: "There are many things that
Indian people are not: They are not and never have been a unified,
homogenous population; they are not represented by the stereotypes of Hollywood or most fiction; they are not people without
history, languages, literatures, sciences, and arts; they are not vanished, and are not vanishing." This comes from the text, written by
Dorris, which accompanies Joseph Farber's black and white photographs in the book, *Native Americans: Five Hundred Years After.*

Dorris has worked over the years to provide his readership with
an expanded vision of what it means to be Native American, by
moving beyond the stereotypes that mainstream Americans are
served with typical Thanksgiving meals, or hear in some commonly
used linguistic expressions like "Indian givers," or use as mascots
for athletic teams like the "Redskins."

A source that enables readers to find high quality books on Native Americans without stereotypes is the 1983 American Library
Association's *Guide to Research on North American Indians.* Dorris

coauthored this book with Arlene Hirschfelder and Mary Gloyne
Byler. The annotations included in this reference book provide a
summary of the work, discusses the period(s) of time covered, and
notes inclusion of maps, artwork, photographs, appendix, and bibliography. The authors note if a work is based on field work or
manuscript files, and indicate if sources are published or unpublished, primary or secondary.

In *The Broken Cord,* another nonfiction book, the author tells
the story of his oldest son, Adam, from birth until he leaves home
at the age of twenty. Adam is at the center of the book and is
accompanied by a huge cast of characters. However, this is also
Michael Dorris's story, the story of a proud, loving father, struggling to come to terms with his adopted son's multiple physical and
mental problems caused by an alcoholic mother. On another level,
The Broken Cord details the tragedy of Fetal Alcohol Syndrome
(FAS), a set of preventable birth defects which are caused as a
direct result of alcohol consumed during pregnancy and passed to
developing babies. By making *The Broken Cord* Adam's story,
Dorris gives FAS the face and name of a person for whom readers
can come to care about. This focus raises the issue above the statistics and facts.

Throughout the book, Dorris mourns what could have been for
his own child and others victimized by FAS, individuals who will
be hindered or prevented from developing a joy for life and a curiosity for what goes on around them. Dorris does not explain as much
as he paints a picture. In describing Adam's legacy, Dorris writes:
"He came from a country that encouraged the farthest sight, but he
forever stood in a well shaped by a bottle." Dorris made the transition from nonfiction to fiction in 1987 with *A Yellow Raft in Blue
Water,* a story told in three voices. An adult novel, it also speaks to
young adults. Rayona, fifteen years old, is the novel's first narrator.
Tall like her largely absent dad and with skin that announces she's a
blend of her African American father and her Native American
mother, Rayona wonders where she will fit into the world. She lives
with her mother, Christine. Mother and daughter have no money
and have no prospects for getting any. They begin a journey home
to the reservation and to Aunt Ida, Christine's mother.

Christine abandons Rayona on the reservation. Aunt Ida becomes all Rayona has. Ida, a large, forbidding woman, whose "real
life is squeezed between the times of her programs on TV," refuses
to speak English with Rayona but instead uses only her native
Indian language. Rayona may know her family's native tongue, but
everything else on the reservation is new and strange to her. She is
forced to deal with a new school and no friends, her enigmatic Aunt
Ida and other relatives whom she meets for the first time, comments
and taunts on her mixed heritage, and the unwanted attention of a
young priest. Fleeing from the priest, Rayona, completely on her
own, finds help, gains confidence, earns money, and later respect.
Rayona exhibits strength and persistence—qualities she has in common with her mother and grandmother, who each tell their own
story before the novel ends.

Multiple viewpoints, intricate family dynamics, and complex
characters keep *A Yellow Raft on Blue Water* absorbing, while allowing the readers to draw their own conclusions as to why the characters are the way they are and what their futures will be.

While continuing to utilize Native American society and culture,
Michael Dorris changes settings and focus in his more recent novels, *Morning Girl* and *Crown of Columbus.* Both books focus on
the effects Columbus's encounter with the indigenous people of the
Americas. Set five hundred years apart, the two novels are directed
toward different audiences.

Morning Girl is Dorris's first book directed at a younger audience, upper elementary through ninth graders. Set in 1492 in the Caribbean, it tells a story of the Tainos, the native people of a small Bahamian island. Michael Dorris won the O'Dell Award for Historical Fiction for *Morning Girl.* Taking turns doing the narration, Morning Girl, a twelve year old Taino, and Star Boy, her younger brother, tell of the beauty and hardships of their lives.

Morning Girl and Star Boy think of themselves as different as night is from day. But, together with their parents, they mourn the miscarriage of a new sibling, miss their deceased grandfather, survive a powerful hurricane and public ridicule, and celebrate life with other community members. Morning Girl and Star Boy may see the world from different vantage points but they grow to appreciate and love each other in their nurturing environment.

Dorris captures the richness of his characters' culture in lyrical language. By depicting the Tainos' life clearly, Dorris helps the readers visualize the people that Columbus names incorrectly and considers only for servitude. Columbus expresses this thought in his diary, and Dorris quotes from the diary to end *Morning Girl.*

In *Crown of Columbus,* which Michael Dorris coauthored in 1991 with his wife, Louise Erdrich, the authors create a fictional couple who wrestle with Columbus's continued influence and the controversy the world faces on the quincentennial anniversary of his voyage. Written as an adult book, it has some appeal for young adults, although the only teen in the book is not fully developed. What *Crown of Columbus* has is adventure, intrigue, and mystery. The novel touches but does not dwell on the destructive elements of discovery and colonization.

Michael Dorris, who earlier combined his writing with teaching and developing the Native American studies program at Dartmouth College, now writes full time. His articles and reviews appear in the *New York Times,* the *Washington Post,* the *Los Angles Times,* and various national magazines. In the future, he plans to publish a volume of short stories entitled *Working Men,* another adult book *Paper Trail,* and a subsequent young adult novel, tentatively called *Guests.*

Dorris explores universal issues such as the quest for personal identity, coming of age, and the importance of personal accountability for behavior. Dorris creates strong characters. He writes with a distinct sense of time and place and presents multiple sides of complex issues. These factors combined with Michael Dorris's skillful use of language and imagery gives readers fiction and nonfiction books that nourish and ask for additional consideration from their audience.

—Karen Ferris Morgan

———

DOUGLAS, Michael. See **CRICHTON, Michael.**

———

DOYLE, (Sir) Arthur Conan. British. Born in Edinburgh, Scotland, 22 May 1859. Educated at the Hodder School, Lancashire, 1868-70, Stonyhurst College, Lancashire, 1870-75, and the Jesuit School, Feldkirch, Austria (editor, *Feldkirchian Gazette),* 1875-76; studied medicine at the University of Edinburgh, 1876-81, M.B. 1881, M.D. 1885. Served as senior physician at a field hospital in South Africa during the Boer War, 1899-1902; knighted, 1902. Married 1) Louise Hawkins in 1885 (died 1906), one daughter and one son; 2) Jean Leckie in 1907, two sons and one daughter. Practised medicine in Southsea, Hampshire, 1882-90; full-time writer from 1891; stood for Parliament as Unionist candidate for Central Edinburgh, 1900, and tariff reform candidate for the Hawick Burghs, 1906. Member, Society for Physical Research, 1893-1930 (resigned). Recipient: LL.D.: University of Edinburgh, 1905. Knight of Grace of the Order of St. John of Jerusalem. *Died 7 July 1930.*

PUBLICATIONS

Novels

A Study in Scarlet. London, Ward Lock, 1888; Philadelphia, Lippincott, 1890.
The Mystery of Cloomber. London, Ward and Downey, 1888; New York, Fenno, 1895.
Micah Clarke. London, Longman, and New York, Harper, 1889.
The Firm of Girdlestone. London, Chatto and Windus, and New York, Lovell, 1890.
The Sign of the Four. London, Blackett, 1890; New York, Collier, 1891.
The White Company. London, Smith Elder, 3 vols., 1891; New York, Lovell, 1 vol., 1891.
The Doings of Raffle Haw. London, Cassell, and New York, Lovell, 1892.
The Great Shadow. New York, Harper, 1892.
The Great Shadow, and Beyond the City. Bristol, Arrowsmith, 1893; New York, Ogilvie, 1894.
The Refugees. New York, Longman, 3 vols., 1893; New York, Harper, 1 vol., 1893.
The Parasite. London, Constable, 1894; New York, Harper, 1895.
The Stark Munro Letters. London, Longman, and New York, Appleton, 1895.
Rodney Stone. London, Smith Elder, and New York, Appleton, 1896.
Uncle Bernac: A Memory of Empire. London, Smith Elder, and New York, Appleton, 1897.
The Tragedy of Korosko. London, Smith Elder, 1898; as *Desert Drama,* Philadelphia, Lippincott, 1898.
A Duet, with an Occasional Chorus. London, Grant Richards, and New York, Appleton, 1899; revised edition, London, Smith Elder, 1910.
The Hound of the Baskervilles. London, Newnes, and New York, McClure, 1902.
Sir Nigel. London, Smith Elder, and New York, McClure, 1906.
The Lost World. London, Hodder and Stoughton, and New York, Doran, 1912.
The Poison Belt. London, Hodder and Stoughton, and New York, Doran, 1913.
The Valley of Fear. New York, Doran, 1914; London, Smith Elder, 1915.
The Land of Mist. London, Hutchinson, and New York, Doran, 1926.

Short Stories

Mysteries and Adventures. London, Scott, 1889; as *The Gully of Bluesmandyke and Other Stories,* 1892.

The Captain of the Polestar and Other Tales. London, Longman, 1890; New York, Munro, 1894.

The Adventure of Sherlock Holmes. London, Newnes, and New York, Harper, 1892.

My Friend the Murderer and Other Mysteries and Adventures. New York, Lovell, 1893.

The Memoirs of Sherlock Holmes. London, Newnes, 1893; New York, Harper, 1894.

The Great Keinplatz Experiment and Other Stories. Chicago, Rand McNally, 1894.

Round the Red Lamp, Being Facts and Fancies of Medical Life. London, Methuen, and New York, Appleton, 1894.

The Exploits of Brigadier Gerard. London, Newnes, and New York, Appleton, 1896.

The Man from Archangel and Other Stories. New York, Street and Smith, 1898.

The Green Flag and Other Stories of War and Sport. London, Smith Elder, and New York, McClure, 1900.

Hilda Wade (completion of book by Grant Allen). London, Richards, and New York, Putnam, 1900.

Adventures of Gerard. London, Newnes, and New York, McClure, 1903.

The Return of Sherlock Holmes. London, Newnes, and New York, McClure, 1905.

Round the Fire Stories. London, Smith Elder, and New York, McClure, 1908.

The Last Galley: Impressions and Tales. London, Smith Elder, and New York, Doubleday, 1911.

His Last Bow: Some Reminiscences of Sherlock Holmes. London, Murray, and New York, Doran, 1917.

Danger! and Other Stories. London, Murray, 1918; New York, Doran, 1919.

Tales of Adventure and Medical Life. London, Murray, 1922; as *The Man from Archangel and Other Tales of Adventure,* New York, Doran, 1925.

Tales of Long Ago. London, Murray, 1922; as *The Last of the Legions and Other Tales of Long Ago,* New York, Doran, 1925.

Tales of the Ring and Camp. London, Murray, 1922; as *The Croxley Master and Other Tales of the Ring and Camp,* New York, Doran, 1925.

Tales of Terror and Mystery. London, Murray, 1922; as *The Black Doctor and Other Tales of Terror and Mystery* (selection), New York, Doran, 1925.

The Case-Book of Sherlock Holmes. London, Murray, and New York, Doran, 1927.

The Maracot Deep and Other Stories. London, Murray, and New York, Doubleday, 1929.

The Conan Doyle Historical Romances. London, Murray, 2 vols., 1931-32.

The Field Bazaar. Privately printed, 1934; Summit, New Jersey, Pamphlet House, 1947.

The Professor Challenger Stories. London, Murray, 1952.

Great Stories, edited by John Dickson Carr. London, Murray, and New York, London, House and Maxwell, 1959.

Strange Studies from Life, Containing Three Hitherto Uncollected Tales, edited by Peter Ruber. New York, Candlelight Press, 1963.

The Annotated Sherlock Holmes, edited by William S. Baring-Gould. New York, Schocken, 1976; as *The Sherlock Holmes Illustrated Omnibus,* London, Murray-Cape, 1978.

The Best Supernatural Tales of Arthur Conan Doyle, edited by E.F. Bleiler. New York, Dover, 1979.

Sherlock Holmes: The Published Apocrypha, with others, edited by Jack Tracy. Boston, Houghton Mifflin, 1980.

The Best Science Fiction of Arthur Conan Doyle, edited by Charles G. Waugh and Martin H. Greenberg. Carbondale, Southern Illinois University Press, 1981.

The Edinburgh Stories. Edinburgh, Polygon, 1981.

The Final Adventures of Sherlock Holmes, edited by Peter Haining. London, W.H. Allen, 1981.

Uncollected Stories, edited by John Michael Gibson and Roger Lancelyn Green. London, Secker and Warburg, and New York, Doubleday, 1982.

The Best Horror Stories of Arthur Conan Doyle, edited by Martin H. Greenberg and Charles G. Waugh. Chicago, Academy, 1988.

The Supernatural Tales of Sir Arthur Conan Doyle, edited by Peter Haining. Slough, Berkshire, Foulsham, 1988.

The Baker Street Dozen, edited by Pj Doyle and E.W. McDiarmid. New York, Congdon and Weed, 1989.

Memories and Adventures. Oxford, Oxford University Press, 1989.

The Red-Headed League. Mankato, Minnesota, Creative Education, 1989.

Sherlock Holmes: Two Complete Adventures. Philadelphia, Running Press, 1989.

Tales for a Winter's Night. South Yarmouth, Massachusetts, Curley, 1989.

When the World Screamed and Other Stories. San Francisco, Chronicle, 1990.

The Adventure of the Solitary Cyclist. Mankato, Creative Education, 1991.

The Adventures of the Speckled Band and Other Stories. Des Moines, Perfection Form, 1991.

The Horror of the Heights and Other Tales of Suspense. San Francisco, Chronicle, 1992.

Six Great Sherlock Holmes Stories. New York, Dover, 1992.

Plays

Jane Annie: or, The Good Conduct Prize, with J.M. Barrie, music by Ernest Ford (produced London, 1893). London, Chappell, and New York, Novello Ewer, 1893.

Foreign Policy, adaptation of his story "A Question of Diplomacy" (produced London, 1893).

Waterloo, adaptation of his story "A Straggler of 15" (as *A Story of Waterloo,* produced Bristol, 1894; London, 1895; as *Waterloo,* produced New York, 1899). London, French, 1907; in *One-Act Plays of To-Day,* 2nd series, edited by J.W. Marriott, Boston, Small Maynard, 1926.

Halves, adaptation of the story by James Payne (produced Aderdeen and London, 1899).

Sherlock Holmes, with William Gillette, adaptation of works by Doyle (produced Buffalo and New York, 1899; Liverpool and London, 1901).

A Duet (A Duologue) (produced London, 1902). London, French, 1903.

Brigadier General, adaptation of his stories (produced London and New York, 1906).

The Fires of Fate: A Modern Morality, adaptation of his novel *The Tragedy of Korosko* (produced Liverpool, London, and New York, 1909).

The House of Temperley, adaptation of his novel *Rodney Stone* (produced London, 1910).

The Pot of Caviare, adaptation of his story (produced London, 1910).

The Speckled Band: An Adventure of Sherlock Holmes (produced London and New York, 1910). London, French, 1912.

The Crown Diamond (produced Bristol and London, 1921). Privately printed, 1958.

It's Time Something Happened. New York, Appleton, 1925.

Poetry

Songs of Action. London, Smith Elder, and New York, Doubleday, 1898.

Songs of the Road. London, Smith Elder, and New York, Doubleday, 1911.

The Guards Came Through and Other Poems. London, Murray, 1919; New York, Doran, 1920.

The Poems of Arthur Conan Doyle: Collected Edition (includes play *The Journey).* London, Murray, 1922.

Other

Contributor, *The Fate of Fenella.* London, Hutchinson, 1892.

Contributor, *My First Book.* London, Chatto and Windus, and Philadelphia, Lippincott, 1894.

The Great Boer War. London, Smith Elder, and New York, McClure, 1900.

The War in South Africa: Its Cause and Conduct. London, Smith Elder, and New York, McClure, 1902.

Works. (Author's Edition). London, Smith Elder, 12 vols., and New York, Appleton, 13 vols., 1903.

The Fiscal Question. Hawick, Roxburgh, Henderdon, 1905.

An Incursion into Diplomacy. London, Smith Elder, 1906.

The Story of Mr. George Edalji. London, Daily Telegraph, 1907.

Through the Magic Door (essays). London, Smith Elder, 1907; New York, McClure, 1908.

The Crime of the Congo. London, Hutchinson, and New York, Doubleday, 1909.

Divorce Law Reform: An Essay. London, Divorce Law Reform Union, 1909.

Sir Arthur Conan Doyle: Why He Is Now in Favour of Home Rule. London, Liberal Publication Department, 1911.

The Case of Oscar Slater. London, Hodder and Stoughton, 1912; New York, Doran, 1913.

Contributor, *What the Worker Wants.* London, Hodder and Stoughton, 1912.

Divorce and the Church, with Lord Hugh Cecil. London, Divorce Law Reform Union, 1913.

Great Britain and the Next War. Boston, Small Maynard, 1914.

In Quest of Truth, Being Correspondence Between Sir Arthur Conan Doyle and Captain H. Stansbury. London, Watts, 1914.

To Arms! London, Hodder and Stoughton, 1914.

The German War. London, Hodder and Stoughton, 1914; New York, Doran, 1915.

Western Wanderings (travel in Canada). New York, Doran, 1915.

The Outlook on the War. London, Daily Chronicle, 1915.

An Appreciation of Sir John French. London, Daily Chronicle, 1916.

A Petition to the Prime Minister on Behalf of Sir Roger Casement. Privately printed, 1916.

A Visit to Three Fronts: Glimpses of British, Italian, and French Lines. London, Hodder and Stoughton, and New York, Doran, 1916.

The British Campaign in France and Flanders. London, Hodder and Stoughton, 6 vols., 1916-20; New York, Doran, 6 vols., 1916-20; revised edition, as *The British Campaigns in Europe 1914-18,* London, Bles, 1 vol., 1928.

The New Revelation; or, What Is Spiritualism? London, Hodder and Stoughton, and New York, Doran, 1918.

The Vital Message (on spiritualism). London, Hodder and Stoughton, and New York, Doran, 1919.

Our Reply to the Cleric. London, Spiritualists' National Union, 1920.

A Public Debate on the Truth of Spiritualism, with Joseph McCabe. London, Watts, 1920; as *Debate on Spiritualism,* Girard, Kansas, Haldeman Julius, 1922.

Spiritualism and Rationalism. London, Hodder and Stoughton, 1920.

Editor, *D.D. Home: His Life and Mission,* by Mrs. Douglas Home. London, Paul Trench Trubner, and New York, Dutton, 1921.

The Wanderings of a Spiritualist. London, Hodder and Stoughton, and New York, Doran, 1921.

Spiritualism: Some Straight Questions and Direct Answers. Manchester, Two Worlds, 1922.

The Case for Spirit Photography, with others. London, Hutchinson, 1922; New York, Doran, 1923.

The Coming of the Fairies. London, Hodder and Stoughton, and New York, Doran, 1922.

three of Them: A Reminiscence. London, Murray, 1923.

Our American Adventure. London, Hodder and Stoughton, and New York, Doran, 1923.

Memoirs and Adventures. London, Hodder and Stoughton, and Boston, Little Brown, 1924.

Translator, *The Mystery of Joan of Arc,* by Léon Denis. London, Murray, 1924; New York, Dutton, 1925.

Our Second American Adventure. London, Hodder and Stoughton, and Boston, Little Brown, 1924.

Editor, *The Spirtualist's Reader.* Manchester, Two Worlds Publishing Company, 1924.

The Early Christian Church and Modern Spiritualism. London, Psychic Bookshop, 1925.

Contributor, *My Religion.* London, Hutchinson, 1925; New York, Appleton, 1926.

Psychic Experiences. London and New York, Putnam, 1925.

The History of Spiritualism. London, Cassell, 2 vols., and New York, Doran, 2 vols., 1926.

Pheneas Speaks: Direct Spirit Communications. London, Psychic Press, and New York, Doran, 1927.

What Does Spiritualism Actually Teach and Stand For? London, Psychic Bookshop, 1928.

A Word of Warning. London, Psychic Press, 1928.

An Open Letter to Those of My Generation. London, Psychic Press, 1929.

Contributor, *If I Were a Preacher.* London, Cassell, and New York, Harper, 1929.

Our African Winter. London, Murray, 1929.

The Roman Catholic Church: A Rejoinder. London, Psychic Press, 1929.

The Edge of the Unknown. London, Murray, and New York, Putnam, 1930.

Works (Crowborough Edition). New York, Doubleday, 24 vols., 1930.

Conan Doyle's Stories for Boys. London, Cupples and Leon, 1938.

Sherlock Holmes: Selected Stories. Oxford, Oxford University Press, 1951.

Sherlock Holmes: A Definitive Text, edited by Edgar W, Smith. Heritage Press, 1957.

Famous Tales of Sherlock Holmes. Dodd, 1958.

The Glorious Hussar: The Best of the Exploits and Adventures of the Brigadier Gerard. New York, Walker, 1961.

The Boys' Sherlock Holmes: A Selection From the Works of A. Conan Doyle. New York, Harper, 1961.

Strange Studies from Life, edited by Peter Ruber. New York, Candlelight Press, 1963.

The Complete Adventures and Memoirs of Sherlock Holmes: A Facsimile of the Original Strand Magazine Stories, 1891-1893, illustrated by Sidney Paget. New York, C.N. Potter, 1975.

Arthur Conan Doyle on Sherlock Holmes. London, Favil, 1981.

Essays on Photography, edited by John Michael Gibson and Roger Lancelyn Green. London, Secker and Warburg, 1982.

Letters to the Press: The Unknown Conan Doyle, edited by John Michael Gibson and Roger Lancelyn Green. London, Secker and Warburg, and Iowa City, University of Iowa Press, 1986.

The Sherlock Holmes Letters, edited by Richard Lancelyn Green. London, Secker and Warburg, 1986.

*

Media Adaptations: *The Adventures of Sherlock Holmes* (film), Twentieth Century Fox, 1939; *The Hound of the Baskervilles* (film), Twentieth Century Fox, 1939; *A Study in Scarlet* (film); *His Last Bow* (film); *The Firm of Girdlestone* (film); *The Exploits of Brigadier Gerard* (film); Doyle's writings have also been adapted for plays, television broadcasts, and filmstrips, as well as numerous other film productions.

Biography: *Conan Doyle: His Life and Art* by Hesketh Pearson, London, Methuen, 1943, New York, Walker, 1961; *The Life of Sir Arthur Conan Doyle* by John Dickson Carr, London, Murray, and New York, Harper, 1949; *Conan Doyle: A Biography* by Pierre Nordon, London, Murray, 1966, New York, Holt Rinehart, 1967; *A Biography of the Creator of Sherlock Holmes* by Ivor Brown, London, Hamish Hamilton, 1972; *The Adventure of Conan Doyle: The Life of the Creator of Sherlock Holmes* by Charles Higham, London, Hamish Hamilton, and New York, Norton, 1976; *Conan Doyle: A Biographical Solution* by Ronald Pearsall, London, Weidenfeld and Nicolson, 1977; *Conan Doyle: Portrait of an Artist* by Julian Symons, London, G. Whizzard, 1979; *The Quest for Sherlock Holmes: A Biographical Study of the Early Life of Sir Arthur Conan Doyle* by Own Dudley Edwards, Edinburgh, Mainstream, 1982, Totowa, New Jersey, Barnes and Noble, 1983; *Arthur Conan Doyle* by Don Richard Cox, New York, Ungar, 1985; *The Unrevealed Life of Doctor Arthur Conan Doyle: A Study in Southsea* by Geoffrey Stavert, Horndean, Hampshire, Milestone, 1987; *Arthur Conan Doyle* by Jacqueline A. Jaffe, Boston, Twayne, 1987; *The Quest for Sir Arthur Conan Doyle: Thirteen Biographers in Search of a Life* edited by Jon L. Lellenberg, Carbondale, Southern Illinois University Press, 1987.

Bibliography: *A Bibliographical Catalogue of the Writings of Sir Arthur Conan Doyle* by Harold Locke, Tunbridge Wells, Kent, Webster, 1928; *The World Bibliography of Sherlock Holmes and Dr. Watson* by Ronald Burt De Waal, Boston, New York Graphic Society, 1975; *A Bibliography of A. Conan Doyle* by Richard Lancelyn Green and John Michael Gibson, Oxford, Clarendor Press, 1983.

Manuscript Collection: Humanities Research Center, University of Texas, Austin.

Critical Study: *The Private Life of Sherlock Holmes* by Vincent Starrett, New York, Macmillan, 1933, London, Nicholson and Watson, 1934, revised edition, Chicago, University of Chicago Press, 1960, London, Allen and Unwin, 1961; *In the Footsteps of Sherlock Holmes* by Michael Harrison, London, Cassell, 1958, New York, Fell, 1960, revised edition, Newton Abbot, Devon, David and Charles, 1971, New York, Drake, 1972; *The Man Who Was Sherlock Holmes* by Michael and Mollie Hardwick, London, Murray, and New York, Doubleday, 1964; *A Sherlock Holmes Commentary* by D. Martin Dakin, Newton Abbot, Devon, David and Charles, 1972; *Sherlock Holmes in Portrait and Profile* by Walter Klinefelter, New York, Schocken, 1975; *The Sherlock Holmes File* by Michael Pointer, Newton Abbot, Devon, David and Charles, 1976; *Sir Arthur Conan Doyle's Sherlock Holmes: The Short Stories: A Critical Commentary* by Mary P. De Camara and Stephen Hayes, New York, Monarch, 1976; *The Encyclopedia Sherlockiana* by Jack Tracy, New York, Doubleday, 1977, London, New English Library, 1978; *Sherlock Holmes and His Creator* by Trevor H. Hall, London, Duckworth, 1978, New York, St. Martin's Press, 1983; *Sherlock Holmes: The Man and His World* by H.R.F. Keating, London, Thames and Hudson, and New York, Scribner, 1979; *Who's Who in Sherlock Holmes* by Scott R. Bullard and Michael Collins, New York, Taplinger, 1980; *The International Sherlock Holmes* by Ronald Burt De Waal, Hamden, Connecticut, Shoe String Press, and London, Mansell, 1980; *A Sherlock Holmes Compendium* edited by Peter Haining, London, W.H. Allen, 1980; *Sherlock Holmes in America* by Bill Blackbeard, New York, Abrams, 1981; *Sherlock Holmes: A Study in Sources* by Donald A. Redmond, Montreal, McGill-Queen's University Press, 1982; Entry in *Dictionary of Literary Biography,* Volume 18, Detroit, Gale, 1983; Volume 70, 1988; *A Study in Surmise: The Making of Sherlock Holmes* by Michael Harrison, Bloomington, Indiana, Gaslight, 1984; *The Complete Guide to Sherlock Holmes* by Michael Hardwick, London, Weidenfeld and Nicolson, 1986; *Sherlock Holmes: A Centenary Celebration* by Allen Eyles, London, Murray, 1986; *Elementary My Dear Watson: Sherlock Holmes Centenary: His Life and Times* by Graham Nown, New York, Ward Lock, 1986.

*   *   *

For the greater part of the century, the contributions of Sir Arthur Conan Doyle to young adult fiction have been at best underrated and at worst obscured by his Sherlock Holmes mysteries. It has been only in the recent past that the science fiction and adventure stories featuring Professor E. Challenger have resurfaced and become recognized for the quality works they are.

The exploits of Professor Challenger, chronicled in *The Lost World,* "The Poison Belt," "When the World Screamed," "The Disintegration Machine," and *The Land of Mist,* bear an important similarity to the Holmes stories. In both series, the escapades of a famous man are narrated from the viewpoint of a lesser man. Professor Challenger's chronicler is generally the young newspaper reporter Edward Malone, but the two are joined in some of their adventures by outdoorsman Lord John Roxton and Professor Summerlee. This larger cast of regular characters is not seen in the other works by Doyle.

The characters who make up the party itself are a great source of material for the author; their personalities and professions are diverse enough to create many an interesting interplay. Their interactions are not always of the civilized Holmes sort, as clashes of opinion and personality are commonplace. Challenger is a far cry from the Holmesian hero. As his title would denote, he is a teacher, a man of science, specializing in zoology. He is characterized as small and somewhat misshapen, but possessing enormous strength. His personality is volatile. He is given to argue with anyone on any subject, to become suddenly terribly violent, and to exhibit an enormous egotism. Given the sheer size and intensity of his personality, the other players can only react to and interact with him; Challenger is always the center of attention. Summerlee, for example, is also a scientist, a zoologist, and argues incessantly with Challenger on any and all scientific topics that arise. Roxton, on the other hand, is a hearty, even-tempered man who competently leads the group in dangerous situations. Lastly there is Malone, the seemingly naive man, who sees all with the wondering eyes of one who is carried along on the coattails of his fellows. It is Malone who reveals most of the joy of discovery and implications of human nature in the stories, and he is an excellent narrator with whom the reader may identify. The personalities of this intrepid group add a unique twist to the peculiar situations in which they find themselves.

Unlike the Holmes stories, Challenger adventures feature a much larger view of the world and deal with topics that are more far-reaching or have a greater bearing on the world at large. While Holmes and Watson rarely leave the microcosm of London, Challenger and his crew journey both the world and their own backyards, encountering many strange cultures and happenings as they go. The exotic locales, coupled with his lively and unusual characters, gives Doyle the freedom to incorporate more exciting adventure and science fiction plot elements. He creates fantasy worlds in these places where the reader is more prone to believe such strange events could occur. Challenger does use a keen sense of observation and superior reasoning skills, as does Holmes, but the added action appeals more to the younger reader.

In some ways, the exploits of Professor Challenger and his party are more complex in structure than their Holmesian counterparts. Along with their broader scope and greater physical action, the Challenger stories show far more wit and ironic humor than is normally seen in Doyle's work. Doyle uses this ironic humor to counter the main events in the story, accenting the gravity and horror of these events with just a touch of the farcical. As Charles Higham, in his biography of the author, *The Adventures of Conan Doyle,* points out, a particular scene of this type occurs in *The Lost World.* Upon returning from South America, Professor Challenger lectures at Queen's Hall on his discoveries, and presents a mysterious box:

Come then, pretty, pretty! [he said] in a coaxing voice.

An instant later, with a scratching, rattling sound, a most horrible and loathsome creature [a pterodactyl] appeared from below and perched itself upon the side of the case. Even the unexpected fall of the Duke of Durham into the orchestra, which occurred at that moment, could not distract the petrified attention of the vast audience.

The Duke's mishap, while comical in itself, serves to further stress the horror of the assembled crowd. More wry humor surfaces in "The Poison Belt," when Challenger expects all the inhabitants of the world to be exterminated by a huge cloud of gas from the heavens. He explains to his manservant, "I'm expecting the end of the world today, Austin," to which Austin replies, "Yes, sir, what time sir?"

Following the popular, if less successful release of "The Poison Belt," Challenger reappeared in the short story "When the World Screamed." In it, the professor believes that the earth is itself a living organism, wholly unaware of the pestilence of the human race upon itself. He drills a shaft through the earth's crust, eight miles down to a soft cortex. One writer suggested that the entire story hinged on a sexual symbolism in which the female earth is conquered by Challenger's penetrating, phallic drill. Challenger also appears in a short story entitled "The Disintegration Machine," in which he foils an evil scientist's plot to develop and sell to the highest bidder the ultimate weapon. Neither story appeared to be particularly popular, the latter having drifted almost entirely into obscurity.

Conan Doyle went on to explore the spirit world in *The Land of Mists.* Himself an avid spiritualist, he brought his beliefs to issue in this last Challenger novella. Spiritualism suffered then, as a science, from the same skepticism with which it is seen today. Edward Shanks, in reviewing the novella for *London Mercury* in 1926, attacked Conan Doyle's conviction of the truth of Spiritualism on the basis of his errors in getting the style and title of the Duke of Pomfret right! Wrote Shanks, "one cannot help feeling that a writer who can go so far astray with the usages of the tangible world might make serious mistakes with those of the intangible."

Along with the sin of being "an incurably inaccurate writer," Doyle was also accused of sinning by omitting a strong love interest in *The Lost World.* Indeed, the reviewer W. M. Payne in *The Dial* could find precious little else to criticize. However, the reviewer for *The Nation,* in 1912, applauded the work, stating: "To deal realistically with a theme of this kind requires no slight art. It would be easy enough to cram up a few books of geology and anthropology, and then imagine some way of getting a modern man back among the wild growths of the past; but to give the real thrill of living adventure to battles with flying elephants and ape-men is another matter. The creator of Sherlock Holmes has done this, and he has made the four adventurers in this lost world genuine men of distinct characters."

The Lost World became, for the most part, a critical and commercial success. Doyle so enjoyed his Challenger character that he dressed as the professor for publicity photos after the publication of the first story. Shortly before his death in 1930, Doyle described Challenger as "a character who has always amused me more than any other which I have created." Doyle's stories of Professor Challenger's exploits are rightly identified as science fiction and compare favorably to the works of Jules Verne. But equally his Challenger stories which have been out of print until recently, still appeal to adolescents today, with their unstuffy, irascible, fun-loving, childish hero.

—Nicholas Ranson

———

DOYLE, Brian. Canadian. Born in Ottawa, Ontario, 12 August 1935. Educated at York Street Public School, Ottawa; Glebe Collegiate Institute, Ottawa; Carleton University, Ottawa, B.A. in journalism 1957. Married Jacqueline Aronson in 1960; one son and one daughter. Journalist. Toronto *Telegram.* Since 1969 high school English teacher at Glebe Collegiate, Ottawa, Ontario, and Ottawa Technical High School, Ottawa, also head of English department at